D0753312

THE SAGE HANDBOOK OF
POLITICAL ADVERTISING

THE SAGE HANDBOOK OF
POLITICAL
ADVERTISING

EDITORS
LYNDA LEE KAID
University of Florida

CHRISTINA HOLTZ-BACHA
University of Erlangen-Nürnberg

SAGE Publications
Thousand Oaks ▪ London ▪ New Delhi

For information:

Sage Publications, Inc.
2455 Teller Road
Thousand Oaks, California 91320
E-mail: order@sagepub.com

Sage Publications Ltd.
1 Oliver's Yard
55 City Road
London EC1Y 1SP
United Kingdom

Sage Publications India Pvt. Ltd.
B-42, Panchsheel Enclave
Post Box 4109
New Delhi 110 017 India

Printed in the United States of America

Library of Congress Cataloging-in-Publication Data

The SAGE handbook of political advertising / edited by Lynda Lee Kaid, Christina Holtz-Bacha.
     p. cm.
Includes bibliographical references and index.
ISBN 1-4129-1795-6 (cloth)
   1. Advertising, Political—Cross-cultural studies. 2. Television in politics—Cross-cultural studies. I. Kaid, Lynda Lee. II. Holtz-Bacha, Christina.
JF2112.A4S24 2006
324.7′3—dc22   2005037852

This book is printed on acid-free paper.

06   07   08   09   10   10 9 8 7 6 5 4 3 2 1

Acquisitions Editor:	Todd R. Armstrong
Editorial Assistant:	Sarah K. Quesenberry
Production Editor:	Laureen A. Shea
Copy Editor:	Catherine M. Chilton
Typesetter:	C&M Digitals (P) Ltd.
Proofreader:	Kevin Gleason
Indexer:	Mary Mortensen
Cover Designer:	Edgar Abarca

Contents

PART VI. COMPARISONS AND CONCLUSIONS

List of Tables

List of Figures

Acknowledgments

The editors would like to thank, first and foremost, the contributors whose individual chapters make this handbook a valuable reference book for researchers, scholars, students, and political professionals around the world.

Some of the work on this volume began and was inspired while Lynda Lee Kaid was a Fulbright Scholar, and she would like to thank the Council for the International Exchange of Scholars for that support.

Several colleagues and assistants at the University of Florida and at the University of Erlangen-Nürnberg helped with different aspects of the project. The editors would like especially to thank Monica Postelnicu and Kristen Landreville at the University of Florida.

The editors also appreciate the continuing support and direct assistance of their spouses, Clifford A. Jones and Salah Bacha. They contributed in hundreds of ways every single day to making this work possible.

PART I

An International Context for Political Advertising

1

Political Advertising in International Comparison

CHRISTINA HOLTZ-BACHA AND LYNDA LEE KAID

Political advertising as understood here only appears in systems in which the distribution of political power is contested and determined in elections and in which parties or candidates compete with each other. Political advertising, then, is a means through which parties and candidates present themselves to the electorate, mostly through the mass media. In contrast to the so-called free media, political advertising is often referred to as paid media. Regular media coverage is called free because it allows candidates and parties to appear in the media without having to pay for it. Because this kind of coverage (e.g., the news) resides within the responsibility of the media and therefore enjoys higher credibility than candidate-sponsored activities, political actors try first of all to get into the free media. The downside of free coverage, however, is that the usual journalistic selection and production criteria apply, and political actors cannot influence when, how long, or how they are covered. Paid media, in contrast, allow candidates, parties, and sometimes other interest groups to decide how they want to present themselves to the voters.

Because the distinction between paid and free media originated in the United States, where candidates are allowed to purchase advertising time on television, electoral advertising on television is classified as paid media. In many cases, other countries do not allow candidates to purchase broadcasting time for their campaign messages. Therefore, instead of classifying campaign channels as either free or paid media, a distinction of *mediated* versus *nonmediated* channels may be more accurate in an international context. This distinction is also sometimes called *controlled media* and *uncontrolled media*, because candidates and parties can control their own advertising messages but do not exercise complete control over the output of media news messages. In this sense, political advertising is a controlled, nonmediated campaign channel, meaning that responsibility for the ads lies with the political actors, and they do not run the risk of their messages being altered by the media production process. Instead, political actors determine how they are presented on television. Although this is the undoubted advantage of

3

political advertising, such communication obviously has a persuasive intent that casts doubts on its credibility. It is, therefore, a challenge for campaign strategists to prevent and overcome the reactance effect that any persuasive communication risks.

Although political actors strive for frequent and ample coverage in the free media, and particularly on television, their interest in political advertising seems clear. In addition to the uncertainty of what the media will do in their campaign coverage, a commercialized media system has made it difficult for politics to compete with more attractive media fare. Political advertising thus gives candidates and parties the possibility to enhance their presence in the media and determine its shape and contents.

In an earlier work on political advertising in Western democratic systems, the editors defined televised political advertising as "moving image programming that is designed to promote the interests of a given party or individual" (Kaid & Holtz-Bacha, 1995, p. 2). Thus the definition incorporates "any programming format under the control of the party or candidate and for which time is given or purchased" (p. 2). As media systems, channels, and formats of communication have expanded and evolved, the central elements of this definition have remained useful, but a more modernized and professionalized definition now suggests that political advertising should be viewed as "any controlled message communicated through any channel designed to promote the political interests of individuals, parties, groups, governments, or other organizations." This broader conceptualization not only implies the controlled and promotional aspect of the message but acknowledges the different formats, channels, and sponsors that may characterize such communications in a given environment.

As political advertising developed in various media environments and as social changes led to a weakening influence of once-powerful social characteristics and subsequent political predispositions, election campaigns became more important. Traditional social structures have lost their meaning for the individual and no longer prescribe individual behavior in a binding way. Therefore, social variables that played a central role in the classical models of electoral behavior no longer predict voting decisions with the same probability that they once did. Instead, political behavior has become unstable and fluctuating (see Holtz-Bacha, 2002). In fact, findings from several Western democracies have shown that party ties are weakening. Voter volatility, as expressed in increasing numbers of floating voters, and voting abstention have been attributed to the so-called dealignment process (see Dalton, 2002). This is a process that seems to be going on in many countries but not at the same time or with the same speed everywhere. With voters thus being more unpredictable and their electoral decisions open to short-term influences, election campaigns have gained new importance. It is therefore not surprising that political leaders would be interested in the use of political communications such as political advertising that provide for the controlled and unmediated conditions that best serve their campaign interests.

Nevertheless, countries differ considerably in the role television advertising plays in electoral campaigns.[1] Although politicians are the lawmakers and could be expected to push for favorable conditions for their advertising campaigns, restrictions apply to electoral advertising in many countries. This seems to indicate that additional variables are at work here, affecting the attitudes toward electoral advertising and the decisions about the respective rules in a given country. Whether electoral advertising is allowed and, if allowed, the way it is further regulated are usually dependent on several systemic variables, including a country's political system, the electoral system, and the media system. Finally, how electoral messages are actually designed is dependent on a country's political culture, which, at the same time, is reflected in political advertising.

Any study of political communication processes in an internationally comparative perspective must therefore consider the differences in political structures and processes, in political culture, and in the organization of the media (Hallin & Mancini, 2004; Swanson & Mancini, 1996). These variables and their specific interrelations provide for a distinctive national background against which the regulations for political advertising, the role of television adverting in campaign strategies, and findings about effects of political advertising have to be interpreted.

This volume only includes countries where the broadcasting of political advertising during election campaigns is allowed in one way or the other. However, there are countries that do not have electoral advertising on television, either because it is prohibited or because political actors (parties, candidates) agree not to use this kind of advertising channel for their campaigns. For instance, Switzerland is one of the countries where political advertising on television and radio is prohibited during election and referendum campaigns. Several reasons are given for the ban on ads in Switzerland. One is the assumption that parties would not have the financial means to pay for the production of the ads or to even purchase broadcasting time, because Swiss parties do not receive any state funding. However, advertising in newspapers plays a major role in Swiss elections, and protection of the print media and their revenue from advertising is another reason given for the ban on television and radio broadcasting ads. The Northern European countries are also reluctant to permit electoral broadcasts on television. Although Finland does not impose any spending or time limits on television ads, political advertising in Sweden is only imported through channels that broadcast from outside the country. Denmark does not have an official ban on ads, but political actors have agreed not to use them for their campaigning. As in Sweden, Norway also has traditionally

had a ban on political advertising, but new regulations are being developed that will require television stations to allot free time segments for the parties.

South Africa, which is represented here with a chapter, also is a remarkable case. Although television does play a role in electoral campaigns and has gained importance over the last decade or so, electoral advertising is restricted to radio. In a way, the reasons given for this decision are similar to the arguments brought forward in Switzerland: Producing ads for television is expensive and would overstretch the financial possibilities of at least some parties. At the same time, television advertising is regarded as a powerful form of persuasive communication and therefore not to be placed in the hands of those striving for power.

As the country chapters of this book illustrate, even where party or candidate spots are allowed, there are many differences in the respective regulation. These differences start at the level of terminology. In the United States, where candidates invest more than half of their campaign budget in television advertising, the usual term is *ads* or *spots*. Electoral ads as we know them in the United States are thus equated with commercial ads and, therefore, "paid media." They are also often associated with *time* being purchased and electoral broadcasts being very short. In other countries, particularly in those where broadcast time cannot be purchased, researchers tend to avoid the term *ads*. In the Western European countries where public broadcasting has long dominated the market and the public service philosophy is still present, parties and candidates are mostly provided with free broadcasting time to be used for their advertising. Researchers from these countries often shrink from calling these electoral messages ads and instead use the term *political electoral broadcasts* (e.g., United Kingdom), *polispots* (Greece), or, in the English translation of the Italian term, *independently produced political messages*

(Italy). However, if a country allows electoral advertising in both public service broadcasting and commercial broadcasting, as in Germany, it still remains an open question whether the broadcasts in both systems are indeed that much different. In fact, German parties tend to use the same ad for both broadcasting systems and only shorten it for broadcasting on commercial television. In any case, the use of different terms can be regarded as one indicator of the diverging attitudes toward political advertising across countries.

POLITICAL SYSTEM DIFFERENCES

The political system and the electoral system go hand in hand with the role of the parties. In almost all countries that are included here, parties play a dominant role on the political scene; the United States is the exception. Although there are other countries with a presidential system (Latin American countries, for instance), it is in the United States that the candidate orientation of the presidential system has led to a decline of parties. Elsewhere, the parties mostly remain in a dominant role. This is definitely the case for parliamentary systems. In spite of trends toward personalization and a focus on individual candidates, campaigning overwhelmingly lies in the hands of parties. This is reflected in Table 1.1, which shows, for a sample of 28 countries from different parts of the world, that during parliamentary elections spots are sponsored by parties everywhere except the United States.

Sponsorship does not necessarily mean that advertising time is paid time. In many countries, advertising time on television is provided free during elections. However, if this is the case, time is allocated to parties and not to individual candidates. Where parties do not have to pay for advertising time in the media, they still have to pay for the production of the spots.

The strong role that parties play in most political systems is also indicated by the fact that even in presidential elections, sponsorship of television advertising does not lie with the candidates. Table 1.1 also gives an overview of sponsorship of spots during presidential elections. Half (14) of the 28 countries listed have direct elections of the president. Among countries that do not elect a president directly, several are monarchies, such as Spain, the Netherlands, and the United Kingdom, where a queen or a king is the nominal head of state. In other countries, the president is not elected by the people directly but instead determined by the parliament or another electoral committee. Campaigning in the real sense of the word and thus electoral advertising can only be expected in those countries where the president is elected directly by the people. In several cases, it is still the parties that are responsible for the sponsorship of ads on television. This is primarily the situation in Europe, where only the new democracies of Middle or Eastern Europe have adopted a system of candidate sponsorship for the spots in presidential campaigns. Candidate sponsorship thus can also be regarded as an indicator of the role the president plays in a political system: In most Western European countries, with France being the clearest exception, the president, though being nominally the head of state, is in fact in a secondary role compared to the prime minister.

The electoral system of a country can be expected to have a major impact on campaign strategies and thus on the design of electoral advertising (Roper, Holtz-Bacha, & Mazzoleni, 2004). For example, strategies may vary according to the number and size of parties running in a race. If elections usually lead to clear majorities and single-party governments or usually end up in coalitions of two or more parties, such a system can also impinge on campaign and advertising strategies because campaigners may, for example, refrain from negative advertising against future or former coalition partners. Thresholds that parties must overcome to be represented in the parliament

Table 1.1 Sponsorship of Spots and Electoral Systems

Country	(Direct) Presidential Elections Held?	Sponsor of Ads	Parliamentary Election Ad Sponsors	Electoral System[a]
Argentina	Yes	Parties	Party	Proportional representation
Australia	No	—[b]	Party	Majority vote
Austria	Yes	Parties	Party	Proportional representation
Belgium	No	—	Party	Proportional representation
Brazil	Yes	Parties	Party	Proportional representation
Bulgaria	Yes	Parties	Party + candidates	Proportional representation
Canada	No	—	Party	Majority vote
Chile	Yes	Parties	Party	Binominal system
Czech Republic	No	—	Party	Proportional representation
Estonia	No	—	Party	Proportional representation
Finland	Yes	Parties	Party	Proportional representation
France	Yes	Candidates	Party	Majority vote
Germany	No	—	Party	Proportional representation
Greece	No	—	Party	Proportional representation
Israel	No	—	Party	Proportional representation
Italy	No	—	Candidates + party	Majority vote
Japan	No	—	Party	Segmented system
Latvia	No	—	Party	Proportional representation
Lithuania	Yes	Candidates	Party	Segmented system
Mexico	Yes	Parties	Party	Segmented system
Netherlands	No	—	Party	Proportional representation
Poland	Yes	Candidates	Party	Proportional representation
Portugal	Yes	Parties	Party	Proportional representation
Russia	Yes	Candidates	Party	Segmented system
South Korea	Yes	Candidates	Party	Segmented system
Spain	No	—	Party	Proportional representation
United Kingdom	No	—	Party	Majority vote
United States	Yes	Parties + candidates	Candidates	Majority vote

a. Source of electoral system: Nohlen (2000).

b. The dash is an indication that there were no presidential elections, so there could be no sponsors.

7

are another factor exerting an influence on the strategies used in campaign advertising. The electoral system may also lay the ground for the allocation method for free advertising time, which can be equal for all parties, proportional according to the strength of a party in earlier elections, or based on other criteria.

Table 1.1 provides an overview of the electoral systems in the countries included in our survey. For the sake of clarity, the variety of electoral systems that exist across the world has been reduced here. As can be seen from the table, the majority of countries follows some kind of proportional representation. However, it should be noted that there is much variation in proportional systems. Only some countries apply a pure proportional system; most combine proportional representation with elements of majority voting. Germany, for example, has developed its own special model of a personalized proportional system, which was adopted by New Zealand in 1993 (Roper et al., 2004). Proportional systems also differ according to the formula (quota) used to distribute seats among parties. In segmented systems (also called parallel systems), two electoral systems are applied separately, with one group of candidates elected according to majority vote and the others according to a proportional system. Finally, Chile has a singular electoral system that more or less forces the parties to form electoral alliances. (For more extensive information, see Blais & Massicotte, 2002; Nohlen, 2000; Powell, 2000.)

ELECTORAL BROADCASTS

In addition to the differences in the political systems, the specific features of the media systems should be of relevance because of the importance of political advertising and its formats in the different countries. This concerns the media system in general and, more specifically, the structure of the broadcasting system, as well as the function or status of the different media from the perspective of the audience.

The countries represented in this book again differ considerably in the historical development of their broadcasting systems, and this has consequences for current structures and, finally, for the regulation of political advertising. Commercial broadcasting and competition among several television companies have a long tradition in the United States, but such systems were only introduced in most West European countries in the 1980s. Today, these countries feature dual systems, with public service broadcasting remaining a major player in the market, and thus the social responsibility philosophy of the public service model is still very much alive. The Eastern European countries, where the media were in the hands of the state or the ruling parties for more than four decades after World War II, restructured the media systems after the political changes of 1989 and have also built up dual broadcasting systems. However, because it did not have the long tradition of public service broadcasting, this part of the system often is in a weaker position than in Western Europe. The public service idea has also been exported beyond the European continent. Chile, for example, reformed its formerly government-run and then military controlled television network according to the BBC model after the end of the Pinochet dictatorship in 1993.

The development of distribution technologies, the emergence of dual broadcasting systems, and the ensuing commercialization process have led to a radical change in the situation of the broadcasting media in general and of political broadcasting in particular. Overall, competition has increased, mostly to the disadvantage of political contents. Where television stations strive to attract the biggest audience possible in the interest of their advertising clients, politics has to adapt to the rules of the game, meaning it must adopt an entertainment format or end up in a marginal role.

With the multiplication of channels, the number of outlets for political advertising has increased. However, those countries in particular

Table 1.2   Purchase of Time on Television

Country	On Commercial TV	On Public TV
Argentina	Yes	Yes
Australia	Yes	No
Austria	Yes	No
Belgium	No	No
Brazil	No	No
Bulgaria	Yes	Yes
Canada	Yes	Yes
Chile	No	No
Czech Republic	No	No
Estonia	Yes	No
Finland	Yes	No
France	No	No
Germany	Yes	No
Greece	Yes	No
Israel	No	No
Italy	Yes	No
Japan	Yes	No
Latvia	Yes	Yes
Lithuania	Yes	Yes
Mexico	Yes	No
Netherlands	Yes	No
Poland	Yes	Yes
Portugal	No	No
Russia	Yes	Yes
South Korea	Yes	Yes
Spain	No	No
United Kingdom	No	No
United States	Yes	No

that have a long tradition of public service broadcasting did not automatically open up the commercial television sector for electoral advertising. Those that did did not necessarily allow candidates or parties to freely purchase broadcasting time. Table 1.2 shows where advertising time can be purchased in the public or commercial television sector.

The picture that emerges here is quite clear. Public television is mostly out of bounds for the purchase of advertising time. Only some countries allow for advertising time to be purchased on public television, and these are countries not in the traditional public service zone of Western Europe. Commercial television, on the other hand, has indeed brought new possibilities for electoral advertising, with many countries giving candidates or parties the opportunity to expand their presence on the screen during election campaigns. It must be kept in mind, however, that these tables only include countries where electoral advertising on television is allowed in one way or the other; countries that do not have any electoral advertising on television at all are not represented.

In addition to, or instead of, allowing for the purchase of advertising time, many countries allocate free broadcasting time to parties or candidates during electoral campaigns. Thus these countries keep campaign broadcasts under control by fixing the time span during which electoral advertising is broadcast, the method of allocation, the amount of time, and

Table 1.3 Provision of Free Political Television Advertising Time

Country	No Free Time	Free Time on Public TV	Free Time on Commercial TV	Free Time on Both Public and Commercial TV
Argentina		x		
Australia		x		
Austria	x			
Belgium		x		
Brazil				x
Bulgaria	x			
Canada				x
Chile				x
Czech Republic		x		
Estonia	x			
Finland	x			
France		x		
Germany		x		
Greece		x		
Israel				x
Italy			x	
Japan	x			
Latvia		x		
Lithuania		x		
Mexico	x			
Netherlands		x		
Poland		x		
Portugal				x
Russia		x		
South Korea	x			
Spain		x		
Switzerland	x			
United Kingdom			x	
United States	x			

the number of slots that are given to campaigners. In some cases, further restrictions apply to the contents of the free-time broadcasts. Table 1.3 gives an overview of which countries provide free air time and if so, if that is on public or commercial television.

Free time provided on public television is the most common model in our sample. There are only a few exceptions, with some countries according parties or candidates no free segments at all or only on commercial television. The provision of free broadcasting time on public television seems to be closely connected with the public service philosophy that still

very much rules the Western European countries. Against this background, the cases of Austria, Finland, Italy, and the United Kingdom merit further discussion because they have chosen a different path. Austria and Finland do not provide free air time on any system but allow parties to buy advertising time on commercial television. Finland, which is therefore regarded as the "odd case" among the Nordic countries (see chapter 11), lifted the ban on paid political advertising and has allowed for purchase of advertising time on commercial television since 1991. Austria only recently changed its law: Until 2002, when a new law was passed that abolished the old regulation, public television allocated free time for parties during election campaigns. However, they are allowed to purchase time on commercial television. The snag is that public television in Austria had a monopoly until a couple of years ago. Now commercial broadcasting is allowed, but still there is only a limited number of private stations and only one with a nationwide schedule. Acquiring party advertising carried by "windows for Austria" on German or other international commercial television channels has thus gained more importance than buying broadcast time on the Austrian commercial outlets.

The history of electoral advertising in Italy is of a more colorful nature. Campaign ads were broadcast by the commercial stations until a new law was passed in 1993 that banned spots during the hot campaign phase. The former regulation allowed for purchase of an unlimited number of spots. In 2000, a new law obliged the local commercial stations to provide free air time and be reimbursed by the state. In addition, it is possible to buy extra broadcast time on the same channels. The public service network, RAI, however, remains completely ad free.

The situation is somewhat similar in the United Kingdom. The "mother of public service broadcasting," the BBC, which does not air any commercial advertising at all, was kept free from political advertising as well, but commercial television provides free air time for electoral broadcasts.

Different models are applied if air time is allocated to parties or candidates. Although election laws or other campaign regulations usually prescribe equal treatment for all competitors, that does not necessarily mean an equal amount of time is given to each of them. In fact, most countries apply a system of proportional allocation, with bigger parties receiving more airtime than the smaller ones.

Ads that must be purchased tend to be very short, but there is much variety in the usual length of the free broadcasts. Some countries provide parties and candidates with long time segments or started out with 20- or 30-minute broadcasts. In the first elections in 1993, Russia gave parties 20-minute slots, which were deemed far too long, and the country therefore cut down the time allocated to campaigners. In other countries, free time for parties is much shorter and approaches the same length that parties use when they have to pay for advertising time. An exemplary case for this development is Germany. Here, parties were allocated 5- to 10-minute slots when political advertising was first introduced on television in 1957. Over the years, the time for individual slots was reduced and has now reached 90 seconds, and 30 and 45 seconds are the usual lengths parties use when they purchase time on commercial television.

In addition to regulations as to where electoral advertising is allowed and whether air time can be purchased, further restrictions apply in most countries. Again, the United States is the exceptional case: Electoral advertising has no limits at all. Several countries impose restrictions on the amount of money the parties or candidates are allowed to spend for their television advertising. Of the countries represented here, this is the case in Argentina, Canada, Latvia, Lithuania, Mexico, Poland, and South Korea. According to Mexican law, for instance, the total amount spent for television advertising should not exceed 20% of the public financing for parties during presidential elections and 12% for congressional elections. It is estimated that candidates and parties spend up to 80% of their public funds for advertising on television. Poland sets a general limit for the advertising campaign in parliamentary elections. Similarly, there is a limit for the total amount of money that parties are allowed to spend for their campaign in Latvia and Lithuania.

There also exist diverse provisions concerning the contents of the electoral broadcasts. These mostly apply to the video part of the ads. In Israel, for example, the broadcasts must be approved by the Central Committee of Election. Broadcasts can be prohibited if they divulge security secrets or if they use soldiers or abusive language. Italy and Japan in general do not allow negative advertising. Electoral ads in Mexico fall under the free speech article of the Constitution and are supposed to avoid any affront, defamation, or slander that may denigrate candidates, parties, or other institutions. However, this provision is infringed easily without being sanctioned in any way. As for advertising in general, Bulgaria does not allow electoral advertising to feature the state's coat of arms and the national anthem. France is particularly restrictive, prohibiting the use of public buildings and the national anthem and restricting the amount of preproduced videoclips that can be used. In Finland, regulations on content are different according to the broadcaster concerned. The biggest commercial broadcaster, MTV3, rules that only image advertising for parties and other organizations can be inserted. Advertising for single candidates is not allowed, to avoid the appearance of a candidate in an ad and in the program following the ad. Although parties and organizations can be judged and compared, negative assessments of electoral candidates are not allowed. These are special regulations MTV3 has put up; the second largest channel (Nelonen) simply applies the regular advertising rules to political advertising as well.

Even if air time can be purchased by parties or candidates, the time period for electoral advertising and the number and length of the broadcasts are often limited. In Mexico, for example, the law prescribes the maximum number of hours of electoral ads in any presidential elections: Ad hours are not to exceed 250 hours on radio and 200 hours on television. This total number of hours is divided proportionately among all presidential candidates according to their party's current percentage in congress. Candidates without any representation in congress receive 4%. Of the remaining number of hours, 30% is distributed evenly to all parties regardless of their percentage in congress and 70% proportionately according to their strength in congress. The same regulation is applied for congressional elections, but advertising time is restricted to 50% of the amount available for presidential elections.

CONCLUSION

This overview of just a sample of 28 countries leaves a mixed picture. The United States stands out, with its complete openness toward political advertising and the great importance that campaigners attach to television ads. The only common characteristic for the other countries is that all have some restrictions. Even where electoral advertising has acquired a major role as a campaign instrument, there are always some limitations. Why electoral advertising is restricted and which limitations apply can in some cases be traced back to influences from the specific political, electoral, or media system. However, even countries with similar contexts differ in their regulation of political advertising.

The same is true for the role television advertising plays in electoral campaigns. In a questionnaire that we used in advance to collect data on the regulation of electoral advertising in the different countries, we also asked our respondents to rate the importance of electoral advertising on television compared to other campaign channels. Ratings were given on a seven-point scale ranging from 1 (not important at all) to 7 (most important). In general, the importance attributed to television ads is rather high in the countries considered here. Compared to other paid media, electoral advertising on television received a mean score of 5.54 (n = 28). However, with a value of 1.66, the standard deviation was quite high. The lowest score (1 = not important at all), for example, was given for Senegal, the highest (7 = most important) for Bulgaria and Mexico. Compared to other campaign channels in general, the overall rating was somewhat lower, reaching 4.81 (n = 28). In this case, the standard deviation was even higher (1.84), thus reflecting the diverse situation of electoral advertising in the countries represented here.

Against the background of this more or less heterogeneous picture, it appears necessary to dig deeper into the history and current situation of political advertising of individual countries. The chapters in this book all follow a similar structure and thus allow for comparison of the development of political advertising across countries. After chapter 2, which provides an overview of the methodologies used to study political advertising, the chapters are organized around the central features of each country or region's use of political advertising. Standing alone in the first section is the United States, the only system in the world wherein all television advertising is provided solely through a private, commercial television system in which time is purchased by candidates and parties, and no time is given free on either commercial or public channels. The second group of chapters discusses the political advertising in countries where the public system of broadcasting provides free time to candidates or parties, but no time can be purchased for political advertising on either public or commercial television. A third grouping of countries represents the dual broadcasting systems in which various combinations of public and private commercial broadcasting can result in candidates and parties both being given free time and purchasing time on a variety of different broadcasting outlets. In the last section, this volume presents review and analysis of how political advertising is evolving in new and developing democracies around the world. A concluding chapter provides some comparisons of research findings on the content and effects of television advertising around the world.

NOTE

1. If not noted otherwise, this overview is based on data provided by the authors of the country chapters in this book. In addition, we thank the following colleagues for information about the situation of electoral TV advertising in their country: Roger Blum (Switzerland), Peter Filzmaier (Austria), Gustavo Martinez Pandiani (Argentina), Fabro Steibel (Brazil), and Stefaan Walgrave (Belgium).

REFERENCES

Blais, A., & Massicotte, L. (2002). Electoral systems. In L. LeDuc, R. G. Niemi, & P. Norris (Eds.), *Comparing democracies. Vol. 2: New challenges in the study of elections and voting* (pp. 40–69). London: Sage.

Dalton, R. J. (2002). *Citizen politics: Public opinion and political parties in advanced democracies* (3rd ed.). New York: Chatham House.

Hallin, D. C., & Mancini, P. (2004). *Comparing media systems: Three models of media and politics.* Cambridge, England: Cambridge University Press.

Holtz-Bacha, C. (2002). The end of old certainties: Changes in the triangle of media, political system, and electorate and their consequences. *Ethical Perspectives, 9,* 222–229.

Kaid, L. L., & Holtz-Bacha (Eds.). (1995). *Political advertising in Western democracies.* Thousand Oaks, CA: Sage.

Nohlen, D. (2000). *Wahlrecht und Parteiensystem* [Electoral law and the party system] (3rd ed.). Opladen, Rhine Province: Leske + Budrich.

Powell, G. B., Jr. (2000). *Elections as instruments of democracy: Majoritarian and proportional visions.* New Haven, CT: Yale University Press.

Roper, J., Holtz-Bacha, C., & Mazzoleni, G. (2004). *The politics of representation. Election campaigning and proportional representation.* New York: Peter Lang.

Swanson, D. L., & Mancini, P. (Eds.). (1996). *Politics, media and modern democracy. An international study of innovations in electoral campaigning and their consequences.* Westport, CT: Praeger.

2

Methodologies for the Study of Political Advertising

ANNE JOHNSTON

Over the past decades, scholars have used a variety of methods to research political advertising. In the individual chapters of this handbook, the authors explore the legal, cultural, political, and communication environments of and the research findings on political advertising in various countries. In this chapter, we turn our attention from what we know about political advertising to how scholars have researched political advertising. This chapter provides a review of some of the methods used in exploring political advertising across the globe, comments on the value of the methods, and offers suggestions for future directions in political advertising research.

Political advertising can include many types of research; therefore, in this chapter, the definition of what counts as political advertising will include those forms of advertising available to candidates, political parties, government entities, and other organizations throughout the world. This will include content, paid for or given as free time, such as political spots, political party broadcasts,

posters, newspaper ads, or, as defined by Kaid and Holtz-Bacha, "any format under the control of the party or candidate and for which time is given or purchased" (Kaid & Holtz-Bacha, 1995, p. 2).

HISTORICAL STUDIES AND OVERVIEWS OF CULTURE AND CONTEXT

Our understanding of political advertising across the globe has been well served by studies providing overviews of the ways in which political advertising has emerged within a particular context and culture. In these studies, the method may be a combination of historical and rhetorical methods, or the study may be more descriptive, outlining how the particular legal, cultural, political, and media or communication environment gave rise to political advertising. In some cases, researchers have used broader concepts of political marketing to discuss the growth of political advertising within a particular country.

Historical studies have laid important groundwork for understanding the role of political advertising in political campaigns, and they have helped scholars understand the evolution of some of the styles and types of ads as well as their functions (Jamieson, 1986, 1996). Researchers have also characterized televised political ads in terms of the communicative functions they perform, placing their functions into discussions about gender, political position, type of ad, and political consulting (Trent & Friedenberg, 1995).

In addition to historical studies of ads, scholars have used exploratory or descriptive methods to connect the political advertising to some broader cultural phenomenon or to identify a context or theory in which to understand the use and influence of advertising. Numerous studies have looked at the style and use of political advertising in various countries to understand the influence of an "American" style of campaigning or a "modernization" of campaign techniques; others have used political marketing as the way in which political advertising is contextualized and understood within a country's legal, economic, political, and media systems (see, for example, Baines, Scheucher, & Plasser, 2001; Dean & Croft, 2001; and chapter 16 in this handbook). Several studies have used product advertising and branding concepts to explore or explain the use of political advertising in a country (see, for example, James & Hensel, 1991; Yen, Coats, & Dalton, 1992).

Other studies have provided overviews of the legal, political, cultural, and communication environments in a country and then described the ads in terms of a variety of characteristics, such as production techniques, settings, themes, and issues mentioned in political broadcasts (see, for example, chapters in Bolivar, 2001; Bowler & Farrell, 1992; Gross et al., 2001; Mazzoleni, 1987; O'Neil & Mills, 1986; Papathanassopoulos, 2000; Swanson & Mancini, 1996). Although there is some discussion of content, the analysis in many of these works is more descriptive than systematic

or more qualitative than quantitative. However, these studies of the cultural, legal, political, and media environment have provided a good foundation for an understanding of the ways in which differences in international communities influence how political advertising develops and forms. For example, by providing a description of some of the video and film techniques used in various campaigns in Europe, Axford and Huggins (2002) examine how political advertising communicates cultural messages. Although the analysis is fairly descriptive, it provides an aesthetic critique of the techniques used in the political ads and how those techniques serve to connect the ads to broader, cultural images and forms. The edited book by Roper, Holtz-Bacha, and Mazzoleni (2004) provides chapters on political advertising strategies and descriptions of some of the global patterns and then discusses how the legal and political contexts necessitate changes in the styles, strategies, and appearance of ads in Germany, New Zealand, Italy, and the United States.

These types of studies have been useful in our understanding of how political advertising fits into particular legal, governmental, cultural, and communication environments. They provide, in many ways, case studies of particular races and campaigns within particular cultures. Because systematic case studies are very important to the understanding, in depth, of some communication event or environment, political advertising research could certainly benefit from more systematically done case studies. Case studies of course provide a way to study a "bounded system . . . over time through detailed, in-depth data collection involving multiple sources of information rich in context" (Creswell, 1998, p. 61). Many of the pieces that have looked at the legal, historical, and cultural environments and then have described or content-analyzed a set of ads could be considered case studies, but future research might build on this initial knowledge of the legal, historical, and cultural environments of a country's political campaigns and look at the ads and their use and role in the campaign. The studies so far have generally done a good job of providing the settings and context of the case, but researchers should consider looking at "multiple sources of information ... [including] observations, interviews, audio-visual material, and documents and reports" (Creswell, 1998, p. 61).

Case studies do exist in political advertising research and have included an analysis of Paul Wellstone's attack ads from his 1990 senate campaign (Pfau, Parrott, & Lindquist, 1992), an analysis of the Canadian Tory Party's advertising in 1993 and the British Labour Party's advertising in 1992 (O'Shaughnessy, 2002), a study of the factors affecting the 1994 Italian elections and the political advertising used (Mazzoleni, 1995), and an in-depth look at U.S. president Eisenhower's first spot campaign (Wood, 1990).

ANALYSIS OF POLITICAL ADVERTISING CONTENT

An important approach in understanding political advertising is analysis of the content of the political poster, advertising, or broadcast. Over the decades and across cultures, contexts, and countries, researchers have tried to uncover the various layers of symbols, styles, appeals, and content in political advertising. Through the use of various methods of looking at content, scholars have been able to document how cultural myths and symbols, how negative and positive appeals, how issue concerns and image characteristics have shaped the nature of what exists in political advertising. Analyses of content have benefited from methods including qualitative content analysis, quantitative content analysis, and critical and rhetorical analyses.

Descriptive and Rhetorical Analysis

Descriptive analyses of political advertising content have typically tried to describe the content in terms of functions they serve or how the content is connected to larger factors and influences in the campaign. Several of these studies have described the content of ads over a course of decades (see, for example, Braund, 1978; Devlin, 1986, 1993, 2001) or from a variety of specific campaigns from Denmark, Finland, the Netherlands, Russia, Belgium, Israel, Australia, and Britain (Acosta & Garcia, 2000; Brants, 1995; Johnson & Elebash, 1986; Leitch & Roper, 1999; Miskin & Grant, 2004; Moring, 1995; Philo, 1993; Siune, 1995; Van den Bulck, 1993; and chapter 18 in this handbook).

Studies using rhetorical analysis have applied a variety of approaches in understanding the content of political ads. For example, rhetorical analysis has been used to study the use of Burke's frames in explaining the images and storylines in U.S. presidential ads (Smith & Johnston, 1991); to identify the rhetorical visions present in the convention acceptance speeches, political ads, campaign posters, and the official political broadcasts during the 1988 presidential elections in France and the United States (Hale, 1991); to analyze political campaign films (Morreale, 1991); to look at the elements of political argumentation present in the television ads featured on Québec television during the 1993 Canadian federal elections (Gauthier, 1994); and to explore the function and rhetorical strategies of political ads over the course of a campaign (Diamond & Bates, 1992). Narrative analysis has been used to study the language and stories present in political advertising (Gronbeck, 1992), and semiotic analysis has provided a way of exploring the meaning of symbols and signs in political advertising. For example, Quéré (1991) looked at posters used during the 1988 French presidential campaign and used semiotics to explore the images, photos, language, slogans, and themes present in the candidates' and parties' posters. Semiotic analysis has also been used to explore ads of major political parties in South African elections (Bertelsen, 1996), to study Dukakis' advertising (Descutner, Burnier, Mickunas, & Letteri, 1991), to understand the hidden myths in the political ads used during a gubernatorial election (Nimmo & Felsberg, 1986), and to analyze Dianne Feinstein's 1990, 1992, and 1994 campaign television advertisements (Sullivan, 1998). In many cases, the overall symbols and structures of the ads are analyzed using rhetorical or semiotic analysis, but in other studies, the researchers have applied more linguistic analysis, looking at sentences and the semantic content of each sentence (not the overall ad) to see the semantic direction (positive, negative, or neutral) of the sentences (for example, de Repentigny, 1999).

Quantitative Content Analysis

Content analysis has been perhaps one of the most popular methods for understanding political ads or broadcasts. As mentioned earlier, sometimes content analysis has been part of a case study approach in looking at the legal, historical, and cultural aspects of a country's political campaigns and then analyzing the ads to understand how those aspects affect the content of ads. Some standard content analyses have included descriptions of issues and image characteristics; the evidence of attacks in ads and the content of negative advertising; the information shortcuts contained in ads; how gender is represented in ads; masculine and feminine styles in ads; the acclaims, attacks, and defenses in ads; the values present in ads; the language and symbols used in the ads; the production components of the ads and the methods of presentation; the narrative elements of the ads; the relation of the content in ads to models of voting or theories of elections; and the intermedia agenda-setting function for ads (Benoit, 2000, 2001; Benoit, Pier, & Blaney, 1997; Boiney & Paletz, 1991; Brazeal & Benoit, 2001; Bystrom, 1996; Dermody & Sullion, 2000; Johnson-Cartee & Copeland, 1991; Johnston & Kaid, 2002; Johnston & White, 1993; Kaid & Johnston, 1991, 2001; Kern, 1989; Lebel, 1999; Lemish & Tidhar, 1999; Lopez-Escobar, Llamas,

McCombs, & Lennon, 1998; Roberts & McCombs, 1994; Romanow, de Repentigny, Cunningham, Soderlund, & Hildebrandt, 1999; Sayre, 1994; Shyles,1986; Stein, 2005; Vavreck, 2001; Wadsworth et al., 1987; Weimann & Wolfsfeld, 2002; West, 2001).

In addition to these and other categories analyzed in content analyses, scholars have dealt with a variety of issues in deciding how to carry out content analyses of political advertising. Several of these issues include the sample of ads used, how the ads are coded and how the content categories are determined, and the comparability of the sample selected between countries and its influence on coding.

Selection of Samples and Categories

In content analyses of political advertising, the samples studied have been fairly diverse. Several studies have used convenience samples (Boiney & Paletz, 1991; Joslyn, 1986; Kern & Edley, 1994), but more have used purposive samples, gathering ads from particular campaigns to study the ads used in a particular election or elections during a particular year (Brazeal & Benoit, 2001; Gronbeck, 1992; Johnston & Gerstlé, 1995; Johnston & White, 1993; Procter, Schenck-Hamlin, & Haase, 1994; Roberts & McCombs, 1994; Tinkham & Weaver-Lariscy, 1995; Trent & Sabourin, 1993; Vavreck, 2001; West, 1994.) Other purposive samples have been chosen to look at issues of gender and have sampled, for example, ads from women candidates who ran for U.S. House, Senate, and gubernatorial seats from 1964 to 1998 (Shames, 2003) or 124 spots from mixed gender Senate and gubernatorial campaigns in 1996 (Robertson, Froemling, Wells, & McCraw, 1999). Purposive samples have also included samples covering several years to look at trends and changes over time (Balloti & Kaid, 2000; Benoit, 2001; Benoit et al., 1997; Brazeal & Benoit, 2001; Johnston & Kaid, 2002; Kaid & Johnston, 1991, 2001; West, 2001) or covering numerous elections in a single year, as in the study by Spiliotes and Vavreck (2002), which analyzed 1000 ads aired by 290 candidates in 153 elections in 37 states during the 1998 U.S. midterm elections.

Researchers have used a variety of methods to collect their samples of ads and have employed several criteria for including or excluding certain ads from the sample. For example, Kern (1989) defined her sample as ads that appeared on air from 6:00 to 9:00 p.m. in four states. Other studies have used samples of ads taped off air (Gunsch, Brownlow, Haynes, & Mabe, 2000) or ads taped off air but during a particular time, such as ads appearing during network newscasts (West, 2001). Some studies have used archival services to provide the sample of ads (Johnston & Kaid, 2002; Kaid & Johnston, 1991). In whatever way the ads are gathered, from archives, consultants, off air, or off the Internet, it is important that researchers explain the criteria for why ads will be included or excluded from their sample. For example, Kaid and Johnston (2001), in their study of presidential advertising from 1952 to 1996, used a political archive to gather their ads and define the boundaries for using the ads as only those ads known to be sanctioned by the candidate or the candidate's election committee. West (2001) studies what he defines as the prominent ads and selects his ads in a variety of ways: either ones that other scholars have identified in their historical studies as important on a variety of criteria or as those aired on a particular news station.

Operationalizing Concepts, Defining Variables, and Coding Categories

Most content analyses of political advertising have clearly defined, at least for their particular study, how a concept would be measured. Also, there have been numerous ways that the topics in political advertising have been operationalized. For example, what

count as issues and images in political advertising has varied in the studies on political advertising across the globe. How and what to code to get at issues and images have also varied. Sometimes researchers have been interested in the frequency of issue mentions in an ad, as well as how often the ad appears. For example, Romanow (1999), in his study of ads appearing on English-language TV during the 1993 Canadian federal elections, noted the "telecast occasions" of ads or how often ads were broadcast. In addition, he noted how many times an issue was mentioned in an ad and coded those as "issue citations." Scammell and Semetko (1995) looked at the total number of seconds that issues were discussed and the percent of time they occupied in the party election broadcasts (PEBs) during the 1992 British general elections.

The debate on what counts as an issue ad or an image ad affects both content analysis and experimental research. Defining what is meant by a negative ad has also been an issue for researchers doing content analyses of political advertising. Several studies have argued that the operationalization of negative advertising is problematic. For example, Richardson (2001) presented a critical review of the academic work on negativity in political advertising, arguing that the definitions have been too broad and too holistic. There have been some studies that have attempted to separate out what makes an image ad versus an issue ad or positive ad versus a negative one by looking at large samples to find commonalities (for example, see Kaid & Johnston, 1991; Johnston & Kaid, 2002). Johnson-Cartee and Copeland (1991) operationalize negative advertising as a type of short story and analyze more than 1000 ads based on what is said in the ads (substance and underlying themes) and how it is said (presentation style or plot).

Early studies of televised political advertising content tended to be interested in verbal content categories or what was being said in the ads. Later studies began to integrate not only what was being said but also how it was said. One of these methods, which has been used over the course of 20 years of political advertising research and in a variety of countries, is "videostyle." Researchers using videostyle code for the verbal content, the nonverbal content, and the film or video production techniques of political ads. First outlined by Kaid and Davidson (1986) in a study of senatorial ads, the approach has been used over the years to look at the style of candidates in their ads and to look at how context, culture, and political position influence the style components a candidate might use in his or her ads. The method has been applied to ads or broadcasts used in a variety of countries, including Germany (Holtz-Bacha & Kaid, 1995) and Italy (Mazzoleni & Roper, 1995) as well as others discussed in the chapters in this volume. (For a complete discussion of the method and theory and for a review of studies using videostyle, see Kaid & Johnston, 2001.)

Research using videostyle has also evolved in accordance with the countries being studied, and researchers have made modifications to the videostyle coding design based on the unique attributes of the political ads or broadcasts being studied. For example, chapter 12 in this handbook looks at the content of the Greek polispots using videostyle but combines this discussion with an analysis of models of voting and frames in the spots. Studies of German spots have modified the videostyle instrument and adapted it to German elections because of the unique characteristics of German spots (chapter 10 in this handbook; see also Holtz-Bacha & Kaid, 1995).

There have been several content studies that have been truly comparative, looking at two or more countries to see what differences or similarities exist in the content of political broadcasts and ads (see, for example, Johnston, 1991; Kaid & Holtz-Bacha, 1995; Tak, Kaid, & Lee, 1997). The strength of these studies has been the researchers' ability to incorporate the differences in the approaches, theories, and cultures

of the countries to compare and analyze the ads. For example, Tak et al. (1997) look at the form and content of political ads in major daily newspapers in South Korea and the United States, as well as at the TV political commercials, during the 1992 elections in both countries. A comparison of spots used in Israel and the United States in the 1992 campaigns highlights the differences in visual imagery (Griffin & Kagan, 1996). In comparing ads in different countries, the way in which to analyze the ads is one issue, but how to sample is another issue. Researchers have tried to make the samples equivalent, not necessarily equal (Tak et al., 1997).

In other studies, available content analysis data in the form of studies from different countries are compared on various dimensions. Carlson (2001) reports the results of a secondary comparative analysis of male/female legislative candidates in the United States and Finland. Data were collected for single country studies (one in the United States and one in Finland) and then the author compared the two studies, discussing in detail how comparable the two content analyses are. Using available data from other studies, Plasser and Plasser (2002) compared videostyle studies from a variety of countries to make comparisons about how styles in ads are different across countries.

Although ways of operationalizing the content categories have been suggested by past research or writing about issues in political advertising, experts have also been used to help researchers decide how to code ads. Several studies have asked panels of experts to help formulate the content categories or to help interpret the categories. For example, Sayre (1994) asked scholars, media experts, and party officials in Hungary to help in the interpretive analysis of visual images used in the political ads. Other researchers have used Delphi panels to help determine themes and patterns in smaller samples of ads to help in future coding (Kern, 1989; Shyles, 1986).

Many content analyses in political advertising have used at least two coders and report an intercoder reliability. In some cases, coders must agree before a category is marked. For example, Lemish and Tidhar (1999) used two trained coders and a consensus coding model in which coders had to talk and agree before only one entry was recorded for each variable. Garramone, Steele, and Pinkleton (1991) also had disagreements between two coders resolved by a third coder in a content analysis of responses to ads. Although most content analyses in political advertising have used human coders, there have been several studies using computerized content analysis to look at language, verbal style, linguistic dimensions, and policy information in ads (Ballotti & Kaid, 2000; Gunsch et al., 2000; Hansen & Benoit, 2002).

Although there have been a variety of techniques and methods used to analyze content, the application of theory to the analysis has been sporadic. It should be noted that research on theory used in content analysis studies in mass communication shows that most of these types of studies lack a theoretical framework (Riffe, Lacy, & Fico, 2005). Political advertising content analyses that use theory or models include those that have connected the content in ads to theories or models of voting or approaches to elections (Boiney & Paletz, 1991; Joslyn, 1986), to gender systematic analysis and theories of gender portrayal and meaning (Lemish & Tidhar, 1999; Shames, 2003), to priming or functional analysis (Benoit, 2000, 2001; Benoit et al., 1997; West, 2001), and to philosophical or cultural theory and differences in comparing content from two cultures (Tak et al., 1997).

Other studies have used approaches that combine theories of communication, politics, or film theory to analyze the content of the ads. One of the ways in which both the quantitative and qualitative content analyses would benefit would be a more systematic discussion of the theoretical elements guiding the research. There are actually now a variety of studies, in a variety of countries, that have

looked at videostyle, for example. Because videostyle is an approach to understanding the languages of political ads, it may now be beneficial for research to step back and look at how the body of research in this area has helped define the stylistic components of ads and determine whether the approach has any predictive or explanatory value. In their book, Kaid and Johnston (2001) set out the major elements of videostyle and how these elements have translated into a presidential style over time and within particular contexts of campaigns and political position. Future studies of videostyle across culture and time could build the theoretical groundwork of videostyle and comment explicitly on what the studies add to our conceptual thinking about that approach.

STUDYING THE EFFECTS OF POLITICAL ADVERTISING

Experiments on the effects of political advertising have provided a wealth of information about what influence political ads have on the public. The topics studied in experimental research in political advertising have included the interrelationships of audience motivation, commercial type, and information processing on candidate image formation (Garramone, 1986); influence of information processing and candidate characteristics (Garramone et al., 1991); the influence of attitudes toward political advertising on information processing of TV political ads (Christ, Thorson, & Caywood, 1994); how adwatches influence the effects of ads (Pfau & Louden, 1994); influence of ads on persuasion, information retention, and issue salience (Groenendyk & Valentino, 2002); reception of political spots and changes in candidate images (Holtz-Bacha & Kaid, 1995; Kaid & Holtz-Bacha, 1993); what is learned from ads and how emotion and structure influence memory of both audio and visual information (Lang, 1991); the priming effects of ads compared to news stories (Schleuder, McCombs, & Wanta, 1991); information seeking (Kaid, 2002); influence on vote and evaluation of candidates (Chang, 2003); moderating effect of attitudinal bond or relationship between voter and candidate to predict how voter will process and respond to a persuasive message (Alwitt, Deighton, & Grimm, 1991); comparing the processing of political commercials to brand commercials, looking at attitudinal responses, not memorial responses (Thorson, Christ, & Caywood, 1991b); the impact of issue and image content in political advertising and the interaction of that content with the audio and visual components of television on memory (Geiger & Reeves, 1991); influence of negative advertising on the political process (Garramone, Atkin, Pinkleton, & Cole, 1990); inoculation from negative advertising, boomerang effects, and black sheep effects of negative advertising (King & McConnell, 2003; Matthews & Dietz-Uhler, 1998; Pfau & Kenski, 1990; Pfau, Park, Holbert, & Cho, 2001; Shen & Wu, 2002); how female voters process ads and how ads using male and female styles are processed (Chang & Hitchon, 2004; Wadsworth et al., 1987); comparisons across six countries of the effects on images of candidates of emotional reactions to political advertising (Kaid & Holtz-Bacha, 1995); and effects of technological distortions in ads (Kaid, 2001; Noggle & Kaid, 2000). (See chapters in this volume for a more explicit discussion of effects findings from individual countries.)

Although most of the experiments have been set in the laboratory and have measured short-term effects, some have been field experiments (e.g., Cappella & Jamieson, 1994) and have looked at delayed effects of ads over repeated exposures (e.g., King & McConnell, 2003).

Factors in Experimental Design

Developing Stimulus Materials

One of the questions for studies trying to understand the effects of advertising has been what ads to use as stimuli and how to gather the ads for the experiment. The question facing researchers in many cases is whether to use actual ads from campaigns and pretest them in some way to determine the validity of what they are measuring; to construct ads and be able to include various dimensions of the independent variable; or to include some combination of these, using real ads from campaigns but manipulating and editing them to incorporate other dimensions. For example, Chang (2003), in his study of newspaper ads, took ads from real campaigns but created and manipulated the content to which the subjects were exposed. Cundy (1986) created a script for an ad that was then read by a professional radio announcer. For studies researching broadcast ads, digital video and editing and the ability to download ads from Web sites have generally made manipulating ad content much easier. Studies that have produced ads or manipulated the content of actual ads for the experiment include Ansolabehere, Iyengar, Simon, and Valentino (1994); Thorson, Christ, and Caywood (1991a); Valentino, Hutchings, and Williams (2004); and Wadsworth et al. (1987).

A critical issue in studying the effects of political ads is defining and operationalizing the variables. Several experiments have used formal content analysis first to define the ads (Lang, 1991; Noggle & Kaid, 2000; Schenck-Hamlin, Procter, & Rumsey, 2000), textual analysis to identify the "textual oppositions" present in political ads (Cronkhite, Liska, & Schrader, 1991), or experts or judges to determine the content of ads before they are used in experiments (Geiger & Reeves, 1991).

Some researchers have used detailed procedures to first ascertain how subjects are interpreting ads by coding responses to ads. In Garramone et al. (1991), subjects were given 3 minutes to list their thoughts about ads they were shown. Trained coders then coded these thoughts into image or issue thoughts. If a subject's thoughts were dominant in one category or the other, that subject was identified as an image processor or issue processor. Then the same subject was shown made-up ads to see how his or her processing style interacted with the attractiveness of the candidate (with a panel of judges also used here to determine attractiveness) in his or her evaluation of the candidates and vote likelihood.

Subjects

As in most studies in mass communication, student populations dominate the subject pools in political advertising studies. Several studies have combined student and nonstudent samples (Chang, 2003; Kaid, Chanslor, & Hovind, 1992). Some researchers have used members of churches, clubs, or community groups or random adult nonstudent groups (Basil, Schooler, & Reeves, 1991; Cundy, 1986; Geiger & Reeves, 1991; Newhagen & Reeves, 1991; Schleuder et al., 1991; Valentino et al., 2004). Other studies have used likely or eligible voters (Ansolabehere et al., 1994; Clinton & Lapinski, 2004; Pfau & Kenski, 1990) or subgroups of voters. For example, Alwitt et al. (1991) used only female voters. The debate about using student versus nonstudent populations in general can be applied to studies of political advertising effects. Lau, Sigelman, Heldman, and Babbitt (1999) found in their meta-analysis that there were no major differences attributable to student subjects versus adult samples, but other analyses have shown that subjects can be a moderating variable in terms of effects and effect sizes from political advertising studies (Benoit, Leshner, & Chattopadhyay, 2005).

Measuring Effects

Typically a pen and paper questionnaire is used to ascertain feelings, attitudes, or information about ads. Several studies have used continuous measurement techniques, through which participants respond to ads using handheld dials linked to computers (Newhagen &

Reeves, 1991; Tedesco, 2002), or have used computer-assisted self-interviewing software (Valentino et al., 2004). Several studies have used the thought-listing approach or the cognitive response tradition, in which subjects are asked to list their thoughts and responses to ads that researchers then put into categories (Meirick, 2002; Pinkleton, Um, & Austin, 2002; Schenck-Hamlin et al., 2000). In some cases, researchers have looked at memory, recognition, and influence from ads by looking separately at the audio content and the visual content of broadcast ads (Geiger & Reeves, 1991; Newhagen & Reeves, 1991; Thorson et al., 1991a) or have looked at visual literacy effects by testing this in a video rather than a written format (Noggle & Kaid, 2000).

Some studies of information processing of ads have used elaborate study designs to test the influence of ads on different types of processors. Garramone et al. (1991) used a two-part study to first content-analyze subjects' cognitive responses to a series of televised ads into image or issue processing. They then exposed the subjects to ads to see how their processing style influenced their evaluations of candidates. Subjects have also sometimes been divided into study cells based on motivations provided by the researcher for watching the ads (Garramone, 1983) or based on context issues during a campaign (Mazzoleni & Roper, 1995). Mazzoleni and Roper (1995) divided their subjects into groups to deal with scandals that had been a part of the 1992 Italian elections. In this case, they divided their subjects into two groups, with one cell instructed to think back to political circumstances surrounding the period.

Embedding Ads Into Other Content

One concern in experimental studies is the setting of the experiment and how the ads are viewed. In several studies, researchers have attempted to naturalize the setting by having the participants view the ads in smaller groups, around a table simulating a living-room experience (Geiger & Reeves, 1991; Lang, 1991; Thorson et al., 1991b). One of the ways in which researchers have tried to naturalize the exposure to ads has been to embed the ads into news programs or content, entertainment programs or content, or filler and consumer ads (Meirick, 2002; Pfau et al., 2001; Valentino et al., 2004).

Although the embedding of political ads into other content is a good way of naturalizing the exposure to the ads, most of the studies have not tested for the effects or influence of the context materials. Although it makes sense to include political ads among other materials in an experiment, it does not make sense to assume that the surrounding material is somehow neutral and will not influence the response to the political ads. Several studies have explicitly looked at the influence of the surrounding material or have asked subjects about their response to the context or surrounding material (Basil et al., 1991; Chang, 2003; Geiger & Reeves, 1991; Kaid, Chanslor, et al., 1992; Schleuder et al., 1991). Looking at how surrounding material influences the response to political ads is a very important way to understand the effects of political ads. Studies should continue to explore the differing effects of content on a variety of types of ads (such as issue and image ads or negative and positive ads) in a variety of media settings (broadcast, print, the Internet). In studies that do embed ads simply to naturalize the exposure, researchers should include questions about the surrounding material simply to lessen the participants' awareness that they are being asked about only the political ads or to give the researchers a way of checking the neutrality of the surrounding content.

Meta-analyses of Effects

Several meta-analyses exist of political advertising effects. For example, Lau et al. (1999) provide a meta-analysis of the effects of negative political advertising. Meta-analyses are valuable in any discipline as a way of quantitatively evaluating and combining findings from several studies (Rosenthal & DiMatteo, 2001). There are a couple of issues that are particularly important to consider when doing meta-analyses of political advertising effects.

One important issue that is mentioned in reviews of this method is the need to look carefully at how the variables in the studies are operationalized and measured. Therefore, meta-analyses of political advertising effects should ask: How are the studies similar or different in how they operationalized the concepts? How did the individual studies measure the dependent variables? As the previous discussion of how effects might be measured in political advertising indicates, we need to be cautious in how we group effect studies, depending on how the content of the ads or the stimuli is determined or operationalized and how the effects, whatever they might be, are measured. In good meta-analyses, these things are comparable.

Most meta-analyses deal with published studies, and this is one of the biggest criticisms of existing meta-analyses (Rosenthal & DiMatteo, 2001). The question that is frequently asked here is, how does one account for the bias in a meta-analysis of reviewing only those studies that have been published and not being able to account for those that have not been published? Do we assume that the published ones are the best? Do we assume that the unpublished ones are the ones with smaller effects or no significant effects (Rosenthal & DiMatteo, 2001)? There are solutions offered for this dilemma (Rosenthal & DiMatteo, 2001), but the important aspect for meta-analyses done on political advertising effects is to acknowledge this issue within the study. The Lau et al. (1999) study of the effects of negative political advertising tried to find the unpublished studies as well as the published studies for their meta-analysis.

UNDERSTANDING THE USES
OF ADS AND SURVEY RESEARCH

Survey research has been an important method for understanding how voters globally use, remember, and interpret information and images in political ads. Survey research has helped scholars understand the general impact of advertising and other media sources during campaigns, understand the effects of negative advertising, measure reactions to negative advertising over time, explore general attitudes toward or information-seeking behavior inspired by political broadcasts or advertising, test whether misleading claims in ads worked, measure learning from ads, and measure believability and value of political advertising and recall of advertising (Faber, Tims, & Schmitt, 1993; Freedman & Goldstein, 1999; Jasperson & Fan, 2002; Marks, 1993; Moring, 1995; O'Cass, 2002; Ohr & Schrott, 2001; Pattie & Johnston, 2002; Siune, 1995; Winneg, Kenski, & Jamieson, 2005; Zhao & Bleske, 1995; Zhao & Chaffee, 1995). Use of available data, typically from the American National Election Survey, has helped in our understanding of recall of ads, effects of ads on vote choice, effects of ads on issue knowledge and salience, and effects of negative advertising on turnout (Ansolabehere, Iyengar, & Simon, 1999; Brians & Wattenberg, 1996; Finkel & Geer, 1998; Goldstein & Freedman, 2000, 2002; Gwiasda, 2001; Holbert, Benoit, Hansen, & Wen, 2002; Kahn & Kenney, 1999). Chapters in this handbook offer other examples of surveys in a variety of settings and countries.

Surveys have also been used to test assumptions about theories, particularly about uses and gratifications and rational choice as they apply to political advertising (Cohen & Wolfsfeld, 1995; Ohr & Schrott, 2001), or to further explore conceptual dimensions of types of political ads. For example, Sigelman and Kugler (2003) looked at data from three gubernatorial campaigns to measure how voters define and interpret "negativity" in political ads.

Although most survey research in political advertising has included adults in the general public or likely voters as the sample, scholars have been interested in understanding professionals' attitudes and opinions about political advertising. Plasser and Plasser (2002) provide a survey of political consultants in the United States, Latin America, Western and Mediterranean Europe, East Central Europe, and other areas to understand the experience and attitudes of political consultants in these areas. (See also Perloff & Kinsey, 1992, for a survey of consultants.) Other samples surveyed in a variety of countries about their opinions on, use of, or reactions to political advertising include children (Rahn & Hirshorn, 1999), journalists (Perloff & Kinsey, 1992), newspaper ad directors (Fletcher, Ross, & Schwietzer, 2002; Ross, Fletcher & Schwietzer, 1994), advertising agency executives (Waller, 2002; Waller & Polonsky, 1996), and politicians (Waller, 2002; Weaver-Lariscy & Tinkham, 1987).

Survey research has also been combined with content analysis in several studies to explore the use and influence of negative advertising or advertising and public policy issues (see, for example, Finkel & Geer, 1998; Gwiasda, 2001; Hansen & Benoit, 2002; West, 1994, 2001) or in conjunction with experimental studies to see how subjects primed by viewing political information might differ from subjects surveyed during the same time (Schleuder et al., 1991).

Most assessments of audiences have used traditional survey research; however, there have been other methods used in studying audiences of political advertising. For example, Mansfield and Hale (1986) used Q analysis to examine the subjective viewpoint of varied audience members about political advertising. Other studies using qualitative approaches have included "participatory action research," used in a study of college students, urban communities, and political party strategists during the 1993 Canadian federal elections (Romanow et al., 1999), and a focus group approach to understand voters' ethical perceptions of political advertising (Kates, 1998).

Qualitative audience studies have provided valuable insights into the ways in which voters (viewers or readers) may process and interpret political advertising. Approaches such as participatory action research allow the researcher to interview, in depth, audiences or professionals without the structure of a survey. As Romanow et al. (1999) explain, there is a lot of care taken in this approach to prevent the researcher's bias from controlling the interview or the answers. In this type of design, research participants are encouraged to associate themselves with the study and to help the researcher interpret the responses.

A similar approach that researchers might find fruitful in doing qualitative research in political advertising would be the long interview method and the grounded theory approach. A grounded theory approach allows for the construction of a "theory closely related to the phenomenon being studied." "The researcher collects primarily interview data, makes multiple visits to the field, develops and interrelates categories of information, and writes theoretical propositions or hypotheses or presents a visual picture of the theory" (Creswell, 1998, p. 56). The long interview, as part of a grounded theory approach, is a method that can help the researcher understand how culture and context may mediate human action (McCracken, 1988). In the field of political advertising, grounded theory and the long interview might prove fruitful in, for example, a study of women politicians to understand how they process, interpret, and use political advertising. Studies of gender differences in the styles and strategies in political advertising content have provided a good foundation for this type of research. A grounded theory study of female politicians might reveal how the female candidates themselves are interpreting and understanding their use of political advertising.

SUMMARY AND CONCLUSION

Globally, political advertising research has been enriched by the variety of methods used by scholars to understand the content, use, and effects of this type of political communication. The historical and legal studies have enabled us to acknowledge and understand the important foundation for the rise and development of political advertising within the context and climate of political, social, and cultural dimensions of the various countries studied. True case studies could be developed even more systematically in this area, to understand a particular election and the use of ads in that election from a variety of information sources. Content analysis has provided details about what form political advertising, broadcasts, and posters might take in terms of the languages available to the medium in which the content appears. Content analysis has also given us some ways of measuring the same variables across time and across cultures, proving that different contexts and cultures require that researchers refine the ways in which they operationalize or categorize variables. Content analysis studies, particularly those using similar approaches or theories, would benefit from increased attention to comparisons across culture, time, and circumstance. Experimental research has also shown that political advertising does affect our reaction to candidates, our vision of our role in our political system, and our attitudes toward the system. Experimental research is continuing to explore new areas: Studies with promise include those looking at the context of how we experience the ads and the content surrounding those ads. Finally, analyses of audience reception and reaction have used methods ranging from survey research to more interpretive analyses to help us understand political advertising's role in our processing of campaign communication. Survey research will continue to refine and help us explore voters', viewers', and readers' reactions to political advertising, but we would also benefit from research that allows not only a breadth of information, as surveys do, but also a depth of information about the interpretive processes of the public or of the political actors using and exposed to political advertising.

REFERENCES

Acosta, M., & García, V. (2000, September-October). La publicidad política por televisión en las elecciones del año 2000 en México [Political advertising on television in the 2000 elections in Mexico]. *Revista Mexicana de Comunicación, 65*, 7–11.

Alwitt, L. F., Deighton, J., & Grimm, J. (1991). Reactions to political advertising depend on the nature of the voter-candidate bond. In F. Biocca (Ed.), *Television and political advertising. Vol. 1. Psychological processes* (pp. 329–350). Hillsdale, NJ: Erlbaum.

Ansolabehere, S., Iyengar, S., & Simon, A. (1999). Replicating experiments using aggregate and survey data: The case of negative advertising and turnout. *American Political Science Review, 93*, 901–909.

Ansolabehere, S., Iyengar, S., Simon, A., & Valentino, N. (1994). Does attack advertising demobilize the electorate? *American Political Science Review, 88*, 829–838.

Axford, B., & Huggins, R. (2002). Political marketing and the aestheticisation of politics: Modern politics and postmodern trends. In N. J. O'Shaughnessy & S.C.M. Henneberg (Eds.), *The idea of political marketing* (pp. 187–207). Westport, CT: Praeger.

Baines, P. R., Scheucher, C., & Plasser, F. (2001). The "Americanisation" myth in European political markets: A focus on the United Kingdom. *European Journal of Marketing, 35*, 1099–1116.

Ballotti, J., & Kaid, L. L. (2000). Examining verbal style in presidential campaign spots. *Communication Studies, 51*, 258–273.

Basil, M., Schooler, C., & Reeves, B. (1991). Positive and negative political advertising: Effectiveness of ads and perceptions of candidates. In F. Biocca (Ed.), *Television and political advertising. Vol. 1. Psychological processes* (pp. 245–262). Hillsdale, NJ: Erlbaum.

Benoit, W. L. (2000). A functional analysis of political advertising across media, 1998. *Communication Studies, 51*, 274–295.

Benoit, W. L. (2001). The functional approach to presidential television spots: Acclaiming, attacking, defending: 1952-2000. *Communication Studies, 52*, 109–126.

Benoit, W. L., Leshner, G., & Chattopadhyay, S. (2005, May). *A meta-analysis of political advertising.* Paper presented at the International Communication Association Conference, New York.

Benoit, W. L., Pier, P. M., & Blaney, J. R. (1997). A functional approach to televised political spots: Acclaiming, attacking, defending. *Communication Quarterly, 45*, 1–20.

Bertelsen, E. (1996). Selling change: Advertisements for the 1994 South African election. *African Affairs, 95*, 225–252.

Boiney, J., & Paletz, D. L. (1991). In search of the model model: Political science versus political advertising perspectives on voter decision making. In F. Biocca (Ed.), *Television and political advertising. Vol. 1. Psychological processes* (pp. 3–26). Hillsdale, NJ: Lawrence Erlbaum Associates, Publishers.

Bolivar, A. (2001). Changes in Venezuelan political dialogue: The role of advertising during electoral campaigns. *Discourse & Society, 12*, 23–43.

Bowler, S., & Farrell, D. M. (1992). *Electoral strategies and political marketing.* New York: St. Martin's Press.

Brants, K. (1995). The blank spot: Political advertising in the Netherlands. In L. L. Kaid & C. Holtz-Bacha (Eds.), *Political advertising in western democracies: Parties and candidates on television* (pp. 143–160). Thousand Oaks, CA: Sage.

Braund, V. (1978). *Themes in political advertising: Australian federal election campaigns 1949-1972.* Unpublished master's thesis, Department of Government, University of Sydney, Australia.

Brazeal, L. M., & Benoit, W. L. (2001). A functional analysis of congressional television spots, 1986-2000. *Communication Quarterly, 49*, 436–454.

Brians, C. L., & Wattenberg, M. P. (1996). Campaign issue knowledge and salience: Comparing reception from TV commercials, TV news, and newspapers. *American Journal of Political Science, 40*, 172–193.

Bystrom, D. G. (1996). Candidate gender and the presentation of self: The videostyles of men and women in U.S. senate campaigns. *Political Communication, 13*, 487–489.

Cappella, J. N., & Jamieson, K. H. (1994). Broadcast adwatch effects: A field experiment. *Communication Research, 21*, 342–365.

Carlson, T. (2001). Gender and political advertising across culture: A comparison of male and female political advertising in Finland and the U.S. *European Journal of Communication, 16,* 131–154.

Chang, C. (2003). Party bias in political-advertising processing: Results from an experiment involving the 1998 Taipei mayoral election. *Journal of Advertising, 32,* 55–67.

Chang, C., & Hitchon, J.C.B. (2004). When does gender count? Further insights into gender schematic processing of female candidates' political advertisements. *Sex Roles: A Journal of Research, 51,* 197–208.

Christ, W. G., Thorson, E., & Caywood, C. (1994). Do attitudes toward political advertising affect information processing of televised political commercials? *Journal of Broadcasting & Electronic Media, 38,* 251–270.

Clinton, J. D., & Lapinski, J. S. (2004). "Targeted" advertising and voter turnout: An experimental study of the 2000 presidential election. *Journal of Politics, 66,* 69–96.

Cohen, A., & Wolfsfeld, G. (1995). Overcoming adversity and diversity: The utility of television political advertising in Israel. In L. L. Kaid & C. Holtz-Bacha (Eds.), *Political advertising in Western democracies: Parties and candidates on television* (pp. 109–124). Thousand Oaks, CA: Sage.

Creswell, J. W. (1998). *Qualitative inquiry and research design: Choosing among five traditions.* Thousand Oaks, CA: Sage.

Cronkhite, G., Liska, J., & Schrader, D. (1991). Toward an integration of textual and response analysis applied to the 1988 presidential campaign. In F. Biocca (Ed.), *Television and political advertising. Vol. 2. Signs, codes, and images* (pp. 163–184). Hillsdale, NJ: Erlbaum.

Cundy, D. (1986). Political commercials and candidate image: The effect can be substantial. In L. L. Kaid, D. Nimmo, & K. R. Sanders (Eds.), *New perspectives on political advertising* (pp. 210-234). Carbondale: Southern Illinois University Press.

Dean, D., & Croft, R. (2001). Friends and relations: Long-term approaches to political campaigning. *European Journal of Marketing, 35,* 1197–1216.

de Repentigny, M. (1999). Political ads on Quebec TV during the 1993 federal election. In W. I. Romanow, M. de Repentigny, S. B. Cunningham, W. C. Soderlund, & K. Hildebrandt (Eds.), *Television advertising in Canadian elections: The attack mode, 1993*

(pp. 75–97). Waterloo, ON: Wilfrid Laurier University Press.

Dermody, J., & Sullion, R. (2000). Perceptions of negative political advertising: Meaningful or menacing? An empirical study of the 1997 British general election campaign. *International Journal of Advertising, 19,* 202–202.

Descutner, D., Burnier, D., Mickunas, A., & Letteri, R. (1991). Bad signs and cryptic codes in a postmodern world: A semiotic analysis of the Dukakis advertising. In F. Biocca (Ed.), *Television and political advertising. Vol. 2. Signs, codes, and images* (pp. 93–114). Hillsdale, NJ: Erlbaum.

Devlin, L. P. (1986). An analysis of presidential television commercials, 1952-1984. In L. L. Kaid, D. Nimmo, & K. R. Sanders (Eds.), *New perspectives on political advertising* (pp. 21–54). Carbondale: Southern Illinois University Press.

Devlin, L. P. (1993). Contrasts in presidential campaign commercials of 1992. *American Behavioral Scientist, 37,* 272–290.

Devlin, L. P. (2001). Contrasts in presidential campaign commercials of 2000. *American Behavioral Scientist, 44,* 23–38.

Diamond, S., & Bates, E. (1992). *The spot: The rise of political advertising on television* (3rd ed.). Cambridge: MIT Press.

Faber, R. J., Tims, A. R., & Schmitt, K. G. (1993). Negative political advertising and voting intent: The role of involvement and alternative information sources. *Journal of Advertising, 22,* 67–76.

Finkel, S. E., & Geer, J. G. (1998). A spot check: Casting doubt on the demobilizing effect of attack advertising. *American Journal of Political Science, 42,* 573–595.

Fletcher, A. D., Ross, B. I., & Schweitzer, J. C. (2002). Newspaper ad directors see political ads as less honest. *Newspaper Research Journal, 23,* 50–58.

Freedman, P., & Goldstein, K. (1999). Measuring media exposure and the effects of negative campaign ads. *American Journal of Political Science, 43,* 1189–1208.

Garramone, G. (1983). Issue versus image orientation and effects of political advertising. *Communication Research, 10,* 59–76.

Garramone, G. (1986). Candidate image formation: The role of information processing. In L. L. Kaid, D. Nimmo, & K. R. Sanders (Eds.), *New perspectives on political advertising* (pp. 235–247). Carbondale: Southern Illinois University Press.

Garramone, G., Atkin, C. K., Pinkleton, B. E., & Cole, R. T. (1990). Effects of negative political advertising on the political process. *Journal of Broadcasting & Electronic Media, 34,* 299–311.

Garramone, G. M., Steele, M. E, & Pinkleton, B. (1991). The role of cognitive schemata in determining candidate characteristic effects. In F. Biocca (Ed.), *Television and political advertising. Vol. 1. Psychological processes* (pp. 311–328). Hillsdale, NJ: Erlbaum.

Gauthier, G. (1994). Referential argumentation and its ethical considerations in televised political advertising: The case of the 1993 Canadian federal election campaign. *Argumentation and Advocacy, 31,* 96–110.

Geiger, S. F., & Reeves, B. (1991). The effects of visual structure and content emphasis on the evaluation and memory for political candidates. In F. Biocca (Ed.), *Television and political advertising. Volume 1. Psychological processes* (pp. 125–144). Hillsdale, NJ: Erlbaum.

Goldstein, K., & Freedman, P. (2000). New evidence for new arguments: Money and advertising in the 1996 Senate elections. *Journal of Politics, 62,* 1087–1108.

Goldstein, K., & Freedman, P. (2002). Campaign advertising and voter turnout: New evidence for a stimulation effect. *Journal of Politics, 64,* 721–740.

Griffin, M., & Kagan, S. (1996). Picturing culture in political spots: 1992 campaigns in Israel and the United States. *Political Communication, 13,* 43–61.

Groenendyk, E. W., & Valentino, N. A. (2002). Of dark clouds and silver linings: Effects of exposure to issue versus candidate advertising on persuasion, information retention, and issue salience. *Communication Research, 29,* 295–319.

Gronbeck, B. E. (1992). Negative narratives in 1988 presidential campaign ads. *Quarterly Journal of Speech, 78,* 333–346.

Gross, A. L., Gallo, T., Payne, J. G., Tsai, T., Wang, Y. C., Chang, C. C., et al. (2001). Issues, images, and strategies in 2000 international elections: Spain, Taiwan, and the Russian Federation. *American Behavioral Scientist, 44,* 2410–2438.

Gunsch, M. A., Brownlow, S., Haynes, S. E., & Mabe, Z. (2000). Differential linguistic content of various forms of political advertising. *Journal of Broadcasting & Electronic Media, 44,* 27–42.

Gwiasda, G. W. (2001). Network news coverage of campaign advertisements: Media's ability to reinforce campaign messages. *American Politics Research, 29,* 461–482.

Hale, K. (1991). The spinning of the tale: Candidate and media orchestrations in the French and U.S. presidential elections. In L. L. Kaid, J. Gerstlé, & K. R. Sanders (Eds.), *Mediated politics in two cultures: A comparative analysis of presidential campaigning in the United States and France* (pp. 195–210). New York: Praeger.

Hansen, G. J., & Benoit, W. L. (2002). Presidential television advertising and public policy priorities, 1952-2000. *Communication Studies, 53,* 284–297.

Holbert, R. L., Benoit, W. L., Hansen, G. J., & Wen, W. (2002). The role of communication in the formation of an issue-based citizenry. *Communication Monographs, 69,* 296–310.

Holtz-Bacha, C., & Kaid, L. L. (1995). Television spots in German national elections: Content and effects. In L. L. Kaid & C. Holtz-Bacha (Eds.), *Political advertising in western democracies: Parties and candidates on television* (pp. 61–88). Thousand Oaks, CA: Sage.

James, K. E., & Hensel, P. J. (1991). Negative advertising: The malicious strain of comparative advertising. *Journal of Advertising, 20,* 53–69.

Jamieson, K. H. (1986). The evolution of political advertising in America. In L. L. Kaid, D. Nimmo, & K. R. Sanders (Eds.), *New perspectives on political advertising* (pp. 1–20). Carbondale: Southern Illinois University Press.

Jamieson, K. H. (1996). *Packaging the presidency: A history and criticism of presidential advertising* (3rd ed.). New York: Oxford University Press.

Jasperson, A. E., & Fan, D. P. (2002). An aggregate examination of the backlash effect in political advertising: The case of the 1996 U.S. senate race in Minnesota. *Journal of Advertising, 31,* 1–12.

Johnson, K. S., & Elebash, C. (1986). The contagion from the Right: The Americanization of British political advertising. In L. L. Kaid, D. Nimmo, & K. R. Sanders (Eds.), *New perspectives on political advertising* (pp. 293–313). Carbondale: Southern Illinois University Press.

Johnson-Cartee, K. S., & Copeland, G. A. (1991). *Negative political advertising: Coming of age.* Hillsdale, NJ: Erlbaum.

Johnston, A. (1991). Political broadcasts: An analysis of form, content, and style in presidential communication. In L. L. Kaid, J. Gerstlé, &

K. R. Sanders (Eds.), *Mediated politics in two cultures: A comparative analysis of presidential campaigning in the United States and France* (pp. 59–72). New York: Praeger.

Johnston, A. & Gerstlé, J. (1995). The role of television broadcasts in promoting French presidential candidates. In L. L. Kaid & C. Holtz-Bacha (Eds.), *Political advertising in western democracies: Parties and candidates on television* (pp. 44–60). Thousand Oaks, CA: Sage.

Johnston, A., & Kaid, L. L. (2002). Image ads and issue ads in U.S. presidential advertising: Using videostyle to explore stylistic differences in televised political ads from 1952-2000. *Journal of Communication, 52,* 281–300.

Johnston, A., & White, A. B. (1993). Communication styles and female candidates: A study of the political advertising during the 1986 Senate elections. *Journalism Quarterly, 71,* 321–329.

Joslyn, R. (1986). Political advertising and the meaning of elections. In L. L. Kaid, D. Nimmo, & K. R. Sanders (Eds.), *New perspectives on political advertising* (pp. 139–183). Carbondale: Southern Illinois University Press.

Kahn, K. F., & Kenney, P. J. (1999). Do negative campaigns mobilize or suppress turnout? Clarifying the relationship between negativity and participation. *American Political Science Review, 93,* 877–889.

Kaid, L. L. (2001). Technodistortions and effects of the 2000 political advertising. *American Behavioral Scientist, 44,* p. 2370–2378.

Kaid, L. L. (2002). Political advertising and information seeking: Comparing exposure via traditional and internet channels. *Journal of Advertising, 31,* 27–35.

Kaid, L. L., Chanslor, M., & Hovind, M. (1992). The influence of program and commercial type on political advertising effectiveness. *Journal of Broadcasting & Electronic Media, 36,* 303–320.

Kaid, L. L., & Davidson, D. K. (1986). Elements of videostyle: Candidate presentation through television advertising. In L. L. Kaid, D. Nimmo, & K. R. Sanders (Eds.), *New perspectives on political advertising* (pp. 184–209). Carbondale: Southern Illinois University Press.

Kaid, L. L., & Holtz-Bacha, C. (1993). Audience reactions to televised political programs: An experimental study of the 1990 German national election. *European Journal of Communication, 8,* 77–99.

Kaid, L. L., & Holtz-Bacha, C. (1995). Political advertising across cultures: Comparing content, styles and effects. In L. L. Kaid & C. Holtz-Bacha (Eds.), *Political advertising in western democracies: Parties and candidates on television* (pp. 206–227). Thousand Oaks, CA: Sage.

Kaid, L. L., & Johnston, A. (1991). Negative versus positive television advertising in presidential campaigns, 1960-1988. *Journal of Communication, 41,* 53–64.

Kaid, L. L., & Johnston, A. (2001). *Videostyle in presidential campaigns: Style and content of televised political advertising.* Westport, CT: Praeger.

Kates, S. (1998). A qualitative exploration into voters' ethical perceptions of political advertising: Discourse, disinformation, and moral boundaries. *Journal of Business Ethics, 17,* 1871–1885.

Kern, M. (1989). *30-second politics: Political advertising in the eighties.* New York: Praeger.

Kern, M., & Edley, P. P. (1994). Women candidates going public: The 30-second format. *Argumentation and Advocacy, 31,* 80–95.

King, J. D., & McConnell, J. B. (2003). The effect of negative campaign advertising on vote choice: The mediating influence of gender. *Social Science Quarterly, 84,* 843–857.

Lang, A. (1991). Emotion, formal features, and memory for televised political advertisements. In F. Biocca (Ed.), *Television and political advertising. Vol. 1. Psychological processes* (pp. 221–244). Hillsdale, NJ: Erlbaum.

Lau, R. R., Sigelman, L., Heldman, C., & Babbitt, P. (1999). The effects of negative political advertisements: A meta-analytic assessment. *American Political Science Review, 93,* 851–875.

Lebel, E. (1999). The role of images in Quebec political advertising. In W. I. Romanow, M. de Repentigny, S. B. Cunningham, W. C. Soderlund, & K. Hildebrandt (Eds.), *Television advertising in Canadian elections: The attack mode, 1993* (pp. 99–116). Waterloo, ON: Wilfrid Laurier University Press.

Leitch, S., & Roper, J. (1999, August). Ad wars: Adversarial advertising by interest groups in a New Zealand general election. *Media International Australia Incorporating Culture & Policy, 92,* 103–116.

Lemish, D., & Tidhar, C. E. (1999, September). Still marginal: Women in Israel's television election campaign. *Sex Roles: A Journal of Research*, 41, 389–412.

Lopez-Escobar, E., Llamas, J. P., McCombs, M., & Lennon, F. R. (1998). Two levels of agenda setting among advertising and news in the 1995 Spanish elections. *Political Communcation*, 15, 225–238.

Mansfield, M., & Hale, K. (1986). Uses and perceptions of political television: An application of Q-technique. In L. L. Kaid, D. Nimmo, & K. R. Sanders (Eds.), *New perspectives on political advertising* (pp. 268–292). Carbondale: Southern Illinois University Press.

Marks, A. (1993). How quickly they forget, if they ever knew. *Psychological Reports*, 72, 1337–1338.

Matthews, D., & Dietz-Uhler, B. (1998). The black-sheep effect: How positive and negative advertisements affect voters' perceptions of the sponsor of the advertisement. *Journal of Applied Social Psychology*, 28, 1903–1915.

Mazzoleni, G. (1987). Media logic and party logic in campaign coverage: The Italian general election of 1983. *European Journal of Communication*, 2, 81–103.

Mazzoleni, G. (1995). "Towards a 'videocracy'"? Italian political communication at a turning point. *European Journal of Communication*, 10, 291–319.

Mazzoleni, G., & Roper, C. S. (1995). The presentation of Italian candidates and parties in television advertising. In L. L. Kaid & C. Holtz-Bacha (Eds.), *Political advertising in western democracies: Parties and candidates on television* (pp. 89–108). Thousand Oaks, CA: Sage.

McCracken, G. (1988). *The long interview*. Newbury Park, CA: Sage.

Meirick, P. (2002). Cognitive responses to negative and comparative political advertising. *Journal of Advertising*, 31, 49–61.

Miskin, S., & Grant, R. (2004). *Political advertising in Australia* (Research brief No. 5 2004–05). Retrieved January 6, 2006, from the Parliament of Australia Parliamentary Library Web site: http://www.aph.gov.au/library/pubs/RB/2004-05/05rb05.htm

Moring, T. (1995). The North European exception: Political advertising on TV in Finland. In L. L. Kaid & C. Holtz-Bacha (Eds.), *Political advertising in western democracies: Parties and candidates on television* (pp. 161–185). Thousand Oaks, CA: Sage.

Morreale, J. (1991). The political campaign film: Epideictic rhetoric in a documentary frame. In F. Biocca (Ed.), *Television and political advertising. Vol. 2. Signs, codes, and images* (pp. 187–202). Hillsdale, NJ: Erlbaum.

Newhagen, J. E., & Reeves, B. (1991). Emotion and memory responses for negative political advertising: A study of television commercials used in the 1988 presidential election. In F. Biocca (Ed.), *Television and political advertising. Vol. 1. Psychological processes* (pp. 197–220). Hillsdale, NJ: Erlbaum.

Nimmo, D., & Felsberg, A. J. (1986). Hidden myths in televised political advertising: An illustration. In L. L. Kaid, D. Nimmo, & K. R. Sanders (Eds.), *New perspectives on political advertising* (pp. 248–267). Carbondale: Southern Illinois University Press.

Noggle, G., & Kaid, L. L. (2000). The effects of visual images in political ads: Experimental testing of distortions and visual literacy. *Social Science Quarterly*, 81, 913–927.

O'Cass, A. (2002). Political advertising believability and information source value during elections. *Journal of Advertising*, 31, 63–74.

Ohr, D., & Schrott, P. R. (2001). Campaigns and information seeking: Evidence from a German state election. *European Journal of Communication*, 16, 419–449.

O'Neil, H., & Mills, S. (1986). Political advertising in Australia: A dynamic force meets a resilient object. In L. L. Kaid, D. Nimmo, & K. R. Sanders (Eds.), *New perspectives on political advertising* (pp. 314–340). Carbondale: Southern Illinois University Press.

O'Shaughnessy, N. J. (2002). The marketing of political marketing. In N. J. O'Shaughnessy & S.C.M. Henneberg (Eds.), *The idea of political marketing* (pp. 209–220). Westport, CT: Praeger.

Papathanassopoulos, S. (2000). Election campaigning in the television age: The case of contemporary Greece. *Political Communication*, 17, 47–60.

Pattie, C. J., & Johnston, R. J. (2002). Assessing the TV campaign: The impact of party election broadcasting on voters' opinions in the 1997 British general election. *Political Communication*, 19, 333–358.

Perloff, R. M., & Kinsey, D. (1992). Political advertising as seen by consultants and journalists. *Journal of Advertising Research*, 32, 53–60.

Pfau, M., & Kenski, H. C. (1990). *Attack politics: Strategy and defense*. Westport, CT: Praeger.

Pfau, M., & Louden, A. (1994). Effectiveness of adwatch formats in deflecting political attack ads. *Communication Research*, *21*, 325–341.

Pfau, M., Park, D., Holbert, R. L., & Cho, J. (2001). The effects of party- and PAC-sponsored issue advertising and the potential of inoculation to combat its impact on the democratic process. *American Behavioral Scientist*, *44*, 2379–2397.

Pfau, M., Parrott, R., & Lindquist, B. (1992). An expectancy theory explanation of the effectiveness of political attack television spots: A case study. *Journal of Applied Communication Research*, *20*, 235–253.

Philo, G. (1993). Political advertising, popular belief and the 1992 British general election. *Media, Culture & Society*, *15*, 407–418.

Pinkleton, B. E., Um, N., & Austin, E. W. (2002). An exploration of the effects of negative political advertising on political decision making. *Journal of Advertising*, *31*, 13–26.

Plasser, F., & Plasser, G. (2002). *Global political campaigning: A worldwide analysis of campaign professionals and their practices*. Westport, CT: Praeger.

Procter, D. E., Schenck-Hamlin, W. J., & Haase, K. A. (1994). Exploring the role of gender in the development of negative political advertisements. *Women & Politics*, *14*, 1–21.

Quéré, H. (1991). French political advertising: A semiological analysis of campaign posters. In L. L. Kaid, J. Gerstlé, & K. R. Sanders (Eds.), *Mediated politics in two cultures: Presidential campaigning in the United States and France* (pp. 85–98). Westport, CT: Praeger.

Rahn, W. M., & Hirshorn, R. M. (1999). Political advertising and public mood: A study of children's political orientations. *Political Communication*, *16*, 387–407.

Richardson, G. W. (2001). Looking for meaning in all the wrong places: Why negative advertising is a suspect category. *Journal of Communication*, *51*, 775–800.

Riffe, D., Lacy, S., & Fico, F. G. (2005). *Analyzing media messages: Using quantitative content analysis in research*. Mahwah, NJ: Erlbaum.

Roberts, M., & McCombs, M. (1994). Agenda setting and political advertising: Origins of the news agenda. *Political Communication*, *11*, 249–262.

Robertson, T., Froemling, K., Wells, S., & McCraw, S. (1999). Sex, lies, and videotape: An analysis of gender in campaign advertisements. *Communication Quarterly*, *47*, 333–341.

Romanow, W. I. (1999). Contextual analysis of political advertising: The attack mode on English-language TV. In W. I. Romanow, M. de Repentigny, S. B. Cunningham, W. C. Soderlund, & K. Hildebrandt (Eds.), *Television advertising in Canadian elections: The attack mode, 1993* (pp. 49–73). Waterloo, ON: Wilfrid Laurier University Press.

Romanow, W. I, de Repentigny, M., Cunningham, S. B., Soderlund, W. C., & Hildebrandt, K. (Eds.). (1999). *Television advertising in Canadian elections: The attack mode, 1993*. Waterloo, ON: Wilfrid Laurier University Press.

Roper, J., Holtz-Bacha, C., & Mazzoleni, G. (2004). *The politics of representation: Election campaigning and proportional representation*. New York: Peter Lang.

Rosenthal, R., & DiMatteo, M. R. (2001). Meta analysis: Recent developments in quantitative methods for literature reviews. *Annual Review of Psychology*, *52*, 59–82.

Ross, B. I., Fletcher, A., & Schweitzer, J. C. (1994). Promises, promises: Advertising directors look at questionable political claims. *Newspaper Research Journal*, *15*, 82–90.

Sayre, S. (1994). Images of freedom and equality: A values analysis of Hungarian political commercials. *Journal of Advertising*, *23*, 97–109.

Scammel, M., & Semetko, H. A. (1995). Political advertising on television: The British experience. In L. L. Kaid & C. Holtz-Bacha (Eds.), *Political advertising in western democracies: Parties and candidates on television* (pp. 19–43). Thousand Oaks, CA: Sage.

Schenck-Hamlin, W. J., Procter, D. E., & Rumsey, D. J. (2000). The influence of negative advertising frames on political cynicism and politician accountability. *Human Communication Research*, *26*, 53–74.

Schleuder, J., McCombs, M., & Wanta, W. (1991). Inside the agenda-setting process: How political advertising and TV news prime viewers to think about issues and candidates. In F. Biocca (Ed.), *Television and political advertising. Vol. 1. Psychological processes* (pp. 263–310). Hillsdale, NJ: Erlbaum.

Shames, S. (2003). The "un-candidates": Gender and outsider signals in women's political advertisements. *Women & Politics*, *25*, 115–147.

Shen, F., & Wu, H. D. (2002). Effects of soft-money issue advertisements on candidate evaluation and voting preference: An exploration.

Mass Communication and Society, 5, 395–410.

Shyles, L. (1986). The televised political spot advertisement: Its structure, content, and role in the political system. In L. L. Kaid, D. Nimmo, & K. R. Sanders (Eds.), *New perspectives on political advertising* (pp. 107–138). Carbondale: Southern Illinois University Press.

Sigelman, L., & Kugler, M. (2003). Why is research on the effects of negative campaigning so inconclusive? Understanding citizens' perceptions of negativity. *Journal of Politics, 65,* 142–160.

Siune, K. (1995). Political advertising in Denmark. In L. L. Kaid & C. Holtz-Bacha (Eds.), *Political advertising in western democracies: Parties and candidates on television* (pp. 124–142). Thousand Oaks, CA: Sage.

Smith, L. D., & Johnston, A. (1991). Burke's sociological criticism applied to political advertising: An anecdotal taxonomy of presidential commercials. In F. Biocca (Ed.), *Television and political advertising. Vol. 2. Signs, codes, and images* (pp. 115–132). Hillsdale, NJ: Erlbaum.

Spiliotes, C. J., & Vavreck, L. (2002). Campaign advertising: Partisan convergence or divergence? *Journal of Politics, 64,* 249–261.

Stein, K. A. (2005). Success discourse in incumbent presidential television spots, 1956-2004. *Public Relations Review, 31,* 285–287.

Sullivan, D. B. (1998). Images of a breakthrough woman candidate: Dianne Feinstein's 1990, 1992 and 1994 campaign television advertisements. *Women's Studies in Communication, 21,* 7–26.

Swanson, D. L., & Mancini, P. (Eds.). (1996). *Politics, media, and modern democracy: An international study of innovations in electoral campaigning and their consequences.* Westport, CT: Praeger.

Tak, J., Kaid, L. L., Lee, S. (1997). A cross-cultural study of political advertising in the United States and Korea. *Communication Research, 24,* 413–430.

Tedesco, J. C. (2002). Televised political advertising effects: Evaluating responses during the 2000 Robb-Allen Senatorial election. *Journal of Advertising, 31,* 37–48.

Thorson, E., Christ, W. G., & Caywood, C. (1991a). Effects of issue-image strategies, attack and support appeals, music, and visual content in political commercials. *Journal of Broadcasting & Electronic Media, 35,* 465–486.

Thorson, E., Christ, W. G., & Caywood, C. (1991b). Selling candidates like tubes of toothpaste: Is the comparison apt? In F. Biocca (Ed.), *Television and political advertising. Vol. 1. Psychological processes* (pp. 145–172). Hillsdale, NJ: Erlbaum.

Tinkham, S. F., & Weaver-Lariscy, R. A. (1995). Incumbency and its perceived advantage: A comparison of 1982 and 1990 congressional advertising strategies. *Political Communication, 12,* 291–304.

Trent, J. S., & Friedenberg, R. V. (1995). *Political campaign communication: Principles and practices* (3rd ed.). Wesport, CT: Praeger.

Trent, J. S., & Sabourin, T. (1993). Sex still counts: Women's use of televised advertising during the decade of the 80's. *Journal of Applied Communication Research, 21,* 21–40.

Valentino, N. A., Hutchings, V. L., & Williams, D. (2004). The impact of political advertising on knowledge, Internet information seeking, and candidate preference. *Journal of Communication, 54,* 337–354.

Van den Bulck, J. (1993). Estimating the success of political communication strategies: The case of the political poster impact in a Belgian election. *European Journal of Communication, 8,* 471–489.

Vavreck, L. (2001). The reasoning voter meets the strategic candidate: Signals and specificity in campaign advertising, 1998. *American Politics Research, 29,* 507–529.

Wadsworth, A. J., Patterson, P., Kaid, L. L., Cullers, G., Malcomb, D., & Lamirand, L. (1987). "Masculine" vs. "feminine" strategies in political ads: Implications for female candidates. *Journal of Applied Communication Research, 15,* 77–94.

Waller, D. S. (2002). Advertising agency-client attitudes towards ethical issues in political advertising. *Journal of Business Ethics, 36,* 347–354.

Waller, D. S., & Polonsky, M. J. (1996). "Everybody hide, an election is coming!" An examination of why some Australian advertising agencies refuse political accounts. *International Journal of Advertising, 15,* 61–74.

Weaver-Lariscy, R. A., & Tinkham, S. F. (1987). The influence of media expenditure and allocation strategies in Congressional advertising campaigns. *Journal of Advertising, 16,* 13–21.

Weimann, G., & Wolfsfeld, G. (2002). The 2001 elections: The election propaganda that made no difference. In A. Arian & M. Shamir (Eds.),

The elections in Israel, 2001 (pp. 105–133). Jerusalem: Israel Democracy Institute.

West, D. M. (1994). Political advertising and news coverage in the 1992 California U.S. senate campaigns. *Journal of Politics, 56,* 1053–1075.

West, D. M. (2001). *Air wars: Television advertising in election campaigns, 1952-1992* (3rd ed.). Washington, DC: Congressional Quarterly Press.

Winneg, K., Kenski, K., & Jamieson, K. H. (2005). Detecting the effects of deceptive presidential advertisements in the spring of 2004. *American Behavioral Scientist, 49,* 114–129.

Wood, S. C. (1990). Television's first political spot campaign: "Eisenhower answers America." *Presidential Studies Quarterly, 20,* 265–283.

Yen, S. T., Coats, R. M., & Dalton, T. R. (1992). Brand-name investment of candidates and district homogeneity: An ordinal response model. *Southern Economic Journal, 58,* 988–1001.

Zhao, X., & Bleske, G. L. (1995). Measurement effects in comparing voter learning from television news and campaign advertisements. *Journalism & Mass Communication Quarterly, 72,* 72–83.

Zhao, X., & Chaffee, S. H. (1995). Campaign advertisements versus television news as sources of political issue information. *Public Opinion Quarterly, 59,* 41–65.

PART II

Political Advertising
in Commercial
Broadcasting Systems

3

Political Advertising in the United States

LYNDA LEE KAID

Considered from an international perspective, political advertising can be seen as an "American invention," and certainly no other country in the world has embraced this tool for political communication more fully than the United States. At almost every electoral level, from local school board elections and the selection of court judges to the selection of the president, political advertising is the predominant form of communication between candidates and office seekers and citizens. Political advertising has developed into the most costly aspect of most political campaigns. In the 2004 presidential election, for instance, George W. Bush, John Kerry, their respective national party organizations, and independent groups supporting and opposing the two candidates spent a total of more than $600 million for television advertising (Devlin, 2005; TNS Media Intelligence, 2004). Millions more were spent for political ads in elections below the presidential level, for Congressional and state and local executive and legislative offices. This chapter describes the history of political advertising in the United States, outlines the laws that apply

to political advertising, and summarizes the academic research on the content and effects of political advertising in the United States.

HISTORY OF POLITICAL ADVERTISING IN THE UNITED STATES

The history of political advertising can be traced to early uses of posters, handbills, and printed materials used in the earliest elections in the United States (Jamieson, 1984), but it was the development of electronic media that made advertising so central to U.S. campaigns. Beginning in the 1920s, political parties and candidates began to use radio as a medium for the distribution of political advertising messages (Kaid & Robertson, 2003), and, although radio advertising is still an important factor in many state and local elections in the United States, television has occupied the preeminent role in U.S. political advertising since the 1950s. The first presidential campaign to use televised political spots was the campaign of Dwight D. Eisenhower in 1952. With a series of question-and-answer spots ("Eisenhower Answers America") and an animated cartoon spot produced by the Walt Disney Studios ("I Like Ike"), Eisenhower reformed his image from that of a cold, military leader into that of a warm and comfortable statesman in whom Americans could place their confidence (Kaid & Johnston, 2001). Eisenhower's opponent, Adlai Stevenson, refused to develop a television campaign, although the Illinois Democratic Committee aired some spots on his behalf. No other presidential candidate from that time on dared to overlook the importance of the new visual electronic forum provided by television.

John F. Kennedy used television spots effectively in 1960 to showcase his policy perspectives and to increase his visibility on a national basis. The presidents and presidential candidates who followed Kennedy also used the television medium extensively for advertising their personal qualities and their issue positions. Candidates for political offices at levels below the president also quickly adopted the television spot format as the best way to communicate their message to large numbers of voters.

As television advertising grew in importance, the news media began eventually to understand that the television advertising campaign deserved coverage as a legitimate campaign forum. In the late 1980s, both the print and electronic press began to cover political advertising as part of the campaign, and this led to increased visibility for spot advertisements and increased scrutiny of their content and claims by journalists (Kaid, Gobetz, Garner, Leland, & Scott, 1993). The newest development in political advertising, of course, has been the migration of television spots to the World Wide Web. Political candidates at all levels have found the Web a low-cost and hospitable medium for the distribution of political messages, and since the mid-1990s, Web advertising has played a role in the distribution of messages about political candidates and about political issues in the United States (Kaid, 2004).

LAWS AND REGULATIONS ON POLITICAL ADVERTISING IN THE UNITED STATES

The United States political system is an election-heavy system, and elections take place every 4 years to select electors[1] for the U.S. president and vice president. The 435 members of the U.S. House of Representatives, apportioned by population among the 50 states, are elected every 2 years, and the 100 U.S. Senate members (two from each of the 50 states) are elected for 6-year terms, which are staggered so that one third of the Senate is up for election (or reelection) every 2 years. The terms of office and election schedules of state and local offices in each of the 50 states are set by state law and differ among the states. The United States does not have a parliamentary system, so the presidency does not depend on the president's party controlling any part of Congress, and party losses do not result in the resignation of a government. For example, from 1994 through 2000, the Republicans controlled both the House and Senate but a Democrat, Bill Clinton, held the presidency.

One of the reasons televised political advertising has become so dominant in the United States can be found in the legal and regulatory structure within which such political messages function in the Unites States. Three areas of law are particularly important: (a) the U.S. Constitution, particularly those parts of the First Amendment relating to free speech and freedom of the press; (b) regulations that relate to broadcasting, particularly the Federal Communications Act of 1934, administered by the Federal Communications Commission; and (c) federal campaign finance rules, represented in the Federal Election Campaign Act of 1971, as amended in 1974 and 1976 and in its latest revisions, embodied in the Bipartisan Campaign Reform Act (BCRA), passed in 2002. Some individual states have laws that govern state and local elections in that state, and these laws may provide additional, specific rules on campaign fundraising, spending, and advertising.

Constitutional Protection of Free Speech

One of the most important aspects of the legal environment in which political advertising operates in the United States is the guarantee of free speech and free expression spelled out in the First Amendment to the U.S. Constitution. Everyone who has studied U.S. history and the formation of the United States as a result of the Revolutionary War in which it broke ties with Britain understands that the right to free speech and free expression played then and plays now a preeminent role in the U.S. system of government. The First Amendment to the U.S. Constitution states in part that "Congress shall make no law . . . abridging the freedom of speech or of the press; or of the right of the people peaceably to assemble, and to petition the government for a redress of grievances."

These First Amendment rights are guarded by the courts to such a great extent and interpreted so stringently in favor of free speech, free press, and free association that any regulation of the content or format or distribution of a political message in any form or any medium is almost unthinkable in the U.S. political system. Regulations on political campaign communications are rare in the U.S. system and must be narrowly focused to avoid conflict with the First Amendment. Because of this stringent interpretation of the First Amendment right to free speech, political advertising occupies a unique position in the U.S. regulatory environment, and there are few rules or regulations of any kind that can be called on to control its content (Kaid & Jones, 2004a). Under some state laws, it is possible to bring a legal action against a candidate or party for "libelous" claims made in political advertising, but the legal requirements for proving such an accusation in the political environment are so stringent and

precise that such actions are rarely successful in punishing the source of a political message.

Broadcasting Regulations Related to Political Advertising

Although the First Amendment to the U.S. Constitution protects the freedom of the press, as well as freedom of speech and association, the broadcast media in the United States are subject to some additional regulatory constraints spelled out in the Federal Communications Act of 1934 (and revisions), which is administered by the Federal Communications Commission. This regulatory structure was enacted initially to protect and allocate the commercial use by private broadcasters of "the public's airwaves." Private broadcasters who sought broadcast licenses for commercial purposes were required to operate their commercial broadcasting stations in the "public interest, convenience, and necessity." There is no strong commitment to or system of public broadcasting in the United States, although a small and limited system of public television (the Public Broadcasting System, or PBS) and radio (National Public Radio, or NPR) receives a small amount of public funding and popular support.

The most significant regulatory aspect of the federal broadcasting regulations on private commercial television stations is the requirement (in § 312 of the Federal Communications Act) that all stations must provide reasonable access to or permit purchase of a reasonable amount of time for the use of the station by all legally qualified candidates for *federal* elective office[2] (National Association of Broadcasters, 1988, 2000). In the allocation of time (or allowance for purchase) to meet this requirement, stations must provide "equal time" (§ 312b) to all candidates, and they must sell the time at what is called "the lowest unit charge."

Although they serve as conduits for political advertising messages sponsored by candidates, parties, or independent groups or persons, private broadcast stations are prohibited from censoring or attempting to alter or control in any way the content of a political advertising message. Even if the station believes the statements or messages in a political advertisement are false or misleading, the station has no right to alter the content of the candidate's message. Consequently, stations themselves are held to be exempt from any claim of libel or slander arising from an advertisement broadcast on their station (WMUR-TV, Inc., 1996).

The FCC can and does require sponsorship identification of political messages, and under the new BCRA rules outlined here, stations must insist that the sponsorship identification be in the form provided by the new law. The FCC does not require that private stations or the low-audience public television or radio systems in the United States (PBS and NPR) provide any free time to candidates or parties seeking elective office.

In the 1996 presidential election, the "Free TV for Straight Talk Coalition," an independent group of political observers, encouraged networks to provide free broadcasting time to the major presidential candidates (incumbent President Bill Clinton and then-Senator Robert Dole) (Holtz-Bacha, 1999; "Imagine a presidential," 1996). Several networks participated in providing these free-time segments (CBS, NBC, Fox, CNN, and PBS) in prescribed lengths and formats (Mifflin, 1996). However, audience viewing statistics confirmed that few people saw the spots and most did not even know they had been televised (Kaid, McKinney & Tedesco, 2000). Given this lack of success, it is unlikely that the free-time idea will become a significant part of the political advertising environment in the United States.

Campaign Finance Regulations and Political Advertising

Until 1971, when Congress passed the Federal Election Campaign Act of 1971

(FECA), campaign fundraising and spending were basically unregulated in the United States.[3] FECA, which has been amended several times (notably in 1974 and 1976), provided the first serious attempt to regulate federal elections by requiring campaigns to report the amounts and sources of campaign contributions; by setting limits on the amount of contributions from individuals, parties, and interest group committees; by banning direct contributions by labor unions and corporations (but allowing political action committees representing corporate or labor union interests to contribute); and by providing limited public funding for presidential campaigns which, because a candidate could reject the money, meant that any candidate who accepted it must also agree to accept limits on expenditure set by the FCC. Many states have adopted similar statutes that govern state and local elections.

There are still no substantial regulations limiting the content of political advertising in the United States, although the latest amendments to FECA in the BCRA, passed in 2002, imposed new restrictions on "electioneering communications" by prohibiting corporations and labor unions, as well as independent, tax-exempt, nonprofit organizations, from sponsoring or indirectly financing communications related to a federal candidate within 60 days of a federal general election (§203). Numerous other specific bans and limits on contributions, spending, and coordination of spending with candidate campaigns are also included in BCRA (Kaid & Jones, 2004a).

Finally, the new campaign regulations imposed by the BCRA provide for one additional regulation that overlaps the spending and media regulation area. The BCRA requires the personal identification and endorsement of a commercial by the sponsoring candidate. Under the new regulations in the BCRA, a candidate's political advertising must include an appearance by the candidate and the candidate's explicit statement of approval. Thus, in each of his presidential commercials, George W. Bush was required to appear and to state personally, "I'm George Bush, and I approved the message." This aspect of the new law was explicitly designed to decrease negative advertising, based on the belief that candidates would do less negative advertising if they were forced to take personal responsibility for the advertising messages (Jones & Kaid, 2004; Kaid & Jones, 2004b).

CONTENT OF POLITICAL ADVERTISING IN THE UNITED STATES

Researchers have concentrated a great deal of attention on assessing the content of political advertising in the United States, and most of this attention has understandably gone to television advertising. From the first uses of political advertising in the United States, two criticisms have been overarching concerns. First, political observers have been concerned that the very nature of television, with its focus on visual imagery and limited amounts of time, would reduce the level of reasoned discourse necessary for campaign decision making. This argument often manifests itself in the concern that television advertising will focus the voters' attention more on the image and personal qualities of a candidate than on the candidate's issue experience and positions. The second concern about content has been concentrated around the concern that televised political spots are too negative, too often accentuating criticism of an opponent and providing too little constructive information about the sponsoring candidate. Researchers have found that neither observation squares well with the facts about U.S. political advertising.

Issues and Images

Political observers have been concerned about the possibility that images override issues in political advertising because the classic democratic model of voting behavior underscores the need for voters to make rational decisions based on a thoughtful and informed consideration of the issues important to the nation (Berelson, 1966). Issue ads are considered to be ads that focus on general issue concerns or policy positions, such as the economy, taxes, foreign policy concerns, social welfare topics, and other such concerns. Image content is related to the personal characteristics or qualities of a candidate, to his or her background, experience, previous personal actions, character, and so on. Although systematic analysis of the content in political television ads has debunked this concern, it persists as a perennial criticism of political advertising.

In 1980, Joslyn analyzed a sample of political spots from a variety of campaign levels and concluded that between 60–80% of the spots focused on issues, rather than on candidate images (Joslyn, 1980). This finding has been repeatedly reinforced by individual studies of political campaigns at the presidential level (Geer, 1998; Hofstetter & Zukin, 1979; Kaid, 1991a, 1994, 1998, 2002b; Kern, 1989; Patterson & McClure, 1976). Kaid and Johnston (2001) analyzed a comprehensive sample of presidential ads from 1952 through 1996 and concluded that 60% of all spots used in presidential general elections have focused primarily on issues. Recent presidential campaigns have pushed the emphasis on issues even higher: 78% of presidential ads in 2000 were about issues (Kaid, 2002b). In 2004, the percentage of issue ads sponsored by George W. Bush was in the 85% to 86% range; issue ads made up 79% to 82% of all John Kerry ads (Kaid, 2005; Kaid & Dimitrova, 2005). Overall, across all years since television advertising began to be used in presidential campaigns in the United States, 69% of all the campaign ads used in general election campaigns by the Republican and Democratic candidates for president have been focused on issues (see Table 3.1). Kaid and Johnston (2001) have shown that the most

Table 3.1   Candidate Use of Spots in the United States, 1952 to 2004

Name	Year	Positive (%)	Negative (%)	Image (%)	Issue (%)
Eisenhower	1952	34	66	40	60
Stevenson	1952	—	—	—	—
Eisenhower	1956	100	0	100	—
Stevenson	1956	67	33	80	20
Kennedy	1960	88	12	82	18
Nixon	1960	92	8	82	18
Goldwater	1964	54	46	81	19
Johnson	1964	52	48	72	28
Nixon	1968	85	15	31	69
Humphrey	1968	67	33	46	54
McGovern	1972	60	40	70	30
Nixon	1972	80	20	54	46
Carter	1976	81	19	64	36
Ford	1976	73	27	49	51
Carter	1980	64	36	45	55
Reagan	1980	65	35	57	43
Mondale	1984	46	54	92	8
Reagan	1984	73	27	47	53
Bush	1988	64	36	44	56
Dukakis	1988	46	54	70	30
Bush	1992	34	66	50	50
Clinton	1992	31	69	67	33
Dole	1996	39	61	62	38
Clinton	1996	32	68	86	14
Gore	2000	38	62	84	16
Bush	2000	63	37	63	37
Bush	2004	42	58	85	15
Kerry	2004	66	34	79	21
Total	1952–2004	59	41	69	31

Note: Total number of spots reviewed = 1535.

frequently mentioned issues in presidential ads are economic concerns, taxes, international and foreign affairs, and military-defense spending. In an analysis of ads aired in the 2004 campaign in the top 75 U.S. markets, Freedman, Franz, and Goldstein (2004) found that "nearly 95% of presidential spots and 90% of all general election ads contain some issue-related content" (p. 727).

Researchers have determined that candidates are likely to stress in their ads the issues over which their political party has perceived ownership, particularly for primary elections, in which the candidates must appeal to voters of their own party (Benoit & Hansen, 2002; Damore, 2002). Thus Republicans are more likely to stress issues related to national defense, foreign policy, government spending and deficits, and taxes, and Democrats emphasize education, health care, jobs and labor, poverty, and the environment. Democrats are overall more likely to dwell on issues in their ads, whereas Republicans show a greater concern for morality and candidate character (Benoit, 2004).

Analyses of presidential primary campaigns have also validated the emphasis on issues in political ads (Shyles, 1983, 1984a, 1984b, 1988). Researchers have come to similar conclusions about the predominance of issue advertising in televised spots used in nonpresidential elections (Elebash & Rosene, 1982; Joslyn,1980; Vavreck, 2001).

Nonetheless, it is also important to note that this overwhelming emphasis on issues in U.S. campaign ads does not mean that each and every spot provides the prospective voter with a substantial amount of policy information or provides the detailed information necessary to evaluate a policy option. Most researchers have found that spots that focus on specific policy alternatives are the least frequently occurring issue ads (Johnston & Kaid, 2002; Joslyn, 1986; Kaid & Johnston, 2001; West, 1993). Further qualification is required in acknowledging that there are difficulties in distinguishing clearly between issues and images in campaign messages (Kaid, 2004). Issues have usually been viewed as statements of candidate positions on policy issues or preferences on issues or problems of public concern; images have been viewed as concentration on candidate qualities or characteristics (Kaid, 2004; Kaid & Johnston, 1991; Kaid & Sanders, 1978). This is not always an easy dichotomy, as issue information in a spot often bolsters a candidate's image (Rudd, 1986) and blends image and issue information (Johnston & Kaid, 2002).

Television spots also stand up well against other formats of political information in conveying issue information to citizens. The preponderance of research clearly shows that political television ads contain more substantive issue information than does television news (Center for Media and Public Affairs, 1996; Lichter & Noyes, 1996; Patterson & McClure, 1976) and may even be superior to televised debates in conveying issues to voters (Just, Crigler, & Wallach, 1990).

Negative and Positive Ads in American Campaigns

The controversy over negativity in American political spots has raged even more fiercely than questions of issue-image emphasis. There is certainly substantial evidence that negativity is a growing aspect of campaign advertising in the U.S. It is unquestionably true that there has been a real increase in the number of negative spots used in presidential campaigns in the past few election cycles. Although the percentage of negative ads in presidential campaigns from 1952 through 1996 is only about 38%, Table 3.1 shows that in the last four presidential election cycles in the United States (1992, 1996, 2000, and 2004), negative ads made up substantial percentages of the advertising content of both major party candidates. Both of Bill Clinton's campaigns (1992 and 1996) established new highs in the number of negative ads in a presidential campaign, with 69% of his ads being negative in 1992 and 68% being negative in 1996. Al Gore's presidential campaign used only slightly fewer negative ads; 62% of his ads were negative, compared to 37% of Bush's ads, but Bush resorted to more negative ads (58%) in 2004, as he defended his presidency against challenger John Kerry, who was able to use fewer negative ads himself because large numbers of independent groups took up the negative fight against George W. Bush in ads aired during the 2004 campaign (Kaid & Dimitrova, 2005).

Negative advertising is also a growing feature of political ads for candidates in elections below the presidential level. However, evidence does not support the conclusion that political advertising is predominately negative in state and local election campaigns. For instance, Kahn and Kenney (2000) analyzed 594 ads from Senate campaigns in 1988, 1990, and 1992 and found that less than half (41%) of all ads contained negative attacks. Vavreck (2001) studied 290 candidate ads in the 1998 elections and found that 64% were positive ads.

It is also important to note that negative ads, like most U.S. political spots (as documented here), are usually focused on issues, not candidate personalities (Johnston & Kaid, 2002; Kaid & Johnston, 2001). In fact, West (1993) concluded after his content analysis of typical and prominent ads that "it is somewhat surprising to discover that the most substantive appeals actually came in negative ads" (p. 51).

Some researchers have suggested relationships between negative spot content and electoral outcomes. For instance, Benoit's functional approach to analysis of political ads (Benoit, 1999) classifies political ads as spots that acclaim (make positive claims about the sponsoring candidate or idea), attack (make attacks on opposing candidate or idea), or defend (offer defense against an attack made by the other side), and suggests that winners are more likely to use positive or acclaim ads than negative or attack ads (Benoit, 1999; Benoit, Pier, & Blaney, 1997). Other relationships between negative ads and other aspects of political advertising include (a) the findings that challengers use more negative ads than incumbents in state and local elections (Goldstein, Krasno, Bradford, & Seltz, 2000; Hale, Fox, & Farmer, 1996; Tinkham & Weaver-Lariscy, 1990) but not in presidential races (Johnston & Kaid, 2002), and (b) Democrats used significantly more negative ads in presidential races from 1952 to 2000 (Benoit, 1999; Kaid, 2002b; Kaid & Johnston, 2001).

Videostyle and Advertising Content

Videostyle (how a candidate is presented through the verbal, nonverbal, and television production content of televised political spots) was first described by Kaid and Davidson (1986). Videostyle has been used to describe characteristics of presidential spots (Kaid, 2002b, 2005; Kaid & Johnston, 2001; Kaid & Tedesco, 1999a), to analyze spot styles of incumbents and challengers (Kaid & Davidson, 1986), and to determine differences in male and female candidate styles (Bystrom, Banwart, Kaid, & Robertson, 2004).

In addition to analyzing the issue or image content and negative or positive content of political ads, work on videostyle has also been concerned with the use of logical, emotional, or ethical proof in political ads. Emotional content, in particular, has been recognized as an important aspect of campaign spots (Hart, 2000; Kaid & Johnston, 2001; Kern, 1989).

The verbal style of political television spots has also been analyzed. Using Hart's (1984) indicators of verbal style (optimism, activity, realism, certainty), Ballotti and Kaid (2000) used computerized content analysis to categorize presidential ads used between 1952 and 1996 and found a decline in language representing realism and certainty in presidential ad discourse. They also found that the language choices of Democrats indicated that they were less willing to take stands and demonstrated less certainty than Republicans and that winners were more likely to use words of activity and optimism (Ballotti & Kaid, 2000).

The misleading or unethical content of political spots has also been a concern in U.S. spots, particularly given the use of new technologies to alter video and audio content of political ads (Kaid, 1991b). Research indicates a growing use of technologically based ethical concerns in ads from 1980 through the present (Kaid, 1996b, 1998, 2002b; Kaid, Lin, & Noggle, 1999; Kaid & Noggle, 1998; Noggle & Kaid, 2000; Vavreck, 2001).

Advertising Content for Female Candidates

Over the past two decades, as increasing numbers of women have sought political office, a substantial body of research has developed on the use of political advertising by female candidates seeking election in the United States. In many ways, this research has documented that female candidates use political advertising in much the same way as their male opponents. For instance, women, like men, emphasize issues more than personal qualities or image characteristics (Benze & DeClercq, 1985; Johnston & White, 1993; Kahn, 1993, 1996). Men and women are even quite similar in the specific issues they choose to emphasize in their commercials, because women seek to find a balance of "masculine" (economy, military defense) and "feminine" (education, health care) issues, and men find themselves supporting "feminine" issues to show their warmth and compassion (Bystrom et al., 2004; Bystrom & Kaid, 2002). The same is true for the emphasis of specific image qualities or traits in their advertising, as summarized by Bystrom and Kaid (2002) when they conclude that both men and women candidates

> emphasize mostly "masculine" traits such as strength, aggressiveness, performance, and experience balanced with such "feminine" attributes as honesty, sensitivity, and understanding. That is, both men and women seem to be presenting themselves as tough but caring—at least when running against each other. (p. 164)

However, voters tend to read gender stereotypes into the information they process, and thus, for a woman to be sure voters are taking her seriously, she must address her ability to deal with masculine issues in an overt and definitive way (Chang & Hitchon, 2004; Hitchon & Chang, 1995; Hitchon, Chang, & Harris, 1997).

This balancing act is more difficult for female candidates when they face the question of whether their advertising can be effective when it attacks their opponents. A great deal of traditional "political wisdom" suggests that female candidates should steer away from negative advertising. However, consistent research findings have shown that female candidates do not differ much from male candidates on this campaign factor; female candidates are just as willing to attack their opponents as are their male opponents (Bystrom et al., 2004; Bystrom & Kaid, 2002; Bystrom & Miller, 1999; Kahn, 1993, 1996; Procter & Schenck-Hamlin, 1996; Procter, Schenck-Hamlin, & Haase, 1994; Robertson, Froemling, Wells, & McCraw, 1999; Trent & Sabourin, 1993; Williams, 1998).

Researchers have found some differences in the videostyles of male and female candidates. For instance, in analyzing nonverbal content of political advertising videostyle, Bystrom and Kaid (2002) found that women candidates are more likely to speak for themselves in their ads, rather than relying on surrogates to speak for them. The authors also discovered differences in the television production techniques used by men and women candidates. For a more detailed analysis of the videostyles of male and female candidates, see Bystrom et al. (2004).

EFFECTS OF POLITICAL ADVERTISING IN THE UNITED STATES

Academic researchers, media reporters, and political professionals share a common interest in the effects of political advertising in the United States. The overriding question for all these political participants is, does political advertising work? Despite a multitude of qualifications and "ifs," the bottom-line answer seems to be that political advertising can and does have measurable effects, both on individual voters and perhaps on the larger political system in the United States. These effects generally fall into four areas: (a) effects on citizen knowledge and information levels, (b) effects on public evaluations of candidates and parties, (c) effects on the all-important variable of voting decisions, and (d) effects on citizen attitudes toward and participation in the political system itself. Research has also shown that ad effects may be related to characteristics and content of ads, differing characteristics of voters, and the different formats and channels of the political advertising.

Effects on Citizen
Information and Knowledge

The measurable effects of political advertising in the United States are the clearest and most strongly identifiable in the area of citizen information and knowledge levels. U.S. citizens in general and voters in particular are not particularly well informed or knowledgeable about politics or politicians (Delli Carpini & Keeter, 1996), and early studies of the sociological, psychological, and political antecedents of voting decisions did not hold out much hope for the development of an "informed electorate" in the United States (Klapper, 1960; Lazarsfeld, Berelson, & Gaudet, 1948). Thus it came as a bit of a surprise when the first empirical studies of the effects of televised political advertising established that voters were, indeed, learning information about candidates and issues from televised spots. The ability of television ads to overcome partisan selectivity was, of course, one of the reasons for this success (Atkin, Bowen, Naiman, & Sheinkopf, 1973; Surlin & Gordon, 1976).

The success of political advertising in communicating knowledge and information to voters has been repeatedly documented by researchers in several major ways. Of particular importance to candidates who are not already well-known political figures is the finding that exposure to political television advertising increases voter awareness of a candidate's name (Kaid, 1982; West, 1994). This simple, straightforward knowledge resulting from advertising exposure is, of course, critical for candidate success at the polls. Exposure to political ads also increases the information voters have about campaign issues and the positions of specific candidates on those issues (Atkin & Heald, 1976; Freedman, Franz, &

Goldstein, 2004; Hofstetter & Strand, 1983; Martinelli & Chaffee, 1995; Pfau, Holbert, Szabo, & Kaminski, 2002; Ridout, Shaw, Goldstein, & Franz, 2004; Valentino, Hutchings, & Williams, 2004).

Beyond the general finding that exposure to political ads increases voter knowledge, research has also provided a great deal of information about the conditions under which such exposure is most likely to be effective at increasing voter knowledge. For instance, research has shown that the type of content in a political ad may relate to the amount that voter knowledge increases. One surprising finding was that image ads often produce greater recall of information (Kaid & Sanders, 1978), particularly when a candidate is less well known to the voters (Schleuder, 1990). Negative ads, however, appear to be the most successful at producing high levels of information recall (Chang, 2001; Johnson-Cartee & Copeland, 1989; Kahn & Kenney, 2000; Lang, 1991; Newhagen & Reeves, 1991). However, in examining political radio ads, Geer and Geer (2003) found that, although positive and negative radio ads generate the same amount of information recall from listeners, negative radio ads elicit more inaccurate recall.

Agenda-setting theory is also important in understanding the information effects of political advertising. The issue agenda content of ads correlates with judgments of issue salience for voters (Bowers, 1973, 1977; Ghorpade, 1986; Herrnson & Patterson, 2000; Kaid, 1976; Roberts, 1992; West, 1993; Williams, Shapiro, & Cutbirth, 1983) and candidate attributes (Sulfaro, 2001). Voter recall of political spots may also be affected by the structure and design of the political ads (Geiger & Reeves, 1991; Lang, 1991; Lang & Lanfear, 1990; Thorson, Christ, & Caywood, 1991a).

The characteristics or predispositions of the voter may also help determine how much is learned from political ads. Citizens with low feelings of involvement in a campaign

(Rothschild & Ray, 1974) and late deciders or undecideds (Bowen, 1994) may benefit the most in terms of knowledge gain from ad exposure. Recall of information and voter knowledge increases resulting from spot viewing can also be affected by the information-seeking intent of the ad viewer (Christ, Thorson, & Caywood, 1994; Garramone, 1983, 1984a, 1984b, 1986).

Mixed findings continue to make it difficult to compare the relative effectiveness of political advertising with other formats and channels of media content. Adding to Patterson and McClure's 1976 finding that voters learned more about issues from television ads than from television news in the 1972 presidential election (McClure & Patterson, 1974; Patterson & McClure, 1976) are findings that exposure and attention to television ads results in higher information gain than attention to television news (Brians & Wattenberg, 1996; Holbert, Benoit, Hansen, & Wen, 2002; Zhao & Bleske, 1995). However, such findings are not unchallenged in the political media mix analyses. Some multivariate analyses have shown that television news is sometimes a better predictor of overall information gain (Chaffee, Zhao, & Leshner, 1994; Weaver & Drew, 2001; Zhao & Chaffee, 1995).

As mentioned earlier, television ads may be superior to other formats for political information, such as television news or debates, in delivering information to voters (Center for Media and Public Affairs, 1996; Just et al., 1990; Lichter & Noyes, 1996; Patterson & McClure, 1976). However, very little research has addressed directly questions about the relative effectiveness of different channels of political advertising in generating voter knowledge.

Effects on Candidate Evaluation

Researchers and political professionals know that political knowledge and information do not translate automatically to favorable views of a candidate or party. However, advertising in the United States has shown great success in this area as well: Exposure to political ads seems to have identifiable effects on voter evaluations of or feelings about candidates. Sometimes this effect is a positive one, and sometimes it can be a negative one, but such effects have been validated using both experimental and survey research methods (Atkin & Heald, 1976; Becker & Doolittle, 1975; Cundy, 1986, 1990; Hofstetter, Zukin, & Buss, 1978; Kahn & Geer, 1994; Kaid, 1991a, 1994, 1997, 1998, 2001; Kaid & Chanslor, 1995, 2004; Kaid, Leland, & Whitney, 1992; Kaid & Tedesco, 1999b; McLeod et al., 1996; Pfau et al., 1997; Tedesco & Kaid, 2003; West, 1993).

As with the knowledge and information effects of political ads, the characteristics of the ad content, receiver or voter characteristics, and communication channels and formats influence the overall effect of political ads on evaluations of candidates. In regard to the effects of ad content or characteristics, research has shown that issue ads are particularly effective in generating more positive candidate evaluations (Kaid, Chanslor, & Hovind, 1992; Kaid & Sanders, 1978; Thorson, Christ, & Caywood, 1991a; 1991b).

An additional area of research on the effect of specific ad content relates to the emotional content of ads. Emotional content in ads clearly generates emotional responses related to candidate evaluations (Chang, 2001; Kaid, 1994; Kaid, Leland, & Whitney, 1992; Kaid & Tedesco, 1999b; Tedesco, 2002; Tedesco & Kaid, 2003).

The greatest amount of research on the effects of advertising content on candidate evaluation has been done in the context of negative advertising. A large body of research has considered whether positive or negative advertising is more effective in altering candidate image evaluations and under what conditions such effects might occur. Only a brief summary of this large body of research is provided here, but for additional analysis, discussion of definitions, and other controversies related to negative and positive ads, see Kaid (1999, 2004, in press c).

Some research has demonstrated that positive ads can be more effective than negative or comparative ads at generating positive attitudes toward candidates (Hill, 1989; Kahn & Geer, 1994; Shen & Wu, 2002). This should not be interpreted to mean that negative ads are ineffective, only that some experimental studies show them to be less effective than positive spots. Many other studies have validated the success of negative advertising in generating the desired negative evaluations of the opponent (Jasperson & Fan, 2002; Kaid & Boydston, 1987; O'Cass, 2002; Tinkham & Weaver-Lariscy, 1993; West, 1994). Although some studies have suggested that negative ads may elicit a backlash against the sponsor of the ads (Garramone, 1984c; Jasperson & Fan, 2002; Lemert, Wanta, & Lee, 1999; Merritt, 1984; Sonner, 1998), researchers have also demonstrated that backlash effects can be avoided or neutralized by using third-party sponsors for the negative ads, thus diverting blame for the attacks from the candidate (Garramone, 1984c, 1985; Garramone & Smith, 1984; Shen & Wu, 2002); by focusing attacks on issue positions of the opponent, rather than on the opponent's personal qualities (Johnson-Cartee & Copeland, 1989; Kahn & Geer, 1994; Kaid & Tedesco, 1999b; Pfau & Burgoon, 1989; Roddy & Garramone, 1988; Schenck-Hamlin, Procter, & Rumsey, 2000; Sonner, 1998); by intertwining negative personality attacks with issues (Budesheim, Houston, & DePaola, 1996); and by using contrast and comparative ads (Meirick, 2004; Pinkleton, 1997, 1998).

Research has also provided some helpful information for candidates who are the target of attack ads. Rebuttal spots can be effective in blunting the effects of an attack ad (Garramone,1985; Kahn & Geer, 1994; Roddy &Garramone, 1988; Sonner, 1998).

Candidates can also reduce the effectiveness of an attack by producing and airing ads that inoculate against the attack. By getting their own message out first and providing their own side of a controversial issue, the sponsoring candidate may reduce the likelihood that voters will believe the negative attack of the opponent (Pfau & Burgoon, 1989; Pfau & Kenski, 1990; Pfau, Kenski, Nitz, & Sorenson, 1990).

In addition to the type of advertisement, the evaluations of candidates as a result of ad exposure may also be related to the level of involvement of the voter. A voter with low involvement may be more affected by the ads than a voter who is highly involved and interested in the campaign (Cundy, 1990; Valentino et al., 2004).

There is also a small but important body of research on the relative effectiveness of differing formats or channels of television ads. Research has clearly documented a channel effect for candidate evaluations. Some candidates are more successful at communicating with voters through one medium than another (Andreoli & Worchel, 1978; Cohen, 1976). This channel superiority question has resurfaced with the increasing use of the Internet as a distribution channel for political messages. In the 2000 campaign, voters exposed to an Internet message gave a higher evaluation of the candidates than voters exposed to the same message in a television format (Kaid, 2003). In the 2004 campaign, Kaid and Postelnicu (2005) found that Kerry received significantly higher candidate evaluations when 2004 campaign ads were viewed on the Internet than when the same ads were viewed on television. On the other hand, respondents evaluated Bush significantly lower when viewing ads on the Internet but not when viewing the same ads on television.

Effects of Political Advertising on Behavior

When considering the behavioral effects of political advertising, most academics and political observers focus on the ultimate behavioral effect, voting for or against a candidate. Although there are other types of behavior affected by political advertising, direct voting effects are considered first. Verifying the direct effects of political advertising exposure on voting behavior is subject to some limitations and qualifications. Voters are often reluctant to admit to the influence of political advertising and have been taught by the media to say they dislike it and are not affected by it (Kaid, in press c). In fact, voters frequently display a "third-person effect" in regard to political advertising, asserting their belief that others are affected by it, although they themselves are not (Cohen & Davis, 1991; Meirick, 2004).

Despite what voters say about their reactions to political advertising, particularly negative political advertising, there is substantial experimental and survey research evidence that exposure to political ads affects candidate vote choices. Some researchers establish the connection by linking voting outcomes to expenditures, either in the campaign in general (because most of the budget in high-level campaigns goes for advertising) or specifically on political advertising (Jacobson, 1975; McCleneghan, 1987; Reid & Soley, 1983; Shaw, 1999; Soley, Craig, & Cherif, 1988; Wattenberg, 1982; Weaver-Lariscy & Tinkham, 1987, 1996; West, 1994). Other research has relied on experimental or survey research to substantiate the voting effects of advertising exposure (Cundy, 1986; Goldstein & Freedman, 2000; Hofstetter & Buss, 1980; Joslyn, 1981; Kaid, 1976; Kaid & Sanders, 1978; Mulder, 1979).

The type of ad to which a voter is exposed can affect voting results. This seems to be particularly true in regard to negative and positive ads. Positive ads can have a positive effect on voting for a particular candidate, and the evidence is very strong on the specific voter choice effects produced by negative advertising (Ansolabehere & Iyengar, 1995; Basil et al., 1991; Kaid & Boydston, 1987; Kaid, Chanslor, et al., 1992; Roddy & Garramone, 1988).

As discussed earlier in regard to information effects and candidate evaluation effects, voter characteristics play a role in the effectiveness of political advertising. For instance, some research suggests that ads are more likely to affect the voting decisions of low-involvement voters (Rothschild & Ray, 1974), but Faber, Tims, and Schmitt (1993) found that high involvement and attention to television news resulted in greater effects for negative ads on vote preference.

Channel variables have not been frequently considered in studies of television advertising effects on voting behavior. However, the advent of the Internet has reinvigorated interest in such study. Kaid (2002b), in studying the 2000 presidential election, found that channel differences (between TV and Web) for political advertising exposure could also relate directly to voting choices between candidates.

Just as the increase in female candidates has caused more interest in the effect of gender on the content of political ads, researchers have been intrigued by questions about the effects of political advertising on voting for male and female candidates. Researchers have discovered that female candidates seem to receive higher vote likelihood scores when they appear in typical masculine settings (Kaid, Myers, Pipps, & Hunter, 1984; Wadsworth et al., 1987), rather than in feminine (home and family) settings. These findings are complemented by research that suggests that when a female candidate emphasizes masculine issues in her ads, she can increase the voters' perception that she is highly competent on male issues, even though this goes against gender stereotypes (Gordon, Shafie, & Crigler, 2003).

Effects of Political Advertising on the Political System

Beyond knowledge, candidate evaluation, and direct vote choice, some political observers have been concerned about other types of effects of political advertising on the U.S.

political system. The most famous of the research findings in this area are those that suggest that exposure to negative political advertising causes voters to eschew voting altogether and thus lessens voter participation and turnout (Ansolabehere & Iyengar, 1995; Ansolabehere, Iyengar, & Simon, 1999; Ansolabehere, Iyengar, Simon, & Valentino, 1994; Lemert et al., 1999).

However attractive journalists and other political observers may find the thesis that negative advertising decreases democratic participation, the evidence disputing these claims continues to mount, as research confirms that exposure to all types of political advertising has no measurable effect on voter turnout (Brader, 2005; Finkel & Geer, 1998; Freedman & Goldstein, 1999; Vavreck, 2000; Watttenberg & Brians, 1999). Increased negativity in a campaign may even drive turnout to higher levels (Kahn & Kenney, 1999). In fact, research on the advertising exposure in the 2000 campaign led to the conclusion that "The answer is unambiguous: in the aggregate, exposure to campaign advertising stimulated turnout, increasing the probability that our hypothetical citizen will vote by as much as 10 percentage points" (Freedman et al., 2004, p. 732).

Exposure to political advertising may also have other effects on the political system, such as increased political cynicism (Ansolabehere et al., 1994; Kaid et al., 2000). However, as with the decreased turnout possibility, evidence on the other side seems stronger (Garramone, Atkin, Pinkleton, & Cole, 1990; Kaid, 2002a; Martinez & Delegal, 1990; Pinkleton, 1998; Pinkleton, Um, & Austin, 2002; Schenck-Hamlin et al., 2000).

Exposure to political advertising may also affect the extent to which a voter seeks out other information about the candidates or issues. Valentino et al. (2004) found that exposure to political advertising reduced information seeking among voters with high political involvement, whereas voters with low involvement scores were motivated to browse the Web for additional information.

Some researchers have attempted to apply meta-analytic techniques to political advertising research in an attempt to discover broad general conclusions, regardless of methodology and measurement differences (Lau, Sigelman, Heldman, & Babbitt, 1999). These studies are too limited in their own methodologies and political advertising sampling to produce any reliable results (for more discussion of the problems with this research approach as applied to political advertising, see Kaid, 2004).

Political Advertising and the World Wide Web

One of the most important developments in political advertising is the increased role of the World Wide Web, or Internet (Tedesco, 2004). The use of the Web as an advertising tool has tremendous advantages for candidates, parties, interest groups, nonpartisan groups, corporations, organizations, and even individual citizens (Kaid, 2005). Web advertising offers complete control of the message and widespread distribution directly to voters at low cost and, in the United States, with almost universal citizen access. Although presidential campaigns made limited use of the Web in the 1992 campaign, the 2004 campaign marked a new level of Web use for campaigns. The media tracking group TNS (2004) documented that $4.2 million had been spent in online advertising in the 2004 presidential campaign, although this was only a fraction of the money spent on televised political advertising.

Web political advertising takes many forms and provides many avenues through which voters may be informed and persuaded. These include (a) use of Web sites as political advertisements; (b) messages or ads originally disseminated in other communication channels, which are transferred to the Web as a channel for additional distribution; (c) fund-raising appeals; (d) original message ads formulated specifically for the Web environment; and (e) blog ads (Kaid, 2006). In the 2004 presidential campaign, the dominant use of Web political advertising was for fund raising, and many ads stressed recruitment and persuasion (Cornfield, 2004). Despite many humorous negative Web messages that received media attention, the messages of the candidates in their Web advertising were predominantly positive (Cornfield, 2004; Kaid, 2006; Klotz, 1997).

Studies of the effects of Web political advertising are still limited, but evidence suggests that exposure to Web advertising can enhance liking for the candidate (Hansen, 2000; Hansen & Benoit, 2002), decrease political cynicism (Tedesco & Kaid, 2000), provide detailed campaign information (Margolis, Resnick, & Tu, 1997), affect candidate evaluations and vote choices (Kaid, 2002a, 2003; Kaid & Postelnicu, 2005), and stimulate information seeking (Kaid, 2003; Kaid & Postelnicu, 2005).

AD WATCHING AND WEB WATCHING

In the United States, journalists began in the late 1980s to advocate journalistic "policing" of political advertising, or ad watches, in an attempt to expose false and misleading advertising (Broder, 1989). By making political advertising part of the news media's coverage of political campaigns, ad watches were meant to help the public understand ads and keep the campaigns "honest" (West, 1992). However, research has shown that media scrutiny of televised political advertising concentrates mostly on negative advertising and has not provided very thorough analysis of the ads (Kaid et al., 1993; Kaid, McKinney, Tedesco, & Gaddie, 1999; McKinnon, Kaid, Acree, & Mays, 1996; Tedesco, Kaid, & McKinnon, 2000; Tedesco, McKinnon, & Kaid, 1999).

Some researchers contend that ad watches can accomplish the goal of making voters more aware of deceptive advertising appeals

(Capella & Jamieson, 1994; Jamieson & Capella, 1997; Leshner, 2001; Min, 2002; O'Sullivan & Geiger, 1995), but most academic research has been less optimistic, demonstrating that ad watches sometimes produce a boomerang effect, further enhancing the ad and benefiting the candidate's campaign strategy (Ansolabehere & Iyengar, 1995, 1996; Just et al., 1996; McKinnon & Kaid, 1999; Pfau & Louden, 1994). In fact, the research findings on media scrutiny of political advertising call

> into serious question the ability of journalistic coverage of advertising to serve as a watchdog for the public. Much of the research seems to suggest that by analyzing and airing the ads to be scrutinized the media may actually be enhancing the intended effectiveness of the ads. (Kaid, 2004, pp. 187)

The growth of the Internet has spawned another type of oversight for political advertising: ad watches on the Web, or Web watches. Like traditional ad watches in the mainstream news media (usually on television, radio, or newspapers), Web ad watches were designed to dissect and analyze political advertising and to expose inaccuracies and misleading claims. On the Web, however, the ad watch role is not the exclusive purview of the mainstream media. Many other participants in the political system have claimed positions as ad watchers on the Web, including independent organizations and educational institutions (such as FactCheck.org at the Annenberg Public Policy Center at the University of Pennsylvania), political parties (the Republican and Democratic National Committees), independent interest groups (such as MoveOn.org), and even bloggers. In an interesting foldback twist, the novelty of Web ads attracted the ad-watching attention of journalists both on and off the Web, thus further magnifying their effects through free news media coverage (Faler, 2004).

CONCLUSION

Political advertising persists as the major form of communication between voters and political candidates, political parties, and other participants in the political system in the United States. The record expenditures of the 2004 campaign bear witness to the continuation of this preeminent form of political communication in American democracy. New campaign regulations have encouraged additional actors, in the form of independent groups, to increase their production of political advertising for direct distribution to voters. As these new voices compete for their own place in the political system and for the attention of the citizen and voter, these groups will, like candidates and parties, continue to distribute their messages through traditional media channels and will find new opportunities for political advertising and for watching and scrutinizing the ads of competing voices on the widening public sphere of the Internet.

NOTES

1. Although the U.S. presidential election appears to use a direct vote for the candidates for president and vice president, in reality the U.S. Constitution dictates a system in which each state chooses electors as required by each state legislature (see Article II, §1 of the U.S. Constitution), and the electors (not individual voters) cast their vote for president when they meet as members of the "Electoral College" in December after the November election. A majority (270) of elector votes is required for a president to win. Because most states apportion their electoral votes on a "winner take all" basis, it is possible for a candidate to win the popular vote without winning the electoral vote. This happens rarely, but it occurred in the 2000 election when George W. Bush received 271 electoral votes to 267 for Al Gore. Bush had lost the popular vote by a margin of 540,520. For more details, see Kaid and Jones (2004a).

2. Although the actual legal language in the Federal Communications Act of 1934 applies only to candidates for *federal* office, the FCC has interpreted it to mean that the access and equal time provisions should apply to all elective offices. On the other hand, the right to equal access applies only to candidates and does not apply to issue advertising or to party advertising. Thus, if an independent political interest group or individual or an organized political party seeks to purchase time, broadcast stations need not allow such purchase (National Association of Broadcasters, 2000).

3. The Corrupt Practices Act (1925) purported to provide some regulation of campaign financing through vague reporting requirements but was considered ineffective and unenforceable. Other statutes prohibited campaign contributions from labor unions and corporations.

REFERENCES

Andreoli, V., & Worchel, S. (1978). Effects of media, communicator and message position on attitude change. *Public Opinion Quarterly, 42,* 59–70.

Ansolabehere, S., & Iyengar, S. (1995). *Going negative: How political advertisements shrink and polarize the electorate.* New York: Free Press.

Ansolabehere, S., & Iyengar, S. (1996). Can the press monitor campaign advertising? An experimental study. *Harvard International Journal of Press/Politics, 1*(1), 72–86.

Ansolabehere, S., Iyengar, S., & Simon, A. (1999). Replicating experiments using aggregate and survey data: The case of negative advertising and turnout. *American Political Science Review, 93*(4), 901–909.

Ansolabehere, S., Iyengar, S., Simon, A., & Valentino, N. (1994). Does attack advertising demobilize the electorate? *American Political Science Review, 88,* 829–838.

Atkin, C. K., Bowen, L., Nayman, O. B., & Sheinkopf, K. G. (1973). Quality versus quantity in televised political ads. *Public Opinion Quarterly, 37,* 209–224.

Atkin, C., & Heald, G. (1976). Effects of political advertising. *Public Opinion Quarterly, 40,* 216–228.

Ballotti, R. J., & Kaid, L. L. (2000). Examining verbal style in presidential campaign spots. *Communication Studies, 51,* 258–273.

Basil, M., Schooler, C., & Reeves, B. (1991). Positive and negative political advertising: Effectiveness of ads and perceptions of candidates. In F. Biocca (Ed.), *Television and political advertising* (Vol. 1, pp. 245–262). Hillsdale, NJ: Erlbaum.

Becker, L. B., & Doolittle, J. C. (1975, Winter). How repetition affects evaluations of and information seeking about candidates. *Journalism Quarterly, 52,* 611–617.

Benoit, W. L. (1999). *Seeing spots: A functional analysis of presidential television advertising from 1952–1996.* New York: Praeger.

Benoit, W. (2004, Spring). Political party affiliation and presidential campaign discourse. *Communication Quarterly, 52,* 81–97.

Benoit, W. L., & Hansen, G. J. (2002). Issue adaptation of presidential television spots and debates to primary and general audiences. *Communication Research Reports, 19,* 138–145.

Benoit, W. L., Pier, P. M., & Blaney, J. R. (1997). A functional approach to televised political spots: Acclaiming, attacking, defending. *Communication Quarterly, 45,* 1–20.

Benze, J. G., & DeClercq, E. R. (1985). Content of television political spot ads for female candidates. *Journalism Quarterly, 62,* 278–283.

Berelson, B. (1966). Democratic theory and public opinion. In B. Berelson & M. Janowitz (Eds.), *Reader in public opinion and communication* (pp. 489–504). New York: Free Press.

Bowen, L. (1994). Time of voting decision and use of political advertising: The Slade Gorton–Brock Adams senatorial campaign. *Journalism Quarterly, 71*(3), 665–675.

Bowers, T. A. (1973). Newspaper political advertising and the agenda-setting function. *Journalism Quarterly, 50,* 552–556.

Bowers, T. A. (1977). Candidate advertising: The agenda is the message. In D. L. Shaw & M. E. McCombs (Eds.), *The emergence of American political issues* (pp. 53–67). St. Paul, MN: West.

Brader, T. (2005). Striking a responsive chord: How political ads motivate and persuade voters by appealing to emotions. *American Journal of Political Science, 49*(2), 388–405.

Brians, C. L., & Wattenberg, M. P. (1996, February). Campaign issue knowledge and salience: comparing reception from TV commercials, TV news, and newspapers. *American Journal of Political Science, 40,* 172–193.

Broder, D. A. (1989, January 19). Should news media police accuracy of ads? *Washington Post,* p. A22.

Budesheim, T. L., Houston, D. A., & DePaola, S. J. (1996). Persuasiveness of in-group and out-group political messages: The case of negative political campaigning. *Journal of Personality and Social Psychology, 70,* 523–534.

Bystrom, D. G., Banwart, M., Kaid, L. L., & Robertson, T. (2004). *The gendering of candidate communication: VideoStyle, Webstyle, and newsstyle.* New York: Routledge.

Bystrom, D., & Kaid, L. L. (2002). Are women candidates transforming campaign communication? A comparison of advertising videostyles in the 1990s. In C. S. Rosenthal (Ed.),. *Women transforming Congress* (pp. 146–169). Norman: University of Oklahoma Press.

Bystrom, D. G., & Miller, J. M. (1999). Gendered communication styles and strategies in campaign 1996: The videostyles of women and men candidates. In L. L. Kaid & D. G. Bystrom (Eds.), *The electronic election: Perspectives on the 1996 campaign communication* (pp. 293–302). Mahwah, NJ: Erlbaum.

Cappella, J. N., & Jamieson, K. H. (1994). Broadcast adwatch effects: A field experiment. *Communication Research, 21*(3), 342–365.

Center for Media and Public Affairs. (1996, May-June). Whose campaign did you see? *Media Monitor, 10*(3), 1–4.

Chaffee, S. H., Zhao, X., & Leshner, G. (1994, June). Political knowledge and the campaign media of 1992. *Communication Research, 21,* 305–324.

Chang, C. (2001). The impacts of emotion elicited by print political advertising on candidate evaluation. *Media Psychology, 3,* 91–118.

Chang, C., & Hitchon, J.C.B. (2004, August). When does gender count? Further insights into gender schematic processing for female candidates' political advertisements. *Sex Roles, 51*(3/4), 197–208.

Christ, W. G., Thorson, E., & Caywood, C. (1994). Do attitudes toward political advertising affect information processing of televised political commercials? *Journal of Broadcasting & Electronic Media, 38,* 251–270.

Cohen, A. (1976). Radio vs. TV: The effects of the medium. *Journal of Communication, 26,* 29–35.

Cohen, J., & Davis, R. G. (1991, Winter). Third-person effects and the differential impact in negative political advertising. *Journalism Quarterly, 68*(4), 680–681.

Cornfield, M. (2004, October). Presidential campaign advertising on the internet. Retrieved November 26, 2005, from the PEW Internet and American Life Project Web site: http://www.pewinternet.org/pdfs/PIP_Pres_Online_Ads_Report.pdf

Cundy, D. T. (1986). Political commercials and candidate image: The effects can be substantial. In

L. L. Kaid, D. Nimmo, & K. R. Sanders (Eds.), *New perspectives on political advertising* (pp. 210–234). Carbondale: Southern Illinois University Press.

Cundy, D. T. (1990). Image formation, the low involvement voter, and televised political advertising. *Political Communication and Persuasion, 7,* 41–59.

Damore, David E. (2002, September). Candidate strategy and the decision to go negative. *Political Research Quarterly, 55*(3), 669–685.

Delli Carpini, M. X., & Keeter, S. (1996). *What Americans know about politics and why it matters.* New Haven, CT: Yale University Press.

Devlin, L. P. (2005). Contrasts in presidential campaign commercials of 2004. *American Behavioral Scientist, 49*(2), 279–313.

Elebash, C., & Rosene, J. (1982). Issues in political advertising in a Deep South gubernatorial race. *Journalism Quarterly, 59,* 420–423.

Faber, R. J., Tims, A. R., & Schmitt, K. G. (1993). Negative political advertising and voting intent: The role of involvement and alternative information sources. *Journal of Advertising, 22*(4), 67–76.

Faler, B. (2004, March 15). Presidential ad war hits the Web. *Washington Post,* p. A10.

Finkel, S. E., & Geer, J. G. (1998). A spot check: Casting doubt on the demobilizing effect of attack advertising. *American Journal of Political Science, 42,* 573–595.

Freedman, P., Franz, M., & Goldstein, K. (2004, October). Campaign advertising and democratic citizenship. *American Journal of Political Science, 48*(4), 723–741.

Freedman, P., & Goldstein, K. (1999). Measuring media exposure and the effects of negative campaign ads. *American Journal of Political Science, 43*(4), 1189–1208.

Garramone, G. M. (1983). Image versus issue orientation and effects of political advertising. *Communication Research, 10,* 59–76.

Garramone, G. M. (1984a). Audience motivation effects: More evidence. *Communication Research, 11*(1), 79–96.

Garramone, G. M. (1984b). Motivational models: Replication across media for political campaign content. *Journalism Quarterly, 61,* 537–541.

Garramone, G. M. (1984c). Voter responses to negative political ads. *Journalism Quarterly, 61,* 250–259.

Garramone, G. M. (1985). Effects of negative political advertising: The roles of sponsor and rebuttal. *Journal of Broadcasting & Electronic Media, 29,* 147–159.

Garramone, G. (1986). Candidate image formation: The role of information processing. In L. L. Kaid, D. Nimmo, & K. R. Sanders (Eds.), *New perspectives on political advertising* (pp. 235–247). Carbondale: Southern Illinois University Press.

Garramone, G. M., Atkin, C. K., Pinkleton, B. E., & Cole, R. T. (1990). Effects of negative political advertising on the political process. *Journal of & Electronic Media, 34,* 299–311.

Garramone, G. M., & Smith, S. J. (1984). Reactions to political advertising: Clarifying sponsor effects. *Journalism Quarterly, 61,* 771–775.

Geer, J. G. (1998). Campaigns, party competition, and political advertising. In J. G. Geer (Ed.), *Politicians and party politics* (pp. 186–217). Baltimore, MD: Johns Hopkins University Press.

Geer, J. G., & Geer, J. H. (2003, March). Remembering attack ads: An experimental investigation of radio. *Political Behavior, 25*(1), 69–95.

Geiger, S. F., & Reeves, B. (1991). The effects of visual structure and content emphasis on the evaluation and memory for political candidates. In F. Biocca (Ed.), *Television and political advertising* (Vol. 1, pp. 125–144). Hillsdale, NJ: Erlbaum.

Ghorpade, S. (1986, August/September). Agenda setting: A test of advertising's neglected function. *Journal of Advertising Research, 26*(4), 23–27.

Goldstein, K., & Freedman, P. (2000). New evidence for new arguments: Money and advertising in the 1996 Senate elections. *Journal of Politics, 62,* 1087–1108.

Goldstein, K. M., Krasno, J. S., Bradford, L., & Seltz, D. E. (2000). Going negative: Attack advertising in the 1998 elections. In P. S. Herrnson (Ed.), *Playing hard-ball: Campaigning for the U.S. Congress* (pp. 92–107). Saddle River, NJ: Prentice Hall.

Gordon, A., Shafie, D. M., & Crigler, A. N. (2003). Is negative advertising effective for female candidates? An experiment in voters' uses of gender stereotypes. *Harvard International Journal of Press/Politics, 8*(3), 35–53.

Hale, J. F., Fox, J. C., & Farmer, R. (1996). Negative advertisements in U.S. Senate campaigns: The influence of campaign context. *Social Science Quarterly, 77,* 329–343.

Hansen, G. J. (2000, November). *Internet presidential campaigning: The influences of candidate*

Internet sites on the 2000 election. Paper presented at the National Communication Association Convention, Seattle.

Hansen, G. J., & Benoit, W. L. (2002, November). *Presidential campaigning on the Web: The influence of candidate World Wide Web sites in the 2000 general election.* Paper presented at the National Communication Association Convention, New Orleans.

Hart, R. P. (1984). *Verbal style and the presidency: A computer-based analysis.* San Francisco: Academic Press.

Hart, R. P. (2000). *Campaign talk: Why elections are good for us.* Princeton, NJ: Princeton University Press.

Herrnson, P. S., & Patterson, K. D. (2000). Agenda setting and campaign advertising in congressional elections. In J. A. Thurber, C. J. Nelson, & D. A. Dulio (Eds.), *Crowded airwaves: Campaign advertising in elections* (pp. 96–112). Washington, DC: Brookings Institution.

Hill, R. P. (1989). An exploration of voter responses to political advertisements. *Journal of Advertising, 18,* 14–22.

Hitchon, J. C., & Chang, C. (1995). Effects of gender schematic processing on the reception of political commercials for men and women candidates. *Communication Research, 22,* 430–459.

Hitchon, J. C., Chang, C., & Harris, R. (1997). Should women emote? Perceptual bias and opinion change in response to political ads for candidates of different genders. *Political Communication, 14,* 49–69.

Hofstetter, C. R., & Buss, T. F. (1980). Politics and last-minute political television. *Western Political Quarterly, 33,* 24–37.

Hofstetter, C. R., & Strand, P. J. (1983). Mass media and political issue perceptions. *Journal of Broadcasting, 27,* 345–358.

Hofstetter, C. R., & Zukin, C. (1979). TV network news and advertising in the Nixon and McGovern campaigns. *Journalism Quarterly, 56,* 106–115, 152.

Hofstetter, C. R., Zukin, C., & Buss, T. F. (1978). Political imagery and information in an age of television. *Journalism Quarterly, 55,* 562–569.

Holbert, R. L., Benoit, W. L., Hansen, G. J., & Wen, W.-C. (2002). The role of communication in the formation of an issue-based citizenry. *Communication Monographs, 69,* 296–310.

Holtz-Bacha, C. (1999). The American presidential election in international perspective. In L. L. Kaid & D. G. Bystrom (Eds.), *The electronic election: Perspectives on the 1996 campaign communication* (pp. 349–361). Mahwah, NJ: Erlbaum.

Imagine a presidential campaign that made people want to go out and vote. (1996, October 1). *New York Times,* p. A9.

Jacobson, G. (1975). The impact of broadcast campaigning on electoral outcomes. *Journal of Politics, 37,* 769–793.

Jamieson, K. H. (1984). *Packaging the presidency.* New York: Oxford University Press.

Jamieson, K. H., & Cappella, J. N. (1997). Setting the record straight: Do adwatches help or hurt? *Harvard International Journal of Press/Politics, 2,* 13–22.

Jasperson, A. E., & Fan, D. P. (2002). An aggregate examination of the backlash effect in political advertising: The case of the 1996 U.S. Senate race in Minnesota. *Journal of Advertising, 31*(1), 1–12.

Johnson-Cartee, K. S., & Copeland, G. (1989). Southern voters' reaction to negative political ads in 1986 election. *Journalism Quarterly, 66,* 888–893, 986.

Johnston, A., & Kaid, L. L. (2002). Image ads and issue ads in presidential advertising: Using videostyle to explore stylistic differences in televised political ads from 1952 to 2000. *Journal of Communication, 52,* 281–300.

Johnston, A., & White, A. B. (1993). Communication styles and female candidates: A study of the political advertising during the 1986 Senate elections. *Journalism Quarterly, 71,* 321–329.

Jones, C. A., & Kaid, L. L. (2004, Spring). After McConnell: Candidate advertising and campaign reform. *Political Communication Report, 14,* 1–4. Retrieved January 25, 2006, from http://www.ou.edu/policom/1402_2004_spring/Jones_kaid.htm

Joslyn, R. A. (1980). The content of political spot ads. *Journalism Quarterly, 57,* 92–98.

Joslyn, R. A. (1981). The impact of campaign spot advertising on voting defections. *Human Communication Research, 7*(4), 247–360.

Joslyn, R. A. (1986). Political advertising and meaning of elections. In L. L. Kaid, D. Nimmo, & K. R. Sanders (Eds.), *New perspectives on political advertising* (pp. 139–184). Carbondale: Southern Illinois Press.

Just, M. R., Crigler, A. N., Alger, D. E., Cook, T. E., Kern, M., & West, D. M. (1996). *Crosstalk: Citizens, candidates, and the media in a presidential campaign.* Chicago: University of Chicago Press.

Just, M., Crigler, A., & Wallach, L. (1990). Thirty seconds or thirty minutes: What viewers learn from spot advertisements and candidate debates. *Journal of Communication, 40,* 120–133.

Kahn, K. F. (1993). Gender differences in campaign messages: The political advertisements of men and women candidates for U.S. Senate. *Political Research Quarterly, 46*(3), 481–502.

Kahn, K. F. (1996). *The political consequences of being a woman: How stereotypes influence the conduct and consequences of political campaigns.* New York: Columbia University Press.

Kahn, K. F., & Geer, J. G. (1994). Creating impressions: An experimental investigation of political advertising on television. *Political Behavior, 16*(1), 93–116.

Kahn, K. F., &. Kenney, P. J. (1999). Do negative campaigns mobilize or suppress turnout? Clarifying the relationship between negativity and participation. *American Political Science Review, 93,* 877–889.

Kahn, K. F., & Kenney, P. J. (2000). How negative campaigning enhances knowledge of Senate elections. In J. A. Thurber, C. J. Nelson, & D. A. Dulio (Eds.), *Crowded airwaves: Campaign advertising in elections* (pp. 65–95). Washington, DC: Brookings Institution.

Kaid, L. L. (1976). Measures of political advertising. *Journal of Advertising Research, 16*(5), 49–53.

Kaid, L. L. (1982, Spring). Paid television advertising and candidate name identification. *Campaigns and Elections, 3,* 34–36.

Kaid, L. L. (1991a). The effects of television broadcasts on perceptions of political candidates in the United States and France. In L. L. Kaid, J. Gerstlé, & K. Sanders (Eds.), *Mediated politics in two cultures: Presidential campaigning in the United States and France* (pp. 247–260). New York: Praeger.

Kaid, L. L. (1991b). Ethical dimensions of political advertising. In R. E. Denton, Jr. (Ed.), *Ethical dimensions of political communication* (pp. 145–169). New York: Praeger.

Kaid, L. L. (1994). Political advertising in the 1992 campaign. In R. E. Denton, Jr. (Ed.), *The 1992 presidential campaign* (pp. 111–127). Westport, CT: Praeger.

Kaid, L. L. (1996b). Technology and political advertising: The application of ethical standards to the 1992 spots. *Communication Research Reports, 13,* 129–137.

Kaid, L. L. (1997). Effects of the television spots on images of Dole and Clinton. *American Behavioral Scientist, 40,* 1085–1094.

Kaid, L. L. (1998). Videostyle and the effects of the 1996 presidential campaign advertising. In R. E. Denton, Jr. (Ed.), *The 1996 presidential campaign: A communication perspective* (pp. 143–159). Westport, CT: Praeger.

Kaid, L. L. (1999). Political advertising: A summary of research findings. In B. Newman (Ed.), *The handbook of political marketing* (pp. 423–438). Thousand Oaks, CA: Sage.

Kaid, L. L. (2001). Technodistortions and effects of the 2000 political advertising. *American Behavioral Scientist, 44,* 2370–2378.

Kaid, L. L. (2002a). Political advertising and information seeking: Comparing the exposure via traditional and Internet media channels. *Journal of Advertising, 31,* 27–35.

Kaid, L. L. (2002b). Videostyle and political advertising effects in the 2000 presidential campaign. In R. E. Denton, Jr. (Ed.), *The 2000 presidential campaign: A communication perspective* (pp. 183–197). Westport, CT: Praeger.

Kaid, L. L. (2003). Comparing Internet and traditional media: Effects on voters. *American Behavioral Scientist, 46,* 677–691.

Kaid, L. L. (2004). Political advertising. In L. L. Kaid (Ed.), *The handbook of political communication research* (pp. 155–202). Mahwah, NJ: Erlbaum.

Kaid, L. L. (2005). Videostyle in the 2004 political advertising. In R. E. Denton, Jr. (Ed.), *The 2004 presidential campaign: A communication perspective* (pp. 283–299). Lanham, MD: Rowman & Littlefield.

Kaid, L. L. (2006). Political Web wars: The use of the Internet for political advertising. In J. C. Tedesco & A. P. Williams (Eds.), *The Internet election: Perspectives on the role of the Web in campaign 2004.* Lanham, MD: Rowman & Littlefield.

Kaid, L. L. (in press). Implications of political advertising research for political campaigning. In S. C. Craig (Ed.), *The electoral challenge: Theory meets practice.* Washington, DC: Congressional Quarterly Press.

Kaid, L. L., & Boydston, J. (1987). An experimental study of the effectiveness of negative political advertisements. *Communication Quarterly, 35,* 193–201.

Kaid, L. L., & Chanslor, M. (1995). Changing candidate images: The effects of television advertising. In K. Hacker (Ed.), *Candidate images in presidential election campaigns* (pp. 83–97). New York: Praeger.

Kaid, L. L., & Chanslor, M. (2004). The effects of political advertising on candidate images. In

K. L. Hacker (Ed.), *Presidential candidate images* (pp. 133–150). Westport, CT: Praeger.

Kaid, L. L., Chanslor, M., & Hovind, M. (1992). The influence of program and commercial type on political advertising effectiveness. *Journal of Broadcasting & Electronic Media, 36,* 303–320.

Kaid, L. L., & Davidson, J. (1986). Elements of videostyle: Candidate presentation through television advertising. In L. L. Kaid, D. Nimmo, & K. R. Sanders (Eds.), *New perspectives on political advertising* (pp. 184–209). Carbondale: Southern Illinois University Press.

Kaid, L. L., & Dimitrova, D. V. (2005). The television advertising battleground in the 2004 presidential election. *Journalism Studies, 6*(3), 165–175.

Kaid, L. L., Gobetz, R. H., Garner, J., Leland, C. M., & Scott, D. K. (1993). Television news and presidential campaigns: The legitimization of television political advertising. *Social Science Quarterly, 74*(2), 274–285.

Kaid, L. L., & Johnston, A. (1991). Negative versus positive television advertising in presidential campaigns, 1960–1988. *Journal of Communication, 41,* 53–64.

Kaid, L. L., & Johnston, A. (2001). *Videostyle in presidential campaigns.* Westport, CT: Praeger/Greenwood.

Kaid, L. L., & Jones, C. A. (2004a). Media and elections: United States of America. In B. P. Lange & D. Ward (Eds.), *The media and elections: A handbook and comparative study* (pp. 25–57). Mahwah, NJ: Erlbaum.

Kaid, L. L., & Jones, C. A. (2004b). The new U.S. campaign regulations and political advertising. *Journal of Political Marketing, 3*(4), 105–110.

Kaid, L. L., Leland, C., & Whitney, S. (1992). The impact of televised political ads: Evoking viewer responses in the 1988 presidential campaign. *Southern Communication Journal, 57*(4), 285–295.

Kaid, L. L., Lin, Y., & Noggle, G. A. (1999). The effects of technological distortion on voter responses to televised political advertising. In L. L. Kaid & D. G. Bystrom (Eds.), *The electronic election: Perspectives on the 1996 campaign communication* (pp. 247–256). Mahwah, NJ: Erlbaum.

Kaid, L. L., McKinney, M. S., & Tedesco, J. C. (2000). *Civic dialogue in the 1996 presidential campaign: Candidate, media, and public voices.* Cresskill, NJ: Hampton Press.

Kaid, L. L., McKinney, M., Tedesco, J. C., & Gaddie, K. (1999). Journalistic responsibility and political advertising: A content analysis of coverage by state and local media. *Communication Studies, 50*(4), 279–293.

Kaid, L. L., Myers, S. L., Pipps, V., & Hunter, J. (1984, Winter). Sex role perceptions and televised political advertising. *Women in Politics, 4,* 41–53.

Kaid, L. L., & Noggle, G. (1998). Televised political advertising in the 1992 and 1996 elections: Using technology to manipulate voters. *Southeastern Political Review, 26,* 889–906.

Kaid, L. L., & Postelnicu, M. (2005). Political advertising and responses of young voters: Comparison of traditional television and internet messages. *American Behavioral Scientist, 49*(2), 265–278.

Kaid, L. L., & Robertson, T. (2003). Radio and politics. In C. S. Sterling (Ed.), *Encyclopedia of radio.* New York: Routledge.

Kaid, L. L., & Sanders, K. R. (1978). Political television commercials: An experimental study of the type and length. *Communication Research, 5,* 57–70.

Kaid, L. L., & Tedesco, J. C. (1999a). Presidential candidate presentation: Videostyle in the 1996 presidential spots. In L. L. Kaid & D. G. Bystrom (Eds.), *The electronic election: Perspectives on the 1996 campaign communication* (pp. 209–221). Mahwah, NJ: Erlbaum.

Kaid, L. L., & Tedesco, J. C. (1999b). Tracking voter reactions to television advertising. In L. L. Kaid & D. G. Bystrom (Eds.), *The electronic election: Perspectives on the 1996 campaign communication* (pp. 233–246). Mahwah, NJ: Erlbaum.

Kern, M. (1989). *30-second politics: Political advertising in the eighties.* New York: Praeger.

Klapper, J. (1960). *The effects of mass communication.* New York: Free Press.

Klotz, R. (1997). Positive spin: Senate campaigning on the web. *PS: Political Science and Politics, 30,* 482–486.

Lang, A. (1991). Emotion, formal features, and memory for televised political advertisements. In F. Biocca (Ed.), *Television and political advertising* (Vol. 1, pp. 221–243). Hillsdale, NJ: Erlbaum.

Lang, A., & Lanfear, P. (1990). The information processing of televised political advertising: Using theory to maximize recall. *Advances in Consumer Research, 17,* 149–158.

Lau, R. R., Sigelman, L., Heldman, C., & Babbitt, P. (1999). The effects of negative political advertisements: A meta-analytic assessment. *American Political Science Review, 93*, 851–875.

Lazarsfeld, P. F., Berelson, B., & Gaudet, H. (1948). *The people's choice.* New York: Columbia University Press.

Lemert, J. B., Wanta, W., & Lee, T. (1999). Party identification and negative advertising in a U.S. Senate election. *Journal of Communication, 49*, 123–134.

Leshner, G. (2001). Critiquing the image: Testing image adwatches as journalistic reform. *Communication Research, 28*, 181–207.

Lichter, S. R., & Noyes, R. (1996). *Campaign '96: The media and the candidates* (Report to the Markle Foundation). Washington, DC: Center for Media and Public Affairs.

Margolis, M., Resnick, D., & Tu, C. (1997). Campaigning on the Internet: Parties and candidates on the World Wide Web in the 1996 primary season. *Harvard International Journal of Press/Politics, 2*(1), 59–78.

Martinelli, K. A., & Chaffee, S. H. (1995). Measuring new-voter learning via three channels of political information. *Journalism & Mass Communication Quarterly, 72*, 18–32.

Martinez, M. D., & Delegal, T. (1990). The irrelevance of negative campaigns to political trust: Experimental and survey results. *Political Communication and Persuasion, 7*(1), 25–40.

McCleneghan, J. S. (1987). Impact of radio advertisements on New Mexico mayoral races. *Journalism Quarterly, 64*(2/3), 590–593.

McClure, R. D., & Patterson, T. E. (1974). Television news and political advertising: The impact of exposure on voter beliefs. *Communication Research, 1*(1), 3–31.

McKinnon, L. M., & Kaid, L. L. (1999). Exposing negative campaigning or enhancing advertising effects: An experimental study of adwatch effects on voters' evaluations of candidates and their ads. *Journal of Applied Communication Research, 27*, 217–236.

McKinnon, L. M., Kaid, L. L., Acree, C. K., & Mays, J. (1996). Policing political ads: An analysis of five leading newspapers' responses to 1992 political advertisements. *Journalism & Mass Communication Quarterly, 73*, 66–76.

McLeod, J. M., Guo, Z., Daily, K., Steele, C. A., Huang, H., Horowitz, E., et al. (1996). The impact of traditional and nontraditional media forms in the 1992 presidential elections. *Journalism & Mass Communication Quarterly, 73*, 401–416.

Meirick, P. C. (2004). Topic relevant reference groups and dimensions of distance: Political advertising and first- and third-person effects. *Communication Research, 31*(2), 234–255.

Merritt, S. (1984). Negative political advertising. *Journal of Advertising, 13*, 27–38.

Mifflin, L. (1996, November 3). Free TV-time experiment wins support, if not viewers. *New York Times,* p. 38.

Min, Y. (2002). Intertwining of campaign news and advertising: The content and electoral effects of newspaper ad watches. *Journalism & Mass Communication Quarterly, 79*, 927–944.

Mulder, R. (1979). The effects of televised political ads in the 1975 Chicago mayoral election. *Journalism Quarterly, 56*, 336–340.

National Association of Broadcasters. (1988). *Political broadcast handbook* (3rd ed.). Washington, DC: Author.

National Association of Broadcasters. (2000). *Political broadcast catechism* (15th ed.). Washington, DC: Author.

Newhagen, J. E., & Reeves, B. (1991). Emotion and memory responses for negative political advertising: A study of television commercials used in the 1988 presidential election. In F. Biocca (Ed.), *Television and political advertising* (Vol. 1, pp. 197–220). Hillsdale, NJ: Erlbaum.

Noggle, G., & Kaid, L. L. (2000). The effects of visual images in political ads: Experimental testing of distortions and visual literacy. *Social Science Quarterly, 81*, 913–927.

O'Cass, A. (2002). Political advertising believability and information source value during elections. *Journal of Advertising, 31*(1), 63–74.

O'Sullivan, P. B., & Geiger, S. (1995). Does the watchdog bite? Newspaper ad watch articles and political attack ads. *Journalism & Mass Communication Quarterly, 72*, 771–785.

Patterson, T. E., & McClure, R. D. (1976). *The unseeing eye: Myth of television power in politics.* New York: Putnam.

Pfau, M., & Burgoon, M. (1989). The efficacy of issue and character attack message strategies in political campaign communication. *Communication Research Reports, 2*, 52–61.

Pfau, M., Holbert, L., Szabo, E. A., & Kaminski, K. (2002). Issue-advocacy versus candidate advertising: Effects on candidate preferences and democratic process. *Journal of Communication, 52*, 301–315.

Pfau, M., Kendall, K. E., Reichert, T., Hellweg, S. A., Lee, W., Tusing, K. J., et al. (1997). Influence of communication during the distant phase of the 1996 Republican presidential primary campaign. *Journal of Communication, 47*(4), 6–26.

Pfau, M., & Kenski, H. C. (1990). *Attack politics: Strategy and defense.* New York: Praeger.

Pfau, M., Kenski, H. C., Nitz, M., & Sorenson, J. (1990). Efficacy of inoculation strategies in promoting resistance to political attack messages: Application to direct mail. *Communication Monographs, 57*, 25–43.

Pfau, M., & Louden, A. (1994). Effectiveness of adwatch formats in deflecting political attack ads. *Communication Research, 21*, 325–341.

Pinkleton, B. E. (1997). The effects of negative comparative political advertising on candidate evaluations and advertising evaluations: An exploration. *Journal of Advertising, 26*, 19–29.

Pinkleton, B. E. (1998). Effects of print political comparative advertising on political decision-making and participation. *Journal of Communication, 48*, 24–36.

Pinkleton, B. E., Um, N., & Austin, E. W. (2002). An exploration of the effects of negative political advertising on political decision making. *Journal of Advertising, 31*(1), 13–25.

Procter, D., & Schenck-Hamlin, W. J. (1996). Form and variance in negative political advertising. *Communication Research Reports, 13*, 147–156.

Procter, D., Schenck-Hamlin, W. J., & Haase, K. A. (1994). Exploring the role of gender in the development of negative political advertisements. *Women & Politics, 14*(2), 1–22.

Reid, L., & Soley, L. (1983). Promotional spending effects in high involvement elections. *Journal of Advertising, 12*, 43–57.

Ridout, T. N., Shaw, D. V., Goldstein, K. M., & Franz, M. M. (2004). Evaluating measures of campaign advertising exposure on political learning. *Political Behavior, 26*, 201–225.

Roberts, M. S. (1992, Winter). Predicting voting behavior via the agenda-setting tradition. *Journalism Quarterly, 69*, 878–892.

Robertson, T., Froemling, K., Wells, S., & McCraw, S. (1999). Sex, lives, and videotape: An analysis of gender in campaign advertisements. *Communication Quarterly, 47*, 333–341.

Roddy, B. L., & Garramone, G. M. (1988). Appeals and strategies of negative political advertising. *Journal of Broadcasting & Electronic Media, 32*, 415–427.

Rothschild, M. L., & Ray, M. L. (1974). Involvement and political advertising effect: An exploratory experiment. *Communication Research, 1*, 264–285.

Rudd, R. (1986). Issue as image in political campaign commercials. *Western Journal of Speech Communication, 50*, 102–118.

Schenck-Hamlin, W. J., Procter, D. E., & Rumsey, D. J. (2000). The influence of negative advertising frames on political and politician accountability. *Human Communication Research, 26*(1), 53–74.

Schleuder, J. (1990). Effects of commercial complexity, party affiliation and issue vs. image strategies in political ads. *Advances in Consumer Research, 17*, 159–168.

Shaw, D. (1999). The effect of TV ads and candidate appearance on statewide presidential votes,1988-96. *American Political Science Review, 93*, 345–362.

Shen, F., & Wu, H. D. (2002). Effects of soft-money issue advertisements on candidate evaluations and voting preference: An exploration. *Mass Communication & Society, 5*, 395–410.

Shyles, L. (1983). Defining the issues of a presidential election from televised political spot advertisements. *Journal of Broadcasting, 27*, 333–343.

Shyles, L. (1984a). Defining "images" of presidential candidates from televised political spot advertisements. *Political Behavior, 62*(2), 171–181.

Shyles, L. (1984b). The relationship of images, issues and presentational methods in televised spot advertisements for 1980's American presidential primaries. *Journal of Broadcasting, 28*, 405–421.

Shyles, L. (1988). Profiling candidate images in televised political spot advertisements for 1984: Roles and realities of presidential jousters at the height of the Reagan era. *Political Communication and Persuasion, 5*, 15–31.

Soley, L. C., Craig, R. L., & Cherif, S. (1988). Promotional expenditures in congressional elections: Turnout, political action committees and asymmetry effects. *Journal of Advertising, 17*(3), 36–44.

Sonner, B. S. (1998). The effectiveness of negative political advertising: A case study. *Journal of Advertising Research, 38*, 37–42.

Sulfaro, V. A. (2001). Political advertisements and decision-making shortcuts in the 2000 election. *Contemporary Argumentation and Debate, 22*, 80–99.

Surlin, S. H., & Gordon, T. F. (1976). Selective exposure and retention of political advertising. *Journal of Advertising, 5*, 32–44.

Tedesco, J. C. (2002). Televised political advertising effects: evaluating responses during the 2000

Robb-Allen senatorial election. *Journal of Advertising, 31*(1), 37–48.

Tedesco, J. C. (2004). Changing the channel: Use of the Internet for communicating about politics. In L. L. Kaid (Ed.), *The handbook of political communication research* (pp. 507–532). Mahwah, NJ: Erlbaum.

Tedesco, J. C., & Kaid, L. L. (2000, November). *Candidate Web sites and voter effects: Investigating uses and gratifications.* Paper presented at the National Communication Association Convention, Seattle.

Tedesco, J. C., & Kaid, L. L. (2003). Style and effects of the Bush and Gore spots. In L. L. Kaid, J. C. Tedesco, D. Bystrom, & M. S. McKinney (Eds.), *The millennium election: Communication in the 2000 campaigns* (pp. 5–16). Lanham, MD: Rowman & Littlefield.

Tedesco, J. C., Kaid, L. L., & McKinnon, L. M. (2000). Network adwatches: Policing the 1996 primary and general election presidential ads. *Journal of Broadcasting & Electronic Media, 44*(4), 541–555.

Tedesco, J. C., McKinnon, L. M., & Kaid, L. L. (1996). Advertising watchdogs: A content analysis of print and broadcast adwatches. *Harvard International Journal of Press/Politics, 1*(4), 76–93.

Thorson, E., Christ, W. G., & Caywood, C. (1991a). Effects of issue-image strategies, attack and support appeals, music, and visual content in political commercials. *Journal of Broadcasting & Electronic Media, 35,* 465–486.

Thorson, E., Christ, W. G., & Caywood, C. (1991b). Selling candidates like tubes of toothpaste: Is the comparison apt? In F. Biocca (Ed.), *Television and political advertising* (Vol. 1, pp. 145–172). Hillsdale, NJ: Erlbaum.

Tinkham, S. F., & Weaver-Lariscy, R. A. (1990). Advertising message strategy in U.S. congressional campaigns: Its impact on election outcome. *Current Issues & Research in Advertising, 13*(1/2), 1–21.

Tinkham, S. F., & Weaver-Lariscy, R. A. (1993). A diagnostic approach to assessing the impact of negative political television commercials. *Journal of Broadcasting & Electronic Media, 37*(4), 377–400.

TNS Media Intelligence. (2004, November 1). U.S. political advertising spending reaches $1.45 billion reports TNS Media Intelligence/CMR (Press release). Retrieved November 28, 2005, from http://www.tns-mi.com/news/11012004.htm

Trent, J. S., & Sabourin, T. (1993). Sex still counts: Women's use of televised advertising during the decade of the 80's. *Journal of Applied Communication Research, 21*(1), 21–40.

Valentino, N. A., Hutchings, V. L., & Williams, D. (2004, June). The impact of political advertising on knowledge, Internet information seeking, and candidate preference. *Journal of Communication, 54*(2), 337–354.

Vavreck, L. (2000). How does it all "turnout"? Exposure to attack advertising, campaign interest, and participation in American presidential elections. In L. M. Bartels & L. Vavreck (Eds.), *Campaign reform: Insights and evidence* (pp. 79–105). Ann Arbor: University of Michigan Press.

Vavreck, L. (2001). The reasoning voter meets the strategic candidate: Signals and specificity in campaign advertising, 1998. *American Politics Research, 29,* 507–529.

Wadsworth, A. J., Patterson, P., Kaid, L. L., Cullers, G., Malcomb, D., & Lamirand, L. (1987). "Masculine" vs. "feminine" strategies in political ads: Implications for female candidates. *Journal of Applied Communication Research, 15,* 77–94.

Wattenberg, M. P. (1982). From parties to candidates: Examining the role of the media. *Public Opinion Quarterly, 46,* 216–227.

Wattenberg, M. P., & Brians, C. L. (1999). Negative campaign advertising: Demobilizer or mobilizer? *American Political Science Review, 93,* 891–899.

Weaver, D., & Drew, D. (2001). Voter learning and interest in the 2000 presidential election: Did the media matter? *Journalism & Mass Communication Quarterly, 78*(4), 787–798.

Weaver-Lariscy, R. A., & Tinkham, S. F. (1987). The influence of media expenditure and allocation strategies in congressional advertising campaigns. *Journal of Advertising, 16,* 13–21.

Weaver-Lariscy, R. A., &, Tinkham, S. F. (1996). Advertising message strategies in U.S. congressional campaigns: 1982, 1990. *Journal of Current Issues and Research in Advertising, 18,* 53–66.

West, D. M. (1992, March). Reforming campaign ads. *PS: Political Science & Politics, 25,* 74–77.

West, D. M. (1993). *Air wars: Television advertising in election campaigns, 1952-1992.* Washington, DC: Congressional Quarterly.

West, D. (1994). Political advertising and news coverage in the 1992 California U.S.

Senate campaigns. *Journal of Politics, 56,* 1053–1075.

Williams, L. (1998). Gender, political advertising, and the "air wars." In S. Thomas & C. Wilcox (Eds.), *Women and elective office: Past, present, & future* (pp. 38–55). New York: Oxford University Press.

Williams, W., Shapiro, M., & Cutbirth, C. (1983). The impact of campaign agendas on perception of issues in the 1980 campaign. *Journalism Quarterly, 60,* 226–231.

WMUR-TV, Inc., 11 FCC Rcd. 12728 (1996).

Zhao, X., & Bleske, G. L. (1995). Measurement effects in comparing voter learning from television news and campaign advertisements. *Journalism & Mass Communication Quarterly, 72*(1), 72–83.

Zhao, X., & Chaffee, S. M. (1995). Campaign advertisements versus television news as sources of political issue information. *Public Opinion Quarterly, 59,* 41–65.

PART III

Political Advertising in
Public Television Systems

4

Political Advertising in the United Kingdom

MARGARET SCAMMELL AND ANA INÉS LANGER

THE POLITICAL ADVERTISING ENVIRONMENT: THE MEDIA SYSTEM

The political advertising environment of the United Kingdom splits into the two sharply demarcated sectors of print and broadcasting. Paid political advertising is permitted in newspapers and on billboards and is restricted only by the normal law of the land and electoral finance rules. By contrast, it is prohibited completely on television; instead, major parties are allocated rationed blocks of free airtime for party political broadcasts (PPBs), which are labelled party election broadcasts (PEBs) during official campaign periods. This dual configuration of unregulated print and regulated broadcasting mirrors the media system and sets the parameters for the overall importance of advertising, both to parties and to voters. It emerges out of a media system that sits between the free-market "liberal" model of the United States and the more regulated "democratic corporatist" orders of Northern Europe (Hallin & Mancini, 2004). It shares with the United States a commitment to free markets, freedom of speech, and self-regulation as the guiding principles for newspapers. It

shares with Northern Europe a history of strong mass-member parties operating in party rather than candidate systems, highly partisan newspapers, and regulated television markets dominated by well-funded public service broadcasters. To get a clearer idea of the overall environment for political communication and the particular development of advertising, it is helpful to analyse United Kingdom media as two distinct markets: national newspapers and television.

Newspapers: Class and Party

Although newspaper circulation has declined steadily from its postwar peak of more than 16 million in the 1950s to about 12.5 million now, it remains relatively high by comparison with Southern Europe and the United States. Approximately 25% of the population over the age of 16 will buy a national newspaper, or more than 50% of all households. The press is characterised by commercial ownership and national circulation, and readership splits much in line with the sociodemographic characteristics of class, education, and income and by political partisanship.

65

These divisions lead naturally to the prime cleavages in the press market. The first is between the elite and the "popular" press. The popular press (the tabloids) dominate the market, with 79% of total circulation, with *The Sun* the clear market leader. The tabloid response to market decline and increasingly intense competition has been ever more sports coverage, celebrity gossip, and scandal.

The second cleavage is by partisanship. Coverage of politics generally, and Parliament in particular, has declined relatively over the last decade, a casualty, at least in part, of the circulation wars. However, the press, and especially the tabloids, remain powerful political players, willing and at times apparently able to shape the political agenda, and they continue to throw their weight behind or against parties and individual politicians at election times. The days are gone when papers would operate virtually as propaganda mouthpieces for their favoured parties (Scammell & Harrop, 2002). However, alignments remain and are taken seriously by the parties. In the postwar period, most, occasionally almost all, national newspapers have supported the Conservative Party. However, Labour brought about a historic shift in 1997, when most titles declared for Tony Blair. The courting of the tabloids, their proprietors, editors, and leading political journalists was the key to Labour's communication strategy. It was determined to avoid the tabloid "assassinations" of previous leaders, Neil Kinnock and Michael Foot, which in Labour mythology were devastating for the parties' chances in the 1980s and early 1990s (Scammell, 2001).

Television: The Decline of Deference

Gradualism and compromise have been suggested as the defining features of British media (Tunstall, 1997, pp. 244–245): "continuous evolution and policy consensus" coupled with compromise between commercialism and public service. This description is apt in significant respects. Television from the outset was designed as a compromise with a publicly funded broadcaster (BBC) and a commercial rival (ITV), within an overall remit of public service obligations. The public service load has been gradually lightened on the commercial sector as it has grown over time; also, despite nervous years in the Thatcher era, the BBC has been accepted by both Conservative and Labour governments as the cornerstone of quality for the system as a whole. Notwithstanding the highly charged dispute between Labour and the BBC over its reporting of the Iraq war, the government appears committed to protecting the BBC as an amply funded domestic broadcasting giant.[1] Slow evolution also characterises the life of political advertising on television; the system of allocating PEBs, first started in 1951, has been retained in principle and adapted in practice as more channels came on stream and some smaller parties, especially the Liberals and the nationalist parties of Wales and Scotland, established themselves in Parliament.

However, beneath the big systemic picture there are changes of detail that reveal a more radically transformed political communication context. By 2004, the long-predicted revolution in the media market seemed to be gathering pace. For more than 40 years, British broadcasting had been dominated by the "big two": BBC1 and the main commercial channel, ITV1 (or Channel 3, as it is now known). Despite the challenge of multichannel satellite in the 1990s, driven by Rupert Murdoch's BSkyB, with its suite of dedicated sports and movie channels, the old "comfortable duopoly" provided the country's most-watched television. However, by 2004, the new technologies of cable, satellite, and digital had massively expanded the number of available channels, from four in 1990 to more than 270 by 2004, and for the first time the new competitors achieved a combined audience share that outranked ITV1 and BBC1 in the ratings (see Table 4.1).

Table 4.1   Annual Percent Share of Audience Viewing (Individuals)

	Channel					
Year	*BBC1*	*BBC2*	*ITV1*	*C4*	*C5*	*Other*
1990	37	10	44	9	—	—
1995	32	11	37	11	—	9
2000	27.2	10.8	29.3	10.5	5.7	16.6
2004	24.7	10	22.8	9.7	6.6	26.2

SOURCE: Broadcasters Audience Research Board (TV facts, 2006).

The media explosion has had a double-edged effect. It has multiplied opportunities to catch political news; viewers of free-to-air digital can now watch three 24-hour news channels and the BBC's dedicated parliamentary channel. However, it has also squeezed the space for political news and documentary in prime time on the mass-audience entertainment channels. ITV1, in particular, has shifted and shortened the time slot of its flagship evening news program to make way for movies and feature-length dramas. At the same time, analysis of the main (ITV1 and BBC1) news over successive elections from 1992 shows, on both channels, a significant decline in political news compared to nonpolitical stories, less visibility for political actors, and a reduction in the length of politicians' sound bites (Semetko & Scammell, 2005). In short, the window for political news in the United Kingdom has been narrowing on both flagship evening news programs, and within that reduced space there is less opportunity for the parties to get their messages across in their own words. These declines are from a relatively high base, as compared to the United States, for example. Nonetheless, the predicted effects of increased competition are biting at last: As Harrison (2002) put it, "television since 1997 has been 'cruel to coverage of politics.'"

The "cruelty" is relative, when considered in the light of a history of at times extraordinary deference to politics. The television era

opened under a voluntary stricture to report, but not interfere with, the processes of politics. The BBC inherited from World War II the "14 Day Rule," which prohibited it from reporting any controversial topic in the 2 weeks preceding debate in Parliament. Although the rule was abandoned soon after the advent of commercial television in 1955, both channels continued to adopt a "sacerdotal" attitude to politics going into the 1970s (Blumler & Nossiter, 1989) and well beyond for election news. The aggressive grilling of politicians in one-to-one interviews did not become staple fare until the 1980s, and the normal public service requirements to deliver impartial and balanced news were interpreted in a particularly strict way for elections. The allocation of PEBs provided the guidelines for appropriate balance between the parties, with both Labour and the Conservatives receiving equal news time. Liberals were apportioned a share according to their ration of PEBs, typically one third to four fifths. The parties and the broadcast organisations timed "balance" with a stopwatch to ensure fair dues. This interpretation meant that television was uniquely vulnerable to politicians at elections, as time quotas had to be filled, regardless of news values. Moreover, it meant that parties could have an effective veto over some stories by refusing to put forward a spokesperson.[2]

The restrictions have been gradually loosened over time. The ITV unilaterally abandoned "stopwatch balance" for the 1992 general election; news values were to deter-mine the bulletins. Changes to electoral law removed the parties' power of veto, even at constituency level, by 2001, and the rise of celebrity television interviewers, of whom the BBC's Jeremy Paxman is the prime example, fuelled a much-imitated style of distinctly non-deferential questioning of political leaders. The result overall has been declining news space for politics and political spokespeople (as noted earlier), more robust interrogation of leaders, and a wide gulf between the news and parties' agendas (Norris, Curtice, Sanders, Scammell, & Semetko, 1999).

It might be thought in these circumstances that parties looking for new ways to reach vot-ers might turn to paid advertising as poten-tially the most effective means to spread their messages. After all, PEBs, even though strictly limited in number, remain the most important direct, journalistically unmediated means of party communication. However, paid political advertising on television continues to be uni-formly opposed by all the major parties and broadcasters.

POLITICAL ADVERTISING: THE REGULATORY ENVIRONMENT

Regulatory debates over the last 50 years have centered on three main aims:

1. Provision of a relatively level electoral play-ing field for the major parties

2. Control of campaign costs

3. Balancing freedom of speech against the other two aims

There has been substantial cross-party con-sensus on all three aims. The first two are closely linked and between them explain the historic and continued reluctance to open the airwaves to paid political advertising. There have been a number of occasions on which paid TV advertising might have been consid-ered as a realistic option. The first was the

advent of commercial television in 1955. However, the broadcasters preferred to take voluntarily the system of party political and party election broadcasts, which had been established by the BBC, extending long-standing radio practice to television. Another opportunity came with the 1990 Broadcasting Act, which encouraged expansion of competi-tion in the television market and reduced the public service burdens on the private sector. Once again, and with relatively minor dissent, the paid advertising option was disregarded; instead, the PEB-PPB system was written into law for the first time. The third opportunity came in 2002-2003, with the Electoral Commission's review of party political broad-casting. In the light of audience fragmentation across an ever-mushrooming media market, the commission inquired whether the system was valuable or indeed viable any longer. It expressly raised the prospect of paid political advertising and questioned whether prohibi-tion might be a breach of the freedom of expression provisions of the European Con-vention on Human Rights. Again, the major parties and broadcasters all opposed paid advertising, frequently citing the "level playing field" argument.[3]

The PPB-PEB system has been protected by law since 1990, and the overarching frame-work is now overseen by the BBC and Ofcom, the new regulator of the commercial broad-casting and telecommunications sectors.[4] Ofcom's Broadcasting Code lays down mini-mum requirements for designated television and radio channels in regard to carrying party broadcasts of specified lengths, currently between just under 3 and 5 minutes. All the main terrestrial channels (ITV, Channel 4, and Channel 5) must air PEBs in peak time for gen-eral elections and national referenda. ITV and Channel 5 must carry broadcasts for European parliamentary elections, and ITV additionally is tasked to transmit PEBs for Scottish, Welsh and local elections and to run nonelection broadcasts for the major parties, scheduled

Table 4.2   Summary of PPB and PEB Rules

	General Elections and Referenda	European Elections	Scottish, Welsh, Local, and Nonelection	Time Spec: PEBs	Regulator	Schedule Guidelines	Allocation and Scheduling Decisions
TV	BBC1 and 2, ITV, Channels 4 and 5	BBC, ITV, Channel 5	BBC, ITV	2:40, 3:40, or 4:40	Ofcom and BBC	Major parties: PEBs must be shown in peak time	BBC and designated broadcasters
Radio	BBC, Classic FM, talk SPORT Virgin 1215	BBC	BBC	Max 2:30		Other parties: between 5:30 and 11:30 p.m.	

SOURCE: Ofcom Rules on Party Political and Referendum Broadcasts (Broadcast guidance: Ofcom, 2004).

around key events in the political calendar (see Table 4.2). The broadcasts must be offered to select "major parties": Conservative, Labour, Liberal Democrat, plus the Scottish Nationalists and their Welsh counterparts (Plaid Cymru) and four parties in Northern Ireland (the Democratic Unionists, Sinn Fein, the Ulster Unionists, and the Social Democratic Labour Party). "Minor" parties may also qualify for PEBs, provided they are registered with the Electoral Commission and contest at least one sixth of all seats up for election.

Thus the PEB rules keep political advertising on television tightly within the party ambit. They prevent "soft" support from semidetached party backers, which was such a feature of the 2004 U.S. presidential campaign. However, at every general election in recent times, there have been a variety of single-issue, special interest and fringe groups willing to meet the costs of the qualification benchmark. The 2001 general election, for example, saw PEBs from the anti-European Union U.K. Independence Party, the Green Party, and two left-wing groups (the Socialist Alliance and Socialist Labour); previous campaigns have aired PEBs from the antiabortion

Pro-Life Alliance, bizarre exhibitions of transcendental meditation from the Natural Law Party, and pop music from the Monster Raving Loony Party.

The Ofcom code sets the guidelines but leaves the detail of allocation and scheduling in the care of the individual "designated" commercial broadcasters. In practice, together with the BBC, they pool their deliberations in the Broadcasters' Liaison Group, which decides how many PEBs each qualifying party should get and at what dates and times they should be shown. By convention since 1964, the Conservative and Labour parties have received five PEBs each per general election and the Liberals not fewer than three, usually four. Allotments to minor parties are based loosely on preexisting strength in Parliament and current strength in the polls but rarely amount to more than one each.

It is not immediately obvious why broadcasters should be granted power of allocation, and the Electoral Commission's review revealed anxiety among many political parties that broadcasters' self-interest might outweigh wider democratic concerns. The minor parties in particular complained that present arrangements favour the status quo and unfairly restrict their opportunities to reach the national audience. The commission recommended that the allocation should be handled directly by Ofcom (Electoral Commission, 2003, p. 21). At the time of writing, the government was considering the recommendation, following a further public consultation, but it seemed unlikely that there would be any major changes. In part, this stems from reluctance to undermine broadcasters' goodwill, without which the entire PPB-PEB system might collapse. Further, successive governments have upheld the principle that Parliament should not interfere with the broadcasters' independence to control the schedules and content of their own services (Electoral Commission, 2003, p. 21).

The second aim, control of costs, has also been a powerful argument in favour of the PEBs and against the introduction of paid political advertising. The ban has "almost certainly" contained the costs of national campaigns, such that "central election spending in Britain is no higher in real terms than in the 1960s and is barely higher than in the pre-war years" (Pinto-Duschinsky, 1992). The standard contrast, which Pinto-Duschinsky makes, is with the United States, where, despite reforms of campaign finance regulations, costs continue to spiral upwards amid the paid television advertising free-for-all. Moreover, the PEBs effectively offer a subsidy in kind, offsetting to some degree the historic fund-raising advantage of the Conservative Party. The Conservatives have at times flaunted their greater financial muscle with heavy spending on newspaper advertising. They spent more than twice Labour's campaign total in the 1983 and 1987 elections, most of it on print advertising. Those campaigns threatened to raise the stakes for campaign spending and exposed the historic anomaly whereby there were tight legal constraints on constituency candidates but no regulation at all of national campaign spending. The rules changed in 2000, when national campaign expenditure was brought under the control of a newly

established independent body, the Electoral Commission. The commission defines the official campaign period—normally 4 to 5 weeks—and sets spending caps for national campaigns, currently just under £16 million per party. Print advertising remains the largest single item of expenditure in the two major parties' campaigns, accounting for 34% of the Conservatives' total 2001 election spending and 46% of Labour's, according to the Electoral Commission's official register.

Freedom of speech is the third regulatory aim, and this is protected in the Ofcom Broadcasting Code, which states that editorial control of PPBs and PEBs rests with the parties. Thus party broadcasts are free from the normal commercial advertising consumer protections of "honesty" and "truthfulness" and are not subject to the complaints procedures that Ofcom adjudicates for regular commercials. However, freedom comes with two caveats: PEBs and PPBs must be announced—"There now follows a party political broadcast from the _____ party"—and the broadcasters are required by law to comply with taste and decency standards. The latter led to a landmark test case by the Pro-Life Alliance against the BBC. The alliance claimed that the BBC had overstepped its powers by insisting, on taste and decency grounds, that graphic images of aborted foetuses be cut from an alliance PEB during the 1997 election. The case was appealed up to the House of Lords, which in 2003 eventually ruled that the BBC had acted within the law. Political freedom of speech in press advertising is near total. Any party, group, or individual may buy advertising in the usual way, and the content is exempt from the complaints process administered by the commercial self-regulatory body, the Advertising Standards Authority.[5]

THE DEVELOPMENT OF POLITICAL ADVERTISING

There are two seemingly opposed ways to tell the story of political advertising in the United

Kingdom. First, the narrative of decline: Advertising has become increasingly marginal to campaigns constructed for television news. Second, the rise of political marketing: Parties rely increasingly on marketing and advertising expertise to map electoral strategy and develop party and leader images. In fact, these two views are not contradictory. Both are true.

Political advertising fails to compete with television news as *the* site of the campaign battle. TV provides the most important and the most trusted source of national news for most people,[6] and given its obligations for impartiality and balance, the major parties can be assured of airtime. Since the 1960s, by which time television had arrived in virtually every home, a succession of party leaders has felt that they won or lost because of television (Scammell, 1995, p. 37). Campaigns have become increasingly dominated by television, to the detriment of some traditional activities, such as local hustings and doorstep canvassing. Leaders' tours have been redesigned around news deadlines and camera-friendly images are *de rigueur* for all facets of the campaign, from the daily round of morning press conferences to evening rallies. Parties compete to influence the television news agenda, to drive their favoured sound bites and issues up the bulletins, and to derail opponents with instant rebuttals and sometimes ridiculous gimmicks. Advertising itself has become a device to influence the news agenda, with the now common practice of combining press conferences with unveilings of billboard posters. At the same time, the parties, especially Labour, have tried with some success to extract news mileage from the PEBs, with private previews for the press and by capitalizing on celebrity, with broadcasts made by film directors and featuring pop stars and other household names.

Given assured opportunities for free publicity through television and partisan press, it is no surprise that relatively costly newspaper advertising has been in long-term decline. The Conservatives' splurge of the 1980s was against the trend and left the party in considerable debt. Since then, newspaper advertising has decreased at every election. Total pages purchased in 2001 were less than one third of the 1997 figure, and Labour was the only major party to advertise nationally (Scammell & Harrop, 2002, pp. 178–179). Print advertising spending has shifted to billboards, which can be targeted more precisely to battleground constituencies and which offer the added benefit of doubling as photo opportunities.

The story of the decline of PEBs is in one sense inevitable, given the history of television. Before the introduction of commercial TV, the PEBs *were* the campaign on television. The BBC was so concerned to appear politically neutral that it eschewed any campaign coverage at all, apart from an election night results service (Scammell & Semetko, 1995, pp. 22-23). Instead, the BBC persuaded the parties to take PEBs, one each for the major parties in the 1951 and 1955 elections. From such unique beginnings, there was really no way but down for the PEBs. However, the true golden age of PEBs came later, from 1959 to 1966, with the arrival of commercial television and the rapid growth of the audience. By 1959, most homes had a set, ITV had transformed political coverage, removing some of the self-denying shackles of the ultracautious BBC, pioneering the reporting of campaigns and rejecting the former BBC custom of supplying an advance list of questions to interviewees. At the same time, PEBs were becoming established as the main campaign tool on television. The allocation gradually increased in number to the current ration of five each for the Conservatives and Labour by the 1964 election. The broadcasts were shown simultaneously on both channels, thus ensuring a huge captive national audience. Initially reluctant, politicians began to adapt to the new monster of TV and to relish its potential power. The 1959 campaign was the watershed, the first "TV election." Labour seized its opportunity to reach over the heads of the mainly Conservative press and talk directly to voters. It produced the first genre-conscious PEBs, using a news bulletin format with a presenter (Labour MP Tony Benn) introducing themes and party spokespersons. However, it was the Conservatives who made the first "great" PEB, one of the few that could ever be said to have had significant electoral influence. It was the last ad of the campaign and featured then–Prime Minister Harold Macmillan alone, standing and speaking directly to the camera. It was rehearsed, with Macmillan tutored for the performance, and, what was highly unusual for the time, it was recorded in advance. Toward the end of the broadcast, Macmillan walked over to a vast globe, spun it, and turned to the camera: "Let me tell you what I'm going to do about the rest of the world," he said. The *Supermac* PEB entered Conservative mythology as an election winner: It was "dramatic," according to future Conservative Prime Minister Ted Heath; "It changed everything" (Cockerell, 1988, p. 74).

Television historian Seymour-Ure (1991) called the period from 1960 through 1974 the coming of age of political broadcasting. From deeply deferential beginnings, television expanded the boundaries of political coverage, but prudently, picking its way toward an appropriate balance between the public's right to know and undue interference in the political process. The emergence of investigative documentary and more direct interviews gave rise to TV's first celebrity political journalists, but the politicians were the real personalities of the screen. Typically, politicians complained at television treatment: Labour Prime Minister Harold Wilson, in particular, felt the BBC was biased against him, and his first period of government (1964-1970) saw the first stirrings of threats to privatise the BBC. However, in retrospect, it is fair to say that the politicians had never had it so good. Parliamentary and political coverage had a protected place in the schedules in peak time. The PEBs had become

institutionalised and were a major part of the campaign on television, broadcast simultaneously on all channels; their allocation set the terms for "balance" in political news. Blumler and McQuail (1968) provided the first in-depth study of broadcasting of an election campaign, and they concluded that PEBs were *too* dominant; they might guarantee balance in political reporting but risked boredom and alienation of viewers. They suggested scrapping the simultaneous transmission of PEBs and urged journalists to make more bold and challenging programs.

In fact, concurrent transmission continued on BBC and ITV until the 1987 general election. However, by then the decline thesis was strongly rooted. Although Blumler and McQuail (1968) found that PEBs were the most significant source of campaign learning for undecided voters in the 1964 campaign, the expansion of news coverage had long since usurped their educational function. Martin Harrison's reviews of broadcasting in every general election from 1974 tell a consistent story of decline. Although by 1974 PEBs had dwindled to less than a tenth of television's election output, Harrison (1974, p. 158) could still comment that they had "a special place in campaign strategy." At every election since then, he has remarked on their withering significance, as they were undermined by continually shortened time slots and loss of audience as the television market expanded out of all recognition. "Election broadcasts have been wasting away for many years" was his verdict on the 2001 offering (Harrison, 2002, p. 149).

The decline thesis is unarguable in some ways. It is undeniable that the value of PEBs has decreased. How could it be otherwise, as we have moved from the time of two channels and captive audiences to an era when there are some 270 television channels and only five of them are obliged to show PEBs? However, it is equally true that advertisers and their crafts of attitudinal research have moved to centre stage in party communication. The Conservative

Party intermittently had employed advertising agencies since the 1929 general election, but it was the hiring of Saatchi & Saatchi in 1978 that broke the mould. At first the difference seemed relatively modest. The agency was tasked to script as well as produce the party broadcasts, thus enabling them to import techniques from product commercials, with the use of actors, music, and voiceovers. Until then, PEBs had largely been controlled by politicians, and the media experts' role was confined primarily to technical advice. Saatchi prepared all advertising and collateral material, such as leaflets for doorstep delivery—again, a small but significant step toward the unified, disciplined communications that have become a defining feature of modern campaigns. Print and television advertising became coordinated, the one to reinforce the message of the other, and all party publicity was linked by common themes, slogans, and visuals. It is no exaggeration to describe much of modern campaigning as one long advertising campaign. Most important, the agency pioneered the use of focus group research that supplemented the quantitative polling that had already become fairly standard for the two major parties. It was a decisive innovation, because the agency's expertise in rendering market data into communication strategy effectively transformed the role of advertisers. It elevated them from technical and tactical advisers to communications strategists and "ensured their involvement in the political machinery to a degree unprecedented for an advertising agency" (Scammell, 1995, p. 274). Labour copied much from Saatchi for the 1987 election, establishing the Shadow Communications Agency, whose leading figure, Philip Gould, remains close to Tony Blair and a key party strategist.

It is no coincidence that nearly all the more memorable party advertising belongs not in the "golden age" but in the Saatchi and post-Saatchi period. With the exception of *Supermac,* few ads of the pre-Saatchi era stand out. The Saatchis transformed the look of

party advertising, adopting commercial production values, radically reducing politicians' speaking appearances, all but abandoning the tired format of politician talking head, and pioneering an aggressive negative style of advertising. Three Saatchi ads stand out in particular; all were controversial, and two can stake claims to electoral influence. The first and their most famous was the summer 1978 poster, "Labour isn't working." This was posted on only about 20 sites nationally but created such strong protests from Labour that it generated millions of pounds worth of free publicity in news stories. Labour complained that the poster's picture of a dole queue snaking into the distance was a fraud, made up not of the genuinely unemployed but of actors or Saatchi staff. As with all individual pieces of advertising, it is virtually impossible to estimate its overall impact on the election. However, some Conservative campaigners believed that it unsettled the then–Labour government, encouraging them to delay for 9 months the general election that had been widely anticipated in the fall of 1978 and thereby squandering their best chance of victory (Scammell, 1995, p. 72). The second striking Saatchi effort was the combined poster and PPB "Labour's Tax Bombshell" offensive for the 1992 general election. Not for the last time, Saatchi's broadcast owed much to U.S. political advertising in use of imagery and sound effects reminiscent of George H. Bush's attack on Michael Dukakis. The "Tax bombshell" became a motif of the Conservative campaign, and again, although it is impossible to be precise about the effectiveness of individual ads, there is some polling evidence that suggests that the issue of taxes leapt in significance as a barrier to a Labour vote (Scammell, 1995, p. 261).

The third Saatchi ad, *New Labour, New Danger,* again a combined print and PPB campaign, came in the year before the 1997 election. It has become colloquially known as "Demon Eyes" because of one ad that depicted Labour leader Tony Blair with a scary smile and crazed, red eyes. "Demon Eyes" achieved infamy by being the only party political advertising to fall foul of the Advertising Standards Authority's (ASA) code of practice. The ASA ruled that Blair had been shown in a dishonest and sinister way and asked for the advert to be withdrawn. The particular Blair poster was withdrawn, but the Conservatives kept a less personalised demon eyes motif. This episode encouraged the ASA to withdraw altogether from adjudication of political advertising, arguing that its integrity would be threatened if it were to be drawn into party political disputes. Instead, it brought the matter up with the Neil Committee on Standards in Public Life, which suggested that parties might agree on a voluntary code of conduct. To date, no progress has been made in that direction. "Demon Eyes" upset the regulator, but it impressed the advertising industry. The trade journal *Campaign* awarded it the "campaign of the year" accolade, claiming it raised effectively the legitimate issue of Blair's character and generated £5 million worth of free publicity on the back of a £125,000 expenditure (Culf, 1997).

The Conservatives' use of shock tactics to whip up news value has been emulated by Labour, most notably in its 1992 weepy, *Jennifer's Ear*. This was a groundbreaker in that it was a minidrama made by a celebrity director, Mike Newell (*Four Weddings and a Funeral*) and purported to be a fictional but true-to-life story of a little girl forced to wait in agony for an ear operation because of Conservative government neglect of the National Health Service. The *Jennifer's Ear* saga became a bizarre news event, as the Conservatives reacted with outrage, the name of the girl on whom the PEB was based was mysteriously leaked to the press, Jennifer's parents gave conflicting accounts of the accuracy of the story, and the media began its own mole hunt to track the source of the leak.

The energetic effort to turn advertising into news has been one of the most impressive features of elections over the last 10 years. Shock is a continuing tactic, especially for the Conservatives, who produced more fear-laden shockers for the 2001 campaign, with scenes of street muggings and truant school children burning cars and taking drugs. However, Labour, in particular, has developed a strategy of capitalizing on the media appetite for celebrity. Mike Newell, again, composed *Angel,* the final broadcast of the 1997 campaign: It was a politician-free zone, a minidrama starring actor Peter Postlethwaite, the working-class hero of the popular British movie *Brassed Off. Lifted,* the party's opening shot of the 2001 campaign, was a pop video–style celebration of Labour's record in government, which stoked media interest with the appearance of former Spice Girl Geri Halliwell. Trevor Beattie, celebrated for his controversial "FCUK" advertising campaign for the fashion chain French Connection, was awarded the Labour account for both the 2001 and the 2005 elections. The hiring of Beattie itself ensured news value, adding the allure of "cool" to Labour advertising and prompting attention from the normally nonpolitical media sectors of fashion and lifestyle.

Chariots of Fire director Hugh Hudson started the trend to celebrity admakers when, in 1987, he made the first biography spot in PEB history, with a 10 minute film of Neil Kinnock, then Labour leader. The acclaim for *Kinnock—The Movie* encouraged politicians to step into previously off-limits territory. In 1983, Margaret Thatcher had rejected Saatchi's offer of a biopic, saying it was too presidential for British taste and the "Grantham tape," a rough cut made by (Lord) Tim Bell, was not authorised for development. However, after Hudson's breakthrough, all three parties have emulated the formula, and the biog PEB is now standard electoral fare. John Schlesinger (*Midnight Cowboy*) produced one for Conservative Prime Minister John Major in 1992, acclaimed documentary film maker Molly Dineen made a home movie portrait of

Table 4.3   Campaign Experiences of the Electorate (2001 British Election)

Q: During the past few weeks, have you. . . ? (If Yes) Which party was that?

	All (1997)	*Conservatives*	*Labour*	*Liberal Democrats*
Received leaflets[a]	69 (89)	43	40	23
Saw TV PEBs	58 (73)	39	43	28
Saw posters	50 (70)	31	35	7
Saw leaders on TV	43 (36)	32	32	23
Saw press ads	37 (na)	23	25	11
Heard radio PEBs	16 (15)	10	10	7
Was called on	14 (24)	6	7	2
Received letter	12 (20)	6	6	2
Was telephoned	5 (7)	2	3	0
Party Web site	2 (na)	1	1	0
Attended meeting	1 (2)	0	1	1
Received party video	1 (na)	0	1	0
Received party e-mail	1 (na)	<1	<1	0

SOURCE: Market and Opinion Research International, Ltd., for 24-30 May 2001 (from Butler & Kavanagh, 2002, p. 214).

Note: PEB indicates party election broadcast.
a. All candidates are enabled by law to post, free of charge, one leaflet to all registered voters in the relevant constituency.

Blair in 1997, and the Liberal Democrats have produced, albeit less celebrated, bio ads of their leaders, Paddy Ashdown and Charles Kennedy, for the 1997 and 2001 campaigns, respectively.

Saatchi's impact and the response from Labour have transformed PEBs such that they now bear little resemblance to the broadcasts of the "golden age." They are documentary evidence of the rise in prominence of the advertiser in British political communication. Even in the early 1980s, commentators might have hesitated before labelling PEBs as advertisements; in the cases of Labour and the Conservatives, at least, there would be few such qualms now. Ironically, although PEBs have indisputably declined as a proportion of the overall electoral information environment, they have significantly raised their profile as news. Moreover, survey data for recent elections indicates that advertising, PEBs, and posters are the most commonly experienced direct party communication with voters (Table 4.3), eclipsing meetings, rallies, phone calls, and doorstep canvassing—in fact, all other campaign material except individual candidates' leaflets, which, by law, are posted free to all registered electors. All these factors have contributed to a recent revival of research interest in the content and effects of PEBs.

POLITICAL ADVERTISING: TRENDS OVER TIME

Overall, the main features of party advertising over the last 10 years may be summarised as follows:

- Reduced length of PEBs
- Cultivation of nonpolitical language and promotional styles
- Dominance of issue advertising
- Conservative negativity within predominantly positive campaigns

Reduced Length of PEBs

The maximum length has declined progressively, from 30 minutes in 1955 to four

Table 4.4   Politicians Speaking in PEBs: Leaders Versus Other Party Spokespersons

Party (Year)	Leader (%)	Other Party Spokesperson (%)
Labour (1992)	29.2	70.7
Labour (1997)	100	0
Labour (2001)	100	0
Conservatives (1992)	81.3	18.6
Conservatives (1997)	100	0
Conservatives (2001)	100	0
Liberal Democrats (1992)	60	39.9
Liberal Democrats (1997)	99.40	0.6
Liberal Democrats (2001)	94.5	5.5

Note: PEB indicates party election broadcast.

minutes 40 seconds for the 2001 campaign. Although Harrison (as noted earlier) interpreted reduced length as evidence of decline, the parties themselves encouraged the trend. The Conservatives once again led the way. In the 1983 election, they decided unilaterally not to fill their then 10-minute full quota but to produce shorter, sharper broadcasts. The 10-minute slot had become the standard from 1970 onwards, but increasingly, parties have opted not to run to the maximum. In 1997, only Labour ran a full-length piece—the biography PEB for Blair. All the other PEBs, from all the three main parties, kept to the minimum prescribed length of just under 5 minutes. The pattern was repeated in 2001, when the maximum time was cut to 4 minutes 40 seconds and the minimum reduced to 2 minutes 30 seconds. Again, only Labour, and only on one occasion, chose the maximum. Declining length was a predictable step as soon as production was put in the hands of agencies: Commercial advertisers are most comfortable with films of less than 1 minute.

Cultivation of Nonpolitical Language and Promotional Styles

This trend is marked in a number of ways but most clearly by the personalisation of the PEBs, as exemplified in the leader-focused biography ads that emphasise personal character

and values rooted in life experience. Moreover, leaders have progressively eclipsed all other party spokespersons. As Table 4.4 shows, speaking appearances by party spokespersons *other* than the leader have all but disappeared in the last two general elections. This is a striking effect of professionalized communications and a stark contrast to the pre-Saatchi era, when it was the norm for the various members of leadership teams to present issues related to their individual portfolios. It is, as a number of researchers have noted (Hodess, Tedesco, & Kaid, 2000; Scammell & Semetko, 1995), an indicator of Americanization.

Less noted but equally striking is an increasing tendency for ads not to use politicians at all. The politician-free PEB was unthinkable in the golden age and well beyond; on the contrary, the PEB was *the* campaign platform through which politicians could talk directly to voters. However, by 1997, we started to see PEBs that did not feature any images of politicians, even nonspeaking ones. The only politicians who now seem assured of speaking parts are the party leaders, and even the leader's place is not sacrosanct; rather, it is contingent upon strategic calculation of his or her vote-winning appeal. Thus Figure 4.1 shows a dramatic plunge in speaking time allotted to William Hague in 2001, as compared to John Major in 1997. The agency

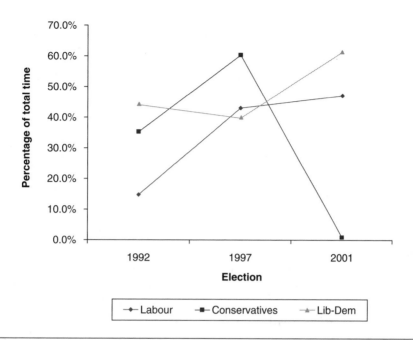

Figure 4.1   Party Leaders Speaking in PEBs (Percentage of Total Time), 1992 to 2001

SOURCE: Based on all 42 PEBs for the three main parties.

Note: Lib-Dem indicates the Liberal Democratic Party; PEB, party election broadcast.

Yellow M replaced Saatchi for the Conservatives for the 2001 campaign, and its PEBs were extraordinary in that they cut back radically on the use of any speech at all, preferring music, sound effects, and inter-titles to carry the message.

These trends, the personalised leader portraits, the absence of other politicians, and the emergence of the politician-free ad are of a piece with the move toward nonpolitical styles of presentation. Blair's Labour has pursued the nonpolitical style with particular vigour. News and documentary have been the predominant formats of PEBs generally over many years, but Labour increasingly has been willing to experiment with genre, using soap opera, romantic drama, spoof horror, satire, and pop video over the last two campaigns. By range of genre, Labour's broadcasts stand

apart from both their main rivals (Scammell & Langer, in press). The Conservatives' genre range has been far more limited: In 2001 especially its PEBs borrowed heavily from the crime and horror genres. In 2001, the Liberal Democrats were the only party that did not stray at all from the news-documentary format.

Dominance of Issue Advertising

Research over successive U.K. elections continues to find that PEBs are informative. They provide a reasonable guide to the main parties' key proposals and to the difference between the party platforms (Blumler & McQuail, 1968; Hodess et al., 2000; Scammell & Semetko, 1995). Content analysis shows that in the 1997-2001 campaigns, 75% of the three

Table 4.5   Information Content in Party PEBs in the Elections of 1997 and 2001

PEB Content	Labour % (n)	Conservatives % (n)	Lib-Dem % (n)	Total % (n)
Emphasis				
Issue	70 (7)	80 (8)	75 (6)	75 (21)
Image	30 (3)	20 (2)	25 (2)	25 (7)
Policy proposals				
Vague	50 (5)	80 (8)	62.5 (5)	64.3 (18)
Specific	30 (3)	40 (4)	62.5 (5)	42.9 (12)

Note: Lib-Dem indicates the Liberal Democratic Party; PEB, party election broadcast.

main parties' PEBs emphasised issues; 43% contained specific policy proposals (see Table 4.5). The influence of professional advertisers has not diluted the dominance of issues. This might seem surprising, given the trends to nonpolitical styles and because commercial advertising itself has shifted from hard-sell, information-based campaigns to soft-sell, entertainment-oriented audience pleasers (Corner, 1995). One might expect that Labour's PEBs, as the most overtly nonpolitical stylistically, might be less issue focussed than the others and, indeed, that is the case. However, it is clear that, for all parties, issues remain the prime tool of differentiation, a finding that conforms to Kaid, Tedesco, Dimitrova, and Williams' (2003) internationally comparative study: Issue-based advertising is the norm in long-established democracies.

Negative Advertising

The dominance of negative advertising and its potential damage to voter engagement has been a major thrust of research in the United States over the last decade (Ansolabehere & Iyengar, 1995; Jamieson, 2000). However, as Kaid et al. (2003) have shown, negative dominance is a peculiarly American problem. Despite clear evidence of U.K. campaigners' willingness to draw lessons from America (Plasser, 2002; Scammell, 1995), they have for the most part declined to go heavily negative. For the three elections from 1992, the PEBs overall have been predominantly positive

(Table 4.6), and both Labour and the Liberal Democrats have become slightly more positive over time. The Conservatives are the persistent exception. Their advertising has become more negative, culminating in the 2001 campaign, which was overwhelmingly attack focussed and contained the most negative series of PEBs yet. Party is the only clear correlation to the propensity to use negative advertising: The Conservatives favoured it whether they were entering the election as the incumbent government (1992 and 1997) or the opposition (2001). Their 2001 campaign, with its horror themes and failure to make any dent in Labour's landslide majority, was heavily criticised after the event. Under the leadership of William Hague, the party had failed to make headway in the polls since 1997 and trailed well behind Labour going into the official campaign, and their negativity was in part a desperate device to try to drive down voter turnout. Although the evidence is not completely conclusive, some research finds that negative content has no effect on U.K. voters (Norris et al., 1999; Sanders & Norris, 2002), and, worse from the Conservative point of view, Pattie and Johnston (2002) suggest that negative ads may backfire on the perpetrator.

PEBs: Do They Work?

PEBs do not enjoy an enviable reputation. An Independent Television Commission (2001) survey of the 2001 election reported

Table 4.6   Negative Appeals in Party PEBs in the General Elections of 1992 through 2001

Dominant Focus	Labour % (n)	Conservatives % (n)	Lib-Dem % (n)	Total % (n)
Positive	67 (10)	20 (3)	75 (9)	52 (22)
Negative	27 (4)	60 (9)	0 (0)	31 (13)
Balanced	7 (1)	20 (3)	25 (3)	17 (7)

Note: Lib-Dem indicates the Liberal Democratic Party; PEB, party election broadcast.

that 57% of respondents turned off or switched channels when PEBs were announced; only 2% found them persuasive, and just 32% said they paid any attention. A survey for the Electoral Commission (2001) presents more dismal findings: 53% of viewers said PEBs were boring, 19% regarded them as dull, and just 13% thought them informative. These results are consistent over time. Audience research carried out for the broadcasting authorities in the 1980s also reported that nearly half the viewer sample found PEBs "boring" (Wober & Svennevig, 1981; Wober, Svennevig & Gunter, 1986). Market & Opinion Research International tracking surveys for the *London Times* over the three elections from 1992 to 2001 reported on each occasion that only about one third of respondents claimed some interest in party broadcasts (cited in Electoral Commission, 2003, p. 12). For all the professional expertise, PEBs have not improved their standing in public esteem.

However, these surveys also provide reasons to suggest that PEBs are potentially valuable opportunities for the parties. The Electoral Commission (2003, pp. 12-13) reported that at least one PEB was seen by between 55% and 62% of the electorate, and although this figure is down from 73% in the 1997 election, all the survey evidence indicates that PEBs still have considerable reach (also see Table 4.3). Moreover, survey respondents claimed that PEBs had been more influential on voting decisions (22%) than opinion polls (13%), posters (10%), and the Internet (4%). Only the news media rated significantly

higher. Thus, the decline thesis notwithstanding, poll evidence suggests that PEBs remain the parties' most important direct campaign tool.

By comparison with media-commissioned surveys, there has been relatively little academic research into PEB effects since the 1960s. Blumler and McQuail's seminal study (1968) confirmed the reinforcement thesis of media effects: PEBs appeared to have little impact on the vote of the two major parties. However, these authors also found that PEBs were important learning resources for undecided voters, that they did influence impressions of parties' competence to govern, and that the Liberals, in particular, benefited. The more uncommitted voters were exposed to Liberal broadcasts, the better their opinion of the party. Pattie and Johnston (2002) revisited PEB effects with an analysis of panel data for the 1997 campaign. Echoing Blumler and McQuail, they found no impact on voting intentions for Labour and the Conservatives but a significant third-party effect: Viewing a Liberal Democrat broadcast increased support for the party. They plausibly explain the third-party effect by simple exposure: Elections provide the only occasions when the party receives high levels of media attention, and the near-equal ration of PEBs assists significantly in raising a third party's profile. Pattie and Johnston also found more general PEB effects: improved assessments of leaders' qualities and, to a lesser extent, overall opinions of parties; also, Labour PEBs (alone) reduced cynicism, encouraging viewers to agree that politicians were interested in more than just buying votes. These authors concluded: "The impact of PEBs is not large . . . but they do have some bearing on election outcomes in Britain" (p. 355).

CONCLUSION: THE FUTURE OF POLITICAL ADVERTISING

Political advertising in the future can be expected to stay on current trend paths: increasingly personalized around leaders on the one hand, politician-free on the other, predominantly issue based, and predominantly positive. Perhaps, if Labour is the trend setter, there will be a further move to more commercial, "nonpolitical" styles and uses of genre. Negative advertising failed for the Conservatives in 2001, and there is little evidence in the United Kingdom to support the thesis that negative campaigns are more effective than positive. As the parties start to gear up for the next election, we can be certain of plenty of attack advertising, especially in print. However, it would be equally surprising if the Conservatives did not wage a more positive PEB campaign.[7] Given declining audiences for the PEB-obliged channels, one would also expect the parties to continue to use a variety of tactics to draw news attention to their advertising. Shock and celebrity are the standards, but Labour in February 2005 gave us a taste of the future with its use of Internet interactivity. A selection of eight posters, all attacking Tory leader Michael Howard, were e-mailed to supporters, who were invited to vote for their favourite. The initiative backfired somewhat after claims that one of the posters was a suspiciously anti-Semitic portrait of Howard. Nonetheless, the use of e-mail and Web sites for the dissemination of advertising looks set to be a new trend.

Will PEBs survive? They seem increasingly anachronistic in a multichannel world, and their chances of being seen at all will diminish as broadcast audiences fragment. They are not well regarded, and one of their major justifications—that they control campaign costs—has been removed by the imposition of national campaign expenditure limits. For all that, they have proved remarkably resilient. They are still the parties' and broadcasters' overwhelmingly preferred alternative to paid political advertising on television, and the latter prospect is nowhere on the horizon. Public opinion, judging by poll evidence, is in favour of retaining PEBs. Even as most claim to be bored with them, a large majority says it is important that they be shown (Electoral Commission, 2003, p. 11). Moreover, and despite broadcast channel proliferation, PEBs are still the most important direct party communication with voters.

They will survive for the foreseeable future, and it is quite likely that they will be protected. In 2003, the Electoral Commission recommended to the government that the obligation to transmit party broadcasts be extended beyond the present narrow group of terrestrial channels and that any TV channel reaching a prescribed threshold of audience share be required to broadcast PEBs. The commission recommended further that parties be given more flexibility and allowed to choose between packages of fewer, longer broadcasts or more, shorter ones. Government responded positively in principle to the recommendations, although by press time it had not produced formal proposals for reform. However, the commission's recommendations seem to be proposals that the parties will find hard to resist. The future thus may well be more and shorter PPBs or PEBs, increasingly in the form of commercial advertising but without the payment. It would be a typically British compromise.

NOTES

1. The BBC operates under Royal Charter, currently renegotiated every 10 years. The charter is due for renewal in 2006. In March 2005, the government made clear that it intended to extend licence fee funding for the BBC, payable by all homes with televisions.

2. Provisions in the Representation of the People Acts ensured that no parliamentary candidate feature in television news without similar opportunity

for his or her competitors. Although this rule has not applied to national leaders talking about national issues, it has been applied strictly to local constituency reports and, indeed, any themes or issues that featured candidates in a nonleadership capacity.

3. There was some minority dissent from some commercial radio organisations and from a professional association, the Institute of Practitioners in Advertising (Electoral Commission, 2003, p. 42).

4. Ofcom was established by the Communications Act of 2003, and it replaced separate regulators for each of the television, radio, and telecoms sectors. The BBC continues to be regulated separately, by a board of governors whose remit is established by Royal Charter, following parliamentary debate.

5. The Advertising Standards Authority opted out of any regulatory control of political advertising following the 1997 election. It argued that it might damage the advertising industry's self-regulatory system if it were seen to have been deployed against one political party but not another. It also felt unable to rule sufficiently quickly to affect an election campaign. Thus its Codes of Practice completely exempt political advertising.

6. The commercial TV regulator is required by law to survey public attitudes about television content, including perceptions of news, its impartiality, and TV's importance as a provider of national and world information relative to newspapers and other sources. These surveys have consistently shown TV to be the most important and trusted source of national and world news.

7. Preliminary analysis of the 2005 election suggests that the Conservatives were less negative than previously, although both Labour and the Liberal Democrats were more negative.

REFERENCES

Ansolabehere, S., & Iyengar, S. (1995). *Going negative.* New York: Free Press.

Blumler, J. G., & McQuail, D. (1968). *Television in politics.* London: Faber & Faber.

Blumler, J. G., & Nossiter, T. (1989). The earnest versus the determined. In I. Crewe & M. Harrop (Eds.), *Political communications: The general election campaign of 1987* (pp. 157–174). Cambridge, UK: Cambridge University Press.

Broadcast guidance: Ofcom rules on party political and referendum broadcasts. (2004, October). Retrieved January 25, 2006, from the Office of Communication Web site: http://www.ofcom.org.uk/tv/ifi/guidance/ppbrules/?a=87101

Butler, D. & Kavanagh, D. (2002). *The British general election of 2001.* Basingstoke, England: Palgrave.

Cockerell, M. (1988). *Live from number 10.* London: Faber & Faber.

Corner, J. (1995). *Television form and public address.* London: Edward Arnold.

Culf, A. (1997, January 10). Demon eyes wins top award. *The Guardian.*

Electoral Commission. (2001). *Election 2001: The official results.* London: Politicos.

Electoral Commission. (2003, January 13). *Party political broadcasting: Report and recommendations.* Retrieved November 30, 2005, from http://www.electoralcommission.gov.uk/templates/search/document.cfm/6718

Hallin, D., & Mancini, P. (2004). *Comparing media systems.* Cambridge, UK: Cambridge University Press

Harrison, M. (1974). Television and radio. In D.Butler & D.Kavanagh (Eds.), *The British general election of 1974* (pp. 146–169). Basingstoke, England: Macmillan.

Harrison, M. (2002). Politics on the air. In D.Butler & D. Kavanagh (Eds.), *The British general election of 2001* (pp. 132–155). Basingstoke, England: Macmillan.

Hodess, R., Tedesco, J., & Kaid, L. L. (2002). British party election broadcasts: A comparison of 1992 and 1997. *Harvard Journal of Press/Politics, 5*(4), 55–70.

Independent Television Commission (2001). *Election 2001: Viewers' responses to the television coverage.* London: Author.

Jamieson, K. H. (2000). *Everything you think you know about politics . . . and why you are wrong.* New York: Basic Books.

Kaid, L. L., Tedesco, J. C., Dimitrova, D. V., & Williams, A. P. (2003, September). *Comparing political advertising around the world.* Paper presented at the Political Marketing Conference, University of Middlesex, London.

Norris, P., Curtice, J., Sanders, D., Scammell, M., & Semetko, H. (1999). *On message: Communicating the campaign.* London: Sage.

Pattie, C. J., & Johnston, R. J. (2002). Assessing the TV campaign: The impact of party election broadcasting on voters' opinions in the 1997 British general election. *Political Communication, 19,* 333–358.

Pinto-Duschinsky, M. (1992, November 30). Labour £10 million campaign closes the gap with the Tories. *London Times,* p. 2.

Plasser, F. (2002). *Global political campaigning.* London: Praeger.

Sanders, D., & Norris, P. (2002, March). *Advocacy and attack.* Paper presented at the Conference of the Euro Consortium for Political Research, Turin, Italy.

Scammell, M. (1995). *Designer politics.* Basingstoke, England: Macmillan.

Scammell, M. (2001). The media and media management. In A. Seldon (Ed.), *The Blair effect: The Blair government 1997-2001* (pp. 509–534). London: Little, Brown.

Scammell, M., & Harrop, M. (2002). The press disarmed. In D. Butler & D. Kavanagh (Eds.), *The British general election of 2001* (pp. 156–182). Basingstoke, England: Macmillan.

Scammell, M., & Langer, A. I. (in press). Political advertising: Why is it so boring? *Media, Culture & Society.*

Scammell, M., & Semetko, H. (1995). Political advertising on television: The British experience. In L. L. Kaid & C. Holtz-Bacha (Eds), *Political advertising in Western democracies* (pp. 19–43). London: Sage.

Semetko, H., & Scammell, M. (2005, September 1–4). *Television news and elections: Lessons from Britain and the U.S.* Paper presented at the annual meeting of the American Political Science Association, Washington, D.C.

Seymour-Ure, C. (1991). *The British press and broadcasting since 1945.* Oxford, England: Blackwell.

Tunstall, J. (1997). The United Kingdom. In Euromedia Research Group (Eds.), *The media in Western Europe* (pp. 244–259). London: Sage.

TV facts. (2006). Retrieved January 25, 2006, from the Broadcasters Audience Research Board Web site: http://www.barb.co.uk/tvfacts.cfm?flag=tvfacts

Wober, J., & Svennevig, M. (1981). *Party political broadcasts and their use for the viewing public.* London: Independent Broadcasting Authority, Audience Research Department.

Wober, J., Svennevig, M., & Gunter, B. (1986). The television audience in the 1983 general election. In I. Crewe & M. Harrop (Eds.), *Political communications: The general election campaign of 1983* (pp. 95–103). Cambridge, England: Cambridge University Press.

5

Election Broadcasts in France

LYNDA LEE KAID AND NATHALIE GAGNÈRE

The role of television in the French election process has evolved as part of a complex public broadcasting system that provides many opportunities for broadcast exposure for political parties and leaders. As in most modern democracies, television has become a dominant medium for information distribution. Television is the major source of information for French citizens: 55 million people in France have television, and 15 million of them subscribe to cable or satellite channels ("Latest French audience," 2005). The average French viewer identifies television as his or her major information source and spends more than 3 hours per day watching television (Cayrol, 1988; Gaouette, 1997; Koch, 1988).

THE POLITICAL AND MEDIA SYSTEM IN FRANCE

The executive power in France includes a directly elected president and a prime minister who serves as head of the government; the legislative branch consists of a bicameral parliament, with the preeminent National Assembly and a lower house, or Senate. Presidents are currently elected for 5-year terms, as are members of the National Assembly, and lower house Senate members are chosen by a group of elected officials for 6-year terms, renewable every 3 years.[1] The directly elected president serves in official capacities, providing policy leadership and national and international representation for France. The French prime minister serves as a day-to-day governmental leader and legislative agenda setter.[2] Consequently, the French system provides the possibility that the president and the prime minister might be of different political parties,[3] and indeed, this situation has occurred several times in the past 25 years, forcing the government to operate on the basis of "cohabitation." For instance, in the 1980s, Socialist François Mitterrand served as president and conservative Jacques Chirac (of the Rassemblement pour la République [RPR;

Authors' Note: The authors would like to thank Stella Darby, Marc Kijner, Laura Rowe, Andrew Paul Williams, and Kaye Trammell for their assistance with this project.

Rally for the Republic] Party) as prime minister. After Chirac was elected president in 1995, he found himself a few years later (1997-2002) facing the reverse situation when a Socialist coalition was able to place Lionel Jospin in the prime minister's seat. The French government was forced to operate on the basis of these uneasy compromises between the two parties and leaders for the sake of maintaining a viable government. However, shortly after his reelection, Chirac's supporters succeeded in bringing together Conservatives, Liberals, and dissidents from the Union pour la Démocratie Française (Union for French Democracy) to form a presidential majority under the flagship of the Union pour la Majorité Présidentielle (Union for the Presidential Majority Party).[4] This strategy allowed the president to secure both executive positions.

Candidates for the National Assembly and the presidency compete in a "first ballot." If no candidate receives a majority vote, the two candidates with the highest vote totals in the first ballot face a run-off election in a "second ballot."[5] This second ballot follows (usually) 1 or 2 weeks after the first ballot, resulting in a total *official* campaign period of about 3 or 4 weeks for both the first and second ballots.[6]

The media system in France is quite complex in that electronic media were traditionally state owned and operated, leading to limited numbers of radio and television outlets in France prior to the 1980s. In the 1980s, however, the government began to reconfigure and deregulate the public monopoly on broadcasting in a controlled fashion (Dyson & Humphreys, 1989; Ehrmann, 1983; Ehrmann & Schain, 1992; Hoffmann-Riem, 1986). Although the media have expanded greatly in the past three decades, and private media, cable, and satellite have greatly increased choices for French citizens, the media system is still highly regulated. The private TF1 channel enjoys the highest ratings of French channel choices, but the public France 2, France 3, and France 5 provide substantial audiences for political programs. News media are charged with covering candidates and parties equally,[7] and in addition to the traditional news formats, popular political shows such as *Mots croisés* (Crosswords), *Cent minutes pour convaincre* (100 minutes to convince) and *France Europe express* play important roles in providing information about political leaders and events (Neveu, 1999). Moreover, in recent years, political leaders and would-be candidates have engaged in new forms of political communication. Like American politicians, they have discovered the art of political "infotainment" in popular talk shows such as *Vivement Dimanche* (Roll on Sunday), *Tout le monde en parle* (Everybody talks about it), and *On ne peut pas plaire à tout le monde* (One cannot be liked by everyone) (Neveu, 2003). As the role of television has grown in French politics, many scholars have cautioned that television's overt predisposition toward dramatization of political events and leaders may be responsible for decreasing public concentration on the political platforms and issues of the parties and candidates (Cayrol, 1997). It is also important to remember that journalists in France often have strong, visible, ideological affiliations that interact with the personalized qualities of the television medium.

ELECTORAL ACCESS TO TELEVISION IN FRANCE

Despite the development of private broadcasting in France, candidates and parties cannot buy time on public or private radio and television stations in France. Instead, candidates are allocated equal blocks of "free" program time on the public television stations: France 2, France 3, France 4, and France 5 (Haiman, 1991; Johnston & Gerstlé, 1995). The time and scheduling of these free "émissions politiques" have changed during the past several election cycles.

As a result of changes to the French Electoral Code in 1985 and the evolution of regulatory interpretations, French candidates were able to use "videoclips" in their free-time television allotments in the 1986 legislative elections (Dauncey, 1999). Prior to this, television time allocated to candidates was characterized by long "talking head" formats that bore little resemblance to modern advertising. Forbes and Nice (1979) described these early French broadcasts as having a "limited televisual repertoire" (p. 42). Thus the 1988 presidential campaign marked a major change in the presidential broadcast formats, allowing presidential candidates to make use of "clips" (Gourevitch, 1989; Johnston, 1991) that consisted of preproduced segments added to various parts of the traditional 5- and 15-minute broadcasts. With their fast-paced edits, visually interesting scene changes, and music, these clips made French candidate broadcasts much more similar to the American campaign style than those used in any previous French campaigns (Johnston, 1991; Kaid, 1991). The French spots moved even closer to the American style in 1995, when spots were produced under new rules that provided for shorter formats and fewer content restrictions.

New regulations governing political campaigns and campaign financing were adopted in France in the early 1990s. These new rules, in effect for the 1995 national elections, not only established new restrictions on campaign finances but banned paid political advertising in all forms of media (television, newspaper, radio, posters, etc.) for 3 months before the election (Maarek, 1997). French regulations governing the presidential election in 2002 provided for precise allocations of broadcast lengths. For the first ballot, each candidate was given, free, on France 2, France 3, and France 5 a set of four "émissions de petit format" (1 minute and 45 seconds each); a set of four "émissions de grand format" (5 minutes each, repeated one time); and one additional broadcast of 1 minute in length (Conseil Supérieur de l'Audiovisuel, 2002b). In the second ballot, each candidate was granted five slots of 2 minutes and five slots of 5 minutes, which were rebroadcast once. Compared to previous presidential elections, the total amount of time allocated to each candidate was actually much smaller, to take into consideration the large number of candidates, as well as time and technical constraints.[8] Candidates had no choice about when their broadcasts would be scheduled, as these slots were also strictly regulated and pronounced in advance after lots were drawn by the Conseil Supérieur de l'Audiovisuel (CSA, 2002a, 2002c, 2002d).

In addition to the number, length, and scheduling of the candidate broadcasts, the regulations set up detailed restrictions on the content of the broadcasts. As set forth in the 2004 regulations (CSA, 2004), candidates must express themselves verbally and visually during the broadcast, and preproduced video or audio segments cannot exceed 50% of the total time allocated to parties or candidates.[9] Outdoor settings can be used, but indoor segments must be produced under very strict rules. For instance, broadcasts cannot be filmed in official public buildings, cannot make use of national and European emblems, and cannot use the music of the French national anthem. Additional restrictions include a prohibition against derision of other candidates or their representative and a ban against using the broadcast to ask for funds. These detailed regulations on time, format, placement, and content of the French political broadcasts are quite restrictive.

HISTORY AND USE OF POLITICAL BROADCASTING IN FRENCH CAMPAIGNS

Like their American counterparts, French politicians have come to see television and successful performance on it as a major factor in presidential elections (Tarlé, 1979). A 1974 public opinion poll, for instance, reported that 64% of the electorate thought television the most useful and efficient means of "choosing a candidate," and 74% thought it best for "knowing what politicians are like" (Grosser, 1975). In fact, television has been cited as playing a major role in establishing the late French president François Mitterrand's image as a statesman (Charlot, 1975; Forbes & Nice, 1979). However, most analyses of the role of television in French politics have focused on the impact of television news formats, which, also like their American counterparts, have been found to concentrate a great deal of time and attention on campaign strategy, or the "horse race" aspects of the campaigns (Gerstlé, Davis, & Duhamel, 1991; Neveu, 1999).

The 1988 Presidential Election

As the first presidential campaign in France conducted under regulations that allowed the use of videoclips within the 5- and 15-minute formats prescribed for the free-time allocations to candidates, the 1988 campaign gave French voters new and more dramatized visual representations of political leaders. The first empirical studies of election broadcasts focused on this election (Gourevitch, 1989; Johnston, 1991; Johnston & Gerstle, 1995; Kaid, 1991).

In 1988, candidates representing nine parties qualified for the first-round ballot, and in the 2 weeks prior to the election on April 24 (first ballot), each was given a 5-minute block at the beginning and end of each of the 2 weeks and four 15-minute blocks during these weeks. The two candidates with the most votes after the first ballot (incumbent president François Mitterrand and Prime Minister Jacques Chirac) were allotted four additional 5-minute slots and four 15-minute slots in the last week before the final balloting on May 8 (Haiman, 1991).

Both Mitterrand and Chirac were able to make use of the shorter, more visually intensive videoclips, which were limited to no more than 40% of the total time of each broadcast. Over the course of both rounds, candidates Mitterrand and Chirac each produced 10 broadcasts; 14 of these 20 broadcasts contained the new and innovative videoclips,

ranging from 4 seconds to 3 minutes (Johnston, 1991). Television audience percentages for these long program formats were not high, accounting for only 5% to 10% of the available audience (Haiman, 1991).

In commenting on the possible comparable use of this format for the French campaign and its similarities to the American style of campaign promotion, Jacques Gerstlé (1989) commented that such dramatizations provide opportunities to construct political reality by transmitting knowledge about the election stakes, crystallizing images, and reinforcing cultural identities. The most unusual and innovative broadcasts in 1988 were those of Socialist incumbent president François Mitterrand, who used in some of his free-time broadcasts a video sequence that presented an 80-second "chronological barrage of 500 images of French history, politics and culture from 1789 to 1988" (Dauncey, 1999, p. 3), providing a visual representation of Mitterrand's campaign slogan, "*La France unie.*" In fact, this clip has been credited with "[leading] the way in modernizing TV political communication" and "[setting] the style of imagery in invoking history, community and unity" (Dauncey, 1999, p. 3). Mitterrand was reelected president with 54% of the vote in the second round of voting.

The 1993 Legislative Elections

Following the 1988 presidential campaign, the French regulatory agency (CSA), citing concern for the low audience numbers attracted by election broadcasts, began to develop new policies for the free broadcasts required by the French Electoral Code (Dauncey, 1999; Johnston & Gerstlé, 1995). These changes governed the 1993 legislative elections, when the public television stations provided a total of 3 hours of broadcast time for the first ballot and 90 minutes for the second ballot, to be shared among all parties. The changes also provided for two other innovations: shorter broadcasts (in two forms, 1-3 minutes and 4-5 minutes) and more frequent airing in more popular time slots on the television channels (Dauncey, 1999). These new formats also allowed additional liberal use of videoclips, which could make up as much as 50% of the shorter time sequences and up to 40% of the longer ones. Broadcast time slots in the legislative elections were allotted to the parties in proportion to their electoral strength in the assembly.

However, the beleaguered Socialist Party candidates were not able to take advantage of the new formats and time slots. They used many of their slots for sober, talking-head presentations. They also used longer spots than other parties and were innovative perhaps only in their use of what Dauncey (1999) labels "vox pox": sequences in which short individual testimonials of ordinary people provide visualization of the culture and values the party wishes to represent.

The RPR party broadcasts took advantage of shorter time sequences; most were 60-second formats. Short sound sequences were "alternated with rapid video sequences backed by appropriately-toned music" (Dauncey, 1999, p. 7). Other parties, although able to take advantage of the new format's possibilities, offered few innovations.

The 1995 Presidential Campaign Broadcasts

In the 1995 French presidential election, with no incumbent president dominating the spotlight, RPR prime minister Jacques Chirac made another bid for the presidency and found himself, in the second round of balloting, facing the Socialist Party candidate, Lionel Jospin. Both party candidates benefited from even more relaxed time, format, and videoclip allowances, but Jospin presented himself in the first round in more traditional question and answer formats and only developed a more dynamic video portrayal in his second-round broadcasts. Chirac, on the other hand, positioned himself as a more modern and dynamic candidate, whose broadcasts in both

the first- and second-ballot time slots epitomized a candidate of substance and policy whose visual symbol of a "fruit-bearing tree" was open to multiple interpretations (Dauncey, 1999).

The 2002 French Presidential Contest on Television

The battle for the French presidency in 2002 was expected to be a fight between the incumbent president, conservative Jacques Chirac, and the sitting prime minister, Socialist Lionel Jospin ("They're just about," 2002). With a president and prime minister from two different political parties, France had been governed jointly by a split arrangement, as in 1997 the Socialist party's parliamentary control accorded them the prime minister's position, resulting in a power-sharing arrangement, or "cohabitation" (Krause, 2000). Leading up to the 2002 election, both Chirac and Jospin enjoyed relatively high respect and approval in opinion polls and were engaged in public communication campaigns designed to mold their images into more positive, sympathetic, and likeable heads of state (Krause, 2000).

However, as the election date in the spring of 2002 grew closer, the French political landscape seemed less settled and more fragmented. The multiparty system in France allowed for 16 presidential candidates, who split the vote along both the left and the right, and neither major candidate (Chirac or Jospin) seemed to engage or excite the electorate. The result was a surprising outcome on the first ballot on April 21, 2002. With the second lowest voter turnout rate in a French presidential race in 37 years, the expected did not happen. Prime Minister Jospin failed to reach the vote level needed in the first ballot to advance to the second ballot run-off. Instead, perennial Front National candidate Jean Marie Le Pen received 16.9% of the votes, sufficient to stand against incumbent president Chirac for the second ballot on May 5 ("Explaining Le Pen's," 2002). The 2-week run-off race turned into an orgy of "stop Le Pen" sentiment, as political leaders from both ends of the spectrum joined labor unions and other groups to ensure that Le Pen did not do well in the final vote (Graham, 2002). Le Pen's victory in the first ballot seemed particularly to energize young voters to protest and to get involved in the system ("Le révolte civique," 2002). On May 2, the leading Paris newspaper, *Le Monde,* did a special layout with many stories about the political leanings and thoughts of young voters ("Ces jeunes qui," 2002).

The first-ballot election result in France also set off a near-hysterical reaction and a media frenzy, not only in France, but throughout Europe. Le Pen was considered a right-wing extremist by many, and his success seemed tantamount to the legitimizing of his entire ultra-right agenda. His advance to the second ballot was labeled cataclysmic, a tornado, a disaster, almost every dramatic phrase that could be called to mind. Known for his anti-immigrant stances, Le Pen was characterized by journalists as "unquestionably France's most rousing orator" (Gourevitch, 1997), given to "roaring flights of populist speech, rich in metaphor, sarcasm, bathos, and a sort of intimacy-building vulgarity ... accompanied by a repertoire of dramatic facial expressions, hand flailings, and full-body thrusts." Le Pen seems to have a "gift for language, especially the sinister kind," remarked a reporter for the *London Times* (Bremner, 2002c, p. 17).

Candidate broadcasts in the 2002 elections reached a large audience. During the first round of the 2002 presidential election, 33 million viewers watched official political programs the first week. The second week, there were some 27 million who saw these broadcasts. This number was even more significant in the second round: Candidate ads on television reached 48 million viewers.[10] Another aspect of the second round of the campaign may have made the party broadcasts even more important than usual in 2002. As mentioned earlier, Chirac's refusal of any kind of direct confrontation with Le Pen meant that, for the first time since 1974, the traditional

debate between the two leading contestants did not happen. Because Chirac did not want to dignify Le Pen's candidacy by appearing on a TV platform with him, the importance of media coverage and party broadcasts took on greater significance. However, despite Chirac's refusal to debate (Bremner, 2002a), he eventually won the second ballot with over 80% of the votes (Johnson, 2002).

RESEARCH ON THE CONTENT AND EFFECTS OF POLITICAL BROADCASTS

Research on the content and effects of French political advertising has been a neglected area in French political communications. Most political communication research has focused on the language and rhetorical style of political leaders (Labbé, 1990), analysis of formal televised debates of the candidates (Nel, 1990), and the political reporting of the campaigns in the news media (Duhamel, 2000; Le Roux, 1993; Maarek, 1997, 2003; Neveu, 1997, 1999). Nonetheless, there have been some descriptive and quantitative analyses of the content of the presidential candidate broadcasts and their effects in the past three election cycles, 1988, 1995, and 2002.

Content and Style of the Presidential Television Broadcasts

The first systematic analyses of the broadcasts were conducted during the 1988 presidential campaign. The innovation of allowing preproduced videoclips made the broadcasts more interesting and more visually dramatic (Gourevitch, 1989). Despite these television production characteristics, however, Johnston (1991) concluded that spots emphasized issues more than images and used more formal settings. French candidates were also more likely to appear in their ads (speaking for themselves) and to use their time to promote their own candidacies, devoting less time than their American counterparts to attacking their opponents (Johnston & Gerstlé, 1995). Holtz-Bacha, Kaid, and Johnston (1994) also found that French

Table 5.1   Content of Ads in 1988 and 2002 French Presidential Campaigns (%)

Ad Content	1988		2002	
	Mitterrand (n = 10)	Chirac (n = 10)	Chirac (n = 5)	Le Pen (n = 5)
Focus				
Candidate positive	100	100	100	80
Opponent negative	0	0	0	20
Negative attack present in ad	0	50	0	80
Ad emphasis				
Issue	100	90	100	60
Image	0	0	0	40
Type of appeal				
Emotional	10	10	40	100
Logical	70	90	80	20
Ethos	20	0	0	80
Character qualities				
Honesty	36	20	0	60
Toughness	73	90	40	80
Warmth and compassion	64	40	40	60
Competence	100	100	100	60
Performance and success	100	80	60	60
Aggressiveness	50	80	0	40
Activeness	82	100	80	60
Qualifications	90	90	20	80

SOURCE: The data for this table were taken from earlier research on the 1988 campaign (Johnston, 1991) and the 2002 campaign (Kaid, Gagnère, Williams, & Trammell, 2003).

Note: Ads include those broadcast before the first and second ballots in 1988, but only those broadcast just prior to the second ballot in 2002.

spots were primarily issue oriented and relied on logical appeals. Similar conclusions were clear in the 2002 campaign (Gagnère & Kaid, 2003).

Table 5.1 shows the content of presidential broadcasts in 1988 and 2002. Overall, French political broadcasts are positive, focusing most of their attention on the issues and programs of the candidate and his party. Although most ads were positive, there was a significant difference in the number of ads in which attacks were made, with Le Pen making some sort of attack on Chirac in 60% of his ads and Chirac remaining above the fray, refraining from any attacks on Le Pen.

This analysis also shows that the presidential candidates primarily use logical appeals to make their case to French voters. In the 1988 campaign, 70% of Mitterrand's broadcasts and 90% of Chirac's programs relied on logical approaches. However, the table also shows that this trend was different in 2002 for the use of emotional appeals. Although neither Mitterrand nor Chirac relied heavily on such appeals in the 1988 campaign, emotion played a much greater role in 2002, because all of Le Pen's spots placed a heavy emphasis on emotion, and even Chirac used emotion in almost half (40%) of his broadcasts.

Effects of Campaign Broadcasts on Voters

Few studies have explored the effects of exposure to French political broadcasts on the voters to whom the spots are addressed. Table 5.2

Table 5.2   Effects of Exposure to Broadcast Advertising in Presidential Campaigns

Ratings of Candidates	Before Viewing (%)	After Viewing (%)
1988		
Mitterrand	58.8	58.9
Chirac[a]	42.0	40.3
1995		
Chirac	48.4	48.8
Jospin	52.8	52.7
2002		
Chirac	41.1	42.9
Le Pen	38.5	31.1

SOURCE: The data for this table were taken from earlier research by the authors (Gagnère & Kaid, 2003; Kaid, 1991; Kaid et al., 2003).

a. *t* test indicates difference between pre- and posttest is significant at p < .05.

Note: Ratings are sum of 12 bipolar adjective pairs (rated 1-7): qualified-unqualified, sophisticated-unsophisticated, honest-dishonest, believable-unbelievable, successful-unsuccessful, attractive-unattractive, friendly-unfriendly, sincere-insincere, calm-excitable, aggressive-unaggressive, strong-weak, active-inactive (Kaid, 1995).

summarizes results from experimental studies from the 1988, 1995, and 2002 French presidential elections. These studies were conducted using young voters at universities in France, whose responses to the presidential candidates were measured before and after viewing sample broadcasts from the respective campaigns.

Overall, these experiments suggest that exposure to the political broadcasts has not been a very important factor in changing voter evaluations of French presidential candidates. The only substantial change documented in Table 5.2 is the significant decrease in positive evaluation of Jacques Chirac following viewing of his broadcasts in 1988. As reported here and in earlier studies (Kaid, 1991; Kaid & Holtz-Bacha, 1995), viewing of the Chirac broadcasts resulted in Chirac being viewed as less *qualified* and less *successful*. No significant effects were observed from similar experimental studies conducted on exposure to television broadcasts by Chirac and Jospin in the 1995 election (Kaid, McKinnon, & Gagnère, 1996). More in-depth analysis of the image dimensions tapped by viewership of the broadcasts, using multiple regression analysis, revealed that the programs had differing influences on Chirac and Jospin supporters and that the broadcasts may have been influential in reconfiguring the image dimensions of the presidential candidates (Cwalina, Falkowski, & Kaid, 2000). Among Chirac's supporters, his own advertisements positively influenced voter feelings, but Jospin's advertisements weakened the relation between his image and voters' attitudes toward him.

Emotional Reactions to French Political Broadcasts

There also seemed to be strong correlations between the emotional content of political broadcasts in France and the effects of the broadcasts on the presidential candidates' evaluations in all three elections, suggesting that the television medium may enhance emotional associations with the candidates (Kaid, 1991; Kaid et al., 1996; Kaid et al., 2003). Although research does show that the French broadcasts have a strong grounding in logical proof and argumentation, the broadcasts also appeared to elicit strong emotional reactions for both candidates in 2002. The difference in these two areas between Chirac and Le Pen was striking. The fact that Chirac focused his broadcasts on issues and was more likely to use logical proof than Le Pen is mirrored in the spot content shown in Table 5.1. This emphasis resulted in a corresponding higher recall of issues for Chirac than for Le Pen by viewers in the experiment, indicating a specific result from spot viewing. For instance, Kaid et al. (2003) found that young French voters recalled an average of 3.9 issues from Chirac's broadcasts but only 2.2 from Le Pen broadcasts.[11] There was no significant difference in the number of image characteristics recalled, but there was a difference in the valence of these image characteristics, suggesting that some aspects of the broadcasts elicited very different emotional responses among the candidates. For instance, respondents recalled more positive characteristics about Chirac and more than twice as many negative qualities about Le Pen as about Chirac, signifying more emotional reactions to the personality qualities of the two candidates. Comments about the candidates volunteered by young citizens who watched the broadcasts also lent weight to this interpretation. Le Pen was called "sneaky" and a "torturer" by several viewers.

Gender Differences in Response to French Political Broadcasts

Some research has suggested that there may be differences between male and female voters in France regarding their reactions to televised political messages. The French 1995 presidential election was one election in which such differences were observed. Men were significantly more positive about Lionel Jospin before viewing political broadcasts than were women, but this difference evened out after seeing the spots: Women became more positive about the candidate (Kaid & Holtz-Bacha, 2000).

Gender differences also played a role in reactions to French presidential candidates in 2002. Although men did not seem to differ in their evaluations of Chirac or Le Pen before or after exposure to their political broadcasts, women experienced a surprising positive increase in the evaluation of Le Pen after seeing his television portrayals (Kaid et al., 2003). Women found Le Pen significantly less *qualified* but more *sophisticated*, more *believable*, more *friendly*, more *excitable*, and more *aggressive* than did male viewers.

In the first round of balloting in France in 2002, Le Pen got a higher percentage of male than female votes, but in his television appearances for the second ballot, he appeared with and featured his wife and daughters and made an effort to soften his macho image. His continued focus on his identification with female French legend Joan of Arc (Bremner, 2002b) may also have appealed to strong-minded female voters.

It is also possible that Le Pen's success with female voters may have been related to his emphasis on particular issues. Norris (1988), in a cross-national comparison of voting behavior and political attitudes of women and men in the member states of the European Community, found significant gender differences in the stands on issues, "with women more left wing on policies such as nuclear energy, unemployment, and defense" (p. 229). She also concluded that issue differences have an impact on voting behavior if the issues become salient during the election campaign. However, an examination of the content in the Chirac and Le Pen broadcast ads in 2002 did not appear to support this conclusion, as it was Chirac who appeared to focus on women's issues, such as children and education, more often than did Le Pen (Kaid et al., 2003).

CONCLUSION

The 2002 campaign was definitely a campaign in which the media coverage of the candidates may have played an important role in the out-come. French independent documentary pro-ducer Michel Boyer commented during the campaign that both Chirac and Le Pen had established their entire political careers on media strategies (Delahaye, 2002). In fact, Le Pen reserved almost all of his time in the last days of the campaign before the second ballot for broadcast opportunities (Vinocur, 2002), including several drive-time radio broadcasts.

In 1988 and 1995, there was little acknowl-edgment in the French media that communi-cation strategies played a role in political campaign outcomes; issues and party plat-forms were considered the overriding factors in electoral outcomes. The atmosphere was very different in 2002, when the media directly attributed Le Pen's success in the first ballot to his successful media strategies: taking his message directly to the people and denouncing the media as conspiring against him (Bacqué & Fabre, 2002). A segment of *Question d'Actu,* a television program on La Chain Info on April 30, 2002, gave considerable time to a panel of historians and journalists discussing Le Pen's "television techniques."

The French political and regulatory environ-ment may have contributed to Le Pen's success, particularly during the first-ballot campaign-ing. Although the press often ignored Le Pen on a day-to-day basis, television was required to give all candidates equal treatment. Such equality of coverage may have endowed Le Pen's candidacy with greater credibility over time, creating an environment in which his own direct messages via television spots were more successful because they were seen as a continuation of a television portrayal already legitimized by regular appearances in more objective news formats. Moreover, starting with the 2001 municipal elections, the media may have prepared the ground for such a legit-imization, because news broadcasts focused significantly on sensitive topics, such as insecu-rity, which just happened to be dear to Le Pen and the National Front (Mercier, 2004).

Other observers have suggested that the media abandoned its own commitment to issues and rational campaign coverage of issues in 2002 when the candidates' campaigns focused on personalities:

> The campaign's focus on personality at the expense of policy had never been that strong for those media covering French elections. . . . This attention to personalities as well as some of the more trivial incidents was a marked feature of the campaign coverage and arguably had some impact on the shock results of April 21st. (Maareck, 2003, p. 21)

What can French voters expect from politi-cal communication in the future? One recent poll suggested that French citizens might be supportive of "re-introducing political adver-tising during electoral campaigns." Results of a 2004 poll asking that exact question found that a majority of young voters (those 34 years old and younger), conservatives, and citizens of the middle working class actually favor a reintroduction of political advertising in the French political environment (Giacometti, 2004).

NOTES

1. Under the French constitution, the presi-dent was originally elected for a 7-year term and senators for a 9-year term, but following a series of constitutional and institutional reforms in 2000 and 2003, those mandates were reduced respec-tively to 5 and 6 years (Embassy of France in the United States, 2005). Both the president and the National Assembly members are directly elected by popular vote (Embassy, 2005); Senate members are selected indirectly by a group of some 145,000 elected officials, including the deputies from the National Assembly, the regional councillors, the general councillors (representing *departments*), and the delegates of French city councils.

2. Under the fifth Republic, the rule of incom-patibility prevents the prime minister and the members of his or her government from holding a mandate in the French Parliament. Once desig-nated, if a prime minister wants to accept a minis-terial portfolio, he or she has 30 days to resign.

3. France has a strong multiparty system. The most active and consistently competitive of these are, from the left to the right: (a) Parti Communiste Français (French Communist Party), (b) Movement des Citoyens (Citizens' Movement), (c) les Verts (the Greens), (d) Parti Socialiste (Socialist Party), (e) Parti Radical de Gauche (Radical Leftist Party), (f) Union pour la Démocratie Française (Union for French Democracy), (g) Union pour la Majorité Présidentielle (Union for a Presidential Majority, including the former Rassemblement pour la République [Rally for the Republic] and Démocratie Libérale [Liberal Democracy] parties), (h) Movement pour la France (Movement for France), and (i) Front National (National Front). In recent years, a series of smaller parties has emerged, disturbing the political scene and even winning some seats in European, regional, and local ballots: (j) Parti des Travailleurs (Workers' Party), (k) Ligue Communiste Révolutionnaire (Revolutionary Communist League), (l) Ligue Opération (Working League), (m) Citoyenneté Action Participation pour le XXIième siècle (CAP 21, a center-right environmental movement), (n) Chasse-Pêche-Nature-Traditions (Hunting, Fishing, Nature, and Tradition), (o) Forum des Républicains Sociaux (Social Republicans' Forum), (p) Rassemblement pour la France (Rally for France), and (q) Movement National des Républicains (National Republican Movement).

4. Like his predecessor, François Mitterrand, in 1981 and 1988, Jacques Chirac took the logical step and dissolved the National Assembly to capitalize on his 2002 presidential victory and capture a new majority with the Union pour la Majorité Présidentielle.

5. In the case of legislative elections, France imposes a threshold of 12.5% of the votes of registered voters on any candidate willing to run for the second ballot. In recent years, this rule has resulted in numerous triangular races.

6. For instance, in 2002, the official presidential campaign lasted from April 8 to April 12 and from April 15 to April 19, but the legislative campaign only lasted from May 26 to June 7 and from June 11 to June 14.

7. The rule of equality applies as soon as the official list of candidates is published in *Le Journal Officiel*. Otherwise, French media simply respect a principle of fairness.

8. As of a 1964 decree, any candidate running for the presidency was supposed to receive 2 hours for each round. Although theoretically it was possible to modify the time allocated to each candidate for the first ballot, in practice it was difficult to implement because of time constraints. In 2001, a new regulation gave the CSA the practical means to truly apply this rule for both rounds and established a minimum of 15 minutes for each candidate.

9. Before the most recent reform (introduced in 2004 for the European Parliamentary elections), these inserts could not exceed 50% of the length of each broadcast.

10. "Cumulated ratings for viewers of 15 years of age and beyond" (CSA, 2002).

11. This difference is statistically significant, $t(37) = 5.73$, $p = .001$.

REFERENCES

Bacqué, R., & Fabre, C. (2002, April 30). Contre Le Pen, les Français descendent dans la rue. *Le Monde*, p. 2.

Bremner, C. (2002a, April 24). Chirac vows to destroy Le Pen to save "France's soul." *London Times*, p. 1.

Bremner, C. (2002b, April 24). Handmaids help macho Le Pen to court female vote. *London Times*, p. 9.

Bremner, C. (2002c, April 27). A talent for sinister blunder gets full play. *London Times*, p. 17.

Cayrol, R. (1988). The electoral campaign and the decision-making process of French voters. In H. R. Penniman (Ed.), *France at the polls, 1981 and 1986: Three national elections*. Durham, NC: Duke University Press.

Cayrol, R. (1997). *Média et démocratie: La dérive* [Media and democracy: The drift]. Paris: Presses de Sciences Po.

Ces jeunes qui sont entrés en politique au soir du premier tour [The young enter politics in the twilight of the first ballot] (2002, May 2). *Le Monde*, pp. 6–8.

Charlot, M. (1975). The language of television campaigning. In H. R. Penniman (Ed.), *France at the polls: The presidential election of 1974* (pp. 227–253). Washington, DC: American Enterprise Institute.

Conseil Supérieur de l'Audiovisuel. (2002a, May 14). *Communiqués de presse no. 490 du 14 Mai 2002: Bilan de la période de campagne officielle pour le premier et second tours de l'élection présidentielle (5 avril–3 mai 2002)* [Press release number 490, May 14, 2002: Assessment of the official campaign period for the first and second ballots of the presidential election, April 5–May 3, 2002]. Retrieved December 1 from http://www.csa.fr/rapport 2002/donnees/chap_annexes/12_liste_commu niq.htm#490

Conseil Supérieur de l'Audiovisuel. (2002b, April 5). *Conseil constitutionel: Élection présidentielle 2002. Campagne radiotélévisée et couverture radiotélévisée de la campagne* [Council constitution: 2002 presidential election. Radio and television campaign and radio and television coverage of the campaign] (Decision no. 2002-201 du 5 avril 2002). Retrieved December 1, 2005, from http://www.conseil-constitution nel.fr/dossier/presidentielles/2002/documents/ csa/2002201.htm

Conseil Supérieur de l'Audiovisuel. (2002c, April 5). *Conseil constitutionel: Élection présidentielle 2002. Campagne radiotélévisée et couverture radiotélévisée de la campagne* [Council constitution: 2002 presidential election. Radio and television campaign and radio and television coverage of the campaign] (Decision no. 2002-202 du 5 avril 2002). Retrieved December 1, 2005, from http://www.conseil-constitutionnel .fr/dossier/presidentielles/2002/documents/csa/ 2002202.htm

Conseil Supérieur de l'Audiovisuel. (2002d, April 23). *Conseil constitutionel: Élection présidentielle 2002. Campagne radiotélévisée et couverture radiotélévisée de la campagne* [Council constitution: 2002 presidential election. Radio and television campaign and radio and television coverage of the campaign] (Decision no. 2002-228 du 23 avril 2002). Retrieved December 1, 2005, from http://www.conseil-constitution nel.fr/dossier/presidentielles/2002/documents/ csa/2002228.htm

Conseil Supérieur de l'Audiovisuel. (2004, November). *Rapport sur la campagne en vue de l'élection des représentants au Parlement européen 13 juin 2004* [Report on the campaign and a look at the election of representatives to the European Parliament of June 13, 2004]. Retrieved December 1, 2005, from http:// www.csa.fr/upload/publication/Parleuro.pdf

Cwalina, W., Falkowski, A., & Kaid, L. L. (2000). Role of advertising in forming the image of politicians: Comparative analysis of Poland, France and Germany. *Media Psychology, 2*(2), 119–146.

Dauncey, H. (1999, May). French culture in party and presidential political spots of the early 1990s. *Web Journal of French Media Studies, 2*(1). Retrieved December 1, 2005, from http://www.wjfms.ncl.ac.uk/daunceWJ.htm

Delahaye, M. (2002, April 27). Une constante à la télé chez le president du FN: Les sequences à scandale [One constant on the television set of the president of the National Front: Sequences of scandal]. *Le Monde Télévision*, p. 5.

Duhamel, A. (2000). *Derrière le miroir: Les hommes politiques à la télévision* [Behind the mirror: Politicians on television]. Paris: Plon.

Dyson, K., & Humphreys, P. (1989). Deregulating broadcasting: The West European experience. *European Journal of Political Research, 17*, 137–154.

Ehrmann, H. W. (1983). *Politics in France* (4th ed.). Boston: Little, Brown & Company.

Ehrmann, H. W., & Schain, M. A. (1992). *Politics in France* (5th ed.). New York: Harper Collins.

Embassy of France in the United States. (2005). *National elections: 2002 elections*. Retrieved December 1, 2005, from http://www .ambafrance-us.org/atoz/elect_nat.asp

Explaining Le Pen's success. (2002, April 25). *Economist*. Retrieved December 12, 2005, from http://www.economist.com/agenda/ displayStory.cfm?story_id=1098317

Forbes, J., & Nice, R. (1979). Pandora's box: Television and the 1978 French general elections. *Media, Culture and Society, 1*, 35–50.

Gagnère, N., & Kaid, L. L. (2003, March). *Political broadcasting in the 2002 presidential election in France: Appeals and effects for young voters.* Paper presented at the European Communication Association Convention, Munich, Germany.

Gaouette, N. (1997, November 4). French turn off the tube. *Christian Science Monitor*. Retrieved March 13, 2003, from http://scmweb2.emcweb .com/durable/1997/11/04/intl.h.html

Gerstlé, J. (1989). La publicité politique: Quelques enseignements de l'expérience américaine [Political publicity: Learning from the American experience]. *Hermès, 4*, 203–213.

Gerstlé, J., Davis, D. K., & Duhamel, O. (1991). Television news and the construction of political reality in France and the United States. In L. L. Kaid, J. Gerstlé, & K. R. Sanders (Eds.), *Mediated politics in two cultures: Presidential campaigning in the United States and France* (pp. 119–143). New York: Praeger.

Giacometti, P. (2004, October). Why French politics needs the return of advertising. *IPSOS Ideas Newsletter, 2*(2), 5–6. Retrieved December 1, 2005, from http://www.ipsos.com/ Ideas/pdf/Global_Ideas_vol4.pdf

Gourevitch, P. (1997, April 4). The unthinkable. *New Yorker, 73*(10), 110-120. Retrieved

January 25, 2006, from http://www.newyorker .com/archive/content/?020422fr_archive05

Gourevitch, J.-P. (1989). Le clip politique [The political videoclip]. *Revue francaise de science politique, 39*(1), 21–32.

Gourevitch, J.-P. (2002a). La récupération du clip par la politique [The revival of the clip in politics]. In R. Cayrol & A. Mercier (Eds.), *Télévision, politique et elections* [Television, politics, and elections] (pp. 15–18). Paris: La Documentation Française.

Graham, R. (2002, April 25). Contest becomes "stop Le Pen" vote. *Financial Times*, p. 2.

Grosser, A. (1975). The role of the press, radio, and television in French political life. In H. R. Penniman (Ed.), *France at the polls: The presidential election of 1974* (pp. 207–226). Washington, DC: American Enterprise Institute.

Haiman, F. S. (1991). A tale of two countries: Media and messages of the French and American presidential campaigns of 1988. In L. L. Kaid, J. Gerstlé, & K. R. Sanders (Eds.), *Mediated politics in two cultures: Presidential campaigning in the United States and France* (pp. 59-72). New York: Praeger.

Hoffmann-Riem, W. (1986). Law, politics and the new media: Trends in broadcasting regulation. *West European Politics, 9*, 125–146.

Holtz-Bacha, C., Kaid, L. L., & Johnston, A. (1994). Political television advertising in Western democracies: A comparison of campaign broadcasts in the U.S., Germany, and France. *Political Communication, 11*, 67–80.

Johnson, J. (2002, May 6). Vote goes against Le Pen rather than for Chirac. *Financial Times*, p. 3.

Johnston, A. (1991). Political broadcasts: An analysis of form, content, and style in presidential communication. In L. L. Kaid, J. Gerstlé, & K. R. Sanders (Eds.), *Mediated politics in two cultures: Presidential campaigning in the United States and France* (pp. 59–72). New York: Praeger.

Johnston, A., & Gerstlé, J. (1995). The role of television broadcasts in promoting French presidential candidates. In L. L. Kaid & C. Holtz-Bacha (Eds.), *Political advertising in Western democracies: Parties and candidates on television* (pp. 44–60). Thousand Oaks, CA: Sage.

Kaid, L. L. (1991). The effects of television broadcasts on perceptions of political candidates in the United States and France. In L. L. Kaid, J. Gerstlé, & K. R. Sanders (Eds.), *Mediated politics in two cultures: Presidential campaigning in*
the United States and France (pp. 247–260). New York: Praeger.

Kaid, L. L. (1995). Measuring candidate images with semantic differentials. In K. Hacker (Eds.), *Candidate images in presidential election campaigns* (pp. 131–134). New York: Praeger.

Kaid, L. L., Gagnère, N., Williams, A. P., & Trammell, K. D. (2003, May). *Political advertising and the 2002 presidential election in France*. Paper presented at the International Communication Association Convention, San Diego, CA.

Kaid, L. L., & Holtz-Bacha, C. (Eds.). (1995). *Political advertising in western democracies*. Thousand Oaks, CA: Sage.

Kaid, L. L., & Holtz-Bacha, C. (2000). Gender differences in response to televised political broadcasts: A multicountry comparison. *Harvard International Journal of Press/ Politics, 5*(2), 17–29.

Kaid, L. L., McKinnon, L. M., & Gagnère, N. (1996, May). *Male and female reactions to political broadcast in the 1995 French presidential election*. Paper presented at the International Communication Association Convention, Chicago.

Koch, M. (1988, March-April). Extra! Extra! French newspapers reach the end of an era. *France Today, 3*(2), 3–4.

Krause, A. (2000, July/August). Squaring off the media image race for the presidency of France. *Europe*, pp. 8–11. Retrieved December 12, 2005, from http://global.factiva.com.lp.hscl .ufl.edu/ha/default.aspx

Labbé, D. (1990). *Le vocabulaire de François Mitterrand* [The vocabulary of François Mitterrand]. Paris: FNSP.

Latest French audience measurement. (2005, July 8). Retrieved December 1, 2005, from the advanced-television.com Web site: http:// www.advanced-television.com/2005/news_ archive_2005/July4_July8.htm#latestfr

Le Roux, P. (1993). Sept sur sept, la célébration repétée d'une admiration mutuelle [Seven on seven, the celebration repeats in mutual admiration]. *Politix, 23*, 113–124.

Maarek, P. J. (1997). New trends in French political communication: The 1995 presidential elections. *Media, Culture and Society, 19*, 357–368.

Maarek, P. J. (2003). Political communication and the unexpected outcome of the 2002 French presidential election. *Journal of Political Marketing, 2*(2), 13–24.

Mercier, A. (2004, May). Télévision et politique [Television and politics]. *Problèmes politiques et sociaux, 900*, 5–8.

Nel, N. (1990). *Le débat televise* [The televised debate]. Paris: Armand Colin.

Neveu, E. (1997). Des questions jamais entendues: Crise et renouvelement du journalisme politique à la television [Of questions never heard: Crisis and renewal in political television journalism]. *Politix, 37*, 25–56.

Neveu, E. (1999). Politics on French television: Towards a renewal of political journalism and debate frames? *European Journal of Communication, 14*(3), 379–409.

Neveu, E. (2003). De l'art (et du coût) d'éviter la politique: La démocratie du talk show version française (Ardisson, Drucker, Fogiel) [Of art (and cost) to avoid in politics: The democracy of the talk show, French version]. *Réseaux, 118*, 129–132.

Norris, P. (1988). The gender gap: A cross-national trend? In C. M. Mueller (Ed.), *The politics of the gender gap: The social construction of political influence*. Newbury Park, CA: Sage.

Le révolte civique de la jeunesse [The civil revolt of the young]. (2002, April 30). *Le Monde*, pp. 1–4.

Tarlé, A. de. (1979). France: The monopoly that won't divide. In A. Smith (Ed.), *Television and political life* (pp. 41–75). London: Macmillan Press.

They're just about off! (2002, February 18). *Economist*, pp. 45–46.

Vinocur, J. (2002, May 2). Le Pen, breaker of taboos. *International Herald Tribune*, pp. 1, 7.

6

Political Advertising in Spain and Portugal

COLLEEN CONNOLLY-AHERN AND JULIO CÉSAR HERRERO

Because they study political communication, analyzing every advertisement, Web site, debate, and speech, scholars might be excused for sometimes forgetting that real-world votes are based on far more than mass-mediated messages. Rather, every vote represents the end-product of a process influenced by myriad forces that must be uniquely weighed and measured by each individual casting a vote. Unfortunately, that message was painfully driven home during March 2004, when a series of bombs detonated in and around the Atocha Railway Station in central Madrid completely changed the context of the Spanish general election. The event, and the fallout from it, led to the greatest upset in Spain's democratic history. It appears that the political advertising messages of the previous 2 weeks were simply drowned out by the terrifying images of the tragedy.

Although it is true that political messages and their effects can at times be overshadowed by events, it is also true that the young—and little studied—democracies of Spain and Portugal offer scholars a unique window into the political communications of countries that are "coming of age" politically. Their electoral campaign laws, particularly those dealing with party financing, resemble those of their more "mature" Western European counterparts, particularly France and Germany (Van Biezen, 2000). However, both Spain and Portugal have taken their own approach to political advertising regulation. In the case of Spain, at least, research indicates that a unique political advertising "style" is developing that reflects that nation's cultural values and particular history.

The purpose of this chapter is to provide an overview of the political advertising environment in both Spain and Portugal. The political and media systems in both countries will be described, to provide context for the discussion of the regulatory environment. Legislation regarding political advertising and campaign finance in both countries will be examined. The small amount of research in the area will be summarized. Finally, a research agenda for interested scholars will be outlined.

POLITICAL AND MEDIA ENVIRONMENT

Spain

With the enactment of the Political Reform Law of 1976, Spain became a parliamentary

97

monarchy. King Juan Carlos I is the titular chief of state, but the government is actually led by the prime minister, currently José Luis Rodríguez Zapatero of the Partido Socialista Obrero Español (PSOE; the Socialist Party).

The Spanish Parliament is bicameral, including a Chamber of Deputies and a Senate. The Chamber of Deputies is home to the representatives of Spain's 52 electoral districts. It is important to note that these districts vary greatly in population, which has important implications for the relative use of political advertising in more populated districts, where face-to-face contact with voters is nearly impossible (Rospir, 1996). The Senate provides for equal representation of all 17 Autonomous Communities that make up the Kingdom of Spain. The parliament is asymmetrical, however, because the Chamber of Deputies has precedence over the Senate as the body charged with supporting a candidate so that a government may be formed.

With regard to the election of the Chamber of Deputies, the Royal Decree-Law of 18 March 1977 outlines the following principles:

1. The minimum percentage of ballots to take part in the distribution of seats is set at 3%; the lowest number of deputies per province is 2. The rest of the seats are distributed according to population brackets.

2. The candidate lists are legally closed and blocked—that is, a single vote is cast for the party's entire slate of candidates.

3. The formula chosen for this distribution of seats is D'Hondt's.

The fact that Spain's candidate lists are closed and blocked has created party-focused electoral campaigns. Spending on propaganda is aimed at highlighting the parties' national agendas, not responding to local concerns (Herrero & Connolly-Ahern, 2004; Rospir, 1996).

Since the adoption of the Constitution in 1978, Spain's press has been free (De Mateo, 2000). The international civil rights organization Freedom House rates Spain's press as free;

however, it notes that the government's war on Basque terrorism has had a chilling effect on the press (Karlekar, 2004). From the earliest electoral campaigns in the young democracy, Spanish political advertising has appeared in print. There are three main national newspapers of record: *El Pais, ABC,* and *El Mundo*. The Spanish press is known to be partisan, with *El Pais* leaning to the left and favoring PSOE; *ABC* more monarchical and conservative; and *El Mundo* covering news in a more sensational way than the other two national print vehicles, focusing on scandals and conflict (Sanders & Canel, 2004). The regional press is particularly important in the non–Spanish speaking regions of the country: Catalonia, the Basque Country, and Galicia. Many local papers are published in various cities as well.

The broadcast picture in Spain has become more diverse in recent years. However, it remains dominated by the state-owned Radio-televisión Española (RTVE), which operates more than 450 public radio stations, the country's public television stations (TVE-1 and La 2), the country's external digital television service (TVE Internacional), and Radio Exterior de España, the third largest shortwave broadcaster in the world after the BBC and Radio Vaticano (De Mateo, 2000). Throughout much of the country, regional governments, known as CCAAs, (Comunidades Autónomas) operate a third public channel, such as TV3 in Catalonia and ETB in the Basque Country. Spanish public television is unusual among its European neighbors, however: Advertising accounts for nearly 80% of revenues (Deiss, 2002).

In addition to the extensive public radio network, Spain hosts hundreds of private radio stations, the majority of which are affiliated with three national radio networks: Sociedad Española de Radiodifusión, Onda Cero Radio, and Cadena de Ondas Populares Española, which is largely owned by the Catholic Church (De Mateo, 2000). Both public and private radio stations can accept political advertising in Spain (Herrero & Connolly-Ahern, 2004).

The Spanish private broadcast network is limited but is growing quickly through augmented digital offerings. Three private terrestrial channels have been operating since 1989: Antena 3, whose primary shareholder is the Spanish telephony provider Telefónica; Tele 5, which is majority owned by the Italian media company Mediaset, founded by Silvio Berlusconi; and Canal +, a French-owned subscription television service. In 1997, these private channels were joined by two large digital satellite operations, Canal Satélite Digital and Vía Digital (De Mateo, 2000). However, as of 2001, 79% of Spaniards still called terrestrial antennas their main mode of television reception; cable and satellite accounted for only 4% and 18%, respectively, which minimizes the impact of these new offerings (Deiss, 2002). This is particularly important because only public television stations, which are available terrestrially, can legally carry political advertising (Herrero & Connolly-Ahern, 2004).

Portugal

With the Revolution of the Carnations' overthrow of the existing dictatorship and the subsequent elections that signaled the beginning of the Third Republic in 1975, Portugal has been a democratic republic. According to the Constitution, governmental power is divided between four entities: the president, who is directly elected by the Portuguese citizens for a 5-year term of office; a unicameral Assembly; the Council of Ministers (also referred to as "the Government"), led by the prime minister; and the Judiciary (Presidency of the Portuguese Republic, 1997). The current president, Jorge Fernando Branco de Sampaio, a member of the Partido Socialista (Socialist Party), was reelected for his second and final term in 2001. The current prime minister, José Sócrates, also a Socialist, took office after a governmental crisis led to a "snap" election in March of 2005.

Portugal's press is characterized as "free" by Freedom House (Karlekar, 2004). In fact, the Portuguese Electoral Law provides for particular protection for freedom of expression during the electoral campaign period. No media company may be sanctioned for the expression of political, economic, or social ideas during an electoral campaign; civil or criminal responsibility cannot be enforced until after election day (Portuguese Electoral Law, 1979). However, the Portuguese population is far less "mediated" than that of its Iberian neighbor, with some of the lowest levels of newspaper readership, television ownership, and Internet access in Western Europe (Correia, 2001; Karlekar, 2004). This historically low use of media has, in turn, had a profound effect on the regulation of, and the campaign tactics and propaganda employed in, Portuguese elections.

Although newspaper media in Portugal has recently exhibited the fastest circulation growth in Europe, at 12.5% in 1999, Portugal remains the least penetrated of Western Europe's newspaper markets, with only 7.4% of the population making a newspaper purchase daily (Correia, 2001). The four largest national newspapers are *Jornal de Notícias, Correio de Manhã, 24 Horas,* and *O Público*; of these, only *Jornal de Notícias* and *Correio de Manhã* had average circulations of more than 100,000 in 2004; the other two were only slightly over 50,000.[1] *Expresso* is the dominant weekly general interest newspaper. All newspapers are privately held. All daily and weekly newspapers have the right to accept political propaganda in Portugal, but they must by law inform the government of their intention to do so (Portuguese Electoral Law, 1979).

The Portuguese broadcast media landscape comprises a mixture of private and public enterprises. The private media are often held by conglomerates, with interests in multiple media formats. In the short period in which private corporations have had access to the airwaves, they have become the dominant voices in the Portuguese market (Correia, 2001). Both public and private broadcast outlets are required to set aside time during the election period for electoral propaganda.

The public broadcast media in Portugal is owned and operated by Rádio e Televisão de Portugal (RTP). The group operates two terrestrial national television networks (RTP 1 and RTP 2), as well as stations with specific geographic focus: RTP Açores, RTP Madeira, RTP Africa, and RTP Internacional. In addition, the corporation has recently launched two new channels: RTPN, with news programming designed to emulate world news players such as CNN and BBC, with an emphasis on news of interest to Portugal, and RTP Memória, which will draw on the 50-year archives of RTP's classic programming (Rádio e Televisão de Portugal, 2005).

The new entries into the public television market were probably forced by the ascendance of private broadcasting, which was introduced into the market in 1992. The two private television outlets, SIC and TV1, were both achieving a higher share of ratings than the public flagship RTP 1 as of June 2001 (Correia, 2001). Changing viewership patterns have probably had little effect on exposure to electoral publicity, however, since in Portugal both private and public television stations are required to carry political propaganda during the election period.

In the area of radio, Radiodifusão Portuguesa is a public entity with a number of channels, including Antena 1, which focuses on general interest programming and news, Antena 2, which has recently been reformatted to include a mix of both classical and contemporary music; Antena 3, a channel targeted at young audiences; RDP Internacional; and the geographically oriented RDP Africa, RDP Madeira (Antena 1 and Antena 3), and RDP Açores (Rádio e Televisão de Portugal, 2005).

The combined offerings of RDP claim about 20% of Portugal's daily radio audiences (Correia, 2001).

In the private radio area, the most important national player is the Roman Catholic Church's Radio Renascença, which owns radio stations in Portugal's major cities, including Lisbon, Porto, and Braga, and controls a 40% share of the Portuguese audience (Correia, 2001). The country is also home to hundreds of private regional and local radio stations. All radio stations are required to carry electoral propaganda.

ELECTORAL CAMPAIGN LEGISLATION

Unlike most of their more mature peers, the Spanish and Portuguese democracies took shape in a mass-mediated world. Radio was present in nearly every home, television in many. The framers of the Spanish and Portuguese constitutions were already familiar with the use of political propaganda—for both good and ill—and saw an immediate need to address the issues in legislation. Thus the conduct of electoral campaigns in both Spain and Portugal has been governed by very specific legal frameworks from the earliest days of these nations' democratic existence.

Spain

The initial regulations by which Spain's electoral campaigns are conducted were set out in Royal Decree-Law 20/1977 of 18th March, which discussed "Electoral Norms." Cruz Bermejo (1993) points out that the almost 40 parties involved in the early formation of the democracy were well aware of the power of television advertising and actively sought the ability to use the medium. Article 40 of Decree-Law 20/1977 (1997) dealt directly with this issue, stating that "Associations, federations, coalitions and groups will be entitled to use the free slots on TV, radio and press of public title." As Herrero and

Connolly-Ahern (2004) note, the original Spanish campaign legislation focused entirely on public media and did not anticipate the development of private media outlets. Thus, when the maturing Spanish parliament revisited the issue of political campaigning in 1985 with Ley Orgánica 5/1985 del Régimen Electoral General (LOREG; Statutory Law 5/1985 of the General Elections System) of June 19 (1985), private television outlets—which did not begin broadcasting in Spain until 1989—remained excluded from the process.

The Spanish electoral period is exactly 15 days, and begins on the 38th day after it is officially announced, as outlined in Article 51 of LOREG. The election period officially ends at midnight of the day prior to the election.

Article 53 of LOREG specifies the times during which electoral publicity may appear. Parties are prohibited from airing any publicity in advance of the official campaign period or after the official campaign period has ended. That means that Spanish citizens receive no mass-mediated advertising messages in the last 24 hours of the campaign. However, there is no requirement that outdoor advertising be removed in advance of elections.

Article 54 deals with a particularly important element of political campaigns in Spain: political rallies. It states that the right to engage in political rallies derives directly from the right of assembly guaranteed by the Spanish Constitution and requires city councils to reserve public spaces in which political parties can hold local rallies free of charge. All city governments must notify regional election authorities about the available venues 10 days in advance of the election; it is then up to the regional election authorities to schedule the venues, dividing them between the candidates equally and keeping in mind both the requests and preferences of the parties, as well as which parties received the most votes from the electoral region in the previous election. This system favors established parties, because the

regional authorities must use past performance as a criterion for assigning venues. New entrants into the political arena are often assigned less attractive venues or given less attractive times at popular venues for their events.

Articles 55 and 56 of LOREG deal with posters, placards, banners, and billboards. The law mandates that city councils set aside specific areas where outdoor advertising can be placed at no charge. The distribution of free outdoor space is based on each party's performance in the previous election of the same type (local, national, or supranational, in the case of the European Union elections). Outdoor spaces include lampposts, which are designed to hold pennants, as well as key areas above streets where large banners can be displayed. It is the duty of the regional election authorities to notify the representatives of each candidate about the outdoor spaces that have been allocated to them within 2 days after the candidates have officially declared their candidacy.

In addition to free public spaces, posters can also be placed in "authorized commercial spaces" for a fee. Political organizations can spend no more than 25% of their advertising budget on such outdoor advertising.

Finally, Article 58 deals with the rights of candidates to access private radio and print during election campaigns. The law mandates that the fees charged for political advertising in private media must be the same or less than those paid by commercial advertisers. The law also mandates that no party may receive preferential treatment from private media entities—all parties must have the opportunity to purchase similar space or time slots. All materials must be clearly labeled as "political advertising."

A number of scholars have indicated that Spanish legislation prohibits the use of televised propaganda during an election campaign (Canel, 1999; Contreras, 1990; Gunther, Montero, & Wert, 1999), but in fact it is only the *purchase* of television advertising that is banned in Spain. Candidates are entitled to use the free airtime that is allotted to them to air political spots that in almost every way resemble the advertisements commonly seen in other Western democracies, such as the United States and the United Kingdom. Gunther et al. (1999) suggest, "Spanish parties and candidates appearing on television are placed in a setting where they actually have to say something about where they stand on the issues" (p. 27); however, content analysis of spots from the two most recent Spanish general elections reveals increasing use of image-oriented strategies by both of the main political parties (Herrero & Connolly-Ahern, 2004). For example, during the 1996 campaign, the Partido Popular produced more than a dozen short spots that emphasized an image of modernity and achievement for the party, although each of the spots focused on a different issue, such as pensions or infrastructure. These spots were professionally produced and unified by an upbeat, modern musical track.

Portugal

Portugal's Parliamentary Electoral Law establishes the official election period as beginning 14 days before the election and finishing 24 hours before the election. Thus, as in Spain, the last day of the Portuguese election cycle is free of broadcast advertising content.

The second chapter of the Electoral Law is entirely dedicated to the use of political propaganda (Portuguese Electoral Law, 1979). The chapter includes very detailed regulations, establishing the rights of candidates to use the airwaves for electoral publicity and offering specific time periods in which publicity will be aired on both radio and television. In addition, the law discusses print advertising, use of entertainment venues, posters, advertising on public buildings, indirect advertising, and the free use of telephone lines for campaign purposes.

Article 61 offers a definition of election propaganda:

All the activities directly or indirectly aiming at promoting candidatures, concerning either the candidates, the political parties, the heads of their bodies or their agents or any other people, particularly with the publication of texts or images that express or represent the content of this activity. (Portuguese Electoral Law, 1979, head. IV, chap. II, art. 61)

In Article 62.1, the law establishes the right of candidates to broadcast time on both private and public radio and television stations. All Portuguese broadcast stations are required to set aside specific slots during the official election period, based on a specific formula:

1. All television stations, both public and private, must reserve 15 minutes between 7:00 p.m. and 10:00 p.m., Monday through Friday, and 30 minutes between 7:00 p.m. and 10:00 p.m. on Saturday and Sunday.

2. Public radio stations must reserve 60 minutes each day of the campaign, 20 minutes of which must come between 7:00 a.m. and noon, 20 between noon and 7:00 p.m., and 20 between 7:00 p.m. and midnight.

3. National private radio stations must reserve 60 minutes each day of the campaign, 20 minutes of which must come between 7:00 a.m. and noon and 40 between 7:00 p.m. and midnight.

4. Regional private radio stations must reserve 30 minutes each day, but no times for these allocations are mandated.

The public radio and television requirements apply equally to RTP's regional and international outlets. Thus, Portuguese citizens living abroad with access to RTP have access to electoral publicity. Article 63 of the law directs the distribution of free airtime, proportionally for national parties using national television outlets and equally for all local parties and constituencies using international and regional outlets.

Although the Portuguese Parliamentary Election Law allows the use of free airtime for political advertising, it is important to note that candidates and parties are forbidden from purchasing any additional commercial advertising time slots for their political messages by Article 72 of the same law. Thus, the total amount of political advertising during any Portuguese electoral campaign period is tightly controlled by law.

Article 64 refers to electoral publicity in print publications. Three days before the campaign period, periodicals with frequencies of more than once every 2 weeks must notify the National Elections Commission of their intention to take political advertising. Without such notification, print vehicles may not accept political advertising, although they are still permitted to accept general election materials, usually reminders for citizens of the importance of exercising their right to vote, from the National Elections Commission.

A novel aspect of Portugal's parliamentary election law is found in Article 65, which deals with propaganda that takes place in entertainment venues; for example, sports stadiums. Ten days before the official election period, owners of such venues are required to notify the civil governor or minister of the Republic about the dates during the campaign that the venues are available for rent; the authorities may requisition the use of the venues if they are needed. The venues must be available to all parties, and the civil governor or minister of the Republic has the responsibility of assuring that each group has access to the venues and that the groups are treated equally with regard to the dates and times available. In the case of two groups requesting the same time and place, the matter is resolved by lottery.

Although hanging posters does not require the authorization of the government, local governments are required to establish official spaces for posters, photographs, wall newspapers, manifestos, and notices. The spaces available must equal the number of candidates running in the area, so that all have equal space for their campaign materials. Article 68

gives authorities the duty of securing the use of public and private buildings for campaign purposes.

Airtime, public spaces, and entertainment venues are assigned by government officials, but Article 67 of the parliamentary election law allows for coalitions to pool the resources that have been assigned to them. Additionally, parties and coalitions may exchange the spaces they have been allotted among themselves.

The compensation of broadcast outlets, print vehicles, entertainment venues, and building owners is discussed in Article 69. The exemption of party organs from carrying advertisements of the opposition is established in Article 70.

The rules governing Portugal's presidential elections are virtually identical to those governing the parliamentary elections, with one major exception. On the last day of the presidential campaign period, each of the candidates is given 10 minutes on the public radio and television stations, between 9:00 p.m. and midnight, to speak directly to the public (Abrantes & Miguéis, 2000). The order of the speeches is established by lottery, to ensure that no candidate has the majority of his or her appeals in unfavorable time periods.

The candidate is the only person who can use this airtime. The candidate may use graphic images, voiceovers, music, and slogans and may even be accompanied by other people, but the candidate must be the main speaker during the 10-minute speech. Under no circumstances are special effects permitted to overshadow the direct appeal of the candidate.

Additionally, the presidential law addresses the importance of public television in the democratic development of Portugal. For this reason, Article 62 of the parliamentary law requires public television and radio outlets to dedicate objective programming for the citizens of Portugal explaining the significance of the elections for the life of the state, as well as the election process in general and instructions for proper voting.

THE ROLE OF ADVERTISING
IN THE YOUNG DEMOCRACIES

A 1993 Spanish Comparative National Elections Project survey indicated that the Spanish population was heavily dependent on television as a source for political information (Gunther et al., 1999). More than 70% of Spaniards indicated they followed politics three or more times per week through television. In contrast, less than 50% said they sought political information through radio, about 30% said they sought political information from newspapers, and only 13% said they sought political information through magazines. It was not surprising that the same study indicated that a plurality of Spaniards considered television the most credible and informative medium, and a majority said it was the easiest medium to understand (Gunther et al., 1999).

No study to date has explored the relative importance of political advertising across media in Spain or Portugal. However, the privileged position held by television for Spanish audiences may indicate the importance of the free airtime given to candidates under LOREG. It may also explain the evolution of Spain's political advertising, from direct statements on issues offered formally by the candidates to the sleek, highly produced, image-building spots used during the 1996 and 2000 general election campaigns.

RESEARCH ON
POLITICAL ADVERTISING

Although political advertising has been present in both Spain and Portugal since the democracies were established, there is surprisingly little literature addressing the content and effects of political communication in general, and political advertising specifically, in the region. However, the topic has recently emerged as the subject of a number of doctoral dissertations in Spain, indicating that scholarly interest in the topic may finally be increasing.

Rospir (1996) appears to have been one of the first scholars to address both the context and content of Spanish political communication. He argues that campaigns are personal, rather than issue oriented, due to Spanish voters' lack of "historical, ideological, or group-based loyalties to parties" (p. 163). Rospir calls television the "principal intermediary between politicians and the public" (p. 164) and suggests that electoral campaigns are scripted to the requirements of the television news cycle, very much as they are in other Western democracies. However, he also notes a unique feature of Spanish political communication: the pre-eminence of the state-owned media in the area of television news delivery, which has left the standing government open to charges of favoritism and cronyism in every election cycle since the beginning of democracy. However, Rospir's case study offers no empirical evidence of bias in the Spanish media.

Semetko and Canel (1997) addressed the issue of balance of coverage directly in their observational study of Spanish newsrooms during the 1996 election cycle. In contrast to Rospir's suggestion that the public nature of Spain's TVE1 left it open to charges of bias, Semetko and Canel's research, as well as a subsequent content analysis by Díez-Nicolás and Semetko (1997), found that TVE1's coverage of the election was highly balanced, especially during the "official" campaign period when government regulations mandated equal coverage. In fact, the authors note that the public servants who worked for TVE1 news felt particular "pressure to be even handed" during the 1996 campaign, due in part to charges of partiality in previous races. Their observations also indicated that the coverage of the private broadcaster Antena3 was more likely to link the campaigns to other news stories than TVE1, probably because of the "stopwatch" mentality that dominated TVE1's coverage of the elections.

Sanders and Canel (2004) looked at the public relations aspects of political communication in Spain as they relate to the private lives of politicians. The authors note that the line between private and public lives, once strictly observed by the Spanish press, has recently begun to blur. They illustrate this point with many examples, including the Aznar family's willingness to allow the celebrity and fashion magazine *¡Hola!* to cover their daughter's wedding. However, Sanders and Canel's qualitative analysis indicates that the level of voyeurism in Spanish political coverage remains lower than that of other countries, such as the United Kingdom and the United States.

Only a few scholarly studies have focused on political advertising in Spain. Herrero and Connolly-Ahern (2004) offered the first comprehensive quantitative content analysis of 1996 and 2000 general elections television advertising in Spain, based on Kaid and Johnston's (2001) videostyle analysis techniques. Their study indicated that, with some notable exceptions, Spanish political advertising in the 1996 election was largely positive in tone. However, since the door to attack advertising was opened in 1996, the landscape of Spanish advertising has changed substantially, with almost all advertising focusing on the party in power, either positively in the party's own advertising or negatively in the opposition's advertising. Spots focus on individuals, not on party affiliation. Fear appeals were common during both election cycles.

Spanish political advertising is characterized by restraint in the area of nationalism, according to Herrero and Connolly-Ahern's research. For example, the Spanish flag was virtually nonexistent in the political advertising of 1996 and 2000. This may be a reaction to the country's authoritarian past, a byproduct of the democracy's relative youth, or even a tacit acknowledgment of the problematic status of the country's Autonomous Regions.

Two recent Spanish doctoral dissertations have examined political advertising in Spain from a qualitative perspective. Rodríguez

Escanciano (2002) looked at communication strategies in television advertising of the Partido Popular (PP) and PSOE between 1989 and 2000, focusing on the rise of image advertising as the primary marketing tool in Spanish elections. Mota Oreja (2002) analyzed the methods employed in Spanish political advertising and propaganda to promote image and minimize the importance of issues as a decision-making factor.

Lopez-Escobar, Llamas, McCombs, and Lennon's (1998) is the only published article dealing with the effects of political communication in Spain. In it, they explore the intermedia agenda during the 1995 regional elections in Navarra. Their analysis includes information about the agenda-setting properties of print and television advertising in those elections. Using cross-lagged correlations, the researchers found an effect of newspaper advertising on candidate attributes in both newspaper and television news coverage, especially in the area of candidate qualifications. Television news influenced later candidate descriptions in televised political advertising. However, there was no indication that television advertising influenced any other media agenda.

It is clear that political advertising is an area of academic interest in Spain, but the field remains largely unexplored, especially from a quantitative perspective. No research could be found in the area of political advertising's effects, for example. In the case of Portugal, an exhaustive search located *no* academic articles focusing on political communication. Clearly, research is needed to understand the persuasive characteristics of political advertising in Spain and Portugal, as well as the impact of political messages on Spanish and Portuguese citizens.

RECENT ISSUES IN POLITICAL ADVERTISING

In spite of the very specific legal requirements for political advertising in both Spain and

Portugal, controversies about the use—and abuse—of political advertising are common in both countries. In addition, new technologies are serving to blur the line between advertising, public relations, and information, at least in Spain. A few recent examples illustrate that Spain and Portugal continue to grapple with the appropriate place for political advertising in the campaign process.

The 2004 general election in Spain was the first in which both parties acknowledged and embraced the power of the Internet. Improving Internet access for Spaniards, who remain among the least wired of Europe's citizens, was a major issue in the campaign (Tapia, 2004). Although the incumbent PP promised all Spaniards ADSL access by the end of 2005, the opposition PSOE reminded voters that 8 years of conservative government had left Spain behind its European neighbors in terms of technology adoption. The PSOE platform included the formation of a new cabinet-level ministry of Education, Science and Technology to remedy the situation (Tapia, 2004).

The PP and the Catalan nationalist party Convergència I Unió experimented for the first time with online keyword marketing, using Google's AdWords service (Tapia, 2004). Search terms such as "elections," "general elections," "Aznar," "Rajoy," and "PP" led surfers to a screen with a Partido Popular or Mariano Rajoy ad on the right side of the screen. Search terms such as "Unio," "Convergencia," and "Duran" led to a paid link for the Convergència I Unió Web site.

Also underscoring the importance of the Internet as a political communications medium, both Mariano Rajoy and José Luis Zapatero created personal Web pages, apart from the official party Web sites. Neither of the politicians shared hit figures for their personal Web sites; however, party spokespeople indicated that journalists were using the sites frequently (Tapia, 2004).

The events of March 11, coming right at the end of the official election period, provided some insight into the possible importance of another new technology in the political arena, namely text messaging. After the Madrid bombings, the prime minister, José Maria Aznar, suspended all campaigning activities out of respect for the dead ("A 21st-century," 2004). This left PSOE with no way to air its opinion that the bombings were related to Al-Qaida and not the domestic terrorist group Euskadi Ta Askatasuna ETA, as the PP government was reporting. In the absence of planned campaign events, citizens mobilized to vent their anger at the government, organizing rallies of thousands in just a few hours by text messaging on their mobile telephones. The March 14, 2004, message read: Today at 6 p.m., Genova Street, to find out the truth. Pass it on" ("A 21st-century," 2004). In response, nearly 5000 people gathered in front of the Partido Popular headquarters to register their mistrust. Responding to the message may have also served to galvanize voters. Although the polls indicated the PP had a comfortable lead on March 10, PSOE won decisively on March 14. According to freelance journalist Ignacio Escolar, the protests gave the left hope that the conservative government could be defeated and drove many who might normally have stayed home to the polls ("A 21st-century," 2004). By some accounts, then, the momentum gained by the text message–induced protests may have turned the tide of the general election.

Recent events in Portugal have illustrated that even the young democracies must continue to adjust their existing campaign regulations to new political realities. Portugal's José Manuel Barroso held the presidency of the European Commission at the same time that Portugal's February 2005 parliamentary snap election campaign was underway, and Barroso chose to appear in an election spot for his compatriots in the Social Democratic Party, which he had led before taking the European Commission position in Brussels. The move was denounced by Martin Schulz, the leader of the Socialist bloc in the European Parliament, who said it demonstrated the "partisanship" of the commission president (Castle, 2005). The incident underscored that there is no clear regulation for the conduct of Portuguese politicians regarding the relationship between performing their pan-European duties and their rights as citizens of Portugal. However, it does not appear that Barroso's appearance in the advertisement broke any Portuguese law.

In any event, if Barroso's spot was an attempt to leverage his clout as a leader in the European Commission to aid his colleagues at home in Portugal, the attempt was in vain. The Socialists took the Portuguese parliament with an absolute majority in 2005, their first in the history of the democracy.

CONCLUSION

It is clear that both Spain and Portugal offer the political advertising scholar a wealth of research possibilities, especially in light of recent political events in those countries. It is also clear that, considering the importance of these two young democracies as members of the European Union, as well as of NATO, the region has not received the attention from scholars that is warranted.

Little is known about the effectiveness of political advertising in either Spain or Portugal. If, as Rospir (1996) suggests, low levels of political interest and party identification give particular importance to the mass media in the formation of political opinions in Spain, then we might say the terrifying and heart-wrenching scenes that dominated the Spanish media in the days between March 11 and March 14, 2004, were the most important of that country's election campaign season. The effect of these images may have been compounded by the Spanish electoral law itself—on the Saturday before the election, the Spanish people saw no campaign messages to counter the images of the bombings themselves.

The use of political advertising in both Spain and Portugal is well-established practice.

However, the content of that advertising has only begun to be described by scholars in Spain. In Portugal, the process has yet to begin. Without significant scholarly content analysis, it is difficult to gauge the significance of political advertising in the region. It is also impossible to say what the impact of that advertising is on the citizens of the two young democracies.

NOTE

1. These data were accumulated and tabulated by the Associação Portuguesa para o Controlo de Tiragem e Circulação ("Imprensa," 2001).

REFERENCES

Abrantes, F., & Miguéis, J. (2000). *Lei electoral do presidente da República, actualizada, anotada e comentada* [Electoral law of the president of the Republic: Actualized, annotated, and with commentary]. Torres Novas, Spain: Almondina.

Canel, M. J. (1999). *Comunicación política* [Political communication]. Madrid: Tecnos.

Castle, S. (2005, February 17). Barroso backs right-wing party in advert. *The Independent (London)*. Retrieved January 25, 2006, from *The Independent* Online Edition Web site: http://news.independent.co.uk/europe/article11499.ece

Contreras, J. M. (1990). *Vida política y television* [Political life and television]. Madrid: Espasa.

Correia, F. (2001). *The Portuguese media landscape*. Retrieved December 3, 2005, from the European Journalism Centre Online Web site: http://www.ejc.nl/jr/emland/portugal.html

Cruz Bermejo, A. de la. (1993). *Comunicación política y elecciones en España (1975-1991)* [Political and election communications in Spain (1975-1991)]. Unpublished doctoral dissertation, Universidad Complutense de Madrid, Spain.

De Mateo, R. (2000). *The Spanish media landscape*. Retrieved December 3, 2005, from the European Journalism Centre Online Web site: http://www.ejc.nl/jr/emland/spain.html

Díez-Nicolás, J., & Semetko, H. A. (1997). *For whom the bell tolls: Television and Spain's 1993 and 1997 general election campaigns.* Paper presented to the annual meeting of the

American Political Science Association, Washington, DC.

Deiss, R. (2002). *The European TV broadcasting market*. Retrieved December 3, 2005, from the Statistisches Bundesamt Web site: http://www .eds-destatis.de/en/downloads/sif/np_02_24 .pdf

Gunther, R., Montero, J. R., & Wert, J. I. (1999). *The media and politics in Spain: From dictatorship to democracy* (Working Paper no. 176). Barcelona, Spain: Institut de Ciències Polítiques i Socials. Retrieved December 3, 2005, from http://www.diba.es/icps/working_ papers/docs/wp_i_176.pdf

Herrero, J. C., & Connolly-Ahern, C. (2004). Origen y evolución de la propaganda política en la España democrática (1975–2000): Análisis de las técnicas y de los mensajes en las elecciones generales del año 2000 [Origin and evolution of political propaganda in the democracy of Spain (1975-2000): Analysis of the techniques and the messages in the general elections of 2000]. *Doxa Comunicación, 2,* 151–172.

Imprensa. (2001). Retrieved January 25, 2006, from the Instituto da Comunicação Social Web site: http://www.ics.pt/index.php?op=cont& lang=pt&Pid=78&area=328

Kaid, L. L., & Johnston, A. (2001). *Videostyle in presidential campaigns: Style and content of televised political advertising.* Westport, CT: Praeger/Greenwood.

Karlekar, K. D. (Ed.). (2004). *Freedom of the press 2004: A global survey of media independence.* Lanham, MD: Rowman & Littlefield. Retrieved December 2, 2005, from the Freedom House Web site: http://www.freedom house.org/pfs2004/pfs2004.pdf

Ley Orgánica 5/1985 del Régimen Electoral General de 19 Junio [Statutory Law 5/1985 of the General Electoral System of June 19]. (1985, June 20). *Boletín Oficial del Estado.* Madrid: Boletín Oficial de la Presidencia.

Lopez-Escobar, E., Llamas, J. P., McCombs, M., & Lennon, F. R. (1998). Two levels of agenda setting among advertising and news in the 1995 Spanish elections. *Political Communication, 15,* 225–238.

Mota Oreja, J. de la. (2002). *Informacion, publicidad y propaganda politica en los procesos electorales* [Political information, publicity, and propaganda in the electoral process].

Unpublished doctoral dissertation, Facultad de Ciencias de la Informacion, Madrid.

Portuguese Electoral Law, Parliamentary Law 14/79 (May 16, 1979).

Presidency of the Portuguese Republic. (1997). *Constitution of the Portuguese Republic. Article 110: Organs with supreme authority* (4th rev.). Retrieved December 2, 2005, from http://www .presidenciarepublica.pt/en/main.html.

Rádio e Televisão de Portugal (Home page). (2005). Retrieved December 2, 2005, from http://www .rtp.pt/

Rodríguez Escanciano, I. (2002). *Estrategias de comunicacion electoral en television durante el periodo 1989-2000* [Electoral communication strategies on television from 1989 to 2000]. Unpublished doctoral dissertation, Facultad de Ciencias de la Informacion, Madrid.

Rospir, J. I. (1996). Political communication and electoral campaigns in the young Spanish democracy. In D. L. Swanson & P. Mancini (Eds.), *Politics, media, and modern democracy: An international study of innovations in electoral campaigning and their consequences* (pp. 155–169). Westport, CT: Praeger.

Royal Decree-Law 20/1977. (1977, March 18). *Boletín Oficial del Estado.* Madrid: Boletín Oficial de la Presidencia.

Royal Decree-Law 20/1977, Article 40. (1997, March 23). *Boletín Oficial del Estado.* Madrid: Boletín Oficial de la Presidencia.

Sanders, K., & Canel, M. J. (2004). Spanish politicians and the media: Controlled visibility and soap opera politics. *Parliamentary Affairs, 57*(1), 196–208.

Semetko, H. A., & Canel, M. J. (1997). Agenda-senders versus agenda-setters: Television in Spain's 1996 election campaign. *Political Communication, 14,* 459–479.

Tapia, B. (2004, March 8). *Internet focus of much campaigning in Spanish elections.* Retrieved December 3, 2005, from the Digital Media Europe Web site: http://www.dmeurope.com default.asp?ArticleID=1146

A 21st-century protest. (2004, March 25). Retrieved December 3, 2005, from the *Guardian* Unlimited Web site: http://www .guardian .co.uk/spain/article/0,2763,1176811,00.html

Van Biezen, I. (2000). Party financing in new democracies: Spain and Portugal. *Party Politics, 6*(3), 329–342.

7

From Electoral Propaganda to Political Advertising in Israel

DAN CASPI AND BARUCH LESHEM

Despite structural and content-related changes throughout the years, the electoral system of Israel has remained basically unchanged; it is an arena where politicians court the electorate, with direct wooing of the electorate involving a widening array of professional "matchmakers." As a result, electoral propaganda has gradually been replaced by political advertising (Jamieson, 1986). This conversion from *electoral propaganda* to *political advertising* may be one of the characteristic signs of enormous changes in political culture over the last few years, and not only in Israel (Kaid & Holtz-Bacha, 1995). How did this change come about?

As in other Western democracies, mainly the United States, semantic changes in Israel have not been coincidental. They have been described by common labels prevalent in academic dialogue and public discourse: professionalization (Caspi & Eyal, 1983), Americanization (Lehman-Wilzig, 1994), personalization (Leshem, 2003), standardization (Caspi, 1999), and so on, each label pointing to a particular trend in the development of electoral propaganda in the Israeli democracy. Consequently, although these changes are not necessarily unique to Israel, they are undoubtedly well anchored in profound changes within Israeli society and political culture.

We will begin by assessing the electoral system and changes incorporated into the system over the years. The heart of our discussion will closely scrutinize changes in electoral propaganda in Israel and its transformation into political advertising. The chapter also evaluates the mutual relationship between changes in electoral propaganda and campaign research conducted in Israel.

THE POLITICAL AND ELECTORAL SYSTEM

Despite external influences, over the years Israel has zealously maintained a multiparty system, based on a general, proportional, national, and secret voting system (Elazar & Sandler, 1992). Nevertheless, for years, comparisons to other political cultures have not ceased. Identifying economic success with an electoral system is apparently responsible for the desire to imitate Western democracies, mainly the United States. In the absence of a broad consensus on changing the electoral system, it seems that leaders were content with the controlled import of components from the American electoral system.

As is customary in a proportional voting system, one votes for a list of candidates without the ability to determine the order of candidates on the list. During the first three decades, internal party procedures such as the "placement committee" (*Vaada Messaderet*), comprising a handful of leaders, determined the final nature of the list (Diskin, 1991). This centralized practice was disrupted in 1977, when most parties began introducing a primaries system, in which party members are able to express their personal preferences for various candidates using the "Hit Parade" system. The more votes candidates received, the higher up on the list they climbed, and vice versa. Internal party elections and the candidate list were usually determined by a central committee of the party, which (allegedly) resembled an American party conference. In smaller parties, assembling the list is the responsibility of members of the party "chamber." In several other cases, parties preferred allowing all members to vote for candidates. Hence, in 1992, two thirds of all 160 thousand members, and, 10 years later, in 2002, 54% of all 110 thousand members, participated in determining the order of candidates on the list of candidates.

The introduction of primaries into the Israeli electoral system has slightly dispelled the sense of lack of personal influence over the composite list for the Knesset, seemingly contributing to democratization within the party. Moreover, over the years, the institutionalization of a primaries procedure reinforced the position of the central committee and its members in particular (Doron, 1996a). The embracing of primaries by more and more parties also redefined the representational balance between the electorate and elected representatives. Candidates were obliged to show evidence of personal achievement to canvass political support. To do so, individual candidates or groups of candidates prepared for the primaries by setting up campaign headquarters equipped with advisors, spokespersons, and surveyors. It should be noted that the personal nature of the elections did not entirely eradicate the system of party factions. Candidates knew they needed to woo votes and prove ongoing personal credentials to win political support. This kind of factional support diminishes the personal basis of election to the Knesset party list. Although factions are just barely in evidence and internal elections are held completely or almost completely on a personal basis, elections remain the sole property of party members.

An additional change in the direction of personal elections took place in 1979 with an amendment to the Law of Elections to Local Authorities differentiating between the election of the mayor or head of the local council and the election of council members. According to this amendment, every citizen votes twice. One envelope contains the vote for the head of the local council. The second envelope contains the vote for the list of candidates to the city council or local authority. Here the vote is for the entire list and does not allow for ranking candidates. A voter can merely support or not support a particular list. This double vote encouraged a split vote or, in other words, support of a candidate for mayor who comes from a party different than that of the candidates for city council. In many cases, a candidate could be elected as mayor even if his or her party had not been successful and was not included in the council's majority list. To be elected, the candidate must win at least 40% of the votes. If no candidate succeeds in this, a second round of elections is held between the two candidates with the most votes. In this arrangement, personal aspects are emphasized as well; candidates are evaluated by character, skills, or personal achievements and not necessarily according to political opinions or ideology.

Perhaps it was the third change that was most significant in reinforcing the personalization of elections in Israel. According to an amendment of the *Basic Law: The Government,* passed in March 1992, the prime minister is to be elected in personal and national elections from the 14th Knesset elections, in the fall of 1996, and onward (Alon, 1995). For the first time in the history of the State of Israel, voters put two envelopes into the ballot box: one for the prime minister and one for the party. This amendment reinstated the principle of a double vote, already in practice in local elections. According to Section 13 of *Basic Law: The Government,* a candidate for the position of prime minister must win more than half of the valid votes and must be a member of the Knesset. If no candidate fulfills these requirements, within 2 weeks a second round of voting will be held to decide between the candidates with the most votes. In this second round, if neither of the candidates wins a majority, special elections are scheduled within 60 days (Nachmias & Sened, 1999). After a brief trial run in March 2001, it was decided to annul this amendment and return to the previous system.

The change in the voting system apparently led to a change in the nature of the parties' approach to propaganda. Whereas during previous elections the two major parties whose leaders were candidates for the office of prime minister turned to their safe constituencies, with the introduction of direct elections, the focus shifted to a struggle for a larger public of voters and, even more clearly, on floating votes that could determine the election of the candidate for prime minister.

Even if a link exists between the voting system and the style of election propaganda, it is difficult to determine which came first—the political process or the communication process. In other words, was it changes in the electoral system that accelerated Americanization of the election campaign or the other way around? Political reform may in itself attest to unease with the existing proportional voting system and aspirations for improvement. The increase in the personal dimension of election propaganda does indeed parallel changes in the electoral system. However, this could also be interpreted as a universal trend toward the standardization of the electoral campaign in various political cultures. Signs of a "New Style" in election campaigns have been widespread and have taken root even in regimes that are not necessarily democratic (Caspi, 1996). Here and there, candidates conduct vigorous election campaigns, including orchestrated rallies with voters, accompanied by an army of journalists, broadcasters, and photographers (Swanson & Mancini, 1996).

Electoral Campaigns

It appears that in addition to the changing rules of the game, media ecology has also left its mark on the electoral system. Over the years, the media map has branched out and been enriched by various media. Simultaneously, the use of media for election propaganda has varied and changed. In general, one can say with a measure of caution that interpersonal media have given way to mass media. However, there has also been a noticeable return to interpersonal media, this time of a different nature, as clarified in Table 7.1.

The printed press and radio enjoyed a relative advantage during the first two decades of Israel's existence. When television was introduced in 1968, it was immediately recruited for election purposes. In fact, ever since then, it has been the major medium of election campaigns and a catalyst of stylistic changes, including the move from propaganda to political advertising, as will be explained further on. For a quarter of a century, propagandists had to make do with a single television channel. It was only in 1993 that a concession was granted to a second, general, commercially

Table 7.1   Comparison of Media Uses in the Election to the Knesset

Electoral Propaganda Campaigns	1950s and 1960s	1970s	1980s	1990s	21st Century
Interpersonal media					
Outdoor public meetings	+++	++	–	–	–
Public hall meetings	+++	++	+	–	–
Campaigning door to door	–	–	++	–	–
Meetings of ethnic and immigrant groups	—	+	++	+	+
Meetings in the workplace	+++	+	–	–	–
Parlor meetings	+++	++	–	–	+
Mass media					
Daily newspapers	+++	+++	+++	++	+
Local newspapers	—	+	+++	++	+
Radio	+	++	++	++	++
Television	—	++	+++	+++	+++
Pirate and foreign broadcasts	–	–	+	++	++
Alternative media					
CDs	—	–	+	+	++
Cassettes	—	–	+	+	+
Videotapes	—	–	–	+	++
Telephone canvassing	–	–	+	++	+++
Mailings	+++	++	+	++	+
Street billboards	+++	+++	+	+	–
Loudspeakers	+++	–	–	–	+
Faxes and the Internet	–	–	–	+	+
Books	–	–	–	+	++
Trips and tours	–	–	–	+	+
Other practices					
Initiating events	–	–	–	++	+++
Speakers and public relations	–	–	+	+++	+++
Public tours with press	–	–	–	++	+++
Street banners	–	–	+	++	++
Animated banners	–	–	–	+++	+++

SOURCE: Based on Galnoor (1982, p. 254) and updated accordingly.

Note: +++ extensive use; ++ frequent use; + little use; – very little use; — no use or almost no use.

funded television station: Channel 2. It, too, was immediately recruited for election campaigning. By 2002, yet another commercially funded channel, Channel 10, had been born.

Election propaganda focuses mainly on television, using both human and financial resources. Lately, however, the appearance of new media, namely the Internet, the cell phone, and the facsimile (fax), have challenged and continue to challenge television's hegemony, with continuously decreasing rates of exposure to election broadcasts only one of the challenges.

The 1950s and 1960s

Many prevalent communication patterns in pre-State Jewish society (*Yishuv*) persisted during the very first election campaign. Various parties efficiently used different social structures, such as new immigrant associations, workplaces, or voluntary associations. These served as communication channels in the elections and also for the Knesset (Galnoor, 1982). The use of social structures for communication purposes allowed politicians personal, focused access to voters. Social changes in the newborn State, including population growth, slightly affected the efficiency of traditional patterns and strengthened the importance of mass media.

During the initial and formative years of Israeli democracy, party leaders persevered in the establishment of direct contact with voters. Election campaigns relied mainly on meetings, at which politicians addressed the masses crowding outdoor places or meeting halls. Oratorical skill was much in demand and highly valued. Gifted orators, such as Menachem Begin and David Ben-Gurion, could fill halls and squares with masses of citizens, regardless of their political leanings. As these were times of mass immigration from Islamic and Eastern European countries, speakers were chosen and sent to speak in new villages according to their fluency in immigrant languages. An election meeting was often a major gathering, attended by nearly every citizen, young and old alike; it resembled gatherings in the Agora of Ancient Greece. Discussions and debates were held in the crowd before the main speech and continued on long after the last speaker had gone.[1] Usually the branch chairman of the relevant party hosted the meeting and delivered a preamble; after the atmosphere had "warmed up," the right of speech was granted to the guest speaker, who was usually a senior personality from the party list.

Electoral propaganda continued to focus on the written word, making use of various printed media—newspapers, pamphlets, posters, and so on. Almost all parties published at least one daily Hebrew newspaper. Sometimes they sponsored, directly or indirectly, a large number of publications in various immigrant languages, such as Arabic, Polish, Hungarian, Rumanian, Yiddish, Spanish, and others. The flourishing party

press served mainly, as it did in the days of the mandate, as an effective ideological organ with which to recruit electoral support (Caspi & Limor, 1999). Party newspapers were distributed to subscribers, and it was possible to identify a reader's political identity by the newspaper she or he received each morning on her or his doorstep. On election eve, political parties were content to publish ads crammed with text and excerpts from their platforms. The ads usually praised their parties' achievements and enumerated their opponents' failures, reaching out to voters for their support. Letters identifying the party list were published in newspaper ads and on city billboards. Ballot slips with the letters of party lists littered the sidewalks in every neighborhood.[2] Citizens stood in front of billboards perusing the platform of each party.

The Knesset Elections Law (Propaganda Methods)—1959 was supposedly intended to guarantee fair play and the neutrality of radio broadcasts and cinema newsreels displayed on the eve of elections. Actually, the law reflected the sense that broadcast and visual messages had an omnipotent impact on individual opinions. The second clause of the law determined limitations and prohibitions on the broadcasting of election propaganda "within a period of 150 days prior to Election Day and on Election Day." Clause 5 of the law prohibited visual coverage of any candidate participating in events within a 60-day period prior to elections. This, naturally, led to the interference of journalistic considerations (Katz, 1999, p. 22). At the time, a ban was placed on weekly newsreels produced at the *Carmel* and *Geva* studios and shown in movie theaters before the movie began. The ban proved even more vital 10 years later, with the introduction of television broadcasts immediately following the Six-Day War. Eventually, due to this clause, television was prevented from broadcasting images of candidates for the Knesset in any form whatsoever within the period defined by law.

As radio broadcasts were organized as a division of the Prime Minister's Office, anchormen could not really conceal their political affiliations. In addition, the prime minister's workforce closely supervised *Kol Yisrael* (Voice of Israel) broadcasts and maintained constant contact with writers and editors in the newsroom (Caspi, 2005). Nevertheless, to guarantee equal access to each party candidate, paragraph 15a of *The Knesset Elections Law (Propaganda Methods)—1959* determined that "each party and its candidates will be granted twenty-five minutes exposure and each party represented in the outgoing Knesset will receive an additional four minutes per Knesset Member."

Thus, as early as the 1961 and 1965 election campaigns, the parties' radio broadcasts were new and stimulating, captivating the interest of listeners. Due to a lack of experience, leaders and spokespeople of the parties tended to shower the public with entire portions of the party platform. In exchange, the general public was fascinated by these broadcasts and by the fact that they did not have to make an effort to go anywhere to listen to candidates. However, as in the earlier public meetings, radio broadcasts required skills in rhetoric and an impressive broadcasting voice to enhance the candidate's image.

The 1970s

The introduction of television broadcasts at the end of the 1960s was a milestone in electoral campaigning in Israel. As expected, legislators adapted to the new medium in no time and immediately began using it to serve election campaigns. Amendment 3 to *The Knesset Elections Law (Propaganda Methods)—1959* regulated the allocation of broadcast time on television by principles similar to those used for radio broadcasts. According to this revision, each party list in the outgoing Knesset was equally entitled to a 10-minute period on broadcast television, with another 4 minutes granted each individual member. Thus, a list of 40 members from the outgoing Knesset was entitled to 185 minutes of radio broadcasting and 170 minutes of television broadcasting, whereas a new list had to make do with the uniform time quota alone.

This arrangement raised much criticism from various sources, if only because it indirectly contributed to the ongoing political status quo and deprived smaller and newer parties of equal time. Moreover, unlike with the Law of Party Financing, which allocates financial resources relative to the size of the party in the elected Knesset, there could be no return of broadcast time—it was not possible to return time retroactively if a party had lost mandates relative to its number in the previous Knesset. In addition, the law discriminates between elections to the Knesset, to local authorities, and to the General Federation of the Israeli Labor Workers Union (*Histadrut Clalit*), all also legitimate arenas of political struggle. As long as the elections for local authorities and for the Knesset were held at the same time, this discrimination was not felt so intensely. However, ever since the elections have been separated, the lack of media presence in local authority elections has grown more intense.

The law determining campaign broadcasting time required that the Head of the Election Committee and the General Manager of the Israeli Broadcasting Authority coordinate to allocate radio and television broadcasting time for parties' campaigns. Election broadcasts were aired at prime time, immediately after the broadcast of the major news program *Mabat*, which was watched by more than three quarters of the population in Israel. Thus the public was, in essence, forced by legislators to be exposed to the electoral campaign on the single television channel that then existed.

Politicians made use of television for the first time in the election campaign of 1969. Due to their inexperience in this medium, candidates appeared on camera as if they were speaking at an election meeting (Gurevitch, 1972). The 1973 electoral campaign was overshadowed by the Yom Kippur War and forced parties to cut down on expenses, so they were unable to allocate resources for the high costs of television (Peri, 1975).

The medium of television was "forced" to wait patiently for another 4 years. In the interim, state-of-the-art television equipment, which had been purchased, enabled the production of propaganda clips rich in visual effects. Professionals at campaign headquarters soon realized the potential of televised broadcasts and recommended the use of short clips rather than on-camera speeches. In the 1977 election campaign, Likud propagandists introduced another innovation: They split the daily time slot into three shorter broadcasts of 3 to 4 minutes each (Elizur & Katz, 1979). Their decision was based on the assumption that one long election broadcast might not capture viewer attention, whereas three broadcasts in one evening, at the beginning, middle, and end of election broadcasts, would create the illusion that the Likud's screen time was longer and that other parties' ads were merely scattered among those of the Likud (Anski, 1977).

It was apparently at this time that the first buds of tension began to sprout between academia and the professionals: Each community aimed at learning from the experience of its colleagues abroad. Professionals sought to emulate propaganda patterns and integrate the television into the electoral campaign as much as possible. Academia, as mentioned earlier, put its efforts into dispelling fears regarding the strong influence of television on electoral preferences. Apparently, the professionals had the upper hand, if only because they were better at persuading politicians as to the validity of their arguments.

The political upheaval (*Hamahapach*) of 1977, which put the Likud movement into the government after many years in the opposition, also marked a change in the style of election campaigns in Israel. For the first time, professionals were engaged officially in party campaign headquarters alongside politicians, and they were instrumental in shaping strategies and propaganda tactics. Campaign headquarters, which previously had been the sacred ground of the party, was now invaded by high-pressure professionals who assured politicians that they had the best "recipes" for appropriate campaign managing. Many of these new experts came from the advertising industry and based their new electoral strategies on their marketing experience. This process, which was similar to one occurring abroad, also accelerated the conversion of electoral propaganda to political advertising (Katz, 1999).

At the command of these new experts, the emphasis in electoral campaigns shifted from the press to broadcasting and later on, more specifically, from radio to television. Propaganda posters were advertised in the printed press and continued to adorn city streets. However, the new consultants recommended that candidates increase their exposure on radio and television, at the expense of more traditional methods. Public meetings became less and less popular and disappeared within the following two decades because of the shift from city square to television studio. Estimates regarding the Americanization of electoral campaigns increased in many research studies and public discussions (Lehman-Wilzig, 1994). The belief in Americanization increased in intensity with the adoption of the television debate as the pinnacle of the electoral campaign.

The television debate between Shimon Peres and Menachem Begin, in the dramatic election campaign of 1977, was probably one of the most fascinating innovations in electoral politics. Media consultants imported the American format and adjusted it to Israeli political requirements. As opposed to the series of debates between the presidential candidates in the United States, in Israel a single televised debate was usually conducted between the leaders of the major lists. The debate was produced at the expense of the parties and took place within the broadcast time framework allocated according to law (Caspi,

1986). In the United States, the television debate is an established part of the presidential election campaign and is held as an open meeting between interviewee and interviewer. In Israel, the parties control the structure of the debate, its content, the identity of the interviewer, the number and length of issues, the broadcasting studio, the directing, and the equal and precise division of time between debaters. How the debate is conducted depends on the good will of candidates and on the recommendations of political consultants (Anski, 1977). Due to these facts, the debate in Israel is a rather structured and boring TV show. It consists of familiar arguments, with each side reciting its own positions and at times ignoring the host's questions. Thus there are, in essence, two unrelated monologues. Nevertheless, preparation for the debate, its filming, and the evaluation of its results capture much interest and are granted in-depth media coverage. The tradition of televised debate was discontinued when former prime minister Ehud Barak adopted the recommendations of his political consultants and refused to debate Ariel Sharon, then the head of the opposing party.

The 1980s

During the second half of the 1980s, cable television broadcasts were introduced, and the single-channel television monopoly was over. Cable television was prevented from broadcasting local news. The monopoly of public television in the provision of information and news in Hebrew held for a few more years, but with one difference. This time, viewers were no longer prisoners to single-channel television. They were able to choose from many cable television channels and could also choose not to watch election broadcasts. The viewing rates of election broadcasts did, in fact, decrease, but remained relatively high. This fortified the status of television and further encouraged the Americanization process of election propaganda.

The increasing involvement of election consultants accelerated processes of professionalizing election campaigns. Small and medium-sized parties also equipped themselves with political consultants. The focus on TV propaganda broadcasts forced almost all party lists to seek the assistance of production studios and advertising firms.

Section 5 of *The Knesset Election Law (Propaganda Methods)—1959* made television news coverage in the month prior to the elections very difficult. The month preceding the elections is particularly intense, with many political displays causing dramatic events of high news value occurring precisely at a time when they cannot receive proper coverage. Thus, the inappropriateness of the limitation was keenly felt just before the elections of 1973, which were postponed because of the Yom Kippur War. Due to compromise and legal revision, permission was granted to cover the negotiations held at Kilometer 101[3] and, later, the Geneva Convention[4] discussions (Cohen & Wolfsfeld, 1995). About three weeks before the elections to the 10th Knesset (June 4, 1981), the summit meeting between Prime Minister Menachem Begin and the president of Egypt, Anwar Saadat, took place at Sharem al-Sheikh. Israeli television cameras documented the entire event, but in the news broadcast, according to law, only half of the frame could be shown—the half in which Begin was not visible. However, the viewer could see the entire frame half an hour later in the Likud's election broadcasts.

It would seem that the printed press benefited from legal limitations on visual coverage. The declining partisan press also helped make widely circulated private newspapers an efficient means of political advertising. As of the 1977 election campaign, to assure visibility and to create an image of the party's power and size, Likud propagandists began publishing full page and even double-spread ads in various newspapers. During the 1980s, nearly every party or list that could afford the expense published huge ads, even though the size of the advertisement actually had a boomerang effect, as more than anything else, it testified to a huge waste of funds. For example, at the outset of the election campaign for the 12th Knesset, Likud propagandists increased their activities and published three-page advertisements, causing a wave of criticism regarding the waste of finances entailed. Unlike advertisements of previous decades, this time the printed propaganda in the newspapers was planned with the assistance of professionals who were well aware of the advent of the era of television. Therefore, research focused on the visual process of printed propaganda, with a multitude of visual components—the size of advertisements, photos, logos, slogans and graphic designs—coming at the expense of a highly diluted text (Caspi & Eyal, 1983).[5]

In March 1992, an amendment to Section 10 of *The Knesset Election Law (Propaganda Methods)—1959* was passed to prevent the trend of large, expensive advertising in print journalism. As a result, various limitations were placed on written propaganda in the daily newspapers, and the size of an election advertisement was limited to 40 inches. A political party was not allowed to publish more than one advertisement in one newspaper per day; an advertisement was not to be printed in more than two colors; a party was not allowed to publish more than 10,000 inches during the 3 months prior to elections.

In the 1980s, consultants discovered the potential of various new technologies, such as audiocassettes and records, and old technologies, such as mailing lists and telephone calls. As of the 1981 election campaign, there were signs of "sobriety" from the intoxication of mass media and a shift toward integrating old and new technologies with interpersonal media. Small parties and political lists, such as *Tami*, whose access to broadcast media was limited, began producing cassettes and distributing them among voters. In the elections to the 12th Knesset (1984), these lists discovered

the advantages of the videocassette. They were distributed among supporters, presented in various social frameworks, and occasionally broadcast on pirate cable television stations.

In the 1988 and 1992 election campaigns, new ways of using existing media were introduced that were similar to those common in United States election campaigns. At the beginning of the campaign, the Labor Party purchased the telephone lists of Bezek (the national telephone company) subscribers. Campaigners telephoned close to 1½ million citizens, to ferret out those who had not yet decided on their vote. A privately owned company even offered computerized telephoning services, which enabled two-way communication with the voters. Any party or candidate could obtain a voice message box with a personal code and record any propaganda they desired. Any citizen could call up the voice box, listen to the message, and respond to it.

Further, several innovative measures refreshed the stale routine of election campaigns. Propagandists distributed stickers with the letter and the slogan of the party list, mainly to stick on car fenders (Bloch, 2000). Live signs (persons holding slogans and banners) were posted at crossroads. Party youth were hired and dressed in shirts and hats lettered with party slogans. They distributed propaganda material and held signs and banners with the list's slogans and pictures of candidates. A study conducted prior to the elections of the 14th Knesset revealed that more than four out of 10 cars (42%) bore some kind of sticker, mainly political. This rate is 10 times higher than that found in a similar study carried out in the United States. The rest of the stickers related to other issues, such as military, road safety, and advertising of products or "personal" statements (Olinski, 1996).

The 1990s

At least two trends accelerated the professionalization process of election campaigns in the 1990s. At the beginning of the decade, a new television channel, Channel 2, started broadcasting, putting an end to the monopoly of one-channel television and a single-channel source of visual information. Waves of mass immigration from the former Soviet Union added new voters to the electorate. As a result, campaign headquarters established departments to campaign in Russian, as a response to the flourishing of immigrant parties.

The addition of a television channel in and of itself may not be considered a dramatic change. However, it served to double broadcast time, and precisely for this reason, the politicians required the aid of media consultants, spokespersons, and public relations officers. An additional television channel could have provided an alternative and an escape from propaganda broadcasts. So, once again, legislators revised the law, this time to obligate commercial channels to allocate free time for election broadcasts. Consequently, in 1993, the law was amended to apply to additional television channels: Channel 2, followed by Channel 10. Toward the end of the decade, the media reality of an abundance of foreign satellite news channels made a mockery of the legal limitations on showing faces of candidates 1 month prior to the elections. What had been banned from viewing on Israeli news editions could be viewed on the foreign news channels. Thus, in March 1992, the period during which broadcasting of election propaganda was banned was reduced to 60 days, and simultaneously, the period during which coverage of events in which Knesset candidates participated was banned was shortened to 30 days before elections. Prior to the 1996 elections, this period was shortened once again to a mere 21 days, and before the elections in 1999, both limitations were totally revoked, enabling a return to regular media coverage (Katz, 1999, p. 22). Researchers lost no time in studying television coverage of the election campaigns, "but there was no indication of preferences," as neither television channel

favored either of the major parties, Labor or Likud (Arian, Weimann, & Wolfsfeld, 1999; Weimann & Wolfsfeld, 1996).

It appears that the new commercial television channels also contributed to a shift from electoral propaganda toward political advertising. After all, the same human resources are involved in both propaganda and advertising. The campaign headquarters of most parties were staffed with experts and consultants. They channeled most financial resources into election broadcasts, thus indirectly contributing to the development of the television industry in Israel. Production companies refurbished studios and hired professional staff, such as scriptwriters, cameramen, and directors, to handle increasing requests. Production standards also improved, and election campaigns resembled commercial clips, with a concise message condensed into a few seconds. Because the parties continued to enjoy the same generous time quotas, broadcasts were aired several times, thus increasing the similarity to commercial clips.[6]

The increasing cost of election campaigns and restrictions on the scope of advertisements called for cheaper creative alternatives. Campaign headquarters resorted to replacing paid ads with productive public relations by initiating news events whose value lay in the fact that they merited free media coverage. To achieve this, campaign headquarters employed spokespersons and public relations officers to work alongside hired propaganda experts, who specialized in disseminating information regarding the election campaign. Public relations officers diverted reporters' attention from messages and contents to events occurring during the election campaign. Results of public opinion polls served as a main tool in shaping electoral strategies (Doron, 1998). They enabled information to be manipulated so that it promoted tactical goals. Party headquarters conducted polls more and more frequently and began to release partial findings from these surveys before the elections, as propagandists saw fit (Shamir, 1986). As of the 1970s, increasing information about data from the polls cultivated an awareness of the need for these data during the campaign. This updated the status of pollsters at the campaign headquarters, some of them acquiring the status of political consultants (Weimann, 1998).

Election results of three campaigns—1988, 1992, and 1996—focused public attention on exceptional achievements of the religious and *Haredi* (ultraorthodox) parties, which excelled at exploiting interpersonal and alternative media. It seemed as though propagandists in these parties rebelled against the Americanization that had been introduced by professionals working for the major parties. The propagandists rediscovered the power of interpersonal media, locating voters via existing social structures in the community, such as synagogues and religious schools, or by making house calls.

On the eve of elections for the 14th Knesset, the distinction between the Sephardi and Ashkenazi Haredi parties was clearly evident. All Haredi parties used alternative media. However, whereas the Sephardi *Shas* party benefited from oral media, such as audiocassettes (Blondheim & Kaplan, 1993), pirate radio stations, and satellite television broadcasts,[7] the Ashkenazi Haredi parties preferred printed media, such as newspapers, synagogue newsletters, and wall posters or notices posted in the street.[8] In all cases, the parties used the media according to the size of their electoral audience, its native language, and its needs (Liebes, Peri, & Grabelski, 1996). Those practices reaffirmed the view of Israeli society as fragmented into cultural enclaves (Sivan, 1991) or tribes (Peri, 2004). Some of these enclaves displayed traditional characteristics, such as a wealth of well-developed, interlocking networks, which provided efficient alternatives to the new mass media.

However, professional campaigners continued adopting innovative media technologies, such as the fax and the Internet, revealing their potential for propaganda. Prior to the 1996

elections, almost all campaign headquarters (although mainly the Likud's) began establishing Internet Web sites for the purpose of public relations and election propaganda.[9] Most party lists introduced Web sites, which proved to have a twofold advantage: It was inexpensive to use the Web site, and it was also an acceptable source of exposure to propaganda messages. Party Web sites turned into portals overflowing with information and propaganda. In addition to information on the party's platform, candidates, parlor meetings, and meetings with candidates, campaigners posted advertising material, such as stickers, posters, ads, and radio and video clips.

In comparison to other traditional and mass media, the construction and use of Web sites involves reaching a wide-spectrum audience at low cost. In addition, visitors to the party Web site are voluntarily exposed to propaganda messages. Consequently, the use of the Internet for propaganda may create new functions and pose a threat to activities at campaign headquarters, because viewers may switch to watching the computer screen more than the television screen. Because the Internet is a less costly medium, it is liable to reduce election campaign expenses, thus causing financial losses to the election industry, in which many make a living from television advertising.

RESEARCH ON POLITICAL ADVERTISING IN ISRAEL

Changes in electoral campaigning have preoccupied researchers and journalists, as well as those responsible for the changes. When Israeli election literature is reviewed, a twofold source of tension can be detected: the first between professionals and journalists and researchers and the second among researchers themselves. Both journalists and professionals provide much information and fascinating description of what goes on inside the campaign headquarters, in a sort of "Making of the President [or Prime Minister]" style. They even emphasize the part played by professionals and the manipulative use of the media, mainly of television.

One of the first accounts relates to the 1977 election campaign, in which, for the first time, as stated earlier, external professionals were instrumental in shaping Likud strategy. One of the journalists on the professional staff documented the tensions between politicians and consultants at Likud campaign headquarters and exposed some of the professionals' considerations, as he saw them (Anski, 1977). This practice encouraged political journalists to document later campaigns. There was hardly an election campaign that did not result in books by journalists and bestsellers that shed light on occurrences in campaign headquarters of the major parties (Azulai-Katz, 1996; Caspit, Crystal & Kfir, 1996; Crystal & Kfir, 1999; Doron, 1996b; Drucker, 2002; Neubach, 1996). In some cases, those who did not succeed in the campaigns found it necessary to issue apologetic arguments (Ben Eliezer, 1997; Diskin, 1988; Levi, 1987; Weiss, 1996).

Compared to journalists and professionals, academic researchers were intent on a more cautious evaluation of the changes in election campaigning and its influence on voter intentions. In the 1960s and 1970s, researchers tended to rely on the findings of the campaign research tradition, significantly easing fears regarding the inclusion of television in election campaigning. They came up with research findings bearing witness to selective exposure to propaganda messages and to limited influence on voter preferences (Caspi, 1984; Katz, 1971).

Thus, in the spirit of the research tradition of the 1977 campaign, it was found that election propaganda was used as a source of orientation for many voters who had not yet made a decision: 44% of the interviewees claimed that the election campaign helped them see which party was closest to their opinions; 23% of them watched television propaganda broadcasts to understand the various platforms and plans (Elizur & Katz, 1979). Initial studies compared the efficiency of differential media exposure of candidates on radio versus television. Findings indicated that the radio favored several candidates, a fact that may have mitigated the misgivings related to the overwhelming impact of television (Cohen & Libo, 1975).

The adoption of the television debate seems to have ignited the fancy of Israeli researchers. In addition to giving juicy descriptions of its birth pangs in the election campaign, conflicts of interest in campaign headquarters between politicians and their consultants, and increasing tensions in preparations for the television debate, several researchers sought to identify the strategies and the rhetorical tactics of debaters. Researchers particularly focused on revealing the polarization tactic of debate rhetoric, which partially reflected and partially created the overall atmosphere of the election campaign (Caspi, 1986; Gertz, 1986).

The reassuring research findings on selective exposure to the election propaganda (Katz & Levinsohn, 1989) did not avert fears of manipulation by professionals, such as the selective publication of polling data or campaign agenda setting. Researchers divided the responsibility of poll misuse between pollsters and journalists and criticized media coverage of poll findings (Weiman, 1984). The increasing use of polls and publication of their findings particularly troubled the academic community, which apparently feared losing the credibility of one of its most popular research tools (Fuchs & Bar-Lev, 1998).

It appears that in the 1990s, the agenda-setting tradition affected the research agenda and overshadowed the campaign tradition (Cohen & Wolfsfeld, 1995). Once again, findings abated fears regarding the significant influence of election propaganda caused by the involvement of professionals:

The tendency is apparently one of heightened struggles over the control of the agenda. As a result, election campaigns are more aggressive, negative and rife with emotion; attempting to nourish themselves by encouraging conflicts of a personal nature. The first personal election campaign conducted during the 1996 elections, for office of Prime Minister, emphasized the personal dimension, as well as the interest of the media in conflicts between the candidates. (Wolfsfeld & Weimann, 1999, p. 22)

After the 1996 elections, two researchers found a clear relationship between the issues in election propaganda and the issues that emerged on the media agenda. Netanyahu's victory has been attributed to the success of Likud broadcasts in setting the agenda for Election Day. Prior to the 1999 elections, as stated, the law prohibiting the screening of politicians' faces for 30 days prior to elections was revised. Researchers believe that this caused a decrease in the ratings of election broadcasts in 1999 and in 2001, as well as a decline in the power of the propaganda broadcasts in setting political campaign agendas (Weimann & Wolfsfeld, 2002; Wolfsfeld & Weimann, 2002).

As more and more journalists and professionals turned to research, the focus shifted more and more to institutional aspects of the electoral campaign that had probably been neglected previously for the sake of research convenience. Researchers have difficulty in gaining access to campaign headquarters and to propagandists, so they focus their efforts on propaganda content and messages. Largely due to their personal experience and access to election campaign headquarters, the "new researchers" praised the "new politics," or "telepopulism," backed by the "new media," namely television, which has endured between elections as well (Ben Eliezer, 2003; Galili, 2004; Leshem, 2003; Peri, 2004; Sheafer, 2001). The "new researchers" challenged the traditional research agenda that had shown only a limited effect of electoral propaganda and, even further, backed the semantic shift from *electoral propaganda* to *political advertisement*.

Simultaneously, their colleagues persisted in relating to electoral propaganda rather than to political advertising, from which they learned about tactics and agenda and underrated the influence of election broadcasts, based on a poll of voters (Cohen & Wolfsfeld, 1995; Wolfsfeld & Weimann, 2002). A poll referring to the election broadcasts' impact on voters in 1996 once again revealed soothing findings: Only 11% reported daily viewing of broadcasts on television, and over three quarters of all those questioned claimed that the broadcasts did not affect their vote in any way whatsoever (Arian & Shamir, 1999a, 1999b).[10]

CONCLUSION: THE NEW POLITICS IN ISRAEL

In the conversion of electoral propaganda to political advertising, at least five main characteristics can be identified: telepolitics, consultants, personalization, "carnivalization," and polls (in Hebrew, the acronym for this is TYPEX) (Caspi, 1999). The TYPEX approach did indeed take shape within election campaigns, but in this era of "unceasing elections," it could also characterize Israeli politics (Caspi, 1999).

1. Telepolitics

Telepolitics refers to vigorous propaganda campaigns conducted in the broadcast media, particularly television, including extensive candidate coverage (Peri, 2004). Press conferences are scheduled to coincide with broadcast hours of radio and television news editions, thus enabling direct and unedited broadcasts. Spin doctors set up events to coincide with broadcasting lineups, choosing from three principal formats.

Combined Press Conference and Election Rally

Candidates, or rather professionals, instigate a press conference by creating a "pseudoevent."

The spokesperson usually declares party or candidate intentions to install a new policy or make a dramatic change in the electoral system. As opposed to the usual press conference, which is limited to the spokesperson, assistants, and journalists, an additional party is now included: the "fan club." The candidate is surrounded by supporters who create a sympathetic atmosphere for the "star of the show" and controlled hostility toward journalists. Anyone who dares ask a provocative question is openly ridiculed, and any declaration made by a spokesperson is warmly supported by the crowd.

Combined Electioneering and Press Conference

Candidates are covered visiting public sites where they "meet the people." They shake hands, kiss children, and talk directly to citizens. These visits are planned and staged for the benefit of news coverage. Here too, professionals make a point of surrounding the candidate with loyal fans who cheer him on. When necessary, these fans silence opponents (who have also been hired to provide opposition). At times the outings are dramatically interrupted for a "spontaneous" press conference, a kind of payback for the journalists accompanying the outing.

Electronic Parlor Meetings

The candidate and his fans, who form a kind of roving campaign staff, schedule a break from their travels at the broadcasting studio for an electronic parlor meeting. The candidate talks with the interviewer in an interpersonal format that takes place in one of the electronic forms of the mass media. As opposed to an actual parlor meeting, the electronic meeting takes place in a studio with a receptive and prefabricated audience. The meeting is quite controlled and is geared to ensure exposure of the candidate to large audiences listening at home.

In recent election campaigns, it was a combination of circumstances that gave telepolitics three significant advantages. First, candidates for prime minister Benjamin Netanyahu, Ehud Barak, and Ariel Sharon, each for different reasons, found in the media, mainly television, an effective alternative to shaky party support, as well as an effective means by which they could directly communicate with the electorate. In an interview following his victory in the Likud primaries, Benjamin Netanyahu declared: "We are holding a revolution here and those who will determine its representatives are the public, without the mediation of party staff or politicians" (Yerushalmi, 1999, p. 10). Second, Benjamin Netanyahu's success was interpreted as a victory for telepolitics. It is a well-known fact that one does not challenge success but rather attempts to emulate it with similar tools (Peri, 2004). Finally, in the political climate following Rabin's assassination, telepolitics facilitated candidate security. A studio is always preferable to a campaign trail.

2. Consultants

Professionals surround candidates closely, taking control of election headquarters and pushing aside tried and true party members and campaign workers, as the professionals have imported the best available know-how on effective and rational campaign management.

The election campaign resembles a horse race between foreign consultants, with each candidate proudly displaying his consultants and extolling their reputations. Hence, in the elections for prime minister in 1999, Ehud Barak prided himself on having three American consultants—James Carville, Stanley Greenberg, and Bob Shrum—who had participated in Bill Clinton's presidential election campaign in 1992, Tony Blair's election as prime minister of Great Britain in 1997, and Gerhard Schröder election as chancellor of Germany in 1998. In contrast with Barak, Benjamin

Netanyahu continued his campaign with the aid of Arthur Finkelstein, well known for his electoral success in the previous election campaign.[11]

3. Personalization

The increasing presence of experts on campaign staffs reduces public debate to a personal confrontation between candidates. The candidates and their personalities take center stage in the election campaign. As most experts are ostensibly armed with the know-how and experience of their American colleagues, they favor electoral propaganda taken from election campaigns for American governors and sheriffs. Personal qualifications, as reflected in the media, take over the campaign. Such personality cults downplay the value of ideological messages and the significance of political parties. Since the first televised debate in 1977, personal contrasts between candidates have acquired more prominence than ideological differences; a trend that intensified after the institution of direct elections for prime minister in 1996.

It appears that in the two major parties, during the election campaigns of the 1980s, party leaders appeared in 10% to 20% of the broadcast time, as opposed to the rest of the party members, who appeared in 40% to 60%. From the 1990s onward, this trend was reversed and peaked in the 2003 elections. In the Labor Party, 70% of broadcast time was devoted to the party leader and 14% to the rest of the party members. In the Likud, 55% of broadcast time was devoted to the leader of the list and about 25% to the rest of the party members (Leshem, 2003).

4. "Carnivalization"

Every political event and election rally turns into a kind of gala carnival, complete with balloons, signs, performers, singing, and dancing. Party conventions become projects for professional producers, who freely mingle entertainment and political speeches. In the last election campaigns, rival parties relied on the services of the same producer, who had a sound reputation in the field of mass entertainment. A political convention, especially when the party executive convenes, has always been a festive and highly significant occasion for discussion, ideological deliberation, and decision making. In the convention's carnival incarnation, political messages are drowned out by the roar of entertainment. External changes in political conventions parallel the erosion of party status as an essential component of election campaigns. Such occasions no longer need be exploited to intensify ideological distinctions between one party and its rivals, as these too are liable to be blurred in favor of personal differences between candidates. Consequently, conventions are used to cultivate candidates' personalities. In the carnival atmosphere, everything is based on the "planned spontaneity" of revelers (activists), with amusements overshadowing political elements.

5. Polls

Polls may well have reached mythological status in the last elections, with every pollster considered an oracle whose word is law. The political weakness that first opened campaign headquarters to outside experts also spurs candidates to commission polls for every move they make (Doron, 1998). Reserved spots, candidate list positioning, addressing or avoiding issues for public debate, and even choice of letters for the party symbol are determined according to poll results. Manipulative publication of partial poll findings has become one of the tactics in political advertisement (Weimann, 1984). Politicians and the media are trapped in a kind of vicious circle that benefits the poll industry: The more polls, the more findings; the more findings, the more differences among them; the more differences, the greater the uncertainty; and so on.

It seems that the main characteristic of electoral campaigns in Israel can be identified by a structured tension between the proportional electoral system and the pressures of economic forces and interest groups pushing for an accelerated Americanization of electoral politics. This tension, which is not just semantic, is well reflected in the research on election campaigns in Israel. It exists between those who consider the political activities of persuasion prior to elections as electoral propaganda and those who relate to it as political advertisement.

NOTES

1. At a conference on Leadership and Media that took place at Ben-Gurion University of the Negev on January 3, 2005, Professor Arie Naor, secretary to the prime minister during Menachem Begin's term of office, revealed that at the Herut Convention that took place in 1968 in the Old City of Jerusalem, Menachem Begin, then chairman of the Herut Movement, had integrated a lengthy portion of Latin into his speech. Even though the crowd did not understand a word of the speech, it resounded accurately with the speaker's rhetoric.

2. A feeling of the atmosphere generated during preelection days can be seen in Ephraim Kishon's film *Fox in the Hen-House*.

3. Talks on the cease-fire agreement held between Israel and Egypt following the Yom Kippur War. The talks, which were held on the Cairo-Suez Road, 101 kilometers from Cairo, were intended to anchor the cease-fire between the sides with a formal agreement. The first meeting between both sides was held at midnight between October 28 and 29. At this meeting, they discussed issues of supply and the besieged Third Army; agreements for maintaining the cease-fire were compiled; and lists of POWs that each side was holding were exchanged. At the end of November 1973, a few more talks were held at the 101st kilometer between leaders of the general headquarters of both armies. At these talks, details of dividing forces and withdrawal of *Tzahal* (the Israel Defense Forces) from the West Bank of the Suez Canal were finalized.

4. A convention, under the auspices of the United States and the USSR and in cooperation with the United Nations, at which negotiations between Israel and Egypt took place. The convention was convened in Geneva on December 21, 1973, following the Yom Kippur War.

5. In the 1981 election campaigns, the use of graphic symbols in written propaganda was seven times higher than that of the 1973 campaigns. In 1981, graphic symbols covered more than 75% of the ads. The frequency of national symbols as well, such as the color blue, the Israeli flag, and the Star of David, were clearly evident and highly used in both written and broadcast propaganda.

6. This trend benefited the smaller lists. They were able to schedule shorter broadcasts in the limited time they were allotted, due to the inverse proportion between the length of broadcast and the number of airings: The shorter a broadcast, the more times it was aired (Leshem, 2003).

7. Following the 1992 elections, Shas began airing live weekly lessons with Rabbi Ovadia Yosef, the leader of the movement. The broadcasts were transmitted from his Yeshiva in Jerusalem via satellite and received in 20 centers all over the country. In 1996, 300 synagogues and community centers were reached, in which 50,000 to 60,000 participants gathered each week. As elections grew closer, more and more political issues were integrated into the framework of religious studies (Liebes et al., 1996).

8. *Sichat Hashavua* (Discussion of the Week) is one of the most popular of all synagogue newsletters. It was published by *Tz'irey Habad* (Young Habad), edited by Rabbi Menachem Broad, and distributed in some 190,000 copies. *Oneg Shabbat* (Enjoyment of the Sabbath) was edited by Shmuel Cohen, published by Likud's newsletter, *Association for Implanting of National Jewish Values*, and 40,000 to 50,000 copies were distributed (Rapel, 1991). Just before the 1966 elections, it included an almost permanent column by Benjamin Netanyahu.

9. See these Web sites, which remained active following the elections:

http://www.likud.org.il/index.html

http://www.avoda.org.il

http://www.moledet.org.il/english/index.html

http://ale-yarok.org.il/home

http://www.shinui.org.il/site

http://www.yachadparty.org.il/ASP/Yachad.Asp?WCI=News_Page&ObjID=1&MenuRef=main&objType=8

10. A more comprehensive impression of election studies in Israel throughout the years, including research on election propaganda in Israel, can be found in the project of Asher Arian, who, after every campaign since the 1969 elections, consistently published a volume of articles in English or Hebrew (Arian, 1972, 1975, 1980, 1983; Arian & Shamir, 1986, 1990, 1995, 1999a, 1999b, 2000a, 2000b, 2004, 2005).

11. "The combination of Netanyahu and an American consultant is ideal. . . . Netanyahu is a well-oiled election machine, a candidate who is able to easily adapt into a new line of explanation, has a more than reasonable acting ability and gives his campaign authorization to make use of his family, wife and children, based on the best of American tradition. This was to the benefit of the Likud." (Noibach, 1996, pp. 160-161).

REFERENCES

Alon, G. (1995). *Direct election* (in Hebrew). Tel Aviv: Beitan.

Anski, A. (1977). *The selling of the Likud* (in Hebrew). Tel Aviv: Zmora Beitan Modan.

Arian, A. (Ed.). (1972). *The elections in Israel—1969.* Jerusalem: Academic Press.

Arian, A. (Ed.). (1975). *The elections in Israel—1973.* Jerusalem: Academic Press.

Arian, A. (Ed.). (1980). *The elections in Israel—1977.* Jerusalem: Academic Press.

Arian, A. (Ed.). (1983). *The elections in Israel.* Tel-Aviv: Ramot.

Arian, A., & Shamir, M. (Eds.). (1986). *The elections in Israel—1984.* Tel-Aviv: Ramot.

Arian, A., & Shamir, M. (Eds.). (1990). *The elections in Israel—1988.* Boulder, CO: Westview Press.

Arian, A., & Shamir, M. (Eds.). (1995). *The elections in Israel—1992.* Albany: State University of New York Press.

Arian, A., & Shamir, M. (Eds.). (1999a). *The elections in Israel—1996.* Albany: State University of New York Press.

Arian, A., & Shamir, M. (Eds.). (1999b). *The elections in Israel—1996* (in Hebrew). Jerusalem: Israeli Institute for Democracy.

Arian, A., & Shamir, M. (Eds.). (2000a). *The elections in Israel—1999.* Albany: State University of New York Press.

Arian, A., & Shamir, M. (Eds.) (2000b). *The elections in Israel—2000.* Jerusalem: Israel Democracy Institute (Hebrew).

Arian, A., & Shamir, M. (Eds.). (2004). *The elections in Israel—2003.* Albany: State University of New York Press.

Arian, A., & Shamir, M. (Eds.). (2005). *The elections in Israel—2003.* New Brunswick, NJ: Transaction Press.

Arian, A., Weimann, G., & Wolfsfeld, G. (1999). Balance in election coverage. In A. Arian & M. Shamir (Eds.), *The Israeli elections of 1996* (pp. 295–312). Albany: State University of New York Press.

Azulai-Katz, A. (1996). *Sisyphus' catch* (in Hebrew). Tel Aviv: Miscal, Yediot Acharonot.

Ben Eliezer, Y. (1997). *The industry of temptations, propaganda and politics, religion and commerce and how they are related* (in Hebrew). Tel Aviv: College of Management, the Management Library.

Ben Eliezer, Y. (2003). *Propaganda and communication* (in Hebrew). Tel Aviv: Beitan/A. S. Media International.

Bloch, L. B. (2000). Mobile discourse: Political bumper stickers as a communication event in Israel. *Journal of Communication, 50*(2), 48–76.

Blondheim, M., & Kaplan, K. (1993). On communication and audiocassettes in "Haredi" Society (in Hebrew, with English abstract). *Kesher, 14,* 51–62.

Caspi, D. (1984). Following the race: Propaganda and electoral decision. In D. Caspi, A. Diskin, & E. Gutmann (Eds.), *The roots of Begin's success: The 1981 Israel elections.* London: Croom Helm.

Caspi, D. (1986). Electoral rhetoric and political polarization: The Begin-Peres debates. *European Journal of Communication, 1,* 447–462.

Caspi, D. (1996). American-style electioneering in Israel: Americanization versus modernization. In D. L. Swanson & P. Mancini (Eds.), *Politics, media and modern society* (pp. 173–193). Westport, CT: Praeger.

Caspi, D. (1999). When Americanization fails? From democracy to demediocracy in Israel. *Israel Studies Bulletin, 15,* 1–5.

Caspi, D. (2005). *Due to technical difficulties: The fall of the Israel Broadcasting Authority* (in Hebrew). Mevasereth Zion: Tzivonim.

Caspi, D., & Eyal, C. H. (1983). Professionalization trends in Israeli election propaganda, 1973–1981. In A. Arian (Ed.), *The elections in Israel—1981.* Tel Aviv: Ramot.

Caspi, D., & Limor, Y. (1999). *The in/outsiders: The mass media in Israel.* Cresskill, NJ: Hampton Press.

Caspit, B., Crystal, H., & Kfir, I. (1996). *Suicide: A party forfeits the administration* (in Hebrew). Tel Aviv: Avivim.

Cohen, A., & Libo, R. (1975). The appearance of the candidates for the eighth Knesset on radio and television: A differential evaluation (in Hebrew). *State, Government and International Relations, 7*, 107–120.

Cohen, A., & Wolfsfeld, G. (1995). Overcoming adversity and diversity: The utility of television political advertising in Israel. In L. L. Kaid & C. Holtz-Bacha (Eds.), *Political advertising in Western democracies: Parties and candidates on television* (pp. 109–124). Thousand Oaks, CA: Sage.

Crystal, H., & Kfir, I. (1999). *The sixth citation: 1999 elections* (in Hebrew). Jerusalem: Keter.

Diskin, A. (1988). *Elections and voters in Israel* (in Hebrew). Tel Aviv: Am Oved.

Diskin, A. (1991). *Elections and voters in Israel.* New York: Praeger.

Doron, G. (1996a). *Election strategies.* Rechovot: Kivunim.

Doron, G. (1996b). *The electoral revolution: Primaries and direct election of the prime minister* (in Hebrew). Tel Aviv: Hakibbutz Hameuchad.

Doron, G. (1998). Surveys as a tool for forming election strategies and making public policy. In C. Fuchs & S. Bar-Lev (Eds.), *Surveys: Some good, some less* (in Hebrew) (pp. 43–61). Tel Aviv: Hakibbutz Hameuchad and Haifa University Press.

Drucker, R. (2002). *Hara-kir—Ehud Barak: The failure* (in Hebrew). Tel Aviv: Miskal–Yediot Acharonot.

Elazar, D., & Sandler, S. (Eds.). (1992). *Who's the boss in Israel? Israel at the polls: 1988–89.* Detroit, MI: Wayne State University Press.

Elizur, J., & Katz, E. (1979). The media in the Israeli election of 1977. In H. R. Penniman (Ed.), *Israel at the polls: The Knesset Elections of 1977.* Jerusalem: Jerusalem Academic Press.

Fuchs, C., & Bar-Lev, S. (Eds.). (1998). *Surveys: Some good, some less* (in Hebrew). Tel Aviv: Hakibbutz Hameuchad and Haifa University Press.

Galili, O. (2004). *The telepoliticians: New political leadership in the West and in Israel* (in Hebrew). Tel Aviv: Ramot.

Galnoor, I. (1982). *Steering the polity: Communication and politics in Israel.* Beverly Hills, CA: Sage.

Gertz, N. (1986). Propaganda style of election ads from 1977 to 1984. In A. Arian (Ed.), *The elections in Israel—1984.* Boulder: Westview Press.

Gurevitch, M. (1972). Television in the election campaign: Its audience and functions. In A. Arian (Ed.), *The elections in Israel—1969* (pp. 220–239). Jerusalem: Academic Press.

Jamieson, K. H. (1986). The evolution of political advertising in America. In L. L. Kaid, D. Nimmo, & K. R. Sanders (Eds), *New perspectives on political advertising* (pp. 1–20). Carbondale: Southern Illinois University Press.

Kaid, L. L., & Holtz-Bacha, C. (Eds.). (1995). *Political advertising in Western democracies: parties and candidates on television.* Thousand Oaks, CA: Sage.

Katz, E. (1971). Platforms and windows: Reflections on the role of broadcasting in election campaigns. *Journalism Quarterly, 48*(2), 304–314.

Katz, E., & Levinsohn, H. (1989). Too good to be true: Notes on the Israeli elections of 1989. *International Journal of Public Opinion Research, 1*, 111–122.

Katz, Y. (1999). *It's a sellers market: Mass media and the marketing of politicians* (in Hebrew). Tel Aviv: Sifriat Hapoalim.

Lehman-Wilzig, S. (1994). The 1992 media campaign: Toward the Americanization of Israeli elections? In D. Elazar & S. Sandler (Eds.), *Israel at the polls, 1992* (pp. 251–280). Lanham, MD: Rowman & Littlefield.

Leshem, B. (2003). *La communication politique en Israël: Le processus de personnalisation dans les campagnes électorales télévisées en Israël de 1984 à 1999 et son influence sur le système politique* [Political communication in Israel: The process of personalization in televised electoral campaigns in Israel from 1984 to 1999 and its influence on the political system]. Paris: L'Universite Paris VIII.

Levi, Y. (1987). *The writing on the wall.* Tel Aviv: Kivunim.

Liebes, T., Peri. Y., & Grabelski, T. (1996, November). The media and the alternative media in Israel's 1996 elections (in Hebrew, with English abstract). *Kesher, 2*, 5–20.

Nachmias, D., & Sened, I. (1999). The bias of pluralism: The redistributive effects of the new electoral law in Israel's 1996 election. In A. Arian & M. Shamir (Eds.), *The elections in Israel—1996* (pp. 269–294). Albany: State University of New York Press.

Neubach, K. (1996). *The race—1996 elections* (in Hebrew). Tel Aviv: Yediot Acharonot.

Olinski, D. (1996). The sticker and the Israeli car (in Hebrew, with English abstract). *Kesher, 20*, 38–48.

Peri, Y. (1975). Television in the 1973 election campaign. In A. Arian (Ed.), *The elections in Israel—1973* (pp. 95–119). Jerusalem: Jerusalem Academic Press.

Peri, Y. (2004). *Telepopulism: Media and politics in Israel*. Stanford, CA: Stanford University Press.

Rapel, Y. (1991). Synagogue newspaper in Israel (in Hebrew, with English abstract). *Kesher. 10*, 109–112.

Shamir, Y. (1986). The prediction errors of the pre-election day polls (in Hebrew). *State, Government and International Relations, 25*, 131–148.

Sheafer, T. (2001). Charismatic skill and media legitimacy: An actor-centered approach to understanding the political communication competition. *Communication Research, 28*, 711–736.

Sivan, E. (1991). On cultural enclaves (in Hebrew). *Alpayim, 4*, 45–98.

Swanson, D. L., & Mancini, P. (Eds.). (1996). *Politics, Media and Modern Democracy.* Westport, CT: Praeger.

Weimann, G. (1984). Every day is election day: Press coverage of pre-election polls. In D. Caspi, A. Diskin, & E. Gutmann (Eds.), *The roots of Begin's success* (pp. 273–295). London: Croom Helm.

Weimann, G. (1998). Stay away from surveys—The review of election surveys in the Israeli media (in Hebrew). In C. Fuchs & S. Bar-Lev (Eds.), *Surveys: Some good, some less* (pp. 123–147). Tel Aviv: Hakibbutz Hameuchad and Haifa University Press.

Weimann G., & Wolfsfeld, G. (1996). Nobody's condemned (in Hebrew). *The Seventh Eye, 5*, 20–22.

Weimann, G., & Wolfsfeld, G. (2002). Struggles over the electoral agenda: The elections of 1996 and 1999. In A. Arian & M. Shamir (Eds.), *The elections in Israel—1999.* Albany: State University of New York Press.

Weiss, S. (1996). *Analysis of the 1996 election results for the 14th Knesset and for the prime minister* (in Hebrew). Tel Aviv: Labor Party.

Wolfsfeld, G., & Weimann, G. (1999, December). The struggle over the 1996 election campaign agenda (in Hebrew). *Politika, 4*, 9–25.

Wolfsfeld, G., & Weimann, G. (2002). 2001 elections: The propaganda that didn't change a thing (in Hebrew). In A. Arian & M. Shamir (Eds.), *The elections in Israel 2001* (pp. 101–126). Jerusalem: Israeli Institute of Democracy.

Yerushalmi, S. (1999, April 23). The activists stayed home (in Hebrew). *Ma'ariv Weekend Magazine,* pp.10–11.

8

Political Advertising and Democracy in Brazil

MAURO P. PORTO

The quality of any democratic system depends on the channels available for political parties and candidates to use in communicating with citizens. The lack of pluralistic media and political environments can create serious obstacles for political deliberation, restricting the range of "shortcuts" that can be used by citizens to form their preferences (Porto, 2001). In the case of Brazil's young democracy, political advertising has become a major democratizing force in the political system, opening new and very effective venues for dialogue between the general public and political elites. This is especially true when one considers the fact that the country's communications system had been historically dominated by a single company, which has played an active political role in national politics.

This chapter is aimed at identifying the main features of Brazil's model of political advertising. The chapter is organized in the following way. First, I introduce the main features of the country's media and political systems. I then provide an overview of political advertising regulations and analyze the model resulting from these statutes. Research on the contents and

effects of political advertising is then discussed, stressing its key role as a source of information for voters. Finally, the conclusions summarize the findings and speculate about future prospects for political advertising in Brazil.

THE BRAZILIAN MEDIA AND POLITICAL LANDSCAPES

To understand the significance and role of political advertising in Brazil, it is important first to consider the main features of the country's political and media systems. Since 1889, Brazil has had a presidential system of government. A president and a vice president are elected directly by the population, and since 1998, the president has been able to run for a second consecutive term. On the same day as the presidential elections, voters choose states' governors and representatives to a bicameral National Congress, which includes a Chamber of Deputies and a Senate. The electoral system adopted for the selection of the members of the Chamber of Deputies is based on proportional representation, resulting in a multiparty system. In the last decades, around

16 political parties have been represented in the Chamber of Deputies. The Brazilian party system is not only fragmented but also weakly institutionalized (Mainwaring, 1999).

Between 1964 and 1985, Brazil was ruled by a military dictatorship, and individual and political rights were severely restricted, if not completely eliminated. After a mass movement demanded direct elections for president in 1984, the military dictatorship collapsed, and the first civil president took office in 1985. Since then, a relatively stable democratic regime has been in place, and competitive, free presidential elections were held in 1989, 1994, 1998, and 2002. A clear sign of greater democratic consolidation was the 2002 election, won by Luis Inácio Lula da Silva, or simply "Lula," the candidate of the socialist-oriented Partido dos Trabalhadores (PT; Workers Party). Despite his leftist identity and his trajectory as a trade union leader, Lula's victory was not followed by political instability or by threats of authoritarian regression.

Since it began, Brazilian broadcasting has been commercially oriented and privately operated. The first legal statutes that emerged in the 1930s to regulate radio established a broadcasting system inspired by the American model. Nevertheless, as in other Latin American countries, no relatively independent regulatory agency was established, and the executive has historically monopolized the power to allocate radio and television licenses. As a result, presidents have used this privilege to buy political support, distributing licenses to sympathizers and excluding opponents.[1]

The Brazilian communications system is characterized by the dominant position of television as a source of information and entertainment. Other media have much more limited penetration. In the case of newspapers, about 40 copies are sold for each 1000 inhabitants, putting Brazil among those countries with the lowest newspaper circulation in the world, behind some of its South American neighbors. Radio has not developed a national

character in Brazil, and audiences prefer television and newspapers as news sources (Straubhaar, 1996, pp. 223-224).

If television is the most pervasive medium in Brazil, Globo Organizations is the dominant force in the communication landscape. The company has been consolidated through processes of vertical and horizontal integration, with business activities in several areas, including the main television network (TV Globo), one of the nation's main newspapers (O Globo), radio stations, a publishing house, a recording company, cable and satellite television, telecommunications, and the Internet, among many other sectors (Amaral & Guimarães, 1994; Brittos, 2000; Lima, 2001; Sinclair, 1999; Straubhaar, 1996). Brazilian television is dominated by TV Globo, the network that controls an absolute majority of the national audience ratings, especially during prime time. TV Globo is also a major player in the global market and has become a major exporter of programming, especially telenovelas (soap operas).

TV Globo has been characterized by an active political role in Brazilian politics. During the military dictatorship (1964-1985), the media owned by the family Marinho, especially TV Globo, developed a close alliance with the military, supporting its project of national and economic integration (Fox, 1997; Lima, 1988; Sinclair, 1999). When democracy was reestablished in 1985 by a coalition of moderate sectors of the civilian opposition and "dissidents" of the military regime, TV Globo changed its political alliances and strategies to support the new power bloc (Guimarães & Amaral, 1990; Lima, 1988; Straubhaar, 1989). In the years that followed, the network was characterized by a consistent pattern of political intervention. It provided support to presidential candidates in electoral processes and to government coalitions once they were established. Studies have shown how TV Globo tended to align itself with the government of the day during key moments of

Brazil's recent democracy, including presidential elections and the impeachment of President Collor in 1992 (Porto, 2003).

As we will see, the role of political advertising in Brazil becomes particularly important when one considers the dominant position of TV Globo in the media system and the weak and fragmented foundations of several political institutions, especially political parties.

THE REGULATION OF POLITICAL ADVERTISING

With the end of President Getúlio Vargas' populist dictatorship in 1945, Brazil experienced almost two decades of democratically elected governments (1945-1964). During this democratic period, legislators turned their attention to the issue of candidates' access to broadcasting. The first legal statute to discipline political advertising in Brazil was the 1950 Electoral Code, which established the norms for paid advertising on radio. In this initial period, candidates' access to radio was limited to the purchase of airtime. The code established that in the 90-day period preceding elections, radio stations needed to allocate 2 hours daily for party propaganda and that the prices charged for airtime needed to be the same for all candidates and parties. Nevertheless, the law did not prohibit radio stations from refusing to sell airtime to specific candidates and parties. As a result, stations were particularly vulnerable to governmental pressure, a factor that contributed to restricted access to the airwaves by oppositional candidates in local and federal elections (Duarte, 1980, pp. 174-175).

Law 4115, approved on August 22, 1962, established a new form of access to the airwaves for parties and candidates: free airtime. This statute reserved 2 hours every day in the 60 days preceding the elections for the free broadcasting of ads in radio and television stations. This was the first regulation to impose mandatory free electoral time, although it did

not prohibit candidates from purchasing extra airtime.

The democratic period was interrupted by a coup in 1964, which established a military dictatorship that progressively eliminated political and civil liberties. The authoritarian regime cancelled presidential elections, abolished the existing political parties, and imposed a two-party system (one progovernment, the Aliança Renovadora National [National Renewal Alliance], and another representing the only opposition allowed, the Movimento Democrático Brasileiro [Brazilian Democratic Movement]). Among the various forms of political manipulation that were established by the military to perpetuate its power, changes in the regulation of political advertising were among the most important. First, Law 9601, approved on August 15, 1974, eliminated the possibility of paid political advertising in broadcasting. Since then, candidates and political parties have not been allowed to purchase airtime on radio and television stations. Moreover, the law severely restricted the purchase of space in newspapers, allowing candidates to print in their ads only their name, number, and a short curriculum vitae.

Another form of political manipulation by the authoritarian regime was introduced in 1976 as a result of an important electoral defeat of its political party (Aliança Renovadora National). In the 1974 parliamentary elections, the only legalized oppositional party (Movimento Democrático Brasileiro) achieved a surprising electoral performance, winning a majority in the Senate despite all the restrictions and coercions imposed by the dictatorship. One of the factors that explains the good electoral performance of the opposition is the creative use of the free political advertising time that was made by its candidates (Albuquerque, 1999, p. 47; Duarte, 1980, p. 182). Following this electoral defeat, the military introduced several restrictions to the political process, including changes in candidates' access to the media. One of the most insidious changes was

Law 6339, known as the *Lei Falcão,* approved on July 1, 1976, and named after Minister of Justice Armando Falcão. The law imposed severe content restrictions on the ads. Candidates were allowed to broadcast only their names, numbers, and brief summaries of their curriculum vitae. In the case of television, candidates could only air a close-up photograph. The use of other images was prohibited. These rules were enforced until the 1982 state-level elections, the last elections to take place during the military dictatorship.

With the return of democracy in 1985, the regulatory framework imposed by the dictatorship was progressively dismantled and replaced by new, more democratic statutes. Law 7332 of July 1, 1985 abolished authoritarian content restrictions on political advertising and gave to the Tribunal Superior Eleitoral (Superior Electoral Court) the prerogative of regulating elections. It also established a curious aspect of the Brazilian system: Congress has to approve a new law for every election, including the regulation of candidates' access to the media. As a result, specific provisions about political advertising change from year to year. For example, different criteria were adopted to divide airtime among the various candidates in the elections that followed (Albuquerque, 1999, pp. 49-50; Schmitt, Carneiro, & Kuschnir, 1999, pp. 289-290).

Although the specific statutes vary from election to election, some features of the Brazilian model of political advertising regulation remain constant. There are five key aspects of the model known as horário gratuito de propaganda eleitoral (HGPE; free electoral political advertising time):[2]

1. Access is free for candidates and political parties. Airtime from radio and television stations cannot be purchased, although candidates and parties can buy space in newspapers. Airtime is "free" for candidates and parties, but since 1986, radio and television stations have the right to deduct from their

taxes the loss of advertising revenues caused by the airing of political advertising (Lima, 1994, p. 200).

2. Airtime is divided in proportion to the number of seats that parties or coalitions have in the lower house of Congress. For example, according to present regulations, the total time of political advertising during presidential elections is divided in the following way: 33% is distributed in equal shares between all registered candidates and 66% is divided in proportion to the number of seats that each party or coalition has in the Chamber of Deputies.

3. There are few content restrictions on political advertising. Since redemocratization (1985), the different electoral laws have tended to reaffirm the principle that no censorship can be exercised over the contents of political advertising. The main exception came in the 1994 presidential election, when Law 8713 of September 30, 1993, prohibited candidates from using images generated outside studios and the presence of any other person than the candidate in their programs (a discussion of candidate programs follows). The law expressed a rationalist bias that conceives of political discourse as verbal and rational, reducing the symbolic appeal of political advertising and making the programs less interesting and meaningful for audiences (Albuquerque, 1999, p. 51; Miguel, 1997; Rubim, 1999, pp. 61-62). These content restrictions were not enforced in the elections that followed.

4. Regulations include the right of reply. Although there are few content restrictions on political advertising, candidates can request the right of reply to the Tribunal Superior Eleitoral whenever they feel that attacks aired by opponents in their programs have injured their reputation. The tribunal considers the appeals and frequently grants candidates the right to appear during the airtime of opponents to respond to previous attacks.

5. The free electoral political advertising time is mandatory and is broadcast simultaneously by all stations in fixed time slots. Current regulations allocate 2 hours per day— 1 hour in the early afternoon (1:00-2:00 p.m.)

and 1 hour at night (8:30–9:30 p.m.)—for the broadcasting of the programs in the 45 days preceding elections.

THE REGULATION OF PARTY PROGRAMS

Besides the HGPE, which grants free access of candidates to radio and television during electoral campaigns, there is another form of free access to broadcasting in Brazil. In nonelectoral periods, political parties have the right to broadcast two annual TV programs, usually 20 minutes long each, which are also aired simultaneously by all stations in fixed time slots. This modality of media access was first established by the 1965 Organic Law of Political Parties. The main purpose is to allow political parties to publicize their platforms, ideologies, and the resolutions of their conventions. No messages targeting elections or promoting candidates can be aired in these programs. Thus, with the exception of a short period during the military dictatorship (July 1977–October 1978), political parties have also enjoyed access to free broadcasting (Lima, 1994).

Although the regulation of party programs prohibits their use for electoral purposes, the lack of specific guidelines has allowed political parties to disregard this rule. In some occasions, such electoral use of party programs has had a major impact on the campaigns. In the first presidential election of the democratic period (1989), the then-unknown candidate Fernando Collor de Mello used his party program and the programs of two other small parties to project his personal image. His use of these three party programs increased the percentage of people willing to vote for him from 9% in March to 43% in June. Collor de Mello then maintained the first place in the polls and became president in November following the second round of the election (Lima, 1993; Porto, 2003).

In the 2002 presidential election, the Partido da Frente Liberal (PFL; Party of the Liberal Front) also used its programs for electoral purposes. Early on in the preelectoral period, the PFL launched the name of Roseana Sarney as a precandidate. After she appeared in the programs that the PFL broadcast in November 2001 and January 2002, Sarney's poll numbers grew dramatically. She jumped to second place in November 2001 and threatened to tie with the front runner, Lula, in February 2002 (Porto, 2004). Nevertheless, a political scandal involving Sarney and her husband emerged in March and had a devastating effect on her candidacy. On April 13, 2002, after a dramatic fall in the polls, she withdrew from the race.

Such cases point to a major blind spot in the Brazilian regulatory framework for the free access of political parties to the media. To avoid problems with the Electoral Court when using programs for electoral purposes, political parties just need to avoid identifying candidates in explicit ways. Nothing prevents them from devoting entire programs to the promotion of individual party leaders during preelectoral periods if they are not identified as candidates and if elections are not mentioned.

THE RISE OF SPOTS: THE AMERICANIZATION OF POLITICAL ADVERTISING?

As we have seen, the main form of access for candidates to radio and television during electoral campaigns is free electoral political advertising time, or HGPE. This form of political advertising involves the daily broadcasting of candidates' programs, which are aired together in two time slots, each 1 hour long (one in the early afternoon, the other at night). Because political advertising time is divided proportionally to the number of seats that parties or coalitions have in the Chamber of Deputies, the time allocated to each candidate can vary considerably.[3]

A new form of access was introduced during the 1996 municipal elections and became part of the Brazilian model of political advertising. Law 9100 of September 29, 1995, created the spots (*inserções*), short announcements aired during regular commercial breaks.[4] Therefore, to the 2 daily hours devoted to HGPE, the law added 30 minutes for the broadcasting of commercials, which can last for 15, 30, or 60 seconds, depending on candidates' preferences (Mendes, 2000). The total airtime of spots is also divided in proportion to the number of seats that parties or coalitions have in the Chamber of Deputies.

Considering the similarities between the format of spots and the U.S. model of political advertising, have Brazilian campaigns become more "Americanized"? As Albuquerque (1999) notes, a first glance would suggest a positive answer, as Brazil seems to be adopting the American format of political advertising. Nevertheless, there are major differences in the "communicative style" of spots in both countries. Albuquerque (1999) argues that there are no significant differences between spots and HGPE in terms of language and in terms of the broader variety of message types that characterizes political advertising in Brazil (p. 67). It is also important to stress that although spots are purchased by candidates in the United States, they are free in Brazil. Because of these and other reasons, the rise of spots cannot be interpreted as a process of Americanization of Brazilian elections (Albuquerque, 1999; Mendes, 2000).

THE MESSAGES OF POLITICAL ADVERTISING

The previous discussion on the regulation of political advertising in Brazil has identified three main forms of access to radio and television stations by candidates and political parties: (a) HGPE, (b) party programs, and (c) spots. How are these spaces used by candidates and parties? Which types of messages do such programs and segments present to voters?

In the case of HGPE, most research has focused on presidential elections. Analyzing the programs aired by three of the main candidates in 1989, during the first presidential election after redemocratization, Albuquerque (1999) argued that the model of political advertising adopted in Brazil is an original one, characterized by a mosaic of types of messages that reflect specific features, including the need to adapt content to the quantity of time each candidate receives, the fact that programs interrupt the regular programming schedule of the stations, and the fact that programs are presented together in a single block (p. 183).

Reflecting this diversity of styles and formats, the Partido dos Trabalhadores developed innovative and quite successful symbolic strategies in the programs of its presidential candidate, Lula, during the 1989 elections. Lula's campaign adopted the format and language of the regular programming schedule of the dominant network, TV Globo. In calling its political advertising program the "People's Network" (*Rede Povo*), PT parodied the dominant television company, "Globo Network" (*Rede Globo*). The program presented PT's political messages by imitating regular programs on TV Globo, as well as commercials. It also included a great number of *telenovela* stars from TV Globo. By adopting this strategy, the PT was not only able to format its programs in a way that was more familiar to audiences but also managed to reduce the "rupture" caused by interruption of regular programming that results from the mandatory, simultaneous broadcasting of free political advertising time.

Scholars have applied a variety of approaches to investigate the contents of HGPE. Based on Joslyn's (1990) concept of "appeals," Porto and Guazina (1999) identified the main symbolic strategies of the six main candidates in the HGPE of the 1994 presidential election. Their content analysis found that the presentation of platforms, or "prospective policy choice appeals" (Joslyn, 1990), was the main strategy, taking 22% of the total airtime of the six candidates. The appeal "situational analysis," in which candidates present an evaluation of the country's situation, came in second place, with 17% of the total airtime. Almost all of this airtime was devoted to the analysis of the new economic plan of the government, the *Plano Real,* which managed to reduce the previously uncontrolled inflation rates. It is interesting to note that negative advertising was not as pervasive as is suggested by some commentators. Negative ads, which included attacks on opponents, the federal government, and other figures and institutions, took only 13% of the total airtime of HGPE, although it was the main appeal of Lula and Brizola, candidates of the leftist opposition (Porto & Guazina, 1999).

Applying the same analytical categories for the analysis of HGPE in the 2002 presidential election, Porto, Vasconcelos, and Bastos (2004) demonstrated that candidates developed different symbolic strategies in their programs. Lula, who was elected president in that election, focused on "situational analysis"; José Serra, the candidate supported by President Fernando Henrique Cardoso, emphasized "retrospective policy performance," especially in terms of his achievements as minister of health and senator.

Along with presidential elections, scholars have investigated the content of candidates' HGPE programs in state and municipal elections (Carvalho, 2003; Rubim, 2002; Silveira, 2002). In the specific case of spots, a content analysis of 258 spots broadcast during the 1996 mayoral elections of the two biggest Brazilian cities, São Paulo and Rio de Janeiro, has identified candidates' main persuasion strategies (Figueiredo, Aldé, Dias, & Jorge, 2000). In both campaigns, incumbents used spots to demonstrate the good situation of the "current world" and stressed the threat of disruption of that world represented by the opposition. Challengers, on the other hand, made the mistake of accepting aspects of incumbents' "current world," a tactic that undermined their

ability to construct a persuasive political alternative. Moreover, when compared to political advertising from other democracies (the United States and France), Brazilian spots tended to present fewer negative ads with attacks on opponents and fewer calls for change on the part of challengers (Figueiredo et al., 2000).

POLITICAL ADVERTISING AND VOTING BEHAVIOR

As we have seen, free political advertising programs and spots have presented a variety of persuasive and symbolic messages. What effect, if any, do these programs have on the broader political system? What is the impact of political advertising on voting behavior?

There has been some debate about the impact of television on Brazil's political system. According to some authors, the rise of marketing techniques, political consultants, and political advertising has transformed old political practices and institutions. For example, Carvalho (1999) studied electoral campaigns in the northern state of Ceará and concluded that HGPE has contributed to the generation of a new media-based marketing pattern in the state's politics. As a result, old forms of campaigning that are characteristic of traditional oligarchic elites have been replaced by "modern" communication strategies centered on political advertising.

There is also a debate about how television in general, and political advertising in particular, have transformed the party system. For some, it appears that television has enabled candidates to bypass party channels and communicate directly to the public, weakening the party system (Avelar, 1992; Lavareda, 1991, p. 169; Lima, 1998; Mainwaring, 1999, pp. 237-240). Others believe that these arguments have ignored the positive influences exerted by political advertising. According to this perspective, party and electoral programs have opposed the individualist tendencies of the electoral system, strengthening party images and party identification (Albuquerque & Dias, 2002; Schmitt et al., 1999). The Brazilian case suggests that free access to radio and television has contributed to the consolidation of an otherwise fragmented and weak party system.

The availability of free access to prime-time radio and television by candidates and parties has been a major factor in electoral campaigns. Several studies have presented evidence about the impact of political advertising on presidential elections, as illustrated by the 1989 contest. As we have seen, the HGPE programs of the Workers Party's candidate, Lula, adopted a very creative format, known as the "People's Network." There are strong indications that Lula's programs had an important impact on the campaign. During the free political advertising time broadcast in the first round of the election, between September and November, Lula doubled his poll numbers. Although Lula would finally lose the election to candidate Collor de Mello, political advertising helps explain Lula's good performance. Survey data suggest that political advertising had a substantial effect on voters' behavior in the 1989 presidential election. Free political advertising time on TV was the second most frequent source of information for choosing a candidate, and the Brazilian audience stayed tuned to the program, expressing a high degree of interest in it (Straubhaar, Olsen, & Nunes, 1993).

The two presidential elections that followed (1994 and 1998) were won by Fernando Henrique Cardoso, candidate of the Partido da Social Democracia Brasileira (Brazilian Social Democratic Party). Unlike the 1989 campaign, voting intentions did not change significantly during the period of free electoral political advertising time. In both elections, Cardoso's successful economic plan, the *Plano Real*, became the main campaign issue. The plan was launched in 1993 when Cardoso was minister of finance and managed to reduce inflation rates and bring economic stability. This conjuncture presented severe constraints for Lula,

Cardoso's main opponent in both elections. Research based on surveys and focus groups suggests that in 1994 and 1998, Lula's political advertising was not able to build a credible political alternative in a scenario in which the economic plan enjoyed broad public support (Almeida, 2002; Veiga, 1998; Venturi, 2000).

POLITICAL ADVERTISING IN THE 2002 PRESIDENTIAL ELECTION

To investigate in more detail the role of political advertising in Brazilian democracy, this section analyzes data from the Estudo Eleitoral Brasileiro (Brazilian Electoral Study; ESEB), a national cross-sectional survey that followed the 2002 presidential election.[5] Table 8.1 presents the factors that were mentioned by voters as the most important for them in the process of choosing their presidential candidate. The data show the importance of television. Debates, political advertising, and news on TV are among the four main factors mentioned by voters. Other media, such as newspapers and radio, have a much less significant position as sources of information. Voters present political advertisement on television as the second most relevant factor in their electoral choices. The same results were found in surveys conducted during the 1989 presidential election (Straubhaar et al., 1993).

Besides considering political advertising on TV the second most important factor in their electoral decisions, voters were also exposed to its messages: 76.5% saw the spots aired by candidates and 79.4% watched the HGPE programs at least one day per week. In regard to HGPE, 15.8% watched the programs at least once a week, 34.8% watched 2 or 3 days per week, and 28.3% watched 4 days or more per week. Thus levels of exposure were very high. A significant part of the electorate also alleged that political advertising affected its electoral choices: 17.3% said that they changed their voting intentions for president because of political ads broadcast on television.

Table 8.1   Most Important Factors in the Choice of Presidential Candidate in the 2002 Election, According to Brazilian Voters (%)

Importance of Factor	Debates on TV	Political Advertising on TV	Chats With Friends or Family Members	TV News	Chats With Friends at Work or School	News From Newspapers	Electoral Polls	Political Rallies	Information From Church	Political Advertising on Radio	News on Radio
1	29.7	16.4	14.2	7.1	6.2	4.8	3.7	3.1	3.0	2.6	1.6
2	16.1	15.2	12.4	12.6	8.4	7.2	4.6	4.5	3.3	2.2	2.8
3	10.8	11.8	11.7	12.6	9.3	7.3	6.0	6.1	2.5	3.1	3.8
Not mentioned	36.9	50.2	55.2	61.2	69.6	74.2	79.3	79.9	84.7	85.6	85.3
Total	100	100	100	100	100	100	100	100	100	100	100
	n = 2040	n = 2039	n = 2039	n = 2041	n = 2039	n = 2049	n = 2041	n = 2039	n = 2041	n = 2038	n = 2040

SOURCE: From Estudo Eleitoral Brasileiro (2002).

Note: The question asked was, "From these factors, which was the most important in your decision on whom to vote for president? Which was the second most important? The third?"

137

As happened in the 1989 presidential election, the 2002 campaign was characterized by a significant level of volatility in voters' preferences, and much of this variation was the result of political advertising. As we have seen, the growth of candidate Roseana Sarney in the preelectoral period had a clear connection to the party programs broadcast by the PFL. Later on, candidate Ciro Gomes also achieved a significant growth in the polls. After appearing in the programs of his party (PPS; Partido Popular Socialista) in June, Gomes jumped from fourth to second place in the presidential race. Nevertheless, after HGPE and spots started in August, candidate José Serra (PSDB; Partido da Social Democracia Brasileira) launched a series of attacks on Gomes. Partially as a result of this negative advertising, especially those aired in the form of spots, Gomes dropped back to fourth place in the polls. The Partido Popular Socialista candidate fell from 26% in August 20, when political advertising programs began, to 9% on October 5, just after they ended (Figueiredo & Coutinho, 2003, p. 106).

The free access of candidates to prime-time television seems to have benefited Lula in a more significant way. He was the candidate with the highest level of growth in the polls during the period of political advertising, when the percentage of the electorate intending to vote for him grew from 34% to 45% (Figueiredo & Coutinho, 2003, p. 106). Lula's programs played a central role in reworking his image, which had been established in his three previous bids for the presidency (1989, 1994, and 1998). During these campaigns, Lula consolidated his reputation as a former trade union leader who represented marginalized sectors of Brazilian society. Nevertheless, his lack of administrative experience and competence was frequently presented as a major personal deficiency.[6] His leftist orientation was also considered a sign of radicalism in some elite sectors. After the hiring of Duda Mendonça, the best known political consultant

in Brazil's political marketing industry, Lula's campaign made a clear attempt to change this image. The new controversial strategy became known as *Lulinha Paz e Amor* (Little Lula Peace and Love) and emphasized Lula's competence as a negotiator who had the necessary skills to unite Brazilian society and solve the country's pressing social problems. Stressing Lula's past as a trade union leader, his campaign reworked the notion of competence in ways that diminished resistance to his persona. It did so by developing the idea that the political situation demanded someone with political competence, not technical or administrative experience (Rubim, 2004).

HGPE was the central stage on which Lula's image was reshaped during the 2002 election. First, his program adopted a "light" tone. He was the candidate who devoted the most airtime to music jingles and the least airtime to negative ads (Porto et al., 2004). Second, Lula always began his programs surrounded by experts and PT political leaders, stressing the technical competence of his team.

The candidates of the opposition, and especially Lula, were also very skillful in using political advertising as an alternative forum in relation to the mainstream media for the discussion of campaign issues. In its coverage of the presidential election, the main newscast of TV Globo, the *Jornal Nacional*, emphasized the economy as the main campaign issue (Porto, 2004). This focus on the economy was related to the difficulties that Brazil was experiencing in the electoral period. The country was facing high levels of distrust on the part of foreign investors, especially Wall Street banks, which led to a significant devaluation of the national currency. In its news coverage, the *Jornal Nacional* consistently supported the interpretive frame that was promoted by the government and its candidate, José Serra. According to this frame, the main cause of the problems in the exchange rate of the national currency and in the declining trust of foreign investors was the fact that the opposition was leading the polls and threatening to change the economic model established by President Cardoso.

As the mainstream media emphasized the economy as the main campaign issue, Lula and other candidates of the opposition used political advertising to discuss Brazil's serious social problems. One key aspect of Lula's programs was the emphasis on the issues of poverty, social inequality, and hunger (Porto, 2004; Porto et al., 2004). He used political advertising not only to emphasize a different set of issues but to frame them in alternative ways. Survey data suggest that this strategy had a major impact on voters' preferences. Higher levels of exposure to the *Jornal Nacional* made voters attribute higher priority to the objective of keeping inflation low and to maintaining the stability of the economy. On the other hand, higher levels of exposure to political advertising made voters attribute less priority to these objectives and emphasize social problems instead (Porto, 2004). Thus political advertising frequently contributes to a widening of the range of interpretive frames to which voters have access, establishing a more pluralistic and diverse process of political deliberation.

CONCLUSION

In this chapter, I have attempted to demonstrate that free political advertising is a key and essential feature of Brazilian democracy. Few countries in the world offer similar levels of access to free time in the media for candidates and parties.[7] Through three main forms of access (HGPE, party programs, and spots), the Brazilian model of free political advertisement is a major democratizing force in the political process, offering citizens a variety of points of view and restricting the influence of money in electoral processes. Political advertising is not only one of the most important sources of information for voters; it also contributes to the establishment of a more democratic and pluralistic public sphere. In a communications system dominated by a single company (TV Globo), political advertising has established an alternative forum for the debate of political and social problems.

Despite the positive contributions of political advertising, the Brazilian mainstream media and other elites have consistently attacked the mandatory broadcasting of the programs and spots as an authoritarian measure. Frequently, these actors argue that Brazilians do not watch political advertising and that they favor its elimination. Such claims are simply false. Audience ratings data from the Instituto Brasileiro de Opinião e Estatística show that about 56% of the households keep their television sets on during HGPE programs, which is the same level of audience as for Brazil's most popular television programs, TV Globo's *telenovelas* and the newscast *Jornal Nacional* (Porto & Guazina, 1999, p. 7). The claim that Brazilians oppose the political advertising model is also not true. When asked if political advertisement programs on TV should continue, two thirds (65.9%) of respondents from the 2002 ESEB survey answered yes and only 31.4% said no.

Finally, it is necessary to consider whether the rise of new technologies, such as paid TV (cable and satellite television) and the Internet, have altered or challenged the Brazilian model of political advertising. This question is important, because the laws that regulate the access of candidates and parties to the media apply to the traditional broadcasting networks but not to pay TV channels. In other words, cable and satellite channels are not subjected to the mandatory free political advertising time. Thus Brazilians who have access to these technologies have other programming alternatives during the periods in which political advertising is broadcast. Nevertheless, the impact of cable or satellite television has been limited in the Brazilian case. Only about 11% of the households in Brazil have access to these technologies.

Candidates have made intensive use of the Internet, but only more recently have scholars started to pay attention to this new modality of political advertising (Carneiro, 2002; Carvalho, 2000). Although the Internet has limited penetration when compared to television, a study of the 2002 presidential election shows that candidates' Web sites were very effective in generating real-time events and controversies that attracted extensive news coverage, thus playing an important agenda-setting role (Aldé & Borges, 2004). Political advertising through the Internet is one of the most open and promising fields of inquiry in Brazil.

Although new technologies will affect Brazil's model of political advertising in important ways, its main features will not change. The centrality of programs and ads aired on television and the free access of candidates to broadcasting will most likely continue, reinforcing one of the most positive aspects of the legal and institutional arrangements that characterize Brazilian democracy.

NOTES

1. The 1988 Constitution established some limits to the ability of the executive to manipulate licenses. For example, it established that licenses needed to be approved by Congress. Nevertheless, the Constitution also established quorum demands and voting rules by which Congress had to abide if it wanted to reject licenses authorized by the executive, making it very difficult for the parliament to reject them (Motter, 1994, pp. 296–297).

2. Albuquerque (2004) correctly points out that the term *political advertising* is not appropriate for the Brazilian model. The literal translation of the Portuguese expression *horário gratuito de propaganda eleitoral* would be "free electoral propaganda time." Nevertheless, the term *propaganda* has a strong negative connotation in English and does not accurately reflect the types of programs aired in Brazil. On the other hand, the term *advertising* tends to suggest the possibility of purchasing airtime, a practice that is not allowed in the Brazilian case. Since *political advertising*

is the term usually used worldwide to designate programming designed to promote the interests of parties or candidates (see Kaid & Holtz-Bacha, 1995), I have chosen this designation to describe the Brazilian model.

3. For example, in the 2002 elections, the programs of presidential candidates took 25 of the 60 minutes allocated to each of the two daily blocks. Candidates for governor, Congress, and State Assemblies took the remaining 35 minutes. The length of the programs of presidential candidates ranged from 1 minute and 23 seconds to 10 minutes and 23 seconds (Porto, 2004).

4. In fact, spots first appeared in the 1993 referendum on the system of government. Voters were called to choose between presidential, parliamentarian, and monarchist systems of government. Three parliamentarian fronts, defending one of the three systems, were organized and were allowed to broadcast short spots during regular commercial breaks (Miguel, 2002, pp. 87-116). In the end, 66% of the voters chose a republican over a monarchist government, and 55% preferred a presidential system to a parliamentarian one. Although the referendum represents the first case in which political spots were used, it was an exceptional event that was not part of the regular electoral calendar.

5. ESEB was a postelection survey conducted with 2513 voters, 16 years old or older, in all states of the country between October 31 and December 28, 2002. The project was coordinated by the Centro de Estudos sobre Opinião Pública, Universidade de Campinas, and DATAUFF research centers.

6. Before his election as president in 2002, Lula had never occupied an executive position at local or state levels. His only experience as an elected official was the term he served as a representative in the Chamber of Deputies (1986-1990). Lula was also discriminated against because he lacked a university diploma.

7. According to Schmitt et al. (1999, p. 291), Brazil is the democracy that allocates the most free time for political advertising in the world.

REFERENCES

Albuquerque, A. de. (1999). *"Aqui você vê a verdade na tevê": A propaganda política na televisão* ["Here you see the truth in TV": Political advertising on television]. Niterói, Rio de Janeiro: MCII.

Albuquerque, A. de (2004, June 22-25). *Advertising ou propaganda? O audiovisual político brasileiro numa perspectiva comparativa* [Advertising or propaganda? A comparative perspective on the Brazilian political audiovisual media]. Paper presented at the 13th Encontro Anual da Associação Nacional dos Programas de Pós-Graduação em Comunicação, São Bernardo do Campo, Brazil.

Albuquerque, A. d., & Dias, M. (2002). Propaganda política e a construção da imagem partidária no Brasil [Political advertising and the construction of party image in Brazil]. *Civitas, 2*(2), 309–326.

Aldé, A., & Borges, J. (2004, July 21-25). *Internet, the press and Brazilian elections: agendasetting on real time.* Paper presented at the Second International Conference on Politics and Information Systems: Technologies and Applications, Orlando, FL.

Almeida, J. (2002). *Marketing político: Hegemonia e contra-hegemonia* [Political marketing: Hegemony and counterhegemony]. São Paulo, Brazil: Xamã.

Amaral, R., & Guimarães, C. (1994). Media monopoly in Brazil. *Journal of Communication, 44*(4), 26–38.

Avelar, L. (1992). As eleições na era da televisão [Elections in the age of television]. *Revista de Administração de Empresas, 32*(4), 42–57.

Brittos, V. (2000). As Organizações Globo e a reordenação das comunicações [Organizations Globo and the reorganization of communications]. *Revista Brasileira de Ciências da Comunicação, 23*(1), 57–76.

Carneiro, L. O. (2002). A eleição através do mouse: Uma abordagem sobre o uso da Internet nas eleições municipais de Salvador em 2000 [Election by mouse: An analysis of the use of the Internet in the 2002 municipal elections in Salvador]. In A. A. Rubim (Ed.), *Mídia e eleições 2002 em Salvador* [The media and the 2002 elections in Salvador] (pp. 401–416). Salvador, Brazil: EdUFBa.

Carvalho, C. (2000). Eleições 98: A campanha dos partidos e candidatos à presidência na Internet [The 1998 elections: The campaign of the parties and candidates for the presidency on the Internet]. In A. A. Rubim (Ed.), *Mídia e Eleições de 1998* [The media and the 1998 elections] (pp. 201–217). Salvador, Brazil: EdUFBa.

Carvalho, R. V. (1999). *Transição democrática brasileira e padrão midiático publicitário da política* [The Brazilian transition to democracy and the model for political advertising in the media]. Campinas, Brazil: Pontes.

Carvalho, R. V. (Ed.). (2003). *A produção da política em campanhas eleitorais* [The production of politics in electoral campaigns]. Campinas, Brazil: Pontes.

Duarte, C. (1980). A Lei Falcão: Antecedentes e impacto [The Falcão Law: Antecedents and impact]. In B. Lamounier (Ed.), *Voto de desconfiança* [The no-confidence vote] (pp. 173–216). Petrópolis, Brazil: Vozes.

Estudo Eleitoral Brasileiro. (2002). Study data and information available from the Universidade Federal Fluminense, Rio de Janeiro, and the Universidad Estadual de Campinas, São Paulo, Brazil.

Figueiredo, M., Aldé, A., Dias, H., & Jorge, V. (2000). Estratégias de persuasão em eleições majoritárias: Uma proposta metodológica para o estudo da propaganda eleitoral [Strategies of persuasion in majoritarian elections: A methodological framework for the study of electoral advertising]. In R. Figueiredo (Ed.), *Marketing político e persuasão eleitoral* [Political marketing and electoral persuasion] (pp. 147–203). São Paulo, Brazil: Fundação Konrad Adenauer.

Figueiredo, R., & Coutinho, C. (2003). A eleição de 2002 [The 2002 election]. *Opinião Pública, 9*(2), 93–117.

Fox, E. (1997). *Latin American broadcasting.* Luton, England: University of Luton Press.

Guimarães, C., & Amaral, R. (1990). Brazilian television: A rapid conversion to the new order. In E. Fox (Ed.), *Media and politics in Latin America* (pp. 125–137). Newbury Park, CA: Sage.

Joslyn, R. (1990). Election campaigns as occasions for civic culture. In D. Swanson & D. Nimmo (Eds.), *New directions in political communication* (pp. 86–119). Newbury Park, CA: Sage.

Kaid, L., & Holtz-Bacha, C. (Eds.). (1995). *Political advertising in Western democracies.* Thousand Oaks, CA: Sage.

Lavareda, A. (1991). *A democracia nas urnas* [Democracy in the ballot box]. Rio de Janeiro, Brazil: Rio Fundo/IUPERJ.

Lima, V. A. de. (1988). The state, television and political power in Brazil. *Critical Studies in Mass Communication, 5*(2), 108–128.

Lima, V. A. de (1993). Brazilian television in the 1989 presidential election: constructing a president. In T. Skidmore (Ed.), *Television, politics and the transition to democracy in Latin America* (pp. 97–117). Baltimore: Johns Hopkins University Press.

Lima, V. A. de (1994). Propaganda política no rádio e na televisão: Notas e questões sobre a legislação brasileira [Political advertising on radio and television: Notes and questions about Brazilian legislation. In H. Matos (Ed.), *Mídia, eleições e democracia* [Media, elections, and democracy] (pp. 191–205). São Paulo, Brazil: Scritta.

Lima, V. A. de (1998). Os mídia e a política [Media and politics]. In M. das G. Rua & M. I. Carvalho (Eds.), *O estudo da política* [The study of politics] (pp. 209–230). Brasília: Paralelo 15.

Lima, V. A. de (2001). *Mídia: Teoria e política* [Media: Theory and politics]. São Paulo, Brazil: Editora da Fundação Perseu Abramo.

Mainwaring, S. (1999). *Rethinking party systems in the third wave of democratization: The case of Brazil.* Stanford, CA: Stanford University Press.

Mendes, S. (2000). Spots eleitorais: As restrições na eleição de 1998 [Electoral spots: The restrictions in the 1998 election]. In A. A. Rubim (Ed.), *Mídia e eleições de 1998* [Media and the 1998 elections] (pp. 175–186). Salvador, Brazil: EdUFBa.

Miguel, L. F. (1997). Mídia e discurso político nas eleições presidenciais de 1994 [Media and political discourse in the 1994 presidential elections]. *Comunicação & Política, 4*(1), 80–96.

Miguel, L. F. (2002). *Política e mídia no Brasil* [Politics and the media in Brazil]. Brasília: Editora Plano.

Motter, P. (1994). *A batalha invisível da constituinte: Interesses privados versus caráter público da radiodifusão no Brasil* [The invisible battle of the Constituent: Private interests versus public character in Brazilian broadcasting]. Unpublished master's thesis, Universidade de Brasília, Brasília.

Porto, M. (2001). *Media framing and citizen competence: Television and audiences' interpretations of politics in Brazil.* Unpublished Ph.D. dissertation, University of California, San Diego.

Porto, M. (2003). Mass media and politics in democratic Brazil. In M.D.A. Kinzo & J. Dunkerley (Eds.), *Brazil since 1985* (pp. 288–313). London: Institute of Latin American Studies.

Porto, M. (2004, July 25-30). *Framing controversies: The role of television in the 2002 Brazilian presidential election.* Paper presented at the 25th Annual Conference of the International Association for Media and Communication Research, Porto Alegre, Brazil.

Porto, M., & Guazina, L. (1999). A política na TV: O horário eleitoral da eleição presidencial de 1994 [Politics on TV: Political advertising in the 1994 presidential election]. *Contracampo, 3,* 5–33.

Porto, M., Vasconcelos, R., & Bastos, B. (2004). A televisão e o primeiro turno das eleições presidenciais de 2002: Análise do *Jornal Nacional* e do horário eleitoral [Television and the first round of the 2002 presidential elections: An analysis of the *Jornal Nacional* and political advertising]. In A. A. Rubim (Ed.), *Eleições presidenciais em 2002 no Brasil* [The 2002 Brazilian presidential elections] (pp. 68–90). São Paulo, Brazil: Hacker.

Rubim, A. A. (1999). *Mídia e política no Brasil* [Media and politics in Brazil]. João Pessoa, Paraíba: Editora UFPB.

Rubim, A. A. (Ed.). (2002). *Mídia e eleições 2002 em Salvador* [Media and the 2002 elections in Salvador]. Salvador, Brazil: EdUFBa.

Rubim, A. A. (2004). Visibilidades e estratégias nas eleições presidenciais de 2002 [Visibility and strategies in the 2002 presidential elections]. In A. A. Rubim (Ed.), *Eleições presidenciais em 2002* [The 2002 presidential elections] (pp. 7–28). São Paulo, Brazil: Hacker.

Schmitt, R., Carneiro, L. P., & Kuschnir, K. (1999). Estratégias de campanha no horário gratuito de propaganda eleitoral em eleições proporcionais [Campaign strategies in proportional elections' political advertising]. *Dados, 42*(2), 277–301.

Silveira, F. (Ed.). (2002). *Estratégia, mídia e voto* [Strategy, media, and the vote]. Porto Alegre, Brazil: EdiPuc.

Sinclair, J. (1999). *Latin American television: A global view.* New York: Oxford University Press.

Straubhaar, J. (1989). Television and video in the transition from military to civilian rule in Brazil. *Latin American Research Review, 24*(1), 140–154.

Straubhaar, J. (1996). The electronic media in Brazil. In R. Cole (Ed.), *Communication in Latin America* (pp. 217–243). Wilmington, DE: Scholarly Books.

Straubhaar, J., Olsen, O., & Nunes, M. (1993). The Brazilian case: Influencing the voter. In T. Skidmore (Ed.), *Television, politics, and the transition to democracy in Latin America* (pp. 118–136). Baltimore: Johns Hopkins University Press.

Veiga, L. (1998). Horário eleitoral, o eleitor e a formação da preferência [Political advertising, the voter, and formation of preference]. *Comunicação & Política, 5*(3), 93–109.

Venturi, G. (2000). Imagem pública, propaganda eleitoral e reeleição na disputa presidencial de 1998 [Public image, political advertising, and reelection in the 1998 presidential race]. In A. A. Rubim (Ed.), *Mídia e eleições de 1998* [Media and the 1998 elections] (pp. 103–124). Salvador, Brazil: EdUFBa.

9

Political Advertising in Chile

MARKUS MOKE

Since democracy was restored in 1989, confidence and interest in politics in Chile have constantly declined. This development particularly affects the political parties as the central actors within the political system (Tironi & Agüero, 1999; Huneeus, 2001). As a consequence, parties and politicians have modified the way in which they present themselves to the electorate. Today, parties and candidates use instruments for advertisement and presentation that include media appearances, as well as combined insertions of themselves in both sophisticated, up-to-date campaign technologies and traditional forms, such as neighborhood gatherings and door-to-door canvassing.

Changes in the way the parties and candidates present themselves have also led in recent years to a huge increase in campaign costs. The expenditure for a candidature for the Senate is estimated to be between $4 and $8 million. In the case of presidential campaigns, this can easily boom to approximately $50 to $100 million, a cost that is far above that in most Western European countries ("U.S. $30 milliones," 1997). This trend favors wealthy parties and candidates; poor ones are at a disadvantage, particularly as Chile is still without a fund-raising act to legitimize sources of money for political parties or to ensure the transparency of campaign expenditures (Arriagada, 1997; Espíndola, 2002).

The importance of the mass media in the mediation of political information means that political players must maintain a constant media presence and employ adequate event management methods on an ongoing basis. Because the Chilean mass media system has developed a commercial character, party advertising is left entirely in the hands of individual campaign managers. Within the media landscape, television has developed an outstanding position. As a corporate medium (Bryant, 1995) it is ideal, in many ways, for broadcasting images. Radio is as popular as it was in the past, reaching people in their family environment or at work. Since the late 1990s, the Internet and e-mail have been implemented on a grand scale; however, the use of these communication tools is still behind that of television and radio. Nevertheless, today, every political party has its own Web site, offering discussion forums and Web logs (blogs). In the late 1990s, the parties had

145

already begun to use this medium to recruit volunteers for campaign activities through blogs, chatrooms, and e-mail.

As in many other Latin American countries, the phenomenon of the "Americanization" of election campaigns in Chile is evident in terms of the engagement of external PR experts and even spin doctors (Plasser, 2000). This also holds true for the growing deployment of scientific methods. Empirical methodologies (e.g., controlling and evaluation measures) that are used to optimize campaigns and to collect information about voters' perceptions have become an indispensable tool for most of the political actors. However, the introduction of new campaign techniques has not displaced, by any means, traditional campaign methods such as the effective door-to-door canvassing, in which groups of candidates' adherents, wearing uniform clothing and equipped with gifts, visit the voters in their districts to inform them about candidates. Aside from such grassroots activities, in recent years the parties have also reactivated the use of neighborhood gatherings, which are always well received and well attended. The candidates regularly visit such events to discuss basic political issues with the voters and the inhabitants of a quarter, with the aim of improving their own public position. The importance of streets and places in party advertising has been shown both during the presidential contest of 1999 and the congressional elections of 2001, during which the Alianza por Chile (Alliance for Chile) and the governing Concertación (Agreement) fought for supremacy (Moke, 2003).

The employment of external political consultants is increasing. Hernán Büchi, the former presidential candidate of the Union Democratic Party, the right-wing successor to Pinochet's right-wing party, was the first to engage British campaign advisors for his presidential campaign, in the early 1990s. As foreign experts have not always been successful with their strategies and activities in Latin America, because of their failure to consider the typical characteristics of a country (Wolfenson, 1997), this approach has only slowly taken root in Chile. Nevertheless, it continues and was demonstrated in Lagos' 1999 first-round campaign when he was advised, among other domestic specialists, by two European experts, Jacques Séguéla (of France) and Jörg Richter (of Germany) (Moke, 2004).

THE POLITICAL SYSTEM IN CHILE

Traditionally, Chile has been one of the more highly politicized countries of Latin America. Although progressive political and social institutions had already emerged in Chile in the form of a sophisticated party system, the country remained economically underdeveloped. The attempt to reduce the gap of this heterogeneity in the 1960s failed, and the hyperpoliticization among political parties and in the population during the Allende era finally led to the breakdown of democracy and resulted in the coup d'état on September 11, 1973.

Chile returned to electoral democracy in the late 1980s. Although the military tried to force the traditional multiparty system to become a two-party system, it was impossible: Even 16 years of harsh dictatorship and almost no political party activity could not smash down the political system that still remained structured to the right, center, and left, as it was before 1973. However, the two-party electoral system that was imposed by the military had forced the parties into large coalitions, primarily within two political blocks. Paradoxically, the political right, which had supported, uncritically, the Pinochet regime through the Unión Demócrata Independiente (UDI; Independent Union Democratic Party) initially and—to a lesser extent—Renovación Nacional (National Renewal Party), was strengthened by this authoritarianism. In particular, the extreme left-wing parties that existed outside of the two political blocks lost much of their influence (Nohlen & Nolte, 1992; Valenzuela, 1995).

Today, Chile is ruled by a center-left coalition that has maintained its official position since the restoration of democracy in 1990. In December 1999, Chile held its third presidential election. As in the two preceding elections, the last contest was won by a representative of the large party coalition, the Concertación. This coalition consists of the leading Partido Demócrata Cristiano (Christian Democrats), Partido Socialista (Socialist Party), Partido por la Democracia (Party for Democracy), and Partido Radical Social Demócrata (Radical Social Democratic Party). In contrast, the political parties of the opposition are more fragmented and are dominated by the political right. The conservative coalition is the right-wing Alianza por Chile, which was formed at the end of the dictatorship by two political parties, Renovación Nacional and UDI. Outside of the two large coalition blocks, there exist several smaller parties, such as the Unión de Centro Progresista (Central Union of Progressive Centrists), Alianza Humanista Verde (Humanist Party), and other independent parties. The spectrum of the extreme left is dominated by the Partido Comunista (Communist Party).

According to its 1980 constitution, Chile is a presidential system in which the president is the executive authority and acts as head of state and government. To be elected, a candidate has to obtain an absolute majority of 50% plus one of the valid votes. The president is elected for a period of 6 years and appoints the cabinet. If no candidate gets the majority, the two candidates with the largest number of votes compete in a second round of voting. This was the case in the 1999 contest, in which no candidate obtained an absolute majority. The close results that were obtained by Ricardo Lagos (Partido Demócrata Cristiano) and Joaquin Lavín (UDI) led to the first runoff election in the history of Chile. In early 2000, Lagos finally defeated Lavín by 51.3% to 48.7% (Garretón, 2000; Silva, 2001).

The legislature is represented by the National Congress, a bicameral congress composed of a Senate and a Chamber of Deputies. The Senate consists of 48 members, 38 of which are elected members from 19 districts. Nine senators are appointed for an 8-year term, and one senator is appointed for life. The Chamber of Deputies consists of 120 deputies, who are elected in 60 districts for 4-year terms.

Even before the military regime had resigned, the *junta militar* had established a two-party electoral system for electing the National Congress. Its structure was defined in 1989, after several articles of the Constitution were reformed. For each district and region, the political parties and electoral alliances present a list of two candidates. The two candidates with the majority of votes are elected. If one list of candidates receives twice as many votes as the runner-up, both candidates will be elected. However, the two-party electoral system produces strong incentives to form large coalitions; consequently, the highest pluralities encourage the formation of two multiparty coalitions and simultaneously prevent the emergence of any third force (Oppenheim, 1999).

THE MASS MEDIA SYSTEM

Today, Chile's media system is characterized by a unique privatization, concentration, modernization, and transnationalization process. The media system follows a commercial logic that developed as a consequence of a neoliberal media policy imposed by the dictatorship and the subsequent transitional process that started in the early 1990s. Aside from television, where up to the present day the state not only acts as the owner of *Televisión Nacional* (Channel 7) but also determines television policy, the official administration plays a deregulative role with regard to the mass media. Even though Chile has a long tradition of an active media closely linked to political parties, today, the mass media in general (and the newspapers in particular) clearly show tendencies of depoliticization in content and an increasing loss of confidence (Moke, 2003), as illustrated in Table 9.1.

Table 9.1   Confidence in News Reports in Chile

Amount of Confidence	Radio	Television	Newspaper	News Magazines
Absolutely or sufficient	59.8	49.1	36.4	24.4
Little or scarcely any	38.1	49.3	58.6	66.3
No indication	2.1	1.6	5.0	9.3

SOURCE: Centro de Estudios Públicos, Santiago, Chile.

Since the restoration of democracy, the people's interest in political information has declined continuously. In 2002, only 12% of Chileans expressed confidence in the parties (Angell, 2003; Saavedra, 1999). This growing political apathy particularly affected the national press. As a consequence, many political newspapers and magazines, amongst others *Análisis, APSI, Fortín Mapocho,* and *Cauce,* disappeared from the market in the early 1990s. Contrary to expectations, the return of civilian rule did not lead to an increment of new publications. In fact, during the dictatorship, the market of daily print media became concentrated in the hands of two powerful groups, the El Mercurio–Edwards Company (owner of the quality newspaper *El Mercurio*) and the Consorcio Periodístico de Chile (COPESA) group (owner of *La Tercera,* the tabloid *La Cuarta*, and the influential political news magazine *Qué Pasa*). Today, *El Mercurio* is by far Chile's leading conservative quality newspaper, dominating the print market and remaining the most influential newspaper in opinion circles. To date, the El Mercurio–Edwards Company, as the most powerful newspaper group in Chile, is closely tied to business groups. Besides its eponymous nationally distributed periodical, with a Sunday circulation of about 340,000, the enterprise owns *La Segunda,* another periodical, which presents balanced and fair reporting. With *Las Ultimas Noticias,* the conglomerate finally holds a stake in the hard-fought market of the daily evening papers. Outside the metropolitan region, the

El Mecurio–Edwards Group owns another 14 regional newspapers. Beyond this "El Mercurio-COPESA duopoly" only the government-affiliated newspaper *La Nación* can be found (Bresnahan, 2003, p. 48).

Apart from television, radio is the most popular medium in contemporary Chile. Unlike TV, radio evolved almost privately and in a decentralized manner, as did the print media. Since the early 1990s, the number of radio stations, particularly smaller FM radio stations, has risen significantly, from about 330 to more than 900 stations at the end of the last decade. This tremendous expansion was the primary cause of the emergence of nationwide radio chains, *cadenas radiales,* in which international investors play an increasingly significant role. At the end of the 1990s, the Colombian *Caracol Network* and the *Iberoamericana Chilena,* with financial support from Venezuela and the United States, managed to form the two most powerful radio consortiums, with a listener share of more than 55% (Castellón, 1999). The growing role of transnational actors, including the Chilean Communication Company (with support from the American Hicks, Muse, Tate & Furts) and the Venezuelan Cisneros group, has transformed many local stations' repertoires into a purely repetitive version of city-based stations' programming. As commercial radio prospered, political programs tended to be less important (Cortés, 1998; Secretaría de Comunicación y Cultura, 1999).

In contrast to other Latin American countries, Chile rejected the U.S. model in

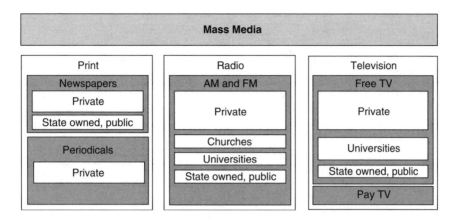

Figure 9.1   Structural Organization of the Chilean Mass Media System

favor of a television system similar to that of European public service broadcasting. Before 1973, television channels were run either by the government, as in the case of Televisión Nacional de Chile (Channel 7; the National Television Network of Chile), or by the universities, such as Universidad de Chile (Channel 11), Televisión Universidad Católica de Chile (Channel 13), and Televisión Universidad de Valparaíso (Channel 5), which tried to promote a certain degree of pluralism and education. The broadcast stations were financed by a mix of subsidies, granted by the government and through advertising.

During Chile's dictatorship, television was—more than any other medium—strictly controlled by the military, the authorities of the networks of the University of Chile, and the National Television Network of Chile. The opposition, in particular, had no access to television. It was only in 1987, in the months before the plebiscite, that the political leaders of the opposition gained limited access to television (Bresnahan, 2003).

Since the early 1990s, the situation has changed. Chilean television underwent a major transformation process when Megavisión (Channel 9), owned by the Pinto Claude Group and directed by Ricardo Claro, and La Red (Channel 4) became the first two privately owned television stations introduced into the national market. In 1993, the Luksic Group entered the private television market, buying a 75% share of Maxivisión, and broadcast in the metropolitan region. Since then, commercial broadcasting and cable television have been transformed into a more U.S.-style model, and television has been opened to foreign, transnational investors. According to an estimate by Consejo Nacional de Televisión (CNTV; the National Television Council), the broadcast stations compete for around $400 million annually in advertising ("Claves explicativas del," 2000; Trejo Ojeda, 2000). This has led, not surprisingly, to the evolution of broadcasting that has an eminently commercial character, lacking in educational and political programs. Without doubt, politics has transformed television news broadcasting through the introduction of several political talk shows. However, the process of the depoliticization of programs has continued, with the effect that political formats (e.g., discussion rounds) are broadcast at marginal times during the night. The expansion of television by cable started in the mid-1990s. Today, nearly 20% of Chilean households receive pay-per-view channels. Only two providers, Metropolis Intercom and Via Transradio Chilena S.A., control nearly 95% of the national cable television market. Figure 9.1 illustrates the structural organization of the media system in Chile.

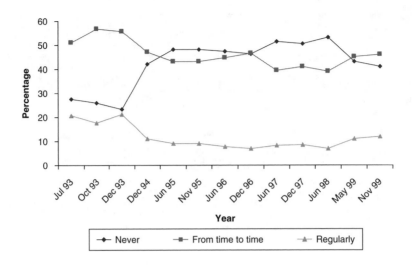

Figure 9.2   Exposure to Political TV Programs in Chile, 1993 to 1999

Both the increasing production costs and the strong competition among privately owned channels have caused a process of concentration that has subsequently led to the emergence of strategic alliances with powerful national and international business groups which have, in turn, transformed Chilean television into an entertainment medium. According to a survey, television reaches 100% of the population, and news is seen by approximately 98% of the viewers (Carvajal Rivera, 1999; García Luarte, 2002). Although a high percentage of Chileans regularly expose themselves to television news, the interest in political programs on TV continues to decrease, as Figure 9.2 shows.

REGULATION OF PARTY SPOTS ON CHILEAN TELEVISION

By Chilean law, free TV is obliged to broadcast political commercials for free. The right for parties to advertise on television is provided for in the law 18.700 Orgánica Constitucional sobre Votaciones Populares y Escrutinios. According to this law, each party that is registered at the Electoral Service for an upcoming election has the right to obtain airtime on TV. The allocation of the time for electoral advertising is legally regulated in Articles 30 through 35 of the law. Electoral propaganda on commercial channels—pay, or cable, TV—is not allowed, nor can political parties purchase airtime (Article 31, paragraph 6). According to Law 18.700, both Asociación Nacional de Televisión (the National Television Association) and all free TV channels are required to provide a block of airtime to political parties for free. The so-called franja política or franja electoral—electoral spots that are shown in this block—are to be transmitted daily, simultaneously, on all channels 30 days prior to an election. Airtime is allocated in proportion to the votes obtained in the previous election. The executive body supervising the allocation of airtime and the compliance of broadcasters with the law is the Consejo Nacional de Televisión (1997a; Servicio Electoral, 1996; Transparency International, 2002).

Article 31, in particular, regulates the distribution of airtime on television for the parties, pacts, coalitions, and independent candidates. According to this article, the channels of the free TV are obliged exclusively to dedicate a certain amount of daily airtime for the transmission of political propaganda. In the case of a presidential and parliamentary election, this amount is raised to 40 minutes (in parliamentary elections without a presidential election, it is 30 minutes).

In this way, Chile, in contrast to Brazil and Argentina, has avoided the paid political advertising on TV that is one of the features of commercial television and often subject to criticism. The regulation is constantly criticized, by television operators in particular; because only free TV channels are obligated to provide airtime free of charge, they reject the current system and criticize it vehemently. They consider these regulations to be inappropriate as long as private commercial stations are not also obligated to provide airtime for electoral advertising. Ironically, the electoral law is specific neither about how allocation of airtime is to be managed nor about when channels must broadcast electoral propaganda during the day.

In Chile, where parties are responsible for their own funding, the discussion in recent years about political broadcasting has raised not only concerns about television stations' legal obligation to broadcast political commercials but also about how the time slots are distributed. Airtime is granted to the political parties and independents in direct proportion to the number of votes received in the previous election. Both the method of distribution and the lack of direction in the legal framework regularly provoke dissatisfaction among the involved actors, and in its maelstrom polemic discussions frequently arise in regard to modifying the law about electoral advertising on television. Nonetheless, politicians, especially those who benefit from the current system, assign importance to it and contribute underlying effects to political commercials broadcast on TV. Jovino Novoa, former president of the UDI, considers the franja electoral essential in that it both transmits images and informs the electorate about candidates and programs. Additionally, even those candidates who are obviously discriminated against by the system

are reluctant to reject the law that provides them with free airtime for their electoral propaganda on television (Miranda, 1997). Although not all political actors are convinced of the effectiveness of televised ads, a certain join-in effect among the political forces is evident, as parties benefit from production costs that are relatively low in comparison to purchased TV airtime. Following Radunski's (1980) evidence that not presenting party posters during an election campaign means a party's capitulation, it may be estimated that the same holds true for those parties that are inclined to reject the chance to broadcast ads on TV.

The political parties are requested to submit an ad to the National Television Council no later than 2 days prior to its transmission on television. The time slots assigned to political parties cannot be modified, transferred, accumulated, or extended. The time slots for electoral propaganda on TV are dependent on the results obtained in previous elections. During the 2001 congressional election campaign, the Christian Democrats, as the major force within the political landscape, were given a time slot of 469 seconds each day. In contrast to this, in 1997 they were given 526 seconds each day. In comparison, both the Liberal Party and the Humanists received only 3 seconds each (Dávila, 2001). During an electoral campaign, commercials can be rebroadcast. Usually, the spots that are shown in the afternoon are transmitted again in the evening or on following days. The political parties are allowed to submit two sets of TV ads; one can be broadcast in the morning and one in the evening. Hence, only a few parties tend to broadcast one spot more than two times. It seems that the political parties make use of the possibility of producing new spots.

Political ads are financed and produced by the political parties themselves. Consequently, the parties are responsible for the content. Broadcast stations can refuse spots only if they do not align with the assigned time, technical specifications, or submission date to CNTV. The franja propaganda is broadcast daily in two blocks of 15 minutes each. Immediately before the ads are transmitted on air they are announced as political propaganda. It is announced that the channels are obliged by law, and in accordance with the agreements with the Asociación Nacional de Televisión and CNTV, to air electoral propaganda. Another message follows, pointing out that the parties are responsible for the content of the ads. It is not only this announcement but also the fact that Chileans already know when electoral propaganda is shown on TV that hampers the effects that commercial advertising is estimated to have (CNTV, 1997a, 1997b; "Consejo Nacional de," 1997).

RESEARCH ON CHILEAN ELECTORAL COMMUNICATION: THE CASE OF TELEVISION

Due to the 16-year-long dictatorship, during which political activities were abolished from daily life and both political and communications departments at universities and other research institutions were either closed or under strong control by the military junta, the research-based approach to political communication and political advertising in Chile is still limited.

In recent years, political advertising on television has attracted only a small amount of scientific attention. Unlike the United States and Europe, where research on political communication, especially in regard to TV, has a long tradition, in contemporary Chile it is still considered a desideratum. Experimental studies that address the production, content, and formal features of effective party spots on television (Holtz-Bacha & Kaid, 1993, 1996; Holtz-Bacha, 2000; Kaid & Holtz-Bacha, 1995) have rarely been carried out in Chile. Earlier scientific contributions have analyzed more of the communicator-oriented aspects of the dissemination process than investigated the

content and style of televised advertising specifically. Hence the majority of the published studies on advertising on television are more hermeneutic or descriptive than empirical. To date, a large number of the existing studies deal with the 1988 plebiscite and the subsequent first democratically held elections of 1990. In *La política en pantalla* (politics on television), Maria Eugenia Hirmas' (1989) chapter analyzes the role of television during the electoral rally by describing the advertising in the months leading up to the 1988 plebiscite. From January to August 1988, the military regime broadcast a total number of 7302 spots, although the opposition was only permitted to broadcast 1156 announcements (M. E. Hirmas, personal communication, November 18, 1997).

The important role that television played within the electoral campaign strategies, in regard to the referendum, was the main topic of Skidmore's (1993) *Television, Politics, and the Transition to Democracy in Latin America*. By using a hermeneutic, descriptive approach, Hirmas (1993) analyzed the content and issues of the commercials produced by both the authoritarian regime and the opposition. Proregime commercials pursued the aim of frightening the public by pointing out the horrors of the Allende administration between 1970 and 1973. In contrast to this, the main strategy of the opposition was to create a feeling of confidence and optimism and persuade the public to vote against a ruling dictator to achieve free elections within the year 1989. The month the franja was broadcast, it became the most widely discussed of events and was viewed by one of the largest TV audiences ever in the history of Chile. Hirmas' results illustrate that political leaders— whether they incline toward the opposition or the government—consider television the most important of the media.

In their contributions, Catalán and Sunkel (1991) and Sunkel (1989) describe the process of the abolition and the renewed rise of politics on television in the preplebiscite period. Their conclusion is that political issues and politicians were consequently stigmatized and led to what Sunkel (1989) has called the retreat of politics from TV, culminating in the "satanization" of politics by the military (p. 16). The relevance of televised ads in the 1988 plebiscite and the subsequent 1989 presidential and congressional elections is the subject of Tironi's (1990) *La invisible victoria* (the invisible victory). This publication is composed substantially of newspaper reports and articles and contributions published in news magazines. It is a description of the communication strategies used by the ruling military and the opposing Concertación. In contrast to this, Catalán and Sunkel (1991) and Tironi and Sunkel (1993) have, in their investigations, stressed both television's role within the process of transition to democratic rules and in the following democratization process. In this context, the authors examine the process of restructuring undergone by a pluralistic media system that had been used as a tool by the military and subsequently forced into the hands of private investors.

An empirical analysis of political ads shown on Chilean television was presented by Piñuel (1990). In *La cultura política del cuidadano y la comunicación política en TV, en la transición política del plebiscito Chileno* (The political culture of the citizenry and televised political communication in the political transition of the Chilean plebiscite), he analyzes the spots of the military and the opposition as part of the political communication process shown on television during the transitional phase.

To date, many of the published articles and contributions concerning political TV advertising in Chile are still of unscientific provenance. It seems that political communication in general, and political propaganda on television in particular, are of more interest to daily newspapers and news magazines than to academic researchers.

METHOD FOR ANALYSIS OF CHILEAN ELECTORAL SPOTS

When compared to political ads that are broadcast in the United States, contemporary Chilean party advertising on TV reveals considerable differences in respect to format, content, length, and style. Chilean spots are normally longer than U.S. spots, and different stylistic formats and topics are used within a single spot. However, because categorical systems developed in the United States refer more to a candidate than to consideration for the diversity of content, the instruments applied to the analysis of party spots had to be changed. Due to the fact that Chilean electoral spots are more akin to those of European countries than to those of the United States, a new instrument had to be introduced for the analysis of the content in electoral ads. This tool was tailored to the particulars of Chilean political advertising on TV and primarily applied to investigation of the first Congressional elections without a simultaneously held presidential contest, in December 1997. Out of a total number of 590 TV spots, 1269 sequences were analyzed (Moke, 2003). Table 9.2 shows the number of spots for each party.

The categorical system used in this survey was adopted from an empirical instrument developed by Lessinger (1997). The categorical system was modified to take into account the specific characteristics of Chilean advertising and to study the explicit formats of the party spots. A pretest indicated that a content-based sequence analysis would be the most appropriate empirical method to use in investigating the spots on their different levels. In this respect, the survey considered not only the content-based and design-based characteristics but also the linguistic and visual levels of the electoral ads. In contrast to using the entire spot, as had been done in previous studies, the spots were coded sequentially according to different levels. Structural data were coded for the whole ad on a specific level, and each

Table 9.2   Number of TV Spots Produced by Parties in Chile

Political Parties	Number of Produced TV Spots
Partido Demócrata Cristiana	26
Renovación Nacional	26
Unión de Centro Centro Progresista	21
Partido Comunista	17
Unión Demócrata Independiente	17
Partido por la Democracia–Partido Socialista	14
Alianza Humanista Verde	13
Partido Radical Social Demócrata	13

Note: Total number of spots = 147.

sequence of a scene was coded following the film theory of Hickethier (1996).

This approach ensured the comparability of the extreme heterogeneous spots. A *sequence* is thereby defined as a continuum that is connected by several criteria (e.g., through a continuum of time, location, constellation of acting figures, filming material). A change in a sequence is indicated when contextual or formal changes can be detected (e.g., changes in the constellation of acting persons or topics, changes with regard to the production techniques). Two sequences are separated from each other through a cut or cross-fading. However, a cut does not necessarily mean that a sequence has changed. The definition of the category "Presentational Formats" is as important as the definition of an actual sequence. Presentational formats are formal categories used to measure whether a politician is presented in a scripted way or a more natural communicative style. A take in which a politician only appears does not necessarily mean that the spot can be categorized as having a presentational format with a politician as a central actor. However, the flash of a candidate giving an interview can be coded as presentational format with a candidate as a central actor. To put it differently: The label of presentational format is assigned to a spot in which a politician appears when there is a specific activity. These formats are used to operationalize the political goals of a party or a candidate.

Altogether, 1269 sequences were analyzed according to a categorical system that represented 130 characteristics. The outcome showed a considerable variety with regard to the number of sequences each spot revealed. This stems particularly from the differences in terms of the length of the spots presented by the political parties. The largest party, the Christian Democrats, used a daily time slot of 461 seconds; the smallest party, the Humanists, only had 20 seconds of airtime. A look at the production techniques provides insight into how the parties adjusted themselves to the principles of television, as well as to the reception habits of the audience. This can be considered an indicator for the state of the art and modernization of political TV advertising. The results reveal that the parties generally tend to shun unusual recording techniques. The reason is that the deployment of special techniques increases production costs. Consequently, parties rely more on traditional filming techniques. With regard to the application of production techniques such as blue-screen, split-screen, and computerized animations, an increasing tendency to mix up different techniques is detected. Alongside the widely applied fading, the parties use more and more computerized production techniques. In accordance with the desire to use different production styles, the spots were filmed using different angles, of which the most popular were total shots and close-ups. With respect to

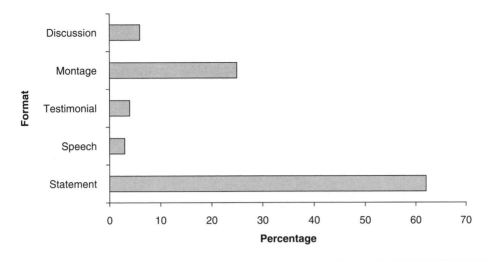

Figure 9.3   Presentational Formats With Candidates

the application of music in Chilean party ads, the results showed that in half of the analyzed sequences music was used in a stylistic way. This result can be linked to the traditional use of political party songs and jingles in electoral spots.

To measure the way in which candidates were presented in the spots, the sequences were divided into two categories: those in which candidates appeared as central actors and those in which either no candidate was presented or, when aired, the person was not the central topic of the sequence. Most of the sequences were coded as presentational formats without a candidate (60%). A closer look at the duopoly of the presentational styles, shown in Figure 9.3, indicates a clear tendency: In sequences in which a candidate was the central topic (40%), the most popular formats used were statements followed by a montage (defined as a series of pictures or scenes that are dissolved into each other).

The cultivation of party images can be seen through the implemented strategies used in the TV ads. In addition to showing politicians standing in front of a camera while giving a statement, the actors in ads were often filmed together with other colleagues and party functionaries. This was a popular strategy because

the majority of the political parties wanted to present themselves as more of a team than a one-man show. In this respect, the presentation of candidates was used to disseminate political issues to the electorate rather than to pursue an explicit personalization strategy. In respect thereof, candidates were presented as being connected to political issues to reduce the growing complexity of political issues. Within the scope of the parties' self-portrayal, as well as within the dialogue with the citizens, the journalistic format (such as interviews) did not play a significant role. The same holds true for such formats as testimonials, discussion rounds, and discourse.

To test the generally expressed assumption that contemporary election campaigns increasingly focus on top candidates with the objective of personalization, whereas the related political parties take more of a back seat, those sequences that presented candidates were analyzed. To measure whether political parties use their candidates to communicate complex political issues or to pick a candidate out as the central topic (with the aim of personalization and to shape a certain image), sequences were analyzed according to whether a candidate was the main topic or not. The results revealed that, indeed, all political parties have presented candidates in their spots. In the majority of cases, however, the strategy used was to connect political issues to candidates to gain better communication with the voters. It was the Christian Democrats in particular, along with the Radical Social Democrats and the Humanists, who refused to use the concept of singling out their top candidates, instead presenting their candidates as part of a crew. Only one political party has pursued a clear personalization and image-constructing strategy in its spots. The UDI used the element of personalization to shape a certain image of their political leaders. The UDI primarily tried to contour the image of their top candidates as hard-working technocrats whose commitment is to serve the Chilean people without any political-ideological imprint.

This strategy was again pursued by the Alianza por Chile in the 1999 presidential contest. The campaign of the UDI "was dominated by the style and themes of Lavín, especially in the media which, with the exception of a couple of radio stations and one television channel, gave him their unrestricted support" (Garretón, 2000, p. 79). The strategy was, like that 2 years before, to depoliticize the campaign, distance Lavín from his party, and discard his former image as a *pinochetista* (Saavedra, 1999).

CONCLUSION

This chapter was designed to provide insight into contemporary Chilean election campaigning, with a focus on the use of television. To provide an impression of what campaigning in Chile is about, the political and media systems, as well as legal aspects of Chilean election campaigns, have been considered, because these systemic variables exert considerable influence on how political advertising is managed.

Although domestic electoral campaigns have not turned into purely televised campaigns to date, the relevance of the audiovisual medium within an overarching and coherent strategy is considered important. The assumption that

television has advanced to become an important medium within national election campaigns is not only endorsed through statements affirmed by political leaders but is also indicated by the space dedicated to it in Law 18.700. Even though the deployment of television within Chilean electoral campaigns is comparatively young, it already claims leadership over the other mass media, especially in comparison to radio. A certain presumed dependency on television is also evident through the expenditures of the parties for the production of TV ads. This, however, is closely related to the financial background of the parties and candidates, as it is their responsibility to provide for the production costs of their ads. Although wealthy actors tend to produce electoral ads on a qualitatively high level that entails costs of $100,000 and up for a single spot filmed in a Hollywood-style format, others refuse expensive production techniques due to economic constraints. However, political actors who lack financial resources tend to invest in television for fear that otherwise their profiles may remain unnoticed by a greater public. Still, there are campaign experts (and even candidates) who confess ambivalent feelings as far as political commercials on television are concerned, even more so if TV spots lack quality, creativity, or content (J. Richter, personal communication, July 21, 2000).

With regard to political advertising on TV, the sequential content-based analysis has revealed that issues and programming topics are primarily communicated via political arguments. This, however, does not mean that parties tend to refuse to present their candidates in the spots. In fact, personalization is still used more to disseminate complex political issues than to construct a certain image (although personalization strategies are increasingly being used to distract from the parties' negative image in the public sphere). The presentation of candidates usually takes place in conjunction with the discussion of political issues. Candidates' private lives are almost ignored, and the parties tend to show their candidates in the role of public servants.

Within the process of selling politics, Chilean parties tend to insert modern political marketing methods. However, the campaign management and decision-making process vary according to the self-estimation of a given party. A shift toward a more candidate-centered and personalized approach was detected during the 1999 presidential contest, during which the conservative Alianza por Chile took a back seat during the campaign of its presidential candidate, Joaquín Lavín. Alianza por Chile's national leaders were not on stage when the top candidate entered the political arena, and even the UDI's national headquarters in the capital showed no visible sign of electoral activity. The campaign and the candidate were separated to reaffirm Lavín's image as a capable technocrat rather than a politician. In contrast to this, within the governing Concertación, the decision-making process was entirely in the hands of the party leaders. The formal direction of the campaign was controlled by prominent Christian Democrats, and the campaign management was in the hands of experts of the Socialist Party and Party for Democracy, which are closely related to Ricardo Lagos (Espíndola, 2002, p. 11).

In Chile, the management of election campaigns is just as modern as it is traditional. Sophisticated, up-to-date campaign methods and techniques, along with increasing professionalism, in no way hamper conventional elements that are considered very important by campaign leaders. More than copying U.S. style on a one-to-one basis, parties and candidates construct a unique marriage: They combine international political marketing techniques with traditional elements. Aside from the door-to-door canvassing, probably still the most important campaign element, parties and candidates tend to be present in the streets and public places. To amplify their presence, they usually cover the streets in the cities with thousands of posters, hanging down from traffic lights and power supply lines, put up in large numbers and long rows. A similar visual impact is guaranteed through the traditional political wall paintings carried out by so-called *muralistas,* adherents who usually paint and spray the names of candidates and slogans onto bridges, pillars, and building walls. The symbiosis of traditional and modern campaign elements and techniques that are applied on a global stage forms a unique Chilean electoral campaign culture.

REFERENCES

Angell, A. (2003, October). *Party change in Chile in comparative perspective.* Retrieved December 12, 2005, from http://www.lac.ox.ac.uk/parties-ips.pdf

Arriagada, G. (1997, December). *El poder de la gente* [The power of the people]. Santiago de Chile: La Red.Bryant, J. (1995). Paid media advertising. In J. A. Thurber & C. Nelson (Ed.), *Campaigns and elections American style* (pp. 84–100). Boulder, CO: Westview Press.

Bresnahan, R. (2003). The media and the neo-liberal transition in Chile: Democratic promise unfulfilled. *Latin American Perspectives, 30*(6), 39–68.

Carvajal Rivera, J. (1999). Das Rundfunksystem Chiles [Chile's broadcasting system]. In Hans Bredow-Institut (Ed.), *Internationales Handbuch für Hörfunk und Fernsehen* [International handbook of sound broadcasting and television] (pp. 638–643). Baden-Baden, Germany: Nomos.

Castellón, L. (1999, July 27-30). *Chile: The unfinished transition.* Paper presented at the Annual Conference of International Association for Media and Communication Research, University of Leipzig, Germany.

Catalán, C., & Sunkel, G. (1991). Comunicaciones y democracia en Chile [Communications and democracy in Chile]. *Diálogos de la Comunicación, 29,* 61–67.

Claves explicativas del comportamiento electoral Chileno 1988-2000 [Explanatory keys to Chilean electoral behavior, 1988-2000]. (2000, September). *Bitácora Electoral, 1,* 1–15.

Consejo Nacional de Televisión. (1997a). *Documento sobre canales de televisión en Chile* [Report on television channels in Chile]. Santiago de Chile: Author.

Consejo Nacional de Televisión. (1997b). *Hábitos y usos de la televisión Chilena* [The habits and uses of Chilean television]. Santiago de Chile: Author.

Consejo Nacional de Televisión: Distribución del tiempo de propaganda gratuita por televisión para las elecciones parlamentarias del 11. de diciembre de 1997 [The National Television Council: Distribution of free propaganda time on television for the parliamentary elections of December 11, 1997]. (1997, September 5). *Diario Oficial de la República de Chile*, p. 4.

Cortés, F. (1998). Modernización y concentración: Los medios de comunicación en Chile [Modernization and concentration: Methods of communication in Chile]. In C. Toloza & E. Lahera (Ed.), *Chile en los noventa* [Chile in the 1990s] (pp. 557–611). Santiago de Chile: Dolmen.

Dávila, L. (2001). Lo que los partidos van a mostrar en su franja del TV [What the parties will show during their TV time slots]. *Primera Linea*.

Espíndola, R. (2002, April 5-7). *The effect of professionalised campaigning on the political parties of the Southern Cone*. Paper presented at the 52nd Annual Conference of the Political Studies Association, University of Aberdeen, Scotland. Retrieved December 12, 2005, from http://www.psa.ac.uk/cps/2002/espindola.pdf

García Luarte, A. (2002, February 8). Desafíos del periodismo televisivo chileno en la era digital [Challenges for Chilean television media in the digital age]. *Pulso del Periodismo*. Retrieved December 12, 2005, from http://www.pulso.org/Espanol/Nuevos/tvdigital chile020208.htm

Garretón, M. A. (2000). Chile's elections: Change and continuity. *Journal of Democracy, 11*(2), 78–84.

Hafemann, M. (2005). Contienda presidencial 2005: El reality show electoral [The presidential contest of 2005: An electoral reality show]. *Revista Ercilla*. Retrieved July 26, 2005, from http://www.ercilla.cl/nanterior/n3269/presidenciales

Hickethier, K. (1996). *Film- und Fernsehanalyse* [Film and television analysis] (2nd ed.) Stuttgart, Germany: Metzler.

Hirmas, M. E. (1989). La franja entre la alegria y el miedo [The place between joy and fear]. In D. Portales, G. Sunkel, M. E. Hirmas, M. Hopenhayn, & P. Hidalgo (Eds.), *La política en pantalla* [Policy on the screen] (pp. 107–158). Santiago de Chile: ILET-CESOC.

Hirmas, M. E. (1993). The Chilean case: Television in the 1988 plebiscite. In T. E. Skidmore (Ed.), *Television, politics, and the transition to democracy in Latin America* (pp. 83–96). Baltimore: Johns Hopkins University Press.

Holtz-Bacha, C. (2000). *Wahlwerbung als politische Kultur: Parteienspots im Fernsehen 1957-1998* [Electoral advertisements as political culture: Party spots on television, 1957-1998]. Wiesbaden, Germany: Westdeutscher Verlag.

Holtz-Bacha, C., & Kaid, L. L. (1993). Wahlspots im Fernsehen: Eine Analyse der Parteienwerbung zur Bundestagswahl 1990 [Electoral spots on television: An analysis of party advertisements during the Bundestag election of 1990]. In C. Holtz-Bacha & L. L. Kaid (Eds.), *Die Massenmedien im Wahlkampf: Untersuchungen aus dem Wahljahr 1990* [The mass media in the election campaign: Investigations from the 1990 election year] (pp. 46–71). Opladen, Germany: Westdeutscher Verlag.

Holtz-Bacha, C., & Kaid, L. L. (1996). "Simply the best." Parteienspots im Bundestagwahlkampf 1994—Inhalt und Rezeption [Party spots in the Bundestag election campaign of 1994: Content and reception]. In C. Holtz-Bacha & L. L. Kaid (Eds.), *Wahlen und Wahlkampf in den Medien: Untersuchungen aus dem Wahljahr 1994* [Elections and election campaigns in the media: Investigations from the 1994 election year] (pp. 177–207). Opladen, Germany: Westdeutscher Verlag.

Huneeus, C. (2001). *El financiamiento de los partidos políticos y las campañas electorales en Chile* [Electoral financing of the political parties and the electoral campaigns in Chile]. Retrieved December 12, 2005, from http://www.cerc.cl/Publicaciones/FINAN_PART_POL.pdf

Kaid, L. L., & Holtz-Bacha, C. (1995). Political advertising across cultures: Comparing content, styles, and effects. In L. L. Kaid & C. Holtz-Bacha (Eds.), *Political advertising in Western democracies: Parties and candidates on television* (pp. 206–227). Thousand Oaks, CA.: Sage.

Lessinger, E.-M. (1997). *Politische Information oder Stimmenfang? Eine explorative Studie zum Kommunikationsstil in Wahlwerbespots der Bundestagswahlen von 1976 bis 1994* [Political information or sound bite? An explorative study of communication styles in electoral advertising spots during Bundestag elections, 1976-1994]. Unpublished master's thesis, Ruhr-Universität Bochum, Germany.

Miranda, C. M. (1997). Juicio a la franja: El síndrome de la campaña del "no" [Judgment on the strip: The "campaign of no" syndrome]. *El Mercurio*, pp. A1-D25.

Moke, M. (2003). *En Campaña: Wahlkampf in Chile zwischen Modernität und Tradition* [In the country: Election campaign in Chile between modernity and tradition]. Münster, Germany: LIT Verlag.

Moke, M. (2004). Wahlkampf in Chile zwischen Globalisierung und Nationaler Identität [Election campaign in Chile between globalization and national identity]. *Kas-Auslandsinformation, 5,* 137–161.

Nohlen, D., & Nolte, D. (1992). Chile. In D. Nohlen & F. Nuscheler (Ed.), *Handbuch der Dritten Welt* [Third World handbook] (pp. 277–337). Bonn, Germany: Dietz.

Oppenheim, L. H. (1999). *Politics in Chile: Democracy, authoritarianism, and the search for development.* Boulder, CO: Westview Press.

Piñuel, R. J. L. (1990). La cultura política del cuidadano y la comunicación política en TV, en la transición política del plebiscito Chileno (Octubre 1988) [The political culture of caution and political communication on TV in the political transition of the Chilean plebiscite (October 1988)]. *REIS: Revista Española de Investigaciones Sociológicas, 50,* 125–237.

Plasser, F. (2000). Proliferación mundial de técnicas americanas en campañas electorales [Worldwide proliferation of American techniques in electoral campaigns]. *Contribuciones, 2,* 123–146.

Radunski, P. (1980). *Wahlkämpfe: Moderne Wahlkampfführung als politische Kommunikation* [Election campaigns: Modern election campaign guidance as political communication]. München, Germany: Olzog.

Saavedra, M. (1999, December 8). *Disenchantment dominates Chilean election campaign.* Retrieved December 12, 2005, from the World Socialist Web site: http://www.wsws.org/articles/1999/dec1999/chil-d08.shtml

Secretaría de Comunicación y Cultura. (1999). *Concorcios radiales en Chile 1999* [Radio and television syndicates in Chile, 1999] . Santiago de Chile: Author.

Servicio Electoral. (1996). *Ley No. 18.700: Ley orgánica constitucional sobre votaciones y escrutinios* [Law 18.700: Constitutional statutory law on voting and investigations]. Santiago de Chile: Author.

Silva, P. (2001). Towards technocratic mass politics in Chile? The 1999-2000 elections and the "Lavín phenomenon." *European Review of Latin American and Caribbean Studies, 70,* 25–39.

Skidmore, T. E. (Ed.). (1993). *Television, politics, and the transition to democracy in Latin America.* Washington, DC: Woodrow Wilson Center Press.

Sunkel, G. (1989). Imágenes de la política en televisión [Images of politics on television]. In D. Portales, G. Sunkel, & M. E. Hirmas, M. Hopenhayn, & P. Hidalgo (Eds.), *La política en pantalla* (pp. 13–28). Santiago de Chile: ILET-CESOC.

Tironi, E. (1990). *La invisibile victoria: Campañas electorales y democracia en Chile* [The invisible victory: Election campaigns and democracy in Chile]. Santiago de Chile: Ediciones SUR.

Tironi, E., & Agüero, F. (1999). Sobrevivirá el nuevo paisaje político Chileno? [Will the new Chilean political landscape survive?] *Estudios Publics, 74,* 151–168.

Tironi, E., & Sunkel, G. (1993). Modernización de las comunicaciones y democratización de la política: Los medios en la transición de la democracia en Chile [The modernization of communications and the democratization of politics: The media in transition in the democracy of Chile]. *Estudios Públicos, 52,* 215–246.

Trejo Ojeda, R. (2000, March). *La indústria audiovisual en Chile: Informe ano 2000* [The audiovisual industry in Chile: Year 2000 report]. Santiago, Chile: Ministry of Education. Retrieved December 12, 2005, from http://www.chileaudiovisual.cl/pdf/trejo.pdf

Transparency International. (2002). *Monitoreo de la cobertura en los medios de comunicación de las elecciones* [Monitoring the coverage of methods of communication during the elections]. Retrieved December 12, 2005 from http://www.transparency.org/tilac/herramientas/2002/dnld/cap3/monitoreo_medios_chile.pdf

U.S. $30 milliones gastarán los políticos en la campaña. (1997, November 2). *El Sur*, pp. 1–9.

Valenzuela, J. S. (1995). Origenes y transformaciones del sistema de partidos en Chile [Origins and transformations of the party system in Chile]. *Estudios Públicos, 58,* 5–78.

Wolfenson, G. (1997). Las campañas electorales en América Latina: Nuevas technologías y viejas tradiciones [Election campaigns in Latin America: New technologies and old traditions]. *Contribuciones, 2,* 53–72.

PART IV

Dual Systems of Public and Commercial Political Advertising

10

Political Advertising in Germany

CHRISTINA HOLTZ-BACHA

Among the three German-speaking countries in Western Europe, Germany is in a unique position as far as political advertising is concerned. Switzerland's political system is a direct democracy in which, in addition to national and canton (state) elections, referenda are held on new laws or other political issues. Such a system increases the willingness of parties to compromise and thus decreases competition among the political actors. Because of the frequent referenda and regular elections, campaigning is also a common feature of Swiss political life, but Switzerland does not allow any electoral advertising on television. The Austrian political system, with a chancellor as head of the government and the central figure in the political process and two chambers exercising federal legislation, is similar to the German system. Both countries are federal republics, and elections are held regularly on the national and state levels. However, although Austria has recently abolished the right of parties to present themselves through television spots, Germany gives parties abundant possibilities for electoral advertising on television during election campaigns.

In this respect, Germany is also more generous than most other countries in Western Europe, but it is still much more restrictive than the United States.

THE POLITICAL SYSTEM: BACKGROUND

National elections are held in Germany every 4 years to determine the representatives for the parliament (the Bundestag), which is one of two legislative bodies (chambers) on the national level. The second chamber (the Bundesrat) is not elected directly by the people but consists of representatives of the state (Land) parliaments. National elections follow the system of a modified proportional election, also called a "personalized proportional election." Each voter has two votes: With the first vote, a party candidate in the constituency is elected, and the second vote is given to a party list. The number of seats a party gets in the parliament is calculated according to the number of party or second votes. These seats are taken either by those candidates who win a constituency or by candidates from the party

163

list. During election campaigns, all parties primarily try to solicit second votes; campaigning on the constituency level is left mainly to the candidates. Given that only the bigger parties have the chance to win the constituency, the first vote cast for a small party risks being a lost vote. Therefore, and due to coalition considerations, more and more people have split their ticket since the 1960s, giving their first vote to one of the big parties and their second vote to a smaller party. As this electoral system, even for German voters, is somewhat complicated and the term "second vote" often leads to the association of its being less important, political campaign advertising is also used to explain the meaning of the two votes. Thus the voting system itself becomes an issue during the electoral campaign, particularly in its last phase, shortly before election day, to remind people that the second vote is decisive (Holtz-Bacha, 2004b, 2004c).

The party receiving the majority of votes, or a coalition of two parties, nominates the chancellor, who is elected by the parliament. The chancellor is the head of the government and is also the one who appoints the ministers for the government. The German president, although the highest ranking representative of the state, has primarily a ceremonial function; the chancellor is the most important figure in the German political system. As neither the president nor the chancellor is elected directly by the people, the Bundestag is the only institution—besides the supranational European Parliament—in which members are directly elected on the national level.

The parties play a central role in the German political system. Their task of "participating in the formation of political opinion and the political will" is even laid down in the constitution and described further in a party law. The main pillars for the financing of German parties are membership dues and subsidies allocated by the government. The amount of these subsidies is dependent on the success of the individual party in elections

(number of votes), and the total sum of other contributions and donations is also taken into consideration. Campaign activities are paid for by these funds.

To take seats in the parliament, parties have to get at least 5% of the votes. Until the 1980s, the German political landscape was dominated by three parties: the conservative Christlich-Demokratische Union/Christlich-Soziale Union (CDU/CSU; Christian Democrats), the Sozialdemokratische Partei Deutschland (SPD; Social Democrats) and the liberal Freie Demokratische Partei (Free Democrats). The largest parties by far have always been the CDU/CSU and the SPD. The German chancellor, therefore, always has been a member of either one or the other of these parties. As usually neither the CDU/CSU nor the SPD wins the absolute majority of the votes, a coalition of (at least) two parties is necessary to push a candidate through as chancellor and to form a government. As a coalition of the two big parties is an exception and has only happened once at the national level, for almost four decades the Free Democrats have played a decisive role in helping one or the other party into government, thus gaining more political weight than is justified by the usually single-digit percentage of votes the party receives in elections. During the 1980s, the Greens, which developed from the roots of an ecological movement, became more and more influential and were thus another possible partner for a coalition. After the election of 1998, the first "red-green" (Social Democrats and Greens) coalition government was formed under the chancellorship of Gerhard Schröder (SPD). The outcome of the 2002 elections allowed the two parties to continue their coalition for another 4 years.

In October 1990, Germany, which had been a divided country as a result of World War II, was reunited. The former German Democratic Republic was dissolved and the five new federal states (Laender) that were formed instead acceded to the Federal

Republic of Germany. The first all-German election in December 1990, and later elections, particularly in the East German states, showed that a fifth force has developed on the German political scene. As a successor to the former German Democratic Republic state party, the Partei des Demokratischen Sozialismus (PDS; Party of Democratic Socialism) has gained a strong foothold in the East German Laender and also has received enough votes to make it into the Bundestag.

THE MEDIA FRAMEWORK

Germany only opened up its broadcasting market for commercial stations in the mid-1980s. Today, the television market in particular is extremely competitive. The average household with a TV, amount and kind of technical equipment notwithstanding, receives 36 channels. The public broadcasters' overall share of the adult audience (14 years and older) is 44%. The commercial broadcasting sector is dominated by two groups, Bertelsmann/RTL and the Sat.1 group, which was recently bought by the U.S. entrepreneur Saban. Each group operates four channels, with an audience share of 24% and 23%, respectively, leaving about 10% to 12% to several other minor stations. Due to the high number of channels and the fact that the programming volume is growing much more rapidly than individual viewing time, audience fragmentation has become a characteristic of the German TV market. Individual channels reach a comparatively low overall audience share. The most popular channel, which in 2004 was the commercial station RTL, has a share of barely 15%.

The most important feature of the German dual broadcasting market is the coexistence of public and commercial broadcasting within the communication system. Under this arrangement, public broadcasting was assigned the task of "basic supply"; that is, to offer a comprehensive and varied selection of formats and content, encompassing the classical broadcasting mandate of information, education, and entertainment. This also included programming for minority groups. The task of basic supply was assigned to public stations because they have a guaranteed income through a broadcasting fee paid by everyone who owns a radio or TV set. The requirement for diversity goes hand in hand with the notion of basic supply. Consequently the Constitutional Court, which has always had an important role in German media politics, ruled that as long as the public stations guarantee a high degree of diversity, such requirements for commercial stations could be lowered, although not completely abandoned. Thus it is in the interest of the commercial stations that public broadcasting remains capable of fulfilling its task, because commercial stations would have to compensate should the public stations no longer be able to deliver the basic supply. Being bound to cater to all interests or, in other words, having to provide more than just a basic level of diversity would deprive commercial broadcasters of their freedom and independence in programming decisions that are otherwise guided mainly by the pursuit of profit. Having to provide comprehensive and diverse programming would run counter to their ratings orientation.

The German newspaper market has traditionally been dominated by regional papers. Of about 135 independent dailies, only six are distributed nationally. Among them are the elite newspapers *Die Welt*, *Frankfurter Allgemeine Zeitung*, *Süddeutsche Zeitung* and *Frankfurter Rundschau*, which—in this order, from first to last—represent the political spectrum. The alternative newspaper *Die Tageszeitung*, perennially struggling for survival, is also distributed nationally. Finally, with a daily circulation of more than three million, the conservative-inclined tabloid *Bild* reaches the widest audience. German newspapers pride themselves on being objective, although readers can usually recognize their partisan leaning, be it right or left. Traditional party newspapers have completely disappeared. During election campaigns, newspapers remain rather critical of both sides and endorsement of candidates is never done. Thus it came as a complete surprise when, in 2002, the *Financial Times Germany* openly recommended a vote for the Christian Democrats.

Commercialization, in the sense that economic reasoning has come to dominate program decisions, has most notably affected the electronic media and thus made it more difficult to convey politics to the audience. Just as with other media offerings, politics today has to prove effective in the market, its success being measured by ratings. At the same time, the multichannel environment has made it easier for the individual viewer to avoid politics on TV. Cumulatively, these developments have challenged the politicians and have compelled them to make greater efforts to gain the public's attention. Politics has, therefore, adopted approaches more familiar in the entertainment industry and that have proven successful in attracting large audiences.

ELECTORAL SPOTS AND THEIR REGULATION

The right of parties to electoral advertising on television and radio is fixed in the Laender broadcasting laws. Although this is rather a general regulation, details have developed over the years through the Federal Constitutional Court when it had to decide about complaints that were brought to the court by the political parties.

Each party registered for an election has the right to obtain free airtime on the two public TV channels. In accordance with regulations for other public services, the equal opportunity rule is the guiding principle for the allocation of advertising time on television. Nevertheless, a system of graded allocation is applied, with smaller parties getting less time (fewer spots) than larger parties. This has been the subject of several cases submitted to the

Federal Constitutional Court, which, however, approved the graded allocation system. To allow for a certain repetition effect, which is regarded as a necessary condition for reaching audience attention, the minimum number of television spots per party was set at two (per public channel).

The number of spots an individual party may broadcast is calculated according to its strength in earlier elections and according to its expected success in the upcoming election. During recent campaigns, when the two big parties were about equally strong, the Christian Democrats and Social Democrats each received 8 time slots on the two public TV channels, adding up to 16 for each party. During the 2002 election campaign, the SPD got eight slots and the CDU was allocated seven because the SPD had fared much better than the CDU in the 1998 election. The smaller parties represented in the Bundestag each got four, and the smallest parties, those that did not make it into parliament, were allocated the minimum quantity of 2 slots each. Since the election of 1998, the maximum length for the individual spot to be broadcast in these time slots was fixed at 90 seconds. Before then, since the 1960s, airtime for each spot had been 2½ minutes. The large number of campaigning parties, which each have the right to obtain at least two time slots, causes a capacity problem for the public stations. During recent campaigns, more than 20 parties were registered. Thus public channels have to provide a lot of airtime for electoral advertising. This is one reason why electoral advertising is not very popular with the public stations, which have adopted a kind of "dissociation strategy" to distance themselves from the ads.

Immediately before the spots are broadcast on German television—on public as well as on commercial channels—they are announced as electoral advertising. At the same time, it is stressed that the stations are obliged by broadcasting law to carry the party spots. Finally, the speaker points out that the parties themselves are responsible for the contents of the ads. Thus, these announcements, which almost give the impression of a warning, weaken the surprise effect that helps the ads in the United States to find their audience. In addition, the public stations in Germany put the spots in a frame during their entire length, with a permanent insert saying "electoral advertising." The two public channels thus make clear that they are obliged to air the ads but that responsibility for the contents lies with the parties (Holtz-Bacha, 2003b).

All parties can purchase additional airtime on commercial television. Although airtime is provided for free on public television, parties have to pay the prime costs on commercial channels. In 1994, this was interpreted as 55% to 60% of the usual spot prices; in 1998, as well as in 2002, it was 45%. As the campaigns since 1990 have shown, only the bigger parties can afford to pay for advertising time. In earlier years, not even all parties represented in the Bundestag bought additional airtime on commercial TV. In fact, 2002 was the first election year when all five parliamentary parties actually purchased airtime for advertising on the commercial channels. However, only the two biggest parties, SPD and CDU, can afford to buy a big amount of airtime; the smaller parties can only purchase a little. Thus, even more than the graded system of free-time allocation, the opportunity to buy additional time on commercial channels has undermined the equal opportunity rule that guided electoral advertising on television for a long time in Germany.

The public channels themselves determine what time the spots will be broadcast. However, it has to be at a time when a wide audience is likely to be reached. Spots are thus usually broadcast in the evening, with the earliest aired around 6:00 p.m. and the latest at about 11:00 p.m. On the public channels, political advertising is not part of the advertising blocs. Regular advertising is not allowed

after 8:00 p.m. on public TV in Germany, but an exception is made for electoral advertising. Even though the spots do not interrupt programs, they reach comparatively large audiences because they are aired immediately prior to and after popular programs. Which specific spot is aired at a given time is decided at random. Viewers are therefore caught by chance by the spots in general and the specific party in particular.

On commercial channels, parties of course can decide at what time their spots should be broadcast. Contrary to the allocation system of public TV, the commercial channels allow parties to choose the specific channel for their advertising and the time or surrounding program. Commercial television thus offers parties the opportunity to address certain target groups. In 2002, for example, the Greens bought airtime on the music channel MTV for a spot that was supposed to address young people in particular.

The parties produce the television spots themselves. The broadcasting stations can refuse spots only if they obviously do not contain electoral advertising or if they contravene criminal law. However, the stations do not have to judge whether a spot is in accordance with the Basic Law (constitution). Equal opportunity for the parties to present their programs is the supreme rule. In some campaigns, the equal opportunity rule has led to problems for the broadcasting stations when they refused to air the spots of extreme right parties containing xenophobic propaganda. The courts always required the stations to broadcast the controversial spots, stressing that equal opportunity has to be given to all parties as long as the party itself is not prohibited. To avoid having to broadcast the spots of the extreme right parties during the election campaign of 1994, some public stations in summer 1993 initiated a discussion about the spots and proposed to change the broadcasting laws to eliminate electoral advertising. Although some politicians supported the initiative, others, in their own interest, remained reluctant, and finally the whole discussion petered out again.

RESEARCH ON
GERMAN PARTY SPOTS

Although electoral ads have been broadcast since the 1950s, little research on content and effects was done until the 1980s. For a long time, discussion of legal aspects was prevalent in publications on party advertising (Becker, 1990; Bornemann, 1992; Franke, 1979; Gabriel- Bräutigam, 1991; Schulze-Sölde, 1994). Only a few German studies addressed questions of creation, content, formal features, or effectiveness of party spots. Dröge, Lerg, and Weissenborn (1969) presented a description of the content and styles of commercials broadcast during the 1969 parliamentary election campaign. Martin Wachtel (1988) analyzed the argumentation content of the 1987 parliamentary election spots. He determined that communicating trustworthiness and competence is the major goal of the political parties in their television spots and that visual qualities of the commercials played an important role in communicating these qualities. Holtz-Bacha (1990) analyzed survey data on the 1989 European parliamentary election in West Germany. Results showed that attentiveness to the spots correlated with attentiveness to other campaign channels—that is, those who noticed political advertising in one medium also noticed advertising in another medium. These data also prove that watching party commercials correlates with a positive opinion about the campaign and also with an improvement in attitude regarding the European Community (EC), German membership in the EC, and the European Parliament. As these attitudes influence a person's intention to cast a ballot, party spots can be judged as affecting voting intentions indirectly.

Research into party advertising finally took off with the beginning of the 1990s when the commercial channels got established on the broadcasting market and, by offering ad time to be purchased, made television advertising a more interesting campaign instrument (Jakubowski, 1998). These studies at first were very much inspired by the extensive research in the United States. By using the category system that had already been used for analyzing ads in the United States and elsewhere, researchers could consider the findings from Germany in the light of international comparisons (Holtz-Bacha, Kaid, & Johnston, 1994; Kaid & Holtz-Bacha, 1995). However, researchers soon realized that the instruments used in the analysis of television ads in the United States had to be changed and adapted to the German situation, for two reasons: First, German electoral ads, at least those broadcast on public television, are longer than ads in the United States. German ads also use several different formats within one spot. Second, category systems developed in the United States refer to candidate ads, whereas German ads are produced by the parties, and individual candidates are not allowed to purchase air time (for a more extensive discussion, see Holtz-Bacha, 2003a).

Therefore, a new instrument was drawn up for content analysis that was adapted to the specifics of German party advertising on television. This was used for a longitudinal study that analyzed German electoral advertising since its introduction on television in 1957 until 1998 (Holtz-Bacha, 2001). The same category system was used to analyze the spots of the most recent German parliamentary election, which was held in the fall of 2002. Thus the findings presented here refer to 13 German campaigns altogether.

Instead of using the whole ad as the coding unit, the German spots were coded on two different levels (Lessinger, 1997). Structural data were first coded for the whole spot, and formats and contents of the spots were then coded according to spot sequences or scenes (for a more extensive description, see Holtz-Bacha, 2001, 2004a). In a definition adopted from

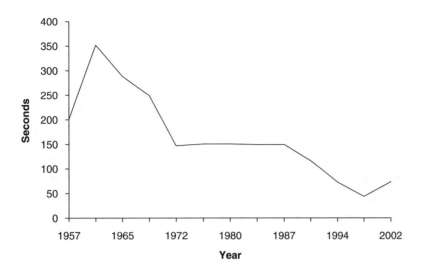

Seconds / Year

Figure 10.1   Length of German Spots

Note: Only the spots of those parties represented in parliament (n = 319) were included.

film theory, a *spot sequence* is a unit containing one or multiple takes (separated by cuts or superimpositions) that constitute a continuum connected to a unit by several criteria. These criteria refer either to the content (e.g., a continuum of location, time, action, the constellation of actors, or the topic) or to the formal features (e.g., a continuum of sound, music, speaker). A sequence changes if the content or formal brackets change and another action, constellation of figures, topic, or other formal features dominate. One sequence is always separated from another sequence through a cut or a superimposition, but a cut is not necessarily the beginning of a new sequence.

The central category for the analysis of the visual strategies here is the presentational style or format. Formats represent the dramatic means used to operationalize the political goals of a party or a candidate (such as montage, videoclip, candidate statement, interview). Instead of coding a format for the whole spot, this analysis assigned a format to each sequence (which functioned as the unit of analysis). A change of format always implies the beginning of a new sequence (scene), although the beginning of a new sequence does not necessarily

imply a change of format. *Format* here is exclusively used as a formal category, and the content of the spot is coded independently.

STRUCTURAL CHANGES OF ELECTORAL ADS FROM 1957 TO 2002

All in all, the long-term analysis shows a trend toward shorter spots and a faster pace. The spots became shorter in two steps. In the early years, the parties were allotted 5- and even 10-minute slots for their campaign advertising. In the 1960s, the public stations shortened the maximum length for the individual spots to 2½ minutes and in 1998 to 1½ minutes. Modifications of the conditions as set by the television stations thus have an effect on spot style. The same applies to ads produced for commercial television: If parties have to pay for airtime, spots are shorter. Figure 10.1 shows how the average spot length decreased over the years. In 2002, the parties bought less time on commercial channels, and this is why the overall mean approaches the length of the spots on public channels in this year.

The shortening of the spots coincides with an accelerated pace, as indicated by cuts. At

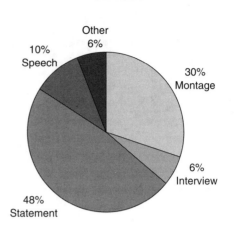

Figure 10.2   Presentational Formats

the end of the 1990, the ads had become much more hectic, displaying a higher number of cuts per spot than in earlier years. However, in 2002, the pace seems to have slowed down again, which also may be due to the overall mean being dominated by spots aired on public television.

Formats here were divided according to whether a candidate was present or not. The most popular formats among those that do not show a candidate as the central political actor are montages and pack shots. A *montage* is produced by dissolving a series of pictures or scenes into each other that can later be separated by either cuts or superimpositions. *Pack shots* (a category derived from economic advertising) are pictures of the product, usually combined with a slogan or the brand name. Here, *pack shot* is defined as a sequence dominated by the party logo that is, in most cases, shown at the end of a spot to reinforce the party name. In addition, it is supposed to remind viewers of which party is responsible and should be associated with the ideas expressed in the ad. Finally, a *signal shot* is a format consisting of one picture only, which serves as a structural element.

Figure 10.2 shows the total shares of the different formats without a candidate for all of the 13 campaigns. Montages account for about one third and pack shots for one fourth of the sequences. This makes sense, because montages mostly convey an emotional feel-good atmosphere, and pack shots emphasize the name of the party. Emotional appeals and stressing the brand name are typical features of consumer ads. It is surprising, however, that signal shots rank third. The testimonial, here coded only as testimonials by nonparty representatives, is used in 8% of the sequences.

The candidate statement is the most frequently used format among those sequences showing a party representative. It accounts for 47% of the sequences. If the length of the sequences is taken into account, more than 50% of the total time falls to the talking head format, which is common in political ads. Smaller parties in particular prefer candidate statements because of the low production costs. The montage showing the candidate carrying out his official duties ranks second with almost one third of the sequences. Clippings from candidate speeches are used in 10% of the sequences.

Personalization of Party Spots

The party-oriented political system does not prevent the personalization of campaigns. When they use a personalization strategy, parties respond to the logic of the media in general and television in particular and at the same time offer voters a reference point in the otherwise rather abstract and complex world of politics (see Holtz-Bacha, Lessinger, & Hettesheimer, 1998). In any case, the top candidates of the parties have always been at the center of the electoral campaigns. Because only the two big parties have a chance to win the chancellorship, they have usually been the only ones to nominate chancellor candidates. As a consequence, their campaigns have taken on the character of a duel between the incumbent chancellor and the competitor. Much of the media's attention is also concentrated on the chancellor candidates (see Wilke & Reinemann, 2000, 2003). For the election campaign in 2002, the Free Democrats, although too small to ever have a chance to fill the position of chancellor, nevertheless nominated their party leader explicitly as a candidate for chancellor, hoping thus to gain adequate attention.

In regard to electoral advertising, the personalization strategy has been reflected in the "image versus issue" dichotomy that has become an ongoing topic of discussion. Many previous studies have regarded an ad as "image oriented" if it concentrates on the presentation of a candidate's personal characteristics. The presentation of a candidate's stand on issues is coded as "issue oriented." Image orientation is often (negatively) associated with personalization and depoliticization (see Shyles, 1986, pp. 111-112). However, campaign strategists also use issue-oriented formats to support the image of a candidate (e.g., Rudd, 1986), and previous research has indeed shown that issue formats can influence a candidate's image (e.g., Geiger & Reeves, 1991; Holtz-Bacha & Kaid, 1996; Kaid & Sanders, 1978). On the other hand, "issue

orientation" does not necessarily mean the extensive discussion of political issues. Instead, issues are often employed to convey a particular impression of the candidate (e.g., Joslyn, 1980). In fact, the "real" informational content of issue-oriented spots (and thus their supposed superiority in comparison to image-oriented spots in conveying information) has rarely been analyzed.

The longitudinal study from which the data presented here were taken used categories that allow for a clear-cut differentiation of the presentation of a candidate, issue presentation, and the conveying of images. This was very much inspired by Shyles (1986), who suggested:

> If we recognize a difference in the meaning of "image" when used to refer to graphic methods or presenting candidates (visual display), versus character attributes of candidates, then we can begin to assess more accurately the relationship between images and issues in televised political spots; perhaps then some of the controversy regarding the value of image and issue content of candidates in televised political advertising can be resolved. (p. 115)

Thus, the candidate is here seen as a topic and used as a category for analysis.

According to these considerations, the sequence analysis differentiated formats with and without the presence of candidates as actors. Overall, formats without a candidate as the central actor dominated the campaigns between 1957 and 2002. With the exception of 1990 only, which was Germany's "unity election," formats without candidates by far outnumbered formats that featured a candidate. Taking the sequences of all spots and of all election years together, only 33% presented formats with candidates as the central actor. Of course, this overall finding also reflects the high number of parties running for election, with many small parties whose personnel are mostly unknown to the electorate and which therefore concentrate their advertising on issues without connecting them to candidates.

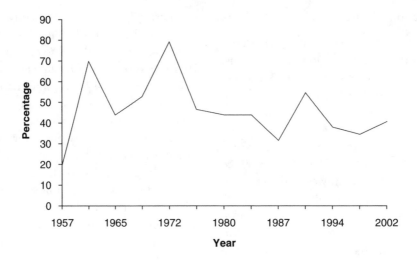

Figure 10.3   Candidates Present in Spots

Note: Spots from all parties were examined (n = 2184).

Focusing the spots on the top candidates can be regarded as one of the main indicators for an increasing personalization of campaign advertising. This study not only coded for the presence of a top candidate but differentiated between the visual or verbal presence, on the one hand, and the "top candidate as issue" (further information is given about the candidate's life, personal characteristics, or activities), on the other. This latter category is used here as an indicator of the image orientation of a sequence.

The comparison over time reveals much variance in the number of sequences that present a candidate in the visuals. Figure 10.3 demonstrates that politicians appeared most frequently in the spots of election campaigns in 1961 (70%), 1972 (79%), and 1990 (55%), whereas candidate appearances were particularly low in the ads of 1987 (32%), 1994 (38%), and 1998 (35%). Even during the most recent election, which was generally regarded as a particularly personalized campaign, the overall presence of candidates in the television ads was comparatively low. The overall mean, as presented in Figure 10.3, is again very much influenced by the high

number of small and mostly unknown parties that do not show candidates in their ads. Most of the candidate appearances originate from parties that are represented in the parliament.

The picture looks different if we regard the results in light of the big parties only. The Christian Democrats and the Social Democrats have the most prominent candidates because the chancellor is always chosen from one of these two parties. Therefore, the presence of the candidates in the ads of these parties gives a better impression of the degree of personalization in German campaigns. Figure 10.4 shows the presence of candidates in CDU and SPD spots over the total period from 1957 to 2002.

Based on the whole sample, 57% of the sequences of the SPD spots feature a party member, whereas only 40% of the sequences of the CDU spots show a member of the political team. Of the sequences that feature a party member, the spots of the CDU and SPD are, naturally, dominated by their top candidate. In fact, 78% of the respective sequences in CDU spots and 81% of the scenes in SPD spots introduce the incumbent chancellor or

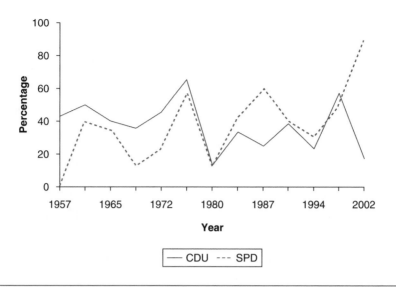

Figure 10.4   Candidates Present in Spots: CDU and SPD

his challenger. If a top candidate is present, he or she is a topic in 46% of the sequences of SPD spots.

Comparing over time how often the chancellor candidates of the CDU or the SPD are mentioned, visually or verbally, or presented with further information reveals interesting differences between the two big parties (see Figures 10.5 and 10.6). Over the whole period of the study, the chancellor candidates of the CDU play a minor role in the ads. The results of the study also demonstrate that there is no overall and homogenous trend toward increased personalization. Instead, the presence of candidates in the TV ads seems to be highly dependent on the personality of the candidate and how much the party is indeed backing its top candidate. This becomes clear by looking at the CDU campaigns under Helmut Kohl between 1983 and 1998. He was not equally present in all campaigns. In 1987, he was almost absent from his party's advertising and was not made the issue of the CDU spots at all. However, because Kohl was regarded as the "father" of German unification, the party focused its campaign on Kohl during the 1990 campaign for the "unity election" and tried to use this same image of Kohl

once more during the following campaign in 1994.

The SPD uses personalization to a greater extent than the Christian Democrats. Figure 10.6 shows the long-term development of personalization in SPD spots. When Willy Brandt was the party's top candidate for the first time in 1961, the Social Democrats already relied on personalization. Almost all sequences that showed an SPD politician dealt with the top candidate, who was the central theme in 57% of the sequences. In the years 1965 and 1969, the personalization of Brandt decreased considerably but went up again in 1972. The SPD spots also concentrated on their top candidate Helmut Schmidt in the election campaigns of 1976 and 1980. However, Schmidt was most prominent in electoral year 1980, when the CDU presented its disputed candidate Franz Josef Strauss more hesitantly. In 1998, SPD spots reached the lowest level of personalization since 1961, but what personalization there was was concentrated exclusively on Gerhard Schröder. During the campaign in 2002, when Schröder was much more popular with the electorate than his party was, all spots featured the incumbent chancellor trying to transfer his popularity to the party.

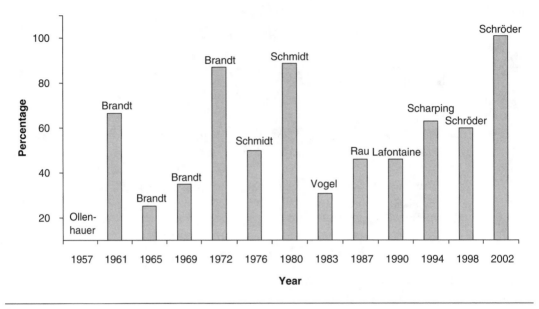

Figure 10.5   SPD Chancellor Candidates

Note: Bars indicate the percentage of sequences in which the candidate was the topic of the sequence. A total of 376 sequences was examined.

In most cases, electoral advertising in Germany is a serious matter. This is underlined by the settings of the spots and the way in which candidates are dressed. In 47% of the sequences, candidates appear inside and in a formal setting, such as their office. Another 22% present the candidate in an official situation outdoors (e.g., meeting other politicians, traveling). The clothing of the candidates is also predominantly official. Most politicians appear in suits, business shirts, and with ties. These are variables that can also be taken as indicators of the degree of privatization, in the sense of showing candidates in their private environment. However, German spots contain only few private scenes, and these do not lend themselves to predicting a trend toward further privatization. In fact, when we find candidates shown in a private setting, it is part of a broader strategy aiming at a specific image to be conveyed. This was the case for SPD chancellor candidate Willy Brandt when he ran for the first time in 1961 as a competitor of the much older incumbent Konrad Adenauer. Brandt was shown with his family

at the coffee table in their garden or in a rowboat with his young sons, thus presenting him as an ordinary citizen and more youthful than Adenauer. When the Christian Democratic chancellor candidate Franz Josef Strauss ran in 1980 and could be seen in the kitchen of his home playing games with his wife and young children, this served to soften the image of the brawny man. In 1994, the only spot that the SPD produced for public television presented the mother and the wife of chancellor candidate Rudolf Scharping and inserted pictures taken from a private video. This was all part of a strategy titled "Mensch Scharping" (man Scharping), launched to make the candidate better known and at the same time humanize the image of a wooden and sometimes awkward politician. All in all, and even though privatization has become the subject of controversial discussion with the image strategies of "media chancellor" Gerhard Schröder, the findings of the longitudinal analysis do not speak for a continuous trend toward personalization in general and privatization in particular. Instead, these strategies appear to be

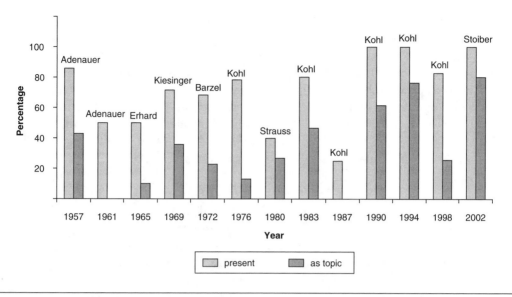

Figure 10.6   CDU Chancellor Candidates

Note: Lighter bars indicate the percentage of sequences in which the candidate was present; darker bars indicate the percentage of sequences in which the candidate was the topic of the sequence. Total number of sequences examined was 225.

dependent on the personality of the candidates and specific aims in the interest of their image.

Reaching the Audience

In a survey (IP Deutschland, 2002) conducted in late August 2002, 4 weeks before election day and 1 day after the spots had started being broadcast on TV, 30% of the respondents said they had already seen party spots. No major differences were found between men and women or among different educational groups. It comes as a surprise, however, that among the four age groups, respondents 45 to 59 years old had not been reached by the spots to the same extent that the two younger groups and voters 60 years and older had. In addition, there was a difference according to the regional origin of the voters: Although 31% of the West German voters had already seen spots, only 25% of the East Germans said that they had encountered political advertising on TV. This difference might be due to TV preferences, which differ between East and West Germany: Public television is

more popular in West Germany, and that is where the spots started airing, earlier than on commercial TV. Therefore West Germans simply might have had a better chance to be reached by the ads during the first days of spot advertising than East German voters.

Considerable differences were shown for respondents according to party preference. The percentage of voters who identify with either of the two big parties (SPD or CDU) or with the Greens and who had already seen party spots did not differ much from the overall mean, whereas voters of the other two smaller parties showed deviant results: Only 26% of those who tended to vote for the Free Democrats said they had already watched party spots. Voters in the PDS, however, stood in sharp contrast to the other groups: 42% of PDS voters had been reached by party advertising by the end of August. The PDS was also the party that attributed the highest relevance to political advertising on public television (IP Deutschland, 2002).

According to telemetric measurements, 61% of the voting-age audience was reached by the spots that were broadcast on public television over the 4-week period. This means that 36 million Germans saw at least one spot during the "run-up" phase (the last few weeks) of the campaign. The average number of spots watched by an individual viewer was 4.4 (D. K. Müller, 2002, p. 624).

Because of their surprise effect, television ads are considered more effective in reaching uninterested voters than other campaign channels. In fact, as a study by Schmitt-Beck (1999) showed, the difference between the number of voters with low political interest and the number with high interest in politics reached by TV spots is lower than that of other campaign channels. Only campaign posters, a medium that simply cannot be avoided, fare better in this respect. Thus, overall, the effectiveness of posters and television ads in reaching the uninterested members of the electorate is above average. The Schmitt-Beck (1999) study also revealed that attention to ads produced either by SPD or CDU is considerably higher than for the smaller parties. This may be an effect of the higher number of slots that the two big parties are allotted on public television. Both parties also buy airtime on commercial channels. Therefore, the chance of catching a spot by one of the big parties is higher than that for the ads by smaller parties. These findings may also be a result of the higher visibility of the big parties in general.

Due to the growing number of television channels in Germany, which has led to a decrease in the overall market share of the individual channels, the audience ratings for electoral ads have also gone down but are still high, particularly when compared to other campaign channels. However, audience ratings alone do not tell us much about acceptance and attention and even less about the effects of campaign advertising. However, little is known about the impact of electoral advertising on voters in Germany. Of course, parties are mostly interested in the ads' influence on voting decisions, but it is almost impossible

to isolate the impact of spots among the many different campaign channels. Asking voters directly whether the ads influenced their voting decision would probably lead to underestimation of the ads' influence, because people usually do not want to admit to being influenced by advertising. In fact, ads ranked only ninth among 14 campaign channels when voters were asked which channel they regarded as "very important" or "important" for their electoral information (Zentrum für Umfragen, Methoden und Analysen, 2002). Against this background, it comes as a surprise that another survey found that about 26% of the voters, asked for the role political ads play for their voting decision, said the spots were "very important" or "important" ("Glotze ohne Einfluss," 2002).

COGNITIVE AND ATTITUDINAL EFFECTS OF TV ADS

Even though the ads reach a good share of the electorate, their direct influence on voting decisions is not very likely. In addition to producing indirect effects through attitudes and images, the ads have proved their effectiveness in providing viewers with information about the campaign and the election and in changing the perception of relevance attributed to campaign issues.

The high number of respondents naming ads when they are asked where they get information about an ongoing campaign speaks to the informational function of television advertising. Television ads, like campaign posters, seem to work almost like signals announcing an upcoming election. The surprise effect of the ads ensures that viewers are caught by ads of parties almost unknown to them. In fact, more than 50% of the respondents in a survey conducted in 1994 agreed that the ads draw their attention to parties and groups about which they have not heard much before. However, this knowledge remains mostly superficial, because only one third said that they also learned about the program of the parties (Kliment, 1994).

Party ads also have an effect in changing the relevance that is attributed to a campaign issue. Against the background that it is one of the main campaign objectives of the parties to put their own issues on the public agenda and to make sure that other issues do not become the subject of discussion, the agenda-setting effect becomes an important function of the ads. A study on the general election campaign in 1990 indeed found that the spots were effective in playing down an issue (Semetko & Schoenbach, 1994).

Schmitt-Beck (1999) also attributed to ads a catalytic function, which refers to the ads' impact on voters' involvement during the campaign. Findings from several studies can be interpreted in this way. During the 1990 election campaign, ads enhanced interest in what was going on in the campaign (Semetko & Schoenbach, 1994). Interest in turn is an important condition for further attention to the campaign and for voting. A similar effect appeared during the European election campaign in 1989, during which viewing of the ads led voters to form an image of the ongoing campaign: Those who had seen spots were more inclined or able to evaluate the campaign as either positive or negative (Holtz-Bacha, 1990).

In addition, the same study showed that viewing the ads can have an effect on attitudes, which could then influence voting or even the direction of the votes. Viewing the ads improved viewers' perspective on the European Parliament; those who did not see the spots regarded the parliament as a less important institution. Similar findings were found for attitudes about EC membership and the speed of European integration (Holtz-Bacha, 1990).

Studies from several parliamentary elections in Germany found that the ads affected viewers' perspective on candidate images, which could be expected to influence voting

intention as well. In experimental settings, viewing the ads in some cases led to changes in overall sympathy for the chancellor candidates. At the same time, respondents changed their evaluation of candidate images on a semantic differential scale. However, the direction of the changes was heterogeneous, with some attributes graded higher and others lower after respondents had seen the ads. Differences seen at the beginning of the 1990s between East and West Germans in pre- and posttest evaluations of the candidates disappeared over the years, but gender differences in reactions to the ads proved to be consistent (Holtz-Bacha & Kaid, 1996; Kaid & Tedesco, 1999). Real-time-response measurements allowed assessment of those parts of the ads that elicited the strongest reactions from the viewers. Findings in Germany confirmed similar results from the United States showing that subjects particularly respond to emotional appeals but not necessarily in a positive way (Kaid, 1996).

CONCLUSION

Due to the German legal framework, electoral TV ads are different in relevance for smaller and bigger parties. Because public channels are obliged to broadcast party spots for free, TV advertising provides a great chance for the smaller parties, particularly for those that are almost unknown to the electorate. Even low market shares guarantee an audience that these parties would never draw with any other campaign event. They are unable to purchase airtime on commercial television, so the slots allotted to them on the public channels provide them with the opportunity to speak to the voters directly. Thus they at least demonstrate that they are present in the electoral contest.

Nevertheless, German regulation of political advertising, in the end, works in favor of the larger, and therefore richer, parties. Although the equal opportunity principle has again and again been emphasized by the courts, they were unable to legislate it, and the system continues to work to the advantage of the big parties, which are allotted more spots on public television and have the means to produce additional spots and buy broadcasting time for discounted spot prices on commercial channels.

In spite of these advantages, the trend seems to indicate that the interest of the larger parties in this campaign channel is decreasing. The reason given by advertising experts concerns the specific conditions under which the individual ads are aired: Both public and private TV stations are unhappy with the obligation to broadcast political advertising. Therefore, they apply a dissociation strategy to emphasize that they do not take responsibility for the content of the ads. The announcements that serve this strategy point to the persuasive character of the spots and counter the surprise effect on the viewers. Thus these disclaimers are detrimental to the interests of the parties. General conditions, however, still predicate nothing about the style and content of German electoral TV ads, and the parties are left with plenty of possibilities in their own advertising strategies, presenting themselves to the voters in the way they think is most effective.

In Germany, electoral advertising on television is only one campaign instrument among several, and it is definitely not the most important. In a survey conducted about 3 weeks before election day in 2002, TV ads ranked ninth among 14 campaign channels when people were asked where they got information about the campaign (Zentrum für Umfragen, Methoden und Analysen, 2002). Another study asked campaign managers about the importance they attributed to TV ads. On the average, TV ads were rated 5 on a scale ranking from 0 to 10 (with 10 being the highest). The same study showed that most campaign managers attributed less relevance to TV ads in 2002 than they did in 1998 (M.G. Müller, 2002). Thus, not only do voters get more information through other campaign

channels (and in Germany they prefer to rely on traditional media reporting and posters), but those who are actually responsible for managing the campaign also do not have much faith in TV advertising. In addition, what confidence there was in TV is on the wane.

REFERENCES

Becker, J. (1990). Wahlwerbung politischer Parteien im Rundfunk [Broadcast electoral advertising by political parties]. In J. Becker (Ed.), *Symposium zum 65. Geburtstag von Ernst W. Fuhr* [Symposium on the 65th birthday of Ernst W. Fuhr] (pp. 31-40). Baden-Baden, Germany: Nomos.

Bornemann, R. (1992). Ideenwerbung im Rundfunk [Ideological advertising in broadcasting]. In Bayerische Landeszentrale für neue Medien (Ed.), *BLM Jahrbuch 92: Privater Rundfunk in Bayern* [BLM yearbook '92: Private broadcasting in Bavaria] (pp. 127–138). München, Germany: R. Fischer.

Dröge, F., Lerg, W. B., & Weissenborn, R. (1969). Zur Technik politischer Propaganda in der Demokratie. Analyse der Fernseh-Wahlwerbesendungen der Parteien im Wahlkampf 1969 [The techniques of political propaganda in a democracy: Analysis of party electoral advertising on television during the 1969 election campaign]. In *Fernsehen in Deutschland. Die Bundestagswahl 1969 als journalistische Aufgabe* [Television in Germany: The 1969 Bundestag elections as a journalistic task] (pp. 107–142). Mainz, Germany: Hase & Koehler.

Franke, E. (1979). *Wahlwerbung in Hörfunk und Fernsehen. Die juristische Problematik der Sendezeitvergabe an Parteien* [Electoral advertising on radio and television: The legal problem of assigning time slots to parties]. Bochum, Germany: Studienverlag Dr. N. Brockmeyer.

Gabriel-Bräutigam, K. (1991). Wahlkampf im Rundfunk. Ein Beitrag zur Problematik von Drittsendungsrechten [The election campaign in broadcasting: A contribution to the problem of third-party rights to a time slot]. *Zeitschrift für Urheber- und Medienrecht, 35*, 466–478.

Geiger, S. F., & Reeves, B. (1991). The effects of visual structure and content emphasis on the evaluation and memory for political candidates. In F. Biocca (Ed.), *Television and political* advertising, *Volume I: Psychological processes* (pp. 125–143). Hillsdale, NJ: Erlbaum.

Glotze ohne Einfluss [The tube without influence]. (2002, August 26). *Focus*, p. 167.

Holtz-Bacha, C. (1990). Nur bei den Wasserwerken Effekte? Eine Studie zur parteipolitischen Spot-Werbung vor Europawahlen [Effects at the waterworks only? A study of party political spots before the European elections]. *Medium, 20*, 50–53.

Holtz-Bacha, C. (2001). *Wahlwerbung als politische Kultur. Parteienspots im Fernsehen 1957-1998* [Electoral advertising as political culture: Party spots on television, 1957-1998]. Wiesbaden, Germany: Westdeutscher Verlag.

Holtz-Bacha, C. (2003a). Political advertising during election campaigns. In P. J. Maarek & G. Wolfsfeld (Eds.), *Political communication in a new era* (pp. 95–116). London: Routledge.

Holtz-Bacha, C. (2003b, May). *To the advantage of the big parties but they seem to lose interest—TV advertising during the 2002 German national election campaign.* Paper presented at the Annual Conference of the International Communication Association, San Diego, CA.

Holtz-Bacha, C. (2004a, June). *Advertising à l'Américaine? The development of electoral TV advertising in Germany and why the U.S. model cannot succeed here.* Paper presented at the Workshop on Internationalization or Political Marketing: Americanization or Plain Globalization?, Paris.

Holtz-Bacha, C. (2004b). Germany: From modern to postmodern campaign. In J. Roper, C. Holtz-Bacha, & G. Mazzoleni, *The politics of representation: Election campaigning and proportional representation* (pp. 77–97). New York: Lang.

Holtz-Bacha, C. (2004c). Germany: The "German model" and its intricacies. In J. Roper, C. Holtz-Bacha, & G. Mazzoleni, *The politics of representation: Election campaigning and proportional representation* (pp. 9–27). New York: Lang.

Holtz-Bacha, C., & Kaid, L. L. (1993). Wahlspots im Fernsehen. Eine Analyse der Parteienwerbung zur Bundestagswahl 1990 [Electoral spots on television: An analysis of party advertising before the 1990 Bundestag elections]. In C. Holtz-Bacha & L. L. Kaid (Eds.), *Die Massenmedien im Wahlkampf. Untersuchungen aus dem Wahljahr 1990* [The mass media in the election campaign: Research on the 1990 elections] (pp. 46–71). Opladen, Germany: Westdeutscher Verlag.

Holtz-Bacha, C., & Kaid, L. L. (1996). Parteienspots im Bundestagwahlkampf 1994—Inhalt und Rezeption ["Simply the best": Party spots in the 1994 Bundestag election campaign—contents and reception]. In C. Holtz-Bacha & L. L. Kaid (Eds.), *Wahlen und Wahlkampf in den Medien. Untersuchungen aus dem Wahljahr 1994* [Elections and election campaigns in the media: Research on the 1994 elections] (pp. 177-207). Opladen, Germany: Westdeutscher Verlag.

Holtz-Bacha, C., Kaid, L. L., & Johnston, A. (1994). Political television advertising in Western democracies: A comparison of campaign broadcasts in the United States, Germany, and France. *Political Communication, 11*, 67–80.

Holtz-Bacha, C., Lessinger, E.-M., & Hettesheimer, M. (1998). Personalisierung als Strategie der Wahlwerbung [Personalization as strategy in political advertising]. In K. Imhof & P. Schulz (Eds.), *Die Veröffentlichung des Privaten—die Privatisierung des Öffentlichen* [The publication of the private—the privatization of the public] (pp. 240–250). Opladen, Germany: Westdeutscher Verlag.

IP Deutschland. (2002, August). (Survey). Berlin: Author.

Jakubowski, A. (1998). *Parteienkommunikation in Wahlwerbespots. Eine systemtheoretische und inhaltsanalytische Untersuchung zur Bundestagswahl 1994* [Party communication in electoral advertising spots: A systems theory and content analysis investigation of the 1994 Bundestag elections]. Opladen, Germany: Westdeutscher Verlag.

Joslyn, R. A. (1980). The content of political spot ads. *Journalism Quarterly, 57*, 92–98.

Kaid, L. L. (1996). "Und dann, auf der Wahlparty . . ." Reaktionen auf Wahlwerbespots: Computergestützte Messungen ["And then, during the electoral party...." Reactions to electoral advertising spots: Computer-assisted evaluations]. In C. Holtz-Bacha & L. L. Kaid (Eds.), *Wahlen und Wahlkampf in den Medien. Untersuchungen aus dem Wahljahr 1994* [Elections and election campaigns in the media: Research on the 1994 elections] (pp. 208-224). Opladen, Germany: Westdeutscher Verlag.

Kaid, L. L., & Holtz-Bacha, C. (1995). Political advertising across cultures: comparing content, styles, and effects. In L. L. Kaid & C. Holtz-Bacha (Eds.), *Political advertising in Western democracies: Parties and candidates on television* (pp. 206–227). Thousand Oaks, CA: Sage.

Kaid, L. L., & Sanders, K. R. (1978). Political television commercials: An experimental study of type and length. *Communication Research, 5,* 57–70.

Kaid, L. L., & Tedesco, J. (1999). Die Arbeit am Image. Kanzlerkandidaten in der Wahlwerbung. Die Rezeption der Fernsehspots von SPD und CDU [Working on the image. Candidates for chancellor in electoral ads: Reception of the SPD and CDU's television spots]. In C. Holtz-Bacha (Ed.), *Wahlkampf in den Medien—Wahlkampf mit den Medien. Ein Reader zum Wahljahr 1998* [The election campaign in the media—campaigning with the media: A reader on the 1998 elections] (pp. 218–241). Opladen, Germany: Westdeutscher Verlag.

Kliment, T. (1994, July). Orientierung im Wahlkampf oder nur Propaganda? Wahlwerbespots im Urteil der Bevölkerung. Eine Repräsentativumfrage in Hessen [Campaign orientation or just propaganda? Electoral advertising spots in the judgment of the people: A representative inquiry in Hessen]. *Media Perspektiven,* 419–427.

Lessinger, E.-M. (1997). *Politische Information oder Stimmenfang? Eine explorative Studie zum Kommunikationsstil in Wahlwerbespots der Bundestagswahlen von 1976 bis 1994* [Political information or just snatching for votes? An explorative study of communication styles in electoral advertising spots in the Bundestag elections of 1976-1994]. Unpublished master's thesis, Ruhr-Universität Bochum, Germany.

Müller, D. K. (2002, December). ARD und ZDF als Werbeträger nach 20.00 Uhr [ARD and ZDF as advertising media after 10:00 p.m.]. *Media Perspektiven,* 623–628.

Müller, M. G. (2002, December). Parteienwerbung im Bundestagswahlkampf 2002 [Party advertising in the 2002 Bundestag election campaign]. *Media Perspektiven,* 629–638.

Rudd, R. (1986). Issues as image in political campaign commercials. *Western Journal of Speech Communication, 50*(2), 102–118.

Schmitt-Beck, R. (1999). *Wirkungen der Parteienwerbung im Fernsehen* [The effects of party advertising on television]. Unpublished manuscript, Mannheim, Germany.

Schulze-Sölde, A. (1994). *Politische Parteien und Wahlwerbung in der dualen Rundfunkordnung* [Political parties and electoral advertising in the dual broadcast system]. Baden-Baden, Germany: Nomos.

Semetko, H. A., & Schoenbach, K. (1994). *Germany's "unity election": Voters and the media.* Cresskill, NJ: Hampton.

Shyles, L. (1986). The televised political spot advertisement: Its structure, content, and role in the political system. In L. L. Kaid, D. Nimmo, & K. R. Sanders (Eds.), *New perspectives on political advertising* (pp. 107–138). Carbondale: Southern Illinois University Press.

Wachtel, M. (1988). *Die Darstellung von Vertrauenswürdigkeit in Wahlwerbespots. Eine argumentationsanalytische und semiotische Untersuchung zum Bundestagswahlkampf 1987* [The presentation of trustworthiness in election advertising: An analysis of arguments and a semiotic study of the 1987 national election campaign]. Tübingen, Germany: Max Niemeyer.

Wilke, J., & Reinemann, C. (2000). *Kanzlerkandidaten in der Wahlkampfberichterstattung. Eine vergleichende Studie zu den Bundestagswahlen 1949-1998* [Chancellor candidates in election campaign reporting: A comparative study of the Bundestag elections of 1949-1998]. Köln, Germany: Böhlau.

Wilke, J., & Reinemann, C. (2003). Die Bundestagswahl 2002: Ein Sonderfall? Die Berichterstattung über die Kanzlerkandidaten im Langzeitvergleich [The 2002 Bundestag elections: A special case? A comparison of the reporting on the chancellor candidates over the long term]. In C. Holtz-Bacha, (Ed.), *Die Massenmedien im Wahlkampf: Die Bundestagswahl 2002* [The mass media in the election campaign: The 2002 Bundestag elections] (pp. 29–56). Wiesbaden, Germany: Westdeutscher Verlag.

Zentrum für Umfragen, Methoden und Analysen. (2002, September 4-17). *Wahlplakate* [Election posters] (Survey). Unpublished raw data, Mannheim, Germany.

11

Political Advertising on Television in the Nordic and Baltic States

TOM MORING

OVERVIEW OF THE POLITICAL SYSTEMS

This chapter will take a comparative look at political campaigning in the five Nordic states and the three Baltic states. It will focus on political advertising on television. Although there is no such thing as a "Nordic political system" or a "Baltic political system," there is an apparent difference between the group of Nordic states and the group of Baltic states. This difference is not only due to recent history but has paralleled the cultural development of Northern Europe. The shared political history of the Scandinavian states has been supported by common rule and mutually intelligible Scandinavian languages. Because of this, the Nordic states form a region that is more internally homogeneous, whereas the Baltic states, due to more recent historical events, form a region that is more homogeneous in its external relations.

The Nordic states will here be treated as one group and the Baltic states as another. The reader should, however, not be misled: The internal differences within these two groups of states are not minor. Quite the opposite—we are talking about eight distinct states with separate historical and societal features. The Nordic states consist of Denmark, Finland, Iceland, Norway and Sweden; the Baltic states are Estonia, Latvia, and Lithuania. Table 11.1 summarizes some of the contextual features that are relevant to the theme of this article.

System Features of the Nordic States

There have been efforts to present the political system of the Nordic states within one systematic framework (Berglund & Lindström, 1978; Peterson, 1984). This is justified during the historical period of party formation, the development of a welfare system, and the development of a modern society from the late 19th century until the 1970s. A main common feature was a multiparty structure, consisting of five parties, with predominant roles for the social-democratic party, the conservative party, and the agrarian party, complemented

Table 11.1 The Nordic and Baltic States in Political Context

State (Type of Government)	Types of Elections (Number of Years Between Elections)	Voting System	Number of Parties in Parliament (2005)	Name of Parliament (Number of Members)	Population in 2003 and Linguistic and Ethnic Distribution (%)
Estonia (Republic)	Local (4) Parliamentary (4) EU (5) Referenda (president elected by parliament, or if this fails, by an electoral body comprising MPs and representatives of local councils)	Proportional List (for compensation mandates) and personal 5% threshold	6	Riigikogu (101)	1.36 million Distribution in 2000: Estonians (67.9), Russians (25.6), Ukrainians (2.1), Belorussians (1.3), Finns (0.9), foreign nationals and non-nationals (20)[b]
Latvia (Republic)	Local (4) Parliamentary (4) EU (5) Referenda (president elected by parliament)	Proportional List (with possibility for preferential indication of candidate) 5% threshold	8	Saeima (100)	2.33 million Distribution in 2000: Latvians (57.7), Russians (29.6) Belorussians (4), Ukrainians (2.7), Poles (2.5), Other (3.7), foreign nationals or non-nationals (26)[b]
Lithuania (Republic)	Local (4) Parliamentary (4) Presidential (5) EU (5) Referenda	Proportional List in a multimember constituency, with 5% threshold Majority and personal in single member constituencies and in presidential elections	7	Seimas (141)	3.46 million Distribution in 2001: Lithuanians (83.5), Poles (6.7), Russians (6.3), Belorussians (1.2), Ukrainians (0.7), Other (1.6), foreign nationals (1)[b]
Denmark (Parliamentary democracy, monarchy)	Local (4) Parliamentary (4) EU (5) Referenda	Proportional Mixed list and personal 2% threshold	7 (+ four regional seats)	Folketinget (179)	5.38 million Distribution in 2002: Danish (ca. 95), Germans (ca. 0.3, as of 1990), foreign nationals (4.9)

(Continued)

State (Type of Government)	Types of Elections (Number of Years Between Elections)	Number of Parties in Parliament (2005)	Name of Parliament (Number of Members)	Voting System	Population in 2003 and Linguistic and Ethnic Distribution (%)
Finland (Republic)	Local (4) Parliamentary (4) Presidential (6) EU (5) Referenda	8	Eduskunta (200)	Proportional Personal (according to the d'Hont system)	5.21 million Distribution in 2003: Finnish (92), Swedish (5.6), Sami (0.03), foreign nationals (2.0)
Iceland (Republic)	Parliamentary (4) Presidential (4) Referenda	5	Althingi (63)	Proportional List and personal 5% threshold (pertains to 9 "equalization seats")	0.29 million Distribution in 2003: Icelandic (96.5), foreign nationals (3.5)
Norway (Parliamentary democracy, monarchy)	Local (4) Parliamentary (4) Referenda	8	Stortinget (165)	Proportional List	4.55 million Distribution in 2004: Norwegian, (ca. 95); Sami (ca. 1; foreign nationals (4.3)
Sweden (Parliamentary democracy, monarchy)	Local (4) Regional (4) Parliamentary (4)[a] EU (5) Referenda	7	Riksdagen (349)	Proportional List (with possibility for preferential indication of candidate) 4% threshold (12% locally)	8.94 million Distribution in 2001: Swedish (90–92); Finnish (ca. 3–5); Sami, Roma, and Yiddish (ca 0.4); foreign nationals (5.3)

a. Local, regional, and parliamentary elections are held simultaneously in Sweden.
b. Data from the 2000 and 2001 population censuses according to *Rahvastiku kodakondsuskoosseisust Eestis ja teistes Euroopa riikides* (The composition of the population in Estonia and other European countries), which is available (only in Estonian) on the Web site of the Statistical Office of Estonia (http://www.stat.ee) under the heading "Statistics/Statistical publications/e-publications 2005."

Note: The statistics for this table were obtained from the National Statistics Offices and official parliament and government Web sites of Denmark, Estonia, Finland, Iceland, Latvia, Lithuania, Norway, and Sweden. In addition, the following sources were used: Article 3 from the *Report Submitted by Denmark* on the Council of Europe Web site (http://www.humanrights.coe.int/Minorities/Eng/FrameworkConvention/StateReports/1999/denmark/Article_3.htm), *Estonica: Encyclopedia About Estonia* ("Local government," 2000; http://www.estonica.info/eng/lugu.html?menyy_id=336&kateg=39&nimi=&alam=48&tekst_id=337), *Eurostat Yearbook 2004* (http://epp.eurostat.cec.eu.int/cache/ITY_OFFPUB/KS-CD-04-001-2/EN/KS-CD-04-001-2-EN.PDF), the LaborLawTalk Encyclopedia ("Elections in Norway," n.d., http://encyclopedia.laborlawtalk.com/Elections_in_Norway), the *OECD Factbook* (http://fiordiliji.sourceocd.org/factbookpdfs/01-02-01.pdf), Baltic Voices (Rose & Berglund, 2005, http://www.balticvoices.org/BVindex.html?estelex.htm), and the Official Gateway to Sweden Web site ("The Swedish population," n.d., http://www.sweden.se/templates/cs/BasicFactsheet_6048.aspx). Immigrant populations have been calculated according to residents with foreign citizenship as a percentage of the entire population. Where available, linguistic divides between nationals have been accounted for separately. All sites were retrievable as of December 20, 2005.

by a smaller liberal party and a left-wing socialist party. Despite a common political culture, the heterogeneity in the international orientation of the Nordic states is striking. Denmark, Norway, and Iceland are members of the North Atlantic Treaty Organisation (NATO). Denmark, Finland, and Sweden are now members of the European Union (EU).

From the 1970s onwards, the Nordic political scenery started to change. With only a few exceptions, the main parties within the old party system have remained but not with the same balance as before. The changes have been only partly uniform. Except in Denmark, liberal parties have been weakened or even disappeared. Except in Finland, centre parties with agrarian roots have lost their role as being among the major players in the political field. New parties have entered the scene; most significantly the green parties and Christian Democrats; but a variety of populist parties on the right have emerged as well—most significantly, the Progress Party in Norway and the Danish People's Party in Denmark.

All Nordic states are multiparty societies, with proportional elections. Compared to the Baltic states, the political stability between parties is very high, although volatile voting has increased during recent decades. As noted earlier, this has also changed the party structure. Denmark, Iceland, and Sweden apply voting thresholds (2%, 5%, and 4%, respectively, of the votes cast, with some modifications in the different states). The number of parties with seats in the parliament has risen to seven (in Iceland, five). In Finland and Norway, which do not apply such thresholds, eight parties have seats in the parliament (see Table 11.1).

Although the political systems of the Nordic states show differences, there are features that some of them have in common. Three states (Denmark, Norway, and Sweden) are parliamentary monarchies, with a traditionally strong position for the prime minister and periods in which the Social Democratic

Party was predominant. These states (and, partly, Iceland) also have list elections, meaning that voters vote for lists presented by the parties (again, with some modifications in each state). Unlike these states, in Finland the voter is required to cast a vote for an individual candidate in all types of elections.

System Features of the Baltic States

The breakdown of the Soviet Union and the subsequent liberation of the Baltic states in the late 1980s and early 1990s brought a shift in the political orientation and political systems of the Baltic states. The development toward democracy took a similar path in the three Baltic states, starting from the reemergence of a political public sphere within the framework of Glasnost during Mikhail Gorbachev's rule, via the establishment of Popular Front movements (in Estonia in April and May 1988 and some months later in Latvia and Lithuania) and other citizens' movements, to restoration of independence in 1990 and 1991 (Lauristin & Vihalemm, 2002). This change was profound and dramatic to the extent that it has been called the "Return to the Western World" (Høyer, Lauk, & Vihalemm, 1993; Lauristin & Vihalemm, 1997).

In their positioning within the international community, the Baltic states took a common path. After establishing democratic systems based on free elections, they simultaneously joined international organizations such as the United Nations (1991), NATO (2004), and the European Union (2004). This uniform behavior on the international scene should, however, not lead the analyst to consider these states to be identical. Quite the opposite: They represent a rich variety in political systems, media systems, and culture, including language and history. In particular, Estonia and Latvia also have a strong subset of ethnic Russians.

For the Baltic states, common system features of the political system are more difficult to establish than for the Nordic states. Since the early 1990s, the party systems have been in constant flux. The volatile vote is considerable, which allows far more room for campaigning effects than in the relatively stable Nordic political systems. Government crises are frequent. Since 1990, the Nordic states have had between six and eight governments; in the same period, Estonia has had 12, Latvia 13, and Lithuania 18 governments.

The Baltic states are multiparty societies, with six to eight parties represented in their parliaments (see Table 11.1). Also, all the Baltic states apply (predominantly) proportional elections. In Estonia and Latvia, there are list elections (with some modifications). Also, in Lithuania, somewhat more than half of the members of parliament are elected in a multimember constituency that applies list election. The other half comes from single-member constituencies with a personalized vote. All three states apply voting thresholds of 5%, and party change and volatility in the parliamentary assemblies have been dramatic since 1990.

The Baltic states are all republics. In Estonia and Latvia, the president is elected by parliament, but Lithuania elects its president on the basis of direct suffrage in a two-round majority system.

THE MEDIA SYSTEMS

Although the media system of the Nordic states is sometimes (after Katzenstein, 1985) said to represent a type of "social corporatism" characterized by a high degree of social organization and respect for the interest of various social partners of the welfare state, the Baltic states have in comparison been called "liberal corporatist" (Balčytienė, 2005, pp. 53-56). In addition to strong protection of freedom of the press, liberal corporatism as Balčytienė (2005, p. 56) understands it is characterized by a liberal system of media regulation.

In the Nordic media market, three conglomerates play an important role in terms of cross-Nordic ownership: Sweden's Bonnier and two Norwegian conglomerates, Orkla and Schibsted. These companies are major players in the Baltic media market as well. The Swedish Bonnier has a strong position, particularly in print media in Latvia. Norwegian Orkla has a strong position in Lithuania and Norwegian Schibsted in print and broadcast media in Estonia (Balčytienė, 2005; Harro-Loit, 2005, pp. 104-109).

The Nordic Media Systems: Stability and Regulation

The Nordic media systems have all grown according to a Northwestern European tradition. To this tradition belongs the predominance of the printed newspaper, which has maintained its relatively strong role in the media market to this day. In terms of sold and subscribed newspapers, the Nordic states rank among the top nations in circulation of printed press per capita. In a worldwide comparison, Norway, with more than 650 daily newspaper copies per 1000 inhabitants, is a leader in circulation, followed by Japan, Finland, and Sweden. These three states also present an extraordinary amount of newspaper titles: 71, 53, and 90 titles, respectively (World Association of Newpapers, 2004). The figures are considerably lower in Denmark and Iceland, partly because of a wide distribution of "free-sheets" of relatively high journalistic standard. Also in the advertising maket, the role of the newspapers is strong in the Nordic states.[1]

Traditionally, this structure has given the press a relatively strong role in election campaigns. In most Nordic states, the press has also been the dominant instrument in political advertising, together with billboards, brochures, and pamphlets. In addition, particularly in Sweden, short trailer-type films have been presented in movie theatres (Carlson, 2000;

Esaiasson, 1990; Pesonen, 1965; Pesonen, Sänkiaho, & Borg, 1993; Vigsø, 2004).

In the Nordic states, the broadcasting media system recently developed into a predominant market. The state monopoly in the broadcasting sector (except, partly, for Finland) made regulations of the media part of the welfare-state. The public service broadcasting sector is also still strong and financed by license fees, paid by all households owning a television receiver. The regulation of broadcasting is comparatively strict, the number of television channels has been kept limited, and there have been tendencies to favor first domestic, then cross-Nordic ownership structures to keep global media conglomerates off the market (Gustafsson, 2003).

There are significant differences in the development of the broadcasting systems in different Nordic states (Syvertsen, 1999), but the publicly owned broadcasting sector, financed by a license fee, continues to play a major role in the Nordic states. Private broadcasting developed in the 1990s and now has a larger audience.

The Baltic Media Systems: Testing the Limits

In the Baltic states, the "corporatist" element is present through systems of media self-regulation and through the ways in which the nation organizes itself as an owner of public service television and a regulator of private broadcasting. With a regained independence and the subsequent fast growth of the market economy in the 1990s, the media sector in the Baltic states was upset, and new structures started to emerge. The political tide was against media regulations, and unlike most of the Nordic states, political advertising on television was not prohibited.

There are several structural features of the media landscapes in the Baltic states that distinguish them from the Nordic states. First and foremost, in comparison to the Nordic states,

the relative position of television as a medium is stronger in all the Baltic states. The relatively weak position of the Baltic press is visible also in its share of the advertising market. In the Nordic states, the newspapers are still clearly market leaders in advertising, but in two of the three Baltic states, namely Latvia and Lithuania, they come in second. In Estonia, the newspapers play a more prominent role than they do in the other two Baltic states. Estonian newspapers have also succeeded in keeping a bigger share of the advertising market than television.[2]

Another structural difference between the Baltic and the Nordic states is the relatively weak position of state-owned broadcast media in the Baltic states. The audience share of daily viewing for public service stations is 34% to 44% in the Nordic states, but only 11% to 17% in the Baltic states.[3]

Unlike the Nordic states, public service television channels in the Baltic states are not financed by a television license paid by the viewers; instead, they have been allowed to carry paid advertising. In 2002, Estonia adopted legislation forbidding paid advertising on the state-owned channel, Eesti Televisioon (ETV) and installed a fee for commercial broadcasters.

The relatively weak economic position of the media, and the rather short tradition of commercial media, have introduced an aspect of bias to editorial independence witnessed by interviewees for this chapter[4] and also mentioned in the literature. Under economically pressing conditions, with little prospect for other revenues, and with weak professional journalistic culture and little attention to media quality, independent journalism is hampered by "strategies applied by various PR companies (especially in political communication)" (Harro-Loit, 2005, p. 113). Straightly put: journalistic attention, such as that seen in interviews, columns, and editorial decisions, is bought and sold on a grey market. In contradiction to expressed principles in the professional

Table 11.2   Political Advertising on Television in the Nordic and Baltic States

Country	Free Slots for Parties on Television	Paid Political Advertising Allowed or Possible	Restrictions of Party Funding
Denmark	Yes	No	No
Finland	No	Yes[a]	No
Iceland	Yes	Yes	No[b]
Norway	No	No	No[b]
Sweden	No	No	No
Estonia	No	Yes[a]	No
Latvia	Yes	Yes	Yes
Lithuania	Yes	Yes	Yes

a. There is no advertising on state or public service television. Political advertising is allowed on commercial channels.
b. Donations from abroad are not allowed.

codes of ethics in all the Baltic states, and in contradiction with regulations, the practice exists in the press and also in broadcast media.[5]

REGULATIONS THAT APPLY TO POLITICAL ADVERTISING

Gradually, television has gained more significance in political campaigning. The design and moderation of campaign television coverage is executed now by professional journalists according to the editorial principles of the media themselves. Public service broadcasters are expected to obey doctrines of fairness and balance in their coverage and to carry specific debates and other presentation programs before state elections.

With some exceptions, the principles setting the context for advertising on television are rather similar in all the states discussed in this chapter. Surreptitious advertising is not allowed; in some states (Denmark, Iceland, Latvia, and Lithuania) public service broadcasters offer some, however limited, access to parties on an equal time base (J. Hansen & R. Karlsson, personal communication, January 2-3, 2006; A. Mellakauls, personal communication, January 28, 2005; "Law amending the," 1992). In the other states, the parties are not allowed free direct access to television. In these states, election programs on television are entirely moderated by journalists (except for paid political advertising, where direct access is allowed) (P. A. Bjerke & A. Lindqvist, personal communication, January 2, 2006; K.-R. Tigasson, personal communication, January 22, 2005). In all states but Iceland, there are rules regarding the transparency of party financing and rules according to which larger donations to parties or candidates must be made public.[6] In 1991, the Nordic consumer ombudsmen and the Directorate of Prices in Iceland together agreed on joint standards for television advertising based on the legislation on marketing practices in the Nordic countries. These rules, however, do not contain specific rules for political advertising (see, for example, "Television marketing," 1991, on the Danish National Consumer Agency Web site: http://www.forbrug.dk/english/dco/guidelines0/televisionmarketing0/). There is a profound difference in the regulation of paid political advertising on television. Table 11.2 shows that paid political advertising on television is not allowed in Denmark, Norway, and Sweden but is allowed in Iceland, Finland, and in all three Baltic states, with very few legal restrictions.

If we revisit the five states where political advertising is allowed, applying the comparative categories of Holtz-Bacha and Kaid (1995, pp. 11-17), we find that the regulatory framework is quite similar: (a) the sponsorship of spots is based on *party and candidate;* (b) the electoral systems include *proportional* elections in all states and *majority* elections in Finland, Iceland, and Lithuania; (c) the number and length of commercial political broadcasts are *unlimited* (although spots are normally 5–30 seconds long), and there are *no* formal restrictions on the content of political advertisements (except for Latvia's and Lithuania's requirements that political advertisements on television be marked to distinguish them from other advertisements).

The Nordic States: Restricted Campaigning on Television

In all the Nordic countries, journalistic autonomy in election coverage on press, radio, and television is the main rule. Before elections, there are party presentations and party leader debates that are moderated by professional journalists or other persons hired by the broadcast media. Even though these broadcasts may be subject to specific regulations,[7] they are still predominantly designed and moderated by professional journalists. In some cases, parties are allowed to run spots presenting their views within such election programs or in various other ways allocated free time on public service television.[8] The allocation of free time is, however, not regulated in the broadcasting legislation.

In spite of regulations prohibiting paid political advertising on television before national elections in Denmark, Norway, and Sweden, the ban has in some cases been broken or bypassed. Parties have been able to buy airtime on channels TV3 and TV5, which broadcast from outside Scandinavia and are distributed via satellite and cable. In Denmark, this loophole was blocked when the parties agreed not to use it. In the other two states, this possibility has been of minor use, as the relatively marginal role of these channels has not encouraged parties to invest in television campaigns. In Norway, the ban against political

advertising has been disobeyed by commercial broadcasters, who have considered the ban to be in contradiction to principles of free speech. The authorities have, however, in each case decided to enforce the rule against political advertising on television. In a Nordic context, Finland and Iceland are the exceptions to the rule. Iceland allows political advertising, with no particular regulations. Although surreptitious advertising and advertising that is deemed to be harmful for minors is prohibited according to the Broadcasting Act, there are no regulations on political advertising on television (Birgisdottir, 2002, pp. 24-25; Icelandic Broadcasting Act, 2000). In certain cases, the parties have tried to make agreements to limit expenditure—for example, by limiting or ruling out advertising on television before general elections—but such agreements have not been made in recent elections (Burgess & Árnason, 2002, p. 8).

With the development toward more deregulated broadcasting and professionalizing of election campaign coverage, in 1991 in Finland the prohibition of broadcasting of political ads on commercial television channels was lifted. Consequently, since then, commercial TV ads have been part of national election campaigns. Advertising on television has established its position in the campaign strategies of both parties and individual candidates in all types of national elections.

The Strictly Regulated States: Denmark and Sweden

In Denmark, the legal position of political advertising has been unclear. Prior to 2003, the parties decided to refrain from using paid political advertising when a ban on television advertising was included in the Radio and Television Act. According to this act ("Bekendtgørelse af lov," 2004, para. 76, § 3), employers organizations, trade unions, religious movements, and political parties are not allowed to broadcast advertising on television.

The act also prohibits sponsoring of programs on television and on public service radio (para. 83, § 2). The formulation of the prohibition of political advertising was still somewhat ambiguous, as it allowed single candidates to advertise. This regulation has been amended so that it also restricts advertising for political movements, elected members, and candidates of political bodies. At the same time, an additional clause was added (para. 76, § 4) prohibiting all advertising of political messages on television from 3 months before the election (or, if less than 3 months, from the moment that the date of the election is declared) until the election is over. This law entered into force in January 2005 ("Lov om ændring," 2004, p. 22).

In the 2005 election campaign, some Danish parties produced advertising spots for distribution on the Internet. Parties have also placed video copies of inserts produced for presentation programs on traditional television on the party Web sites (Krog, 2005). The display of banners in connection with, for example, sport events that are broadcast on television has been debated, and at least on one occasion this has led to a parliament complaint (Nødgaard, 1986). This complaint, however, did not lead the Danish government to take any further action on the matter.

In Sweden, the prohibition against political advertising on television derives from the radio and television law (Radio- och TV-Lag, 1996, chap. 6, § 5). According to paragraph 5, broadcasts that fall under regulations of impartiality cannot include messages that are broadcast on behalf of somebody else and aim at gaining support for political or religious opinions or opinions on matters of interest in the labor market. In Swedish commercial television broadcasters' license to broadcast, a particular clause is included that explicitly applies this paragraph to the broadcaster in question (for example, the license to broadcast of TV4, TV4:s sändningstillstånd, § 1, para. 1). Swedish parties have also been active on the Web, for example with Web videos that

presented candidates and campaign events in the EU campaign in 2004.[9]

Emerging Change?
TV Advertising in Norway

In Norway, political advertising on television is forbidden under their broadcasting act. According to this act (as amended in 1999), "broadcasters may not broadcast advertisements to promote belief systems or political ends on television" (Broadcasting Act, 2005, § 3-1, para. 3). However, in the local election campaign in Norway 2003, the commercial TV2 and a local TV station, TVVest, aired some ads for the right-wing Progress Party. TV2 interrupted the campaign when the Norwegian Mass Media Authority intervened with a fine (70,000 NRK). TV2 has referred to basic international rights and declared that the channel considers the prohibition unlawful and will ask for reparations because of lost income. TVVest interrupted its campaign when the media authorities threatened to withdraw its license.

TVVest brought the case to court as an infringement of the fundamental right of freedom of speech in accordance with the Norwegian Constitution and with Article 10 of the European Convention on Human Rights. The Norwegian Supreme Court found that the Norwegian Mass Media Authority's decision did not represent an infringement of the Norwegian Constitution regarding freedom of speech. The Supreme Court also made an assessment in relation to Article 10 of the European Convention on Human Rights and found that the decision was not in defiance of the convention. TVVest has forwarded this case to the European Court of Human Rights (European Platform of Regulatory Authorities, 2005).

Political television ads were aired "by mistake" in a campaign for the same party by TV2 in the late 1990s, with the explanation that the channel did not know that political advertising was prohibited. This campaign, too, was interrupted when the authorities intervened. The TV spot of the Progress Party from 2003, presenting the party leader, has been put on display on the Internet.[10]

In 2004, a commission assessing party financing in Norway was given the additional task of looking into alternative ways to regulate political advertising on television in case the general prohibition was lifted. In November 2004, this commission submitted a proposal to relax the ban on political advertising during a fixed time before elections (Norges offentlige utredninger [NOU], 2004).

The commission particularly looked at four alternative solutions, if the general ban against political advertising were lifted: (a) a system in which all who wish to would be allowed to publish political advertising during a fixed period[11] before elections, (b) a system in which only parties and candidate lists would be allowed to advertise during this period, (c) either system a or b with quantitative restrictions, and (d) a system based on allocation of free time to political parties during a fixed period before the elections (NOU, 2004, pp. 133-134).

The commission raised serious objections to the last alternative (allocation of free time). It noted that this system would be based on an obligation restricted to the public service company NRK. The main arguments against this solution were that it would be difficult to determine which parties were going to be given free time (and the amount of time for each party) and that it would be an infringement against the editorial freedom of the broadcaster.

Regarding possible quantitative restrictions, the commission would prefer an equal basis for all rather than restrictions based on the size of the party. The commission did not suggest particular content restrictions of a regulative character but rather saw it as the parties' duty to enter into an agreement of fair conduct in political advertising campaigns on television (NOU, 2004, p. 145).

In May 2005, the Norwegian Ministry of Culture and Church Affairs presented a different proposal. Instead of allowing limited advertising rights during the election campaign, political advertising would be banned for a limited period before elections (European Platform of Regulatory Authorities, 2005; Høringsbrev, 2005).

The Nordic Exceptions: Political Advertising on Television in Finland and Iceland

Compared to the other Nordic countries, Finland and Iceland are clearly deviant cases. In these states, advertising time can be purchased on commercial television channels for political advertising in all types of elections. There are no regulations on content or format (although there are certain self-regulatory principles imposed by the biggest broadcaster in Finland). Neither are there regulations regarding rights of third-party interests (individuals, groups, corporations) to purchase time for political advertising (again, some self-regulations are imposed by the broadcasters).

In both states, political advertising generally resembles commercial advertising. It is also aired within the same slots and without any obligatory markers that note its political nature (Moring, 2004; T. Broddason, personal communication, September 29, 2005).

In Finland, the ban against political ads was included in the internal rule system of the license holder (at the time of the ban, the Finnish Broadcasting Company was still the only license holder for on-air television broadcasts, and there was only one on-air commercial broadcaster, MTV). The ban was lifted when these rules were changed in 1991. At the same time, the commercial broadcaster bound itself to certain rules of conduct (Moring, 1995, p. 168): (a) Slots would be sold only to registered parties, (b) spots could include comparative and critical elements but not negative assessments of single candidates, and (c) political advertising should not contain other advertisement messages, such as names of sponsors or financers, logos, or products (J. Miettinen, personal communication, January 24, 2005). With the exception of the first rule, these rules were maintained when MTV got its own license to broadcast in 1993 and continued broadcasting on its own channel under the name MTV3. However, during presidential elections, slots have been sold to larger campaign organizations that have been formed, often by several parties, or as independent support groups, to support particular candidates. Later, civic movements that were not parties (e.g., labor unions), were allowed to participate and air political advertising in other election campaigns. Thus the first rule is not applied in practice, at least not in a strict sense. The second and third rules still stand as a self-regulatory system for MTV3.

According to the internal principles of MTV3, in connection with election programs (debates, etc.), only image advertising for parties or organizations can be inserted, not advertising for single candidates. No party or organization can buy exclusive rights to appear in connection with an election program. MTV3 offers all parties a discount similar to the introductory discount offered to first-time advertisers on television (ca. 20%). There are no specific rules regarding equal pricing for political advertising, but the Finnish Communications Regulation Authority monitors fair conduct in the pricing of all advertising on television (J. Miettinen, personal communication, January 24, 2005).

In practice, the second nationwide commercial channel (Nelonen) follows the same rules but without any formal self-regulatory system. The reason for this is that MTV3 is the market leader, and separate spots have still been produced only rarely just for airing on other channels. Nelonen, however, does not have a formalized rule of conduct but applies the general ethical code for advertising in Finland to political ads (H. Edin, personal communication, August 15, 2003). Thus, in theory, a

party or candidate could produce personal attack ads to be aired on Nelonen that could not be aired on MTV3. This has, however, not happened in practice.

In addition to these self-imposed rules and general ethical rules and legislation, there are no separate rules for political advertising on television in Finland. The sole limiting factors are the comparatively high price of television advertising and a new regulation that obligates candidates to make public the relevant sources of their campaign financing. According to some of the campaign leaders of the parties (Moring, 2005), the new regulation has somewhat decreased the willingness of some sponsors to contribute to the fund-raising of candidates.

In a legal sense, it remains unclear whether political advertising on television and radio in Finland is to be considered advertising at all. When a general regulative framework was installed in 1998 to adjust Finnish media legislation to the EU's Television Without Frontiers Directive (European Parliament & Council of 30, 1989), an effort was made by the authorities to include issue and ideological advertising within this framework. In the government proposition, such advertising was included within the definition of paid advertising. The Constitutional Law Committee, however, argued that this was against the principles of freedom of expression in Article 10 of the Finnish constitution, and the specific mention of issue and ideological advertising was left out of the law.

Thus it remains an open question what the supervisory body in Finland would do if political advertising broke the advertising rules set by the Television Without Frontiers Directive (European Parliament & Council of 30, 1989). So far the commercial broadcasters have followed these rules for political advertising. They have not exceeded the maximum time limits for political advertising and have refrained from broadcasting political advertising outside slots designated for commercial breaks. Also, the Finnish Communications Regulation Authority treats political advertising like any other type of advertising, according to those regulations falling under the directive (Moring, 2004).

A Free-Market Model: Political Advertising on Television in the Baltic States

The culture of commercial advertising (as it is known in older market economies) is still rather weak in the Baltic states. This partly explains why the border between paid and editorial contents is often blurred (I. Brikše, personal communication, October 24, 2005). The rule system, however, is today well adapted to a market economy. As part of the accession process and to harmonize with the legislation of the European Union, advertising in the Baltic states has been regulated in accordance with the principles included in the Television Without Frontiers Directive (European Parliament & Council of 30, 1989). This has brought the regulative frame of advertising in general into relative conformity. There are limits set for the amount of advertising and rules of placement requiring advertising to be distinguishable from other program content.

In the Baltic states, political advertising does not fall under media or advertising legislation. This fact is explained by the specifics of the development of the legislation in the Baltic states (Golovanov, 2005, pp. 3-4): There were plans in the early 1990s to treat political advertising in the same way as commercial advertising and to regulate it under advertising legislation. However, in practice, the law developed in another way, and political campaigning became part of electoral legislation instead.

For example, in Latvia, campaigning (the term *agitation* in law[12] means the same as *campaigning*) is considered a candidate's right. The main instruments that in practice regulate political advertising strive to equalize the input of resources of parties and candidates. Thus, in the electoral legislation of Lithuania and

Latvia, there are different instruments that regulate the amount of expenditure for different parties.[13] With some exceptions, in the Baltic states, paid political advertising is, in practice, broadcast as advertising in general. In this sense the situation is the same as in Finland and Iceland. However, media in the Baltic states are more affected by surreptitious advertising.

According to the questionnaires made for this study (see the introductory chapter to this volume), a common feature of all the Baltic states is that paid political advertising on television has become a major campaign instrument for the political parties. The campaign techniques have become professionalized, and in their presentation, the ads increasingly take on features resembling product advertising (Tigasson, 2003).

Time can be purchased on all television channels, except, as of 1998, for the public service channel ETV in Estonia (H. Šein, personal communication, February 1, 2005). In Latvia and Lithuania, political spots must be distinguished from other television advertising by labeling. Otherwise, there are few restrictions on content or form. Third parties, such as individuals, groups, or corporations, are allowed to purchase time for political advertising (although in Latvia the sponsor must be mentioned). The same rules apply to all types of elections.

The main regulatory instruments used to limit political advertising on television in the Baltic states are the rather detailed limitations regarding campaign expenditure that are applied in Latvia and Lithuania. In Latvia and Lithuania, free time is allowed but on state-owned television only. The rules for allotting free time vary. Estonian television no longer allots free time to parties or candidates.

Estonia: Coming to Terms With Media Ethics

In Estonia, since the reestablishment of independence, there have been no specific regulations on paid political advertising as such. The purchase of advertising time on private broadcasting channels has been unlimited. Separate and strict rules have been enacted only for the allocation of free slots and the length and placement of paid political ads on public service broadcasting during three elections in the 1990s.

In 1992, Estonian public service television (ETV) allowed political parties 5 to 30 minutes of free broadcast time, depending on the number of candidates. Single candidates were allowed 3 minutes each. In 1999, each party was allowed a flat 15 minutes, and single candidates were not allowed broadcasting time. In 1992 and 1995, ETV sold additional advertising time, although there was a limitation of only one spot per day. The channel also limited the length of ads to 75 seconds in 1992 and 30 seconds in 1995. Since 1997, after an agreement was made with the private broadcasters, there has been no paid political advertising on ETV. This is, however, due to a general abstention from advertising by the public service broadcaster and is not specifically an arrangement about political advertising (Tigasson, 2003, pp. 3-5). Also, the system allocating free slots on public service television was dropped after the 1999 election.

Article 6 in the Ringhäälinguseadus, the Estonian Broadcasting Act (1994), states that a broadcaster, upon granting transmission time to a political party or a political movement, shall also provide an opportunity to grant transmission time in the same program service for other political parties or movements without undue delay. There is, however, no obligation for commercial media to treat political parties equally when selling broadcast time. This gives big parties an advantage because of volume discounts and also has opened possibilities for favoritism. Airtime has been purchased to broadcast programs copying the format of normal news programs on TV. There have also been payments for participating in popular TV shows. Thus the

distinction between advertisement, sponsorship, and independent media content has been blurred (Tigasson, 2003, pp. 4-5). On the other hand, professional consciousness among journalists is reported to be on the rise, which reduces the impact of this feature in factual programs (predominantly broadcast on ETV) (H. Šein, personal communication, February 1, 2005).

Although television remains largely unregulated, outdoor advertising was regulated in Estonia after the EU parliamentary elections, during which this type of advertising was extensively debated. The new law prohibits the display of images of independent candidates, political parties, and persons running on a party ticket; party logotypes; and other symbols on the walls of buildings, vehicles of the public transport system and cabs, and other political outdoor ads. This law, however, remains in dispute within the government (Raudsaar & Tigasson 2006, p. 407; see also the *Baltic Times* Web site, n.d.). Estonian election legislation prohibits campaigning on Election Day. Public broadcasting rules also prohibit political campaigning on Election Day ("Rules for the employment," 1992, Article 2.5; Riigikogu Election Act, 1994, Article 8). Public discussion is ongoing regarding the possible need to further regulate media involvement in elections (Tigasson, 2003, p. 2).

Estonia's 1994 Law on Political Parties imposes some regulation on the transparency of party financing. Parties must regularly submit information on sources of income, and 30 days after elections, political parties must submit reports to the National Election Committee on preelection campaign expenditures and the sources of monies received. However, there have been allegations against parties for trying to circumvent this rule by establishing bogus companies (Tigasson, 2003, pp. 5-6). In addition, there have been legislative initiatives to further regulate party financing in Estonia.

Latvia: A Divided Society Merging

Regulations pertaining to political advertising in Latvia mainly concern financing and pricing. Disclosure of who has paid for the ad must be aired immediately before or after the ad is broadcast. Latvia's public service broadcaster is obligated to publish its price list for advertisements 270 days before the elections. Commercial broadcasters are obligated to give equal terms to all parties and candidates. Broadcasters are obligated to report their incomes from the parties 2 weeks after the election. Although there have been informal complaints regarding discounts to parties, and there are television stations (broadcasting in Latvian as well as in the Russian language) that in practice favor particular parties or groups of parties in their programs, no formal complaints have been raised.

The preelection laws (see note 12) regulate against advertising by broadcasters operating outside Latvia. These regulations have, however, not been enforced in practice, and Latvia's advertising regulations are circumvented by broadcasters that operate from Russia. This situation allows favoritism and has thus created inequalities between parties advertising in the Russian language. The impact of broadcasts from abroad has, however, become less substantial in Latvia with the increasing popularity of the First Baltic Channel among Russian speakers. This Latvian-based channel broadcasts in Russian over satellite and cable to all Baltic states (B. Cilevics, personal communication, January 29, 2005).

The restrictions in Latvian radio and television law apply equally to political and commercial advertising. The maximum advertising time allowed per hour (stemming from the Television Without Frontiers Directive, European Parliament & Council of 30, 1989) is, however, extended by 10% during the election campaign, beginning 40 days before the election (A. Mellakauls, personal communication, January 28, 2005). In Latvia, advertising

must also obey special language regulations. The main principle is that a broadcast is scheduled and executed in one language only. Those broadcasts that are not specifically marked as allowed to be in another language must be dubbed or subtitled in Latvian. This rule pertains also to advertising. This law is important, as Latvia has a considerable Russian-speaking population.

All television channels, including the state-owned public service channels LTV1 and LTV7, have been selling advertising time. In addition, parties have been allowed free time on the two state-owned channels. In the last parliament election, parties were allowed to use two 10-minute slots in the preelection period. The parties were allowed also to divide the 10-minute slots into smaller sections.

The main regulations affecting political advertising on television are, however, embedded in rules regarding campaign financing. According to the Law on Financing of Political Organizations (as amended in 2004), there are limits on the total amount of money that the parties may spend for their preelection campaigns, including advertising. A party may not spend more than 0.20 LVL (about € 0.28) per voter in the area the election concerns (the whole state, or regions where the party has candidates). This limit concerns the entire campaign and does not distinguish between types of media used ("Analysis of the political," 2005, p. 10).

Before this legislation was enacted, Latvian election expenditure skyrocketed, with an estimated cost of 2.80 LVL per eligible voter (compared to $1.71 in the United States and £0.40 in the United Kingdom). Five parties exceeded the current limit; the most expensive campaign cost 0.90 LVL per eligible voter (Čigāne, 2002a). The new legislation was enacted in the municipal elections of 2005. The financial limits for the campaign were in some cases exceeded (particularly by one party, Latvian First Party, that used more than double the allowed amount), and some fines were handed out where it was deemed necessary. According to estimates based on the tracking of advertisement volumes, however, the total party expenditure for the election campaign had shrunk to half of the expenditure in the previous election campaign in 2002 ("Analysis of the political," 2005, pp. 9-12; I. Brikše, personal communication, October 24, 2005). Neither were there any immediate signs in the opinion polls taken during the campaign of any gain for the Latvian First Party that would come even close to the party's exceeded investments in television advertising ("Analysis of the political," 2005, p. 26).

As in Estonia, there is a history of surreptitious advertising in Latvia. Recent research, however, has shown that hidden advertising has started to decrease. During the 13 days before municipal elections in 2001, an analysis of hidden advertising on television revealed a total of 215 instances of possible hidden advertising. In the 2002 parliamentary election, during a time period three times as long (39 days), 22 instances of possible hidden advertising on television were found. Although there was a general decrease in surreptitious advertising in the press, the cases in the print media were clearly more numerous than in the broadcasting media.[14] The trend continued in the 2005 municipal election; most surreptitious advertising was found in Russian language newspapers, in some Latvian language newspapers, and on one particular Russian radio station. With the exception of one commercial television channel broadcasting regionally in Latvian, the trend in television broadcasting has been toward less surreptitious advertising. The analysts note that surreptitious advertising today occupies certain lacunae in the media and that only some parties lean on it to any relevant extent anymore. On state-owned television (LTV), almost no such advertising occurred in 2005. The analysts conclude that this development is a consequence of public discussion, active involvement by the National Broadcasting Council of Latvia,

increasing journalistic professionalism, and the ethics codes recently introduced in the state radio and television broadcasting companies ("Analysis of possible," 2005; Čigāne, 2002b). On the other hand, comparing the cases of surreptitious advertising that did occur and the election results, they conclude that this advertising had some effect on the election results in 2005, as some of the parties active in this field did gain votes. The analysts point out, however, that this finding needs to be qualified by further research ("Analysis of possible," 2005, p. 18).

Lithuania: Regulated and Yet Not Regulated

Lithuania recently adopted regulations regarding fair conduct of political advertising. During the 1990s, little regulation was in place. However, with the EU accession process, new regulation started to emerge (L. Ubavičius, personal communication, January 27, 2005). Political advertising on television is allowed at any time within the 30-day period before the election, but it must be distinguished from other television advertising by special labeling on each ad. This regulation was applied in the EU parliamentary election in 2004, although it was not yet part of the legislation. There is a comprehensive monitoring system covering all the national television channels, carried out by the Lithuanian Radio and Television Commission in cooperation with TNS Gallup. Political advertising is, however, exempted from the time constraints imposed by the Television Without Frontiers Directive (European Parliament & Council of 30, 1989) (N. Maliukevičius, personal communication, January 27, 2005).

Parties are allowed free time on state-owned public service television as a part of discussion programs. According to Article 51 of the Law on Elections to the Seimas ("Law amending the," 1992), the Central Electoral Committee shall allocate time for the programs following principles of equality. Each list of candidates shall be allocated no less than 1 hour of state (national) radio time and no less than 1 hour of state (national) television time for a debate with other lists or with representatives from other lists. Each candidate who has been nominated or has nominated himself or herself in a single-member constituency shall be allocated at least 5 minutes of state (national) radio time. In such radio programs, candidates shall participate in a debate held for the candidates of an appropriate single-member constituency. If only one candidate participates in a program, he or she shall have a discussion with a radio program host.

In Lithuania, as in Latvia, the main instrument for regulating political campaigning is embedded in campaign financing regulations. There is a very specific system for regulating campaign financing in Lithuania that gives the Central Electoral Committee immediate control over election accounts. Similar laws exist for all types of elections (parliamentary, EU, presidential, local, and referenda). Here, the aforementioned Law on Elections to the Seimas is followed.

Campaigning in parliamentary elections is regulated according to the Law on Financing of Political Parties and Political Campaigns and Control Over Financing.[15] According to this law, additional financing from the funds received from parties or candidates for the Seimas is accumulated in a special election account opened by the Central Electoral Committee. The maximum permitted amount of money in this account is limited in parliamentary elections to 50 times the average monthly worker's wage for a candidate in a single-member constituency and 1000 times the average monthly wage for a list of candidates in a multimember constituency.

Parties (and candidates in single-member constituencies) must report their funds and expenditures within 25 days (15 days for single-member constituency candidates) after the election. A similar system applies to presidential campaigns. In presidential elections, the maximum allowed expenditure for election campaigning is calculated according to a formula limiting the expenditure for each candidate to the number of voters on the voter list, multiplied by 1.5 Lithuanian litas[16] (Law on Presidential Elections, 1992). In addition, candidates for the office of president of the Republic are paid from federal funds on an equal-shares basis for time on Lithuania's state radio and television networks, the printing of the candidate's campaign poster, and the publishing of an election program.

In Lithuania, the impartiality rule may be circumvented by privately owned media (including television channels) if they declare themselves to be supporters of a certain party or candidate. Such a declaration has to be announced 5 days before the starting date of the campaign, normally 30 days before the election (V. Bacevičius, personal communication, January 27, 2005). Also in Latvia, voices have been raised in favor of this kind of open partiality (B. Cilevics, personal communication, January 29, 2005).

POLITICAL ADVERTISING CONTENT IN FINLAND, ICELAND, AND THE BALTIC STATES

In those Nordic states that allow paid political advertising, and in the Baltic states, political advertising has come to resemble commercial advertising in general. Spots are usually less than 1 minute long, although there have been exceptions, such as the occasional longer ads in Latvia.

Another common feature is that professional advertising agencies are commonly in use, particularly by the bigger parties. In some cases, foreign consultants have been invited to design campaigns. Professionals are also involved in designing ad placement strategies to target specific audiences. In Finland, the total expenditure going into political television advertising has remained rather stable, but in the Baltic states it has tended to grow (there were no numbers available for Iceland).

Table 11.3   Share of TV Advertising Costs for the Four Largest Parties in the 2003
Parliamentary Election in Finland (in Euros)

	National Coalition Party	Center Party	Social Democratic Party	Left Alliance	Total
Campaign budget	750,000	670,000	620,000	466,000	2,506,000
TV advertising	230,000	280,000	300,000	266,000	1,076,000
Share of TV advertising (%)	31	42	48	57	43

SOURCE: Moring, 2005.

Finland: TV Ads as the Image Backbone of the Campaign

The political parties in Finland started actively to use paid political advertising on television as soon as it was allowed. The attention value of political television advertising was also high from the start. Surveys show that in domestic elections, from 1995 onwards, 70% to 80 % of the voters were able to identify ads from all three big parties (e.g., Moring & TNS Gallup Finland, 2003). Ads were designed by advertisement agencies that followed the format of product advertising. Spot lengths normally vary between 5 and 30 seconds.[17] In later years, a popular combination has been a longer party ad (about 20 seconds) followed by a "tail" for a regional candidate (5 seconds).

In content assessments, the ads were found to be predominantly image oriented (Moring & Himmelstein, 1993). This coder perception has been verified in a series of interview studies conducted by TNS Gallup Finland and the University of Helsinki since 1991. For example, in the survey conducted after the parliamentary election in 2003, 75% of the respondents said they found the ads to be predominantly image oriented, whereas 6% found them to be factually oriented and 1% did not know (Moring & TNS Gallup Finland, 2003). Although images and issues are not exclusive categories, the campaign managers generally consider television advertising to be an image-making tool,

providing a backing for more factually oriented advertising in other media.[18]

Political advertising on television has been more important in presidential and national parliamentary elections than in local elections or elections for the EU Parliament. For example, in the EU parliamentary election in 2004, all parties except one (the Social Democratic Party) decided not to use television advertising, as they considered the campaign candidate driven. The candidates, again, could not afford a television campaign that met the requirement of ad repetition necessary to make an impact. Thus political advertising on television was at a very low level in this election.

Table 11.3 shows party expenditures for television advertising in the 2003 parliamentary elections in Finland. Although the parties in parliamentary elections use around 40% of their campaign budget for advertising on television (Moring, 2005), candidates use only 15% to 20% (Venho, 1999, p. 33). Because the cumulative campaign budgets of the candidates are considerably bigger than the budgets of the parties, the total amount of money going into political advertising on television divides almost equally into not quite half for the candidates and slightly more than half for the parties.

All in all, in a national parliamentary election, the amount of money going to political advertising on television amounts to about € 2 to 2.5 million. Around 85% of the advertising revenues go to the biggest commercial channel (MTV3), and most of the rest to the second biggest channel, Nelonen (TV4). A small amount goes to various other channels, such as local or entertainment channels (J. Miettinen, personal communication, January 24, 2005). In 2003, when only one election (the national parliamentary election) was arranged, the share of political advertising on television was 1% of all advertising on television and 0.2% of all media advertising.[19]

Iceland

There is no research available regarding political advertising on television in Iceland. This advertising is, however, a well-established part of the campaign of parties and candidates. Advertising on television tends to be more positive than negative in tone, whereas advertising and campaign coverage in the press has sometimes been extraordinarily negative. This was particularly the case during the presidential elections in 1996, when a systematic negative campaign was financed in the press by the opponents of the leading (and in spite of the campaign, winning) candidate Ólafur Ragnar Grímsson (Blöndal, 1996; T. Broddason, personal communication, September 29, 2005).

There is little regulation of party or campaign financing in Iceland. The only legal restriction is the aforementioned rule that foreign individuals, institutions, and embassies are not allowed to support political parties. As the parties are not expected to report their expenditure, little is known about how the campaign costs are allocated between media.

Estonia: Issues and Material Values Enter

Although it was allowed in Estonia in the parliamentary election in 1992, buying broadcast time was not yet widespread among parties. By the next parliamentary election, in 1995, five commercial TV channels had been established, and party and candidate lists rapidly began to use paid airtime on private broadcasting channels. Subsequently, expenditures for political advertising have grown constantly and faster than the Estonian advertising market in general. The share of political advertising on television of the total advertising market rose from 2.8% in 1995 to 6.1% in 2002. In the campaign leading up to the European Parliamentary Election in 2004, the Estonian political parties invested about €1.3 million in the campaign, mainly on outdoor advertising and TV spots. A total of 41 TV spots with a medium length of 24.5 seconds were broadcast 1965 times, reaching more than 90% of the population. In election years, the political parties are among the most advertised "brands" (Tigasson, 2003, p. 4; Raudsaar & Tigasson, 2006, pp. 394-395).

Since 1995, the influence of various advertising and PR experts and opinion polls has grown considerably. In 1999, almost all the larger political parties used the services of public relations agencies and professional campaign managers. The services of an international political consulting firm were also used by one party in this campaign. In addition, party campaign staff has generally been professionalized. Although the importance of electronic media in election campaigns has grown continuously in Estonia, there still remains a balance between television and printed media. Professional assessments, however, indicate that the role of television among the different campaign channels has become predominant (Tigasson, 2003, pp. 7-8).

An analysis of contents shows that issue orientation in political advertising on television increased, and ads became more informative from 1992 to 2002. In 1992, issues were almost absent from the ads. The appeals were mostly based on national imagery. Gradually, political advertising has started to refer more and more to material benefits, first (in 1999) by introducing issues of taxation and economic policy, and later (in 2002) by promising direct economic benefits for the individual voter.[20] The parties have also changed their portrayal of the ethnic and linguistic cleavages in Estonia. In the beginning of the 1990s, ethnic Russians were still presented as a threat to Estonian independence. In the last two elections, the advertising has turned to an integrative strategy, emphasizing the incorporation of Russians into Estonian society (Tigasson, 2003, pp. 10-17). In the European parliamentary election in 2004, advertising returned to a national and predominantly EU-critical agenda (Raudsaar & Tigasson, 2006, p. 395; Tigasson, 2005, p. 310).

Latvia and Lithuania: Campaigns Dominated by Television

As noted, in Latvia and Lithuania the predominance of television over other types of media is stronger than in Estonia or the Nordic states. Although it is clear from interviews with analysts in the field that the Latvian and Lithuanian election campaigns are dominated by television and that political advertising plays a major role, there is no comprehensive research available that covers the development of political advertising on television (L. Čigāne, A. Mellakauls, V. Bacevičius, L. Ubavičius, personal communications, January 27-28, 2005). Considerable efforts have instead been made in research to analyze surreptitious advertising, including hidden political advertising before elections. The efforts to decrease this type of advertising have been at least partly successful.

No detailed analysis is available, but from advertisement statistics in Latvia and data describing the development in campaign expenditure, one may deduce that paid political advertising is responsible for a lion's share of the increase in advertising expenditure. Before the enactment of new legislation to reduce campaign costs in 2004, the election campaign expenditure in Latvia increased by a factor of 1.6, from the local election in 2001 to the parliamentary election in 2002 (Čigāne, 2002a, p. 7). Parties use 50% to 70% of their campaign resources for political advertising,

and television has been a major advertising medium (Čigāne, 2004, personal communication, January 28, 2005).

Researcher Lolita Čigāne (2004) has characterized advertising on television in Latvia so far as simple, impressive, and emotional but effective. The effect of television advertising is explained by a weak political tradition, reflected in lack of party loyalty, low level of membership in political parties, and a contrast between hopes and outcomes, which has led to disillusionment. She also found the voters to be focused more on image and less on substance.

The relatively sharp division between the Latvian and Russian parts of the population has led to a divided political market. It has also brought particular problems related to cross-border viewing and involvement of Russian television in Latvian election campaigns (B. Cilevics, personal communication, January 29, 2005). The magnitude of this problem is, however, not systematically charted.

Advertising spots in general in Latvia are not longer than in the other nations covered in this chapter. In 2002, on average they were 30 to 60 seconds, the shortest ones ranging from 10 to 13 seconds; in 2005, the average length was 25 seconds. However, as noted earlier, Latvian parties also air some longer ads: Shortly before elections, there have been ads lasting up to 360 seconds (6 minutes) (L. Čigāne, personal communication, January 3, 2006). The aforementioned limits in party financing have recently changed focus somewhat in Latvia, toward direct advertising through mail and outdoor advertising (I. Brikše, personal communication, October 24, 2005).

In Lithuania, systematic research on political advertising on television is scarce. Data from TNS Gallup, however, shows that political advertising has achieved an economically important role in the advertising market. Three election campaigns in 2004 were, for example, the main factor behind a general growth in advertising revenues of 20% during that year. In 2004, political campaigning rose to fifth place in media advertising (V. Bacevičius, personal communication, January 27, 2005; "Politicians fill advertising," 2004). Interviews with representatives of Lithuanian parties and politicians confirm that a main argument for maintaining free political advertising on television is its economical importance to the media (V. Bacevičius and L. Ubavičius, personal communications, January 27, 2005).

The monitoring of political advertising labeling on television, carried out by the Lithuanian Radio and Television Commission, has gradually led to obedience to this rule. Representatives of the commission consider that market dynamics have solved the problem of equal price conditions.

By the Lithuanian media regulator, however, the right of media openly to support parties or candidates is seen as a problem that jeopardizes the equal opportunity rule (N. Maliukevičius, personal communication, January 27, 2005). This question remains under debate also in Latvia, where such support is not allowed. An equally critical view against introducing broadcasters' rights to openly support parties is maintained by the representative of the National Broadcasting Council of Latvia (A. Mellakauls, personal communication, January 28, 2005). As noted above, however, this question also remains debated in Latvia.

THE EFFECTS OF TV POLITICAL ADVERTISING IN FINLAND AND THE BALTIC STATES

A Low-Impact Case: Finland

A longitudinal study that started in 1991 (Moring & TNS Gallup Finland, 2003) shows few changes in Finnish political culture that could be traced back to the rather dramatic deregulation of Finnish media and the introduction of paid political advertising on television. In the first Finnish EU parliamentary election in 1996, there were signs of more "American-style" voting than in local and national parliamentary elections. Since then, such behavioral patterns have been assumed to occur because of mediatization, and they have stabilized or even decreased. We find several indications of this: a relatively low volatility in the electorate in parliamentary elections;[21] stability in the timing of the voting decision (in recent elections, voters have not changed their decision as the election gets closer); and the choice of party over person, which has begun to regain popularity (Moring, 2006).

When seeking information to support their voting decision, most voters exhibit a marked preference for news media of the conventional type. When considering the (in a Scandinavian context) unusual level of deregulation of Finnish broadcast media (Moring, 2004), this is somewhat counterintuitive. The position of traditional sources such as television news and current affairs programs, as well as newspapers, has been strong not only among older voters but among young voters as well. The importance of TV ads has remained low. Since 1991, 20% to 30% of voters say they based their voting decision on information from news and current affairs programs on television ("much" or "very much" influence, on a four-point scale), and approximately the same share say they based their decision on newspaper writings. Usually only 5% to 10% say they based their decision on political advertising on television. Only in two elections during the 1990s (the EU parliamentary election in 1996 and the national parliament election in 1999) did the importance of TV ads reach more than 10%; since then, it has fallen to around 5%.

In comparison with the other types of elections, presidential elections in Finland are a special case. According to postelection studies conducted since 1991, television advertising appears to have had the same low impact in presidential elections as in other elections so far. However, opinion polls show rapid variations in the support for different candidates during the last 6 months before the elections.[22] Television campaigning may potentially increase its impact on the volatile electorate in these highly personalized elections.

The impact of television is, however, not easy to control. During the Finnish presidential election campaign in 2006, NBC talk show host Conan O'Brien repeatedly made jokes about an alleged similarity in appearance between himself and Tarja Halonen, the Finnish incumbent president and candidate, and also appeared in fake ads for Halonen that were broadcast on his show. The show appeared on one of the commercial channels in Finland, where it attracted much attention. A postelection study, however, shows that the program divided the voters equally into those who thought it had a favorable impact (24%) and those who thought it to be unfavorable (25%); 51% had no opinion. Young voters as well as supporters of Tarja Halonen predominantly tended to consider the effect as favorable, whereas it backfired among older voters and supporters of the competing candidate, Sauli Niinistö (Moring & TNS Gallup Finland, 2006).

Presumably High-Impact Cases:
The Baltic States

In the Baltic states, there is so far little research on the actual impact of political advertising on television. A study by the Latvian Center for Public Policy Providus (Čigāne, 2004) shows a remarkable correlation of political advertising and party support in the 2002 election. As the main advertising platform in this election was television, this would indicate that TV ads had a considerable impact. Čigāne, however, notes that disillusionment with politics has been an important factor in elections.

A compilation by the Baltic Institute of Social Science of longitudinal data covering the election campaign (Zepa & Koļesņikova, 2002) shows a mismatch between the support for parties in power and increased exposure to advertising and a match between support for parties in opposition and increased exposure to advertising in the 2002 election campaign.

This would support a conclusion that facility for voter volatility *in combination* with a high level of political advertising increases the impact of advertising. However, advertising in itself may be quite unsuccessful if there are factors such as a general disillusionment with the government working against the advertising party. All in all, it still remains unclear to what extent political advertising on television as such contributed to the development in support of Latvian parties in 2002, as the heat of the campaign was present in society and media in many other ways as well.

As has been noted in the introductory chapter to this volume, electoral advertising on television has risen to an undisputed number one position in Latvia and Lithuania, whereas its importance is somewhat lower in Estonia and still lower in Finland.

An assessment of the relative importance of electoral advertising on television was made with the help of the interviewees for this chapter. In Latvia and Lithuania, on a seven-point scale, television advertising was considered to be most important both in comparison to other paid media (as, e.g., posters, ads in newspapers, leaflets) and in comparison to other campaign channels in general (free and paid media). In Estonia, it was considered to be of more than average importance in comparison to other paid media and of average importance in comparison to other campaign channels in general. In Finland, television advertising was considered to be of average importance compared to other paid media and of less than average importance compared to other campaign channels in general.

RESEARCH OVERVIEW

In addition to the studies quoted in this chapter, there is little research available on the relative role of political advertising on television in the Baltic and Nordic states. For obvious reasons, research interest in the field has not yet emerged in states that do not have such advertising (Denmark, Norway, and Sweden). In Norway, the Norwegian state committee report on party financing (NOU, 2004) contains a comprehensive research overview and an overview of the campaign modes in all Nordic states. In Iceland, there has been no particular research on political campaigning that has focused on political advertising on television.

In Finland, the main part of research focusing particularly on political advertising on television has been done in two milieus. At the University of Helsinki, work has been done through the Swedish School of Social Science (see, for example, Moring, 1995, 2004, 2005, 2006; Moring & Himmelstein, 1993, 1996). Research based partly on the same data has been conducted at the Åbo Academi University (for example, Carlson, 2000, 2001).

The primary contributions in this field from the Baltic states are based on research conducted at Tartu University in Estonia (Raudsaar & Tigasson, 2006; Tigasson, 2003, 2005), SPC Providus in Riga, Latvia (with financing from various sources, such as the European Union, the Soros Foundation, the Society for Openness ["Delna"], the Embassy of Great Britain in Latvia, and the U.S. Embassy in Latvia; see Čigāne, 2002b, 2004; "Analysis of the possible," 2005, "Analysis of the political," 2005), and the Baltic Institute of Social Science in Riga (Zepa & Koļesņikova, 2002). As noted earlier, the development of advertising revenues is continuously charted by TNS Gallup, and the monitoring body of the Lithuanian Radio and Television Commission ensures that ads are marked as required. Media statistics for Lithuania, Latvia, and Estonia are published by the Media House, operating in the Baltic states and the nation of Belarus.

FUTURE TRENDS

The particularities of political advertising on television in those Nordic states that allow it, and in the Baltic states, vary. Not to note the smooth development in this field in Finland and Iceland would be a breach of the golden rule of a researcher. As it has been noted in many instances in this chapter, however, political advertising on television is not a very dramatic story in these two states. Neither has the openly paid political advertising on television in Estonia been a major affair; more attention has, during recent years, been given to surreptitious advertising. Also, outdoor advertising has been more debated and recently restricted by legislation.

In Latvia and Lithuania, the situation is different. In both states, strict regulations on party campaign financing have been introduced. One evident reason for this is the wish of the legislative body to restrict the use of political advertising on television. At least to some extent, this way of limiting excessive use of television advertising also seems to have been successful.

In Lithuania, the rules for campaign financing were made stricter after a political scandal that unfolded in spring 2004. It turned out that the president, Rolandas Paksas, had received a substantial donation from a Russian businessman in the 2002-2003 election campaign. President Paksas had later returned the favor by illegally granting Lithuanian nationality and revealing confidential information to the donor. He was, surprisingly, elected president of Lithuania in January 2003, with 54.9% of the vote (the incumbent, Valdas Adamkus, received 45.1%). After a Constitutional Court ruling, Paksas was forced to resign in April 2004 ("Lithuania president loses," 2004; Deloy, 2004).

In Latvia, stricter rules on campaign financing have been introduced as part of an effort to keep skyrocketing campaign costs down. In this state, there have also been allegations (although not official complaints) regarding surreptitious advertising and widespread favoritism in the media. Similar allegations have been directed at the possible interference of Russian television channels that can be viewed in Latvia (B. Cilevics, personal communication, January 29, 2005). On the other hand, as has been noted, efforts in the Baltic states to improve standards of media performance seem to have been at least partly effective.

In the future, political advertising on television in the Nordic and Baltic states will most likely maintain much of the diversity we see today. There are no signs that stricter regulations will be imposed on political advertising on television in Finland, Iceland, or the Baltic states. If successfully enacted, stricter campaign financing rules in Latvia and Lithuania are likely to decrease expensive television advertising. This may mean that other channels and formats of advertising, such as direct mail, outdoor advertising (where allowed; it could be noted that in addition to the recent Estonian prohibition mentioned above, recent amendments of the Lithuanian legislation introduced further restrictions of outdoor advertising [see "Law amending the . . . ," 1992]), and the Internet, will gain prominence. Also, in states that prohibit political advertising on television (Norway, Sweden, and Denmark), video presentations on the Web have become part of the campaign. In Denmark, parts of these presentations resemble political advertising spots on television.

In Norway, deregulation of political advertising is pending. The complexity of the situation is illustrated by the two diametrically opposed suggestions for future development being discussed at the moment in Norway. The Norwegian State Committee Report on Party Financing proposes that political advertising on television be allowed for a set period covering the most intensive election campaign and prohibited at other times. The Opinion Circulated for Comment by the Cultural and Church Department proposes that political advertising be allowed on television most of the time but prohibited during the most intensive part of the election campaign. By March 2006, no formal follow-up had been made to this proposal. Taking into consideration the political basis of the three parties forming the

Norwegian government at this time, it seemed unlikely that the legislation would move in a more liberal direction.

A new phenomenon that emerged in Finland in the national parliamentary election of 1999 and increased in popularity in the 2003 parliamentary election and the 2004 EU election was the so-called candidate selectors on the Web. The selectors allow voters to match their preferences on a set of key questions with the preferences of the candidates running in the election. A growing proportion of younger voters actively sought information from these selectors to support their voting decision (Moring & Mykkänen, 2005). As sources of information for young voters, these selectors have reached the same level of influence or even passed traditional media such as newspapers or news and current affairs programs on television.

One basic observation that underpins the analysis in this chapter expresses what could be deemed its main conclusion. The relevance of political advertising is a function not only of advertising strategies and the state of development of campaigning skills; a major feature determining its impact is the level of political stability in society as a whole. From this rises the expectation that, with the development of more stable political conditions in the Baltic states, the influence of political campaigning will decrease and approach the proportions it has in Western Europe. One possible scenario, for the Baltic states, would be that although political advertising on television will continue to play a role, this role will become less dramatic, more as it is in Finland or Iceland today.

On the other hand, there is another possible scenario, applicable also to the quite personalized presidential elections in Finland and Iceland: that advertising will become more aggressive and adversarial. This could increase its importance and perhaps lead politicians in those states that today have few rules in this field to consider the need for stricter regulation, in line with the debate going on in Estonia today.

NOTES

1. The market share ratio between television and newspapers in 2004 in Denmark was 19 and 26; in Finland, 20 and 49; in Norway, 31 and 48; and in Sweden, 25 and 40 (Denmark: Dansk Oplagskontrol, n.d.; Finland: TNS Gallup Oy, n.d.; Norway: AC Nielsen Reklame-Statistikk, 2004; Sweden: Institutet för Reklam-och Mediestatistik, 2005).

2. In Estonia, the market share ratio between television and newspapers in 2003 was 26 and 44; in Latvia, 34 and 33; and in Lithuania, 41 and 30 (Media House, 2004).

3. In 2003, the daily reach of ETV in Estonia was 47%; of LTV 1 and LTV7 in Latvia, 35% and 23%, respectively; and of LTV and LTV2 in Lithuania, 48% and 4.5%, respectively. The share of the audience of the public service companies was 16.6% in Estonia (as of 2001), 11% in Latvia (as of 2002), and 12.2% in Lithuania (as of 2003) (Media House, 2004; Radio and Television in Lithuania, Retrieved July 22, 2005, from http://www.media-house.com/company_news.php; H. Šein, personal communication, February 1, 2005). In 2004, the share of daily viewing time of the Danish TV network DR was 34% and the daily reach of its two channels was 52% and 12%. The daily viewing time share of the Finnish Yle was 44%, and the reach of its two channels was 58% and 54%. In Norway, the daily viewing time share of NRK was 43%, and the reach of its two channels was 59% and 21%. In Sweden, the daily viewing time share of SVT was 41%, and the reach of its two channels was 47% and 36% ("Media trends and," 2005).

4. The author gratefully acknowledges the following people, without whose contributing information it would not have been possible to complete this study:

Denmark: Jes Hansen, political journalist, DR

Estonia: Professor Hagi Šein, Tallinn University, and Külli-Riin Tigasson, researcher, Tartu University

Finland: Direktor Jorma Miettinen, MTV3, and Executive Vice President Hans Edin, Nelonen

Iceland: Professor Torbjörn Broddason, director of the Department for Media Studies, University of Iceland; Ragnar Karlsson, researcher, Statistics Iceland

Latvia: Andris Mellakauls, member of the National Broadcasting Council of Latvia; Lolita Čigāne, researcher, SPC Providus; Boris Cilevics, MEP, People's Concorde Party, Latvian Representative to the Committee on Legal Affairs and Human Rights of the Parliamentary Assembly of the Council of Europe; and Professor Inta Brikše, University of Latvia

Lithuania: Vaidotas Bacevičius, member of the Central Electoral Committee, Homeland Union; Executive Director Nerijus Maliukevičius, Radio and Television Commission of Lithuania; and Laimonas Ubavičius, specialist of the Information Society Development Department, Ministry of Culture

Norway: Per Arne Bjerke, political journalist, NRK

Sweden: Anders Lindqvist, political journalist, SR.

5. Article 8 of the Estonian Advertising Act, article 22 of the Latvian Law on Radio and Television, article 8 of the Lithuanian Law on Advertising (Bærug, 2005, p. 58).

6. In Estonia, Denmark, Norway, and Sweden, these rules pertain particularly to parties (in Sweden, based not on legislation but on an agreement between the parties in 1980), but in Finland, due to the individualized voting system, elected candidates must declare their campaign incomes after the election. Only in Iceland are the parties not obligated to publish their incomes (NOU, 2004, pp. 49-53, 66-71; Tigasson, 2003, pp. 5-6).

7. For example: the Administrative Council of the Finnish Broadcasting Company, appointed by the parliament, approves the outline for election programs to be aired on the Finnish Broadcasting Company (Yle). Commercial television in Sweden is bound to an impartiality clause in conducting its programs.

8. For example, Danish public service television in the 2005 parliamentary election allowed each party a 5-minute presentation in the election programs that presented the party. Many parties made these spots available on their Internet sites. As of December 22, 2005, they could still be seen via the Danish Parliament party link site (Partiernes Websider, n.d.; http://www.ft.dk/?/system/partier/partifrm.htm).

9. See, for example, the site of the Swedish Social Democratic Party (Socialdemokraterna, 2005, http://www.sap.se/).

10. The spot can be viewed at the Progress Party's Web site: http://www.frp.no/Innhold/FrP/Temasider/Valg/Valg_2003/FrPs_reklamefilm/?module=Articles;action=Article.publicShow;ID=13115.

11. The commission does not specify what it means by a fixed period but does mention either a period of 4 weeks before the election or a fixed number of weeks before the election in combination with a ban during the last week, to let the voters "rest" (NOU, 2004, p. 134).

12. The Law on Preelection Agitation Before Municipal Elections, adopted March 31, 1994, and the Law on Preelection Agitation Before Saeima and European Parliamentary Elections, adopted August 9, 1995. These laws are available only in Latvian.

13. In Estonia, in the same way as in the Nordic states, the regulation of campaign financing is limited to rules about the transparency of party or campaign financing (Tigasson, 2003, pp. 5-6).

14. In national newspapers in the Latvian language, there were 54 cases; in national Russian-language newspapers, 238 cases; in Latvian-language regional papers, 133 cases; and in Russian-language regional newspapers, 94 cases. A special case was the Russian-language regional radio station, Radio PIK, in Riga, which alone was found to have broadcast 100 surreptitious ads (Čigāne, 2002b). Also, in the municipal elections in 2005, this station stood out as a special case, with 148 cases of surreptitious advertising during a 47-day period. The station did not change its mode of conduct despite the radio authority's decision to close down the station for 3 days ("Analysis of possible," 2005, p. 12).

15. See the Web page of the Central Electoral Committee (http://www.vrk.lt/2004/seimas/agitacija_e.htm).

16. In October 2005 1 euro equalled 3.45 LTL.

17. One prominent exception was the spot aired by presidential candidate Paavo Väyrynen, Center Party, in the 1994 presidential election. At the end of the campaign, he aired a spot more than 10 minutes long (more of an *election video* type) on off-peak-hour commercial television.

18. The campaign managers Juha Kirstilä (National Coalition Party), Vesa Mauriala (Social Democratic Party), Markku Rajala (Center Party), Aulis Ruuth (Left Alliance), Ari Heikkinen and Panu Laturi (Green League), and Berth Sundström (Swedish People's Party) were interviewed after the parliamentary election in 2003 and again after the EU parliamentary election in 2004 (Moring, 2005).

19. This estimation is based on the interview with Jorma Miettinen from MTV3 (January 24, 2005), the party interviews done for Moring (2005), and overall advertising figures provided by the Finnish Association of Marketing Communication (*Mainonnan Määrä Suomessa,* 2003).

20. Tigasson (2003, p. 12) gives a series of examples from the campaign in 2002, including the Centre Party's promise that if they won the elections, all retired people in Tallinn would receive 500 kroons (€ 32) per year from the municipality and the Pro Patria Union's promise of 1000 kroons (€ 64) to every child. The Reform Party promised to decrease the income tax of every individual from 26% to 20%.

21. According to Paloheimo and Sundberg (2005, p. 198) the share of party-loyal voters in parliamentary elections has decreased from 55% to 60% of the electorate in the 1970s to 44% in 2003. The increase is, however, in the group of nonvoters, whereas the party switchers have remained at the same level, 25% to 30% of the electorate.

22. The long-time opinion poll favorite before the presidential election in 2000, Elisabeth Rehn, had more than two thirds of the support 6 months before the election. She ended up with less than 10% support. Four months before the election, the winning candidate Tarja Halonen had less than 20% support and came in last in a comparison of four main candidates (Helsingin Sanomat, 2005).

REFERENCES

AC Nielsen Reklame-Statistikk. (2004). Retrieved December 22, 2005, from the medienorge Web site: http://medienorge.uib.no/Main.cfm?ID=155&Medium=Avis&vis_resultat=YES

Analysis of the political party expenditures prior to the 2005 municipality elections. (2005, May 18). Riga, Latvia: Public Policy Center Providus. Retrieved January 26, 2006, from http://www.politika.lv/polit_real/files/lv/prieksvelgala_zin_2005_en.pdf

Analysis of possible cases of hidden advertising in media prior to 2005 municipal elections. (2005, May 12). Riga, Latvia: Public Policy Center Providus. Retrieved January 26, 2006, from http://www.politika.lv/polit_real/files/lv/Hidden%20advertisement%20final1.pdf

Balčytienë, A. (2005). Types of state intervention in the media systems in the Baltic states and Norway. In R. Bærug (Ed.), *The Baltic media world* (pp. 40–57). Riga, Latvia: Flēra.

Baltic Times. (2005). Retrieved December 22, 2005, from http://www.baltictimes.com/estonia.php

Bærug, R. (2005). Hidden advertising and TV journalism in the Baltic countries and Norway. In R. Bærug (Ed.), *The Baltic media world* (pp. 58–89). Riga, Latvia: Flēra.

Bekendtgørelse af lov om radio- og fjernsynsvirksomhed [the Danish radio and television law] (Lov. no. 506). (2004, June 10). Retrieved July 28, 2005, from http://www.kum.dk/sw13939.asp

Berglund, S., & Lindström, U. (1978). *The Scandinavian party system(s): A comparative study*. Lund, Sweden: Studentlitteratur.

Birgisdottir, G. (2002). *The evolution of new advertising techniques: Iceland*. Brussels, Belgium: Bird & Bird. Retrieved December 15, 2005, from http://europa.eu.int/comm/avpolicy/stat/bird_bird/pub_iceland.pdf

Bloomberg.com. Retrieved April 24, 2005, from http://www.bloomberg.com/apps/news?pid=10000085&sid=a_TUenSnSHQI&refer=europe

Blöndal, K. (1996, Winter). Ólafur Ragnar Grímsson, Iceland's new president. *Scandinavian Review*. Retrieved December 22, 2005, from http://www.findarticles.com/p/articles/mi_qa3760/is_199601/ai_n8748164

Broadcasting Act of 4 Dec. 1992 no 127 (as amended June 17, 2005, no. 98). (2005, September). Retrieved December 26, 2005, from the Medietilsynet Web site: http://www.smf.no/sw261.asp

Burgess, K. G., & Árnason, Á. P. (2002). *Country reports on political corruption and party financing: Iceland*. Retrieved December 22, 2005, from http://www.transparency.org/in_ focus_archive/policy/download/case%20studies/political_corruption_party_financing_iceland.pdf

Carlson, T. (2000). *Partier och kandidater på väljarmarknaden: Studier i finländsk politisk reklam* [Parties and candidates in the market for voters: Studies in Finnish political television advertising]. Åbo, Finland: Åbo Akademi University.

Carlson, T. (2001). Den politiska reklamen—konflikternas scen? [Political advertising—a scene of conflict?]. In H. Hvitfelt & L. Karvonen (Eds.), *Demokratins konflikter (Mitt i Opinionen no 5)* [Conflicts of democracy (in the center of Opinion no. 5] (pp. 78–87). Sundsvall, Norway: Demokratiinstitutet.

Čigāne, L. (2002a). *Analysis of political party expenditure and revenue before the 8th Saeima elections*. Retrieved January 29, 2006, from http://www.policy.lv/index.php?id=102629&lang=en

Čigāne, L. (2004, December 2-3). *Political advertising as an electoral campaign element in Latvia*. Paper presented at the Workshop on EU TV Regulation (IM 10514), Riga, Latvia.

Čigāne, L., with Gņedovska, E., Marteņuka, Z., Mence,L.,Ādamsone,A.,Jesina,I.,etal.(2002b, October). *Analysis of possible occurrences of hidden advertisements in the media before the 8th Saeima elections* (Mimeo). Paper presented at the conference "Openly about 8th Saeima Election Campaign Finance," Joint Project between the Soros Foundation Latvia and the Society for Openness "Delna," Riga, Latvia.

Dansk Oplagskontrol [Home page]. (n.d.). Retrieved December 22, 2005, from http://www.do.dk/

Deloy, C. (2004, June 13). *Presidential election: 13th June 2004*. Retrieved December 22, 2005, from the Fondation Robert Schuman Web site: http:// www.robert-schuman.org/anglais/oee/lituanie/presidentielle/default.htm

Elections in Norway. (n.d.). Retrieved December 26, 2005, from the Encyclopedia on Labor Law Talk Web site: http://encyclopedia.laborlawtalk.com/Elections_in_Norway

Esaiasson, P. (1990). *Svenska valkampanjer 1866-1988* [Swedish election campaigns, 1866-1988]. Stockholm, Sweden: Publica.

European Parliament & Council of 30. (1989). Council directive of 3 October 1989 on the coordination of certain provisions laid down by law, regulation or administrative action in member states concerning the pursuit of television broadcasting activities (as amended July 30, 1997, Directive 97/36/EC). Luxembourg: Office for Official Publications of the European Communities. Retrieved December 26, 2005, from http://europa.eu.int/eur-lex/en/consleg/pdf/1989/en_1989L0552_do_001.pdf

European Platform on Regulatory Authorities. (2005, May 12). *Hearing on the proposal to change the regulation of political advertising in television in Norway*. Retrieved December 22, 2005, from http://www.epra.org/content/english/index2.html

Eurostat yearbook 2004: The statistical guide to Europe. (2004). Luxembourg: Office for Official Publications of the European

Communities. Retrieved October 15, 2005, from http://epp.eurostat.cec.eu.int/cache/ITY_OFFPUB/KS-CD-04-001-2/EN/KS-CD-04-001-2-EN.PDF

Golovanov, D. (2005). Regulation of advertising in the broadcasting sector in countries of the former USSR. *IRIS Plus—Legal Observations of the European Audiovisual Observatory, 2005*(4). Retrieved December 24, 2005, from http://64.233.179.104/custom?q=cache:71XLe CxTjqgJ:www.obs.coe.int/oea_publ/iris/iris_plus/iplus4_2005.pdf.en+Golovanov&hl=en& ie=UTF-8

Gustafsson, K. E. (2003). Karl Erik Gustafssons fyra teser [The four theses of Karl Erik Gustafsson]. Retrieved January 26, 2006, from the Medier i Norden: Fokus Web site: http://www.nordicmedia.info/nmn/Nordisk/03-1fok.htm

Harro-Loit, H. (2005). The Baltic and Norwegian journalism market. In R. Bærug (Ed.), *The Baltic media world* (pp. 90–120). Riga, Latvia: Flēra.

Helsingin Sanomat (Opinion poll results, TNS Gallup, Finland). (2005, September 25). Available from TNS Gallup Oy, Itätuulenkuja 10, PL 500, FIN-02101 ESPOO.

Høringsbrev. Forslag til endringer i lov 4. desember 1992 nr. 127 om kringkasting (kringkastingsloven) om reklame for livssyn og politiske budskap i fjernsyn [Proposal for comment on an amendment in the Norwegian broadcasting law of December 4, 1992, no. 127, concerning advertising on television regarding view of life and political messages]. (2005, May 4). Retrieved December 24, 2005, from the Odin Web site: http://odin.dep.no/kkd/norsk/dok/hoering/under_behandling/043061-990105/ram001-bn.html#ram1

Høyer, S., Lauk, E., & Vihalemm, P. (Eds.). (1993). *The Baltic media's long road to freedom*. Tartu, Estonia: Baltic Association of Media Research, Nota Baltica.

Icelandic Broadcasting Act No. 53/2000. (2000, May 17). Retrieved January 3, 2006, from the Ministry of Education, Science and Culture Web site: http://eng.menntamalaraduneyti.is/Acts/nr/2429

Institutet för Reklam- och Mediestatistik (Home page). (2005). Retrieved December 24, 2005, from http://www.irm-media.se/irm/(nsomz2alt2g1igqhs23rqf45)/lilla_reklamkakan.aspx

Katzenstein, P. (1985). *Small states in world markets: Industrial policy in Europe*. Ithaca, NY: Cornell University Press.

Krog, A. (2005, January 25). *Partier på banen med politiske tv-reklamer på nettet* [Parties on track with political ads on the Web]. Retrieved October 15, 2005, from http://www.comon.dk/index.php/news/show/id=20867

Latvian Radio and Television Law, 24 August 1995 (as amended December 31, 2005). Retrieved January 4, 2006, from http://www.epra.org/content/english/press/papers/Current_Broadcasting_Law_latvia.pdf

Lauristin, M., & Vihalemm, P. (2002). The transformation of Estonian society and media: 1987-2001. In P. Vihalemm (Ed.), *Baltic media in transition* (pp. 17–64). Tartu, Estonia: Tartu University Press.

Lauristin, M., & Vihalemm,P., with Rosengren, K. E., & Weibull, L. (Eds.). (1997). *Return to the Western world: Cultural and political perspectives on the Estonian post-communist transition*. Tartu, Estonia: Tartu University Press.

Law amending the law on elections to the Seimas (No. I-2721; as amended November 17, 2005, No. X-397). (1992, July 9). Retrieved December 26, 2005, from the Lietuvos Respublikos Seimas Web site: http://www3.lrs.lt/pls/inter3/dokpaieska.showdoc_l?p_id=269821&p_query=political%20advertising

Law on presidential elections (No. I-28; as amended April 15, 2004, No. IX-2134). (1992, December 22). Retrieved December 26, 2005, from the Lietuvos Respublikos Seimas Web site: http://www3.lrs.lt/cgi-bin/preps2?Condition1=232111

Lithuania president loses ruling. (2004, March 31). Retrieved December 22, 2005, from the BBC News Web site: http://news.bbc.co.uk/go/pr/fr/-/1/hi/world/europe/3586709.stm

Local government: Theoretical bases of local government. (2000). In *Estonica: Encyclopedia about Estonia*. Retrieved December 24, 2005, from http://www.estonica.info/eng/lugu.html?menyy_id=336&kateg=39&nimi=&alam=48&tekst_id=337

Lov om ændring af radio- og fjernsynsloven (Politiske reklamer og forlængelse af programtilladelser) [Law on the amendment of the radio and television law (Political advertising and prolongation of permit)] (Lov. no. 1437). (2004, December 22). Retrieved July 28, 2005, from http://www.kum.dk/sw18323.asp

Mainonnan Määrä Suomessa 2003-tutkimus. [Amount of advertising in Finland in 2003: Research report]. (2004, April 6). Retrieved

December 26, 2005, from the Finnish Association of Marketing Communication Companies Web site: http://www.mtl.fi/easydata/customers/mtl/files/main_ma/mainonnantiedote.pdf

Media House (Home page) (2004). Retrieved December 26, 2005, from http://www.mediahouse.com/company_news.php

Media trends and media statistics in the Nordic region. (2005). Retrieved December 26, 2005, from the NORDICOM Web site: http://www.nordicom.gu.se/eng.php?portal=mt

Moring, T. (1995). The north European exception: Political advertising on TV in Finland. In L. L. Kaid & C. Holtz-Bacha (Eds.), *Political advertising in Western democracies* (pp. 161–185). London: Sage.

Moring, T. (2004). Finland: A reality check—10 years of political advertising on TV. In S. Nikoltchev (Ed.), *IRIS special, 2004 edition: Political debate and the role of the media. The fragility of free speech* (pp. 81–86). Strasbourg, Alsace: European Audiovisual Observatory.

Moring, T. (2005). Europawahlkämpfe in Finnland. Eine vergleichende Analyse [European election campaigns in Finland: A comparative analysis]. In J. Tenscher (Ed.), *Wahl-Kampf um Europa. Analysen aus Anlass der Wahlen zum Europäischen Parlament 2004* [Election campaigns in Europe: Analysis and causes of the 2004 European parliamentary elections] (pp. 269-292). Berlin: Verlag für Sozialwissenschaften.

Moring, T. (2006). Between medialization and tradition: Campaigning in Finland in a longitudinal perspective. In M. Maier & J. Tenscher (Eds.), *Campaigning in Europe—Campaigning for Europe: Parties, campaigns, mass media and the European parliamentary elections 2004* (pp. 81–99). Berlin: LIT.

Moring, T., & Himmelstein, H. (1993). *Politiikkaa riisuttuna. Kampanjakulttuuri murroksessa televisioidun politiikan aikaan* [Politics in the nude: A political campaign culture in transition in the age of television]. Helsinki, Finland: Oy Yleisradio Ab.

Moring, T., & Himmelstein, H. (1996). The new-image politics in Finnish electoral television. In D. L. Paletz (Ed.), *Political communication research: Approaches, studies, assessments* (Vol. II, pp. 171–141). Norwood, NJ: Ablex.

Moring, T., & Mykkänen, J. (2005, May 26-30). *Voter choice and political mediation: Net-based candidate selectors in Finnish elections.*

Paper presented at the 55th Annual Conference of the International Communication Association, New York.

Moring, T., & TNS Gallup Finland. (2003). *The changes in Finnish TV election campaigns: Project data base.* Tampere, Finland: Finnish Social Science Data Archive.

Moring, T., & TNS Gallup Finland. (2006). *The changes in Finnish TV election campaigns: Project data base.* Tampere, Finland: Finnish Social Science Data Archive.

Norges offentlige utredninger. (2004). *Penger teller, men stemmer avgjør. Om partifinansiering, åpenhet og partipolitisk fjernsynsreklame* [Money counts but votes decide: On party financing, transparency, and party political television advertising] (State committee report). Oslo, Norway: Statens forvaltningstjeneste, Informasjonsforvaltning.

Nødgaard, P. (1986). Spm. nr. S 1986. (14/2 03) [Question no. S 1986 (February 2, 2003)]. Retrieved December 15, 2005, from the Folketinget Web site: http://www.ft.dk/Samling/20021/spor_sv/S1986.htm

Organisation for Economic Co-operation and Development. (2005). Population migration. Retrieved December 17, 2005, from the *OECD Factbook* Web site: http://fiordiliji.sourceoecd.org/factbookpdfs/01-02-01.pdf

Paloheimo, H., & Sundberg, J. (2005). Puoluevalinnan perusteet [Basis for party choice]. In H. Paloheimo (Ed.), *Vaalit ja demokratia Suomessa* [Elections and democracy in Finland] (pp. 169–201). Helsinki, Finland: WSOY.

Partiernes Websider. (n.d.). Retrieved December 22, 2005, from the Folketingets Web site: http://www.ft.dk/?/system/partier/partifrm.htm

Pesonen, P. (1965). *Valtuutus kansalta* [Authorization from the people]. Porvoo-Helsinki, Finland: WSOY.

Pesonen, P., Sänkiaho, R., & Borg, S. (1993). *Vaalikansan äänivalta* [The voting power of the electorate]. Helsinki, Finland: WSOY.

Peterson, O. (1984). *Folkstyrelse och statsmakt i Norden* [Popular rule and state power in the Nordic countries]. Uppsala, Sweden: Diskurs.

Politicians fill advertising market. (2004, July 27). Retrieved December 22, 2005, from the Compiler Trade Portal: http://www.compiler.fi/tradestation/baltics/lithuania/lt-archive/lt-archive2004/lt.week31.html

Radio and televison in Lithuania. (2003-2004). Retrieved July 22, 2005, from the Media

House Web site: http://www.media-house .com/company_news.php

Radio- och TV-Lag (1996:844) [Radio and TV law (1996:844)]. (1996).Retrieved December 26, 2005, from http://www.grn.se/PDF-filer/ ovrigt/Radio-%20och%20TV-lagen.pdf

Rahvastiku kodakondsuskoosseisust Eestis ja teistes Euroopa riikides [The composition of the population in Estonia and other European countries]. (2005). Retrieved January 26, 2006, from the Statistical Office of Estonia Web site: http://www.stat.ee

Raudsaar, M., & Tigasson, K.-R. (2006). The European parliament elections in Estonia 2004: Party spots and the effects of advertising. In M. Maier & J. Tenscher (Eds.), *Campaigning in Europe—Campaigning for Europe. Political parties, campaigns, massmedia and the European parliament elections 2004* (pp. 387–407). Berlin: LIT.

Report submitted by Denmark: Article 3. (1999). Retrieved December 22, 2005, from the Council of Europe Web site: http://www.humanrights .coe.int/Minorities/Eng/FrameworkConvention/ StateReports/1999/denmark/Article_3.htm

Riigikogu Election Act, passed on 7 June 1994 (RT I 1994, 47, 784). Retrieved January 4, 2006, from http://www.legaltext.ee/text/en/ X60044K2.htm

Ringhäälinguseadus [Estonian Broadcasting Act]. (1994, May 19). Retrieved December 24, 2005, from http://www.legaltext.ee/et/andme-baas/tekst.asp?loc=text&dok=X30069K8& keel=en&pg=1&ptyyp=RT&tyyp=X&query= Ringh%E4%E41inguseadus

Rose, R., & Berglund, S. (2005). *Baltic voices.* Retrieved December 26, 2005, from http://www .balticvoices.org/BVindex.html?estelex.htm

Rules for the employment of the Estonian national television and national radio in the election campaign for the Republic of Estonia Riigikogu (parliament) and president. (1992). Retrieved December 24, 2005, from the University of Essex Web site: http://www2 .essex.ac.uk/elect/database/legislationAll.asp? country=estonia&legislation=eemed

Socialdemokraterna (Home page). (2005). Retrieved December 15, 2005, from http:// www.sap.se/

The Swedish population. (n.d.). Retrieved December 26, 2005, from SWEDEN.SE: The official gateway to Sweden Web site: http:// www .sweden.se/templates/cs/BasicFactsheet____60 48.aspx

Syvertsen, T. (1999). The many uses of the "public service" concept. *Nordicom Review, 20*(11, Special issue), 5–12.

Television marketing. (1991, August). Retrieved January 26, 2006, from the Danish National Consumer Agency Web site: http://www. forbrug.dk/english/dco/guidelines0/television-marketing0/

Tigasson, K.-R. (2003, September 18-21). *Political advertising in Estonia, 1992-2002.* Paper presented at the European Consortium for Political Research Conference, Marburg, Germany.

Tigasson, K.-R. (2005). Wahlkampf gegen Europa. Die Wahlen zum Europäischen Parlament in Estland 2004 [Election campaign against Europe: The European parliamentary election in Estonia 2004]. In J. Tenscher (Ed.), *Wahl-Kampf um Europa. Analysen aus Anlass der Wahlen zum Europäischen Parlament 2004* [Election campaigns in Europe: Analysis and causes of the 2004 European parliamentary elections] (pp. 293–315). Berlin: Verlag für Sozialwissenschaften.

TNS Gallup Finland. (n.d.). Retrieved December 26, 2005, from the TNS Gallup Web site: http://www.mdc.fi/

TV4:s sändningstillstånd. [TV4 Transmission License, Sweden]. (2006). Retrieved January 4, 2006, from http://tv4.se/263626.html

Venho, T. (1999). *Tutkimus vuoden 1999 eduskun-tavaaliehdokkaiden kampanjarahoituksesta. Vaalirahoituskomitean mietinnön liite 2* [Research report on the campaign financing of parliamentary election candidates in 1999: Annex 2 to the report of the Committee on Election Financing]. Helsinki, Finland: Oikeusministeriö.

Vigsø, O. (2004). *Valretorik i text och bild: En studie i 2002 års svenska valaffischer* [Electoral rhetoric: A study of text and image in the posters of the 2002 general election in Sweden]. Unpublished Ph.D. dissertation, Uppsala University, Sweden. Retrieved December 26, 2005, from http://www.diva-portal.org/diva/getDocument?urn_nbn_se_uu_ diva-4705-2__fulltext.pdf

World Association of Newspapers. (2004). *World press trends 2005.* Paris: Author.

Zepa, B., & Koļesņikova, K. (2002). *Politisko partiju priekšvēlēšanu reklāma un vēlētāju atbalsts* [Preelection advertisement of political parties and voter support]. Retrieved December 26, 2005, from http://www.bszi.lv/downloads/ publications/pol_partiju_reklama.ppt

12

Polispots in Greece

Between Partisanship and Media Logic

ATHANASSIOS N. SAMARAS AND
STYLIANOS PAPATHANASSOPOULOS

The advent of televised political advertising spots (or polispots) in Greece is associated to a certain extent with deregulation of the broadcasting system and the entry of private commercial channels. The emergence of the private channels has been significant in a number of ways. It has not only removed the television broadcasting system from direct state control but has also come to dominate the broadcasting sector in terms of ratings and advertising revenue. Equally significant has been its more commercial approach toward politics (Papathanassopoulos, 1997, 2000). Most important, the private channels have dominated not only state channels (in regard to news) but also the newspapers, because the onslaught of private television has exacerbated the crisis in the press, drastically changing the ways in which the public acquires information (Papathanassopoulos, 2001). Moreover, the state lost control of the broadcasting deregulation process, and this resulted in the lack of an overall regulatory framework, which meant that parties and candidates were initially absolutely free to purchase as much airtime as they could afford.

The Greek experience may thus be regarded as a case study in which to test some generalizations that have been offered to analyze political advertising in modern democracies. Greek political advertising is interesting for three reasons: (a) contrary to the United States, where the candidate-centered campaign produces candidate-centered spots, the Greek party-centered campaign produces party-centered spots and thus supports rather than undermines the political parties (Samaras, 1999). (b) The gradual erosion of partisanship at the level of the electorate has reduced the partisanship in the content of the spots. This took place not because the parties lost control of the format but because they adapted to the new developments in the formulation of their campaign strategy. (c) In the Greek context, the polispots incorporated media logic resulting from the deregulation of the television system.

This chapter is divided into three sections. The first section explores the relation between "partytocracy" (control of political life and society by political parties), media logic, and polispots. The second section presents the regulatory framework, and the third analyses the attributes of the polispots.

PARTY AND MEDIA CONTEXT OF POLITICAL ADVERTISING IN GREECE

The Greek state initially played a decisive role in the media sector, especially in regard to broadcasting. Unlike most other Western European countries, in Greece, the electronic media were traditionally under the total and tight control of the state, or, in effect, the government of the day. The general pattern of the broadcasting media in this state monopoly era was that a transfer of political power was followed by an equivalent changeover in the state media institutions' executives. News and editorial judgments consequently followed state policies (Papathanassopoulos, 1990). With the deregulation of Greek broadcasting, on the other hand, the state lost its gatekeeping function in the construction of mediated communication.

However, the importance of the parties as managers of the state ensures that their position of significance is structurally guaranteed. Parties are simultaneously instruments of conflict (because they promote conflicting policies) and instruments of integration, to the extent that this conflict organizes political life (Diamandouros, 1993). Thus their power is directly related to their ability to polarize opinion (Wattenberg, 1991). The conflict element of the *interparty frame*[1] performs the double function of polarizing and defining (Samaras, 1998). The major interpretative poles constituting this frame, center right (Nea Dimokratia, ND) and center left (Panellinio Sosialistiko Kinima, PASOK), have been defined by their antitheses, often personalized by the party leaders.[2]

The polarization and content of the media function as a conduit for the diffusion of the polarity of party structure in the electorate. However, the demands of the media's logic means that overtly partisan political discourse has been replaced with a neutral and occasionally (not very) covert antipolitical discourse and nonpolitical news items. This approach also results in depoliticization of the audience. Private television channels publicize and encourage instances of intraparty conflict. The *intraparty conflict frame* presents the party as an institution in crisis, a problem rather than a solution. In this sense, the private media compete with the interparty frame in news agenda and actively undermine the role and image of the parties.

Under this new way of structuring communication with the public, candidate-controlled communication formats were clearly affected. Candidate-controlled time on Greek television traditionally took the form of party election broadcasts (PEBs) allocated by an interparty committee during the campaign period and broadcast by the state stations. The balance of power in the Parliament was reproduced in the pattern of allocation of PEBs, with the exception of a limited amount of time allocated to parties not represented in the parliament. The rapid decline of the audience for state channels after broadcasting deregulation undermined the importance of this persuasive format. The PEB that "inhabited" state broadcasting in campaign periods was functionally displaced by the political advertising spot, which emerged along with private broadcasters.

Figure 12.1 shows the relationship of polispots to media logic, a taxonomy of television campaign formats comprising two sets of categorizations: (a) according to the degree of journalistic mediation, considering both mediated and unmediated communications,[3] and (b) according to the degree of money involved, considering both paid and free media.[4]

In using a "money-involvement" categorization, we demonstrate that the rise of polispots signifies the commodification of candidate-controlled communication. The

	Unmediated	Mediated
Free	Party election broadcast	News, talk shows
Paid	Polispot	Paid appearance on news and talk shows

Figure 12.1 Taxonomy of Greek Televised Campaign Formats

PEB is time allocated for free, and its duration and timing are decisions imposed on the media structure by the political system. The polispot, on the other hand, constitutes time bought by the party or candidate from the channel. Control over the format is conditioned by capacity to pay rather than by the institutional role of the political actor. Thus, from this point of view, the commodification of candidate-controlled communication further subjects politicians and parties to the rationale of the media (Samaras, 2002). On the other hand, the polispot can be seen as one of the means the parties have available to bypass newscasts organized according to media logic. Polispots allow for direct communication with the audience, communication unmediated by journalists.

The taxonomy of television campaign formats highlights another more implicit process of displacement. The amount of time devoted to any one story in television news is short, increasing the "price" politicians have to "pay" to appear in it.[5] Furthermore, limited access to the news media forces politicians to employ paid formats (Samaras, 2003).

In countries like Greece, where there are now more private stations than the market can sustain (Papathanassopoulos, 1993, 1997), excess supply has resulted in the relatively low and declining commercial value of broadcasting time. In such circumstances, decisions are taken in terms of cost minimization rather than profit maximization: Cheap talk shows and current affairs programs tend to displace expensive entertainment, and the drama and entertainment functions of programming are satisfied through politics. For instance, the long duration of newscasts results in more opportunity for political candidates and parties to receive coverage and thus undermines the need for communication via paid media. The incentive to use a 30-second polispot is much higher in the United States, where the average sound bite a candidate receives in the news is 8 seconds—in Greece, it is 55 seconds (Samaras, 1998). Consequently, polispots are employed for a more limited range of functions.

REGULATORY FRAMEWORK FOR POLITICAL ADVERTISING IN GREECE

Polispots appeared with the breakup of the state monopoly in broadcasting. They were regulated as part of the imposition of a regulatory framework on private broadcasters. During the 1989-1990 elections, polispots, like all the other aspects of private stations, were totally unregulated. During the 1993 election, private stations remained off limits to the regulatory authorities. The regulatory body, the National Broadcasting Council, was restricted to regulating campaigning on state broadcasters, but it could only issue recommendations to the private stations.

For the 1996 elections, a regulatory framework was put in place. According to Decree 52135/12.9.1996 of the Ministry of the Interior and Public Administration, the state and the private channels are obliged to give

5 minutes to each party for the presentation of their programs. Thus, although the polispot was not prohibited, the necessity to provide time for party election broadcasts appeared to be imposed on private stations. However, the following article of the law established that private broadcasters might satisfy this requirement by organizing programs in which representatives of more than one party participated. Private stations preferred to choose the (journalistically) mediated rather than the unmediated format. The current campaign regulations are set forth in Law 3032/2002.

In discussions of political advertising in Greece, the most important issue seems to be not the advertisement's content or its persuasive capacity but the fact that the high cost of advertising increases campaign expenditures. Such increased spending is believed to make the "siren songs" of the vested interests more appealing to the ears of candidates and parties. The high cost of media advertising cannot be interpreted the same way for individuals seeking office as it can be for corporations selling products. The "investment return" is not comparable, because the corporation intends to recoup its advertising costs in sales to the public, whereas the only thing a candidate has to sell to recover the cost of advertising is his subsequent vote on public policy decisions (Johnston, 1991). This interpretation of the role of advertising costs means that the regulation of the polispot in Greece has been seen as related to campaign finance regulations.

Campaign finance law was designed to increase the openness and accountability between politicians and their sponsors and to decrease the dominance of the latter. The parties are sponsored with an annual percentage of 1.2% of the national budget and 0.5% for every election. The annual total cannot exceed 1.7% regardless of the number of elections that take place in a year. Parties have to publish their balance annually, and there is a maximum allowed expenditure for parliamentary candidates that is in proportion to the size of their constituency.

Although political advertising was not prohibited by this law, its use for individual members of parliament (MPs) was limited by the allowed expenditures. Even in the largest constituency, Greater Athens (the city of Athens plus certain suburbs), the total amount of allowed expenditure is adequate for the broadcasting of only 18 repetitions of a 20-second spot.[6] Furthermore, Decree 52135/12.9.1996 limited the number of broadcasts to one per channel for each candidate MP. The decrease of the number of allowed repetitions increased the production cost of spots to the extent that no polispots for individual MPs appeared in 1996. The prohibition of the polispots for candidate MPs became explicit with the subsequent law, 2817/2000.

Thus, under the current regulations, television political advertising is prohibited for politicians campaigning for the parliament but allowed for political parties. However, there is a ceiling to the amount of political advertising. No more than 20% of the total campaign expenditure allowed for each party can be allocated to the purchase of political advertising.

Elite Perceptions of Political Advertising

Analysis of Greek polispots from 1993 to 1996 demonstrates that the content of the Greek spots was organized optimally for the parties and might thus counter the representation of politics projected via newscasts (Samaras, 1999). However, the Greek political elite perceived them in terms of cost rather than benefit. The analysis of the parliamentary discussion of Law 2429/96[7] indicated minimal references to the content of the polispots, although the *vested interests frame* was dominant (Samaras, 2000). This frame has developed in response to the involvement of certain entrepreneurs in media ownership and the resulting reversal of the relationships between politicians and entrepreneurs such that the latter were transformed from clients to patrons. The foundation of this frame shows a convergence of entrepreneurial and media power that, combined, has the capacity to make politicians lose control of the allocation of public resources.[8]

Between 1993 and 1996, the vested interest frame came full circle. It emerged from the blame games of ND leadership in the aftermath of the 1993 defeat (Massavetas, 1996), reached maturity as part of the discourse on broadcasting re-regulation, and was finally integrated into campaign rhetoric during the 1996 campaign (Samaras, 1998). The previous uses loaded the vested interest frame with negative connotations and turned it into a dominant demonization method, to be employed in symbolic conflicts. Denouncing the vested interests became a strategy for constructing an image of honesty, a claim that, like patriotism and economic development, is available to all political and social actors. Thus, the parliamentary discussion of Law 2429/96 was intended to increase openness and accountability in campaigning as a means to restrict vested interests. Political advertising was perceived in terms of its high cost, which, because it increases the expenditures of the campaign, is assumed to make the candidate or MP more vulnerable to vested interests.

CONTENT ATTRIBUTES OF GREEK POLISPOTS

West (1993) argues that polispots cannot be explored in isolation from leadership behavior, the flow of information, and the narratives of political campaigns. He suggests a "contextual model" (p. 5) for political advertising, incorporating considerations on the nature of the electoral system, the particularities of the campaign, the operation of the news media, and models of information processing and persuading. In this project, a contextual approach was employed; the focus, however, changes from "studying ads in context" to studying political context and structures through ads. This involves decontextualization from the

peculiarities of a particular campaign and considers instead the structural, positional, and format-related parameters of the advertising.

In the content analysis, a version of the elements of videostyle (Kaid & Johnston, 2001) adapted to the peculiarities of the Greek case and the necessities of the partycentric system was employed. All the spots produced and broadcast by ND and PASOK in the general elections of 1993, 1996, and 2000, as well as those from the European Parliament elections of 1994 and 1999, were analyzed. Also included is the census of the spots of the minor parties (Kommounistiko Komma Elladas, Synaspismos, Politiki Anixi, and Dimokratiko Kinoniko Kinima) for the general elections of 1996 and 2000 and the European Parliament elections of 1999 (N = 224). Intercoder reliability was assessed on a sample of 20% of the spots and averaged +.84 for all categories[9] (Samaras, 2003).

Partisanship of the Greek Polispots

Wattenberg (1996) argues that in the United States, "television coverage of politics virtually ignores parties, as acquaintance with personalities is much easier to convey through the visual media than knowledge about abstractions such as political parties" (p. 91). Subsequent research proves that the candidate-centered character of the campaign has had reverse effects on the partisanship of the polispot. Boiney and Paletz (1991) argue that advertisers seem to feel partisanship is a cue relied on less and less by voters. Actually, the candidate-centered organization of the U.S. campaign is mirrored by the attributes of the format. Just and colleagues (1996) identified three patterns concerning partisanship in U.S. polispots: "messages explicitly reinforcing partisan orientation were virtually non-existent; explicit attacks on the opposition party were rare. Criticism of the opposition was directed at individual office holders within the party rather than the party itself" (pp. 66-67).

Table 12.1 Party Versus Candidate Emphasis in
Greek Polispots (%)

Emphasis	1993	1994	1996	1999	2000
Party	98	100	92	65	46
Partisanship of candidate	0	0	1	6	40
Candidate	2	0	7	15	14
No specific emphasis	0	0	0	15	0

SOURCE: Data from Samaras, A. N. (2003). *Television political advertising: A quantitative research on Greece.* Athens: IOM.

In the case of the Greek spots, the effects of partytocracy become obvious through the use of party slogans and symbols. In the polispots of 1993 to 1996, party slogans appeared in 86% of the spots, and the party symbol was the symbol most often employed, present in 100% of party-sponsored spots. After 1996, a slight decrease in the use of party slogans and symbols can be seen. In the 1999 European Parliament elections, the party logo and party slogan appeared in 71% and 85%, respectively, of the spots. In the general elections of 2000, 78% of the polispots contained a party logo, and the party slogan appeared in 94%. The decrease in these percentages was even more dramatic in the case of ND-sponsored spots, as the ND abstained from the use of the party logo in spots in 1999 and used it in only 25% of its spots in 2000. The reduced use of its logo by the ND was caused by two simultaneous phenomena: the party tag was being deliberately undermined as part of the party rebranding process and negative spots were deliberately left unidentified in 1999 to minimize the backlash effect.

To further examine the partisanship of the spots, a continuum of mutually exclusive codes, organized according to the lines of partisanship, was constructed. The spots were differentiated according to (a) emphasis on the party, (b) emphasis on the partisanship of the candidate, and (c) emphasis on the candidate. What is measured in this categorization is the focus on the projection of "us" in the spot.

Table 12.1 shows that from 1993 to 1996, the predominance of the party was overwhelming in party-sponsored spots: Party was the focus in 98% of 1993 spots, 100% of the Europarliament spots, and 87% of 1996 spots. Higher numbers of spots emphasizing the partisanship of the candidate (3%) or the candidate himself (11%) appeared in 1996 as a result of the appearance of new party leadership.

In the 1999 and 2000 elections, the depoliticization of the audience seemed to affect the content of the spots, because the emphasis in the construction of identity in the spot shifted from the party to the candidate. The emphasis on the party declined dramatically, from 92% in 1996 to 65% in 1999 and to 46% in 2000. This dialectic between public opinion and the content of the spots seems to be mediated by strategic considerations: (a) opinion polls consistently showed that the leaders of the two major parties were more popular than their respective parties, and (b) the use of the new leader was considered essential to the rebranding of the party. This process did not affect the overall emphasis of the spots in 1996, but in 2000, Konstantinos Karamanlis seems to have replaced the party tag of the ND as the dominant reference point of partisan identification.

Issues and Images in Polispots

One of the main dichotomies that organizes the analysis of spots is the distinction between

Table 12.2   Issue and Image Emphasis in Greek Polispots (%)

Emphasis	1993	1994	1996	1999	2000
Issue	51	85	42	44	47
Image	49	15	58	56	53

SOURCE: Data from Samaras, A. N. (2003). *Television political advertising: A quantitative research on Greece.* Athens: IOM.

Table 12.3   Specificity of Issue References in Greek Polispots (%)

Issue Specificity	1993	1994	1996	1999	2000
Contains issue reference[a]	71	100	74	77	75
Does not contain issue reference[a]	29	0	26	23	25
Candidate's issue concern[b]	69	100	77	62	67
Vague policy reference[b]	5	0	9	4	0
Specific policy proposals[b]	26	0	14	34	33

SOURCE: Data from Samaras, A. N. (2003). *Television political advertising: A quantitative research on Greece.* Athens: IOM.

a. N = total polispots.
b. n = polispots containing issue references.

image and issue. *Image* is defined as character attributes of a candidate; an *issue* is a current topic or civic concern linked to the national interest (Shyles, 1983, 1991). Flanigan and Zingale (1991) note that party images may have important effects on candidate images. The nature of the political system in which the polispot appears affects the working definition of the image. In the U.S. candidate-centered system, *image* refers to the personal traits of the candidate (Cundy, 1986), and issue statements are employed to support this image. In party-centered, parliamentary systems, "party image" is much more important than "party leader image" (Johnson & Elebash, 1986, p. 311). Thus, in Greece, the party leader's image may become a synecdoche of the party's image, merging with references to policy issues to construct the overall image of the party campaign.

There seems to be an equal distribution between spots emphasizing images and those emphasizing issues in general elections: 51% and 49%, respectively, in 1993; 58% and 42% in 1996; and 47% and 53% in 2000, as shown in Table 12.2. In the polispots used in U.S. presidential campaigns from 1952

through 1996, the rate is two thirds issue focused and one third image focused (Kaid & Johnston, 2001). The difference between the two countries may be due to the fact that issue ownership patterns are employed in the U.S. spots as implicit cues for party activation. Since the Greek parties lack clear-cut patterns of issue ownership, they tend to operate with more explicit patterns of party activation.

Hacker (1995) suggests not viewing issues as isolated from candidate personality assessments. At the level of polispot content, issue and image may merge when policy preferences are employed to build the image of a candidate. Even though many commercials contain information about issues, very few present substantive policy propositions because, very often, issues are important only as a means of selling an image (Kaid & Davidson, 1986).

Often, issue references are mere references to candidates' issue concerns combined with emotional appeals, to construct images. This was considered by examining the specificity of issue references, seen in Table 12.3.

Although three quarters of the Greek polispots contain issue references, these tend

Table 12.4   Focus of Polispots in Greece (%)

Focus	1993	1994	1996	1999	2000
Candidate positive	14	92	55	56	77
Opponent negative	65	0	29	29	23
Balance	20	7	16	15	0
Contains negativity or attack	90	31	55	59	40

SOURCE: Data from Samaras, A. N. (2003). *Television political advertising: A quantitative research on Greece.* Athens: IOM.

to be predominantly vague candidate issue concerns employed for image-making purposes. Policy specificity in a polispot is an autonomous factor that maximizes source credibility. A candidate who is willing to have his program examined in detail, and thus exposes himself before the electorate, is giving people a chance to see his flaws (Popkin, 1997). Specificity equals credibility for another reason: It cuts through the ambiguity that is often perceived by the electorate as covering or lying. Although specific references (verbal and visual) to what the government party has done build credibility retrospectively, specific policy proposals perform the same function through future references for the main opposition party. A number of such spots presenting very specific measures appeared in the 1996 and 2000 ND party campaigns, and high issue specificity by PASOK was shown in its detailed and explicit references to its governmental record.

Positive Versus Negative Polispots

Some of the political negativity in Greece derives from the direct opposition of those two main parties that alternate in power; some comes from the minor parties and is focused against the bipartisan nature of political power and the minor parties' electoral marginalization. In effect, two different vocabularies of negativity exist: (a) negativity produced as part of bipolarism (bipartisan political power contest) and (b) negativity incorporated into the image-making process of a party. The polispots of PASOE and ND during the 1993,

1996, and 2000 general elections, as well as those in the 1999 European elections, fall into the first category. The spots from the European Parliament campaign, as well as the spots of minor parties in 1996, are representative of the second case. The construction of negativity in bipartisan opposition involves attacks on the opponent personally; attacks on performance in past positions; and attacks on partisanship, as well as negative associations and name calling. These aspects are intimately related to the nature of the binary opposition (one major party vs. another major party) and are not shared by the minor parties.

In terms of the purpose of the attacks, it is noteworthy that of all the polispots containing negative messages in the first-order elections (national general elections of 1993, 1996, 2000), 52% included negative references to the opposing party; 37%, attacks on the opposition's performance; 32%, attacks on the image of the opposition's leader; 28%, attacks on issue stands or the consistency of the opposition; and 15%, negative references to the partisanship of the opposition (see Table 12.4). The last indicates a strategy of reversing, by counter-conditioning, the rebranding of the opposing party by transferring positive connotations from the leader's image to the party's image. Although negative references to the opposing party is the technique most often employed, there has been a continuous decrease in this technique, from 66% in 1993, to 55% in 1996, to 24% in 2000. This is a clear indication of the gradual loss of the capacity of parties to mobilize the electorate through negativity.

Table 12.5   Retrospectivity in Greek Polispots (%)

Retrospectivity	1993	1994	1996	1999	2000	Total
The past, negative, focused on the opponent	68	31	28	70	27	43
The past, positive, focused on the candidate	20	15	13	29	37	23
The future, negative, focused on the opponent	22	8	24	9	2	15
The future, positive, focused on the candidate	35	46	62	74	71	59
The historical past of the country	2	0	1	0	0	1
The future of the country	8	92	34	47	77	43
Dominant retrospectivity						
Past	57	15	32	47	37	40
Future	22	85	55	32	46	44
Balanced	14	0	11	18	14	13
None	6	0	3	3	4	3

SOURCE: Data from Samaras, A. N. (2003). *Television political advertising: A quantitative research on Greece.* Athens: IOM.

Note: For the categories of retrospectivity (excluding those for dominant retrospectivity), the results do not add to 100% because each spot may contain more than one kind of reference and may thus be coded in more than one category.

In 82% of the attack-containing spots in the general elections, the attack is conducted by an anonymous announcer. Greek polispots seem to incorporate the American dictum that the candidate should avoid presenting attacks him- or herself, to minimize backlash. Given the party-centered nature of the Greek polispots, the anonymous announcer operates as the party voice, and this suggests that the conflict is not between persons but between political blocs— between "us" and "them." There seems, however, to be a steady fall from attacks in 95% of the spots in 1993, to 88% in 1996, to 53% in 2000. The gradual depreciation of party politics led to an increase in the use of voters to deliver the attack, from 20% in 1999 to 47% in 2000.

Retrospectivity

Another important attribute of the polispot is *retrospectivity*, the degree to which the spot refers to the past. Boiney and Paletz (1991) consider the retrospectivity of the spot as an indication of the advertisers' presumption of retrospective voting. These researchers found that the dominant assumption is that retrospective voting is the norm, with prospective voting virtually nonexistent. In the sample of spots they examined, 75% referred primarily to the past and 18% primarily to the future; 68% did not refer to the future at all.

To examine specific attributes, the researchers supplemented the elements of videostyle with two taxonomies. The first examined the presence of references made to the past or to the future combined with references to the focus of the spot. This taxonomy incorporated six categories: negative or opponent-focused references to the past, negative or opponent-focused references to the future, positive or candidate-focused references to the past, positive or candidate-focused references to the future, references to the historical past of Greece, and references to the future of Greece. The second taxonomy examined the overall focus of each spot in the past or in the future.

The aggregate results, displayed in Table 12.5, suggest that there is an overall equilibrium between retrospective and prospective spots. In the total number of polispots examined from 1993 through 2000, 40% focused on the past and 44% on the future. Retrospective references in Greek spots were fed by negativity and prospective references by positive or candidate-focused appeals.

In 1993 there was a double retrospective election:[10] Both PASOK and ND focused on each other's recent past, hoping that voters would select the "lesser evil." This resulted not only in an extremely negative campaign but also in high levels of retrospectivity—57% of the spots focused on the past. The conflict between Konstantinos Mitsotakis and Andreas Papandreou that personalized electoral competition between the ND and the PASOK during the 1993 elections carried with it 30 years of intensely personal, and at the same time highly publicized, animosity.

This past history maximized the use of negative retrospective references. In 1996, the rise of new leadership, Konstantinos Simitis in PASOK and Miltiadis Evert in ND, led to a 25% decrease in retrospectivity, from 57% retrospective spots in 1993 to 32% in 1996, and a 40% decline in the spots containing opponent-focused references to the past. The 1999 Europarliament elections operated as a prepropaganda session for the forthcoming general elections. ND and the Dimokratiko Kinoniko Kinima employed negative retrospective arguments to deconstruct the image of Prime Minister Konstantinos Simitis, and PASOK employed similar references, using the 1990-1993 ND governmental record as a tool to undermine the rebranding of the ND. This resulted in a greater number of spots containing candidate-focused references, from 28% in 1996 to 70% in 1999, as well as of retrospective spots, from 32% to 47%.

Noteworthy is the 1994 campaign for the Europarliament. This campaign took place 1 year after the 1993 campaign and was used as an image-making exercise. The circumstances of the elections did not activate a personalized party conflict framework and resulted in 85% of the spots focusing on the future; only 15% focused on the past.

Fiorina (1981) argues that the depoliticization of the electorate makes retrospective evaluations of candidate performance more important. Boiney and Paletz (1991) argue that this results in high levels of retrospectivity in the spots. In Greece, despite the gradual depoliticization of the electorate from 1993 to 2000, the levels of retrospectivity in the spots fell. The explanation here may be that partisanship was activated through negativity that required large amounts of retrospection. Thus, retrospective references were fed by negativity rather than by instrumental actualization of the past. This (partial) incapacitation of an essential element of the vocabulary of Greek politics resulted in prospective electioneering: Spots containing positive references to the candidate rose from 35% in 1993 to 71% in 2000, and those containing references to the future of the country rose from 8% to 77%.

Polispots and Intraparty Conflict

As the U.S. experience suggests, the effect polispots have on the representation of politics is conditional on the existence of an electoral context that allows competition between candidates of the same party. Such a condition is institutionalized in the United States, where the primaries result in open intraparty conflict at the highest level. On the other hand, the potential for intraparty conflict is minimized in counties with small constituencies and only one candidate from each party (e.g., the United Kingdom). The Greek system has a variety of constituencies, some extended, with multiple candidates from each party, and others smaller. This creates a context of intraparty friction between aspiring MPs during the campaign period. Of course, the potential for such intraparty friction at the MP level exists independent of polispots. The question is to what extent the polispot is integrated into this conflict. If polispots are used to voice attacks against candidates of the same party, and thus to perpetuate the image of intraparty negativity right into the electoral period, then the campaign period will lose its character as a unifying ritual for the party.

Three factors have restrained this situation: First, the electoral system that minimizes the tendencies of individual MPs and maximizes the role of the parties sets limits on the levels of friction between MPs. Second, during the 1993 elections, when use of polispots by candidate MPs was unregulated, the area of dominant influence of the national media was much more extensive than any one constituency, thus making the use of polispots in the national media feasible only for candidates of the Greater Athens constituency. Third, in the national elections of 1996, the total amount of polispot advertising per candidate per television station was set by law (Law 2429/96, and also Decree 51529/4.9.1996 of the Ministry of the Interior and Public Administration) at 1 minute on television and 3 minutes on radio for the whole duration of the campaign. This, in effect, prohibited the employment of polispots by individual candidates.

At the level of the party-sponsored polispots, attack strategies with the potential to undermine the interparty frame are rarely used: Only 5% of the negative spots used statements by a member of the other party that attacked the member's own party's leadership. The purpose of this strategy was to communicate the image of intraparty conflict in the opposition party. This is an interesting case of the merging of frames: The intraparty conflict frame appears embedded within the interparty frame. The coexistence of the two frames creates the potential for different interpretations for the audience.

Despite their rarity, spots projecting intraparty conflict in the opponent party are very powerful. In 1993, PASOK's spot comprised leading members of ND, one after another, expressing their discontent with the political situation, juxtaposed with a statement by Mitsotakis saying that his "has been the best government of the last 45 years." The focus of discontent in the testimonials was not very explicit, in the sense that the ND's member did not name Mitsotakis, but this was easy to infer from the overall context and structure of the spot. To counter it, ND produced three spots that employed leading party members expressing their satisfaction with the government and

attacking the opponent in a ritualistic demonstration of party unity. In reality, ND's administration (1990-1993) was devastated by intraparty conflict. The government actually fell because of the defection of its MPs. Thus the employment of the intraparty conflict in the polispots has been rather limited in relation to the actual intraparty conflict and has paled in comparison to the representations of intraparty conflict portrayed in television news.

Antipolitics Frame

The emergence of the private broadcasting media in Greece gave rise to the *antipolitics frame*. This frame incorporates polarized communication and populist deliberation. It projects the antithesis between politicians and the media. Journalists and media owners are presented as genuinely representing the people, and politicians, the parties, and the party sector are presented as incompetent or corrupt, thus undermining their relationship of representation with the electorate.[11]

Parties rotating in power have less motivation to employ the antipolitics frame than small parties, which tend to benefit from the disillusionment of the electorate with the two larger parties and voters' fear of the manipulatory potential of power. All minor parties in Greece have explicitly employed the "vote for us to balance the power of the major parties" argument in their negative spots. Thus, permanent minor parties, as well as parties of protest, benefit from projecting an all-inclusive negativity as the antithesis between the two major parties takes the form of a binary opposition that contains negativity and is adverse to the use of the antipolitics schema, as illustrated in Table 12.6.

Although the polispots of PASOK and ND never contain the antipolitical frame, the construction of negativity in the minor parties may evoke it. In all minor parties, negativity is combined with an overall ambiguity that takes the form of general and unspecified attacks on politicians. This occasionally evolves into

Table 12.6　　Focus of Attacks of Major and Minor Parties in Greek Polispots (%)

Focus of Attack	1996		1999		2000	
	Major Parties	Minor Parties	Major Parties	Minor Parties	Major Parties	Minor Parties
Direct attack against another politician or candidate	60	0	45	11	62	0
Direct attack against another party	37	0	36	11	25	0
Direct attack against bipartisanship	0	29	0	56	0	0
More general direct attack against government and other parties	0	14	0	0	0	0
Indirect or implicit attack without specific reference to object of attack	3	57	18	22	13	100

SOURCE: Data from Samaras, A. N. (2003). *Television political advertising: A quantitative research on Greece.* Athens: IOM.

Note: Spots examined were, for the major parties, an aggregate of ND and PASOK spots; for the minor parties in 1996, an aggregate of Kommounistiko Komma Elladas, Synaspismos, and Politiki Anixi; in 1999 and 2000, an aggregate of Kommounistiko Komma Elladas, Synaspismos, and Dimokratiko Kinoniko Kinima.

more explicit attacks and may result in the injection of cynicism. Overall, however, this frame usually does not reach the level of explicitness necessary for the formulation of the antipolitics frame as it is seen in the United States. There are two reasons for this: (a) the inherent lack of explicitness in Greek spots, which derives from the structural and connotative stability of the setting, and (b) the partisan control of the messages provides stabilizers, minimizing the chances of an explicit use of the antipolitics frame. In the United States, on the other hand, the loose control of the party over the candidates' messages results in an optimal environment for citizen disillusionment with politics, to be voiced in candidate-controlled communication.

CONCLUSION

As mentioned earlier, there are two main keys to interpretation of the attributes of political spots in Greece:

1. The Greek political parties completely control the content of the polispots. In other words, the political structure has affected the content resulting in party-centered spots.

2. The erosion of partisanship at the level of the electorate, manifested both as a positive sense of affect upon the supporting party and, in the negative sense, as the rejection of any opposing party, have negatively affected the partisanship in the content of the spots. This took place not because the parties lost control of the format but because they incorporated the new developments into the formulation of their campaign strategy.

The content of Greek polispots is organized optimally for the parties in the sense that it perpetuates the interparty frame that is the hermeneutic pillar of partytocracy. In Greece, the polispot entered electioneering through the political parties, which shape the message content of spots. For the same reason, there is no employment of either the intraparty conflict frame or the antipolitics frame in Greek polispots. The absence of these two frames differentiates the Greek polispot both from its U.S. counterpart and from Greek newscasts.

Political conditions since the restoration of the Parliament (1974) have elevated the party to a permanent and significant element of the Greek political system, more stable and more permanent than the personality contests between party leaders. This was obvious in the polispots of election campaigns of 1993 and 1996. The rise of new leaderships in both major parties and the use of spots for rebranding the party affected the partisanship of the spots negatively. The transfer of positive attributes from the image of the new leader (Simitis for PASOK and Karamanlis for ND) to the image of the party led to a decline in the emphasis of the party. This is not tantamount to the rise of personality politics, as is characteristic of the U.S. model. In Greece, the party leader personifies the party and thus operates within the partisan context.

The gradual erosion of partisanship at the level of the audience affected the capacity of the parties to activate partisanship through negativity. This affected certain attributes of the spot: a decrease in retrospection and in the negative references to the opposing party, as well as a reduction in the use of the anonymous announcer, who operated as the party voice. On the other hand, there was an increase in the use of ordinary people (i.e., voters) to deliver the attack. It seems that the vocabulary of binary opposition that shaped negativity in the early and middle 1990s has been gradually eroding.

Last, but not least, although in the past, political advertising in Greece was blamed as a negative force in the political system, since the 1990s it has been legitimized and has acquired an important status. To a certain extent, the development and growing dominance of private television and the subsequent media logic that is now the modus operandi of the Greek communication system led to this acceptance of political spots. The relation of polispots and media logic is an intimate one, not only structurally but also perceptually. In the final analysis, however, polispots provide the parties with the potential to circumvent journalistic mediation and to achieve unmediated communication with the audience. However, the development of the regulatory framework failed to incorporate this dimension, focusing instead on the need to "increase accountability" and provide a level playing field to reduce the potential influence of vested interests.

NOTES

1. *Frame* is defined as a schema of interpretation that enables individuals to locate, perceive, identify, and label occurrences (Goffman, 1974). The process of framing involves selecting certain aspects of a perceived reality and making them more salient in a communicating text to promote a particular definition of a problem, causal interpretation, moral evaluation, or treatment recommendation (Entman, 1993).

2. The party system of Greece comprises the following parties: Nea Dimokratia (New Democracy), Panellinio Sosialistiko Kinima (Panhellenic Socialist Movement), Kommounistiko Komma Elladas (Communist Party of Greece), Synaspismos tis Aristeras kai tis Proodou (Coalition of the Left and Progress Party), Dimokratiko Kinoniko Kinima (Democratic Social Movement), Politiki Anixi (Political Spring). The center-right ND won the general elections of 1974, 1977, 1990, and 2004, and the center-left PASOK won the general elections of 1981, 1985, 1993, 1996, and 2000. ND governed from 1974 to 1981, 1990 to 1993, and 2004 onwards; PASOK governed from 1981 to 1989 and from 1993 to 2004, with two interim coalition governments between 1989 and 1990.

3. For simplicity's sake, we have not differentiated between degrees of journalistic mediation.

4. The concept of "paid" does not necessarily refer to monetary transaction; it may also relate to implicit forms of favoritism.

5. This price may be (a) direct, in the form of "give and take" transactions between politicians and media professionals and owners, or (b) indirect, in the form of intense transformations of the behavior of politicians that are necessary for the latter to conform to the requirements of newsworthiness

6. See the statements of Kefalloyiannis, MP of ND ("Parliamentary discussion," 1996).

7. Titled "Financing of Political Parties, Publicity, and Control of the Finance of Political Parties and Candidate MPs: Statements of the Financial Position of Politicians, Public Servants, and Owners of Mass Media and Other Directives," this law was designed to regulate campaigning and electioneering.

8. Critical political economy abounds with such analyses. The qualifying difference of the vested interest frame in Greece is that it has not been contained in academia but has emerged as a popular frame, with multiple uses.

9. Reliability has been computed using the formula suggested by North, Holsti, Zanninovich, and Zinnes (1963): R = 2(C1,2)/C1 + C2, where C1,2 = the number of category assignments both coders agree on and C1 + C2 = total category assignments made by both coders.

10. On double retrospective elections, see Wattenberg (1991).

11. On the media-constructed antipolitical news in the 1996 campaign, see Samaras (1998).

REFERENCES

Boiney, J., & Paletz, D. L. (1991). In search of the model model: Political science versus political advertising perspectives on voter decision making. In F. Biocca (Ed.), *Television and political advertising. Vol. 1. Psychological processes* (pp. 3–26). Hillsdale, NJ: Erlbaum.

Cundy, D.T. (1986). Political commercials and candidate image. In L. L. Kaid, D. Nimmo, & K. R. Sanders (Eds.), *New perspectives on political advertising* (pp. 234–292). Carbondale: Southern Illinois University Press.

Diamandouros, N. P. (1993). Politics and culture in Greece, 1974-91: An interpretation. In R. Clogg (Ed), *Greece, 1981-89: The populist decade* (pp.1–25). London: Macmillan.

Entman, R. M. (1993). Framing: Towards clarification of a fractured paradigm. *Journal of Communication, 43*(4), 51–58.

Fiorina, M. P. (1981). *Retrospective voting in American national elections.* New Haven, CT: Yale University Press.

Flanigan, W. H., & Zingale, N. H. (1991). *Political behavior of the American electorate.* Washington, DC: Congressional Quarterly Press.

Goffman, E. (1974). *Frame analysis.* New York: Harper and Row.

Hacker, K. L. (1995). *Candidate images in presidential elections.* Westport, CT: Praeger.

Johnston, A. (1991). Political broadcasts: An analysis of form, content, and style in presidential communication. In L. L Kaid, J. Gerstlé, & K. R. Sanders (Eds.), *Mediated politics in two cultures: Presidential campaigning in the United States and France* (pp. 247–260). New York: Praeger.

Johnson, K. S., & Elebash, C. (1986). The contagion from the right: The Americanization of British political advertising. In L. L. Kaid, D. Nimmo, & K. R. Sanders (Eds.), *New perspectives on political advertising* (pp. 293–323). Carbondale: Southern Illinois University.

Just, M. R., Crigler, A. N., Alger, D. E., Cook, T., Kern, M., & West, D. M. (1996). *Crosstalk, citizens, candidates and the media in a presidential campaign.* Chicago: University of Chicago Press.

Kaid, L. L., & Davidson, D. K. (1986). Elements of videostyle. In L. L. Kaid, D. Nimmo, & K. R. Sanders (Eds.), *New perspectives on political advertising* (pp. 184–209). Carbondale: Southern Illinois University Press.

Kaid, L. L., & Johnston, A. (2001). *Videostyle in presidential campaigns: Style and content of televised political advertising.* Westport, CT: Praeger.

Massavetas, G. (1996). *Overthrow Mitsotakis* (in Greek). Athens: Evroekdotiki.

North, R. C., Holsti, O., Zanninovich, M. G., & Zinnes, D. A. (1963). *Content analysis: A handbook with applications for the study of international crisis.* Evanston, IL: Northwestern International Press.

Papathanassopoulos, S. (1990). Broadcasting politics and the state in socialist Greece. *Media, Culture & Society, 12*(3), 387–397.

Papathanassopoulos, S. (1993). *Liberating television* (in Greek). Athens: Kastaniotis.

Papathanassopoulos, S. (1997). *The power of television: The logic of the medium and the market* (in Greek). Athens: Kastaniotis.

Papathanassopoulos, S. (2000). Election campaigning in the television age: The case of contemporary Greece. *Political Communication, 17,* 47–60

Papathanassopoulos, S. (2001). The decline of newspapers: The case of the Greek press. *Journalism Studies, 2*(1), 109–123.

Parliamentary discussion on law 2429/96. (1996). In *Records of parliamentary proceedings* (p. 7319). Athens: Greek Parliament.

Popkin, S. L. (1997). Voter learning in the 1992 presidential campaign. In S. Iyengar &

R. Reeves (Eds.), *Do the media govern? Politicians, voters, and reporters in America* (pp.171–180). Thousand Oaks, CA: Sage.

Samaras, A. N. (1998). *Broadcasting deregulation and political communication in Greece: From party to media logic.* Unpublished doctoral thesis, University of Sussex, Brighton, U.K.

Samaras, A. N. (1999). Party-centered campaigns and the rise of political advertising spots in Greece. In L. L. Kaid (Ed.), *Television and politics in evolving European democracies* (pp. 187–206). Commack, NY: Nova Science.

Samaras, A. N. (2000, September). *The meta-communication discourse of polispots.* Paper presented at the Congress of British Political Studies Association "On Message: A Conference on Political Communication and Marketing," Loughborough, U.K.

Samaras, A. N. (2002). Political marketing, party-tocracy and the transformations of the political communications system. *Journal of Business and Society, 15*(1-2), 158–173.

Samaras, A. N. (2003). *Television political advertising: A quantitative research on Greece* (in Greek). Athens: IOM.

Shyles, L. (1983). Defining the issues of a presidential election from televised political spot advertisements. *Journal of Broadcasting, 27,* 333–343.

Shyles, L. (1991). Issue content and legitimacy in 1988 televised political advertising: Hubris and synecdoche in promoting presidential candidates. In F. Biocca (Ed.), *Television and political advertising. Vol. 2. Signs, codes and images* (pp. 133–162). Hillsdale, NJ: Erlbaum.

Wattenberg, M. P. (1991). *The rise of candidate centered politics.* Cambridge, MA: Harvard University Press.

Wattenberg, M. P. (1996). *The decline of American political parties 1952-1994.* Cambridge, MA: Harvard University Press.

West, M. D. (1993). *Air wars: Television advertising in election campaigns, 1952-1992.* Washington, DC: Congressional Quarterly Inc.

13

Sure to Come, But Temporarily Delayed

The Netherlands in Search of the Political Ad

KEES BRANTS

When uncertainty about the media's representation of politics grows, so do the need and desire of political parties to control and reduce it. Such is the situation in the Netherlands, where in the last decade the competition between media, an increasingly volatile electorate, and a rocked and shocked political culture has created an uncertain environment for political communication. Under such circumstances, the media are more driven by a need to reach as large a public as possible with as attractive and savvy a programme as the system allows for. "Mediademocracy," "mediatization," and "media logic" are all labels that have been attached to the new situation, but whatever the neologism, the traditionally consensual political system in the Netherlands and the remnants of corporatist "pillarization" (described later) have been virtually replaced by the contours of a more media- and performance-driven audience democracy (Manin, 1997).

The ubiquitous access that Dutch political parties used to have to the free publicity of public broadcasting and the public interest–oriented press is slowly giving way to a relationship of mistrust—parties and media are moving from symbiosis and respect to suspicion and struggle. Even though such a sketchy introduction might do violence to the much more intricate and complicated situation that is political communication in the Netherlands (described in more detail later), most political parties feel a growing urge to focus more on paid publicity, in which they have more control. At the same time, the political culture and the financial context do not seem to be ready for this. Election campaigns are still characterized by relative amateurism and low budgets, and public opinion seems to resist business and other sponsorship of political parties. Political advertising thus is caught up between a professional need and desire, on the one hand, and limited opportunities to realise this, on the other. Still, it is a reality waiting to happen.

THE CHANGING CONTEXT OF POLITICAL COMMUNICATION

The Netherlands, in the post–World War II period, has always been renowned for its specific form of consociational democracy. "Pillarization," "accommodation," and "pacification" were the labels for an arrangement of peaceful coexistence between disparate groups within a vertically segmented society living apart together in potentially conflictual "pillars" based on religion or ideology: Catholic, Protestant, socialist, and liberal-conservative. Although each of those pillars had their own separate associations (ranging from trade unions to the school system), as well as media and political parties, the elites of the different pillars pacified and accommodated potential conflict through often secret and usually invisible negotiation and compromise. The result was consensus and paternalism at the top and tolerance, or rather acceptance of each other's culture, at the bottom (Lijphart, 1968).

The media more or less formed the mouthpieces of the pillars' elites. They were partisan and more lap dog than watchdog in the process of political communication, fairly uncritically providing a platform for that information the social and political establishment wanted the rank and file to know. Although this was a relatively closed system, access for the elite to their own platform was easy because interlocking directorships between the political and the media elites guaranteed an open door. The media thus were part and parcel of the process of accommodation and pacification and so performed an integrating role within the pillar. The combination of pillarization and an internally focused political communication system also explains why the "rules of the consensus game" were accepted and internalised. Through the symbiotic (if somewhat one-sided) partisan

relationship, the media confirmed and reinforced, as well as justified, trust among the population at large that the coalition of parties in government was acting not on the basis of their partisan interests but in the interest of society as a whole.

As such, pillarization as a social and political system did not survive the "roaring sixties." Although it kept on resonating in the consensual and pragmatic political culture of "polder politics" (a complicated system of agreements and negotiations metaphorically defined by the Netherlands' complicated geographical relationship of land and sea) and "regulated tolerance" (hot potatoes such as prostitution and soft drugs kept on being criminalized, but for all practical purposes were not prosecuted), loyalty within the pillars, obedience to the political elite, the culture of secrecy, and the pedagogic paternalism all came under pressure. In the following decades, the landscape of government politics and media-political parallelism changed substantially. The electorate, especially the young, who were leaving the Catholic and Protestant churches in droves, began to float and to object to automatically copying their parents' political behaviour. Political parties could thus no longer count on the loyalty of a self-evident following but had to campaign for the vote. However, the unquestioned access to partisan media had begun to dwindle as well.

With the depillarization of the 1960s, the more or less closed political communication system disappeared as well. The media severed their direct links with political parties and distanced themselves from the intimate symbiosis and dependency these entailed. Journalism was emancipated and became an independent and critical profession but with a sense of coresponsibility for the well-being of the political system and the democratic process. The media identified no longer with a specific political party but with the public interest and thus began to address their readers, listeners, and viewers as citizens instead of as the "subjects" they had considered them in the paternalistic past. Michael Schudson (1999, pp. 119-120) has described this shift to a cultural pedagogic approach as a "trustee model," in which journalists provide the news they deem useful for the public to know so citizens can make sense of and fully participate in a complex democracy.

Toward a Media Logic

Determining the exact boundaries of a period is always difficult, if not impossible, but the end of media-critical depillarization was more or less heralded by two, historically rather different but in time (1989) coincident, occasions: the introduction of commercial television in the Netherlands and the fall of the Berlin wall. The first strengthened (or triggered) an increasing competition between media, and the second triggered (or accelerated) the decline in the importance of ideology as the cement that binds society and the political system. The waves were felt in politics, the media, and the public.

The relationship between political parties and the electorate, already loosened by depillarization, changed even more dramatically. At each election, voters now decide whether to turn out or not, and if so, what party to vote for. This creates tremendous uncertainty for political parties and how to plan coalition formation after the election. The choice for the voters is further complicated because parties position themselves more and more in the electoral centre, and the substantial difference between party manifestos and political stances has become blurred. Party loyalty thus decreases, and party membership has fallen to one of the lowest in Europe, creating a problem for the recruitment of parliamentarians, the employment of volunteers in the campaign, and the legitimacy of parties' claims to representation. At the same time, membership in single-issue movements, albeit often in the form of "checkbook activism," grew to one of

the highest in Europe. Until the turn of the 21st century, there were few indications that the idea of consensual democracy itself was not still regarded as the most suitable vehicle for Dutch sociopolitical arrangements; still, the need for campaigning and for personalization grew.

The consequences in the media of a growing competition (at the beginning of 1988 there were only two public TV channels, but at the beginning of 2005 there were three, plus around eight national commercial channels) is a development toward what Altheide and Snow (1979) have dubbed "media logic." Under such circumstances, the content and kind of news is decided by the frame of reference through which media make sense of facts and people. In such a commercialization-driven logic, media identify less with the public interest than with what the public is interested in or enjoys watching. Out go the readers, listeners, and viewers; in come the media consumers. Journalists become central performers who combine a critical stance with informing as well as entertaining their audience. They interpret and frame what goes on in an election campaign on the basis of what they assume the strategies of politicians and parties are—on the basis of the conflicts and scandals that make the election attractive and the news more saleable. Research in the United States claims that such political reporting often results in a spiral of cynicism, media malaise, and a politically cynical and turned-off voter (Cappella & Jamieson, 1997; Patterson, 1993; but for a European critique, see Newton, 1999; Norris, 2000). Although media do not (yet) set the campaign agenda in the Netherlands and a spiral of cynicism has not been observed, research does show declining substance in media reporting in the last election campaigns (especially in commercial television and the press), increasing journalistic dominance, and specific conflict and strategy framing (Brants & Van Praag, 2005). The uncertainty about how commercialised media will portray the party, politicians, and politics outside and during the election campaign is a drive toward controlled communication.

Finally, there are changes with the public, where we can see an increased individualization and fragmentation. The first is characterised by a consumer orientation in which the government is paradoxically expected to keep its distance but at the same time solve the ills of a society at risk and respond more to individual demands. Political performance is also increasingly judged on the basis of the question "What's in it for me?" At the same time, media audiences become more and more fragmented. Young people especially, with the remote control in hand, surf in search of pleasure and satisfaction, often avoiding political content. Moreover, where a single exposure in the main TV news would have been enough some 15 years ago, to reach their electorate now, political parties need the stage of every channel and each programme in which they can possibly appear. With such changes in the electorate, media strategies become a necessity for political parties.

Dead Man Talking

Perhaps even more dramatic than these structural changes was the appearance in mid-2001 of populist politician Pim Fortuyn, who openly and loudly criticised the political elite and consensual Dutch politics, introducing an adversarial tone, style, and culture that until then had been considered anathema in the Netherlands. He focused particularly on the questions of asylum, immigration, and integration, blaming the government for too lenient a policy and successfully linking a generally felt sense of insecurity with both anti-immigration discourse and the "back-room" politics of the political establishment. His outspoken naming and blaming, the blunt language he used, the antiestablishment sentiments he professed in his debates with other vested politicians, his alignment with the assumed plight of the ordinary people, all

made him an instant, although controversial, success. He combined his populist appeal with a lavishly stylish appearance and an openly gay and nonconformist lifestyle.

Fortuyn was murdered 9 days before the parliamentary elections in May 2002. Huge and emotional demonstrations followed. The "people's voice" was gone, and what the media described as "an outpouring of national grief" was reflected in the election result: The party that was named after him (Lijst Pim Fortuyn, or LPF) became the second party in the land, close on the heels of the Christen Democratisch Appèl (Christian Democrats; CDA). It was as if the dead man were still talking. Although the subsequent cabinet in which the LPF participated fell within 100 days of the elections and the party was subsequently decimated in the elections of 2003, negative campaigning was no longer considered "not done" in Dutch political culture. During the election campaign, vested party leaders called each other liars, and a generally more negative tone seemed to characterise political communication.

Declining trust in political institutions, increasing numbers of floating voters, and growing importance of personal and performance characteristics as a measure of success are all favourable prerequisites for negative campaigning, a rougher campaign culture, and the use of more elaborate forms of controlled communication.

A Slowly Changing Campaign Culture

Until 2002, campaigns in the Netherlands could be described as dull, amateurish, and cheap (Van Praag, 2005). Political parties "fought" each other using a rather businesslike tone, which excluded personal attacks and, certainly, attempts at character murder. Politicians kept their private life to themselves, and journalists generally respected that. There had been exceptions, such as the elections of 1956, when the Partij van de Arbeid (labour party; PvdA), whose symbol is a red rooster, seemed to do well in the Catholic south of the country, which led to drastic reactions. The Katholieke Volkspartij (Catholic people's party; KVP), published a pamphlet with illustrations of their own pillarized institutions (school, hospital, the broadcasting organization KRO) on fire. The suggestive caption read "When the red rooster cries victory." Audio cables were cut during the campaign, PvdA members covered a church altar with posters, and the Social Democratic newspaper opened with a labour minister accusing the KVP of lying and using "Goebbels' methods" (Van Praag, 2005); certainly this was 10 years after the war, but even now that would be considered the ultimate insult.

The year 1956 was unusual, definitively within the consensual period of pillarization. Pim Fortuyn revived memories of that campaign. His strategy in 2002 was to attack the political establishment wherever and as hard as he could; this often included vested political journalists as well. In an almost sadomasochistic reaction, even when insulted, the media were even more attracted by these techniques. Fortuyn also practised the old feminist creed of "the personal is political." He invited the cameras into his house, combining his charismatic style with extreme openness (when asked what he knew about the criminal tendencies of young Moroccans, he jokingly answered: "Everything; I sleep with them") and lavish dandyism: a Bentley, two cuddly dogs in the front seat next to the chauffeur, and a huge and very expensive house. Although the election campaign of 2003 was of a different tone, there are clear indications that politicians more easily used the attack mode, calling each other liars if only because it guaranteed media exposure.

The amateurism in the election campaigns had already begun to change in 1994, when for the first time PvdA employed a (part-time) researcher and the CDA modernised and personalised its campaign, focusing on the performance of its leader and employing a media strategy that included the gossip press as much as the traditional serious media. Since then, electoral research and a carefully considered media strategy are part of each party's campaign. Such professionalization, however, is not more than a hesitant attempt to join the league of modern democracies. Few countries have campaigns that are so short (usually not more than 3 weeks), still so relatively businesslike, and so much an internal party affair: campaign managers, media strategists, and even researchers are all loyal party members and are rarely hired from the world of campaign professionals.

There are cultural and historical reasons for that (pillarization combined with an antipropaganda tradition) but also a financial one. Political parties have, or at least spend, little money for campaigning. Put differently: Campaigns in the Netherlands are relatively cheap. In the 1990s, the political parties combined spent less than 50 Eurocents per voter, with only PvdA using more than a million. There is no money for expensive advertising campaigns, as almost all of it must come from the party itself; around 40% of the campaign budget goes to paid publicity. That was never considered a real problem, because access to the channels that gave free publicity was usually easy. The first impression was that Pim Fortuyn would change all that. He announced that he had raised €3.5 million, mostly from property developers, but that money never seemed to materialise. The campaign of 2002 was certainly more expensive than that of 1998 (€7.8 million, or 65 Eurocents per voter), but it never reached the expected high. After Fortuyn was killed, 9 days before the election, the political parties agreed to stop campaigning, although they had planned to invest most in the last week. With the elections of 2003 less than a year later, the party budgets were hardly up to scratch, making that election more than €1 million cheaper than that of the year before.

A SHORT HISTORY
OF THE PARTY SPOT

Political broadcasts, based on a system of proportionality and sponsored by government money, have existed on radio since 1925 (Brants, 1995). The 1959 elections saw the first experimental TV spots: 10 minutes freely allocated twice to each political party regardless of electoral support. In 1962, party broadcasts were officially introduced when the government claimed regular time for the political parties on what was then the only TV channel. Party political broadcasting thus became part of the information function of public service broadcasting.

With television reasonably well established at the beginning of the 1960s, weekly political broadcasts were introduced, alternating so that each party would have about five 10-minute programmes per year. Parties represented in Parliament had equal time as a matter of principle; and in the weeks prior to national elections, parties with candidates in all electoral districts (often amounting to more than 20 different parties) were also allowed a 10-minute slot twice. Studio and camera facilities were freely provided by the public broadcaster NTS (later NOS), and the government subsidized the 10-minute programmes with Dfl 400 (€181) each. This system has remained virtually intact, with a few not unimportant differences. The government subsidy has been raised over the years, to €15,375 in 2003; with three public channels, political parties were allowed some 20 broadcasts per year, plus an extra six in the last 2 weeks of an election campaign; and the length of the broadcasts has been reduced to 3 minutes each, which make them somewhat comparable to a "real" political ad, or halfway between a spot ad and an informercial.

In the pillarized system, and even when, after the 1960s, the link between political parties and broadcasting organisations was severed, these political broadcasts were considered an extravagant, even unnecessary luxury. There are enough public broadcasting channels that have felt not only the need to inform the viewers but also to offer parties and politicians a stage from which to address (in journalistic interviews, but still) the electorate. Because there are no legal limitations on content or on (extra) money spent, this free time still occupies a marginal position in the campaign strategies of the political parties. Even during the European elections, which are usually reported in a relatively low-key style (and the campaign thus could do with some extra publicity), the same opportunity for party political broadcasts is gracefully but uninterestedly accepted. One should not look a gift horse in the mouth, as the saying goes.

The coming of commercial television in 1989 was expected to change all that, but it was more than 10 years before the change materialised. Shortly before the 1998 elections, SBS6, a commercial broadcaster, and STER, the noncommercial foundation that broadcasts blocks of advertisements on the three public channels, decided to open up their channels for political advertising. Coming from SBS, this was no surprise, but it was greatly surprising coming from STER, which had to change its own rules, which originally did not allow political advertising. Already in 1994 the larger commercial channel RTL had decided against political ads. It was afraid the other advertisers might not like to be next to party spots, and the channel was afraid to lose its neutral image if only a few parties advertised. In 1998, RTL still did not offer political advertising, but in 2002 it changed its mind.

Because the decision to allow political advertising was made at such a late stage, only two parties—Democraten 66 (liberal democrat; D66) and Socialistische Partij (socialist; SP)—jumped on board; the others did not want to change their campaign budget. D66 was a surprise, because in prior discussions it had always objected to introducing political advertising in the election campaign. One reason it saw to change its mind was that it, correctly, saw a publicity spinoff if it did. The liberal democrats spent just over €80,000 (15% of their campaign budget) on a 15-second spot that was broadcast 47 times. SP's choice was considered amazing: Radical socialism and commercialisation were not expected to mix that well. However, already in 1989, the socialists had been the first to advertise on radio and in 1994, on local TV. In 1998, they spent €33,000 on TV ads.

After this hesitant start, it was expected that in 2002, political advertising would be seen as a normal part of electoral communication—normal, but not without mixed feelings. When Pim Fortuyn announced that he would use most of his €3.5 million budget for political advertising, the other parties not only got nervous but accused the populist politician of introducing unwelcome influence in the campaign from "organised interests." The social democrats, who at the time were doing well in the polls, proposed to ban external funding and purchasing of advertising slots, but the others would only agree that transparency as to who receives how much from whom was desirable. A government regulation to that effect was more or less promised, but as of 2005 it had not materialised. Political parties and pressure groups are free to purchase advertising time and, within the limits of the law, there are no restrictions as to ads' content or format.

In spite of the initial discussions, all 10 (serious) election contenders reserved some 40% of their campaign budgets, or €3 million, for TV advertising. SP was the frontrunner (€400,000), but the Social Democrats, Christian Democrats, Liberal Democrats, and Liberals also had substantial budgets. The LPF, Pim Fortuyn's party, in the end professed to no more than a mere €238,000. Most parties invested also in radio advertising, especially with music channels, which could give access to that most treasured of species: the young voter. Unlike radio ads, TV spots are usually expensive, especially when continually repeated. The cost of purchasing TV advertising time, however, is dependent not only on the number of ads and repeats but on the time of broadcast and the (expected) audience ratings. The cheapest transmission was recorded by LPF (€27.50), but this was in the middle of the night, just before a home shopping programme. An average 15-second ad, a one-off at prime time, costs a minimum of € 5000.

A substantial part of the advertising budget of the parties in 2002 was never spent. Fortuyn's murder and the subsequent silencing of the election campaign meant that many political ads, most of which had been planned for the last 10 days, were never shown. The new elections, 8 months later, in January 2003, gave a similar picture. Organisationally and financially they came too soon for most parties. Several parties decided against TV ads. PvdA limited itself to local stations. Only SP, the Volkspartij voor Vrijheid en Democratie (People's Party for Freedom and Democracy; VVD), and LPF did advertise, and so, for the first time, did the Christian Union, which had previously had religious objections to advertising. The money spent by all parties on TV advertising in the end totalled 2.4 million.

THE CONTENT OF PARTY BROADCASTS AND POLITICAL ADS

Because of the aborted campaign in 2002 and the financial reluctance of the parties in 2003, political advertising remained in its infancy. In describing the content of and trends in spots, we will thus focus mainly on party political broadcasts, which have a long tradition. Where possible, information about party ads will be presented, but they are too recent for us to present a longitudinal picture of them, and there were too few in the 2002 and 2003 elections for us to present quantified data on them.

The first party spots in the 1960s—that is, of what still exists in the archives or what

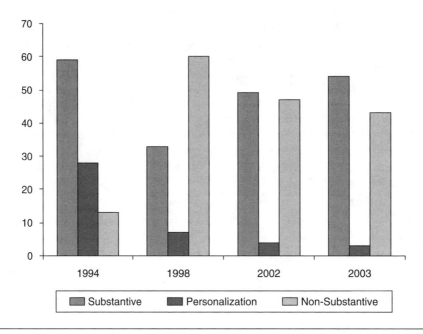

Figure 13.1   Content of Party Political Broadcasts in the Netherlands

observers at the time can remember—were generally dull and more a form of visual radio: talking heads, sitting behind a table on which a vase with flowers tried to indicate colour in a black and white picture, the politician nervously looking in and around the camera, unfamiliar and uncomfortable with the new medium. It was more like Dutch uncles preaching to their own parish. Whenever there was a reference to other parties, the tone could be critical but was seldom attacking. In general, one addressed one's own electorate; if other denominations watched, that was fine. Sometimes documentary film was used to convince the electorate about the seriousness of politics and the party's awareness of postwar issues such as housing shortages and the Cold War. The Catholic KVP filmed a short series of staged allegories, using fictional elements to dramatise the issues they wanted to portray.

In the 1970s and early 1980s, the focus in party broadcasting was cognitive, with the type of content depending partly on the time of broadcasting. Spots at election time had a more propagandistic function, promoting the

party's manifesto issues and its slogan. In the period between elections spots were more informative, carrying views on issues of that moment. Interviews by journalists were sometimes used to overcome the credibility problem most party political broadcasts have with the viewers, but often the TV journalists were still associated with the party's pillar.

Analysing the broadcasts of the four main parties (CDA, PvdA, VVD, and D66) over a period of 10 years and four elections, we see a rather fluctuating picture as to the level of informative content and the substantiveness of the message communicated (see Figure 13.1). In 1994, just under 60% of the spots focused on the issues the different parties deemed important and their stands and positions on them. In 1998 this percentage was almost halved, only to return to around 50% in the following two elections. It should be noted, however, that issues in the spots are usually not discussed and solutions not presented— mentioning them is the most parties normally do. It is probably not surprising that the party ads in 2002 had less informative content than

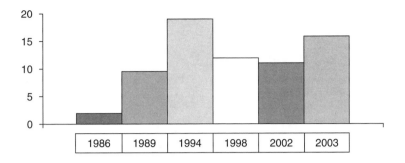

Figure 13.2   Number of Shots per Minute in Netherlands Party Broadcasts

the party political broadcasts, although half a year later, both have equal amounts.

The relative substantiveness of the political broadcasts does not mean that the emphasis lies on the personal (nice, kind) and political (expertise, a real leader) qualities of the candidate or the qualities of the party in terms of style (reliable, helpful). With the exception of 1994, the Big Four focus on content, although the text of the broadcasts is neither informative nor image oriented. The political ads show the same picture. The personal qualities of the politician are (still) rarely displayed in this form of controlled communication. The big exception in 1994 was the party broadcast of the eventual prime minister Wim Kok, who "suffered" from a cold and not very social image. The party attempted to warm it up by showing the Social Democratic Party leader walking, arm in arm with his wife, along the streets of the town of his birth, telling about his poor background and hard-working father and how family and solidarity had always been the leading lights in his life.

The polarised campaign of 2002 did not result in more negative campaigning in controlled publicity. In that year, Pim Fortuyn and CDA strongly criticized the parties that had formed the government for years, but it was only parties and not politicians that received the wrath of the populist politician or that of the prime minister to be, Peter Balkenende. To show how exceptional negative advertising is, in 1994, VVD had openly and strongly criticized

the labour party and the Christian Democrats, mentioning and showing specific ministers. A subsequent study showed that that was the only spot that year that most viewers disliked (Boer, Brants, Neijens, & van de Weyer, 1995). Parties in Dutch political culture have always been very hesitant to use negative campaigning. If the elections of 2003 are anything to go by, we do not see that controlled communication has entered a new, adversarial era. Only PvdA, in its political broadcast, and LPF, in its party ad, showed a negative tone that year.

The Relative Modernity of the Spot

Looking at the picture and format aspects of party broadcasts—how much they resemble modern advertising and videoclips or, more, the traditional "talking head"—we see some indication of modernity, but not across the board (Blanksma & Brants, 2005). The clearest development is the faster pace, as shown by the number of shots and changes of pictures per minute (see Figure 13.2). The upswing, which made the spot look more like an advertisement, coincided with the introduction of commercial television and particularly with the shortening of the broadcasts from 10 to 2 and 5 minutes (later to 3 minutes). The comparison, over a period of almost 20 years, based on the four main parties (CDA, PvdA, VVD, and D66) and giving averaged data, indicates that after 1994 there was a relative

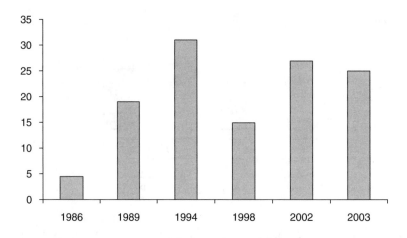

Figure 13.3   Music in Party Broadcasts in the Netherlands (%)

return to the old, somewhat slower pace. Looking at the 15-second ads in 2002 and 2003, however, we can clearly see the influence of general advertising: In both years, the number of shots was 25 per minute, making the political ad almost twice as fast as the party political broadcast.

Another indication of modernity is the use of music in the spot. In the 1960s and 1970s, the party political broadcasts were predominantly text based, although under the text music could be heard (Brants, 1995). In the course of the 1980s and beyond, we see an increase of music as the only means of communication in the spot (see Figure 13.3), although 1998 shows a dip again. The CDA spot of 1993 is notorious: Half a year before the elections, when the then-leader Lubbers handed over the party leadership to his successor Brinkman, the succession is filmed in slow motion, with revolving camera and blue filter, and the communication is totally nonverbal. The viewer hears only Neil Diamond's "One by One, Two by Two." In 2002 there are two notable extremes, showing, in near-ideal types of these styles, the traditional talking head and the modern videoclip: on the one hand, the SP spot (a 15-second version was used as political ad), which was filled with Dutch pop musicians who sang to a cheering audience in a bus

about the evils of the Cabinet; on the other hand, LPF, in which Pim Fortuyn was filmed addressing a conference, followed by two other LPF candidates who talked about their ideas. The modern populist party was clearly not ready for a modern party broadcast. The few political ads hardly differ in their use of music.

Looking at the form and filmic aspects of the recent party political broadcasts and, to a lesser extent, of the political ads, we can distinguish three stylistic formats. First is the *documentary* style, which is most popular with the parties. The leader is followed by the camera, sometimes in a fly-on-the-wall style, or interviewed by a respectable journalist, and tells about his or her worries and ideas. This format was first used by D66, when, in a *nouvelle vague* style, the young and charismatic party leader was filmed walking along Amsterdam's canals and driving a car, explaining in a voiceover the Democrats' solutions to the problems of the day. This format is also linked to the more substantive spot. Second, there is the *feature film* format. This was used by the Catholic KVP in the 1960s, but we rarely see it now. In 1989, filmmaker Theo van Gogh (who was killed by a Muslim fanatic in 2004) shot the PvdA spot, and in 2002, he proposed to do the same for LPF.

Pim Fortuyn refused, as Van Gogh wanted him to play an immam in a djellaba. In 2003, LPF did use the feature format: A woman is mugged in the street and a man, coming to her aid, is attacked (the voiceover says: "To raise your voice, you need guts").

Finally, there is the *videoclip* format, which is increasing in popularity. The pop singer in the SP spot (used in both 2002 and 2003, and extracts of it were used in the political ads) is the most obvious example. In 2003, the Christian Democrats applied split-screen techniques, VVD used a shaking camera and blue filter, and the Green Left party mixed colour with black and white and low-pixel pictures. This format is usually, although not always, linked to the personal and image aspects of political advertising.

The Disappearing Audience

Available data at the time indicate that in the early stages of party political broadcasting, nearly half of those with a television set—particularly the old and the less educated—watched. When there was only one channel, high scores could usually be explained by preceding or following popular programmes, such as news, feature films, or televised soccer matches. Whether people actually watched could not be detected by the rating techniques at the time, but even the political parties doubted the validity of the figures.

It seemed that it was the novelty of it that attracted the wide audience, because they did not stay long. Between 1963 and 1968 the ratings dropped from 43% to 26% (when a second channel was introduced), a steady decline that only continued in the following decades. In the multichannel reality that was established in the 1990s, audience ratings were around 2%, or some 250,000 viewers. Contrary to the picture of parties preaching for their own parish, however, research seems to indicate that parties reach beyond their loyal electorate, albeit mostly to viewers

with a high interest in politics. With three public and eight Dutch-language commercial channels—not to mention another 20 foreign, local, and special-interest channels—the audience these days is extremely fragmented, a situation that will get worse with the (further) introduction of digital television, the Internet, and multiapplication mobile phones. In 2002 and 2003, the ratings for party political broadcasts averaged 1% and 1.9%, respectively. There are moments that viewers can, by way of speaking, be counted on the fingers of one hand; at other times, a rise to 5% or more can be detected. This is dependent on the programme in the vicinity of which the party broadcast is scheduled, something the political parties have no say in. The regulator *Commissariaat voor de Media* decides the timing by lottery.

With political advertising, the parties can choose to the minute the time their ads will be aired, allowing them to target specific groups of viewers (the young watching a music programme; housewives watching a coffee show), even if high ratings do cost more. Compared to the party broadcasts, the ads hardly present a shinier picture. In 2003 the ratings for LPF, SP, and VVD averaged 1.3, 2.7, and 3.7, respectively. The Dutch national voters study, however, which measured the cumulative reach of all broadcasts as reported by the respondents, seemed to suggest that by the end of the campaign, more than half of the Dutch electorate had seen at least one party spot (Blanksma & Brants, 2005).

In light of the growing antipathy to programme-interrupting ads and advertising in general, the appreciation for the party political broadcasts and party ads is surprising (see Table 13.1; 1998 data are based on six and 2002 data on seven parties). Around a third of the viewers seem to like the spots, and only 14% consider them bad. The majority is clearly more moderate in its opinion. There are substantial differences between parties: In 2002, the LPF spot was clearly appreciated

Table 13.1 Appreciation of Party Broadcasts and Ads in the Netherlands (%)

Rating	1998	2002
Good	33	31
Moderate or reasonable	53	55
Bad	14	14

SOURCE: Irwin, van Holsteyn, and De Ridder (2005).

(46%), and in 1998, PvdA (47%) stood out (Blanksma & Brants, 2005, p. 191).

What to Expect Next

The need for a strategic and controlled form and style of political communication seems evident and irresistible. Political journalism is adhering more to a media logic than to a professional approach of substantive reporting about the ins and outs of parties' campaigns during an election. Voters increasingly are floating, exchanging traditional loyalty for a more consumerlike approach. Young voters especially, who are "audiovisually fragmented," are turning away from politics and political information altogether. New political parties come and go rapidly and are less moulded by a consensual political culture.

One might thus have expected a grateful continuation of that cheap means of communication, the party political broadcast, and an intensifying focus on political ads. The content of the latter especially would have reflected the changes in political culture and style, emphasizing more the personalities in the campaign than the issues and party stands. In a style more resembling the video clip than the serious talking head, changes in content and format would be particularly likely to attract the politically less interested youth. The unusual and exciting election campaigns of 2002 and 2003 saw only a glimmer of all that. With both the party broadcasts and the advertising spots, personalization was minimal, the style

fairly traditional, and the viewers far and few between and not very appreciative.

There are at least two reasons for the parties' reluctance to use paid political advertising. First, the domain of free publicity is still seen as the place where voters can be convinced and won. Unlike paid publicity, news is considered by the viewers as more reliable—not the intended propaganda of the political party, but the result of independent professional journalism. Even with critical and framing journalists, political parties deem news and current affairs programmes more relevant stages. Moreover, the public and private broadcasters also have talk shows with a possibly less-critical interviewer and with a large and, one can hope, open-minded audience. Second, in spite of the midnight bargains, political advertising is costly, and the political parties in the Netherlands (still) do not have the money for as much as they need. In the United States, if more than two thirds of the campaign budget of a presidential candidate is spent on TV advertising, that still leaves dozens of millions for other necessary expenses, such as research and staff. A simple cost-benefit analysis has taught the Dutch party pundits that money spent on very small percentages of audiences (viewers who might also use those advertising minutes to do other things) is not necessarily money well spent.

Moreover, political parties have a new alternative: the Internet. In the 2002 and 2003 elections, all parties had party and candidate Web sites, and many leaders and candidates had their own blogs, in which they philosophized about what they would do, once elected, and what disasters might happen if they were not. Controlled communication on the Internet turned out to be much more personalised than other forms of communication. All sites also were well visited, especially by the young (Voerman & Boogers, 2005). Internet advertising is an opportunity still to be used by political parties, but resistance to banner ads might well be a reason to stick to the good old Web site. A new medium to be discovered here might well be the mobile phone. Young people nowadays spend more time in front of the computer screen and the mobile phone display than they do in front of the TV set.

In spite of the alternatives and the reluctance, political parties could have a good reason for turning to TV ads: Other means of controlled communication are dwindling. The party poster in the window—the traditional street sight in cities, towns, and villages—has virtually disappeared; folders, especially those aimed at target groups, are far and few between; billboards have always been rather unusual in the Dutch campaign landscape; the full page, last-day ad in national newspapers is now rarely used; and the cheap radio ad leaves political parties with money to spare. However, production costs for the TV ad, the endless repeats for impact, and the preference for prime time are bound to have a price-pushing effect on limited party budgets. It may be a price too high for the political ad to break through, or it may be an extra push for the parties to find other sources that will professionalize the election campaign.

REFERENCES

Altheide, D., & Snow, R. (1979). *Media logic.* Beverly Hills, CA: Sage.

Blanksma, A., & Brants, K. (2005). De uitgestelde doorbraak van de politieke spot [The delayed coming of the political ad]. In K. Brants & Ph. van Praag (Eds.), *Verkoop van de politiek. De verkiezingscampagne van 1994* [Selling politics: The election campaign of 1994] (pp. 173–195). Amsterdam, Holland: Het Spinhuis.

Boer, D. den, Brants, K., Neijens, P., & van de Weyer, B. (1995). Politieke communicatie in een plaspauze [Political communication during a sanitary stop]. In K. Brants & Ph. Van Praag (Eds.), *Verkoop van de politiek. De verkiezingscampagne van 1994* [Selling politics: The election campaign of 1994] (pp. 193–209). Amsterdam, Holland: Het Spinhuis.

Brants, K. (1995). The blank spot: Political advertising in the Netherlands. In L. L. Kaid & C. Holtz-Bacha (Eds.), *Political advertising in Western democracies* (pp. 143–161). Thousand Oaks, CA: Sage.

Brants, K., & Van Praag, Ph. (Eds.). (2005). *Politiek en media in verwarring. De verkiezingscampagnes in het lange jaar 2002* [Politics and media in confusion: The election campaigns in the long year 2002]. Amsterdam, Holland: Het Spinhuis.

Cappella, J., & Jamieson, K. (1997). *Spiral of cynicism: The press and the public good.* New York: Oxford University Press.

Irwin, G., van Holsteyn, J., & De Ridder, J. (2005). *Dutch parliamentary election studies 2002, 2003.* Amsterdam, Holland: Rozenberg.

Lijphart, A. (1968). *The politics of accommodation: Pluralism and democracy in the Netherlands.* Berkeley: University of California Press.

Manin, R. (1997). *The principles of representative government.* Cambridge, England: Cambridge University Press.

Newton, K. (1999). Mass media effects: Mobilization or media malaise? *British Journal of Political Science, 29*(4), 577–599.

Norris, P. (2000). *A virtuous circle: Political communication in postindustrial societies.* Cambridge, England: Cambridge University Press.

Patterson, T. (1993). *Out of order.* New York: Knopf.

Schudson, M. (1999). What public journalism knows about journalism but doesn't know about "public." In T. Glasser (Ed.), *The idea of public journalism* (pp. 118–134). New York: Guildford.

Van Praag, Ph. (2005). De veranderende Nederlandse campagnecultuur [The changing Dutch campaign culture]. In K. Brants & Ph. Van Praag (Eds.), *Verkoop van de politiek. De verkiezingscampagne van 1994* [Selling politics: The election campaign of 1994] (pp. 21–44). Amsterdam, Holland: Het Spinhuis.

Voerman, G., & Boogers, M. (2005) Digitaal informeren en personaliseren [Digital information and personalisation]. In K. Brants & Ph. Van Praag (Eds.), *Verkoop van de politiek. De verkiezingscampagne van 1994* [Selling politics: The election campaign of 1994] (pp.195–218). Amsterdam, Holland: Het Spinhuis.

14

TV Political Advertising in Italy

When Politicians Are Afraid

GIANPIETRO MAZZOLENI

For more than a decade, Italy's political and electoral communication has been deeply marked by the presence in government and in active politics of a media mogul that epitomizes in himself the world of marketing and advertising: Silvio Berlusconi. In the domestic collective imagery, he represents the icon of "going commercial" in the television industry, as well as in the lifestyle of millions of Italians. After all, he was the one who, in the early 1980s, changed the nature of broadcasting and radically transformed the TV consumption patterns of the national audience. A deluge of advertising invaded the private TV channels, thus reinforcing the impression that commercial breaks that interrupted films, series, shows, and so on were the symbols of the newly born commercial television—of which Silvio Berlusconi was the master and commander.

The inauguration of commercial television occurred in coincidence with a parallel process that interested the political arena as well: the commercialization of political communication.

According to some analyses (Mazzoleni, 1992), it was not just a matter of coincidence, because the phenomena could be spotted also in other national contexts and had been described as "Americanization" of political communication. In Italy, the commercial drift of political communication received a big thrust from commercial television. By making its space and technology available to politicians and political candidates, commercial television served as a huge "gym" in which to train new office seekers, imposed new language schemes on traditional political and electoral discourse, and simply made it easy for candidates and parties to disseminate their messages.

The concept of "mediatization" is strictly connected with the process of commercialization (Mazzoleni & Schulz, 1999). Indeed, in Italy there was a rapid and strong transition to mediatized forms of communicating politics and even of doing politics, especially after the media tycoon himself stepped into the political fray.

241

All this notwithstanding, Italy's politics and political communication cannot be reduced to a concert of commercial messages. Hard politics is still performed in the "old," Machiavellian ways, often behind the scenes of the political spectacle. A lot of political communication focuses sharply on real, and often dramatic, issues that divide the nation's public opinion. Still, campaigns turn easily into pageantry, giving in to the most trite commercial, show-biz imperatives. The "Berlusconi factor" is critical in all this: The tycoon is one of the wealthiest entrepreneurs in Europe, owns a media empire of three successful television networks and the largest publishing house in the country, and controls the flow of domestic advertising spending. In a word, Berlusconi is a political competitor who can rely on enormous financial and organizational resources that no adversary can match.

Berlusconi has used his resources lavishly in all of the campaigns since he entered the political arena in 1994, and, apart from the general election of 1996, he has scored a series of clear-cut electoral successes (Mazzoleni, 2004). Berlusconi's communication resources soon became a source of anxiety for his opponents. The political forces of the Center-Left Coalition took advantage of being in power in 2000 to pass restrictive legislation that required the media to achieve "equal treatment" of all competitors in election campaigns. This is the legislation described in the following pages.

OVERVIEW OF THE POLITICAL AND MEDIA SYSTEMS IN ITALY

The Political System

Understanding the Berlusconi factor is pivotal to the understanding of the Italian political system and its peculiar dynamics. Berlusconi is the product of radical changes in the domestic political marketplace and at the same time the most relevant actor; he affects both the nation's life (whether he is in power or in the opposition) and the strategies of his adversaries (competitors).

The turning point for the Italian political system can be traced back to the early 1990s, when the fall of the Berlin wall represented also the shattering of long-lasting balances in the domestic political arena. For four decades, the pure, proportional system allowed the coexistence of a large Christian Democratic party (Democrazia Cristiana; DC), which maintained power for the entire period; several smaller satellite parties that were long allied with the DC, and Western Europe's largest Communist Party, which never succeeded in seizing power (mostly because of the Cold War ban on communists in the West).

This rigid scheme, which privileged the governing coalition parties and, to some extent, made them untouchable, thanks to their being shields against "the communist threat," allowed a sort of impunity for the several cases of corruption and worked until 1992, when a pool of prosecutors from Milan started to investigate political corruption. It was the beginning of the flood. For more than a year, all top politicians that had governed the country and had occupied the political stage for decades, one after the other, were incriminated in several charges of corruption, primarily for illegal funding of their political parties. Such corruption had been a tolerated practice for a long time but clearly was no longer acceptable when the parties' task of containing communism was done. In the same period, in the media, there was a mounting antiparty campaign against the "old political class" and a rising demand for a broad revision of the rules and players of the political game. A referendum showed that Italian public opinion supported the switch to a plurality (majoritarian system), as voters assumed that the proportional voting system had been a source of coalition and government instability and an alibi for corrupt practices.

In 1993, Parliament passed the electoral reform that introduced a mixed system: 75%

pluralist, 25% proportional. "The change in the electoral system came at a moment of crisis and of significant transformation in the political system, marking such a major break with the past that observers spoke of a transition to a 'Second Republic'" (Perrucci & Villa, 2004, p. 4). A similar reform, geared to giving more power to the mayors in city elections, was introduced and immediately applied in 1993, with strong approval from the voters. The reform of the parliamentary and mayoral elections was indeed a revolution in traditional domestic political customs, as it privileged performance over ideological patterns in the voters' assessment of candidates.

The reforms touched upon the electoral dimensions of politics but left largely untouched the existing political institutions, in spite of a strong wave of Italian public opinion that pushed in the direction of a broader change at all levels. An attempt to change some articles of the Constitution failed in the mid-1990s, and thus the Italian Republic is still headed by a president elected by and in Parliament, Parliament has a Chamber of Deputies with 630 seats and a Senate with 330 seats, and the prime minister is not elected directly by the voters but selected by Parliament. Italy has 20 regions with their own presidents, governments, and regional parliaments, elected every 5 years.

However, the most tangible and dazzling effect of the electoral reforms was to take place in the general election of 1994. Because of the vast empty space in the political system left by the old, prereform political party system, there was plenty of room for new entries. On the left side of the political spectrum, the Communist Party had changed its name (it is now the Democratic Party of the Left]) and converted to pluralist democracy; on the right, the ex-neofascists also changed their name and outlook (they are now the Alleanza Nazionale [National Alliance]). Astonishingly, at the center, there was no new power, as the former Christian Democrats and Socialist Democrats

were still in disarray. Suddenly, in January 1994, only 3 months before election day, Silvio Berlusconi launched a brand-new party, Forza Italia, through a bombardment of TV commercials in which he marketed the new political force and presented himself as the "architect of a new Italian miracle." He appealed to the voters of the center, who had remained anchorless following the crumbling of the Christian Democrats' regime. Three months later, at the ballot box, Berlusconi, who had invented himself as a politician and created a new party from scratch, scored an unexpected electoral success and eventually was appointed prime minister.

The shockwaves of such an event in the Italian political system are still palpable after a decade, as this political earthquake was not simply unexpected but hardly plausible, in terms of political analysis. In other words, no commentator would have thought such a dramatic change was possible in so short a time. The critics pointed to Berlusconi's media power, and to a certain extent that helped him in launching his own party, but other systemic reasons were later taken into account to explain the electoral victory, such as the tycoon's ability to address the center (i.e., the moderate voters) and to make alliances with the new right and the neopopulist and antipolitical Northern League. The Berlusconi cabinet did not last long, due to conflicts within his coalition. Nevertheless, Berlusconi's electoral performance demonstrated that in the new electoral system, a polarization of the voting dynamics on the axis of center-right versus center-left is possible, and this permitted the inauguration of the "alternation" between coalitions. As a matter of fact, in the subsequent elections, in 1996, it was the center-left who gained power and, in 2001, the center-right again. Political analysts (Itanes, 2001) have welcomed this true novelty in a political system that had been famous for its incredible instability (Italy had had about 50 governments in 45 years).

Table 14.1   Political Parties in Italy: Chamber of Deputies (Proportional Vote, 2001)

Party	Number of Votes (Proportional)	%
Forza Italia	10,923,146	29.4
Alleanza Nazionale	4,459,397	12.0
CCD-CDU	1,193,643	3.2
Lega Nord	1,461,854	3.9
Nuovo PSI	352,853	1.0
Other minor	26,951	0.1
Total center right	18,417,844	49.6
DS	6,147,624	16.6
Margherita	5,386,950	14.5
Girasole	804,488	2.2
Comunisti Italiani	619,912	1.7
Other minor	33,313	0.1
Total center left	12,992,287	35.0
Rifondazione Comunista	1,868,113	5.0
Democrazia Europea	887,037	2.4
Lista Di Pietro	1,443,271	3.9
Pannella-Bonino	831,199	2.2
Fiamma Tricolore	142,894	0.4
Other minor	518,179	1.4
Total chamber of deputies	37,100,824	100.0

SOURCE: Data provided by the Ministero dell'Interno.

The map of the Italian parties represented in Parliament since the last general election (2001) appears in Table 14.1.

The Media System

It may seem surprising that presenting the main features of the media system brings one once again to the Berlusconi factor. Indeed, Berlusconi is pivotal also in the media world, as indicated earlier. His corporate policies affected the development of the entire media system for years to come. Incidentally, this mingling of both political and industrial interests in a single person is a major source of widespread concern in the future of democracy in Italy. It was a serious problem from the very beginning of the political adventures of the media tycoon: his mastering of a huge media power clashes with a balanced democratic game in which opposing forces compete

for power with similar resources. Parliament has tried for a decade to pass legislation to force Berlusconi to either sell his media assets or to place them in a blind trust for the time he is in office. A very limited law eventually was approved in 2004 that left the core of the problem unresolved. The conflict of interest remains at the heart of media-politics relations while Berlusconi is in power.

The presence of the tycoon in the Italian media industry goes back to the times when, after striking gold in the real estate business, Berlusconi moved his interests to commercial broadcasting. It was the mid-1980s, and Berlusconi, a good friend of socialist Prime Minister Bettino Craxi, gained his support for ad hoc legislation that allowed Berlusconi to extend his three TV networks to the entire national landscape. It was the beginning of a fierce and mounting competition with the Radio Audizioni Italiane (public broadcasting;

RAI) channels. RAI had to compete, increasing its own commercialism, stirring the protest of several political forces and intellectuals because it was thought to be losing its public service outlook in favor of low-quality programming.

The establishment of the three Berlusconi networks and the strengthening of the three RAI channels took place in a situation of virtual laissez faire, because governments and parliaments were unable to pass comprehensive deregulation and liberalization plans. The situation was nicknamed the "Wild West" of Italian broadcasting: no real competition—the law of the strongest prevailed. That was the beginning of what has later been euphemistically named the "mixed system," or rather "duopoly." The first law to attempt to regulate the system was No. 223/1990, which did actually introduce measures to stop cross-media ownership but also legitimated the status quo; that is, the duopolist division of the broadcasting sector: Berlusconi (three channels) versus RAI (three channels). No subsequent attempts by governments to introduce tougher constraints and ensure more competition were successful. In 1997, the center-left government passed a law (No. 249/1997) that was intended to oblige RAI and Mediaset (Berlusconi's holding) to give up one channel, but because of legal complications that goal was not attained. The duopoly has thus continued through the 2000s, well beyond the reform law recently passed by the Berlusconi cabinet (No. 112/2004), which left the situation unchanged. The device worked out by the new law to overcome the duopoly standstill was the launching of digital terrestrial television, which was supposed to bring forth a new frontier of competition for new players that had been unable to break the old duopoly of generalist, analog television.

In an electronic media marketplace, where Berlusconi controls the aggressive and richest commercial channels, there stands the further complication of Berlusconi being at the same time prime minister, an office that exerts a lot of influence on the policies of public broadcasting. Critics have decried this amassing of media control and power in one man's hands. Berlusconi actually and virtually rules the entire television system of the country. Once again, conflict of interest, unresolved by law, surfaces in paradoxical situations such as this one.

In brief, the map of the television system in Italy is as follows:

A. Public broadcasting: three generalist networks, all carrying news shows
   1. RAI Uno, with the most popular news show, Tg1
   2. RAI Due, with Tg2
   3. RAI Tre, with Tg3 plus 20 editions of regional news shows, one for each region

B. Commercial broadcasting
   1. Canale 5, Mediaset's flagship, carrying the very popular Tg5
   2. Rete 4, owned by Mediaset, with Tg4, a news show overtly pro-Berlusconi
   3. Italia 1, owned by Mediaset, with *Studio Aperto* (a daily news show)
   4. La7, owned by Telecom Italia media, an independent company, running the news show Tg7
   5. A number of minor networks, compete for the remaining 8.8% of the national audience

Table 14.2 shows the audience share of each station in Italy.

Public television is financed by the licence fee (a tax on the public) and by advertising. Commercial television relies almost completely on advertising. Together, RAI and Mediaset have a dominant 85% share of the revenues of the entire television advertising market.

This duopolistic control of the advertising resources has often been an object of investigation and disapproval by state authorities. In particular the Competition Authority in the mentioned report on "Fact-finding

Table 14.2   Audience Share by Television
                Station in Italy (%)

Channel	2003	2002
RAI Uno	24.2	24.4
Canale 5	23.2	22.8
RAI Due	12.0	13.0
Italia 1	10.5	10.1
RAI Tre	9.5	9.9
Rete 4	9.5	9.4
La7	2.3	1.9
Other	8.8	8.5

SOURCE: IP International Marketing Committee
(2004, p. 178).

investigation into the sale of television commercials" of 26 November 2004 stated that the harvest of advertising investments in Italy has a concentration unparalleled in other EU countries. (EU Monitoring and Advocacy Program, 2005)

In addition to terrestrial broadcast television, there is a growing sector of satellite television, actually owned by one company, Rupert Murdoch Sky Italia, that scored the record of 3 million subscribers at the end of 2004. Like many other postindustrial countries, Italy has a saturation of television consumption. In fact, 98.5% of households in Italy have televisions (a total of 21,320,000 households), and 70% of the population receive 9 channels (IP International Marketing Committee, 2004, p. 174).

REGULATION OF POLITICAL ADVERTISING

In Italy, the Latin phrase *par condicio* (equal treatment) has become very popular since the early 1990s, when the president of the Republic at the time urged legislators to pass a law to guarantee all political parties equal access and equal treatment on television and triggered a debate that is still heated after a decade. Today, par condicio is the phrase that stands for regulation applying to political and electoral television broadcasts and to political advertising. The regulation was codified by Law No. 28/2000. Its aim was to secure freedom of choice for voters by guaranteeing them the opportunity to assess and select effectively among various political viewpoints. "Freedom of choice" implies the existence of a real competition between a plurality of parties and candidates, in a condition of parity and equal treatment.

Law No. 28/2000 was passed after heated discussion in and out of Parliament. The law, a bit paradoxically for a campaign context, forbids the airing of paid political commercials. The rules forbidding parties and candidates to buy television time for their electoral publicity can be understood within the frame of a sort of distrust of this type of political communication. The political majority that passed the law (the center-left) clearly manifested a sort of ideological bias against political commercials, considering this form of communication intrinsically inadequate to express the complexity of political debate on issues.

The law also provides an operational definition of the entire complex of political communication activities in and out of regular campaign periods. *Political communication* is defined as "the dissemination on broadcast media of programs containing political opinions and judgments" (Article 2), thus distinguishing it from (political) news diffusion and, at the same time, from what the law identifies as "independently produced messages (free or paid)."

To understand the intricacies of this law, one must clarify the particular meanings adopted in the distinction between political communication, information, and independent messages. The expression *political communication* is used as a synonym for *political propaganda*, usually performed in "party broadcasts, debates, confrontations, interviews, and every other kind of broadcast where the expression of political opinions and judgments is important" (Perrucci & Villa, 2004, p. 14). The law requires that all stations (public as well as commercial) ensure equal treatment of candidates and issues of political and campaign debate, as well as equal access for all. In addition, the channels must offer free political programs, which must comply with the principle of "balanced opposing views." Furthermore, for the entire period of the campaign, the presence of politicians in office and candidates is forbidden in nonpolitical broadcasts (such as entertainment, sport, lifestyle programs, etc.). The term *information* means, in this case, *newscasts*; that is, the normal journalistic coverage of political events and actors, which is acknowledged as free from any limitation outside the period of an election campaign. However, when the campaign starts, the law sets a series of strict rules for news coverage:

- Journalists must avoid giving, even indirectly, indications of how to vote and must not disclose their own political outlooks and preferences (Article 5.2).
- Directors and program conductors must behave correctly and impartially, so as to avoid influencing, even surreptitiously, the voters' choice (Article 5.3).
- In the last two weeks of the campaign, the media may not disclose figures from any opinion polls on voting intentions and trends (Article 6.1).

On examination, the distinction made in the law between *political communication* and *political information* appears confusing and affects the actual implementation of the related norms. A number of talk shows aired by both public and commercial channels have been under inspection by the regulatory bodies (i.e., the Parliament's Board of Vigilance on RAI and the Authority for Communications), which at times contradict one another in identifying a program either as "political communication" or "political information," with all the imaginable implications in terms of the efficacy of the law. "This difficulty in making

a sharp, precise distinction between information programs and political communication is probably one of the weak links in the legislation, posing, above all, problems as to sanctions" (Perrucci & Villa, 2004, p. 17).

More clear-cut appears the further distinction made and definition given by Law No. 28/2000 of "independently produced political messages" (Article 3). These messages, either paid or free, lasting 1 to 3 minutes on television, carry the motivated exposition of a political stance. The messages cannot interrupt other featured programs but should be concentrated in ad hoc advertising breaks or similar time slots in the program schedules. These spaces should be made known to the regulatory authorities at least a couple of weeks before the messages are aired (Article 3.3).

Television stations bear no responsibility for the contents and are simply carriers of these "independent" messages. The national networks can air only free messages, making available equal time to all political subjects. The choice of the time slot in which the messages are to be aired is made by lot. The local stations can charge for the airing of the messages but must discount the normal cost of advertising airtime by 50% (Article 3.7). Outside the election campaigns the law forbids the airing of this type of message on the national networks but allows them on the local stations.

These independently produced political messages can be considered the closest program genre Italy has to the better known spot ads or commercials. They are definitely longer than the average spot of 15 to 30 seconds, to comply with the principle of a "motivated exposition," and they are freely aired by the networks, to ensure that all parties and candidates be allowed to diffuse their messages, independent of their personal wealth. As mentioned, the par condicio law was voted in by the anti-Berlusconi political majority of 2001-2006 and was intended to contain the tycoon's well-known affluence and lavish expenditure for political commercials. His party had been launched in 1994 by means of an unexpected and unprecedented deluge of commercials in the total absence of any regulation.

Finally, in an era of virtual "permanent campaigning," the legislature tried also to set clear boundaries to the campaign period in which the regulations apply. Thus, in Italy, the election campaign is understood as the period between the day when the "electoral rallies [comizi] are called" and election day; that is, 45 days. In its turn, the period is divided into two phases: phase 1 is the first 2 weeks after the calling of election rallies and phase 2 is the last 30 days, beginning with the publication of the candidate lists. For each of these two phases, the law foresees different norms: In the first period, broadcasting times are allotted among the parties and candidates who are part of the assemblies (Parliament, regional, etc.) to be renovated; in the second period, the times are allotted according to the principle of "equal opportunity" for the competing coalitions and lists of candidates (Article 4.2).

The par condicio law undergoes different applications, according to the type of elections: European, general, regional, provincial, city, referendum. The Authority for Communications issues specific regulations that apply to the different types and to the different election mechanisms of the election called. Parliament itself intervened in 2003 with a new law (No. 313) to lift some limitations regarding the possibility for local stations to sell airtime to parties and candidates. Local stations that air free spot ads even get reimbursement from the State.

The Authority for Communications is also entrusted with control over the application of the par condicio regulations. In case of violation, the authority

sets up a procedure of complex, precisely organized interventions that must be brought to a conclusion in very short time (brief preliminary investigation, rebuttal of facts, eventual acceptance of counter-deductions within 24 hours after the accusation, sanctions applied within 48 hours after the ascertained violation). The sanctions are intended to reassert the balance among the political parties. (Perrucci & Villa, 2004, p. 18)

In practice the authority's intervention is far from timely. Often, if any sanction is assessed by the regulators, it comes months after election day.

Prime Minister Silvio Berlusconi has, on various occasions, announced his personal aversion to legislation that he defines as "illiberal," and put pressure on Parliament to abolish the par condicio law. Berlusconi's interventions, however, have boomeranged, as some of his own (smaller) allies in the "House of Liberties" coalition have fiercely defended the existing law, lest the next general election of 2006 (in April) be dominated by Berlusconi's powerful communication machine.

HISTORY AND DEVELOPMENT OF THE USE OF POLITICAL ADVERTISING

Long before the introduction of the par condicio law in 2000, Italian campaigns introduced paid political commercials in the late 1970s, along with the development of commercial television. The first time was in the general election of 1979, when a few private stations carried a number of spot ads of candidates in some cities (Mazzoleni, 1987). After that inauguration, the phenomenon was "in crescendo," soon to become a feature of the modern and postmodern campaign (Norris, 2000). The growing resort to this type of political publicity mirrors the expansion of television in the political arena. Television has taken on a centrality in the political process, becoming the "place" where most politics is performed publicly. The reference here is to the well-known processes of spectacularization and personalization of politics, of the importance of personalized leadership vis-à-vis a weakening of the traditional links to ideologies and to the partisan allegiances of the electorates. The politicians themselves adjust to the new imperatives of show biz and political spectacle. Communication patterns undergo a rapid and intense change and reflect the language and syntax of television discourse. "Mediatization of political communication" implies more professionalization in organizing and managing election campaigns and more resorting to external expertise (political consultants).

In Italy, campaign broadcasts were inaugurated in 1960, only 6 years after the introduction of television in the country. It was anything but a success, in today's terms, as television in those years was still to become a popular medium. However, Italian voters for the first time could see and watch the party leaders debate and quarrel not in the usual rallies in the city squares, but in the muffled sound of a television studio. Since then, all election campaigns have been fought—at times fiercely—also on television, and a new program genre was invented, the so-called *Tribuna politica*, a generic term for different kinds of broadcasts: roundtables, debates, interviews of leaders, voters' question-and-answer sessions, one-sided propaganda, and other formats.

Paid commercials were inaugurated in the 1979 general election, but they hit the headlines as a widespread custom in the subsequent general election of 1983. It was mostly the parties, rather than single candidates, who resorted massively to paid commercials. The commercials were carried only by private television networks, as the public company, RAI, is forbidden to air paid political publicity. There were 39 different commercials, produced on behalf of the various competitors by the most important advertising agencies: seven for the DC, six for the Communist Party, 12 for the Socialist Party (the most active on this front), seven for the Republican Party, six for the Socialist Democratic Party, and one for the Liberal Party. In general, these first spot ads were based on films, with a very simple narrative structure in which the party represented its conflict with competitors or depicted the

difficulties of the country and proposed solutions (Pezzini, 2001, pp. 34-39).

The commercialization of campaign communication reached its height in the 1987 general elections, labeled the "TV campaign par excellence." The private television networks were in their most successful phase, following the liberalization granted by the Craxi government in 1985. Parties and candidates exploited extensively the firepower made available by the new channels. Dozens of new television formats were attempted, all focusing on intense personalization of political leaders and candidates. This campaign was characterized by the confrontation between two opposing leaders, Socialist Bettino Craxi and Christian Democrat Ciriaco De Mita. Dozens of spot ads were commissioned by parties and candidates from advertising agencies and other image-building professionals. The contents were a mix of emotion and argument. The DC resorted to the poetic representation of a happy and united family, the Socialist Party to listing the accomplishments of the Craxi government and appealing to voters to defend them.

The election campaigns between 1989 and 1992, including the European and local campaigns, were characterized by uniform growth in advertising investment and by a substantial homogeneity in "selling" strategies, almost to the point of a certain "routine." The mediatization of electoral discourse was tangible in all parties' (and candidates') propaganda. Candidates exposed themselves personally, making public bits of their private and professional lives, accepting the rules of the television spectacle.

The 1994 general elections represented a dramatic turning point in the national history of politics and campaigning. Commentators agree in defining this as the transition from the "First" to the "Second Republic," because they coincided with the collapse of the old political establishment and the appearance on the domestic political stage of a series of new parties and political figures, such as Silvio

Berlusconi, with his brand-new party, Forza Italia. Berlusconi's campaign was dominated by marketing strategies and management. It was the first example of a scientifically planned campaign, the best example of Americanization of Italian campaign propaganda (Swanson & Mancini, 1996).

However, the case of 1994 remained a unique instance of the process of commercialization of Italian campaigning, characterized by the lack of clear regulations. The astonishing victory by Berlusconi rang the alarm in the political domain, and new norms started being outlined for future campaigns. In fact, in the 1996 general elections, provisional rules were introduced that later were named par condicio, as described earlier. The 1996 elections were won by the center-left coalition, and the new prime minister was Romano Prodi, who was later appointed president of the European Union Commission. Prodi was personally unsympathetic to political commercials in his coalition's campaign. He largely preferred talk shows and debates (even a great debate with his opponent Berlusconi), a sign of a return to a more policy-oriented type of campaign discourse. However,

> It is worth noting that politicians and leaders had devised a clever way to circumvent the *par condicio* constraints: by kicking off their actual campaign warfare months ahead of the official campaign start date. Berlusconi aired his own and his coalition's commercials in the pre-campaign months, and Prodi rode the "Olive Tree bus" throughout Italy, securing daily news coverage from the many journalists following his campaign trail. (Roper, Holtz-Bacha, & Mazzoleni, 2004, p. 136)

A new peak in paid commercials was reached in the European election of 1999: Several parties invested in paid spot ads, especially Forza Italia and the Radicals, with their prominent candidate, Emma Bonino (later appointed EU commissioner). Both parties engaged in a very long campaign, started well ahead of the official period.

The 2001 general elections saw the return to power of Berlusconi. The par condicio law was circumvented once more by the two front runners, who resorted to commercials outside the official campaign days. However, it was not so much the commercials that characterized the campaign as the huge street posters (3×6 meters). Berlusconi literally inundated Italy with thousands of

> posters portraying his younger close-up photo with catchy phrases such as "Less taxes for all" and "Safer cities." He also utilized assertions like "A president-worker to change Italy," "A president-entrepreneur to launch great infrastructures," "A president-friend to help those who can't make it." (Roper et al., 2004, p. 139).

Berlusconi clearly dominated the entire campaign, leaving his opponent lagging behind him. The tycoon controlled also the commercial (his own) as well as the public channels (RAI), refusing to confront his opponent in a "great debate," claiming that Rutelli did not deserve free publicity from the match with him and especially by appearing at the very end of the campaign in the most popular talk show (*Porta a Porta* [Door to Door]) to sign, live, his "Contract With the Italian People" before a national audience. Berlusconi scored a sweeping victory, ensuring for his coalition a large majority in both the Chamber of Deputies and the Senate and his own return to the premiership.

RESEARCH ON THE CONTENT AND EFFECTS OF POLITICAL ADVERTISING

Contrary to what one might expect—that the popularity of political commercials on private television would have prompted a great deal of academic research on the phenomenon—the existing literature in Italy is anything but copious. Election campaigns as a whole, the journalistic coverage, and the interaction of the media and politicians have attracted most of the attention of Italian researchers. Overall, one can count no more than a dozen contributions on political advertising, most of which concentrate on the early stages of the phenomenon, with preference for a semiotic approach. The passing of the anticommercials legislation (par condicio) in 2000 contributed to loss of interest in this political communication tool in the last few years. Even the virtual permission for the national networks to air free commercials and independently produced messages did not cause politicians to turn to them. The networks found it uneconomic to dedicate free airtime to political advertisements. Thus there has been no activity of this sort on national commercial channels since 2001.

In earlier campaigns, Italian political advertising shared similarities with the spots in many other democracies. For instance, an analysis of ads from the 1992 general election found that most of the ads concentrated on campaign issues but often contained more emotional than logical arguments (Mazzoleni & Roper, 1995). Looking back at the last time election spot ads were used (i.e., 1999-2000, when the European election [1999] and the local elections [2000] were called), one can identify a typology of paid political advertising on Italian commercial TV networks. In the campaign for the EU elections, the Mediaset channels aired 1173 spots, spending a total of about U.S.$5 million: Forza Italia (Berlusconi's party) was responsible for 803 of those; the Lista Bonino (a single independent candidate engaged in a very active, personalized campaign), 217; Alleanza Nazionale, the ex-neofascist party, 69; the Christian Democrats, 49; the center-left Democrats, 15; and other minor candidates, 20 (Guarino, 2001, p. 78).

The Forza Italia commercials relied on the party's main asset: Berlusconi's political image and personal charisma. Long before the start of the official campaign, the propaganda was addressed to the key sectors of the center-right electorate: senior citizens, the young, and women. The films display the same format

(people speaking of Berlusconi's successes), and all contain a strong invitation to change. In the case of the commercial for women, the closing moments show a towering Berlusconi hugging a group of women (each of whom uttered a short statement), symbolically taking them under his personal protection.

The other commercials, more explicitly focused on the EU elections, present a more traditional Berlusconi addressing the audience directly, smiling, in a typical pose, sitting at his table in his office with photos of his family—very much like the early commercials of 1994, when he launched Forza Italia.

In between the 1999 EU elections and the spring 2000 local elections, Mediaset's channels aired two spot ads with "season's greetings" offered by Berlusconi to the Italian people and to the young. The first one, 30 seconds long, showed a close-up of the former premier making this statement:

> In this blessed period we listen deep in our heart to what is true, right and good. These sentiments should urge us all to work together to solve the many problems that distress our country. This is the best way to enter into the new millennium and guarantee to all, especially to those who suffer, to those who are in need, a better life. I'll do my best. With this hope and this promise I wish you all a Merry Christmas and a happy new year!

The title of the message is "good sentiments," one preferred by Berlusconi, together with that of his records' list.

In spring 2000, the new par condicio law (No. 28) was passed by the center-left government. Before the enforcement of the ban on paid political TV commercials, Forza Italia aired the very last spot ad it could before the free of charge "independently produced political messages" were all that could be aired. Once again, Berlusconi—who would not be a candidate in the local elections—was the message: From his office, he addresses the electorate and invites voters to choose between two Italys: "the one stricken by unemployment, low pensions, high taxes, unsafe and in fear, and the other one, that knows love, that is free, right, generous, that you and I envision."

Overall, the paid political advertisements presented by Forza Italia, besides being the most numerous and the most frequently broadcast to Italian electors, visualize the image, sentiments, remarks, appeals, and the face of "the" leader himself: Berlusconi becomes an icon of himself, is a fixed and at the same time reproducible image and symbol of a world—his own world. "The TV tycoon, also in the political ads uses a language that is more television than advertising loaded. . . . People are asked to vote for him and to be like him" (Guarino, 2001, p. 89).

The application of the law stopped all paid advertisements, which were replaced by the more old-fashioned free propaganda spaces, swiftly exploited by candidates and parties to the maximum length allowed by law: 3 minutes. The new free messages, according to experts, are products that "do not reflect the codified genres, and are unable to appeal to the viewers" (Guarino, 2001, p. 100). Their inaugural use in the campaign for the 2000 local elections was anything but brilliant: The messages appeared sloppy, homemade, and, overall, boring. The obligation to place the messages in defined time slots (outside prime time) penalized their impact factor. These shortcomings, observed in 2000, are still pointed out by critics of the par condicio legislation today.

Nevertheless, when the free messages are produced using external and professional expertise, they can display a significant capacity to reach and speak to voters, if not necessarily to convince them. In the 2000 campaign, the prime minister in office, Massimo D'Alema, addressed the national audience by means of a message judged excellent and well constructed. The communication strategy was indeed sophisticated and innovative compared to D'Alema's traditional image, in support of

which he usually spoke aloofly, at a seeming distance from the people. This time he agreed to walk among the ordinary people and get involved in their problems (Guarino, 2001, pp. 106-107). Still, this new communication scheme did not pay in terms of persuasion. D'Alema—even though he was not himself a candidate—resigned from office following a clear defeat of his center-left coalition in the local elections.

EFFECTS OF POLITICAL ADVERTISING

As we have noted, there is limited scholarly research on the stimulus (i.e., senders and contents) of political advertising. There is even less investigation of the diverse psychosocial effects that electoral spot ads might trigger in the voters. Of the several reasons that might explain this, two stand out as major obstacles to investigation: on the one hand, a clear difficulty in tracing any individual effect back to a specific stimulus, especially in the short run, and on the other hand, the preferred concentration of most domestic research on overall campaign effects on political knowledge and voting behavior. The actual abolishment of the electoral spots ads on national TV channels through Law No. 28/2000 has also overshadowed the possible impacts of the phenomenon in campaign dynamics.

Clearly, this is not to say that election spot ads are considered a weak means of communication or that they do not have a significant effect on voters' attitudes. In an experimental study of ads used in the 1992 general election, findings indicated that exposure to the ads actually resulted in a decline in the image of the Christian Democrat candidates and that strong emotional reactions and feelings were stimulated in viewers as a result of their watching the spot ads (Mazzoleni & Roper, 1995).

The launching of Forza Italia in 1994, as mentioned earlier, by means of a bombardment of commercials on the Berlusconi channels, was certainly effective. Similarly, the

Table 14.3 Most Important Reasons to Vote (2001 Election Campaign; in %)

Most Important Reason	June 2000	May 2001
Trust in the candidate	41.1	31.1
Defense of my interests or values	33.6	32.1
My vote is crucial to the outcome	15.2	19.6
My vote helps to contain the adversaries	5.7	10.1
Interesting campaign	1.5	1.5
Other	29.0	56.0
Total	100.0	100.0
Number of subjects	2993	3596

SOURCE: Mannheimer (2002), p. 185.

Table 14.4 The Most Important Medium to Use in Keeping Informed About Politics (%)

Medium	1990	1994	1996	2001
Television	62.1	72.9	72.4	77.4
Informal networks				7.7
Newspapers	19.7	16.3	22.3	6.4
Radio	2.6	5.8	2.7	1.0
News magazines	.9	1.4	.8	.4
Internet				.1
Other				.5
None of the above or no answer	14.7	3.6	1.8	6.4
Total	100.0	100.0	100.0	100.0

SOURCE: Legnante (2002), p. 245.

stunning personal consensus gathered in the European elections of 1999 by Emma Bonino, an outsider from the mainstream political establishment, was undoubtedly secured by means of an intense multimedia campaign based on several commercials. Giovanni Sartori, a prominent political scientist and political analyst for the daily *Il Corriere della Sera*, has often acknowledged that political commercials aired in a campaign are effective in helping undecided voters to make a decision. However, no figures have ever been produced to support empirically the widely shared conviction that spot ads are not synonymous with wasted money for candidates and their parties.

Available research data from the general elections of 2001 provide a useful frame for the systemic evidence and for speculation among scholars about the efficacy of political advertising.

One piece of information is particularly noteworthy: Panel interviews with voters revealed that the campaign is never among the first three motivating factors that send voters to the polls (see Table 14.3).

The fact that television in Italy is synonymous with competition between public service channels (RAI) and commercial networks (Mediaset) has implied also an ideological confrontation: On the public side, the channels have been, to a significant degree, identified

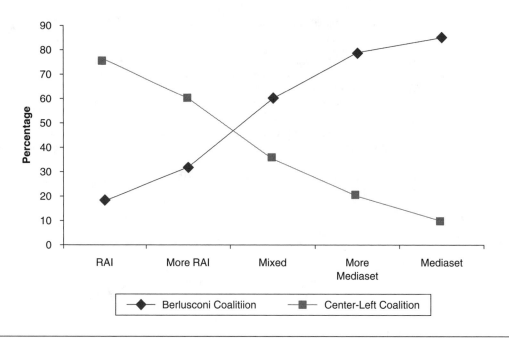

Figure 14.1 Votes for the Berlusconi Coalition and the Center-Left Coalition, Based on Viewing Patterns of Networks and News Shows (%)

SOURCE: Legnante (2002), p. 255.

with the center-left political spectrum, and the Mediaset network with the political colors of the Berlusconi coalition (center-right). Researchers have measured a strong correlation between the viewing patterns of voters in the Italian audience and their political outlook and behavior. Figure 14.1 displays the clear split of votes between the consumers who prefer commercial channels (who tend to cast their ballot in favor of the networks' master and political leader Berlusconi) and those who are loyal to the public channels and tend to vote for the center-left coalition.

The evidence represented in the figure refers to the 2001 election campaign; that is, to a campaign in which, because of the par condicio law, political commercials were banned. One cannot thus infer a hypothetical contribution of political advertising to the overall effect. However, this "channel-political congruence" has been noticed and tracked by scholarly research since the late 1990s (Sani,

2001). If one considers that political advertising in the traditional sense (paid commercials) was carried only by commercial networks and that between 1994 and 2000 a large majority of the spot ads was produced by the Berlusconi party and coalition, one can reasonably speculate that paid commercials enhanced to some extent the channel-political congruence.

CONCLUSION

The era of paid political TV advertising in Italy seems to be over, with the par condicio regulation. The legislature has ruled that political communication is a serious business that must be performed with respect for the rules of balanced and reflective public debate among all the players of the electoral game. The legislature's stance appears to be based on the desire to guarantee all parties equal opportunity, especially considering competitors (e.g., Berlusconi) who can command huge media power. This was the rationale behind the center-left government's policy in 2000. This rationale has been, significantly, accepted by all parties, including those that stand in Berlusconi's center-right coalition, and has only been rejected by Berlusconi's own party, Forza Italia.

Until the 2005 local elections, the ban on paid political advertising on national television channels was maintained and strictly applied. The regulation seems to have been effective in setting limitations on Berlusconi's super-powers in regard to TV.

Nevertheless, there is a growing skepticism about the real capacity of the law to ensure balanced campaign warfare, for a series of reasons that have to do with (a) the duration of the campaign, (b) attempts to disregard the rules, and (c) migration to alternative means and outlets of communication. First, in terms of the campaign duration, the rules speak of advertising 30 to 45 days before election day. However, not only in Italy, nowadays, is politics characterized by a "permanent campaign" that makes it difficult—and a bit artificial—to set time limitations. The implication regarding the Italian case is that parties, politicians, and prospective candidates start to look at the elections long before the kick-off of the regular campaign, and all accordingly initiate their propaganda activities to exploit the space that law does not regulate. Players have the opportunity to wage a long political battle using the actual weapons in their possession, without the shelter offered by the law in the very last period on the eve of elections. This means that Berlusconi (or any other powerful political subject) can really conduct the game for months and years, at the expense of the weaker players.

The second issue is circumvention of the law. The Web site of the Authority for Communications (http://www.agcom.it) provides accounts of hundreds of cases of attempts by parties and candidates to violate or "freely interpret" the par condicio law.

There is no major case of violation worthy of being studied. However, the sheer number of those attempts (or allegations of violation by opposing parties)—all dealt with by the authority in terms of preliminary investigations, rebuttal of facts, acceptance of counterdeductions, rulings, or sanctions (very few)—reveals that the existing regulation is structurally weak and full of holes. If one considers the distinctions worked out by legislators between *political communication*, *independently produced messages*, and *political information* (as discussed earlier), one cannot help but recognize that these definitions are not only artificial but also hard to implement in terms of concrete norms.

Finally, the use of alternative media is an important concern. Two different strategies are pursued by political communicators who cannot rely on a campaign of TV commercials: One has to do with the classical media and the other with the new, online media. The former strategy founds itself on the conviction of national parties, key leaders, and prominent candidates that it is possible to affect the attitudes and opinions of the electorate by pursuing significant public visibility in the media through news shows, talk shows, front pages, interviews, and the like. Staging events that attract the attention of the media is also a common tactic, preferred by, for example, minority, protest, and populist movements in search of free publicity (Mazzoleni, Stewart, & Horsfield, 2003). Italian politicians have invested heavily in the exploitation of these alternative ways to broadcast their political message, and the media has always been keen to cater to the demands of the political system, very much according to the "sacerdotal model" of media-politics relations (Semetko, Blumler, Gurevitch & Weaver, 1991). With the political capital built up by stable media coverage between elections, there is little need to resort to a short bombardment of (paid) TV commercials, even if it is intensive.

These remarks do not exclude the possibility (which has been true in a few cases in the recent elections in Italy) that political subjects with large financial resources will engage in direct propaganda activities, such as the one mentioned earlier in which the country was covered with giant posters and stands months before the official start of the campaign. Resorting to new and online media is a recent phenomenon in Italy, at least on a large scale. The 2001 campaign marks the inauguration of a significant activity by interested parties and candidates. Out of about 4000 candidates for Parliament, 552 Web sites were counted, meant for a substantial band of Internet users (about 12 million). These Web sites had the prevalent functions of (a) providing information, (2) mobilizing potential voters, and (3) networking. Fund raising, press relations, and administrative facilities were more typical of the Web sites of the political party organizations and the two front runners. Generally, all sites carried standard Internet communication tools such as e-mail, chat rooms, forums, newsletters, bulletin boards, and the like (Bentivegna, 2001). However, besides being themselves a propaganda tool, overall, the Web sites of Italian candidates do not yet seem able to replace TV political advertising. The diffusion of broadband Internet will certainly change the present scene, making possible the carrying and the downloading of short films. Future research on the intensity and quality of the use of information and communication technologies will tell whether political commercials will return, to become a typical feature of the domestic election campaigns with new production forms and fruition patterns.

The possibility should also be considered that future political majorities may eliminate the par condicio legislation and liberalize political advertising. If this is done, it will be because media tycoon and prime minister Silvio Berlusconi is no longer a menace to a balanced political and electoral competition. Considering the flow of events on the eve of the 2006 general elections, this seems uncertain.

REFERENCES

Bentivegna, S. (2001). La prova generale del 2001: Candidati ed elettori nel mare di Internet [The general elections of 2001: Candidates and voters in the sea of the Internet]. *Comunicazione Politica*, 2, 183–204.

EU Monitoring and Advocacy Program. (2005). *Television across Europe: Italy country report.* Budapest, Hungary: Open Society Institute.

Guarino, P. (2001). Gli spot politici: 1999-2000 [The political spots]. In I. Pezzini (Ed.), *Lo spot elettorale* [The electoral spot] (pp. 75–119). Rome: Meltemi.

IP International Marketing Committee (2004, October). *Television 2004. International Key Facts.*

ITANES [Italian National Election Studies Program]. (2001). *Perché ha vinto il centro-destra* [Why the center-right won]. Bologna, Italy: Il Mulino.

Legnante, G. (2002). Tra influenza e incapsulamento: Cittadini, comunicazione e campagna elettorale [Between influence and encapsulation: Citizens, communication, and electoral campaigning]. In M. Caciagli & P. Corbetta (Eds.), *Le ragioni dell'elettore* [Voters' reasons] (pp. 233–274). Bologna, Italy: Il Mulino.

Mannheimer, R. (2002). Le elezioni del 2001 e la "mobilitazione drammatizzante" [The elections of 2001 and the dramatization of mobilization]. In G. Pasquino (Ed.), *Dall'ulivo al governo Berlusconi* [From the center-left coalition to the Berlusconi government] (pp. 179–198). Bologna, Italy: Il Mulino.

Mazzoleni, G. (1987). The role of private television stations in Italian elections. In D. Paletz (Ed.), *Political communication research* (pp. 75–87). Norwood, NJ: Ablex.

Mazzoleni, G. (1992). *Comunicazione e potere* [Communication and power]. Napoli, Italy: Liguori.

Mazzoleni, G. (2004). With the media, without the media: Reasons and implications of the electoral success of Silvio Berlusconi in 2001. In I. Blondebjerg & P. Golding (Eds.), *European culture and the media* (pp. 257–266). Bristol, England: Intellect.

Mazzoleni, G., Stewart, J., & Horsfield, B. (Eds.). (1993). *The Media and neo-populism: A contemporary comparative analysis.* Westport, CT: Praeger.

Mazzoleni, G., & Roper, C. S. (1995). The presentation of Italian candidates and parties in television advertising. In L. L. Kaid & C. Holtz-Bacha (Eds.), *Political advertising in Western democracies* (pp. 89–108). Thousand Oaks, CA: Sage.

Mazzoleni, G. & Schulz, W. (1999). Mediatization of politics: A challenge for democracy? *Political Communication, 16,* 247–261.

Norris, P. (2000). *A virtuous circle.* Cambridge, England: Cambridge University Press.

Perrucci, T., & Villa, M. (2004). Italy. In P. Lang & D. Ward (Eds.), *The media and elections* (pp. 1–23). New York: Erlbaum.

Pezzini, I. (2001). *Lo spot elettorale* [The electoral spot]. Rome: Meltemi.

Roper, J., Holtz-Bacha, C., & Mazzoleni, G. (2004). *The politics of representation: Election campaigning and proportional representations.* New York: Lang.

Sani, G. (Ed.). (2001). *Mass media ed elezioni* [The mass media and elections]. Bologna, Italy: Il Mulino.

Semetko, H. A., Blumler, J. G., Gurevitch, M., & Weaver, D. H. (1991). *The formation of campaign agendas: A comparative analysis of party and media roles in recent American and British elections.* Hillsdale, NJ: Erlbaum.

Swanson, D. L., & Mancini, P. (Eds.). (1996). *Politics, media and democracy.* Westport, CT: Praeger.

15

Political Advertising in Mexico

JOSÉ-CARLOS LOZANO

On July 2, 2000, Mexican voters elected, for the first time in 71 years, a candidate from an opposition party. This electoral result ended a complex process of political transformation that had started in 1968 with a student revolt in Mexico City that was brutally repressed by the government. The push to a truly free electoral process became more resolute in the late 1980s and the 1990s, culminating in the 2000 elections. Although Americanization of the campaigns had started formally in the presidential elections of 1994, with the first televised debate among the different candidates and the use of more aggressive and competitive political ads, the 2000 election was definitely the turning point in the adoption of the new model of political campaigning in Mexican electoral processes.

Mexico is a federal republic, composed of 31 states and the Federal District. Governmental powers are divided between executive, legislative, and judicial branches. Suffrage is universal for those older than 18 years, and voting is mandatory. The legislative branch has a Senate of 128 members, three from each state and the Federal District and 32 more

members selected by proportional representation from a single national circumscription. There is also a Chamber of Deputies, with 300 members elected in the same number of electoral districts and 200 selected in proportion to the votes received by each political party. Senators serve 6-year terms, and deputies serve 3-year terms. Members of the legislature cannot be reelected for the immediately succeeding term.

For 71 years, Mexico was ruled by a single political party, the Partido Revolucionario Institucional (PRI). Founded in 1929 to stabilize the country and allow an institutional way in which the veteran generals and leaders of the Mexican civil war (Mexican revolution) could accede to power, the party contributed to the development of a political system characterized by power that was overwhelmingly in the hands of the president, vertical corporativism, institutionalized clientelism, and electoral processes controlled by the government (Salazar, 1995, p. 342). For decades, the PRI never lost a state or federal election, and it lost only a few at the local level. In the late 1970s and early 1980s, some modifications to the

259

electoral law allowed for more representation of opposition parties in the Mexican Congress. In the presidential election of 1988, for the first time, the PRI's candidate faced strong competition from both the right-of-center Partido de Acción Nacional (PAN) and a coalition of left-of-center parties promoting the candidacy of a former PRI politician, Cuauhtémoc Cárdenas, who was also the son of an influential expresident of Mexico. The crisis of legitimacy that arose from the dubious triumph of the PRI's candidate, Carlos Salinas de Gortari, forced the new administration to make more fundamental reforms to the political and electoral systems, in particular the creation in 1990 of the independent Federal Electoral Institute. The next presidential election was even more competitive, and although the PRI candidate again won the presidency, for the first time the ruling party lost control of the lower House of Congress. By the year 2000, the opposition parties controlled 12 out of the 31 states and the Federal District. The transformation of the political system reached a climax when Vicente Fox, a candidate from the opposition right-of-center party PAN, won the presidential election of 2000.

During all the time the PRI remained in power, the mass media tended to be subservient to that power, praising the government, avoiding any type of criticism, and refusing any access to dissenting voices and opposing parties or candidates. In his review of Latin American journalism in the early 1980s, Alisky (1981) included Mexico in his list of nations with "media guidance," arguing that it represented the "nation in Latin America with institutionalized control mechanisms from a political and economic establishment that can permit relative press freedom but still guarantee support for the Revolutionary coalition which has dominated Mexican public life for more than sixty years" (p. 27).

This was mostly the case for print journalism, although there were some independent and critical newspapers and magazines.

Electronic journalism, on the other hand, was even more supportive of the ruling party and government, due in part to legislation allowing the government to take away licenses from grantees if it believed they were not doing a proper job. There were other more subtle and illegal mechanisms as well that produced censorship and self-censorship. According to Hughes and Lawson (2004), Mexican television was dominated at that time by private entrepreneurs who received subsidies and concessions in exchange for favorable coverage: "Televisa [at that time, Mexico's only national television network] . . . provided the regime with the sort of relentlessly positive coverage that one might expect from a government-controlled outlet. Opposition parties were dismissed or denigrated, although candidates of the ruling party were treated with deference and enthusiasm" (p. 85).

During the transformation of the political system, the Mexican mass media also started to change, but only after a crisis of legitimacy and credibility, because their unconditional support of the government for so many decades started to affect their ratings. One turning point was in 1988, when different civic organizations carried out a careful and in-depth monitoring of electoral coverage in the main print and electronic news media, exposing the evident bias in favor of the ruling party (Arredondo, Fregoso, & Trejo Delarbre, 1991). After that year, many of the mass media moved gradually to a more open and balanced coverage of electoral processes. In the early 1990s, the government privatized a network of state-owned television channels, allowing the creation of a second major national network, Television Azteca, the first private competition for Televisa's quasimonopoly. In 1996, significant electoral reforms provided opposition parties with more funds and with regulations that made electoral processes fairer (Hughes & Lawson, 2004, p. 86). By 1997, at the beginning of the elections for governor of Mexico City, the anchor of Televisa's main evening news program explained to viewers that his newscast would grant exactly the same amount of time to every candidate, starting each day with the oldest political party and ending with the newest. Although the news program did grant equal time to all candidates, the qualitative presentation of each segment was still biased in favor of the PRI candidate (for example, his segment showed positive shots of his acceptance by the masses) and against the other candidates (whose segments included close-ups in big public assemblies instead of showing the response of the followers, their focus on organizational problems, and so on), as a study of the Mexican Academy for Human Rights showed (Acosta, 1997). By the election of 2000, however, the news programs on both Televisa and TV Azteca were much more balanced in quantitative and qualitative terms (Lawson, 2003), although they had embraced completely the model of infotainment and tabloidization in their coverage of the electoral process (Lozano, 2001; Lozano et al., 2001). Local stations in the different Mexican states, however, continued to show partisan bias in favor of the party in control of the state (Hughes & Lawson, 2004, p. 87).

HISTORY AND DEVELOPMENT OF POLITICAL ADVERTISING IN MEXICO

For many decades, political advertising in Mexican television was not relevant for voters. Because of their initial relationship with the government and the ruling party, TV stations would provide in-depth coverage of the ruling party's candidates in their news programs, making political ads unnecessary (Aceves, 2000). The few advertisements these stations transmitted were for pretense, not for mobilizing voters in favor of the candidate.

In 1968, the government imposed a tax of 25% on the profits of all Mexican private radio and television stations. The next year, the broadcast companies agreed to pay that

tax to the government not in cash, but through 12.5% of their transmission time. That time would be used by the government for any content it might find useful for audience members. In January 1973, a new federal electoral law established for the first time that part of that 12.5% of programming time should be granted to all political parties so they could promote their candidates and their programs (Granados Chapa, 1981, p. 27). This turned out to be a cosmetic opening, as the lack of independence and freedom of the political parties and the actual time granted to them made these transmissions irrelevant. In the electoral campaign of 1976, the opposition parties decided not to participate in the presidential election because of the flagrant inequality and their lack of real access to the media; only the candidate of the ruling party had real access. This situation, and the emergence of some terrorist organizations for the first time in Mexican history, forced the government in 1977 to promote sweeping political reforms and to pass new legislation mandating that private broadcasting systems run weekly programs providing access to all political parties (Aceves, 2000, pp. 14-15). Each party had 15 minutes in which it could broadcast, at the official times, its own produced spots or programs to promote its candidates or its programs. Very soon, however, the television stations started to transmit these programs outside prime time, choosing times in which ratings were almost nil. This legislation, in addition, left out any provision for the purchase of commercial time for ads, leaving media owners free to decide whether they would sell time to opposition candidates.

In 1993, new regulations were passed finally eliminating the discretionary power of television owners to decide whether to sell time to opposition candidates (Aceves, 2000, p. 16). In the 1988 presidential elections, the two leading opposition candidates had openly denounced their lack of access to the media and the media bias in favor of the PRI candidate.

Manuel Clouthier, the candidate from the PAN, even asked the voters to boycott Televisa's programs, products, and sponsors. During the campaign, the private TV stations rejected the attempts of Clouthier and the other opposition candidate, Cuauhtémoc Cárdenas, to buy time to broadcast electoral ads (Arredondo, 1991, pp. 69-70).

Important electoral reforms in 1996 provided opposition parties with a large amount of public funds for their electoral campaigns. By 1997, these parties were spending more than 150 million pesos, the bulk of it on TV ads. In contrast, the ruling PRI spent only 111 million pesos that year. In the presidential elections of 2000, public funds were again available for all parties, allowing a more balanced number of electoral ads in the approximately 25 hours of advertising on the two main networks bought by the three main candidates (Hughes & Lawson, 2004, p. 86). In the midterm elections of 2003, the coalition of the PRI and the Partido Verde Ecologista Mexicano (Green Party) aired a total of 2756 spots on television, in contrast with 405 aired by the PAN (the party of the current president of Mexico) and 489 aired by the left-of-center Partido de la Revolución Democrática (Democratic Revolutionary Party). The estimated cost of all the spots was around 468 million pesos, or U.S.$44,570,000 ("Acaparan spots PVEM," 2003).

The Código Federal de Instituciones y Procedimientos Electorales (Federal Code of Electoral Institutions and Procedures) regulates electoral advertising in television. According to this code, each political party has 15 free minutes per month to promote its candidates and programs. Also, during presidential campaigns, TV stations must provide a total of 200 free hours for all the parties. In midterm federal elections, TV stations must provide 100 hours. In addition, during electoral campaigns, the Federal Electoral Institute buys 400 twenty-second spots per month and distributes 30% of them evenly among all political parties and 70% proportionately to each party. Finally, political parties are able to buy time individually (although they must inform the Federal Electoral Institute and ask for its authorization), according to their own economic resources. Different sources point out that most parties spend up to 60% of their campaign funds on television ads.

EFFECTS OF TELEVISION ADVERTISING IN MEXICAN ELECTIONS

In the electoral campaign of 2000, for the first time in the modern history of the country, voters experienced an openly aggressive dispute between candidates through radio, television, and the press. Candidates criticizing their opponents openly and strongly received extensive coverage in newspapers and news programs on a daily basis, and access for all parties seemed, for the first time, completely balanced and fair. After 71 years of officialism and self-censorship in the vast majority of the mass media, opposition candidates not only received coverage on radio and television stations but were able to criticize, openly and harshly, the current president of Mexico and the candidate of the ruling party. Some of the opposition candidates, in particular Vicente Fox, participated also for the first time in comedy shows and sketches, tolerating the irreverence of the anchors and actors and the frivolity of the content so that they could reach important segments of the public not reached by the news media. During the campaign, fierce criticism of opponents, populist acts, photo opportunities, sound bites, and debates among the main contenders were the rule.

Many analysts agree that political marketing (including television advertising) exercised a powerful influence over voting behavior in the presidential campaign of 2000 (Lawson, 2003; Lozano, 2001; Toussaint, 2000; Trejo Delarbre, 2002). Also for the first time in Mexico, political ads in the presidential race were used in widespread and complex strategies of political marketing that resorted to dramatization and personalization (Lozano et al., 2001). Francisco Labastida, the PRI candidate, and Vicente Fox, the candidate of a coalition formed by the PAN and the Green Party, were the two contenders, out of the total of six candidates, who used the most aggressive and innovative political ads, including a significant number of very negative ones. Taking into account the historical context, in which private and public television stations had never transmitted ads from the opposition either praising candidates or criticizing the ruling party or current administrations, the numerous ads attacking the PRI's candidate as belonging to a corrupt party monopolizing power for 71 years and the ads praising the personal qualities of Fox surprised potential voters and had a definite impact on them.

In the midterm elections of 2003, voters started to show signs of being tired of negative television ads, and in some instances, candidates for the Chamber of Deputies or for governorships had to stop using them. This was the case in the race for the governorship of Nuevo Leon, one of the most powerful and important states in Mexico: The candidate from the PAN had to pull his negative television ads against the PRI candidate abruptly due to public outcry and criticism for using "dirty" tactics. A survey of potential voters done by the prestigious newspapers of Grupo Reforma in Mexico City, Monterrey, and Guadalajara found that the majority were fed up and rejected the use of negative ads on radio and television (Moreno, 2003). However, an unprecedented number of ads full of personalization and dramatization continued to be transmitted, showing that this kind of political ad had become a staple of electoral campaigns in the country.

The actual impact of campaign ads in the outcome of the elections of 2000 and 2003 is not clear, however. Not a single comprehensive study looking at the influence of political ads on

voters has been carried out, and academic research on audiences in the field of political communication has been almost nonexistent.

SCARCITY OF ACADEMIC RESEARCH ON POLITICAL ADVERTISING

Despite its overwhelming presence in federal elections from 1994 to the present day, political advertising is one of the less-studied topics in Mexican academic research on media and politics. The Documentation Center in Communication Sciences, the best database in communication research in Mexico, has only one work with the words "political advertising" in its title. One of the few studies about the impact of political propaganda on voters, done in 1973, concerned the influence a particular political propaganda program, *Diálogo Político*, had on its viewers (León Martínez, cited in Aceves, 2000, p. 23). Looking for evidence of changes in voting behavior among the viewers, Martínez found that watching that program had had no traceable effect. Many years later, Vega (2000) used qualitative interviews to explore the influence of the coverage of the television news programs on Televisa and TV Azteca on Mexico City housewives in the local elections of 1997. Again, the study did not find evidence that the televised political information had any kind of impact on the voting behavior of the sampled women. According to the women interviewed, their voting decisions had been made before the start of the campaign and did not change despite their exposure to the political coverage of the two networks. Although this second study, unlike Martínez's, was not about political ads or political propaganda, it illustrates the difficulties Mexican scholars have in finding direct evidence that televised political information has any influence on voters.

Some empirical studies about exposure to political news help us understand the importance political ads may have for Mexican audiences. A national survey carried out by the

Ministry of the Interior in 2003 found that 80% of Mexicans say they learn about politics through television, in contrast with 29% who say they learn through radio and only 18% who learn through newspapers (Secretaría de Gobernación, 2002, p. 7). Another survey, carried out in Guadalajara in 1994, found that 73% of voters in that city used television to get political information and considered this medium the best, the most reliable, and the most complete in the provision of political news (Aceves, 1998, p. 39). Although neither study included specific questions about exposure to political ads or about their impact, both point out the importance television has in the voter's search for information.

A detailed descriptive analysis of the political ads transmitted on nine television channels in the 2000 presidential elections is the best report yet on the specific role played by political advertising in Mexico (Acosta & García, 2000). According to this report, between May 8 and June 30 (The last 2 months of the campaign), a total of 2316 spots were broadcast on those nine channels: 51% of that number represented ads sponsored by political parties, 34% were sponsored by local and federal governments, and 15% were sponsored by electoral authorities (pp. 7-8). Acosta and García found an unprecedented balance between the total airtime occupied by ads for each of the three top presidential candidates: 1:43 minutes for the ruling party contender Francisco Labastida, 1:37 for Vicente Fox, and 1:20 for Cuauhtémoc Cárdenas (p. 8). Of course, the greatest percentage of ads (47%) was concentrated on one particular channel: Televisa's channel 2, the highest in rating and national coverage of all sampled channels. Unfortunately, Acosta and García focus exclusively on a descriptive presentation of the data and provide no critical analysis of the implications of their results or the impact of these political spots on the outcome of the election.

One of the very rare studies that takes into account the actual impact of political advertising on television audiences is based in the findings of a survey of voters in the state of Puebla during the electoral process of 1988 (González Molina, 1990). According to the author, voters in that Mexican state lacked information about and interest in the political process, perceiving it as an event with almost no credibility, legitimacy, or respectability (p. 127). González Molina concluded, however, that the political advertising of the opposition candidate for the governorship of the state, which focused on the possibility of a political change, had had a significant impact on voters: "What counts for the voter in these circumstances is his/her perception of the implications of a political change and not so much his/her knowledge and party affiliation" (p. 131). Unfortunately, the study did not report the specific way in which political ads helped audience members to decide how to vote in the election and did not explain anything else about political ads or the reactions of the voters.

GOVERNMENTAL SPOTS IN ELECTORAL CAMPAIGNS

One of the major controversies related to political advertising in Mexican elections has been the abundant transmission of political ads by the current government during electoral campaigns that boast of its achievements. In contrast with other countries, in Mexico it is common for federal, state, and local governments, even for congress and the judiciary, to use official time or to buy commercial time to "inform" the citizenship about their accomplishments. Although they may broadcast these ads at any time, frequently they increase the number of ads during electoral campaigns to help their candidates convince voters that their parties should remain in power.

For years, the PRI was the only party using this strategy, and opposition parties would question and denounce (unsuccessfully) the use of public resources. The analysis of Acosta and García (2000) mentioned earlier highlighted the large presence of political ads sponsored by the federal government during the 2000 presidential campaign to promote the achievements of the PRI administration and boost the image of the ruling party. Despite criticism by the opposition parties and other political actors, the government devoted 5 hours and 41 minutes (four times the average of each candidate's total time) to institutional messages trying to convince the audience members that PRI administrations were the best deal for the people.

Now, elected officials of all political parties use this questionable practice, from the current president of México, Vicente Fox, to the Partido de la Revolución Democrática, PAN, and PRI governors of the 32 states. In the midterm elections of 2003, the Fox administration used 15,260 hours (over all the commercial channels) of political ads to publicize its accomplishments and to ask people to vote (Villamil, 2003), and many governors from different parties acted in the same fashion, despite demands by the Federal Electoral Institute that they stop (López, 2003).

Despite the obvious unfairness, there are currently no clear regulations in Mexico that can stop these abuses. Villanueva (2005), one of the leading experts in media regulation of electoral processes, has recently asked for urgently needed reform that would prohibit the airing of government spots related to the inauguration of public works, introduction of new government social programs, and so on from the first day of the electoral campaign to election day: "The use of public funds for the promotion of the image of public officials or their parties may be legal at this moment, but it is clearly illegitimate and immoral," argues Villanueva. At the state level, some progress has been made. The local electoral laws of the states of Mexico, Chihuahua, and the Federal District prohibit this type of public advertising for a period of 20 to 30 days before Election Day. At the federal level, however, the government is still free to advertise whatever it

considers fit. Currently the issue is in the agenda of topics to be discussed for the 2006 presidential elections, and we can hope that political actors involved in the negotiation for new, more equitable rules may find ways to adopt new regulations ensuring fairer democratic contests.

CONCLUSION

For the first time in Mexico's history, political advertising has become a definitive factor in election campaigns. The most visible part of the adoption of political marketing strategies in presidential and midterm elections, as well as state and local elections, political ads started timidly in the 1994 presidential election, grew in the 1997 midterm elections, and exploded in the 2000 presidential election, becoming the most important element in the success of the first opposition candidate in 71 years.

The system of providing political parties with large sums of public funds to buy time from the networks and TV stations has allowed the electoral process to become more competitive and balanced. Now, major and minor opposition parties have systematic access to television time, and viewers receive a more diverse spectrum of information and proposals from different political actors, a dramatic improvement from the inequities of former years. However, the lack of regulations concerning free access of candidates and parties to television time and the discretionary power of television networks and channels to charge candidates and parties differently according to their own ideological preferences are still major obstacles to fair electoral contests. Initiatives such as the one rejected recently in the Mexican Chamber of Deputies asking for free time on television for electoral ads may need to be posed again and again until they are approved, if real progress is to be made in this matter.

Public funds for electoral campaigns is another issue that needs to be addressed in the near future in Mexico. Sums are extremely high, around 5400 million pesos (U.S.$478 million) per electoral process, and although they allow for more balanced contests, citizens are not voting more or becoming more interested in politics. Some congressmen and congresswomen have tried to pass new regulations to lower these funds in recent years, but the powerful lobby of television owners has not allowed this to happen. Public debate in the country will most likely feature this issue very prominently in the next election.

The adoption of political marketing strategies and the use of modern political ads are too recent in Mexico for anyone to determine whether the boom of ads observed in the presidential elections of 2000 and in the midterm elections of 2003 is going to continue. In particular, it is difficult to assess whether the apparent decline seen in 2003 in the use of negative ads is going to last or if it may represent only an adjustment after the excess experienced in 2000. More likely, after having gone to both extremes, the parties will continue to use negative political ads in a more restricted way. Mexican voters can hope to see fewer of the really mean, derogatory ads like those in the 2000 presidential campaign and more issue-oriented ads useful for helping them make up their minds.

Finally, it is important for Mexican scholars to start paying more attention to political advertising because of the relevance it has achieved in the last few years. The research agenda includes all types of issues, from the political-economic issues such as regulations, subsidies, costs, and schedules, to tendencies, characteristics, topics, and formal features, to the differentiated uses of the ads by audiences.

REFERENCES

Acaparan spots PVEM y el PRI [PVEM and PRI take most spots]. (2003, June 5). *El Norte,* p. A1.

Aceves, F. (1998). Información mediática, usuarios y acontecimiento político [Mediated information, users, and political events]. *Comunicación y Sociedad, 32,* 29–47.

Aceves, F. (2000). La investigación académica sobre el papel de los medios de comunicación en los procesos electorales en México [Academic research on the role of mass media in Mexican electoral processes]. *Comunicación y Sociedad, 37,* 11–36.

Acosta, M. (1997). Las elecciones federales de 1997 según Televisa y TV Azteca [The federal elections of 1997 according to Televisa and TV Azteca]. *Revista Mexicana de Comunicación, 49,* 21–23.

Acosta, M., & García, V. (2000, September-October). La publicidad política por televisión en las elecciones del año 2000 en México [Political advertising on television in the 2000 elections in Mexico]. *Revista Mexicana de Comunicación, 65,* 7–11.

Alisky, M. (1981). *Latin American media: Guidance and censorship.* Ames: Iowa University Press.

Arredondo, P. (1991). Los medios de comunicación en la lucha político-electoral [The mass media in the political-electoral struggle]. In P. Arredondo, G. Fregoso, & R. Trejo Delarbre (Eds.), *Así se calló el sistema: comunicación y elecciones en 1988* [And the system failed: Communication and elections in 1998] (pp. 47-77). Guadalajara, Mexico: Universidad de Guadalajara.

Arredondo, P., Fregoso, G., & Trejo Delarbre, R. (Eds.). (1991). *Así se calló el sistema: Comunicación y elecciones en 1988* [And the system failed: Communication and elections in 1988]. Guadalajara, Mexico: Universidad de Guadalajara.

González Molina, G. (1990). ¿En qué piensa el elector cuando vota? Comunicación política y polarización electoral [What does the voter think about when he votes? Political communication and electoral polarization]. *Comunicación y Sociedad, 9,* 123–144.

Granados Chapa, M. A. (1981). 1979-1976, un sexenio de comunicación [1970-1976: The media during a presidential term]. *Connotaciones, 1,* 25–35.

Hughes, S., & Lawson, C. (2004). Propaganda and crony capitalism: Partisan bias in Mexican television news. *Latin American Research Review, 39*(3), 81–105.

Lawson, C. (2003). Television coverage, media effects, and the 2000 elections. In J. I. Domínguez & C. Lawson (Eds.), *Mexico's pivotal democratic election: Candidates, voters, and the presidential campaign of 2000* (pp. 187–210). Stanford, CA: Stanford University Press and Center for U.S.-Mexican Studies, University of California, San Diego.

López, M. (2003, June 13). Abre SEGOB cabildeo por spots [The Ministry of the Interior lobbies for spots]. *Mural*, p. 11.

Lozano, J. C. (2001). Espectacularización en la cobertura informativa de las elecciones mexicanas a la presidencia [Infotainment in the coverage of Mexican presidential elections]. *Comunicación y Sociedad, 14*(1), 29–49.

Lozano, J. C., García, H., López, G., Medina, J., Mendé, B., Smith, C., et al. (2001). La espectacularización en las elecciones mexicanas del 2000 [Infotainment in the 2000 Mexican elections]. *Revista Mexicana de Comunicación, 14*(71), 34–37.

Moreno, A. (2003, March 3). Ven campañas negativas [They see the campaigns as negative]. *Reforma*, p. A6.

Salazar, L. (1995). Agotamiento de la hegemonía revolucionaria y transición política [Depletion of the revolutionary hegemony and political transition]. In *México a fines de siglo* [Mexico at the end of the century] (J. Blanco & J. Woldenberg, compilers; Vol. 2, pp. 342–376). México City: Fondo de Cultura Económica.

Secretaría de Gobernación. (2002, August). Conociendo a los ciudadanos mexicanos [Learning about Mexican citizens]. *Este País,* pp. 1–24.

Toussaint, F. (2000). Las campañas electorales del 2000 en televisión: El caso mexicano [Electoral campaigns in 2000 on television: The case of Mexico]. *Revista Mexicana de Ciencias Políticas y Sociales, 44*(180), 39–56.

Trejo Delarbre, R. (2002). Reporte sobre los medios en México—2002 [Report on the media in Mexico, 2002]. In *Internationales Handbuch Medien 2002/2003* [International media handbook] (pp. 897-903). Baden-Baden, Germany: Nomos Verlagsgesellchaft.

Vega, A. (2000, February-April). Los procesos electorales en México y su relación con el comportamiento político de las amas de casa: El caso de 1997 en el D.F. [Electoral processes in Mexico and their relation to the political behavior of housewives: The case of 1997 in the Federal District]. *Razón y Palabra, 17.* Retrieved January 5, 2006, from http://www.cem.itesm.mx/dacs/publicaciones/logos/anteriores/n17/17avega.html

Villamil, J. (2003, July). La mediatización de las campañas: Muchos spots, poca política [Mediation of campaigns: Many spots, little politics]. *Periódico Zócalo, 41.* Retrieved January 5, 2006, from http://www.periodicozocalo.com.mx/cabeza/anteriores/2003/julio/index.html

Villanueva, E. (2005, March 22). Publicidad: Criterios gubernamentales [Advertising: Governmental criteria]. *Proceso.* Retrieved January 7, 2006, from http://biblioteca.itesm.mx/nav/contenidos_salta2.php?col_id=infolatina

16

Political Advertising in Australia and New Zealand

JULIANNE STEWART

OVERVIEW OF THE POLITICAL SYSTEMS IN AUSTRALIA AND NEW ZEALAND

Australia and New Zealand, both previously colonies of the former British Empire, are constitutional monarchies based on the Westminster system of the separation of powers, or arms of government. The judiciary is completely separate from any electoral process, and each country's head of state is a governor-general, an individual normally recommended by the prime minister but formally appointed by the queen of the United Kingdom of Great Britain and Northern Ireland (who is also queen of Australia and of New Zealand). The queen and the governor-general are politically neutral in both countries and are not involved in the political contest.

The system of government in each country is that of a parliamentary democracy (for a breakdown of Australia's parliamentary system, see Figure 16.1). Both countries have a House of Representatives, and Australia also

has a Senate (House of Review).[1] In both cases, the national government is formed by the party (or parties in coalition) that has a majority of seats in the House of Representatives. The leader of the government party or coalition is the prime minister.

Although Australia became an independent nation only in 1901 and New Zealand in 1907, each country began holding elections in the mid-1800s.[2] In Australia and New Zealand, elections are normally held every 3 years, with Australia's most recent federal elections held in 2004 and New Zealand's in 2005. Voting is compulsory in Australia but optional in New Zealand. However, the latter has a very high level of voter participation, with around 75% of eligible adults turning out at the polls. Australia has preferential voting in the 150 electorates of its House of Representatives and proportional representation in the state-based Senate. New Zealand has had what is termed "mixed-member proportional representation" (MMP) since 1993.[3] Under this system, which is based on the German electoral system, the

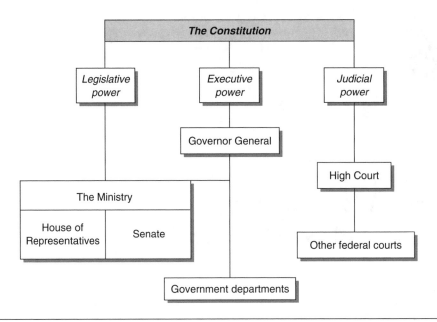

Figure 16.1   Diagram of Australian Parliamentary System

SOURCE: Parliament of Australia: Education (2005).

120 New Zealand electorates are made up of 62 from general electorates, seven from Māori electorates, and 51 from party lists. Māori voting uses the "first past the post"[4] system. Non-Māori voters vote twice, once for a constituency candidate and once for a party. Parties appoint their own candidates to take up seats once that party's number of seats is known, and this number is derived using the Sainte Laguë method of calculating proportionality. Usually the party with the most candidates elected is also the majority party and the one that forms a government. Unless the proportion of list seats of the winning party falls below 40% of the total vote, the MMP system virtually guarantees that the party with the most votes gets the most seats (Vowles, Karp, Banducci, Aimer, & Miller, 2002, p. 188).

In addition to national elections, both countries also have local government elections every 3 to 4 years, and Australia also has three or four yearly elections for parliaments in each of its six states and two territories. The structure of the Australian state and territory parliaments is generally similar to that of the national parliament. The rules governing political advertising are the same for state and territory elections as for national ones. The bodies in each country responsible for implementing these rules are the Australian Electoral Commission and the Electoral Commission (New Zealand), respectively. Both are independent statutory government bodies.

OVERVIEW OF THE MEDIA SYSTEMS

Both countries have a generally free media system that works within a broad regulatory framework. Australia, with a population of around 20 million people, has three commercial and two publicly funded free-to-air[5] television channels,[6] as well as two major commercial pay-television providers. It has numerous local newspapers,[7] but only one national daily newspaper, *The Australian*, owned by Rupert Murdoch's News Corporation. Each state capital outside of Sydney and Melbourne has only one daily newspaper. The circulation of all the Australian daily state and national newspapers is 2.3 million, 3.5 million for Sunday papers (Department of Foreign Affairs and Trade [DFAT], 2004). There are around 265 commercial radio stations and more than 300 community (publicly funded) radio stations (Given, 2001, p. 10), as well as two government-funded national radio networks (the Special Broadcasting Service and the Australian Broadcasting Commission). Almost all households have free-to-air television, but only around 25% have pay television (DFAT, 2004). Not all households can receive all five free-to-air channels; universal coverage is not always available in rural and remote areas.

There is a great concentration of media ownership in Australia, as News Corporation controls two thirds of the capital city's daily newspapers (Given, 2001, p. 11), as well as most pay television via its interest in the Foxtel company. The Packer family's Publishing and Broadcasting Limited has also long been a major media player in Australia, owning both a free-to-air commercial television network and a large proportion of the magazine industry. Cross-media ownership laws have tended to restrict media ownership to one kind of media (either television, radio, or newspaper) within the same license area (for example, Sydney, or regional Queensland) (Given, 2001, p. 3). In addition, a person is prohibited from controlling television licenses that cover more than 75% of the total Australian population.

However, although these laws have a history dating back to the 1930s, when they were enacted to restrict the number of radio licenses a person could control, they are currently being challenged by the industry and are made less meaningful with the advent of the Internet. Furthermore, the current Liberal-National conservative coalition government has, since it was first elected in 1996, desired to relax the ownership laws, with the major stumbling block being opposition from the Senate. In the elections of October 2004, the coalition government finally gained control of the Senate, taking effect in July 2005. It therefore seems likely that the laws will be relaxed, suggesting that a further reduction in media diversity in Australia is very likely. This legislative relaxation is, paradoxically, likely to be combined with the current legislative protection of the interests of the existing free-to-air television stations within the new digital television broadcasting environment that forbids new entrants "in the medium term" (Jackson, 2002).[8]

A similar lack of media diversity exists in New Zealand. Servicing a population of around 4 million, four companies dominate the news media in that country, with a "near duopoly in each of the three main media" (Rosenberg, n.d., p. 1). Of the four major television stations, two (TV1 and TV2) are government owned and two (TV3 and C4) are owned by Canadian company CanWest. There are also a number of regional television stations, many of them owned by Prime, an Australian company that also owns regional television stations in Australia. Apart from digital broadcasts from News Corporation's Sky Television, which controls pay television and is received in 34% of homes (Norris, 2005, p. 48), digital television has been slow to develop in the free-to-air market.

There is no national daily newspaper in New Zealand, although there are three national Sunday papers. Each major city has at least one daily newspaper, the largest of which is Auckland's *New Zealand Herald*. In addition, most provincial towns have their own daily newspaper. John Fairfax Holdings, an Australian newspaper company, owns daily newspapers in New Zealand comprising almost half the circulation of all newspapers.

REGULATIONS GOVERNING POLITICAL ADVERTISING

Australia and New Zealand are two of the few countries in the world that allow paid political advertising on electronic media during election campaigns. In New Zealand, legislation governing political advertising is covered by the Electoral Act of 1993 and the Broadcasting Act of 1989. These acts restrict broadcast-based political advertising by registered political parties during election campaigns to that which can be purchased from fixed public funding and to that which is allocated as free broadcasting time on Television New Zealand and Radio New Zealand.[9] Such public funding is proportional to the party's performance in the previous national election and is allocated by the Electoral Commission (Elections New Zealand, 2005). It can only be used for broadcast media advertising. Additionally, broadcasters are not permitted to charge different rates to different parties for political advertising. The process is made transparent by the requirement for both broadcasters and parties to report in detail to the Electoral Commission on their dealings in this area. The New Zealand government funding to parties has not been indexed to inflation and remains fairly low—around NZD 2 million divided among all parties. Additionally, New Zealand has regulations against misleading political advertising (covered by the Broadcasting Act of 1989) and tends to apply the Advertising Standards Authority's Advertising Code of Ethics (which regulates advertising in general) to political advertising as well as other forms of advertising. New Zealand also has strict controls on the spending and timing of political ads.

In Australia, political advertising is regulated (to the extent that it is actually regulated at all) by the Electoral Act of 1918 and the Broadcasting Services Act of 1992. The act that regulates all forms of advertising other than political advertising is the Trade Practices Act of 1974. In contrast to electoral advertising regulation in New Zealand, there are few restrictions of any kind on political advertising in Australia. For example, Australia puts no limits at all on the amount spent on political advertisements or the volume of political advertising. Geddis (2003) comments that without controls such as those that exist in New Zealand, access to expensive broadcast media, particularly television, is limited to those who can afford it. This generally means the major parties, and in a democracy, questions of unequal access to all forms of political communication are serious ones and need to be addressed. Furthermore, Australia has no requirement to file election expenditure returns (Miskin & Grant, 2004). Restrictions that are in place include the fact that all political ads must contain the name and address of the ad's producer (similar to New Zealand), and there is a "blackout" on television- and radio-based political advertising (but not print advertising) during the 3 days immediately before an election day. (Elections are always held on a Saturday, and the blackout commences at midnight on the previous Wednesday). In New Zealand, no such blackout exists, except on the election day itself, and the advertising can begin as soon as the election writ has been promulgated.[10]

In the 2001 Australian election campaign, the public purse funded political parties to the amount of AUD 32 million, of which 84% went to the three major parties. Thus, to compare the funding of two major parties in each country, the New Zealand Labour Party receives only 4% of the amount of public funding received by its trans-Tasman counterpart, the Australian Labor Party,[11] and this party was permitted to raise as much additional funding to spend on its election campaign as it wished to augment its public funding. The implications of this practice in Australia, together with the fact that parties pay regular market prices for their political advertising, are that increasingly, candidates and parties need a great deal of money to compete equally during elections. Currently in New Zealand there are recommendations (from a parliamentary committee) to increase the political advertising funding to parties to NZD 3 million and to simplify the guidelines for parties on election expenses and advertising rules, especially the distinctions between party advertising that promotes electoral candidates and candidates' ads that promote their party (Elections New Zealand, 2004, p. 2).

In Australia, in addition to public funding subsidies for election campaigns, the national broadcasters, the Australian Broadcasting Commission and Special Broadcasting Service, make freely available a 30-minute time slot and six 5-minute slots for each of the government and opposition parties during the election campaign. Rarely do minor parties qualify for this free time. In New Zealand, the length of the free broadcasting time allocations for parties on TV New Zealand and Radio New Zealand is at the discretion of the broadcasters themselves, although the broadcasters must commit to this time and table their allocations in the parliament as soon as possible prior to an election period. This free time is only to be used for the opening and closing addresses of each political party during the election period.

Young (2004) makes the point that in Australia, the generous public funding of election campaigns is not matched by any restrictions on the content of political advertising. The only two restrictions on content are (a) material may not be defamatory of the character of a candidate if the material is not true (Commonwealth Electoral Act,1918, § 350 [1]) and (b) the content of an advertisement may not mislead a voter in relation to the actual casting of his or her vote (Commonwealth Electoral Act, 1918, § 329 [1]). This latter regulation refers to the technical process of marking the ballot paper and is thus very specifically related only to this process.

There have been several attempts to regulate political advertising in Australia, but these have generally failed. Two notable attempts occurred in 1984 and 1991. In February 1984, the Commonwealth Electoral Act of 1918 was amended to make it an offence to make misleading or deceptive statements in electoral advertising in any form. However, this amendment was repealed 8 months later (Miskin & Grant, 2004). The major argument against the amendment was that it would lead to numerous injunctions during election campaigns that would seriously disrupt the campaign. In 1991, the national parliament attempted to ban paid political advertising in the electronic media altogether and passed the Political Broadcasts and Political Disclosures Act, which came into effect in January 1992. This legislation was initially applied to various state elections held during 1992 and proved so unpopular that the High Court ruled it unconstitutional (on grounds that the act restricted an implied right of political communication within the Constitution) in August of that year.

The most recent (and some would argue, complete) liberalization of the content of Australian political advertising occurred in the 2004 federal election, when the Federation of Australian Commercial Television Stations[12] ceased its self-appointed role of scrutinizing the content of political ads for veracity after discovering that the requirements of the Trade Practices Act of 1974 did not apply to political advertising.

In terms of who is allowed to make political broadcasts, there are no restrictions on this in Australia, as long as the broadcasts have the name and address of the producer clearly indicated. However, in New Zealand, there are specific restrictions. Only parties and candidates can broadcast actual ads for those candidates and parties, but electoral agencies may broadcast official ads, broadcasters may make nonpartisan ads relating to election issues as a community service, and "other individuals or organizations may publish or broadcast an advertisement which is not an election programme but which relates to an election" as long as they do not name or appear to promote a particular candidate or party. Again, the name and address of the "person for whom or at whose direction it is published and their address must also be stated in the ad" (Elections New Zealand, 2005, § 40).

The lack of controls on political advertising volume and spending in Australia, coupled with public subsidies of this spending, has resulted in a marked increase of spending, particularly by the three major parties, in each successive election. This puts a great deal of pressure on minor parties and independents, who find it difficult to compete with the advertising budgets of the major parties.

HISTORY OF POLITICAL ADVERTISING AND THE EVOLUTION OF DIFFERENT MEDIA FORMATS

Political advertising has been a feature of the democratic process in both countries since their colonial days, when elections formed part of early representative government in the middle of the 19th century, with a limited male franchise. Because, in both countries, there were initially no political parties, the predominant form of advertising during the 19th century was the newspaper ad placed by individual candidates. These tended to be long-winded and acknowledged the fact that an ad could say very little, compared to a live public meeting, in which each candidate could speak for up to two hours (Young, 2004, p. 29). In fact, prior to 1901, Australian electoral campaign advertising was dominated by public meetings and supported extensively by "newspaper advertisements, posters, leaflets and handbills" (Young, 2004, p. 32). Young also comments on the importance of the candidates' colors during this early period—colors that would be used on posters, worn as ribbons by the candidates, adorn their carriages and their dogs, and be used in banners.

Both countries faced problems with bribery and drunkenness during the election campaigns of these early years. In New South Wales (Australia), one person was killed during the very first election campaign, leading to calls to regulate political advertising and, in some states, to ban ribbon wearing, banner flying, and music playing during campaigns. The New Zealand response to similar behavior was to pass an Act of Parliament in 1858 prohibiting both bribery and the use of alcohol-licensed premises for either campaigning or as polling booths (Atkinson, 2003). As early as 1885, limits were also placed on New Zealand candidates' campaign spending.

In regard to the relationship between the Australian Constitution (which came into being upon the federation of the former Australian colonies in 1901) and the practice of political advertising, Sarah Joseph (2001) states that the Constitution has always "protected this form of political expression" (p. 48). In 1918, the Electoral Act was made law, and it was largely this act that governed electoral advertising until it was joined by the various broadcasting acts, most recently the Broadcasting Services Act of 1992, which governs elements of broadcast political advertising.

In Australia, cinema advertising, which began in 1925, as stilted and long-winded (each silent ad lasted at least 10 minutes) as it was, did, however, show the importance of the visual medium in electoral advertising. Mills (1986, p. 133) states that this medium's ability to show the human face led to a focus in political advertising (and indeed in other forms of political communication) on the appearance of the leader.

However, the 1930s and 1940s saw radio embraced as a key medium for political advertising in both Australia and New Zealand. In Australia, radio began to replace public meetings as a source of political information for voters (Young, 2004, p. 33). In New Zealand, although radio was introduced in the early 1920s, it was not until 1938 that the first (strictly regulated) political broadcasts were allowed. In that year, the advertising was limited to a few speeches from MPs representing major parties and independents, according to a quota, and commercial stations were only permitted to broadcast brief announcements of public meetings, up to a maximum of 15 minutes each day (Atkinson, 2003).

The first use of television for political advertising in New Zealand was in 1963. This was an uninspiring 2 hours of prerecorded speeches by candidates uncomfortable with the new medium, on each of the four regional television stations, at a period when radio broadcasting of political ads had increased to 24 hours. Hayward and Rudd (2003, p. 2) argue that historically, New Zealand's regulations restricting political advertising on television tended to make newspaper advertising more important than it otherwise might be after the advent of television, and this trend has persisted in the early 21st century. In their analysis of the 1996 New Zealand election, Vowles, Aimer, Banducci, and Karp (1998) note that although television has certainly become more important in recent years, the newspaper is still extremely important as a source of election news and advertising. Coupled with this, different parties spend proportionally more on some formats than on others. For example, during the 1996 campaign, the Nationals spent 44.2% of their advertising budget on printed materials, compared to only 21.5% on radio or television. The Labour party, by contrast, spent 47.9% on radio and television and only 29.8% on printed matter. This difference reflects what media each party believes its constituents are more likely to be exposed to.

Television appears to have made a much greater impact on political advertising in Australia than in New Zealand. Young (2004) notes that in Australia, between 1949 and 2001, there was a great decline in the number and variety of political advertisements placed in newspapers (from 118 different ads in 1949 to 10 in 2001). Thus the decline in newspaper advertising predated the arrival of television in Australia in 1956. Young attributes this decline, both in variety of ads and in the use of newspapers for Australian political advertising, to an increasing centralization of control

over political campaigns since 1949 and the concomitant reduction in regional differences. This, in turn, has been seen as a function of the increasing cost of using professional advertising companies and the need to maximize the value of the campaign dollar. Nowadays, 90% of voters are exposed to political advertising on commercial television, compared to only 70% for either press or radio (Young, 2004, p. 38), so television advertising, in spite of its much higher cost, has come to take precedence over other formats. Between the elections of 1958 (the first for which television was available) and 1996, the amount spent on television advertising has gone from virtually nil to almost AUD 9 million. However, there is no correlation between the amount spent on television advertising and electoral success (Young, 2004, p. 41).

RESEARCH ON POLITICAL ADVERTISING IN AUSTRALIA AND NEW ZEALAND

Little academic interest was shown in political advertising in either Australia or New Zealand prior to the latter part of the 20th century. Hayward and Rudd (2003) state: "There has been very little research on political advertising in New Zealand despite the importance of advertising in political party campaigns" (p. 2). What has been written in both countries has often been local or specific to a particular time period; for example, "Election Advertising in the *Otago Daily Times*, 1946-2003" (Hayward & Rudd, 2003) and "Themes in Political Advertising: Australian Federal Election Campaigns 1949-1972" (Braund, 1978). Much of the focus has been on the regulatory regimes in each country, often within a comparative framework (Geddis, 2003; Joseph, 2001; Legislative Assembly of Queensland Legal Constitutional and Administrative Review Committee, 1996; Williams, 1997). Political advertising literature often comprises short newspaper articles or official reports to or from the respective electoral commissions in each country (see especially Miskin, 2005; Miskin & Grant, 2004) or occurs incidentally in works on other electoral issues (see recent work by Vowles et al. in New Zealand).

Australian political advertising has been discussed by journalists O'Neil and Mills (1986), who traced its historical roots and analyzed particularly the 1984 Australian election advertising. They regard paid political advertising as a significant, even "dominant," aspect of political campaigning in Australia (p. 337). Young (2002, 2004) believes that academic study of Australian political advertising is gradually changing and points to new Ph.D.s and the opening up of new courses in political communication in Australian universities as cause for optimism. In fact, Young has recently established the Political Advertising Archive at the University of Melbourne, a repository of hundreds of print and electronic political advertising materials, both historical and contemporary, and her recent work (2004) is a much more comprehensive analysis of political advertising in Australia than anything previously written. *The Persuaders* critically focuses on the role played by political advertising in the construction of what Young calls "the PR State," with its tendencies toward secretive practices rather than the open and transparent practices required for healthy democratic processes. Young, who has also written shorter articles on political advertising (Tucker & Young, 2001; Young, 2002), notes that the "PR State" is an outcome of a move to intensive media management that began during the early 1970s under Labor's brief period of government and has increased exponentially since then. Young estimates that 4000 journalists are employed by various levels of government across the country, and all major political parties employ media advisors in increasingly large numbers. Young also notes the rise in media monitoring by parties of anything that is said about them in the

media and criticizes the intimidatory tactics employed to keep the media in line. Thus, according to Young, electoral advertising in Australia has become just another part of the ongoing process of monitoring public opinion and presenting one's party and leader in the best possible light, both during and between election campaigns.

In New Zealand, a recent book edited by Hayward and Rudd (2004) looks at several aspects of political advertising in that country, but under the broader heading of "political communications," reiterating Young's implication that it is necessary to see political advertising within the broader framework of communications and marketing. In commenting on mediatizing trends in New Zealand political campaigns, Vowles, Karp, Banducci, and Miller (2002) suggest that, as in most other democracies, New Zealand "news coverage mediates the election experience" (p. 48). However, this has largely resulted in an increasing framing of the elections as a "horse race" and has not led to an undue focus on the personalities of the leaders.

Both countries' electoral commissions provide useful analyses and discussions in simplified formats on their Web sites for general information. Some discussion of political advertising has occurred in relation to recent changes in New Zealand's system of voting to proportional representation (see especially Banducci & Vowles, 2002; Denemark, 1998). Of the few studies done of effects of political advertising, that by O'Cass (2002) in the Australian context, focused on voter believability of negative versus positive election campaigns (both equally believable) and also found that electors valued unpaid political news during election campaigns more highly than paid advertising.

One of the first major academic studies of political advertising in Australia was that of Braund (1978), which examined themes in political advertising between 1949, when the Liberal (conservative) government first came to power, and 1972, when it finally lost to the Australian Labor Party. Braund's study (a master's thesis) reveals a propensity for both major parties to adopt an "aggressive style" (p. 369) of campaigning and the fact that both parties have always (during this period at least) claimed to be the "people's party." She argues that the advertising during this period constructed the electorate as gullible, as advertisers frequently resorted to fear tactics and hyperbolic descriptions of what life was or would be under the other party. Other themes that dominated election campaign advertising during this period were fear (of communism and of economic disaster) and the importance of good management. Both parties constructed themselves as having "vision, vitality and vigour" (p. 363), and there was very little to differentiate the parties in terms of the benefits the electorate was promised if they voted for that party. The Liberal party predominantly used themes of threat and fear in its campaigns, whereas Labor, being in opposition the whole of that time, tended to focus more on the mismanagement of the government, as well as adopting a defensive stance against Liberal charges of communist and undue union influence. However, in the later years of the 1960s and early 1970s (building up to their electoral win in late 1972), Labor campaigning changed to emphasize its new unified national vision for Australia, which needed still to be seen against a background of Liberal mismanagement and increasing disunity.

In New Zealand, the New Zealand Election Study has been conducted during each election campaign in that country since 1990 by Jack Vowles at the University of Auckland and his colleagues, and from this research a number of books and articles have been published (Vowles & Aimer, 1993; Vowles, Aimer, Catt, Lamare, & Miller 1995; Vowles et al., 1998, 2004; Vowles, Karp, Banducci, Aimer, et al., 2002; Vowles, Karp, Banducci, & Miller, 2002). Although these studies do not address political advertising in particular, they do

assess the match between issues identified as important by voters and the extent to which they believe the parties have addressed these issues in their campaigns. Vowles (2003) does analyze the 2002 New Zealand election campaign and finds that the surprising outcomes of reduction in support of both major parties was caused by a failure of both parties to mobilize effectively on the issues of importance to the people.

In New Zealand, Hayward and Rudd's 2003 study of political advertising in the regional newspaper *The Otago Times* found little change over a 58-year period. Although recent ads may have acquired a 21st-century slickness, their level of detail and ability to inform voters did not change over that time.

The topics of adversarial advertising and negative campaigning have been the focus of academic writing in both countries. Leitch and Roper (1999) studied a campaign waged during the 1996 New Zealand election by a major workers' union and an employers' federation. This campaign was clearly one of ideological adversaries, and contrasted with the campaigns of the major political parties, which both fought for the middle ground. The authors found that the less overtly ideological stance of the parties made their campaigns more effective than those of the union and employers' groups. Miskin and Grant (2004) have written on the allegations in Australia about an increasing trend toward negative electoral campaigning. They assert (with Braund, 1978) that far from being a recent phenomenon, electoral advertising in Australia has always tended to focus on negative attributes of the opposing party. In fact, Miskin and Grant detect a pattern of positive campaigning during the first few weeks of Australian election campaigns followed by quite negative advertising late in the campaign. These attacks can be quite personal and usually name key members of the opposing party. Recent examples were Labor's attack on Treasurer Peter Costello as representative of the "mean and tricky" attributes of his government in the 2001 campaign, and the Liberals' particular targeting of Labor leader Mark Latham during the 2004 elections.

KEY EVENTS IN THE DEVELOPMENT OF POLITICAL ADVERTISING

It would be difficult for any electoral advertising practice in contemporary Australia or New Zealand to replicate the bribery, drunken violence, shocks, and controversies of election campaigns during the colonial days noted earlier in this chapter. Probably the first controversial political advertising campaign in Australia in more recent times was in the 1949 elections, when Robert Menzies became the first Australian politician to seriously (and successfully) exploit the electronic news media (radio) and managed to overturn the Labor government by using their own tactics. Mills (1986) quotes Menzies:

> If we are going to match the Labor Party, let us face up to the fact that the Labor Party has a clever set of advertising tradesmen at work in the centre. . . . The Labor Party's advertising always had a bite in it. They have no mealy-mouthed ideas of the kind we suffer from. They say to themselves, "How do you knock him over?" They reply, "By saying he's a stinker." Then they say it, and they say it so forcibly that people think he is. They always attack. It is these attacking advertisements that are read. (p. 89)

Menzies then employed one of Labor's "clever advertising tradesmen" to work for his newly formed Liberal Party. One of the key strategies was an 18-month-long radio program presented by the fictitious John Henry Austral, a typical "thinking Australian," who in honeyed tones berated the Labor government's "socialist sins" at a time of growing suspicion of communism.

Another noteworthy Australian electoral advertising campaign was the one that finally brought down the Liberal government in 1972

after 23 years in office. Gough Whitlam's "It's Time" advertisements used new forms of suggestive, policy-free advertising to promote the image and person of the Labor leader. Young (2004) quotes the ad company responsible for the campaign, Spectrum International, as taking the "soft-sell" approach to give voters "not the reality but an image which would fit with their desires" (p. 15). These ads took the form of television commercials, balloons, t-shirts, buttons, stickers, and even matchboxes (Young, 2004, p. 17). Young claims that this campaign was decisive, if not in its effect on voters (Labor's margin of victory was not large), then certainly in its effect on politicians on both sides who believed it had worked. Young claims that the assumed success of Whitlam's media campaign tactics, which foregrounded marketing and television advertising, "led to a system based on a scramble for cash in order to purchase the most expensive media management techniques" (p. 22).

Young (2004) provides evidence of the Americanization of Australian political advertising in the use of the "flip-flop" ads of recent years. Flip-flop ads use old media material to show where politicians in opposing parties have been inconsistent, contradicted themselves, or can be shown not to have followed through on a promise during a campaign. An example is a 1993 ad produced by the then Liberal opposition in which two photographs of the then Labor prime minister, Paul Keating, were placed side by side, each captioned with contradicting quotes from Keating: (a) "We won't let there be a recession," and (b) "This is the recession we had to have." Nowadays, Web-based editing techniques permit even more sophisticated manipulation of images and sound.

In New Zealand, Americanization of political advertising began as early as 1925, when the Reform Party's Bert Davy developed a presidential-type campaign using all the latest techniques borrowed from commercial advertising. Simple slogans replaced the previous detailed explanations of policies, and the personality of the prime minister was promoted rather than the policies of the party (Atkinson, 2003).

In terms of key events in New Zealand political advertising, the 1996 election, the first under the new system of proportional representation, about which Vowles et al. (1998) asserted that "the new tactical imperative of maximizing party votes across all 65 electorates, parties' ability to command news coverage and to place their ads before large audiences across New Zealand assumed even greater importance than in past elections" (p. 87). This favored, for example, advertisements placed on television stations with national reach (such as TV1) rather than specific regional ads.

It is interesting that in that same 1996 election, New Zealand's political parties continued disproportionately to target marginal seats, even though the strategic reasons for doing so were much less relevant than under the previous system of "first past the post" voting. Vowles et al. (1998) explain this paradox in terms of all parties' unfamiliarity with campaigning for the safe seats held both by themselves and by their political opposition and, hence, a continued bias in favor of marginal seats. What Karp, from the team led by Vowles, (2002) did observe as a likely function of the move to proportional representation was that parties diverged more on key issues than they had under the previous voting system: "As a result, voters have greater representation and more choice than in the past" (p. 145). However, this is an outcome of the change to the voting system, not to specific political advertising strategies.

The 1999 New Zealand elections were unusual in that the election was contested by two major parties each led by a woman: the Nationals, led by Jenny Shipley, and Labour, headed by Helen Clark. Such a contest did not lead to a campaign focus on women's issues, such as child care or gender equity; these actually tended to be avoided in favor of the promotion of "family friendly" policies. In fact, health and education remained the most important issues of New Zealand election campaigns during the whole decade of the 1990s.

FUTURE DIRECTIONS

As noted earlier, the probable relaxation of the media ownership laws in Australia, combined with the protection of existing free-to-air commercial channels within the new digital television environment, should increase the already high concentration of media ownership in that country. Changes to Australia's media ownership laws may also have an effect in New Zealand, as some of the same people own media companies in both countries (Brown, 2005). The effect of such changes on political advertising can only be guessed. It is unlikely that any form of cross-media ownership laws will be applied to new media, such as pay television and the Internet.

In common with many countries in recent decades, Australia and New Zealand have both seen an enormous increase in the amount, cost, and professionalization of news management by political parties, the so-called spin-doctoring (McGregor, 1996a, 1996b; Tiffin, 1989). Political advertising during election periods needs to be viewed within such a framework of sustained news management. Thus the dividing lines between some forms of political news and political advertising must blur at some point. What is interesting is the extent to which the media may become complicit in the management of news by political newsmakers. McGregor (1996b) discusses an incident in the 1993 New Zealand elections in which the media (in this case commercial TV3) actively cooperated with the Labour Party's Mike Moore to ensure that a banner with the party's campaign slogan was shown to advantage on television interviews with Moore.

In terms of newer forms of distribution of electoral advertising, the Internet, direct marketing assisted by computerized databases, and mobile (cellular) telephones are perhaps the main areas of interest. Of the three, it is the Web that is the least used format. Although in Australia about 50% of federal parliamentarians have a Web site, those using the Web to find out political information are still a small minority. Web-based advertising usually depends on the actions of the voter to seek out political advertising, because such advertising is largely confined to the specific Web sites of parties. Such sites usually provide larger quantities of and more detailed information than that provided via the traditional broadcast or print media, but you have to be keen to access it. Once at the site, the voter can also sometimes choose to ask the politician (usually the party leader) questions and to post their own views, but, as the leader of the Western Australian Labor Party, Geoff Gallup, typically advises on his party's Web site, "Because of the volume of contacts, I will not always be able to reply immediately, but I will take note of your views and ideas"(Australian Labor Party, 2005). This capacity for interaction tends to be available only during election campaigns, not at other times.

In New Zealand, the National Party Web site (2005) provides short biographies of the candidates, including the leader, and provides their e-mail addresses without actually inviting voters to send queries or ideas. The New Zealand Labour Party site has a link to monthly "live chat" lines with MPs, including the prime minister, deputy minister, and education minister. Such chats seem aimed at young people, and the site at which they may be accessed is titled "Heads Up" and focuses on the interests of young families, young workers, and students (New Zealand Labour Party, 2005). Barker (2004) discusses the impact of party Web sites on electoral advertising practice in New Zealand, noting that access to the Internet (used by less than 50% of New Zealanders) is still a barrier to this form of political communication for many citizens. She also notes that the Labour Party Web site is frequently offline for revisions and that smaller parties, such as the Greens, make the best use of the Web. This point is reiterated by Middleton (2004), who, commenting on the use made by minor party ACT New Zealand, states that the Internet is also used to assist with offline aspects of this small party's campaigning.

Web sites can (and do) provide links to sites informing voters how to update their details on the electoral rolls, how to vote abroad, and other information that will help them to vote, as well as how to contact the party, how to make donations, and so on. Voters can also access media releases from the party, as well as find out details about individual candidates. Mostly this information is as brief as other electoral advertising material (such as mailed brochures), echoing the assumptions made in respect of television advertising—that less is more.

During the 2004 Australian elections, however, the techniques of spamming and of chain e-mails assisted in spreading access to Web-based advertising. Prime Minister John Howard and several other Liberal MPs used Howard's son's Internet company to send e-mail spam to their electorates. Political and religious organizations are exempt from recently enacted antispamming legislation in Australia. Chain e-mails (when e-mails are sent to a few people with something humorous or satirical about a politician, with the request to "e-mail this to five friends") were popular in Australia during the same election campaign, especially with minor parties. Within the e-mails are contained links to party and activist group Web sites, which, obviously, contain more serious political content. This technique was employed during 2004 particularly by the minor centre-left party, the Australian Democrats. However, another minor party, the Greens, found that the Internet was better used as a tool for mobilizing existing supporters rather than for getting new voters (Miskin, 2005).

In Australia in recent elections, the controversial technique of recorded political messages sent to telephone numbers, especially in marginal electorates, was used by the Liberal Party leader and his deputy, Peter Costello. Although some voters found the calls annoying, especially when in some cases they had to pay for them themselves, the Liberals believed they were effective in helping them to win some six marginal seats. Attempts by the Labor Party to complain about the Liberals because they did not carry the appropriate authorization failed when it was discovered that this requirement in both the Commonwealth Electoral Act of 1918 and the Broadcasting Services Act of 1992 only related to traditional media advertising and did not apply to newer media and communication formats (Miskin, 2005). This technique can reach more of the targeted voters than more traditional media, and its efficacy is enhanced by the existence of answering machines and mobile phones.

The role of bloggers during election campaigns has to be noted: In the 2004 Australian campaign, these sites attracted more visitors than the official party sites.

Direct mail is increasingly used in Australian campaigns, especially since the availability of increasingly accurate databases that allow detailed targeting of the "swinging voters" in marginal seats. A study in 2001 found that direct mail was the "primary source of policy information for 41% of those canvassed" (Miskin, 2005). Such techniques tend to favor incumbent parliamentarians, because they have the taxpayer-funded resources to research, print, and mail the material to their electorates.

Greater use of newer electronic means of communication by political parties has benefits and disadvantages for democracy. The benefits are that these are relatively low-cost methods of reaching voters directly and can thus be employed equally by large and small parties, governments and oppositions alike.

The disadvantages are that, increasingly, political advertising (and even policy formulation) takes the form of finely tuned targeted marketing, and only a few in the electorate are among those whose interests are targeted.

NOTES

1. New Zealand's Legislative Council (upper house) was abolished in 1951.

2. Australia's first election, for the newly formed New South Wales Legislative Council, was held in 1843, and New Zealand's first election was held in 1853 for its General Assembly, which comprised a House of Representatives and a Legislative Council.

3. Prior to 1993, New Zealand had "first past the post" voting.

4. "First past the post" is a system of voting in which the candidate who gets the most votes wins. No preferences are allocated, as each voter only votes for one candidate. This system is inherited from the British voting system.

5. "Free-to-air" means that the viewer receives this station free of charge, rather than paying a subscription. Free-to-air stations may or may not carry commercials.

6. These are the Australian Broadcasting Commission and the Special Broadcasting Service.

7. There are 35 regional daily newspapers and 470 other regional and suburban papers (DFAT, 2004).

8. This was legislated under the Television Broadcasting Services (Digital Conversion) Act, 1998.

9. The free time only applies to parties. Advertising for constituency candidates must be paid for.

10. In New Zealand, election broadcasts may not be transmitted on Sunday mornings and on certain public holidays.

11. The Australian Lab*or* Party spells labour differently from that of the New Zealand Lab*our* Party.

12. Now called Free Television.

REFERENCES

Atkinson, N. (2003). *Adventures in democracy: A history of the vote in New Zealand.* Dunedin, NZ: University of Otago Press, in association with the Electoral Commission.

Australian Labor Party [Home page]. (2005). Retrieved January 6, 2006, from http://www.alp.org.au.

Australian Labor Party. (2005). *Ask Geoff.* Retrieved January 6, 2006, from http://www.betterfuture.com.au/ask.html

Banducci, S., & Vowles, J. (2002). Elections, citizens, and the media. In J. Vowles, P. Aimer, J. Karp, S. Banducci, R. Miller, & A. Sullivan (Eds.), *Proportional representation on trial: The 1999 New Zealand general election and the fate of MMP* (pp. 34–49). Auckland, NZ: Auckland University Press.

Barker, L. (2004). Party websites. In J. Hayward & C. Rudd (Eds.), *Political communications in New Zealand.* Auckland: Pearson Education New Zealand.

Braund, V. (1978). *Themes in political advertising: Australian federal election campaigns 1949-1972.* Unpublished master's thesis, Department of Government, University of Sydney, Australia.

Brown, R. (2005). Going west? *New Zealand Listener, 197*(3381). Retrieved March 15, 2005 from http://www.nzlistener.co.nz/printable,3461.sm

Denemark, D. (1998). Campaign activities and marginality: The transition to MMP campaigns. In J. Vowles, P. Aimer, S. Banducci, & J. Karp (Eds.), *Voters' victory? New Zealand's first election under proportional representation* (pp. 81–100). Auckland, NZ: Auckland University Press.

Department of Foreign Affairs and Trade. (2004). *Australia now: The media in Australia.* Retrieved January 5, 2006, from http://www.dfat.gov.au/facts/media.html

Elections New Zealand (2004, April). *Electoral brief* (No. 27). Retrieved January 21, 2005, from http://www.elections.org.nz/pandr/electoral_brief-apr-04.pdf.

Elections New Zealand. (2005). *Interim guide to broadcasting at parliamentary elections 2005.* Retrieved January 27, 2005, from http://www.elections.org.nz/esyst/interim_broadcasting_guide.doc

Geddis, A. (2003). Reforming New Zealand's election broadcasting regime. *Public Law Review, 14*(3).

Given, J. (2001, February). Media ownership in Australia: The laws, the players. Retrieved January 27, 2005, from the Centre d'Etudes sur les Medias Web site: http://www.cem.ulaval.ca/CONCAustralia.pdf

Hayward, J., & Rudd, C. (2003, April). *Election advertising in the* Otago Daily Times, *1946-2002.*

Paper presented at the Political Science Association Conference, Leicester, UK. Retrieved January 6, 2006, from http://www.psa.ac.uk/journals/pdf/5/2003/Janine%20Hayward.pdf

Hayward, J., & Rudd, C. (Eds.). (2004). *Political communications in New Zealand.* Auckland: Pearson Education New Zealand.

Jackson, K. (2002, January 3). *Digital television and datacasting.* Retrieved January 6, 2006, from the Parliament of Australia: Parliamentary Library Web site: http://www.aph.gov.au/library/intguide/sp/digdata.htm

Joseph, S. (2001). Political advertising and the Constitution. In G. Patmore (Ed.), *The BIG makeover: A new Australian Constitution* (pp. 48–59). Annandale, NSW: Pluto Press.

Karp, J. (2002). Members of Parliament and representation. In J. Vowles, P. Aimer, J. Karp, S. Banducci, R. Miller, & A. Sullivan (Eds.), *Proportional representation on trial: The 1999 New Zealand general election and the fate of MMP* (pp. 130–145). Auckland, NZ: Auckland University Press.

Legislative Assembly of Queensland Legal Constitutional and Administrative Review Committee. (1996, December). *Truth in political advertising* (Report No. 4). Brisbane, Queensland: Author.

Leitch, S., & Roper, J. (1999, August). Ad wars: Adversarial advertising by interest groups in a New Zealand general election. *Media International Australia Incorporating Culture & Policy, 92,* 103–116.

McGregor, J. (1996a). Hidden hands: The news manipulators. In J. McGregor (Ed.), *Dangerous democracy? News media politics in New Zealand* (pp. 120–134). Palmerston North, NZ: Dunmore Press.

McGregor, J. (1996b). Spinning the news. In J. McGregor (Ed.), *Dangerous democracy? News media politics in New Zealand* (pp. 135–148). Palmerston North, NZ: Dunmore Press.

Middleton, G. (2004). *Better campaigning through technology.* Retrieved January 6, 2006, from the Hillwatch.com Web site: http://www.hillwatch.com/Publications/Research/Campaigning_Through_Technology.aspx.

Mills, S. (1986). *The new machine men: Polls and persuasion in Australian politics.* Ringwood, Victoria: Penguin.

Miskin, S. (2005, February 8). *Campaigning in the 2004 federal elections: Innovations and traditions* (Research note No. 30 2004–05). Retrieved January 6, 2006, from the Parliament of Australia Parliamentary Library Web site: http://www.aph.gov.au/library/pubs/RN/2004-05/05rn30.htm

Miskin, S., & Grant, R. (2004). *Political advertising in Australia* (Research brief No. 5 2004–05). Retrieved January 6, 2006, from the Parliament of Australia Parliamentary Library Web site: http://www.aph.gov.au/library/pubs/RB/2004-05/05rb05.htm

New Zealand Labour Party. (2005). *Heads up.* Retrieved January 6, 2006, from http://www.headsup.co.nz

New Zealand National Party [Home page]. (2005). Retrieved January 6, 2006, from http://www.national.org.nz

Norris, P. (2005, November). Public broadcasting in the digital age: Issues for television in New Zealand. *Media International Australia Incorporating Cultural Policy, 117,* 43–63.

O'Cass, A. (2002). Political advertising believability and information source value during elections. *Journal of Advertising, 31*(1), 63–74.

O'Neil, H., & Mills, S. (1986). Political advertising in Australia: A dynamic force meets a resilient object. In L. L. Kaid, D. Nimmo, & K. R. Sanders (Eds.), *New perspectives on political advertising* (pp. 314–337). Carbondale: Southern Illinois University Press.

Parliament of Australia: Education. (2005, March 22). *Parliament: An overview.* Retrieved January 5, 2006, from http://www.aph.gov.au/parl.htm#house

Rosenberg, B. (n.d.) News media ownership in New Zealand. Retrieved January 6, 2006, from http://canterbury.cyberplace.org.nz/community/CAFCA/publications/Miscellaneous/mediaown.pdf

Tiffin, R. (1989). *News and power.* North Sydney, Australia: Allen & Unwin.

Tucker, D., & Young, S. (2001). Public financing of election campaigns in Australia: A solution or a problem? In G. Patmore (Ed.), *The BIG makeover: A new Australian Constitution* (pp. 50–71). Annandale, NSW: Pluto Press.

Vowles, J. (2003, April). *Before and after: Campaign influences on voting choices at the 2002 New Zealand election.* Paper presented at the New Zealand Political Studies Association Conference, University of Auckland. Retrieved January 6, 2006, from http://www.nzes.org/docs/papers/APSA_2003_Vowles.pdf

Vowles, J., & Aimer, P. (1993). *Voters' vengeance: The 1990 election in New Zealand and the fate of the fourth Labour government.* Auckland, NZ: Auckland University Press.

Vowles, J., Aimer, P., Banducci, S., & Karp, J. (Eds.). (1998). *Voters' victory? New Zealand's first election under proportional representation.* Auckland, NZ: Auckland University Press.

Vowles, J., Aimer, P., Banducci, S., & Karp, J. (Eds.). (2004). *Voter's veto: The 2002 election in New Zealand and the consolidation of minority government.* Auckland, NZ: Auckland University Press.

Vowles, J., Aimer, P., Catt, H., Lamare, J., & Miller, R. (1995). *Towards consensus? The 1993 election in New Zealand and the transition to proportional representation.* Auckland, NZ: Auckland University Press.

Vowles, J., Karp, J., Banducci, S., Aimer, P., & Miller, R. (2002). Reviewing MMP. In J. Vowles, P. Aimer, J. Karp, S. Banducci, R. Miller, & A. Sullivan (Eds.), *Proportional representation on trial: The 1999 New Zealand general election and the fate of MMP* (pp. 175–191). Auckland, NZ: Auckland University Press.

Vowles, J., Karp, J., Banducci, S., & Miller, R. (2002). *About the New Zealand election study.* Retrieved January 6, 2006, from the New Zealand Election Study Web site: http://www.nzes.org

Williams, G. (1997). *Truth in political advertising legislation in Australia.* Law and Bills Digest Group. Research Paper 13, 1996-97. Retrieved March 10, 2006, from http://www.aph.gov.au/library/pubs/rp/1996-97/97rp13.htm#HISTORY

Young, S. (2002). Spot on: The role of political advertising in Australia. *Australian Journal of Political Science. 37*(1), 81–97.

Young, S. (2004). *The persuaders: Inside the hidden machine of political advertising.* North Melbourne, Australia: Pluto Press.

17

Political Advertising in Japan, South Korea, and Taiwan

JINYOUNG TAK

Elections are occasions when the nature of a nation's life is put to the test, and campaigns are inherently interesting, even fascinating, events in and of themselves. Unlike voters in times past, today's voters are increasingly dependent on the media for their political information, and political advertising serves many functions and offers many opportunities for candidates to be competitive. Among the functions of political advertising (particularly of televised political spots), the two most important are helping the candidate define or redefine his or her image and providing a forum in which campaign issues can be explained and developed (Johnston & Kaid, 2002).

Different parameters in different cultures can differentially promote or constrain political communication roles and behaviors within those cultures. Far from overlooking political differences, a comparative approach to the analysis of political communication offers the means of distinguishing unique from more generic phenomena. During the 1990s, political

communication researchers increasingly paid attention to cross-national aspects of political advertising. However, those studies are mostly reflections of Western culture and, accordingly, focus on the context of Western election campaigns. This suggests an emerging need for an alternative way of looking at political advertising by comparing differences and similarities among various political structures, political processes, and media systems. This perspective can provide guidelines for studying political value transferences and adaptations. Further, a careful analysis of the similarities and differences in election campaigns between nations might yield useful insights into the process of political campaigns and provide a competitive edge for the development of more reliable political systems.

The major concern of this chapter is the cultural aspect of political advertising. I present a case for the viewpoint that political advertising mirrors the culture, be it in Western or non-Western countries. Because it is almost impossible in a single chapter to examine political advertising within all Asian countries, three major East Asian countries have been purposely selected. In terms of countries that can be compared in regard to Americanization, Japan, South Korea, and Taiwan stand out as interesting cases. These countries are selected not because they are the most dominant nations in terms of power but because they are the most observable Eastern democracies that have outstanding democratic traditions of their own, and they share many basic democratic principles. Moreover, because it is almost impossible to introduce and compare political advertising at all levels of elections, this study will explore the general election in Japan and presidential elections in South Korea and Taiwan.

Whatever form it takes, political advertising, as a special type of political communication, now plays an essential role in election campaigns in these three nations. With regard to the nations under study, I am well aware of the difficulty of isolating any one aspect of a country's campaign from its total political culture, therefore making it harder to pinpoint the relationships of political advertising. However, based on the assumption that divergences exist among the nations, I have viewed these divergences as differing in degree or in emphasis rather than as strict divisions.

Unlike most previous comparative political advertising studies, this study's major focus was not on the overall messages and strategies of particular countries but in how political ads were systematically alike and different in accordance with particular cultures. This chapter shows, first of all, indigenous political structures and some background of each country, followed by an examination of each country's media system. Next, I discuss the history and current regulations of political advertising in each country and, finally, suggest possible future discussions and directions for scholarship, with consideration of neglected areas of political advertising research in this part of the world.

POLITICAL STRUCTURES AND BACKGROUNDS

We can assume that different parameters in political and media systems will differently promote or constrain roles and behaviors of political advertising within those systems (Gurevitch & Blumler, 1990). A particular difficulty in the comparison of political advertising lies in the presidential-parliamentary divide, the fundamental contrast among the three countries analyzed here. South Korea and Taiwan have the presidential system, but Japan uses the parliamentary system, in which a prime minister takes charge of the assembly.

Japan

Japan functions as a representative democracy. The head of state is the emperor, and the head executive is the prime minister. The prime minister is chosen by a ballot of the Diet (parliament) and appoints a cabinet, a majority of whose members must also be members of the Diet. The bicameral Diet comprises the House of Representatives (the more powerful lower house), whose 480 members are elected every 4 years, and the House of Councilors (the upper house), whose 247 members are elected for 6-year terms, with half of its number elected every 3 years. There are 300 single-seat constituencies and 180 seats filled by proportional representation in the House of Representatives.

The Diet is the highest organ of the state. It is responsible for designating the prime minister. Although the emperor is the head of state, his function is purely symbolic. The party-political structure is dominated by the conservative Liberal Democratic Party (LDP), which has ruled Japan either alone or in coalition for most of the years since 1955. Japanese politics have been characterized by one-party rule for over four decades, with the sole change being which clique within the party presides over decision making (Richardson & Flanagan, 1984).

Japan's modern political era began in 1868 with the overthrow of the Tokugawa shogun state and the establishment of a unified state under the authority of Emperor Meiji. It was not until the Diet was opened in 1890 that nationwide political activities started in earnest. The first parliamentary election was held in 1890, for an electorate restricted to male property owners—just 1% of the total population. Spurred by Japan's rapid economic development and by the democratizing influence of World War I, the Diet's power grew steadily in the first 25 years or so of the 20th century. The foundations of Japan's young democracy were, however, undermined in the 1920s by growing economic difficulties at home and abroad. As Japan's economic problems grew, so too did the influence of the military in the country's political life. By the end of the 1930s, after the onset of the war with China, the military's grip on Japan's political life was complete, and in 1940 all political parties were disbanded (Economist Intelligence Unit, 2004a).

During Japan's occupation by the United States and its allies from 1945 to 1952, a new constitution was written and a whole range of new political reforms was initiated, including universal suffrage (International Research Center for Japanese Studies, 2003). At the end of 1955, Japan's two main conservative political parties, the ruling Democratic Party and the Liberal Party, merged to form the LDP. The LDP enjoyed nearly 40 consecutive years in power. Inevitably, one consequence of this long period of dominance by the LDP was a high level of corruption, particularly in the party's upper echelons, as its various factions vied with each other for influence (Thies, 2002). Since the LDP's fall from single-party power in 1993, Japan's political scene has become highly fluid. One sign of this has been the large number of prime ministers (10) since 1993.

The Japanese government has seen a gradual trend toward increasing political competition and reform over the past decade.

Although no longer able to govern without the support of other parties, the LDP remains by far Japan's largest political party and continues to dominate the political landscape. Furthermore, the results of the 2003 general elections brought changes to the party system in Japan, from single-party dominance to a two-party system, as the LDP and its coalition partners managed only a slim margin over the opposition party (Rosenbluth & Thies, 2004). The election results have convinced many observers that Japan is finally on its way to a genuine two-party system (Lee, 2004). However, the pattern of Japan's interaction with other countries in Asia is still influenced by the bitter legacy of its colonial past. Many Asian countries believe, not without justification, that Japan has never accepted responsibility for the atrocities committed in the region by its troops in the 1930s and 1940s.

The personalism and localism of Japanese political organization and election campaigning impose an enormous financial burden on Diet candidates and produce problems of political corruption that are well known (Richardson, 1997). Political life in Japan is extraordinarily expensive, especially for LDP politicians. As campaigning is perennial, despite legal stipulations to the contrary, and because a Diet member or aspirant must build his or her own political factions to cultivate voter support, a tremendous amount of time and energy is put toward raising money (Curtis, 1988). No one knows precisely how much money the Japanese electoral process consumes. Although the Political Funds Regulation Law requires politicians, political parties, and other political organizations to submit annual income reports, it is an open secret that income reported is only the tip of an enormous iceberg of political contributions (Curtis, 1999).

South Korea

In Korea, there is a single race, a single language, common cultural assumptions, and no minority group of significant size. The official name of the country is the Republic of Korea, and the country uses a presidential system. The president and the National Assembly are directly elected, based on a "first past the post" system. The president (elected for a single term of 5 years) appoints the rest of the State Council (cabinet), which is composed of the president, prime minister, and between 15 and 20 ministers. However, the State Council is not entirely composed of members of the National Assembly. In the unicameral National Assembly, which is composed of 299 members, who are elected for 4-year terms, currently 243 seats are filled by direct election, and the remaining 56 seats are distributed between parties in proportion to their share of the vote.

Reflecting the past influence of the armed forces on South Korea's political life, the constitution stipulates that the armed forces must maintain political neutrality. Between 1961, when Park Chung-Hee seized power, and 1988, when Chun Doo-hwan relinquished it, the government party existed in the National Assembly and in the country to support the president, but the power base of the regime lay elsewhere—in the military. Moreover, opposition parties in the National Assembly, although they might criticize government policies, could not safely challenge the constitutional basis on which the government was established, at least not until the mid-1980s (Lee, 1990).

Since its founding, South Korea's overriding external preoccupation has always been with North Korea and its threats of renewed aggression. Whether in the form of its alleged nuclear program or its stockpile of chemical weapons, North Korea's terrorization has never truly ceased. From time to time, this theoretical threat has also been reinforced by acts of terrorism by North Korea against South Korea. However, South Korea, for its part, proclaims the ideal of peaceful unification, and cannot afford to abandon it, as there are still today millions of Koreans separated from immediate members of their families by the war in 1950-1953. The threat from North Korea has determined that South Korea's principal external tie should be a military alliance with the United States, which still has troops stationed between Seoul and the Demilitarized Zone as a guarantee of U.S. involvement from the first hours of any renewed inter-Korean conflict.

Upon liberation from Japan in 1948, Korea was divided into two independent republics. The division into North and South Korea along the thirty-eighth parallel was supposed to be a temporary military measure, yet it still remains in force today. The politics of the divided Korea is in many ways the outcome of a contest between the leaders of North and South Korea and of the clash of their political wills. Korean politics is a high-risk system: The stakes of political conflict are very high, as the winner takes all and the loser gets nothing (Kihl, 1984). Although the political form was Western, the way in which politics in Korea actually worked during its first four decades owed more to traditional political culture than to imported ideas (Clough, 1987).

Party politics in South Korea has been largely a tale of power struggles among conservative parties and component factions, devoid of conflicting ideological contentions. Further, the fact of divided nationhood seems to have accentuated these elements in Korean political culture (Kihl, 1984). However, Korea today is facing the monumental task of transforming its centralized political system into a decentralized system. Democratization in Korea since 1987 has led to the gradual establishment of a diverse set of institutional arrangements— competitive electoral systems, local autonomy, freedom of the press, and freedom of association—that facilitate the articulation of political interests (Lim & Tang, 2002).

South Korea's relations with Japan are prickly, mainly as a result of lingering bitterness over Japan's harsh 35-year (1910-1945) rule over the Korean peninsula. Ties between the two countries are, however, growing stronger, notwithstanding continued diplomatic spats, such as the row that ensued in late 2001 when Japan's prime minister paid an official visit to the Yasukuni shrine in Japan, where Japan's war dead are honored. Closer ties reflect both continued security concerns relating to North Korea and an appreciation of the advantages for both countries in enhanced economic cooperation.

Taiwan

The division of China into mainland China and Taiwan along the Taiwanese strait was also meant to be a temporary solution, and yet it too remains in force today. Both governments have been struggling with this matter for more than 50 years. Taiwan had been a declared province in its own right only since 1886, just 9 years before it was ceded to Japan at the end of the Sino-Japanese war. The island remained under Japanese occupation—albeit of a less barbarous variety than that which characterized Japanese rule in Korea and Manchuria—until the end of World War II. In 1945, Taiwan was restored to Chinese sovereignty under the rule of the Kuomintang (the KMT). However, many people in Taiwan viewed the mainland Chinese regime as just another colonial oppressor, feckless and corrupt. Facing defeat with the civil war against the Chinese Communist Party in 1949, the KMT retreated to Taiwan with the remnants of its army and the Republic of China government, which had been established in 1912 following revolution in the previous year.

Taiwan's official name is the Republic of China, and the head of state is the president. It is hard to say whether Taiwan has adopted a presidential or parliamentary system of government, because it has an unusual political system. The system is semipresidential, with the executive power shared by the president and the legislature. In this sense, Taiwan's

system resembles the French Fifth Republic. However, in Taiwan, the relationship between the president, prime minister, and parliament is less defined than it is in France (Rawnsley, 2003). The president, who is directly elected for a term of 4 years, nominates a premier to preside over the Executive Yuan (cabinet). Taiwan's constitution is based on that of the Republic of China, promulgated in 1947. This lays out a government structure consisting of the president, a National Assembly, and five branches (Yuan) of government: the Executive, the Legislative, the Judicial, the Examination, and the Control Yuan. In recent years, the policy-making powers of the Legislative Yuan have increased relative to the National Assembly, as the island moves toward a unicameral parliamentary system. The 225-seat Legislative Yuan, formerly a rubber-stamp parliament, has in the past decade become a more powerful body.

The story of Taiwan between 1949 and the 1980s is one of spectacular economic growth set against a backdrop of authoritarian rule. Political freedoms were suppressed. Martial law, imposed in 1949, was not lifted until 1987. Although supplementary elections were held periodically after 1969, martial law permitted full elections only at the local level. The only legal political parties were the KMT and two small progovernment parties, although independent candidates were allowed to compete in elections. The KMT had overwhelming advantages in terms of patronage and financial resources in the bureaucracy, the military, and the media. Although the KMT did not lose power until 2000, its transformation since 1991 has been so great that it is the equivalent of a change in the ruling party (Fell, 2001). From 1992, the Democratic Progressive Party (DPP) and dissidents within the KMT began focusing their attacks on the KMT's vote buying, links to gangsters, and public works corruption. As a series of scandals began to tarnish the KMT's public image, the KMT moved toward political liberalization. In 1987, martial law was lifted and political prisoners were released. Opposition parties were gradually legalized over the next 2years. The political reforms began with an election of the National Assembly in 1991. This was followed by the election of the Legislative Yuan in 1992, the first full election since 1949. Further, reform of the executive branch led to Taiwan's first direct presidential election in 1996.

The arrival of democratic debate in Taiwan brought the sovereignty issue to the forefront (Chang, 2003). By the end of the 1980s, the majority of the population favored maintenance of the status quo, under which their newfound prosperity and democracy could be preserved without prompting conflict with China. These changes led Taiwan's leaders to embark on a strategy of renouncing the country's long-standing goal of reconquering the mainland. This daring effort was not enough for the KMT's candidate to be reelected in the 2000 presidential election, which was won by a DPP candidate, Chen Shui-bian. The Democratic Progressive Party, officially formed in 1986, made inroads in local government and Taiwan's legislature and took the presidency in 2000. The major political challenge for both parties was dealing with mainland China, which asserts that Taiwan is a renegade province and maintains a standing threat to invade the island. The KMT has traditionally favored unification with China, whereas the DPP advocates independence. The DPP again won the presidential election in 2004.

MEDIA SYSTEMS

Japan

If China draws international power from the sheer size of its population, Japan, the other potent force in Asia, draws power from its economic well-being. Daily newspaper circulation of 580 copies per 1000 people, the highest in the world, means that the average family gets more than one paper. By 2002, the *Yomiuri* was the only paper in the world to boast a circulation of over 10 million. Japan has five national dailies, *Yomiuri, Asahi, Mainichi, Nihon Keizai,* and *Sankei Shimbun.* The explanations for the high circulation figures may lie in the broad-based content of the newspapers, which have something for everyone, from comics to fact-laden news stories (Yin & Payne, 2003). Along with newspapers, the Japanese have thousands of monthly and weekly magazines to read. Unlike newspapers, they are sold in stores, not by subscription.

In Japan, the electronic media operate under a dual broadcasting system—one public broadcaster (Nihon Hoso Kyokai, NHK) and several commercial broadcasters. The NHK, unabashedly modeled on the BBC when it was established in 1926, became Japan's sole public broadcaster. It is independent of both government and corporate sponsorship and relies almost entirely on household reception fees. NHK began television service in 1953 after the occupation ended. The autonomy of NHK derives partly from its ability to set and collect its own fees, although the legislature does review fee proposals (Chen & Chaudhary, 1991). Moreover, the NHK has complete freedom in programming. However, the prime minister does appoint NHK's board of 12 governors. Japan has five major commercial channels (Nihon TV, TBS, Fuji TV, TV Asahi, and TV Tokyo) and many other local commercial stations (about 100 stations). Japan's broadcast law reflects both political needs and cultural values. It stipulates that programs should not disturb public security, good morals, or manners; should be politically impartial without distorting facts; and should clarify different points of view on controversial issues (Yin & Payne, 2003).

South Korea

Ever since the military takeover in 1961, press freedom has taken on various shades of gray. Further, martial law in 1980 brought with it the repressive Basic Press Act and the biggest press purge in the history of the nation: 172 publications were closed and 683 journalists were dismissed. In late 1987, however, a new constitution was put in place and a new press law enacted. Along with changes in the number of periodicals came changes in content. More aggressive reporting has led citizens, rather than the government, to criticize journalists whose stories they disliked (Chen & Chaudhary, 1991). Korea has four major dailies, with a circulation of more than 1 million each. The largest and most prestigious papers are *Chosun-Ilbo* and *Dong-A Ilbo*, both founded in 1920 and with a circulation of more than 2 million each. All these major national dailies target the elite and the conservative class and are mostly probusiness (Yin & Payne, 2003).

The electronic media operate under a dual broadcasting system (public and commercial). The newspaper system is governed on free enterprise principles, but electronic media have traditionally been state owned and operated. Since 1992 there has been some expansion and privatization of broadcasting stations in Korea, but the systems are still highly regulated. There are two public networks (KBS and MBC) and one commercial network (SBS) in South Korea. It also has one government-owned educational broadcasting network, EBS. Korean broadcast programming focused on national and political interests until the 1980s, but since then programs have become more commercial (Yin & Payne, 2003). KBS has 48 affiliated stations, and MBC has 18 stations. In addition, Koreans are being serviced by numerous local commercial stations, cable television stations, and satellite television (Sky TV).

Taiwan

Striking parallels exist between Taiwan and South Korea, although one should not forget important differences, such as the role of religious media in South Korea (Chen & Chaudhary, 1991). In Taiwan, significant changes occurred in 1987, when martial law was ended and the restrictions on print media were lifted. With the restrictions in force, newspapers had to have licenses to publish and could print only 12 pages. Despite these restrictions, the opposition party launched a newspaper in 1987. Under martial law, the *China Times* and the *Central Daily News* had more than 80% of the nation's daily newspaper circulation and more than 70% of newspaper advertising (Chen & Chaudhary, 1991). The number of pages has increased from 12 to more than 50 over the weekend for big papers. Because press freedom is relatively new in Taiwan, the industry has yet to adjust to the new environment. Today, the *United Daily News* and the *China Times* share about 60% of daily newspaper circulation and more than 75% of advertising (Yin & Payne, 2003).

In Taiwan, although the press is now mostly free, there is still control over the electronic media. The law stipulates that all programs are subject to prior censorship except for news (Yin & Payne, 2003). In the same vein, drama series have proved so popular that government regulations now limit the number of episodes in a series and the number of series in any one evening. With the end of martial law in 1987, restrictions on television eased somewhat. In 1989, the government even agreed to consider a request from the three networks to drop the ban on direct satellite transmissions from mainland China. For a long time, Taiwan had three television stations, owned by the government, the army, and the KMT. In 1997, a new TV station, *Formosa TV*, came into being with financial support from the opposition party. In 1998, Taiwan's public television station went on the air. Although three of the five television stations (CTV, TTV, and CTS) and a large number of the radio stations are owned by the government, the army, and the KMT, many of them are commercial in nature (Yin & Payne, 2003).

Table 17.1   Media Indexes in Japan, South Korea, and Taiwan

Index	Japan	South Korea	Taiwan
Population (in millions)	124.5	44.8	20.9
Daily newspaper	108	60	149
TV sets (per 1000 people)	707	346	258
TV system	Public and commercial	Public and commercial	Public and commercial
Network TV stations	6	4	5
Internet users (in %)	31	35	29
Government control of content	Almost none	Moderate	Moderate

SOURCE: Plasser and Plasser (2002) and Yin and Payne (2003).

For a comparative summary of the various elements in these three countries' media systems, see Table 17.1.

HISTORICAL DEVELOPMENTS OF POLITICAL ADVERTISING

Japan

Japan had no political advertising through the mass media until the 1928 election. The major form of political advertising during the prewar period existed in the form of print: newspapers and editorials. There have been many constraints in Japanese election law for providing the institutional devices for political advertising. It can be said that this resulted from Japan's political traditions, such as the emphasis of party over candidates. Consequently, although both electronic and print media saturate Japan, the regulations that prevent parties from advertising their candidates and candidates from advertising their party severely constrain the use of the media as a campaign tool. The historical development of Japanese political advertising can be divided into four phases, according to the changes in the election laws and the role of campaign advertising.

The first era can be viewed as "the birth of political advertising" (1928-1951). For the first time, in the election of 1928, primitive types of newspaper political advertising appeared. However, political ads of this phase are characterized by factual descriptions and

lack of advertising concept. Two major parties, the Association of Political Friends and the Constitutional Association, ran small-scale visions of ads; however, this daring effort was discontinued once the military government took political power.

The second phase is the "the revival of political advertising" (1952-1968). During the elections of 1952, there was a flood of various types of political advertising through mass media channels, including television. In addition, this is when advertising agencies first became involved in major parties' election campaigns. In this era, although party and candidate political advertising were permitted, political advertising itself was unrefined in nature, compared to commercial advertising.

The third phase is "the developmental struggle over political advertising" (1969-1995). The elections of 1969 opened a new era of election campaigning in Japan. The LDP tried to imitate the 1968 American presidential election campaigns, using the experiences of political consultants for the first time ever. In this election, Japanese politics witnessed full-page newspaper ads, technicolor TV spots, and an emphasized usage of TV spots. In addition to this, television speeches were first introduced in this campaign. The enthusiasm for media advertising waned, however, once it became evident that party ads were of scant help to voters trying to decide which particular candidate to vote for (Kim & Cho, 2000).

The last era is called "toward the maturity of political advertising" (since 1996). Japanese politics never realized the importance of this new trend in campaigning because of the LDP's single-party dominance, which lasted until 1996. However, the ruling party began to realize the necessity of political advertising, because its electoral fortunes had steadily declined from the mid-1970s to the early 1990s. In 1996, Japanese politics crossed an important threshold. Because of changes in both law and society, political candidates could no longer rely on personal voter contact, past party loyalty, or group ties to ensure election (Holden, 1996). A new system of representation, coupled with the changing dynamics of Japanese society, meant that media, and especially television, were now the central organizing device in politics. The LDP began to realize the importance of forming a favorable image of party leaders in the minds of the people, and it began to apply more sophisticated campaign strategies and a more Americanized style in its political campaigns. As a result, its utmost concern became the construction of a favorable candidate image, based on the marketing strategies. These efforts were fully developed with the aid of big advertising agencies and political consultants (Holden, 1999). Big advertising firms have been important in creating television commercials for the ruling LDP and, to a lesser extent, for the opposition parties (Thies, 2002). Since then, electronic mediation (in particular, television ads) has played a more prominent role in electoral politics (Holden, 1999). With television predisposed to dramatic and visual imagery, Japanese party leaders have come to rely heavily on constructing favorable images.

South Korea

Korea had no political advertising in the electronic media until the 1992 election campaign. The major form of political advertising through mass media channels was in newspapers.

In general, Korean politics could not fully develop political advertising because of various regulations and the lack of understanding of the importance of political advertising in modern politics. There have been many constraints in the laws governing presidential elections on providing the institutional devices for political advertising. It can be said that this resulted from the deviant political situation in South Korea (consider that under military rule, there were no party politics). The lack of professionals in political advertising led to a stereotyped and monotonous advertising style in which the forms and contents were not creative. The historical development of Korean political advertising can be divided into three phases, in accordance with the special inclusion of mass-mediated political advertising in the presidential election laws and the development of sophisticated advertising strategies (Tak, 1993).

The first era is "the birth of political advertising" (from 1948, the founding of the Republic, to 1962). Primitive types of political advertising had appeared from the beginning of the Republic in 1948. However, political ads in this phase are characterized as mere repetition of candidate names and factual descriptions without advertising concept.

The second phase is "the developmental struggle over political advertising" (1963-1986). The presidential elections of 1963 opened a new era of election campaigns in Korea. The revised presidential election law provided a legal basis for newspaper political advertising for the first time ever. In this election campaign, though they were unrefined in nature, the concept of targeted audiences, cartoon ads, poster-type ads, display ads, and concise headlines appeared. However, this progressive movement was banned in 1972 by the new constitution. Although the 1981 election was an indirect election, newspaper political advertising was partially allowed again in this election.

The third era is called "toward the maturity of political advertising" (from 1987 onward).

Korean politics never realized the importance of this new trend in campaigning until the 1987 election. The December 1987 presidential election in Korea was historic because it took place under a new constitution that was the result of a rare compromise between the ruling and opposition parties. Korea had a peaceful presidential succession in 1987 for the first time ever. Korean politics began to apply more sophisticated campaign strategies and a more Americanized style of political advertising in this presidential election than ever before (Lee, Kaid, & Tak, 1998). As a result, the utmost concern became the construction of a favorable candidate image, based on the marketing strategies. These efforts were fully developed in the 1992 presidential election campaign. There was political advertising in the electronic media (a total of 10 ads) in the election of 1992 for the first time ever.

The degree to which the focus of advertising had shifted to television was shown by the fact that the election law allowed 30 television spots for each candidate in 1997. The landmark 1997 presidential election pinpointed the maturity of Korea's democracy, when the ruling party's 40-year reign finally ended. In addition, it was the first time in Korean politics that the management of election campaigns was handed over to the public. Governments began to subsidize partial campaign expenditures for each candidate in proportion to their obtained votes. As members of a new democracy, the citizens of Korea were introduced to Western-style campaign advertisements slightly reminiscent of American-style ads (Tak, 2000). However, these ads were different from American ads because of the incorporation of unmistakable Korean cultural imagery.

The December 2002 presidential election in Korea was also historic because it took place within a new political phenomenon that was the result of the voluntary involvement of the younger generations (Lee & Benoit, 2004). Until this election, the political party system was under the absolute influence of the conservatives. Never before had the citizens of Korea enjoyed popular participation in government affairs. There was a peaceful political upheaval that called for a change in Korean politics and the election in 2002 of a liberal candidate over conservative politicians and the old generation. It was triggered by a candle-light parade in the heart of Seoul for the innocent death of a young girl killed by American soldiers and the successful welcome of the 2002 Fédération Internationale de Football Association World Cup. For the first time, in the 2002 presidential election, Korean politics experienced successful campaigning without the help of political parties. Young voters, called the "net generation," showed more political participation than ever before through the use of the Internet.

Taiwan

During the 1950s and 1960s, the KMT ruled the island with an iron fist. Gradually, however, the KMT opened up the political system. Election campaigning in Taiwan has developed in parallel with this political maturation (Rawnsley, 1997). Political advertising in mass media in the election campaigns was not allowed in Taiwan's election until the late 1980s, when Taiwan underwent drastic political reforms. As late as the 1989 election, advertising was banned in Taiwan; since then, the intensity and scope of election advertising has increased. The historical development of Taiwanese political advertising can be divided into three phases, according to the changes in the presidential election laws and the development of television political advertising.

The first era is "the darkness of political advertising" (1949, the retreat of the Republic to Taiwan, to 1986). There was no political advertising, because Taiwan suffered under martial law until 1987. Furthermore, there existed a one-party system under the absolute influence of the KMT, and there were no free elections.

The second phase is the "developmental struggle over political advertising" (1987-1999). In the Legislative Yuan election of 1989, restrictions on the use of mass media as campaign vehicles were loosened. Therefore, candidates began to run political ads in newspapers and magazines but not in the electronic media. These restrictions were again relaxed, and Taiwanese politics experienced the emergence of television party broadcasts in the 1991 National Assembly election. The format was similar to the party political broadcasts used in the United Kingdom: Taiwan's Central Election Commission allotted parties free time on three government-controlled broadcast stations (TTV, CTV, and CTS) in accordance with the number of candidates nominated. Further, Taiwanese politics experienced cable television political ads for the first time ever in the 1995 Legislative Yuan election. Finally, the presidential elections of 1996 opened a new era of election campaigns in Taiwan. The 1996 presidential election was the first direct presidential election, and the combined opposition forces had a chance to win. The 1996 election was the first presidential campaign in which TV advertising was the main campaign method, and without the CEC-sponsored free TV time, all the ads were aired on cable. Opposition parties pushed to loosen governmental control over broadcast media and searched alternative media for ways to air their messages. It was through this desperate search of outlets for political voices that privately owned cable television became a critical campaigning medium for the opposition party (Chiu & Chan-Olmsted, 1999). As cable television grew, political candidates' access to this medium became crucial in the design of their campaigns. Although each presidential candidate spent most of his or her media campaign budget (Chang, 2000), the lack of professionals in political advertising led to a stereotyped and monotonous advertising style in which the forms and contents were not creative (Gross et al., 2001). Interestingly enough, cable's growth as a popular medium for political campaigns was also the result of a legal loophole created by an election law that prohibited political parties and their candidates from engaging in any campaign activities or airing commercials on broadcast television networks (Chiu & Chan-Olmsted, 1999). Because the election law does not explicitly outlaw political advertising on cable, and the authorities are hesitant to tackle this highly sensitive issue, more and more candidates are appealing to the electorate through cable ads.

The third era is called "toward the maturity of political advertising" (since 2000). Taiwanese politics never realized the importance of this new trend in campaigning until 2000. The 2000 presidential election in Taiwan was historic, because Taiwan had a peaceful presidential succession for the first time in its political history. Further, the revised presidential election law provided a legal basis for television political advertising for the first time ever. Nevertheless, it was not surprising that the KMT's campaign advertising tended to be old fashioned and was not especially creative (Gross et al., 2001). However, the DPP's campaign ads were influenced by Western values and experiences, especially those of the United States. In the 2000 presidential election, Taiwanese politics applied more sophisticated campaign strategies and a more Americanized style of political advertising (Gross et al., 2001). Further, Taiwanese election campaigns have become more marketing oriented since the 2000 presidential election (Chen & Chen, 2003). These efforts were fully developed in the 2004 presidential election campaign. In this election, trends from previous elections continued, with increasing amounts of TV ads.

CURRENT REGULATIONS AND POLITICAL ADVERTISING

Japan

Japanese political democracy and many important aspects of its electoral system and campaign practices have their roots in the political system of the prewar period. These aspects and practices have evolved out of a long and quite distinctive tradition (Curtis, 1988). One significant sign of continuity with the prewar period is the presence in Japan's election law of extensive restrictions on campaign practices. Many present-day regulations, such as limits on the duration of the formal campaign period (12 days for the lower house and 17 days for the upper house) and restrictions on campaign spending were first introduced in the period between the two world wars. These prewar controls on campaign activity were eagerly sought by the conservative parties, in large part because they were expected to disadvantage the fledgling working class parties (Curtis, 1992). Strict regulations on campaign practices also draw broad support from Japan's Diet members, regardless of party affiliation, because these regulations make it difficult for new and relatively unknown politicians to get their names and messages out to voters—thus strengthening the reelection prospects of incumbents (Curtis, 1992).

In 1975, Japan revised its laws regulating campaigning in ways that distinguish sharply between party and candidate campaigns (Flanagan, Kohei, Miyake, Richarson, & Watanuki, 1991). It did so in an effort to weaken the role of individual candidates in obtaining votes and to strengthen the vote-mobilizing role of political parties. In its political reforms, Japan tried to counteract the trend toward increasingly personalized campaigning that has become characteristic of virtually all advanced democratic countries in recent years. However, a consequence of the impact of modern mass media on the Japanese style of party organization and personalized campaigning is that both are considered useless in Japan, and Japanese of all political persuasions tend to be convinced that they reflect the peculiar backwardness of Japan's political culture (Flanagan et al., 1991). In an effort to force politicians' behavior to accord more closely with a model of modern party politics,

the election law has tightened restrictions on candidate campaigns and loosened or even eliminated many limits on the campaign activities of political parties (Curtis, 1999). It should also be noted that the Japanese election laws distinguish between official party candidates and independent candidates. Independent candidates are confronted with far more restrictions regarding their campaign activities than are official party candidates.

A vast array of legal restrictions and prohibitions regulate candidate campaigns in Japan (Central Election Commission, 2002). Since the legal changes made in 1975, however, political parties are free to engage in a great variety of campaign activities prohibited to individual candidates. In addition to a ban on all campaigning outside of the official period, house-to-house canvassing is banned, and both of these restrictions apply to candidate and party alike. The limits on campaign budgets for individual candidates, depending on the size of the district, are strict. Japanese candidates still rely more on traditional campaign tools, such as postcards, handbills, newsletters, posters, and bullhorns than they do on mass-mediated campaign materials. In addition, personal and street speeches from automobiles and boats are important parts of their election campaigning. However, the size and quantity of these traditional materials are also restricted by law. For example, candidates can display the limited number of campaign posters they are allowed only on government-provided poster boards.

Individual candidates are prohibited from purchasing any advertising time on television or radio or space in magazines. Instead, the government provides each candidate with funds to publish a limited number of newspaper ads of specified length (no color ads) and makes possible television and radio appearances for short self-presentation speeches and broadcasting about each candidate's past records. These pieces, however, are broadcast one after another early in the morning and late in the evening during the short campaign period. They are literally "appearances" in that candidates are prohibited from using film footage, props, or any other paraphernalia. In so doing, the legal restrictions have discouraged variability in the way the candidates present themselves to the electorate (Krauss, 2000). The time and quantity of political speeches for each candidate are based on the conditions of broadcasting stations. However, the government provides 10 radios and one television for the lower house and five radios and one television for the upper house so members can watch the short pieces about each candidate's past records. It is interesting that the election law also attempts to discourage negative campaigning by imploring candidates to act responsibly in avoiding statements in these media appearances that would damage the reputation of other candidates, parties, or political organizations. Therefore, televised spots lack the hard-hitting approach of political TV spots in the United States (Krauss, 2000).

Nevertheless, political parties have begun to rely heavily on mass-mediated campaign tools over traditional campaign materials in recent times. Although there are no limits on the quantity and time of political party paid advertisements on television or radio or in newspapers (colored ads permitted) or magazines, none of these ads may mention the name of any individual candidate except party leaders. However, the type, the content, and the financing of those ads are still strictly restricted in Japan. Party leaders and other Diet members may appear in these advertisements only in the context of their party roles, as the alleged purpose of the advertisements is to promote the party's policies, not to publicize its candidates. Mention of the fact that these party leaders will themselves be running in the election, much less a personal appeal for voter support, is a violation of the law. Parties are also provided with free newspaper ads: between eight and 88, depending on the type of election and the party's number of

candidates. There is no limit on political parties' campaign budgets, and parties can run television ads any time outside official election periods at their convenience. Further, political parties can contribute to individual candidates as well as to other political organizations without restriction (Sejong Institute, 2001).

South Korea

Korea's political instability is primarily the result of an imbalance in its economic, social, and political development, compounded by its undemocratic political culture. Thus the very speed of its economic growth and urbanization and educational development was bound to create strains, raising the political expectations of the middle class and younger generation. However, Korean politics is moving toward greater democracy and maturity.

Korean politics and many important aspects of Korea's electoral system and campaign practices have their roots in its divided nationhood and have evolved out of a long and quite distinctive tradition (Tak, 1993). This can be seen in Korea's extensive restrictions on campaign practices. Many present-day regulations, such as limits on the duration of the formal campaign period and restrictions on types and quantities of political advertising that are legitimate and commonplace in the United States and elsewhere, were a consequence of the country's obsession about security matters. These controls on campaign activity were eagerly sought by the conservative ruling parties, in large part because they were expected to disadvantage the opposition parties. Strict regulations on campaign practices also draw broad support from Korean voters, regardless of party affiliation, because most of them are concerned about the serious problem of campaign expenditures.

When Korea reformed its election laws in 1997, it gave a new twist to its long history of extensive campaign restrictions (Park, 2002). It has revised its laws regulating campaigning and has adopted a system of "public management" of the election campaign. It has done so in an effort to provide an equal chance for election to all candidates, to decrease the total amount of campaign expenditures, and to induce candidates to engage in campaigning through the mass media, especially television (Kang & Jaung, 1999). In its political reforms, Korea has tried to cut off the dark connection between politicians and big private corporations, because unofficial election expenses have reached astronomical figures in every presidential election campaign. In an effort to force politicians' behavior to accord more closely with this model of public management, election laws have tightened restrictions on candidate campaign spending and provided official campaign financing for eligible candidates (proportional financial support based on their obtained votes) after the election. No candidate is allowed to spend private monies on political expenses anymore.

A vast array of legal restrictions and prohibitions still regulate candidate campaigns in Korea (National Election Commission, 2004). In addition to a ban on all campaigning outside an official period (14 days for the presidential election), house-to-house canvassing and street speech or any kind of outdoor mass rally are prohibited, and these restrictions apply to candidate and party alike. The limits on campaign budgets of individual candidates, depending on the size of the district, are very strict. Korean election campaigns are now relying more on mass-mediated campaign materials than traditional campaign tools such as postcards, handbills, newsletters, and posters. However, the format, content, and quantity of these mass-mediated campaign tools are also restricted under the strict laws. Further, any candidate who wishes to run a political advertisement has to report to the National Election Commission in advance to get a letter of certification.

Although any candidate is now able to buy television time or newspaper space for political advertisements, within limits, since the reform in 1997, magazine political ads are not allowed, unlike in Japan. Candidates may purchase 70 newspaper ads, 30 television ads (1 minute long), and 30 radio ads (1 minute long) for their campaigns. Eleven television and radio appearances (20 minutes long) for political speeches are allowed for each candidate or supporter. However, these must literally be "appearances" in that candidates or supporters are prohibited from using film footage or any other paraphernalia. In addition, the public broadcasting station (KBS) broadcasts informational segments about each candidate's past records more than eight times. These broadcasts, however, are aired one after another early in the morning and late in the evening during the short campaign period. Further, KBS airs campaign debates between presidential candidates more than three times. Although since the 1997 reform, online campaigning is an important part of election campaigning, political advertising through the Internet is still totally prohibited in Korea. The election law also attempts to strictly discourage negative campaigning: In all media outlets, statements that would harm the reputation of other candidates and parties must be avoided.

Taiwan

Many important aspects of the Taiwanese electoral system and campaign practices have their roots in the division between mainland China and Taiwan along the Taiwanese strait and have evolved out of a long and quite distinctive tradition. Many present-day regulations, such as the limits on the duration of the formal campaign period (28 days for the presidential election) and the restrictions on campaign spending, were first introduced in 1949. These controls on campaign activity were eagerly sought by the members of the authoritarian party (the KMT), in large part because they were expected to disadvantage the opposing parties (Gross et al., 2001).

Taiwan's election law, which puts moderate restrictions on campaign practices, has developed in parallel with the lifting of martial law in 1987 (Hsieh, 2002). Since that time, Taiwan has reformed its extensive campaign restrictions in favor of the KMT, and candidates are free to engage in a great variety of campaigning activities that formerly were prohibited. It has revised its laws regulating campaigning in ways that strengthen the opportunity for individual candidates to obtain votes. It has done so in an effort to adopt the trend toward increasingly personalized campaigning. In an effort to force politicians' behavior to accord more closely with this model of modern politics, Korea has tightened restrictions on campaign expenditures and loosened or even eliminated many limitations on the campaign activities of individual candidates (Chen & Chen, 2003).

In the current election law, only minor legal restrictions and prohibitions regulate candidate campaigns in Taiwan (Central Election Commission, 2003). In addition to a ban on all campaigning outside an official period, house-to-house canvassing is banned, and these restrictions apply to candidates and parties alike. Taiwanese election campaigns still rely on traditional campaign tools, such as newsletters from the Central Election Commission, posters, banners, and personal and street speeches. However, candidates are not allowed to hang or erect slogans, billboards, banners, or other advertising materials at roads, on bridges or partitions, in schools, or in other public buildings, to ensure public safety and traffic order. In addition, political speeches are regulated on the basis of their content (it is prohibited to incite another to commit offenses against the security of the state or to undermine the social order), and all campaign activities are allowed from 7:00 a.m. to 10:00 p.m. only. Other regulations and restrictions on campaign practices concern legal limits on the number of vehicles that may be used by the candidate; publication

of public opinion polls, which may not occur 10 days prior to election day; and overall campaign expenditures. As negative attacks on opponents are part of the cultural tradition, there are no rules or legal provisions counteracting the negative tone of campaign advertising (Hsieh, 2002).

The limits on the campaign budgets of individual candidates, which depend on the number of registered voters, are somewhat strict. However, the limits frequently exceed the amount defined by law (Hsieh, 2002). The maximum amount of campaign expenditures is the sum of 70% of all registered households multiplied by the basic amount of NT$20, plus NT$100 million. In an effort to force politicians' behavior to accord closely with the public management model for election campaigning, the election law has tightened restrictions on candidates' campaign spending but has provided some official campaign funding for eligible candidates (proportional financial support based on obtained votes) after the election. The election law provides that any candidate shall be subsidized to the amount of NT$30 for each ballot exceeding one third of the ballots sufficient to win a seat.

Individual candidates began to rely heavily on mass-mediated campaign tools over traditional campaign materials after the 1996 presidential elections. Candidates could freely buy television and radio time or newspaper and magazine space for political advertisements within the limits of campaign expenditures. However, television and radio broadcasting stations offering chargeable political advertising time must allow equal and impartial access to political parties or candidates. For the presidential and vice presidential elections, the CEC provides public funds for political-view presentation meetings, which are aired on national wireless television stations. Candidates are allowed at least 30 minutes of time during each meeting. In addition, if two or more candidates agree, individuals or groups may hold a national wireless television

Table 17.2   Political Advertising Indexes in Japan, South Korea, and Taiwan

Index	Japan	South Korea	Taiwan
Political system	Parliamentary	Presidential	Presidential
Campaign duration	3 weeks	2 weeks	4 weeks
Parliamentary system	Bicameral	Unicameral	Bicameral
First major use of network TV	1969	1992	2000
TV ads	Unlimited (party only)	30 times	Unlimited
Radio ads	Unlimited (party only)	30 times	Unlimited
Print ads	Unlimited magazine and newspaper (party only); free limited newspaper ads (candidate and party)	Newspaper only (70 ads)	Unlimited (newspaper and magazine)
Free TV time	Candidate only	Candidate and party (11 times)	Candidate only
Free radio time	Candidate only	Candidate and party (11 times)	None
TV debates	Major parties only	More than 3 times	No more than 3 times
Campaign restrictions	Somewhat strict	Strict	Moderate
Expenditure limits	Somewhat strict	Strict	Moderate
Dominant campaign media	TV and mass rallies	TV	TV and mass rallies
Public finance	Some	Almost	Some
Opinion polls	Announcement prohibited	Announcement prohibited	Prohibited from 10 days before the ballot
Internet campaigning	Weak	Strong	Moderate
Internet ads	None	None	None

debate with the financial support of the CEC. Although there are three presidential television debates and one vice presidential television debate, each candidate is limited to 30 minutes in each debate.

For a comparative summary of the various elements in these three countries' systems of political advertising, see Table 17.2.

RESEARCH ON THE CONTENT OF POLITICAL ADVERTISING

The observation that personalization and candidate orientation are indications of Americanization in political advertising in Japan, Korea, and Taiwan has been subjected to little empirical research. Although the actual electoral processes of each country are quite different, the variations in electoral campaigns have been narrowing in recent years because of these trends toward Americanization (Chang, 2000; Holden, 1999; Lee et al., 1998). In particular, the television spot focused on a candidate is typical of the political campaigning in these Asian cultures and, certainly, a sign of Americanization in Asia.

In studying the "videostyle" (Kaid & Johnston, 2001) and content of 1992 Korean presidential campaign advertising on television, researchers (Lee et al., 1998; Tak, Kaid,

& Lee, 1997) have identified patterns of verbal content that suggest Korean political advertising uses less negative advertising than American campaigns, but Korean ads were also less likely to focus on issues. Although they did not provide detailed comparisons with American ads, Lee and Benoit (2004) confirmed the use of fewer issues and less negativity in their functional analysis of the 2002 Korean ads. Tak, Kaid, and Khang (2004) also found that Korean spots relied more on candidate image cues than on issues and less on negative ads in their study of 352 political television spots from campaigns in both the United States and Korea between 1992 and 2002 (1992, 1996, and 2000 for the United States and 1992, 1997, and 2002 for Korea). For instance, American candidates were more likely to talk about issues such as the economy, education, and taxes, and Korean presidential candidates tended to emphasize their personal images and viability as a leader in the spots. The researchers suggest that these differences should be interpreted in terms of cultural norms in the two countries. In a high-context culture such as Korea, most information is encoded in the physical context or internalized in the person, and there is little information in the coded or explicit message (Hall, 1976). In addition, Korea has a high uncertainty avoidance culture—communication is centered on rules, norms, moralities, and proper behaviors (Hofstede, 1983)—so candidates were also more likely to use ethical or source-credibility appeals that gave emphasis to authority figures. As a probable result of cultural patterns, Korean ads mainly aim at affect and emotional elicitation and avoid the expression of conflict or dissatisfaction openly (Hofstede, 1983).

Content analysis of Korean television spots has also found differences in the nonverbal behavior of Korean candidates (formal address, fewer expansive gestures) and television production techniques (more low-angle shots and fewer special effects) that may arise

from the desire for proper behaviors in the Korean culture, along with the greater emphasis on the social aspects of *che-myon*, or face-saving (Tak et al., 2004).

Studies of the content of political advertising in Taiwan (Chang, 2000, 2003) have illustrated the importance of cultural variables, but researchers have also found that content in Taiwan's political ads also shows some transference of principles related to Americanized styles of campaigning. Similar analyses of Japanese political television advertising are not yet available.

DISCUSSIONS AND FUTURE DIRECTIONS

This description provides an opportunity to gain better understanding and insight into how political phenomena are related to cultural orientation by comparing and contrasting the televised political advertising in three major Asian democracies. Although Japan, South Korea, and Taiwan represent typical Eastern cultures, these countries also demonstrate critical differences embedded in cultural and political values. However, Plasser and Plasser (2002) observe that "the imperatives of personal politics and candidate-centered styles of campaigns seem to favor approaches toward television personalization observable in most of the areas studied worldwide" (p. 277).

Examination of Japanese election campaigns reveals that political reforms have tried to counteract the trend toward the increasingly personalized campaigning that has become characteristic of virtually all advanced democratic countries in recent years. Even individual candidates are prohibited from purchasing any advertising time on television or radio or space in newspapers and magazines. Korea is the strictest case among the three countries: It allowed no political advertising in the electronic media until the 1992 election, and many restrictions remain on types and quantity of political advertising. These controls on campaign activity were eagerly sought by Korea's conservative ruling parties, in large part because they were expected to disadvantage the opposition parties. In regard to campaign expenditures, Korea has exercised full public oversight of election campaigns since the 2002 presidential election.

Taiwan boasts Asia's most liberal election laws, and an affluent society has led to media- and money-driven electoral campaigns (Schafferer, 2004). Political ads on network television are still illegal in parliamentary elections, whereas the presidential election law does not restrict political advertising at all on any mass media. Because the election law does not explicitly outlaw political advertising on cable, and the authorities are hesitant to tackle this highly sensitive issue, more and more candidates are appealing to the electorate through cable TV ads. Privately owned cable TV plays an increasingly significant role in Taiwan's election campaigns, which makes Taiwan extremely unusual among nations.

By the end of the 20th century, political marketing appeared to be a global phenomenon, with more and more election campaigns resembling those of the United States. Comparative research has shown the existence of a so-called Americanization of election campaign practices in other democracies (Schafferer, 2004). The reason behind this worldwide proliferation of U.S.-style campaigning may be, in part, transnational diffusion and implementation of American concepts and strategies of electoral campaigning. The liberalization and democratization processes of such countries intensified political competition and the way in which election campaigns were conducted (Schafferer, 2004).

There are a number of environmental constraints on the design of election campaigns that must be considered. At the same time, we should also evaluate the impact of structural factors in building a new approach to election campaigning (Rawnsley, 2003). The information revolution and the growing popularity of the Internet especially have allowed candidates to explore innovative campaign techniques that have brought to the surface new forms and methods of interaction between candidates and voters (Morris, 2003). However, the use of the Internet is sometimes overshadowed by dependence on more traditional mass-mediated campaign methods, because there is no political advertising through the Internet in those three countries. The evidence shows that political use of the Internet is, despite the hype, still in its infancy but that more extensive use will lead to changes in the style and mode of campaign communications in those countries.

In the case of the Internet, Korea ranks first in use for political campaigns, followed by Taiwan. This new resource began to be used in Korean politics after the 1997 presidential election, and a more systematic use took place in the 2002 election campaign. Young voters, called the net generation, showed more political participation than ever before through the Internet. Consequently, in 2002, Korea became the first country in the world where the Internet played a crucial role in the election of a president to office.

In Taiwan, systematic use of the Internet first took place during the 2000 presidential campaign. All the candidates had Web sites devoted to them and their platforms. Political use of the Internet in Taiwan is still in its infancy, but it certainly offers the possibility that it may become another channel for political advertising, as Web sites are already being consulted for campaign information during presidential campaigns (Hong & Chang, 2002; Wang, 2002). On the other hand, Japan has shown a reluctance to explore this new campaign device. This reluctance to develop Internet campaign practices draws broad support among Japan's old politicians regardless of party affiliation because it makes it more difficult for new and relatively unknown politicians to get their names and messages out to young voters and thus strengthens the reelection prospects of incumbents.

Further insight into the relationship between media representations of candidates and cultural values in these three countries might be provided by comparing campaign news coverage and candidate presentations through other media formats. A great limitation in pursuing research in this area is, of course, the lack of English-language research articles and data concerning political advertising in these countries, especially in Japan. Although political advertising research in Taiwan is relatively well established and covers a wide variety of issues and concerns, it also lacks the research devoted to the analysis of the contents and effectiveness of political advertising (Chang, 2003). Future research needs to provide more exhaustive information about the relationship between political advertising and cultural orientations in those countries.

There seems to be little doubt that culture plays an important role in the perception and use of political advertising. However, political advertising in non-American countries does not reflect the indigenous cultures alone but a mixture of those cultures and some selected American cultural traits (Tak et al., 1997). Certain fundamental differences across cultures call for the use of sensitized political advertising strategies or appeals in non-American countries. Even though evidence is clear of increasing Americanization in our three countries, deep-seated Asian cultural values still remain distinct. Thus considering American political advertising styles alone, without comparisons of the cultural values between countries, might be dangerous.

REFERENCES

Central Election Commission. (2002). *Public official election law of Japan.* Retrieved January 26, 2006, from the Sejong Institute Japan Center Web site: http://www.sejongjapan.com

Central Election Commission. (2003). *Presidential and vice presidential election and recall law of Taiwan.* Retrieved January 26, 2006, from the Lawbank Web site: http://db.lawbank.com.tw/eng/

Chang, C. (2000). Political advertising in Taiwan and the US: a cross-cultural comparison of the 1996 presidential election campaigns. *Asian Journal of Communication, 10*(1), 1–17.

Chang, C. (2003). Party bias in political advertising processing. *Journal of Advertising, 32*(2), 55–67.

Chen, C., & Chen, J. (2003). The construction of electoral marketing modes in Taiwan. *International Journal of Management, 20*(2), 143–155.

Chen, A. C., & Chaudhary, A. G. (1991). Asia and the pacific. In J. C. Merrill (Ed.), *Global journalism: Survey of international communication* (2nd ed., pp. 205–266). New York: Longman.

Chiu, P., & Chan-Olmsted, S. M. (1999). The impact of cable television on political campaigns in Taiwan. *Gazette, 61*(6), 491–509.

Clough, R. N. (1987). *Embattled Korea: The rivalry for international support.* Boulder, CO: Westview Press.

Curtis, G. L. (1988). *The Japanese way of politics.* New York: Columbia University Press.

Curtis, G. L. (1992). Japan. In D. Butler & A. Ranney (Eds.), *Electioneering: A comparative study of continuity and change* (pp. 222–243). Oxford, England: Clarendon Press.

Curtis, G. L. (1999). *The logic of Japanese politics.* New York: Columbia University Press.

Economist Intelligence Unit. (2004a, August). *Country report: Japan.* Retrieved December 20, 2004, from http://www.eiu.com

Fell, D. (2001). The evolution and role of campaign issues in Taiwan's 1990s elections. *Asian Journal of Political Science, 9*(1), 81–94.

Flanagan, S. C., Kohei, S., Miyake, I., Richardson, B. M., & Watanuki, J. (1991). *The Japanese voter.* New Haven, CT: Yale University Press.

Gross, A. L., Gallo, T., Payne, J. G., Tsai, T., Wang, Y, Chang, C., et al. (2001). Issues, images, and strategies in 2000 international elections. *American Behavioral Scientist, 44*(12), 2410–2434.

Gurevitch, M., & Blumler, J. G. (1990). Comparative research: The extending frontier. In D. Swanson & D. Nimmo (Eds.), *New directions in political communication: A sourcebook* (pp. 305–325). Newbury Park, CA: Sage.

Hall, E. T. (1976). *Beyond culture.* Garden City, NY: Doubleday.

Hofstede, G.(1983). *Culture's consequences: Comparing values, behaviors, institutions and organizations.* Beverly Hills, CA: Sage.

Holden, T. J. M. (1996). How can we say it in fifteen seconds? Assessing Japan's first mass mediated election. *Japanese Society, 2*, 77–97.

Holden, T. J. M. (1999). Commercialized politics: Japan's new mass-mediated reality. *Japanese Studies, 19*(1), 33–47.

Hong, Y.-H., & Chang, R. (2002). Who's on and why are they there? A study of visitors to electoral candidates' Websites in Taiwan. *Asian Journal of Communication, 12*(2), 30–49.

Hsieh, J. F. (2002). Continuity and change in Taiwan's electoral politics. In J. F. Hsieh & D. Newman (Eds.), *How Asia votes* (pp. 32–49). New York: Chatham House.

International Research Center for Japanese Studies. (2003, September). *Japan Review 2003: Political overview.* Tokyo: Author.

Johnston A., & Kaid, L. L. (2002). Image ads and issue ads in U.S. presidential advertising: Using videostyle to explore stylistic differences in televised political ads from 1952 to 2000. *Journal of Communication, 52*, 281–300.

Kaid, L. L., & Johnston, A. (2001). *Videostyle in presidential campaigns: Style and content of televised political advertising.* Westport, CT: Praeger.

Kang, W., & Jaung, H. (1999). The 1997 presidential election in South Korea. *Electoral Studies, 18*(4), 599–608.

Kihl, Y. W. (1984). *Politics and policies in divided Korea: Regimes in contest.* Boulder, CO: Westview press.

Kim, C., & Cho, J. (2000). A comparative study of political advertising between Korea and Japan. *Advertising Research, 47*, 189–219.

Krauss, E. S. (2000). Japan: News and politics in a media-saturated democracy. In R. Gunther & A. Mughan (Eds.), *Democracy and the media: A comparative perspective* (pp. 266–302). New York: Cambridge University Press.

Lee, C., & Benoit, W. L. (2004). A functional analysis of presidential television spots: A comparison of Korean and American ads. *Communication Quarterly, 52*(1), 69–83.

Lee, H. (2004, Spring). Seats reserved: Political upheaval in Japan. *Harvard International Review, 25*(1), 8.

Lee, M. (1990). *The odyssey of Korean democracy.* New York: Praeger.

Lee, S., Kaid, L. L., & Tak, J., (1998). Americanization of Korean political advertising: A comparative perspective on televised political spots in the 1992 presidential campaign. *Asian Journal of Communication, 8*(1), 73–86.

Lim, J., & Tang, S. (2002). Democratization and environmental policy-making in Korea. *International Journal of Policy, Administration, and Institutions, 15*(4), 561–582.

Morris, D. (2003). The future of political campaigning: The American example. *Journal of Public Affairs, 3*(1), 14–20.

National Election Commission. (2004). *Public election law of South Korea.* Retrieved January 26, 2006, from http://www.nec.go.kr:8080

Park, C. W. (2002). Elections in democratizing Korea. In J. F Hsieh & D. Newman (Eds.), *How Asia votes* (pp. 118–146). New York: Chatham House.

Plasser, F., & Plasser, G. (2002). *Global political campaigning: A worldwide analysis of campaign professionals and their practices.* Westport, CT: Praeger.

Rawnsley, G. D. (1997). The 1996 presidential campaign in Taiwan: Packaging politics in a democratizing state. *Harvard International Journal of Press/Politics, 2*(2), 47–61.

Rawnsley, G. D. (2003). An institutional approach to election campaigning in Taiwan. *Journal of Contemporary China, 12*(37), 765–779.

Richardson, B. M. (1997). *Japanese democracy: Power, coordination, and performance.* New Haven, CT: Yale University Press.

Richardson, B. M., & Flanagan, S. C. (1984). *Politics in Japan.* Boston: Little, Brown.

Rosenbluth, F., & Thies, M. F. (2004). Politics in Japan. In G. A. Almond, G. B. Powell, Jr., K. Strom, & R. Dalton (Eds.), *Comparative politics today: A world view* (8th ed., pp. 316–365). New York: Longman.

Schafferer, C. (2004). *Newspaper and television advertising in 2004 Taiwan presidential election* (Working paper). Retrieved January 26, 2006, from the School of Oriental and African Studies, University of London Web site: http://www.soas.ac.uk/taiwanstudiesfiles/conf042004/papers/panel2shaferrerpaper.pdf

Sejong Institute. (2001, June). *Political finance and democracy in East Asia: The use and abuse of money in campaigns and elections* (Conference summary). Seoul, South Korea: Sejong Institute and the National Endowment for Democracy

Tak, J. (1993). *A cross-cultural comparative study on political advertising between America and Korea: A content analysis of presidential* campaign ads from 1963 to 1992. Unpublished doctoral dissertation, University of Oklahoma, Norman.

Tak, J. (2000). A study on the changes of Korean political advertising: Americanization and similarities of political advertising styles. *Advertising Research, 48,* 27–44.

Tak, J., Kaid, L. L., & Khang, H. (2004, August). *The influence of cultural parameters on videostyles of televised political spots in the U.S. and Korea.* Paper presented at the Association for Education in Journalism and Mass Communication Conference, Toronto.

Tak, J., Kaid, L. L., & Lee, S. (1997). A cross-cultural study of political advertising in the United States and Korea. *Communication Research, 24,* 413–430.

Thies, M. F. (2002). Changing how the Japanese vote: The promise and pitfalls of the 1994 electoral reform. In J. F Hsieh & D. Newman (Eds.), *How Asia votes* (pp. 92–117). New York: Chatham House.

Wang, T.-L. (2002). Whose "interactive" channel? Exploring the concept of interactivity defined in Taiwan's 2000 presidential election online campaign. *Asian Journal of Communication, 12*(2), 50–78.

Yin, J., & Payne, G. (2003). Asia and the Pacific. In A. S. De Beer & J. C. Merrill (Eds.), *Global journalism: Topical issues and media systems* (4th ed., pp. 342–398). New York: Addison-Wesley.

PART V

Political Advertising Developments in Evolving Democracies

18

A Spiral of Post-Soviet Cynicism

The First Decade of Political Advertising in Russia

SARAH OATES

From the rantings of rabid nationalists to the dignified images of the pro-Kremlin forces, Russian political advertising can illuminate important issues relating to the role of power, television, and electoral choice in society. The central lesson from Russian political advertising is that allowing parties voices in a post-authoritarian state does not necessarily lead to a democratic dialogue. Rather, this can encourage elements that work directly counter to democracy: promotion of demagogic figures, strident threats that drown out rational statements, a preference for catchy slogans over real policy alternatives, and noisy nationalism that can slide easily into xenophobia and prejudice. As a result, both paid and free political advertising have done little to contribute to the growth of real political choices in Russia. Although there are some notable exceptions to this trend (e.g., the careful use of free advertising time by the Communist Party of the Russian Federation to delineate meaningful policies), both free and

paid political advertising in Russia generally have echoed the needs of the elite forces in society rather than made an attempt at genuine communication with the electorate.

In addition to the form and content of political advertising, it is critical to consider the context in which it operates. In Russia, this environment has changed somewhat since the first elections in 1993, in particular as enormous power has consolidated around the administration of Russian President Vladimir Putin at the expense of political parties. Although there were few constraints on political advertising—and this political communication tool was usually broadly available—it appeared to have contributed little to the construction of democratic alternatives. Over time, the democratic features of political advertising, such as relatively equal access, have faded. In addition, studies provide compelling evidence that messages from political advertising cannot compete with the influence of television news in the Post-Soviet environment. Instead of informed voters seeing clearly demarcated political spots before or after the news on state-run television, the news itself has become a long, permanent political spot for the Putin regime.

The content and tone of political advertising is problematic in many countries (Ansolabehere & Iyengar, 1995; Kaid & Holtz-Bacha, 1995), but the particular failures of Russian political advertising are underlined by the systemic problems in the consolidation of a party-based democracy. Although Russia adopted a new constitution in 1993 that featured elections based heavily on the involvement of political parties, political parties have failed to emerge as significant political institutions in their own right, despite several election rounds (Hutcheson, 2003; Smyth, 2004). At the same time, major media outlets suffered the same fate as political parties. Rather than developing as independent political institutions, most major television outlets, newspapers, and radio stations have now become mouthpieces for the Putin regime (Oates, 2006). The Internet, which possibly could serve as an alternative outlet for political advertising and information dissemination in Russia, has been hampered from development primarily for economic reasons. How did a relatively liberal constitution and broad provisions for political advertising fail to safeguard against this situation? How did political advertising contribute to these problems? To understand the role of political advertising in the failure of Russian democracy, it is important to consider how parties used advertising, how the audience responded to it, and how openness does not always lead to freedom.

AN OVERVIEW OF POLITICS, THE MEDIA, AND POLITICAL ADVERTISING IN RUSSIA

After more than 70 years of rule by the authoritarian Communist Party of the Soviet Union, the Soviet Union collapsed in 1991. Although the repressive nature of Soviet society varied

somewhat over the decades, in general it was a society in which a "dictatorship of the proletariat" and an enormous state apparatus oversaw virtually every aspect of economic and social life in the vast country. In theory, the country was ruled to protect the rights of the workers. In practice, a narrow circle of elite citizens dictated policy and lived relatively privileged lives in urban centers. Political parties other than the Communist Party were deemed detrimental to society. Those who attempted to start political parties would be arrested, imprisoned, or possibly sent to psychiatric wards against their will. In fact, the Communist Party was not a "party" but an oligarchic state bureaucracy. However, as it was assigned the "leading role" in the Soviet constitution, it was the only legitimate political organization in the country. By the same token, the mass media were tasked with educating the people about the Communist Party to foster support for the regime. The job of the journalist was not to disseminate information but to spread propaganda. To this end, television broadcasts, radio, and the newspapers were saturated with exaggerated stories of Soviet successes and the evils of Western capitalism.

Soviet politics and the mass media started to change dramatically in 1985, with the introduction of *glasnost* by Communist Party leader Mikhail Gorbachev. *Glasnost* translates as "publicity" or "transparency"; it was supposed to bring greater accountability and popularity to the Soviet administration. However, once the Soviet people were given a small voice, it quickly became a loud outcry against the injustice and repression of Soviet society. A series of regional and national elections from 1989 to 1991 brought real opposition into power, against the Communist regime. With a raucous debate over the Soviet past as well as the country's future in the media—combined with political opposition at televised Soviet congresses—the Soviet Communist Party's monopoly on power collapsed. It was during *glasnost* and the heady days of the attempted coup that Soviet television in particular showed its power as a political tool (McNair, 1991; Mickiewicz, 1999; Wedgwood-Benn, 1992). The Soviets had come to rely heavily on television as a means of disseminating propaganda. At least three quarters of all households across the vast Soviet territory had television sets by the end of Soviet rule, and the typical audience for the main nightly news program was 80% of the adult population (Mickiewicz, 1988, p. 8). Only about 5% of the Soviet population could watch television in 1960, but by the 1990s, at least one channel was available to about 99% of the country (even though 60% of homes still lacked a phone, according to official Soviet statistics). By the early 1980s, there were two large national television networks on Channels 1 and 2. Many in the country also could see broadcasts from the Moscow or St. Petersburg (then Leningrad) channels. As news organizations pushed the limits of *glasnost,* the audience became particularly enthralled with catching up on seven decades of scandal, sleaze, and information.

Once the euphoria of the end of the Soviet regime faded, the media found themselves covering a deeply divided Russia. Fighting between Russian president Boris Yeltsin and rebel parliamentarians ended when Yeltsin ordered the army to storm the Parliament building and oust the protesting deputies by force in October 1993. Yeltsin's advisers then drafted a new constitution and called for the immediate election of a new Parliament with roots in new political parties. Under the terms of the 1993 Russian constitution, both parties and the mass media would have important roles to play in elections to the new Parliament.[1] Half of the 450 seats in the Parliament's lower house (the Duma) were elected through party lists, in which voters chose their favorite party across the country. If a party won more than 5% of the popular vote, it received seats in Parliament in proportion to its percentage of

the vote. In addition, the other 225 Duma seats were chosen in "first past the post" races, as voters picked their favorite candidate in Russia's 225 single-member districts (the law was changed after the 2003 Duma elections; now all seats are allocated to parties winning at least 7% of the party list vote). In 1993, individuals could choose to run with or without party affiliation in elections for both chambers. At all levels of this complicated race, candidates and parties are given free airtime, as well as the opportunity to buy paid political advertising. Presidential elections have been held about every 4 years, starting in mid-1996, with similar rules regarding free and paid advertising. In 2005, Russia passed a law that changed the way Duma members are elected, eliminating the single-member district races and distributing all seats via the party-list race.

Given the incentive of winning seats in Parliament, many Russian political parties organized to compete in the 1993 elections. In the end, 13 parties ran for seats in Parliament, including promarket movements that supported Yeltsin, a newly reformulated Communist Party, a nationalist party named the Liberal-Democratic Party of Russia, a coalition of female politicians, and several others, including a youth party. However, the elections did not have the expected effect of consolidating political forces. Rather, as only a handful of political parties won seats through the party-list contest and more candidates have chosen to run as independents in each parliamentary election, parties have fragmented rather than coalesced. As a result, a staggering 43 parties stood for parliament in 1995, 26 in 1999, and 23 in 2003. The fragmentation of the opposition to the presidential administration has meant that there has been little political balance and dialogue in Russia. The only party with a strong grassroots organization, a relatively coherent ideology, and significant popular support has been the Communist Party of the Russian Federation.

Table 18.1   National Television Channels and Viewership in Russia

Channel	Name	Ownership	Daily Reach (%)[a]
1	The First Channel	51% owned by the state, 49% by a mix of public and commercial corporations	84
2	Russian Television and Radio	State owned	71
3	TV-Center	Funded primarily by the City of Moscow	16
4	NTV	Commercial but now controlled by state interests	53
5	Culture	State-owned cultural channel created by presidential decree in 1997. Only national television channel that may not carry paid advertising	8
6	TV-6	Sports channel. Formerly a commercial station carrying some news, briefly inherited the NTV news team before financial takeover by state interests in 2002	20

a. Figures on daily audience are taken from the April 2001 survey (2000 respondents across Russia). NTV and TV-6 have changed ownership since that time, and TV-6 has switched from a commercial news and entertainment outlet to a sports-only channel.

The Communists, however, have been systematically attacked and denigrated by most of the mass media. When other centrist parties led by reputable, elite citizens have arisen in elections, they have been attacked, pressured, and ultimately discredited or cajoled into linking with the presidential administration. Meanwhile, the presidential administration has used its power to promote "parties" in the parliamentary elections that are little more than branches of the Kremlin administration functioning as marketing vehicles for themselves (Oates, 2003; Smyth, 2004). Over time, the progovernment parties have come to dominate in the Russian Duma elections. Although nationalists and communists have won sizable amounts of the party-list vote over the years, the share of the vote to progovernment parties rose from about 15% of the party-list vote in 1993 to almost 50% in the most recent Duma election in 2003.[2]

What sort of television system has Russia offered for information dissemination during elections in 1993 and beyond? (See Table 18.1.) Although the Soviet media were dedicated to the dissemination of propaganda rather than information, there were still a broad range of media outlets and high consumption of the mass media (all state owned). As in Soviet times, state-run television on Channels 1 and 2 remains extremely popular.[3] Commercial television developed quickly in Russia, and the nation's largest commercial channel, NTV, was founded in 1993, although it had little reach in the 1993 elections. By 1995, NTV could reach 75% of Russian's population of roughly 140 million people. The print media initially flourished in the welter of political debate at the end of the Soviet era but were hit hard by rising production costs and plunging sales due to unemployment and inflation in the early 1990s. Many titles folded or cut back drastically. Although the structure of this system has changed little since the early days of the Russian Federation, its nature has shifted dramatically. Some dissent and criticism of the central leaders were tolerated in the young Russian state, but state-run television in particular has become increasingly biased and filled with propaganda about the Putin regime (Oates, 2006). At the same time, financial pressure, legal tactics, intimidation, and the lack of a strong sense of journalistic professionalism have led to less and less openness in the Russian media, including information on critical subjects such as elections and the war in Chechnya.

Russian political advertising should be viewed against the development of election news coverage in Russia from 1993 onward. In developed democracies, political spots and the news often are seen as complementary, in that parties and candidates are able to put across their messages in either free or paid spots unmediated by journalists. Thus voters have both news reports and more direct messages from the parties or candidates themselves. There is occasional synergy between political spots and news, as political spots raise issues or accusations that are then aired on the news. In Russia, this relationship is not the same. News outlets, particularly television, have more often used their news programs as vehicles of propaganda rather than information sources for voters. This is particularly true of state-run television in Russia, although numerous studies have found commercial media to be slanted as well (European Institute for the Media, 1994, 1996a, 1996b, 2000a, 2000b; Organization for Security and Co-operation in Europe/Office of Democratic Institutions and Human Rights, 2004a, 2004b; Oates, 2006). Russian television has *never* played the role of public watchdog or champion in election campaigns, and this lack of oversight has increased over time. Although news in most countries would be viewed as more or less separate from political advertising (although incumbents tend to use the news as an electoral platform), in Russia the news must be considered as a political tool rather than a professionalized information source.

THE RULES FOR POLITICAL ADVERTISING IN RUSSIA

The law regarding political advertising in Russia is quite generous, although rules have been tightened somewhat since 1993. All political parties and candidates in national elections are entitled to free broadcast time on state-run television channels (as well as space in state-run print media). They can buy paid time, if they do not spend more than their overall campaign-funding limit. In addition, they can attempt to win editorial coverage and are technically now guaranteed fair coverage on state-run media (but this rule has never been followed on Russian television).

The original free-airtime provision for parties was extraordinarily generous. The amount of time was set in each election by the Central Election Commission and then divided equally among the parties and the candidates. For parliamentary elections, all parties in the contest received an equal amount of free airtime. This means even tiny parties with virtually no resources received the same amount of airtime on national state television as large parties backed by the Kremlin. However, Russian lawmakers eventually decided that not all parties were equal. By the 1999 parliamentary elections, parties that did not gain at least 2% of the party-list vote were having to pay the state back for their "free" time. As most parties do not get even 1% of the vote on the crowded party ballot for the Duma, this change had the effect of virtually eliminating free advertising for small, impoverished parties. In addition, by 1999, the electoral commission had become more aggressive about requiring parties to spend at least part of their free airtime in a group format (e.g., debating or discussing policies with other parties). This was quite unpopular with both parties and television stations (who had to organize the events). However, an improvement in the free airtime provision was that the original, unwieldy 20-minute blocks of time were broken into smaller segments for parties. Presidential candidates received the free time directly, as many candidates (including Yeltsin and Putin) did not run on party tickets. Putin, however, has never used his free airtime allotment or bought paid advertisements.

Although the format of free broadcasts has changed over the course of elections from 1993 to 2004, the timing of the blocks for viewers has not. Viewers see two blocks of political advertising of about half an hour each, one in the morning and another in the evening. Instead of seeing one party for 20 minutes, as in 1993, however, viewers now see a range of parties within the block, each with a shorter segment. In addition, all candidates and political parties may buy advertising in both print and broadcast media. Political advertising is limited to the 30 days before the polling date. There is no particular spending limit on paid advertising, although there are two constraints: (a) a party or candidate may not exceed overall spending limits, and (b) media organizations must charge all parties and candidates the same rate. This rate is now announced in advance of the campaign. Although the rules seem reasonable, they are actually fairly meaningless in the campaign. Tracking of paid political advertising shows that pro-Kremlin forces have an inordinately large number of ads (European Institute for the Media, 1994, 1996a, 1996b, 2000a, 2000b). The financing of the campaign is unclear, although it is fairly obvious that state resources are diverted to political campaigns for parties that support the Kremlin. In addition, journalists and analysts acknowledge that "hidden" advertising is an enormous problem.[4] This usually takes the form of a favorable newspaper article about a candidate or political party that has been written in the guise of news (European Institute for the Media, 2000a). Journalists often are offered bribes to make a positive mention of a party or candidate in a television broadcast (European Institute for the Media, 2000a; Oates, 2006).

Until 1999, there was little policing of overall spending limits, which is particularly apparent from the large amount of money spent by pro-Kremlin political parties in 1993 and 1995 (as tracked by the European Institute for the Media). In addition, media outlets have refused to sell space or time to candidates or parties with which they were not in political sympathy (European Institute for the Media, 1994, 1996a, 1996b, 2000a, 2000b).

There are relatively broad legal restrictions on the content of electoral advertising. My research has found that these laws rarely come into play. However, television producers have complained over the years of the problems of working with myriad amateur parties, who have little of interest to say and poor production skills.[5] The laws have become more specific in recent years, although the content of political advertising has never been a major issue in Russia. The 2002 law dealing with Duma elections states that political advertising (free or paid) "shall not contain calls for seizure of power, violent change of the constitutional system and violation of the integrity of the Russian Federation, warmongering" and the spots cannot incite "social, racial, national, religious hatred or enmity" ("On the election of deputies," 2002, Art. 64, § 1). It is possible that this law could be interpreted rather widely to target those who were attacking the current rulers. However, as is discussed later, the Putin administration has been far more focused on spreading propaganda about the regime than on complaining about specific political ads.

Perhaps the greatest departure in practice from the theory of political fairness takes place with the heavy involvement of the central government in their progovernment parties during each Duma election. The Duma elections remain the only relevant elections involving political parties. The two successful presidential candidates, Yeltsin and Putin, both declared themselves "above" party politics and ran without party affiliations. Although the Communist Party was an important player in the 1996 presidential elections, that election was the only presidential election in which a party played a significant role. It is interesting to note that it is directly forbidden by Russian law for the central government to be involved in political advertising in parliamentary campaigns: "federal bodies of state power, bodies of state power of Russian Federation subjects, other state bodies, bodies of local self-government" ("On the election of deputies," 2002, Art. 57) cannot be involved in political advertising. Still, state power and key government ministers (often including the prime minister) have dominated political advertising and campaigning in every Duma election from 1993 through 2003. In addition, the news coverage of the government is subverted into a full-blown campaign for the progovernment parties in each election on central state-run television (European Institute for the Media, 1994; Oates, 2006; Organization for Security and Cooperation in Europe/Office of Democratic Institutions and Human Rights, 2004a).

Thus Russian parties, the mass media, and the voters leapt into the electoral fray with a lot of opportunity for political advertising in 1993. What did the first Russian foray into political advertising look like? The 1993 free-time advertising was dominated by talking heads (Oates, 2006). By Western standards, the spots were dull and hard to watch. It was often difficult to distinguish between the different party messages. The 20-minute segments (three for each party over the month-long campaign) were extraordinarily long for political advertisements. Parties had few resources and little time for organization, as the elections were called just weeks before the campaign started. Progovernment and prore-form parties offered somewhat bland speeches during their free time, but nationalist Vladimir Zhirinovsky was unafraid to make extravagant promises in his energetic spots for the Liberal-Democratic Party of Russia. Among his suggestions were closing off Russia's borders to the "criminal element" from the Caucasus, giving schoolchildren free lunches, and restoring all former Soviet territories to Russia. In addition, he promised apartments to 200,000 officers and an abundance of inexpensive vodka.[6] At the same time, other major parties in the elections, including Russia's Choice, Yabloko (which means "apple"), and the Communist Party, were not very successful at making recognizable policy statements during their free time on *The Voter's Hour*. For example, although Russia's Choice argued for a market economy in its electoral platform, party leader and Russian prime minister Yegor Gaidar failed to take any meaningful position or state any policy on the market during his free 20-minute spot. His only comment on the economy was a remark that inflation must be brought under control, and his comments on social-welfare guarantees were also vague. The Russia's Choice programming included pop stars, an uneasy juxtaposition with the serious Gaidar. Well-known market economist and party leader Grigory Yavlinsky also failed to articulate concrete policies during his appearance for promarket Yabloko. Even in this first election, it was clear that candidates and parties would use their free time in ways that the government had not envisioned when designing the law to provide media access for parties and candidates during election campaigns. In particular, Yabloko and the Communist Party used their spots to attack the government and its plans to rush through a new constitution instead of discussing only their own party policies (this was long before the 2002 law that explicitly forbade parties to do this).

In addition to many hours of free broadcasting time, there were 15 hours and 28 minutes of paid political advertising during the month-long Duma campaign (European Institute for the Media, 1994, p. 117). Progovernment parties such as Russia's Choice bought the most time, followed by the Liberal Democrats. Perhaps it is more interesting that successful parties, such as the promarket Yabloko party and the Communist Party, bought little or no paid time. Prices for television advertising ranged from 150,000 rubles per minute (about U.S. $123 in late 1993) to 6 million rubles per minute (about U.S. $4900), suggesting that some parties were offered better bargains by television channels (European Institute for the Media, 1994, p. 35). However, much of the fluctuation could be due to whether the advertising was placed in popular time slots. There were some large sums spent on television advertising, which suggests that parties had access to private money, backing from businesses, money raised for the campaign, or state funds illegally diverted for the use of the campaign. Russia's Choice spent 224 million rubles (about U.S. $183,000) for airtime, more than any other party in 1993 (European Institute for the Media, 1994). The Liberal Democrats were third, spending 154 million rubles (about U.S. $126,000).

Zhirinovsky favored personal appeals in his ads for the Liberal Democrats. Russia's Choice used slicker graphics and a softer sell to market the party. Russia's Choice tended to market the party like a Western product. In one advertisement, legs clad in jeans walk by a small child and a dog sitting on the household floor. A hand reaches down to pin a Russia's Choice campaign button on the child's shirt and he lisps "We can't vote for Russia's Choice because we're too small" as he hugs the dog. This type of cute advertisement is in stark contrast to the rough, ragged, personal appeal made by Zhirinovsky for the Liberal Democrats.

Surveys in 1993 incorrectly predicted that progovernment parties such as Russia's Choice would dominate in the elections and control the new Parliament. The Liberal Democrats, with their charismatic leader and xenophobic message, swept into power with 23% of the party-list vote. The progovernment forces did relatively poorly in the party-list vote, with Yeltsin's favorite party gaining just 16% of the vote but doing well in the single-member districts. The Communists, who had no paid advertising at all, did almost as well as the best progovernment party, with 12% of the party-list vote. Overall, the election was a sharp lesson to promarket, proreform politicians that the electorate either had not heard their messages—or had heard them and rejected them in large numbers. It is true that political advertising in developed democracies can push or pull small numbers of voters in relatively modest directions in most circumstances, but in this case it would appear that political advertising had almost unprecedented power to articulate political positions and capture political territory. The proreform forces failed to capitalize on their large resources, and smaller parties that were considered marginal wound up central in Russian political preferences. It is, however, impossible to determine whether parties such as the Liberal Democrats *created* political preferences or merely *articulated* them. After all, the Communists did relatively well with no paid political advertising. However, it could be argued that it was the political imagery and posturing of Zhirinovsky that brought somewhat latent feelings of Russian nationalism to life in electoral politics in the new nation.

In the 1995 Duma election campaign,[7] this "Zhirinovsky effect" was quite clear. A review of party manifestoes showed that the Russian political parties had become more hawklike, less oriented toward the West, and less market friendly between the two elections (Oates, 1998). The political advertising of the parties also reflected this trend.

New rules set out by the electoral commission on September 20, 1995 provided new detailed guidelines for campaigning in the parliamentary elections ("Instruktsiya: O poryadke," 1995). State-funded media such as Channel 1 were required to refrain from bias in their news coverage (this rule has been ignored). The guidelines also delineated rules for debates and roundtable discussions, although candidates and parties almost all declined to participate in them during the 1995 campaign. Rather, much like their Western counterparts, they favored press conferences and rallies in which they could stick to limited topics, most of them vague and noncontroversial. As in 1993, the national television and radio channels were required to distribute 1 hour of free time daily, to be split equally among the parties (this time 43) on the ballot. In this campaign, however, parties were given shorter spots. Parties could buy additional time, although they were limited by law to an overall campaign-spending ceiling of U.S. $2.4 million per party. However, the suspiciously large amount of paid advertising for progovernment groups, such as Our Home Is Russia, suggests that these rules were broken by those with powerful government ties (White, Rose, & McAllister, 1997, p. 213). The cost of advertising had risen substantially since 1993, with broadcast time now costing between U.S. $10,000 and U.S. $30,000 per minute, depending on the time slot (European Institute for the Media, 1996a, p. 32).

There was a marked increase in both paid advertising and editorial coverage of the parties from 1993 to 1995. Despite the steep rise in price, the volume of paid advertising almost doubled, jumping from 15 hours and 28 minutes in 1993 to 30 hours and 40 minutes in 1995 (European Institute for the Media, 1996a). Although there were three times as many parties in the race this time, the increase came mostly from the rise in television advertising for 10 of the parties in 1995. This was also true of editorial coverage. News coverage of parties increased almost threefold (from about 16 hours in the 1993 campaign to about 45½ hours in 1995), but it was still the major parties, particularly the central progovernment party, that dominated the election news.

As the main 1995 pro-government party, Our Home Is Russia benefited from the heavy exposure of party leader and Russian prime minister Viktor Chernomyrdin. One of the most frequent paid advertisements for the party showed sparks flying in a metal works; a rocket launch; an airplane that had been rescued from hijackers; children marching off to their first day of school, clutching flowers; and a family group voting. In another advertisement, Our Home Is Russia attacked the communists, showing staged man-in-the-street interviews in which attractive, rational people said they would vote for Our Home Is Russia and ragged, ranting people said they would vote for the Communist Party.[8] Our Home Is Russia's free-time broadcasts were less well polished than the party's paid advertising. During its Channel 1 free time, the party featured its leaders talking about the country's need for their party, yet little was said about definite policy or promises.[9]

Zhirinovsky repeated his charismatic performance from the 1993 elections and created rather more interesting free spots for the Liberal Democrats. In the spots, Zhirinovsky portrayed himself as the outspoken opponent of the Yeltsin administration, although the Liberal Democrats actually tend to cooperate with the Kremlin on issues when they are in power. This duplicity has never been discussed seriously by the Russian broadcast media during campaigns. According to the European Institute for the Media (1996a), Zhirinovsky's party bought the third-largest amount of advertising time (almost 3 hours, or 10% of the total) and garnered more than 7% of the editorial time on television in the 1995 campaign. Other parties tried various approaches, including the attempt by the promarket Yabloko party to play on its "apple" name by featuring ads with Sir Isaac Newton getting hit on the head by an apple. The Communist Party had virtually no paid advertising on television in the 1995 elections. However, it could be argued that the communists' use of free time was somewhat better than most, as it was an attempt to inform viewers about policies rather than merely to introduce leaders or engage either in dull speeches with little meaningful content or stunts such as those favored by Zhirinovsky.

In a detailed analysis of media and the 1995 parliamentary elections, the European Institute for the Media (1996a) found that the electoral commission had a difficult time overseeing the editorial coverage on state-owned broadcasting networks such as Channel 1. In addition, the institute's quantitative and qualitative analysis of editorial time on five television networks found a strong bias toward the progovernment Our Home Is Russia and promarket Democratic Choice of Russia. The institute also found that Channel 1's news avoided criticism of the government, often ignored the nationalistic trend in party politics, overlooked the smaller parties' advocacy of swifter reforms, and frequently gave communists, as well as nationalists, negative coverage. On the other hand, commercial channel NTV's main news program provided more balanced coverage, but there was less of it, as the commercial channel focused on reporting on the atrocities of war in Chechnya rather than the Duma election campaign.

The 1996 Russian presidential campaign marked one of the low points in media transparency in the young Russian state. Media heads of both state-run and commercial television made the decision to ignore problems with Yeltsin's health as well as the unpopularity of his administration. Rather, the news organizations joined forces—with the president of NTV taking an active role in the Yeltsin campaign—to present the ailing, unpopular president as the only alternative for Post-Soviet Russia (European Institute for the Media, 2000b; Mickiewicz, 1999; Oates & Roselle, 2000). The communists had surged ahead in the polls, leaving open the possibility of the election of a communist president and a return to a Soviet-style regime. Yeltsin ran against several contenders in the first round and barely edged ahead of Communist Party candidate Gennady Zyuganov. In the second round, Yeltsin managed to win convincingly,

with 54% of the vote to Zyuganov's 40%. Analysis of the 1996 presidential election coverage showed that the nightly news on Channel 1 and NTV had changed significantly, particularly on the commercial channel. There was some voice given to Zyuganov, but it was overwhelmed by the positive gloss on Yeltsin. This coverage ignored the serious health problems of the president as well as corruption problems in his administration. Yeltsin was given more exclusive coverage and was framed as an effective leader who was in touch with the problems of the country.

The 1996 Russian presidential campaign was the only one in which paid and free airtime were important tools for the incumbent leader. Yeltsin's campaign ran an evocative "I trust, I love, I hope" campaign, in which common citizens spoke of their support for Yeltsin. The choice was framed starkly: Elect Yeltsin or return to Soviet repression. This, along with some changes in policy, including a ceasefire in Chechnya, proved enough for Yeltsin to scrape a narrow win in the preliminary round and a convincing win in the final round a few weeks later. It is clear that in these presidential elections, in which Yeltsin had an approval ranking in the single digits 6 months before polling, the marketing and "spin" of the president mattered a great deal. Although both free and paid political ads played a role, the marketing effort subsumed a far wider part of the media and political system. The entire broadcast system, including the newly influential commercial television station NTV, was deployed to present Yeltsin as something he was not—a capable, healthy, democratic president who could control the forces of disintegration and corruption in Russia. It is particularly disappointing that NTV, which had made a reputation for integrity with its unflinching coverage of the atrocities and Russian military blunders in the first Chechen war, chose to play political favorites rather than to support the democratic system.

The 1999 Duma campaign marked the final real struggle for power in Russia, and as a result, it was a loud and dirty contest. The political advertising tells only a small part of this story. As usual, there was a range of ads, from the earthy messages of the nationalist Liberal Democrats to the more measured tone of the Communist Party's free spots discussing social needs. The real battle, however, was between two "parties of power"—with government ministers fronting a pro-Putin party called "Unity" and some regional leaders launching the Fatherland–All Russia party. The regional leaders hoped their new party would give them significant power in the Duma and a platform from which one of their party leaders could run for president in 2000. The mudslinging in this campaign was intense and included scandalous accusations against Moscow Mayor Yuri Luzhkov and his running mates on prime-time news shows on Channel 1. *Kompromat,* which comes from the abbreviation for "compromising materials" in Russian, is a political technique in which politicians accuse opponents of a list of crimes but give little real evidence or chance for rebuttal. By 1999, this was immensely popular with politicians and viewers alike in Russia. Understandably, it contributed to a very low level of political dialogue in the campaign. In addition, a new trend emerged in political spots in which images started to replace words. Although the policy statements of progovernment parties (which have changed names in every Russian Duma election) have always been vague and often untenable, by 1999, the progovernment parties were tending to avoid words altogether. One spot for Unity showed the three party leaders (two government officials and an Olympic wrestling champion) in turn in army gear, chasing criminals and throwing an opponent to the ground. There is a single party slogan at the end and no other words at all. In the end, Fatherland–All Russia did not garner enough voters to mount either a serious challenge to the Kremlin or to launch a viable presidential opponent. Soon after the 1999 elections, Fatherland–All Russia joined a coalition with Unity.

Yeltsin, who had heart surgery soon after his reelection in 1996, resigned on New Year's Eve, 1999. He designated Putin (then prime minister) as acting president for the final months of his term. The 2000 presidential election campaign offered even less of a chance for a discussion of issues. By this time, support for the communists had eroded to the point that even well-known Communist Party leader Zyuganov posed no realistic challenge to Putin. Putin, who lacks Yeltsin's somewhat tolerant acceptance of political PR, did not use his free airtime and did not purchase paid airtime. Rather, the Channel 1 news promoted him relentlessly during the campaign, showing him in his judo costume and piloting a MiG jet (with help). Putin was framed continually as the effective, authoritative leader as he met with a series of officials on a daily basis. State-run news covered a wide range of the most routine meetings, often in great detail. The other contenders were covered, but often in a negative way (European Institute for the Media, 2000b). For example, presidential candidate and Yabloko leader Yavlinsky—closer in age and image to Putin than the more staid Zyuganov—came in for a considerable amount of *kompromat* during the March 2000 presidential elections. This included speculations about whether he had plastic surgery or, more seriously, whether the West had funded his campaign. Yavlinsky was the only main candidate to advertise on four of the main Russian television stations. The total paid political advertising (most of it on Channel 1) bought by all the candidates was 190 minutes. In keeping with his strategy of being above the political fray, Putin purchased no political advertising during the 3 weeks of the campaign (European Institute for the Media, 2000b, p. 57). In point of fact, he did not need political advertising, as Channel 1 news functioned as an infomercial for his campaign.

It is important to note that by the 1999 campaign, television no longer spoke with a unified voice. Although NTV had colluded with the Kremlin for Yeltsin's reelection, the station was more critical of the regime than the more sycophantic state television. However, this does not mean that NTV was providing unbiased information to the public. NTV favored its "own" candidates and causes and, as a result, no major television station has given a reasonable amount of disinterested coverage to the Communist Party (European Institute for the Media, 2000b; Oates, 2006). Arguably, the Communist Party may never have been able to attract a commanding part of the electorate. However, the party did particularly well in 1999, with 25% of the vote despite negative coverage on state-run television and little coverage on commercial television. It is interesting to speculate how the party might have fared on a more even political communication playing field.

By the 2003–2004 election cycle, political advertising had not come full circle to Soviet propaganda, but it had arrived at a Post-Soviet style of form over substance. The central ads for the main pro-Putin party (now a coalition of the two elite parties of Unity and Fatherland–All Russia from the 1999 contest) were more like travelogues than political messages. The ads showed a series of sun-drenched and glowing images of Russian buildings, peoples, and landscapes. The voiceover was the same for these ads, although sometimes it was dropped in favor of just the haunting music of the Russian national anthem:

> Each has his own Russia, that you see, that is right next to you; for some it is factories, for some it is fields—your corners, your school, your harvest, the light in the home opposite you . . . your place to gather mushrooms, your neighbors. We all have our own little Russia. And if we put it all together, the picture becomes united and we see how great and rich Russia is. We will do everything to build a worthy life for all.[10]

The main political slogan of this party (dubbed "Unified Russia") was merely "Together with the President!" This progovernment party dominated the Duma elections. In the presidential election that followed 3 months later in March 2004, there was little contest, although the Channel 1 news continued its heavy emphasis on Putin. Putin won his second term handily, with more than 70% of the vote. Once again, he did not use his free airtime allotment or buy any paid advertising— but this would have been completely unnecessary, given that the primary news program in the country devoted a huge amount of time to promoting his candidacy.

CONCLUSION: WHAT DOES THE RUSSIAN AUDIENCE THINK?

Political advertising is often unpopular or even annoying to voters. In addition, it is in many ways meant to be more dull and reassuring about the political process than exciting, novel, or particularly engaging (Scammell & Langer, 2004). Focus groups and surveys suggest, however, that Russians are particularly turned off by political advertising. In the first place, paid advertising in general is not well accepted by the Russian public. In focus groups, Russians complain that they find television advertising not only annoying but also socially damaging, in that it promotes luxury products that many cannot afford.[11] In addition, they are deeply suspicious of the relationship between business and broadcasting. Given the reliance of the Soviets on television for state propaganda, Russians continue to see television as an authoritative arm of the state. As such, it should not be trivialized by advertisements—or worse, influenced by the advertisers themselves. This notion of television as part of the state, rather than a voice for the people or even a watchdog of the government, means Russians tend to have different expectations from the broadcast medium (Oates, 2006). They expect it to lead them or help bring order to society, not to present them with a bewildering and possibly destabilizing array of choices. As a result, they particularly dislike political advertising. Some find it demeaning for politicians, voters, and the political process. Others find it boring and pointless. Very few—in either focus groups or public opinion surveys—cite either paid or free spots as important for their political education or choices.[12]

Even if the spots are not important to them, television itself remains central to the political education and orientation of Russians. State television, although markedly more biased than commercial television, is one of the most trusted institutions in the country (Oates, 2005). A study of voting behavior in the 2000 presidential elections found support for Putin and Channel 1 viewership to be closely intertwined (White et al., 2005). As the Channel 1 news has become a propaganda platform for Putin and his regime, it has immense power as a political "advertisement." The situation in Russia suggests that a closer look is needed at our understanding of political spots in campaigns worldwide. With the careful control of "spin" in modern campaigns, the ability to frame events in political campaigns often rests more in the hands of the parties and candidates than in those of the journalists. This means an erosion of the traditional boundaries between news and political advertising, which can create a worrying deficit in the amount of useful political information available to the voters.

NOTES

1. The 198 members of the upper house of the Russian parliament (the Federation Council) were elected via single-member district races in 1993, but the elections were never held again. The upper house is now appointed. This chapter does not discuss the Federation Council elections.

2. This information is based on my calculations using election results from the Central Election Commission and assessment of party orientation based on party documents, leader statements, news coverage, and political advertising.

3. The name of the media organization that broadcasts on Channel 1 has been changed twice

since 1993. Previously known as Ostankino, 49% of the station was privatized in 1995, and it became Obshchestvennoe Rossiiskoe Televidenie (Public Russian Television). It has since been renamed the First Channel. It will be referred to in this chapter as Channel 1 to avoid confusion. Throughout the reorganizations, the editorial direction of the main news has been directed by pro-Kremlin forces, and it is best described as "state-run" television, as it is no longer completely owned directly by the state.

4. This information comes from interviews I conducted with journalists, producers, media analysts, and party officials in 1995, 1996, 1999, and 2003, in addition to reports by the European Institute for the Media over several elections.

5. This information comes from interviews I conducted with Russian television producers in December 1999, as part of fieldwork for the European Institute for the Media report on the 1999 Duma elections.

6. These two promises were reported in *Izvestiya* (Feodanov, 1993).

7. The 1993 Russian Constitution called for the first Duma to sit just 2 years and then regularly for 4 years. The Duma can be dissolved by the president, in which case early elections will be necessary; however, this has yet to happen, and Duma elections have been held in 1993, 1995, 1999, and 2003.

8. Our Home Is Russia campaign organizer Sergei Popov reported that the individuals in this advertisement were actors (personal communication, March 1996). This type of "man in the street" ad continues to be popular with various Russian political parties.

9. This occurred during free political broadcasts on Channel 1 November 22, November 23, December 5, and December 6, 1995.

10. My translation.

11. These comments are based on information from 24 focus groups held in 2000 in Moscow, Ulyanovsk, and a hamlet near Voronezh, as well as a series of 10 focus groups in Moscow and Ulyanovsk in 2004. The focus groups, which I commissioned, were funded by grants from the British Economic and Social Research Council and carried out by Russian Research Ltd.

12. These comments are based on surveys of Russians about their attitudes toward the mass media and politics. The surveys were funded by the British Economic and Social Research Council and carried out in 2001, 2003, and 2004. For more information on these surveys, please see White, Oates, and McAllister (2002, 2005).

REFERENCES

Ansolabehere, S., & Iyengar, S. (1995). *Going negative: How attack ads shrink and polarize the electorate.* New York: Free Press.

European Institute for the Media. (1994). *The Russian parliamentary elections: Monitoring of the election coverage of the Russian mass media.* Düsseldorf, Germany: Author.

European Institute for the Media. (1996a, February). *Monitoring the media coverage of the 1995 Russian parliamentary elections.* Düsseldorf, Germany: Author.

European Institute for the Media. (1996b, September). *Monitoring the media coverage of the 1996 Russian presidential elections.* Düsseldorf, Germany: Author.

European Institute for the Media. (2000a, March). *Monitoring the media coverage of the December 1999 parliamentary elections in Russia: Final report.* Düsseldorf, Germany: Author.

European Institute for the Media. (2000b, August). *Monitoring the media coverage of the March 2000 presidential elections in Russia: Final report.* Düsseldorf, Germany: Author.

Feodanov, Y. (1993, November 26). Gospoda Zhirinovsky i Govorukhin derzhat izbiratelei za polnykh idiotov [Mr. Zhirinovsky and Govorukhin treat the voters like real idiots]. *Izvestiya,* p. 1.

Hutcheson, D. (2003). *Political parties in the Russian regions.* London: RoutledgeCurzon.

Instruktsiya: O poryadke predostavleniya efirnogo vremeni na kanalakh gosudarstvennykh teleradiokomanii izbiratel'nym ob"edineniyam, izbiratel'nym blokam, kandidatam v deputy Gosudarstvennoi Dumy Federal'nogo Sobraniya Rossiiskoi Federatsii i publikatsii agitatsionnykh predvybornykh materialov v periodicheskikh pechatnykh izdaniyakh s gosudarstvennym uchastiem [Instruction: On the proper implementation of broadcast time on government television and radio channels for electoral movements, electoral blocs, candidates, and candidates for deputy of the government Duma of the Federal Assembly of the Russian Federation and publication of campaign material in government-supported press periodicals]. (1995). *Vestnik Tsentral'noi izbiratel'noi komissii Rossiiskoi Federatsii [News of the Central Election Commission of the Russian Federation],* (6), 78–90.

Kaid, L. L., & Holtz-Bacha, C. (Eds.). (1995). *Political advertising in Western democracies: Parties and candidates on television.* London: Sage.

McNair, B. (1991). *Glasnost, Perestroika and the Soviet media.* London: Routledge.

Mickiewicz, E. (1988). *Split signals: Television and politics in the Soviet Union.* New York: Oxford University Press.

Mickiewicz, E. (1999). *Changing channels: Television and the struggle for power in Russia* (2nd ed.). Durham, NC: Duke University Press.

Oates, S. (1998). Party platforms: Toward a definition of the Russian political spectrum. *Journal of Communist Studies and Transition Politics,* 14(1-2), 76–97.

Oates, S. (2003). Television, voters and the development of the "Broadcast Party." In V. L. Hesli & W. M. Reisinger (Eds.), *The 1999-2000 elections in Russia: Their impact and legacy.* Cambridge, England: Cambridge University Press.

Oates, S. (2005). Media and political communication. In S. White, Z. Gitelman, & R. Sakwa (Eds.), *Developments in Russian politics* (6th ed.). Durham, NC: Duke University Press.

Oates, S. (2006). *Tuning out democracy: Television and elections in Russia.* London: RoutledgeCurzon.

Oates, S., & Roselle, L. (2000). Russian elections and TV news: Comparison of campaign news on state-controlled and commercial television channels. *Harvard International Journal of Press/Politics,* 5(2), 30–51.

On the election of deputies of the State Duma of the Federal Assembly of the Russian Federation (Fed. Law No. 175-FZ, 2002, December 20).

Organization for Security and Co-operation in Europe/Office of Democratic Institutions and Human Rights. (2004a, January 27). *Russian Federation elections to the state Duma: OSCE/ODIHR election observation mission report.* Warsaw, Poland: Author. Retrieved April 22, 2005, from http://www.osce.org/documents/odihr/2004/01/1947_en.pdf

Organization for Security and Co-operation in Europe/Office of Democratic Institutions and Human Rights. (2004b, June 2). *Russian Federation presidential election 14 March 2004: OSCE/ODIHR election observation mission report.* Warsaw, Poland: Author. Retrieved January 11, 2006, from http://www.osce.org/documents/odihr/2004/06/3033_en.pdf

Scammell, M., & Langer, A. I. (2004, September). *Political advertising in the UK: Avoiding disbelief, inviting boredom.* Paper presented at the Annual Meeting of the American Political Science Association, Chicago.

Smyth, R. L. (2004, September). *What we have here is a failure to consolidate: Explaining Russia's political development in comparative context.* Paper presented at the Annual Meeting of the American Political Science Association, Chicago.

Wedgwood-Benn, D. (1992). *From Glasnost to freedom of speech: Russian openness and international relations.* London: Pinter.

White, S., Oates, S., & McAllister, I. (2002). Was it Russian public television that won it? *Harvard International Journal of Press/Politics, 7*(2), 17–33.

White, S., Oates, S., & McAllister, I. (2005). Media effects and the Russian elections, 1999-2000. *British Journal of Political Science, 35*(2), 191–208.

White, S., Rose, R., & McAllister, I. (1996). *How Russia votes.* Chatham, NJ: Chatham House.

19

Political Communication and Advertising in Poland

WOJCIECH CWALINA AND ANDRZEJ FALKOWSKI

In every democratic system, parties and candidates face the fundamental problem of how to communicate with voters and influence them so that the voters will accept their leadership. Until 1989, the countries of Central and Eastern Europe were hardly aware of this problem. The totalitarian communist system imposed by the Soviet Union on this part of the world ruled out any possibility of real and free political competition based on the rules of the market.

In 1989, the world marked the triumph of democracy and the fall of the order established in Yalta that had divided the world into two blocs of states. The communist and authoritarian regimes in the countries of Eastern and Central Europe were gradually eliminated, and processes of democratic reconstruction were initiated (Agh, 1991; Connor & Ploszajski, 1992; Staniszkis, 1992). Social order began to be restored, including the freedom of speech and opinions; the freedom to establish social, economic, and political organizations; and the freedom to conduct free elections.

June 4, 1989, the day when the first, not yet fully democratic parliamentary elections took place in Poland, can be said to mark the birth of political marketing in postcommunist states. For the first time in 40 years, political groups faced the need to develop voting strategies and conduct professional electoral campaigns to win the support of the electorate. The citizens acquired the right to make political decisions that had actual influence on who came to power (Falkowski & Cwalina, 2004; Cwalina, Falkowski, & Kaid, 2000).

Together with the political changes, a number of changes took place in the ways the media operate (see Ballentine, 2002; Cwalina, Falkowski, & Roznowski, 1999; Kaid, 1999b). These changes concerned both the legal regulations about the media market and its opening up to commercial broadcasters and the introduction of new technologies and improving broadcast quality. According to Diamond and Bates (1992), the development of television production, marketing methods, and public opinion polls led to the

325

establishment of today's high-tech political communication.

These developments led Blumler and Kavanagh (1999) to announce a "third age" of political communication, in which modern and efficient political communication must follow and react to a number of changes taking place all the time in the media and social environment. These changes are mainly about *modernization* and are connected to increased social differentiation, specialization, interests, and identities and proliferating, diverse lifestyles and moral stances. Thus candidates look for specific media and communication channels (e.g., 24-hour information channels, the Internet) to reach all segments of society with their message.

An important challenge in political communication is growing *individualization*. Citizens' personal views, beliefs, and aspirations are becoming increasingly important. Various traditional institutions (the family, for instance) and value systems are losing their importance.

Another social trend that modern political communication takes into account is *secularization*. This contributes to the decreasing importance of ideological divisions and, as a consequence, the marginalization of political parties. It also impairs the authority of political power. Blumler and Kavanagh (1999) claim that as a result of secularization, the distance between the elite and the masses decreases, and the masses become increasingly important. Secularization fosters the development of political and media populism.

The importance of issues connected with the economy is also on the rise. The *economization* of life manifests itself through the growing importance of economic factors to the functioning of political agendas and the possibility that an agenda will be carried out. The political sphere is constantly being made to conform to the will of institutions with financial capital.

According to Blumler and Kavanagh (1999), social life has also been undergoing *aestheticization*. As a result of this, political communication has more and more to do with popular culture and the entertainment industry. This can be illustrated by the fact that television news stations are adopting tabloid news magazine production techniques for newscasts. They reflect sensational news practice, or "infotainment," in which production style overpowers substantive information (Grabe, Zhou, Lang, & Bolls, 2000).

More emphasis is also put on *rationalization*. In political communication, it forces one to adopt a marketing orientation based on facts and citizens' opinions instead of politicians' intuition. The main focus here is on following public opinion and presenting the views of ordinary citizens rather than politicians.

The last element of social changes that Blumler and Kavanagh (1999) point to is *mediatization*. The mass media have moved into the center of all social processes and begun to reconstruct the public sphere and the world of politics.

Public broadcasting has played a dominant role in political communications in many countries. This is because technology has permitted only one, or a limited number, of television and radio channels. Whereas it has been possible—given the political freedom and the will—to create numerous publishing outlets of all sizes, broadcasting has remained a natural, or near, monopoly. Furthermore, television and radio have emerged in recent decades as by far the most popular and influential forms of communication (Pinto-Duschinsky, 1997). In Western and Eastern European democracies, television is the main medium used by the parties to get their particular messages across. Newsprint features high in these areas also, as does radio to a lesser extent. There are basically three types of media coverage: free access for candidates and political parties, paid access for both groups, and editorial coverage through radio, television, or newspapers and magazines (Lasham, 1998). However, new technologies are changing this situation. In some countries, cable television has meant that there are now numerous alternative channels.

The political market is divided into two camps: those who compete for various positions and those who vote for them. Those seeking power perform an active and creative role in this market. Advertising strategy becomes here the most fundamental strategy of political communication. According to Negrine (1994), political advertising always has particular ideological implications. It creates a "dreamt-up" world that distorts reality and thus prevents people from understanding the actual situation. The voters become part of the world of advertising's symbolism, which masks and distorts the actual relation between power and dominance (see Shapiro & Lang, 1991). The goal of the creators of political advertising is to present a candidate as *the* person who can most completely satisfy citizens' needs. To achieve that, political advertising uses any available technical, sociological, and psychological means. Combining them in a creative way determines the content of advertising and is the foundation of potential electoral success.

There are more and more regulations in each country aimed at curbing the intermingling of the world of politics and media. Usually they concern the ways of conducting elections.

Such regulations not only control the course of elections, they also limit, at least to some extent, the free political market. They set limits on candidates' and political parties' access to mass media. In this way, they influence the course and specificity of political campaigns in individual countries.

Legal regulations concerning the use of the media during election campaigns seem to be particularly important for "young democracies." In the countries of Eastern and Central Europe, such as Poland, mass media still depend to a significant degree on centers of political power. Despite the fact that many years have passed since the countries became democratic, the so-called "independent" media still do not seem to fulfill the hopes that societies have for them.

POLISH PARLIAMENTARY ELECTION CAMPAIGNS AND MEDIA

The Polish parliament has two chambers. The Sejm is composed of 460 deputies chosen for 4-year terms of office according to the principle of proportional representation. There are 100 senators, who are also elected to 4-year terms on the principle of majority vote. Terms of office in the Sejm and the Senate begin on the day on which the Sejm assembles for its first sitting and continue until the day preceding the assembly of the Sejm of the succeeding term of office. Elections for the Sejm are ordered by the president of the Republic no later than 90 days before the expiration of the deputies' term of office.[1]

Polish parliamentary elections are based on *The Act of 12 April 2001 on Elections to the Sejm of the Republic of Poland and to the Senate of the Republic of Poland,* with subsequent amendments.

The election is held on a nonworking day (Sunday). Voting is held in the polling stations of the district electoral commission. The National Electoral Commission establishes the aggregated results of voting throughout the entire country and determines which election committees have crossed the "electoral threshold" (5%, and 8% for coalition election committees). An election committee represents either one party or several parties (a coalition). If the committee represents one party, that party's representatives get into Parliament if the committee has won at least 5% of the vote. On the other hand, if the committee represents more than one party, the coalition's representatives enter Parliament if the committee has gained at least 8% of the vote.

Campaigning starts on the day the president of the Republic makes the election proclamation and ends 24 hours before the polling day. From the end of the election campaign up to the conclusion of voting, it is forbidden to publish the results of public opinion polls (preelection surveys) on probable voting behavior and election results.

During the campaigning, Polish Television and Polish Radio are required to provide the National Electoral Commission with the opportunity for cost-free presentation on nationwide television and radio channels of information, explanations, and communications connected with the elections and with the regulations of the election law in force.

Election committees have the right to free broadcast of their election platforms on radio and television in the form of broadcasts and election programs. The total free airtime they are allowed is (a) on nationwide channels, 15 hours of broadcasting by the Polish Television Joint-Stock Company, from 5:00 p.m. to 11:00 p.m., and 20 hours by Polish Radio, and (b) on every regional channel, 10 hours of broadcasting on state channels and 20 hours by regional broadcasting companies.

An election committee has the right to free broadcast of its election materials on nationwide channels if it has registered constituency lists in at least nine electoral constituencies and on regional channels if it has registered a constituency list in at least one electoral constituency. Airtime for broadcasting election materials is divided into equal parts among the election committees. The editors-in-chief of the respective national television channels, including Television Polonia (Poland's international TV channel), regional stations, and radio stations, draw up the sequence of election programs to be broadcast each day. They must do this no later than the 18th day before the actual election and in the presence of the persons who submitted the lists.

Regardless of the time assigned for election programs, each committee can run their paid election advertisements on radio and television at the beginning of the election campaign. The fee for election advertisements and airtime has to be the same for all election committees and must be set according to the price list effective on the day when the date of the election was announced.

PRESIDENTIAL ELECTION CAMPAIGNING IN POLAND AND THE MEDIA

The president of the Republic of Poland is elected for a 5-year term by the people. Presidential elections follow the regulations included in *Law on the Election of the President of Republic of Poland of September 27, 1990,* with the latest amendments passed in 2004.

Presidential elections are ordered by the marshal of the Sejm no sooner than 7 months and no later than 6 months before the current president's term expires, and the date of election must be a nonworking day, prescribed by law, no sooner than 100 days and no later than 75 days before the current president's term expires. A president may be reelected only once.

The election campaign starts on the day the marshal of the Sejm proclaims the decision to hold elections. Campaigning is prohibited 24 hours before the polling day and throughout the polling day until the conclusion of the vote.

From the 15th day before polling day up to the day ending the election campaign, Polish Television and the Polish Radio must broadcast, on nationwide channels, free election programs prepared by election committees. The total time of the free broadcasts amounts to 25 hours for Polish Television, including up to 5 hours for TV Polonia, and 35 hours for Polish Radio, including 5 hours broadcast for listeners abroad.

Editors-in-chief of the respective nationwide television channels, including Television Polonia, as well as the editors-in-chief of Polish Radio, determine the sequence of each day's broadcasting of election programs by drawing lots in the presence of election agents. This must be done no later than the 18th day before polling day.

The broadcasting time limit assigned to an election committee cannot be transferred to another committee. Polish Television or Polish Radio may not interfere with the intent or timing of committee programs unless there is a relevant, final court ruling.

In the event that a second ballot has been ordered, within the period beginning from the ninth day before polling day up to the day ending the election campaign preceding the second round, Polish Television and Polish Radio must broadcast free election programs, prepared by the election committees, about each of the two candidates. The total time of these programs amounts to 6 hours for Polish Television and 8 hours for Polish Radio.

Notwithstanding the length of time allotted for the broadcast of cost-free election programs, each election committee may broadcast, between the 15th day before polling day and the day ending the election campaign, paid election programs on public and nonpublic radio and television channels. The total time assigned for paid broadcasting can be up to 15% of the total time allotted to a committee for its free broadcasts. Rates charged for the broadcast time of election advertisements cannot exceed 50% of rates for commercial advertisements and must be fixed on equal terms for all participants in accordance with the price list in force on the day of the proclamation of elections.

Election committees must cover their own expenses. The expenditures of a committee must not exceed the sum of 12 million zlotys. Committee campaign expenditures for advertising, including press advertising (within the meaning of the press law), may not exceed 80% of this sum.

Election campaign expenditures may not be met from sources derived from (a) the state budget; (b) state organizational units; (c) the budgets of local government units, municipal unions, or self-government councils; (d) state-owned enterprises or other economic subjects in which participants include the State Treasury, units of local administration, municipal unions, other municipal legal persons, associations, or other corporations of units of local administration (excluding public companies); (e) legal entities and organizational units, excluding political parties, which have used public funds within 2 years of the proclamation of the election; or (f) "dependent subjects" (as defined in the Act on Public Trading in Securities).

The Role of the Media in Polish Political Campaigns

Despite clear quality standards for information distributed by mass media, its real quality, and thus its influence on society, does not necessarily meet these standards. The reasons for this discrepancy are connected with the uncertainty about what information is appropriate or reliable; that is, what information should be available in every news service and what information should not be distributed. Also, there is still controversy about what constitutes "objectivity of information presentation" (McQuail, 1994), and mass communication researchers often make distinctions between the "real world" and the "news world" (Wu, 2000).

Managing a candidate's presence in the media during election campaigns is connected with shaping this "news world." In other words, the goal is to limit voters' perception area to only those aspects that are objects of media reports. Political marketing specialists and, particularly, public relations specialists try to influence the media in such a way that the media will focus on particular subjects and particular politicians and not others. They assume that although the mass media may not determine what voters *think* about a given subject, they do determine what voters think *about*. Therefore, if the media focus on issue ownership in regard to a given political party or politician, that party's or candidate's chances of success in the elections increase considerably simply because of the exposure the media have given them (Petrocik, 1996).

Politicians' teams and aides can influence the message the media puts out because of their connections to politicians in power and because media institutions are dependent on politicians and their environment for information. Politicians and those connected to them recognize the power of the mass media in shaping citizens' voting behaviors. The point is for every party and candidate to promote their own agenda through the media (McCombs, 1981; McCombs, Llamas, Lopez-Escobar, & Rey, 1997; McCombs & Shaw, 1972), prime the media to focus on particular content (Iyengar & Kinder, 1987; Iyengar & Simon, 2000; McGraw & Ling, 2003; Miller & Krosnick, 2000), and develop news framing for selected aspects of the perceived political reality (Jamieson & Waldman, 2003; Semetko & Valkenburg; 2000).

The basis for determining whether the media are objective in their presentation of political candidates is the equality of their presentation of candidates' views and positions, something that is easy to determine in two-party political systems. However, when there are more political forces participating in an election, the situation gets more complex. Therefore, it is difficult for voters to spot a bias in the media's presentation of candidates (D'Alessio & Allen, 2000).

Despite that, analyses of the time slots and duration of appearances of particular politicians, particularly on television information programs, are conducted in practically all democratic countries (see, e.g., Butler & Kavanagh, 1992). In Poland, such research activities are conducted by the Instytut Monitorowania Mediów (Institute of Media Monitoring; see their Web site at http://www .instytut.com.pl). The institute monitored the Polish presidential campaign of 2000 (*Kampania*

prezydencka 2000, 2000), and from August 1 to October 6, 2004, all the television programs of four stations, TVP1, TVP2, Polsat and TVN, were analyzed. The researchers focused on the number of appearances of all 13 presidential candidates on television programs and on how long their presentations were. The same analyses were performed for the presentations of their aides and spokespersons. In addition, the number and duration of programs dedicated to the candidates and to the main subjects of their campaign were registered.

The unquestionable leader in the media during this period, given the frequency of his appearances, was the incumbent, President Aleksander Kwasniewski, who appeared on television more than 300 times. Marian Krzaklewski was far behind him (approximately 160 appearances), as was Lech Walesa (more than 120) and—the second person in the voting struggle—Andrzej Olechowski (more than 110).

The duration of the candidates' presentations was distributed slightly differently. Although the leader here is still Aleksander Kwasniewski, he owes his position mainly to the public media. TVP1 and TVP2 gave almost as much time to Jaroslaw Kalinowski and Lech Walesa as they did to Kwasniewski.

This breakdown shows clearly that the media's presentations of the presidential candidates in the presidential campaign of 2000 were biased. Television stations, both private and public, had their favorites and sentenced the other politicians to "non-existence." However, in the case of Aleksander Kwasniewski, one should remember that the media's presentation of him was the result of an overlap between his function as the then president in office and presidential candidate. His appearances in one or the other role changed proportionately as the election campaign progressed. In August, 60% of his appearances were connected with his office, whereas in September and October it was 51%. One of the subjects he raised most often was that of the Olympic games in Sydney.

Most of these statements were made on the public television channels that broadcast the games. Thus viewers had a chance to hear Aleksander Kwasniewski's statements on the Olympic games (see Cwalina & Falkowski, 2005).

The Influence of Political Communication on the Perception of a Candidate's Image

Every citizen wants his country ruled by the best candidate, an almost ideal political leader. However, the following questions arise: What is this ideal? What features should it have?

Studies on social perception demonstrate that in voters' minds, an "ideal" political leader is a kind of prototype, an example of the category of people professionally dealing with politics (Kinder, 1986; Sullivan, Aldrich, Borgida, & Rahn, 1990). Such cognitive schemas are a reference point for people when they judge candidates running for a certain office or when they make voting decisions.

According to Leary (1996), it is extremely important for a political leader to possess five specific features: competence, the ability to evoke sympathy, morality, power, and the ability to embarrass others. Possession of all these attributes contributes to a leader's charisma and improves his or her chances for electoral success.

One of the ways of discovering what voters dream about is simply to ask them this question. In experimental studies conducted between the first and second rounds of presidential elections in Poland in 1995 and 2000, Cwalina and Falkowski (2000, 2005) checked the conformity of the features mentioned in answers to open questions about Aleksander Kwasniewski, Lech Walesa, Andrzej Olechowski, and Marian Krzaklewski. The prototype of an "ideal president" was also analyzed during the presidential elections that followed.

The task of the respondents was to write down the features that an ideal president should have, those that characterized individual candidates, and those that the respondents could infer based on the particular politician's spots. The questions were open, so the respondents could list any number of characteristics. All the characteristics they wrote down were counted and categorized according to their content similarity and the number of the same characteristics that were mentioned.

The results obtained for the ideal president and for candidates participating in the presidential elections in 1995 are presented in Table 19.1.

An analysis of the features presented in the table demonstrates the importance of creating the right image for a candidate if he or she is to be evaluated as matching the prototype of an ideal president. The key features that an ideal president should possess include honesty and credibility, competence and professionalism, education, appearance and attractiveness, intelligence, efficiency, power and determination, and an openness to people and the world. Aleksander Kwasniewski was perceived as having power and determination, good appearance and attractiveness, intelligence and clarity, and eloquence. The dominant features of Walesa's image included honesty and credibility and power and determination.

The results of the studies conducted during the 2000 presidential election campaign in Poland are presented in Table 19.2.

In 2000, the ideal president was characterized by honesty and credibility, appearance and attractiveness, education, competence and professionalism, intelligence, caring about others and the country, power and determination, and openness to people and the world. Aleksander Kwasniewski's image included such features as honesty and credibility, professionalism and competence, openness to people and the world, and power and determination. His main opponent in the presidential fight, Andrzej Olechowski, was characterized by honesty and credibility, power and determination, education, and openness to people and the world. The most important features in Marian Krzaklewski's image

Table 19.1   Comparison of Features Attributed to Ideal President and Main Candidates
in Poland's 1995 Presidential Elections (%)

Feature	Ideal President	Aleksander Kwasniewski	Lech Walesa
Honesty, credibility	80.3	15.8	49.3
Competence, professionalism	47.3	17.2	10.8
Education	37.4	7.4	0.0
Appearance, attractiveness	33.5	25.6	0.0
Intelligence	33.0	25.1	0.0
Efficiency	31.0	9.9	6.4
Power	29.6	29.6	24.1
Openness to people and world	26.6	11.3	5.9
Clarity, eloquence	17.2	24.1	3.5
Wisdom, reason	13.3	12.3	1.5
Activity	11.3	13.8	1.0
Calmness, self-control	11.3	9.4	0.5
Conscientiousness, reliability	9.9	0.0	1.0
Authority, charisma	7.9	2.5	10.3
Caring about others and the country	6.9	0.0	3.0
Responsibility	6.7	2.0	5.2
Seriousness	5.9	7.4	0.5
Independence, objectivity	5.4	1.0	0.0
Fairness	4.9	0.0	0.0
Being a believer	4.4	0.0	6.4
Being known abroad	3.0	0.0	15.8
Friendliness	0.5	6.9	3.0

included honesty and credibility, being a believer (Catholic), education, and caring about others and the country.

In both presidential elections, it is easy to see the discrepancy between Poles' expectations of an ideal candidate and their images of particular politicians. Along with a qualitative analysis of the features that form a politician's image, a quantitative analysis was conducted, using Wilcoxon's Z-test, that compared the profiles of an ideal president and the candidates. The results suggest that the structure of the category "ideal president" in 1995 and 2000 differed considerably from all the candidates competing for presidency in the elections. Clearly, none of the candidates was close to achieving the image that was attributed to the ideal. From a marketing perspective, this means that the campaigns of all the candidates were unsuccessful in meeting voters' needs.

Another conclusion coming from the research is connected with the dynamics of change in the images. Both a politician's and an ideal president's image are characterized by internal changeability, meaning that in time, one's perception of the features of the same object undergoes significant change. The most characteristic shift relative to the changes in the image of an ideal candidate over 5 years (1995-2000) concerned appearance and attractiveness, which moved from fourth to second position. An important shift can also be observed in the category "caring about others and the country" (6.9% indications in 1995 and 21.2% in 2000), "responsibility" (respectively, 6.7% and 18.6%), and "independence" (5.4% and 18.2%). On the other hand, some features of an ideal president became less important. In 1995, 47.3% of the respondents stressed the importance of competence, whereas 5 years later it had fallen to

Table 19.2   Comparison of Features Attributed to Ideal President and Main Candidates
in Poland's 2000 Presidential Elections (%)

Feature	Ideal President	Aleksander Kwasniewski	Andrzej Olechowski	Marian Krzaklewski
Honesty, credibility	89.6	30.6	32.8	34.8
Appearance, attractiveness	36.7	8.9	10.9	4.8
Education	32.2	3.2	21.3	28.7
Competence, professionalism	24.2	28.2	12.6	3.9
Intelligence	23.1	8.1	10.3	2.6
Caring about others and the country	21.2	18.6	5.8	20.0
Power	19.7	21.0	29.3	10.0
Openness to people and the world	19.7	27.4	21.3	2.6
Responsibility	18.6	4.0	4.0	1.3
Independence, objectivity	18.2	11.3	7.5	0.9
Efficiency	16.3	4.8	1.2	3.5
Fairness	14.8	4.0	1.2	1.3
Clarity, eloquence	13.6	11.3	8.1	1.7
Activity	13.3	4.0	5.6	0.9
Conscientiousness, reliability	12.9	5.7	5.2	1.7
Wisdom, reason	8.7	8.1	15.5	2.6
Being a believer	7.2	0.0	1.7	29.1
Seriousness	5.3	7.3	9.2	0.9
Calmness, self-control	3.8	16.1	9.2	0.9
Being known abroad	3.0	1.6	1.2	0.0
Friendliness	2.7	16.9	12.1	2.2
Authority, charisma	1.5	4.8	12.1	0.9

24.2%. A similar situation could be observed with efficiency (31% and 16.3%) and intelligence (33% and 23.1%).

It can be stated that the results of the research suggest that, despite the efforts of marketing experts, the politicians running for the Polish presidency between 1995 and 2000 did not meet the categories of an ideal politician as defined by the voters. However, the prototype of an ideal president is dynamic: In time the relevance of particular attributes changes and so does voters' agreement as to what attributes are relevant for an ideal president.

CONTENT OF POLISH POLITICAL ADVERTISING

Diamond and Bates (1992) point to the 1960s as the beginning of political campaigns that relied on television spots and precise marketing strategies. According to these researchers, the development of TV production, marketing methods, and public opinion polls laid the foundations for modern high-tech political communication. It has become an important indicator of "the third age of political communication" (Blumler & Kavanagh, 1999).

Polish election campaigns were the subject of several research projects conducted by Cwalina and Falkowski (1999a, 2000, 2003, 2005; Cwalina, Falkowski, & Kaid, 2000, 2005; Cwalina, Falkowski, & Roznowski, 1999; Falkowski & Cwalina, 1999). The research focused primarily on the influence of political advertising on citizens' voting preferences. In addition to that, these analyses of Polish political campaigns focused on the content of political spots.

Content analysis is a standard research technique; it is used to better describe mediated communications. According to McQuail (1969), it is a quantitative and "near-objective" approach. The results of such analyses are the basis of hypotheses for research on the influence of mass media's message, and they also disclose the specific cultural characteristics with which a given message is created. McQuail believes that the main advantage of content analysis is that it is a standardized research procedure that can be used in the same form for many years. It is also independent from cultural influences, which allows researchers to use it in conducting comparative international studies. Such a standardized analysis procedure for political advertising was proposed by Kaid and Johnston (1991; see also Kaid, 1999b; Kaid & Holtz-Bacha, 1995b).

Content analysis was used to analyze a political advertising campaign in the 1995 Polish presidential elections. In that year, the campaign on television started on October 20. TVP1 broadcast 14 blocks of spots; TVP2, 6 blocks; and TV Polonia, which reaches many countries of the world, 2 blocks. Each block consisted of 13 spots in the first round of the election (it would have been 17 spots, but four candidates withdrew) and two spots in the second round. The broadcast spots had two different lengths: 3 minutes 30 seconds, and 5 minutes 10 seconds. Each of the 13 candidates was presented in the spots 16 times, and each of two candidates who advanced to the second round was presented in 6 additional spots. Two candidates purchased time for additional 30-second spots: Jan Olszewski bought airtime for 2 spots and Waldemar Pawlak for 10 spots. Regional channels and Polsat TV were not allowed to broadcast political advertisements.

Discussions with candidates were presented for a whole week, except on Sunday; each day, in both the first and the second rounds of the elections, one candidate was interviewed. These discussions lasted 20 minutes on TVP1 and a full hour on TVP2. They were also aired on the commercial Polsat TV stations once a week. The broadcasting campaigns for the first and the second vote ended in "electoral evenings"

broadcast live by TVP1 on the election days of November 5 and 19 (Cwalina et al., 1999).

Cwalina and Falkowski (1999b; see also Cwalina et al., 1999; Kaid, 1999a) carried out content analysis on 81 out of 220 spots broadcast by the three public television channels during the 1995 presidential election. This selection was made to ensure a diversity of spots for each of the candidates. Particular attention was given to the spots of those candidates who received at least 5% of votes in the first election round. The spots were coded by three trained coders, and the coding instrument for the spots was developed from earlier studies of Western European countries (Kaid & Holtz-Bacha, 1995a; Kaid & Johnston, 1991).

The advertising format most frequently used in the 1995 presidential election had an introspective style characteristic of 36% of all the analyzed spots. The format was based on the candidate's presenting himself to the voters. The message provided facts from the politician's life and familiarized the viewers with his achievements and voting program. The introspective format was predominant in the spots of candidates who were not very well known to the general public. Another commonly used advertising format was the documentary style (32% of the spots). As with the introspective message, the message in the "documentary" provided voters with basic information about the candidate. In this case, however, the information was presented by an announcer, not the candidate himself.

The analyzed spots from the presidential campaign of 1995 showed that the dominant style of political advertising (emotional appeal) was attractive to the voters (67% of the spots). Almost all candidates used it. There were very few spots that included a discussion of the issues. Appealing to voters' logic could be found in 21% of the spots. Messages referring to ethical arguments, including such elements as reliability or credibility, could only be found in 12% of the spots.

The results obtained during the analysis of Polish political spots prepared by the

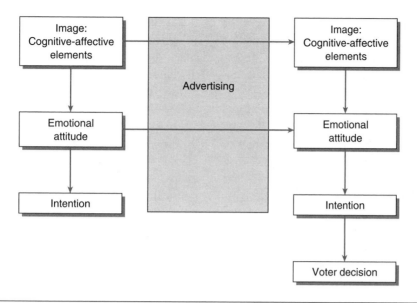

Figure 19.1   Sequential Model of the Influence of Spots on Voters' Behavior

13 candidates for president in 1995 show that they are not very different from spots developed in other countries. Despite the fact that democratic processes are still developing in our country, as far as political marketing is concerned, it is easy to see that American and Western European models are being used to prepare media campaigns.

When it comes to production techniques and ways of appealing to the voters, Polish political advertising seems closest to French political advertising (see Cwalina & Falkowski, 1999b, 2005; Johnston & Gerstlé, 1995). In both countries there are more spots about problems than about image. The person whose voice is used in the soundtrack is the candidate himself, and the most popular technique of filming the candidate involves having him speak straight to the camera.

THE INFLUENCE OF POLITICAL ADVERTISING ON VOTING PREFERENCES

The dominance of political advertising in political campaigns has increased the importance of determining how candidate images are formed (Diamond & Bates, 1992). The ability to elicit affective connections may be central to the voters' image formation process (Abelson, Kinder, Peters, & Fiske, 1982; Cwalina et al., 2000, 2005; Falkowski & Cwalina, 1999; Kaid & Holtz-Bacha, 1995b). In this context, the image means creating a particular representation that, by evoking associations, adds extra value to the object and thus contributes to its affective reception.

Studies conducted in many countries confirm that political advertisements influence voters' image of the candidate and may lead to a reconfiguration of the structure of image attributes (e.g., Falkowski & Cwalina, 1999; Kaid & Chanslor, 1995). An example of this type of research is represented by the studies on the influence of television political advertisements on politicians' image by Cwalina et al. (2000; see also Falkowski & Cwalina, 1999). These researchers proposed a sequential model of the influence of spots on voters' behavior (see Figure 19.1).

The model includes four causally connected components, which allow one to predict citizens' voting behavior: (a) cognitive-affective elements (candidate image), (b) general feelings toward the candidate, (c) intention to vote for a particular candidate, (d) decision to vote for a particular candidate. The image is operationalized by a semantic differential that consists of a dozen or so seven-point scales (for details, see Cwalina et al., 2000). Emotional attitude toward the candidate is measured by a thermometer of feelings, on a scale of 0 to 100 degrees. With voting intention and decision, the task of the subjects is to mark the presidential candidate they were going to vote for during the elections.

The model was empirically tested during the 1995 and 2000 presidential elections in Poland, the 1995 presidential elections in France, the 2004 presidential election in the United States, and the 1994 parliamentary elections in Germany (Cwalina & Falkowski, 1999a, 2003, 2005; Cwalina et al., 2000, 2005; Falkowski & Cwalina, 1999). The obtained results suggest that its predictive power is high. Based on these results, the researchers propose a number of detailed practical suggestions about what attributes political marketers should focus on to create an effective and attractive image of political candidates.

From the marketing point of view, it is important to determine what attributes a politician needs "enriched" for his image to more easily produce positive attitudes toward him. One of the methods used to distinguish important attributes in a politician's image is multiple regression analysis (MRA). The dependent variable here is emotional attitude toward the candidate, and the independent variables are particular scales of the semantic differential—attributes of the image. The practical value of such analysis may be higher if the perceived attributes of each candidate in given elections are tested among the candidate's supporters *and* opponents. Separate analyses of measurements made before and after the spots are shown will help to establish precisely the influence of the spots on subjects' emotional attitude toward the studied candidates. In this way, one can obtain indicators of spot efficiency for particular candidates.

An analysis of the influence of political advertising on the forming of voting preferences based on the experimental design described here was conducted during the 2000 Polish presidential election (Cwalina & Falkowski, 2003, 2005; Cwalina et al., 2005). The experiment consisted of three stages. At the first stage, an experimental group completed a research questionnaire (pretest) anonymously. Then the group watched four political advertisements. The advertisements presented were chosen at random from the advertisements that each of the candidates used in his television campaign. Subjects were exposed to two advertisements for each of the candidates (Aleksander Kwasniewski and Andrzej Olechowski) in an alternating sequence. After the subjects had watched the spots, the experimenter handed out research questionnaires (posttests).

MRA was used for analysis of the data. Four MRAs were conducted for feelings toward each candidate among his supporters and opponents, before and after showing of the spots. The results of the MRAs are shown in Table 19.3. The partition of the sample into two "electorates" was based on voting intention.

In Kwasniewski's electorate, the mean values of R^2 for "own" candidate (Kwasniewski) and opponent (Olechowski) are 0.38 and 0.52, respectively. In Olechowski's electorate, these values are 0.66 for the appraisal of Kwasniewski's image and 0.53 for Olechowski's. In the case of both electorates, the percentage of the explained variance is smaller for own candidate than for opponent. This may imply that the affective attitude toward own candidate is dependent to a lesser degree on his image and to a larger degree on the opponent's attributes (e.g., his political program, party affiliation, system of values). The opponent is monitored more carefully, mainly to find his negative attributes or attributes that discredit him as a potential president. In the case of both electorates, a strong polarization of convictions about individual candidates can be seen. However, the spots did very

Table 19.3 Adjectives Accounting for the Variance of the Feeling Thermometer

Candidate's Supporters	Target	Attributes (Pretest)	Beta (Standard error)	Attributes (Posttest)	Beta (Standard error)
Kwasniewski	Kwasniewski	Attractive	−.50 (.13)	Attractive	−.30 (.14)
		Aggressive	−.40 (.14)	Successful	−.34 (.16)
		$R^2 = 0.43$		$R^2 = 0.33$	
	Olechowski	Honest	.52 (.12)	Friendly	.48 (.18)
		Successful	−.45 (.14)	Sincere	.36 (.15)
		Believing Christian	−.32 (.12)		
		Attractive	−.26 (.12)		
		$R^2 = 0.55$		$R^2 = 0.49$	
Olechowski	Kwasniewski	Attractive	−.48 (.16)	Qualified	−.42 (.19)
		Friendly	.59 (.23)	Passive	−.33 (.16)
		Honest	.46 (.19)		
		Believable	.50 (.21)		
		$R^2 = 0.62$		$R^2 = 0.70$	
	Olechowski	Strong	−.76 (.25)	Honest	,75 (.18)
		Passive	−.56 (.24)	Passive	−1.07 (.33)
				Successful	−.56 (.24)
		$R^2 = 0.39$		$R^2 = 0.66$	

Note: Based on multiple regression analyses of data from the 2000 Polish presidential election campaign. All parameters are significant at $p < 0.05$.

little for the relation between candidate's image and emotional attitude. The R^2 values are, in fact, similar before and after the spots were shown.

The percentage of the explained variance in the thermometer of feelings by differential adjectives is relatively high, which points to the possibility of controlling affective attitude toward candidates by careful emphasis on the candidate's relevant attributes. There appears to be a reconfiguration of the politicians' images that is due to the influence of their spots. The set of significant adjectives explaining the temperature of feelings about a given candidate is different after the exposure. It seems clear that after watching the spots, subjects' images of the candidates have been changed within the overall cognitive behavior, which links all the components of the model: image, feeling, and intention. In other words,

after watching the spots, the voter is sensitive to different adjectives. We can "warm up" or "cool down" the feeling toward the candidate by manipulating selected characteristics of the candidates' images in a promotional advertising strategy (see Cwalina et al., 2000).

To get answers to questions concerning the causal relationship of cognitive and emotional processes in creating voting preferences (see Figure 19.1), structural equation modeling was applied. The specificity of the causal relationship obtained by the structural equation methodology allows us to put forward some practical suggestions regarding a general strategy for electoral campaigns. A hypothesized structural model is presented in Figure 19.2.

To simplify the data structure from the semantic differential and to distinguish perception dimensions of the candidates' image, two principal component analyses

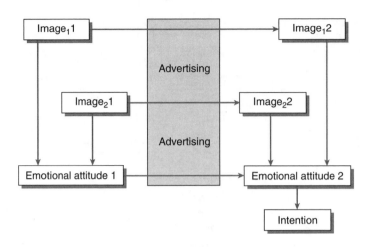

Figure 19.2   Hypothesized Structural Equation Model of Voter Behavior

were conducted, one for each politician (Kwasniewski and Olechowski). In each case, a two-factor solution was obtained. With reference to Kwasniewski, two factors accounted for 53.6% of total variance. Factor 1, "leader's abilities" (42.5% of variance), included such attributes as qualified, open to the world, believable, successful, sophisticated, calm, not aggressive, strong, friendly. Factor 2, "morality" (11.1% of variance), consisted of honest, attractive, active, believing Christian, sincere.

In the case of Olechowski, the factors explained 52.4% of the total variance. Factor 1, "leader's abilities" (42.3% of variance), consisted of the following attributes: qualified, open to the world, believable, successful, attractive, strong, and active. Factor 2, "sociability" (10.1% of variance), consisted of the following attributes: honest, sophisticated, calm, not aggressive, believing Christian, and friendly.

According to the sequential model, the image, operationalized by two factors (Image$_1$ and Image$_2$), influences the general feelings in the first sequence. In the second sequence we can see that after viewing the advertisements, some image reconfiguration and change in affect take place in the voters' minds. According to the constructivist approach, one can assume both an effect of image on affect within the sequence and an effect of image on

image, as well as affect on affect, between the sequences.

The results of the structural equation analyses of each of the candidates on his supporters according to the constructivist approach are shown in Figure 19.3. The partition of the sample into two partisan groups was based on declared voting intention.

The models present specific arrangements of causal relationships, obtained empirically, connecting image with affects and voting intentions for particular candidates. Despite slight differences in the parameters of the paths, the model explains, in similar ways, the voting behavior of Kwasiewski's and Olechowski's supporters. Initial emotional attitude toward the two candidates depends on their evaluation by the voters in their two dimensions of image: leader's abilities and morality for Kwasniewski and leader's abilities and sociability for Olechowski. However, the influence of these evaluations on final voting intentions is lost when political advertising comes into play. It turns out that the voters' positive attitude toward a candidate depends only on the "soft" characteristics of that candidate's image. Political advertising appears to draw voters' attention to the social and moral virtues of politicians, pushing to the background the importance of their competence and professional preparation for performing the function of a president.

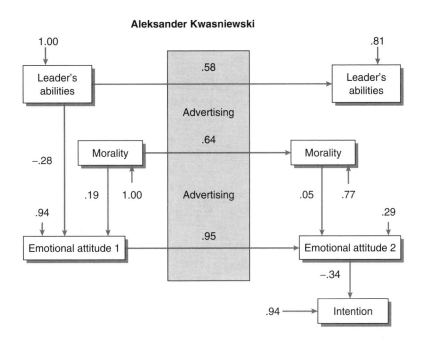

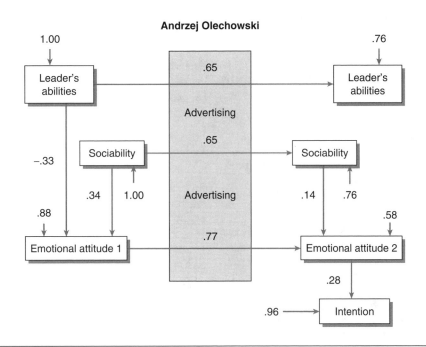

Figure 19.3   Structural Equation Empirical Models: Polish 2000 Presidential Election

CONCLUSION

Although the countries of Central and Eastern Europe liberated themselves from totalitarian systems and entered the road to democratization at the same time, there are still differences between them and established democracies such as the United States or countries of the "old"

European Union. Despite the fact that elections take place in each of these countries on a regular basis, all follow different rules. There are also differences in the rules for conducting election campaigns and the role of the mass media.

As a result, these differences influence the specific nature of promotional activities and events taking place during election campaigns. Naturally, in different countries, one can find different models steering citizens' voting behaviors (see Cwalina et al., 2000, 2005; Cwalina, Falkowski, Newman, & Verčič, 2004; Dalton & Wattenberg, 1993).

What seems common to each of the countries of Eastern and Central Europe and to established democracies is the fact that political advertising has become an inseparable part of the strategy of political communication. Besides, as the results of the research prove (Cwalina et al., 2000), political advertising does have some influence on the formation of citizens' voting preferences. It is possible to distinguish three types of influence:

1. Advertisements may strengthen already existing voting preferences. The supporters of a given candidate consolidate themselves in their support for their candidate, whereas the opponents consolidate themselves in their opposition. In other words, the polarization of voting convictions increases. Political advertising can also be connected with a certain reconfiguration of the candidate's image in the minds of his or her supporters.

2. Advertisements may weaken already existing voting preferences and, in extreme cases, may even change them. We are speaking here of influence that leads to an increase in uncertainty among voters about whom to support. This situation is usually accompanied by a reconfiguration of the candidate's image in the voter's mind. After watching the advertisements, viewers find that certain features of the candidate, other than the ones they had perceived as important before, become relevant for that candidate. They must thus reconsider previously made decisions.

3. Advertisements may neither weaken nor strengthen political preferences but may lead to the reconfiguration of the candidate's image in voters' minds. This type of influence can be called cognitive influence, because, as a result of it, the arguments that led to a previously made decision do change, but the direction and certainty with which the decision was made do not. From the point of view of political marketing, and thus from the point of view of the shaping of political preferences, this type of promotional influence during a presidential or parliamentary campaign can be treated as inefficient. However, leading voters to change their perception of a politician's image can be treated as a first step in the strategy preparing him for the fight for power.

The young democracies of Eastern Europe, as Klingemann and Wattenberg (1992) suggest, can be seen as more similar to the United States than to other European countries because of their greater concentration on candidates than on political parties and their programs. This type of focus is particularly likely to occur when parties are formed around leaders (as was and is still the case in many Eastern European countries) instead of expecting leaders to "emerge" from political parties. Charismatic leaders around whom parties have formed have included, for example, Lech Walesa, Andrzej Lepper, and Stanisław Tyminski in Poland. However, this hypothesis requires further study, not only on the influence of promotion strategies on voting behaviors but also on the relevant social changes taking place in the countries of Eastern Europe.

NOTE

1.   For more details about the election process and information on current elections, see the Sejm Web site at http://www.sejm.gov.pl.

REFERENCES

Abelson, R. P., Kinder, D. R., Peters, M. D., & Fiske, S. T. (1982). Affective and semantic components in political person perception. *Journal of Personality and Social Psychology, 42*, 619–630.

Act of 12 April 2001 on Elections to the Sejm of the Republic of Poland and to the Senate of the

Republic of Poland. (2001). *Dziennik Ustaw*, (46), ¶ 499; (74), ¶ 786.

Agh, A. (1991). The democratic challenge in Central Europe. *Politics and the Individual*, 1(1), 3–19.

Ballentine, K. (2002). International assistance and the development of independent mass media in the Czech and Slovak Republics. In S. E. Mendelson & J. K. Glenn (Eds.), *The power and limits of NGOs: A critical look at building democracy in Eastern Europe and Eurasia* (pp. 91–125). New York: Columbia University Press.

Blumler, J. G., & Kavanagh, D. (1999). The third age of political communication: Influences and features. *Political Communication*, 16(3), 209–230.

Butler, D., & Kavanagh, D. (1992). *The British general election of 1992*. London: Macmillan.

Connor, W. D., & Ploszajski, P. (Eds.). (1992). *Escape from socialism: The Polish route*. Warsaw, Poland: IFiS.

Cwalina, W., & Falkowski, A. (1999a). Decision processes in perception in the political preferences research: A comparative analysis of Poland, France, and Germany. *Journal for Mental Changes*, 5(2), 27–49.

Cwalina, W., & Falkowski, A. (1999b). Reklama polityczna podczas wyborów prezydenckich w 1995 roku: Analiza treści i technik realizacyjnych [Political advertising during the presidential elections in 1995: Content analysis and realization techniques]. In P. Francuz (Ed.), *Psychologiczne aspekty odbioru telewizji* [Psychological aspects of television broadcast reception] (pp. 99–125). Lublin, Poland: TN KUL.

Cwalina, W., & Falkowski, A. (2000). Psychological mechanisms of political persuasion: The influence of political advertising on voting behavior. *Polish Psychological Bulletin*, 31(3), 203–222.

Cwalina, W., & Falkowski, A. (2003). Advertising and the image of politicians: National elections in Poland, France, and Germany. In F. Hansen & L. B. Christensen (Eds.), *Branding and advertising* (pp. 205–231). Copenhagen, Denmark: Copenhagen Business School Press.

Cwalina, W., & Falkowski, A. (2005). *Marketing polityczny. Perspektywa psychologiczna*. [Political marketing: A psychological perspective]. Gdansk, Poland: Gdanskie Wydawnictwo Psychologiczne.

Cwalina, W., Falkowski, A., & Kaid, L. L. (2000). Role of advertising in forming the image of politicians: Comparative analysis of Poland, France, and Germany. *Media Psychology*, 2(2), 119–146.

Cwalina, W., Falkowski, A., & Kaid, L. L. (2005). Advertising and the image of politicians in evolving and established democracies: Comparative study of the Polish and the U.S. presidential elections in 2000. *Journal of Political Marketing*, 4(2/3), 29–54.

Cwalina, W., Falkowski, A., Newman, B. I., & Verčič, D. (2004). Models of voter behavior in traditional and evolving democracies: Comparative analysis of Poland, Slovenia, and U.S. *Journal of Political Marketing*, 3(2), 7–30.

Cwalina, W., Falkowski, A., Roznowski, B. (1999). Television spots in Polish presidential elections. In L. L. Kaid (Ed.), *Television and politics in evolving European democracies* (pp. 45–60). Commack, NY: Nova Science.

D'Alessio, D., & Allen, M. (2000). Media bias in presidential elections: A meta-analysis. *Journal of Communication*, 50(4), 133–156.

Dalton, R. J., & Wattenberg, M. P. (1993). The not so simple act of voting. In A. Finifter (Ed.), *The state of the discipline II* (pp. 193–218). Washington, DC: American Political Science Association.

Diamond, E., & Bates, S. (1992). *The spot: The rise of political advertising on television*. Cambridge: MIT Press.

Falkowski, A., & Cwalina, W. (1999). Methodology of constructing effective political advertising: An empirical study of the Polish presidential election in 1995. In B. I. Newman (Ed.), *Handbook of political marketing* (pp. 283–304). Thousand Oaks, CA: Sage.

Falkowski, A., & Cwalina, W. (2004). Political marketing in evolving European democracies. *Journal of Political Marketing*, 3(2), 1–5.

Grabe, M. E., Zhou, S., Lang, A., & Bolls, P. D. (2000). Packaging television news: The effects of tabloid on information processing and evaluative responses. *Journal of Broadcasting & Electronic Media*, 44(4), 581–598.

Iyengar, S., & Kinder, D. R. (1987). *News that matters: Television and American opinion*. Chicago: University of Chicago Press.

Iyengar, S., & Simon, A. F. (2000). New perspectives and evidence on political communication and campaign effects. *Annual Review of Psychology*, 51, 149–169.

Jamieson, K. H., & Waldman, P. (2003). *The press effect: Politicians, journalists, and the stories that shape the political world*. New York: Oxford University Press.

Johnston, A., & Gerstlé, J. (1995). The role of television broadcasts in promoting French presidential candidates. In L. L. Kaid & C. Holtz-Bacha (Eds.), *Political advertising in Western democracies: Parties and candidates on television* (pp. 44–60). Thousand Oaks, CA: Sage.

Kaid, L. L. (1999a). Comparing and contrasting the styles and effects of political advertising in European democracies. In L. L. Kaid (Ed.), *Television and politics in evolving European democracies* (219–236). Commack, NY: Nova Science.

Kaid, L. L. (Ed.). (1999b). *Television and politics in evolving European democracies*. Commack, NY: Nova Science.

Kaid, L. L., & Chanslor, M. (1995). Changing candidate images: The effects of political advertising. In K. L. Hacker (Ed.), *Candidate images in presidential elections* (pp. 83–97). Westport, CT: Praeger.

Kaid, L. L., & Holtz-Bacha, C. (1995a). Political advertising across cultures: Comparing contents, styles, and effects. In L. L. Kaid & C. Holtz-Bacha (Eds.), *Political advertising in Western democracies: Parties and candidates on television* (pp. 206–227). Thousand Oaks, CA: Sage.

Kaid, L. L., & Holtz-Bacha, C. (Eds.). (1995b). *Political advertising in Western democracies: Parties and candidates on television*. Thousand Oaks, CA: Sage.

Kaid, L. L., & Johnston, A. (1991). Negative versus positive television advertising in U.S. presidential campaigns, 1960-1988. *Journal of Communication, 41*(3), 53–63.

Kampania prezydencka 2000 [Presidential campaign 2000] (Research report). (2000). Retrieved July 31, 2000, from http://www.instytut.com.pl/raporty/wybory_prezdent_2000

Kinder, D. R. (1986). Political character revisited. In R. R. Lau & D. O. Sears (Eds.), *Political cognitions* (pp. 233–256). Hillsdale, NJ: Erlbaum.

Klingemann, H. D., & Wattenberg, M. P. (1992). Decaying versus developing party systems: A comparison of party images in the United States and West Germany. *British Journal of Political Science, 22,* 131–149.

Lasham, C. (1998). *Regulation of media.* Retrieved January 16, 2006, from the Administration and Cost of Elections Project Web site: http://www.aceproject.org/main/english/em/emc08.htm

Law on the Election of the President of Republic of Poland of September 27, 1990 (1990/2004). *Dziennik Ustaw,* (25), ¶ 219.

Leary, M. (1996). *Self-presentation.* Boulder, CO: Westview Press.

McCombs, M. E. (1981). The agenda-setting approach. In D. D. Nimmo & K. R. Sanders (Eds.), *Handbook of political communication* (pp. 121–140). Beverly Hills, CA: Sage.

McCombs, M., Llamas, J. P., Lopez-Escobar, E., & Rey, F. (1997). Candidate image in Spanish elections: Second-level-agenda setting effects. *Journalism & Mass Communication Quarterly, 74*(4), 703–717.

McCombs, M. E., & Shaw, D. L. (1972). The agenda-setting function of mass media. *Public Opinion Quarterly, 36*(2), 176–185.

McGraw, K. M., & Ling, C. (2003). Media priming of presidential and group evaluations. *Political Communication, 20*(1), 23–40.

McQuail, D. (1969). *Towards a sociology of mass communications.* London: Collier-Macmillan.

McQuail, D. (1994). Mass communication and the public interest: Towards social theory for media structure and performance. In D. Crowley & D. Mitchell (Eds.), *Communication theory today* (pp. 235–253). Cambridge, England: Polity Press.

Miller, J. M., & Krosnick, J. A. (2000). News media impact on the ingredients of presidential evaluations: Politically knowledgeable citizens are guided by trusted source. *American Journal of Political Science, 44*(2), 301–315.

Negrine, R. (1994). *Politics and the mass media in Britain.* London: Routledge.

Petrocik, J. R. (1996). Issue ownership in presidential elections, with a 1980 case study. *American Journal of Political Science, 40*(3), 825–850.

Pinto-Duschinsky, M. (1997). Public broadcasting allocations. Retrieved January 16, 2006, from the Administration and Cost of Elections Project Web site: http://www.aceproject.org/main/english/pc/pce03.htm

Semetko, H. A., & Valkenburg, P. M. (2000). Framing European politics: A content analysis of press and television news. *Journal of Communication, 50*(2), 93–109.

Shapiro, M. A., & Lang, A. (1991). Making television reality: Unconscious processes in the construction of social reality. *Communication Research, 18*(5), 685–705.

Staniszkis, J. (1992). *The dynamics of breakthrough in Eastern Europe.* Berkeley: University of California Press.

Sullivan, J. L., Aldrich, J. H., Borgida, E., & Rahn, W. (1990). Candidate appraisal and human nature: Man and superman in the 1984 election. *Political Psychology, 11*(3), 459–484.

Wu, H. D. (2000). Systemic determinants of international news coverage: A comparison of 38 countries. *Journal of Communication, 50*(2), 110–130.

20

Political Advertising in Hungarian Electoral Communications

JOLÁN RÓKA

The election campaigns of the last decade prove that mass media play a fundamental role in shaping and modifying social reality in Hungary. Most of the information Hungarians have about the presidential and party candidates comes from the mass media, which are able to influence citizens' ideological, political, and aesthetic views, concepts, and values through visual and verbal means of manipulation, which make partisan agenda-setting possible. That function of the media (especially the audiovisual media, telecommunications, and multimedia) which forms public opinion can be followed most clearly in political campaigns, where the tactics and strategies that are aimed at the ideological persuasion of the citizens would surely be ineffective without their proper media presentation—in the form of political advertisements. This statement can be illustrated by the outcome of Hungarian parliamentary elections since the democratic régime change in 1990.

AN OVERVIEW OF THE HUNGARIAN POLITICAL SYSTEM

In the Hungarian political system, the most prominent state and representative organ is its 386-member parliament, the Hungarian National Assembly. Its legal status and functions are regulated by the Constitution. Members of the Parliament are elected every 4 years in the course of a regular election campaign, and the winning party or coalition then has the legal right to nominate the prime minister, who formulates the program of the government. The head of the state is the president of the Republic, who is elected by the members of the Parliament for 5 years (Gallai & Török, 2003, pp. 347-369).

Democracy was institutionalized in the Republic of Hungary between 1987 and 1989, as a result of which a multi-tier system came into being and state power gained a totally new legal frame of operation: the parliamentary democracy. The first democratically elected government began abolishing the centrally planned economy to develop a new market-based economy.

> From among the three basic governmental systems found in modern democracies—the presidential, the semi-presidential and the parliamentary—the system formed in Hungary with the democratic transition belongs unambiguously to the last. As we shall see, however, Hungarian parliamentarism in the 1900s is a limited parliamentarism possessing many unusual characteristics. (Körösényi, 1999, p. 147)

Among the unusual characteristics of Hungarian parliamentary democracy mentioned by Körösényi are (a) the parliamentary, institution-oriented concept of politics; (b) liberalism as the ruling political concept; (c) nationalism; (d) two versions of the emancipatory-normative concept of politics (institutionalist and anti-institutionalist); (e) a depoliticized concept of the public interest; (f) an antipolitical approach in Hungarian political thought; and (g) a consensus-oriented approach to politics (Körösényi, 1999, pp. 152-157). Körösényi considers the political parties to be the main actors in Hungarian politics and the formation of public opinion. "By the early 1990s, three political camps had formed—the liberal, the national-conservative/Christian and the socialist. The parliamentary parties all belonged to one of these camps" (Körösényi, 1999, p. 31). The socialist camp included the Hungarian Socialist Party, the liberal camp the Alliance of Free Democrats and the Federation of Young Democrats (Fidesz), the national-conservative and Christian camp the Hungarian Democratic Forum, the Independent Smallholders' Party, and the Christian Democratic People's Party.

> During the second half of the 1990s, some change occurred in this structure, with Fidesz moving from the liberal camp to the national-conservative camp. The extra-parliamentary parties and the parties formed by defections from the larger parties were also, for the most part, associated with one of these camps. Each camp was tied together not only by common political and ideological orientation, but also by the very similar socio-cultural composition of their core political élites and electoral bases, and by shared political attitudes and world-views. (Körösényi, 1999, p. 32)

ASPECTS OF MEDIA SYSTEM STRUCTURES AND REGULATIONS

The media in Hungary had become a political institution in their own right well before the first free elections. They started to build themselves a derivative role in political processes as a means of social power. Their significance has been clearly represented in politics, especially in election campaigns. In the Republic of Hungary, TV, among all the media institutions, has gained crucial importance in shaping the political process as one of the most powerful means for political influence. In 1993, the situation became quite dramatic, as TV had become the target of the parties' political struggle. There was no media law officially accepted by the Parliament that could regulate the functioning of Hungarian television until 1996. The Parliament finally passed the new Media Bill on December 21, 1995, and it came into force on January 1, 1996. The Media Law of 1996 regulates the system of supervision of public media (Hungarian Radio, Hungarian Television, Danube Television). The law regulating print media had been created 10 years earlier, in 1986. Law No. 1 about radio and television broadcasting defines what advertising is in general: It is an item during a program announced as public information for some counter-value or counter-performance, or it is program time placed at the disposal of an agent that contributes to the disposal (e.g., sale) of specified or described goods (e.g., products, services, property, rights, obligations) or to its use for some counter-value or to the achievement of a desired effect.

This law also defines the meaning of *political advertisement:* It is a program that attempts to influence; calls for support by participation in the elections of a party or political movement, its successful actions, its candidate, its initiative for a plebiscite; and popularizes a party or movement's name, activity, aims, slogan, emblem, and image. In the paragraph about restrictions and bans on advertising, the law decrees:

> In election periods, political advertisements can be broadcast according to the orders of the laws about the election of members of Parliament, the local and regional candidates, and the mayors. In any other period, political advertisements can only be communicated in connection with a decreed plebiscite. It is prohibited to announce political advertisements in any programs broadcast to foreign countries. Although another person or institution is sponsoring the political advertisement, this does not decrease either the responsibility or the freedom of the broadcaster, and neither the sponsor nor the broadcaster may change the content or placement of the program because of the ad, just the timing. The broadcaster is not responsible for the content of the political advertisement. A political advertisement must be visually and acoustically separated from other pieces of the program, with a special announcement about its character before and after the ad is broadcast. (Jany, Ilosvai, & Bölcskei, 2000)

POLITICAL AND REGULATORY SYSTEMS FOR POLITICAL ADVERTISING

The Hungarian Political System

Parliamentary elections between 1990 and 2002 were based on Act No. 34 of 1989 on the Election of Members of Parliament (1994), enacted by Parliament on October 20, 1989. This law defines a complicated electoral system: a combination of single-member or direct constituencies and proportional representation or list system, with a share of 176 single-member mandates and 210 list mandates (i.e., 152 regional list mandates and 58 national list mandates).

The distribution of Parliament's 386 seats is accomplished by using a combination of majority and the proportional electoral systems; 176 seats in the individual constituencies are distributed through the majority system. In the first round of voting, a candidate becomes an MP if he or she has obtained more than half of the votes validly cast, provided that more than half of the eligible voters of the constituency have cast their votes (Hungary uses an absolute majority system). Political parties may nominate lists in the regional constituencies (in 19 counties and in the capital). In these regional constituencies, 152 seats are distributed in proportion to the valid votes cast for the party lists. Mandates that cannot be distributed due to the mathematical formula prescribed by law and the mandates of regional constituencies where both electoral rounds are invalid are added to the mandates to be distributed among the national lists. The remaining 58 seats, completed with those previously mentioned, are distributed among the national compensation lists. (For more details, see "Constituencies and electoral," 2002).

Regulatory System

Act No. 34 contains the regulations concerning suffrage, the electoral system (members of Parliament, nomination, determination of election results), and electoral procedures (electoral campaign, polling, electoral bodies, polling wards, registration of voters, publicity of electoral procedures, legal remedies, by-elections, and final provisions). Article 11 in chapter 4 ("Electoral Campaign") of the act briefly defines the media presentation of the campaign:

1. Until the day preceding election at the latest, the Hungarian Telegraph Agency, Hungarian Radio, and Hungarian Television shall carry on an equal footing the electoral calls

of parties putting forward candidates. Each party with a candidate shall be given at least one electoral program free of charge. This same duty shall devolve upon the local studios in their respective area of broadcast with regard to the electoral programs of candidates. Other advertisements that go toward making a party or any of its candidates more popular can only be broadcast with a clear message declaring such publicity "Paid Electoral Advertising."

2. During the 30 days preceding the election, Hungarian Radio and Hungarian Television shall cover the parties presenting national lists on an equal footing in their news of electoral events and, in their electoral reports, in proportion to the candidates nominated.

3. On the last day of the electoral campaigns, Hungarian Radio and Hungarian Television shall broadcast the electoral summary reports prepared by parties presenting national lists, under equal program conditions for all parties, for equal lengths of time, and without comment (Act No. 34, 1994, p. 25).

The key concepts in the act are *equality and proportionality in media presentation of the parties and the candidates*. These principles guide the application of the regulatory system to campaigning.

AN OVERVIEW OF PRIOR RESEARCH ON POLITICAL ADVERTISING IN HUNGARY

The emergence of political communication and political marketing (including the study of political advertising) as a distinct domain of publication, a professional endeavor, and a teaching area goes back to 1990 in Hungary. Publications on political advertising, especially televised advertising, were limited to only a few. One of the first published studies on Hungarian political advertising was the analysis of values in party programs by Ágnes Kapitány and Gábor Kapitány (1990). They continued their studies of political programs

during the second, third, and fourth democratic elections in 1994, 1998, and 2002 (Kapitány & Kapitány, 1994, 1998, 2002a).

The goal of their analysis was mainly to answer some questions that the voters were concerned about and that might have had a decisive effect on the outcome of the elections. One of the authors' basic interests was determining what kinds of values the different parties emphasized (e.g., Europe, nation, property, party image, attitude about the communist past), what the main differences and similarities were among the parties in that respect (the quantity and quality of the mentioned values), and what sorts of verbal and nonverbal means of communication the parties used to represent those values (e.g., the form of the party program, the political candidates as performers in the programs, the situation, background music, style and language usage). As a result of their analysis, an "inventory" of the political values used in the election campaign was prepared that led to the conclusion that the political success of a party lies in shared values between the party and the voters.

In 1994, 1998, and 2002, Kapitány and Kapitány performed a similar task in analyzing a sample of the political programs. They were interested in the explicit and implicit values the parties emphasized, the frequency of emphasis, tendencies (trends) in the programs, the influencing and modifying role of the different components of the programs, such as music; background; number of participants; their sex, character, and style; the symbolic meaning of the values; the means of agenda-setting; parties and cultures; and differences and similarities between the parties according to the analyzed values. A cluster analysis of the value groups and party groups shed light on some tendencies that could be categorized as key values for political success: the existence of identical values between the party and the citizens.

I came to a similar conclusion concerning the success of election campaigns (Róka, 1997). The main objective of my research project was to elaborate possible ways of inter-action between media agenda and public agenda in political campaigns from a cross-cultural perspective, taking into account the dynamics of agenda-setting and agenda-building in public opinion formation. The basic theoretical paradigm of the study, offered in an article by Gabriel Tarde (1922),was based on the assumption that newspapers impose the majority of their daily topics upon conversa-tion. In doing so, they activate, direct, and nour-ish first individual, then public, opinion, thus shaping social relationships and acts. After ana-lyzing several election campaigns, I can propose that the difference between the impact of the media and of political communication on the formation of public opinion is this: Successful media communication must be based on agenda-building; in political communication, the emphasis must be on agenda-setting.

I also analyzed the verbal and visual aspects of the 1994 Hungarian election campaign (Róka, 1994) and the growing importance of communication technologies on shaping pub-lic opinion (Róka, 1999a). In the Hungarian parliamentary elections of 1990 and 1994, I studied the role of political commercials (Róka, 1999b), and in the campaigns of 1998 and 2002, marketing strategies (Róka, 2004).

Some studies on the Hungarian election campaigns of 1990, 1994, 1998, and 2002, in their general discussions of the campaigns, have referred to televised political advertisements. For instance, László Kéri, who has evaluated party campaigns (including political programs) since 1990, in one of his most recent publications (Kéri, 2005) analyzed the permanent political campaigns between 2002 and 2004. Some papers in the annual *Political Yearbook of Hungary* (16 volumes) also deal with present and future tendencies of political communi-cation in the era of digital technology (Magyarország politikai évkönyve 2003, 2004). Many studies are devoted to the study of voters' behavior and the role of infocommunication in political processes (Angelusz & Tardos, 2005).

HISTORY AND DEVELOPMENT OF THE USE OF POLITICAL ADVERTISING IN HUNGARY

The growing importance of communication technologies in the political process can be seen by examining election campaigns taking place in different political and media systems and in different time segments. This chapter summarizes the main conclusions of analyses carried out on the 1990, 1994, 1998, and 2002 party election campaigns plus the 2004 European parliamentary elections in Hungary.

The intentional application of marketing techniques in political campaigns is a relatively new phenomenon in Western democracies. More than 10 years have passed since the first marketing-based election campaign in the United States. Bill Clinton was the first American president whose successes and victo-ries in 1992 and in 1996 were due partly to the introduction of a new type of campaign man-agement and partly to the personality and physical endowments of the presidential can-didate, who was apt and talented at using nontraditional campaign methods (Newman, 1999). This new type of American campaign management had a profound impact on Eastern and Central European political cam-paign conventions, and as a result they changed radically in the middle of the 1990s. In the Republic of Hungary, the marketing approach to parliamentary election campaigns has been applied since 1998. The switch to the marketing approach meant that politics became business, where success depends mainly on professional communication skills and unique public relations strategies. The final goal of this approach is to project the most positive image possible of the political candidate and the party and to sell them with the biggest possible "profit." The profit in this case is voter support and the winning of the elections.

What are the most widely used tools and channels for gaining citizens' attention in political campaigns? Since the advent of electrovisual media, television has played the most prominent role in political communication, and one of the major components of any candidate's campaign is good television usage, including televised advertisements and the broadcast of the candidates' debate. Among the new technological advances, the Internet has a crucial influencing potential. In Hungary, the multimedia, in the form of the Internet, became part of the political skirmish in 1998. In 2002, new possibilities provided by the latest advances in telecommunication technology arose, and short message service (SMS) messages transmitted through mobile phones were added to the mix.

EVALUATION OF HUNGARIAN ELECTION CAMPAIGNS FROM 1990 TO 1998

Hungary's first free elections were held in 1990, and this is considered to be a turning point in Hungarian political history. In the spring of that year, a multiparty Parliament was elected (six parties entered Parliament: the Hungarian Democratic Forum, the Independent Smallholders' Party, the Christian Democratic People's Party, the Alliance of Free Democrats, the Alliance of Young Democrats, and the Hungarian Socialist Party), and a coalition government came into power. The Hungarian Democratic Forum built a coalition government, led by Prime Minister József Antall, with the Independent Smallholders' Party and the Christian Democratic People's Party. The coalition had a 59% majority in Parliament. The coalition government represented the national-conservative, Christian Democratic political center, in opposition to the social-liberal and social democratic centers.[1]

In 1994, very much as in 1990, none of the parties had a real chance for victory, so they were forced to form coalitions. There were too many parties coming forward without clearly outlined political programs or with clear overlaps in their platforms. It is obvious that the more parties, the more divided the political agenda must be, and it becomes more difficult for any party to win the elections. The final result of the second democratic election campaign was the formation of a left-wing liberal governing coalition. After 1990, the political culture had undergone a fundamental change: Parties waged disturbing, violent, often rude and negative campaigns against each other, which surely rendered the formation of a coalition government more difficult after the elections. In 1990, almost all the different parties formed an ideological unity against the former communist ideology, but in 1994, there was no really threatening power after the collapse of communism. There were, however, a lot of different parties competing for the voters' support. This, of course, led to an increase in negative campaigning, political arrogance, and populist offers, and to a bigger role for political extremists. Instead of the party's image, the politician's image received greater attention. On the whole, the political culture became more corrupt. That was the reason why the number of voters with uncertain party preference increased (approximately 2 million citizens, or 40% of the electorate). According to the public opinion polls, the majority of citizens were sure only about their opposition to the government of that time because of the high unemployment rate, the drastic economic situation, and worsening public safety.

In 1998, Hungary faced a balanced competition between the right-wing liberals and the left-wing liberals that broke ground for a two-way purification process leading to the formation of the classical "democratic" (or rather social democratic) and "republican" party model. In 1998, this process led to a slight victory for the right-wing coalition.

The parliamentary elections of 1998 differed from the campaigns of 1990 and 1994 in that a basically different political culture could be seen in 1998: The goal, the campaign strategies, the slogans, the atmosphere—every aspect of the political culture was different. The goal this time was not the completion of the change of the regime, as in 1990, nor the replacement of the conservative government, as in 1994, but the continuation of the social liberal progress and the promise of rapid economic and social development. The parties differed in their respective approaches to economic growth and social progress (including the market economy and joining NATO and the European Union). Consequently, the agenda changed, and it required a less negative political culture.

The election campaign of 1998 also created the tradition of the politicians' public debate. This kind of debate was unusual in Hungarian political life: It was adapted from the United States and was thus more liable to draw in the younger generation, which was well acquainted with Anglo-Saxon political tradition. This is the positive side of the campaign. Negative phenomena include the appearance of politically motivated, physical attacks (explosions, the dramatic spread of crime). The 1998 election campaign also brought about another new phenomenon; namely, the energetic participation of the Catholic Church in the campaign. All in all, the parliamentary elections of 1998 introduced a more balanced, tolerant, peaceful political culture despite some unusual, irritating omens (more details are available in Böhm, 2000).

The electrovisual media were the forum for political ads and roundtable discussions. The number of televised ads radically decreased in comparison to 1994. In 1998 (unlike in 1994), the parties were allowed to broadcast only paid advertisements. These ads were short in length (15-30 seconds), which is why they had to aim to achieve maximum impact and also the perfect mixture of verbal, nonverbal, and visual elements. The number of ads broadcast was low,[2] the ads were scheduled in TV programs in a disorganized fashion, and only one or two commercial channels broadcast them.

Great differences could be seen from party to party in regard to the verbal, visual, nonverbal, and auditory methods applied in the ads. The Alliance of Young Democrats differed from the other parties by not using a narrator; instead, it created an atmosphere and shaped meaning with musical accompaniment in its videoclip-like spots, using rapid cuts. In the clips of the Hungarian Socialist Party, the Alliance of Free Democrats, the Independent Smallholders' Party, and the Hungarian Democratic People's Party, the party president himself addressed the voting citizens in studio or live spots. The Hungarian Democratic Forum, the Christian Democratic People's Party, the New Alliance, and the Union all employed narrators, and the Workers' Party used a combination of narration and direct addresses by the party president. The narrators were, without exception, men with decisive, articulate voices. There were significant differences in different parties' advertising spots in regard to the quality and professionalism of production.

The verbal style used by the different parties became simpler and more understandable, reflecting a conversational style in almost all cases. They tried to avoid a high-flown, archaic style full of pathos. As a result of an analysis of cue words and sentences, a hierarchy of social values can be set up that, even in 1998, puts first the ideas of the Hungarian people, the nation, and homeland. There are other values mentioned that are connected with the ideas of democracy, Christianity, family, safety, and economic growth. The key words and slogans are as follows:

- Alliance of Young Democrats: "Choosing the future," "Freedom and wealth: Civic existence for everyone," "What the citizens believe will be realized"
- Hungarian Socialist Party: "Responsible governing," "We want a safe Hungary," "Give Hungary a chance!"
- Alliance of Free Democrats: "Raise your head, Hungary!" "There is still much to do, but we are on the right path"

- Hungarian Democratic Forum: "Order, safety, growth," "1848 Responsible government in Pest! 1998" (This refers to 150 years of "responsible" government in the city of Pest)

In the election campaign of 1998, print advertisements were represented mostly by posters and leaflets. Radio ads served as memory images: They were the appropriate means by which to emphasize party slogans, accompanied by music suitable to the party's image. There were two new strategies applied in the elections, both of which indicated the increased role of telecommunications in the process of political communication. The Internet, as an information forum, became part of the campaign, announcing party programs alongside current events, the locale of election meetings, and the most important information about the candidates. The home pages of the separate parties were carefully balanced with party images (e.g., parties chose Web site colors that could be identified with their logos). One successful, but unusual and unconventional, idea made the 1998 election campaign memorable. The campaign strategy of the Alliance of Young Democrats included an effective performance in this novelty: The president of the party carried out a one-sided phone call with the citizens of the country. Although only a few of the audiovisual advertisements used the format of direct address, this unusual strategy of the Alliance of Young Democrats was based on this format. It was adequate for popularizing, or at least for making known, the party's program by the different layers of society.

The 2002 Hungarian Parliamentary Elections

As a result of the Hungarian parliamentary elections after the change in regime in 1989, the citizens removed the governing coalition on every occasion and replaced them with the opposition. It is also true that all the four democratically elected governments filled the legally provided official time, which indicates a good balance of stability and dynamism in the political system. That is the positive side of the change. On the negative side is a new social phenomenon, namely that the country and its citizens were radically divided into two opposing ideological groups. The country was ripped in two (the right wing and the left wing), and this brought about social turbulence and a never-ending negative campaign. The direct consequences may be seen in the parliamentary election campaign of 2002. But what actually happened?

The 2002 campaign was the fourth time the Hungarian people had chosen their government since the move away from the one-party communist system. The general elections, as usual, took place in two rounds. In 2002, the Hungarian Socialist opposition won a tight first round in the national elections, with a record turnout of over 71.19% of the country's 8.1 million eligible voters. In the second round, the turnout was even higher: 73.5%. Four years earlier, voter turnout was less than 50% in the first round. A large turnout tends to favor large parties, especially on the left. In 1998, the Alliance of Young Democrats came in second in the first round, beating the Socialists decisively only in the second round. In 2002, the Socialists had polled 42.03%, against 41.11% for the right-wing governing coalition; in the third place, at 5.56%, were the liberal Free Democrats.

As a result of the parliamentary elections of 2002, the Hungarian Socialist Party and the Alliance of Free Democrats (who had already governed together from 1994 to 1998) formed a coalition government. It was a narrow victory for the Socialists but a dramatic failure for the Young Democrats. Some communication experts and political scientists claimed that the failure was due partly to the aggressive communication style and overstrained, negative campaign of the Alliance of Young Democrats and partly to image problems: The campaign seemed to be a one-man, dynamic campaign by Viktor Orbán, who concentrated just on the rural areas and neglected the capital city.

Since 1990, this has been the campaign with the lowest standards: it was about small-minded political matters, accusations, and splitting the nation, not about political programs or the future. The crucial question throughout the campaign was *Who will fail?* not *Who will win?* The voters could do nothing but decide whether to support the fear campaign of the Alliance of Young Democrats or the hope campaign of the Hungarian Socialist Party.

The three main strategies used in the 2002 Hungarian election campaign were the debates of the candidates for prime minister, the symbolism in the political advertisements, and the use of new possibilities provided by the Internet and mobile communication (SMS).

Debate

Debate is not traditionally an organic part of Hungarian election campaigns. In 1998 there was a debate between Gyula Horn (the incumbent prime minister and a member of the Hungarian Socialist Party) and Viktor Orbán (candidate for prime minister), but the debate in 2002, the first one since 1998, was only the second political debate ever between candidates for prime minister. The televised debate took place on April 5, 2002, after a long reconciliation between the two opposing parties. The Alliance of Young Democrats was confident in their superiority due to the excellent communication skills of Viktor Orbán. However,

> Viktor Orbán, and Fidesz, misread the voters' mood on a number of crucial points. Mr Orbán's high-handed attitude during a debate with Péter Medgyessy displeased leftwing voters: when the wooden, uncharismatic socialist did far better than had been expected, a tired Mr Orbán had denied

himself the option of having the government-friendly press engage in a damage control exercise after the debate. (Kliphuis, 2002)

Symbolism of Political Advertisements

Symbols are an essential part of politics, as they concentrate the most characteristic features and images of parties and politicians.

> An important feature of symbols is that the political knowledge involved in them does not contain empirical facts, but beliefs and convictions. Their function is not to describe reality but rather to create possibilities for the desired identification and to direct activities. The symbol wants to orient and integrate, saying: realize, identify, follow! From an intellectual point of view, every symbol is a pure simplification on the one hand; on the other, it is a political emotional concentrate. (Galló, 2002, p. 91)

In Hungary, for example, those citizens who wore rosettes from March 15, 2002, until the election day demonstrated their support for the governing coalition.

In any political campaign, symbolic values are attached to political commercials, street posters, leaflets, and icons. In contrast with the 1998 campaign, which was boring and short, started late, and featured average and ordinary political ads, the 2002 campaign was dynamic and unusually arrogant, aggressive, and intense. The coalition of the Alliance of Young Democrats and the Hungarian Democratic Forum broadcast most of the electrovisual advertisements, followed by the Hungarian Socialist Party.

The campaign of the Young Democrats was built on testimonial-like commercials. These ads showed "talking heads" of carefully chosen social types whose speech evoked the feeling that he or she was "one of us." The chosen person mentioned one or two elements from the political program of Young Democrats as if it were his or her own personal desire. The short messages were easy to remember. The setting resembled an interview, and the advertisement was very much like a report. Among the talking heads were entrepreneurs, agricultural workers, intelligentsia, and clerks, but the majority belonged to students. The Alliance of Young Democrats' slogan in 1998 exhibited the same youth-oriented symbolism: "There is another choice. The choice of future." In 2002, the party used a new slogan: "The future has started." In their interpretation, *future* was equal to *youth*. The talking heads (among them, this time, famous personalities) did not speak much about the future program of the party but about some of its already-achieved results. (The new slogan and the verbal statements were often contradictory.) Both in 1998 and in 2002, the viewers were treated to "the success story of Viktor Orbán," which showed the politician in his family circle, among his children, on the football field, among his friends, delivering speeches to huge audiences, and shaking hands with German Chancellor Helmut Kohl.

The opposition, the Hungarian Socialist Party, started its campaign in 1998 with the slogan "Growth, chance and safety." In 2002, the Socialist Party's clips were very much alike: They showed people going to vote as a narrator spoke about the wishes of different social layers; at the end, one could see Péter Medgyessy, the candidate for prime minister, walking in the street (as people gathered behind him), drinking coffee, saying good-bye to his wife, and taking a seat at the end of a long conference table with the members of the new government. There was real chaos in the party's leaflets, even in the color symbolism, and there were a lot of communication errors in the chosen slogans: "Hungary belongs to all of us!" "Together for the future!" "In agreement with the nation," "Hungary deserves more," and more of the same. In the Socialist Party's campaign in 2002, voter mobilization did not take place, and the Socialists failed to do with Péter Medgyessy what the Young Democrats had done with Viktor Orbán in emphasizing his personality. The Young

Democrats' message about the image of the enemy inspired the Socialists to introduce a program of peace, but it was not a strategic program: it was messy, visually incoherent, and missing political symbolism. The Alliance of Free Democrats made an attempt to introduce a negative campaign that was humorous, full of witty ideas and with less arrogance. They used several slogans, including "Change the government!" "The country is with us!" "Change style, change government!" and "Stop stealing!" The Free Democrats' campaign emphasized their party leader's image, and their campaign humor was successful in the short term, but it was not suitable for building the overall symbolism of the campaign and clarifying the party's image (for more details, see Hargitai, 2002).

The main manifestations of the specific symbols used by the different parties are political advertisements. In 2002, just eight parties (those who managed to get on the national list) could prepare political ads.[3] In previous campaigns, the clips had been about 5 minutes long; in 2002, they lasted for just 1 minute. Ágnes Kapitány and Gábor Kapitány (2002b), as a result of their thorough analysis of the campaign clips, drew the following conclusions: the main social values mentioned in the clips were family, children, youth, wealth, advancement, upswing, support, help, trustworthiness, education, the Hungarian people, homeland, and nation. The governing coalition often mentioned future, energy, success, optimism, activity, and openness. Certain values were characteristic of the right-wing parties only: family estate (farm) and defense of Hungarian land. The opposition (left-wing parties) preferred using values such as democracy, liberty, secure employment, improvement of the public health system, opposition to corruption, clarity in public life.

In the 2002 election campaign, the parties used explicit and implicit values. The Alliance of Young Democrats–Hungarian Civic Party emphasized much more explicit values than any other parties: supported argumentation, realization of goals, family, children, big family, family economy, staying focused, loving children, togetherness, human openness, powerfulness, a chance for life, maturity, continuity, self-awareness, advancement, security, youth, victory, progress, fight, determination, validity, the vision of 21st century fulfilling its promise, future, persistence, concreteness, enthusiasm, upswing, defense of Hungarian land, a worthy life, bigger apartment, money is not everything, no restricting measures, optimism, happiness, civic duty, help, success, pleasantness, education, no tuition fee, support, talent, wish to act, conscious action, venture, intelligibility. Values in written form included future, belief in the power of love and union, tremendous enthusiasm, and action first—words second. Implicit values included activity, importance of family, economic results, importance of traditions, fighting, holding on, high spirits, soundness, the importance of the future, being Hungarian, trustworthiness, huge contrast between old and new, international reputation, independence, help, success, sportsmanship, love, importance of education, mass support, role of religion, happiness, support of rural areas.

The Hungarian Socialist Party pointed out many fewer explicit values than the Young Democrats: happy old age, democracy, united nation, authenticity, trustworthy person, fairness, security of welfare, prosperous change of regime, profitable agriculture, modern education, calmness, liberty, support, new jobs, leader followed by the whole nation, flourishing country, country in which everyone is at home. Values in written form included widening support for family, modern education, higher income, reasonable old-age pension, new agricultural system, and "the country is with us!" Implicit values included happy youth and old age, central importance of family (children), unity, elegance, soundness, balance, calmness, union, professionalism, and the role of religion.

The Alliance of Free Democrats used the following explicit values: reduction of taxes,

envisioning but not bluffing, democracy, clarity in public life, a public health system worthy of the human being, advancement, young democracy, wealth, stopping corruption, realistic economic policy, living according to one's own beliefs, being successful, liberty, more money, real reforms. Values in written form included reduction of taxes, reform of public health system, stopping corruption, "the Alliance of Free Democrats is guaranteed," evaluation of knowledge, and "let's change government." Implicit values included financial security, democracy, health, fearlessness, progress, being determined, humor, being critical, and realism (Kapitány & Kapitány, 2002b, pp. 22-27). The list of explicit and implicit values shows continuity from campaign to campaign in the applied symbolism of the main parties, with a bit more emphasis on typically Hungarian symbols (such as the rosette), family, and attitudes in the 2002 campaign.

Online and Mobile Communication

In the era of digital information technology, telecommunications and multimedia are essential parts of the political process. They were first applied in Hungarian election campaigning in 1998, but they obtained real importance in 2002. In Hungary, 23 of the 144 parties registered by the Hungarian Supreme Court have official Web sites. The main political parties were able to create effective interactive communication with the citizenry through the Internet, which means that online communication became a new qualitative feature of political participation (although online and offline communications of the different parties did not differ much strategically, all communications represented the general conventions, manners, and rules of the party communicating), but it has not yet been proven to what extent online communication contributes to the success of a party.

In 2002, mobile communication came forward in the form of an SMS-campaign

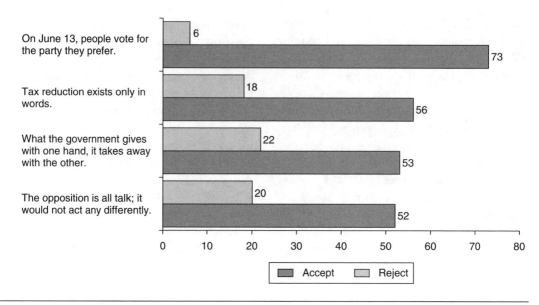

Figure 20.1   Hungary: Key Attitudes Toward the Government and the Opposition

SOURCE: Kód Piac- és Közvéleménykutató Intézet (2004).

technique between the two rounds of the elections when the campaign started deteriorating. In the fourth Hungarian democratic elections, SMS messages were part of the aggressive, rude, indecent campaign on the part of both the left-wing and right-wing parties.

Strategic Political Marketing Implications of the 2004 European Parliamentary Elections in Hungary

As in the majority of European Union member states, in Hungary the most powerful opposition party won the elections. The right-wing Alliance of Young Democrats–Hungarian Civic Alliance obtained the most favorable result in all the 25 European Union countries, with its 42.43% share of the votes. Turnout at the EU elections was lower than at the national parliamentary elections held every fourth year, yet Hungary still came in third in terms of turnout, compared with its newly joined counterparts in other East-Central European countries[4] (Gyévai, 2004, p. 15).

The results of public opinion polls showed that most of the eligible voters considered

voting on June 13, 2004, as a vote of confidence against the present governing coalition. It meant that the citizens tended to vote for the party that they would have liked to have in government. Kód Piac- és Közvéleménykutató Intézet (the Code Market and Public Opinion Research Institute) carried out a monthly survey using a 1200-person sample evaluating the dynamics of the political market, how parties' and politicians' images changed, changes in political agenda, and the application of political strategies and tactics. The surveys showed a general trend toward citizen disappointment with government policy, resulting in political and economic pessimism among voters (Kód Piac- és Közvéleménykutató Intézet, 2004). The message of the Socialists' EU campaign (their slogan was "while the government works, others just talk") failed to strengthen the confidence of citizens toward government, as illustrated in the poll survey results outlined in Figure 20.1.

From among the four parliamentary parties, the Alliance of Free Democrats started the campaign first and conducted the most intense campaign. It used all the means of communication available for campaign purposes: television spots, radio ads, street posters, and leaflets. The TV spots were mostly talking heads representing ordinary people who answered the same question: "What do you need in life?" They shared their ideas about individual freedom, religious tolerance, and tax reduction. The party president and the mayor of Budapest (the leader of the party nomination list), as talking heads, summarized the main message of the party, saying, "We liberals believe in the personal freedom of the individual, and this individual is you. If you choose us, you choose yourself. A new beginning is coming." The 22-week campaign was addressed to those supporters with liberal values.

The Hungarian Democratic Forum used, as a marketing tool, outdoor advertising facilities. Besides street posters, they prepared only a few radio and some television spots. Their campaign was built on the party president's personality and image: Ibolya Dávid spoke up for a corruption-free Hungary, which was emphasized by the slogan "For a normal Hungary! For fairness in public life!" The Hungarian Socialist Party (the major party of the governing coalition) applied a peculiar strategy: At the beginning, they hardly campaigned at all, but later, toward the end, the party campaigned intensively. They initiated a "roadshow" and television and street poster campaigns. The messages did not contain promises, just a laconic implication about their activity: "They don't talk, they act." The main character in their political ads, which were simple in design, was the ordinary citizen. The slogan used did not reveal any further details about the party agenda, except to repeat the same mantra: "Because others just talk! On June 13 [vote for the] Hungarian Socialist Party." It was a typical governing party slogan, and they used it to address the main core of their supporters. Although the Hungarian Socialist Party had announced that they would conduct a positive campaign, after a series of attacks from the Alliance of Young

Democrats, they changed to a negative campaign, using the key phrase "Lie production" and the slogan "Together, let's stop the lie factory of the Alliance of Free Democrats."

The Alliance of Young Democrats created a two-step campaign. In March, they announced their "National Petition," which touched on the most problematic social spheres and topics: health care, agriculture, employment, housing, and growing energy prices. The advertising campaign, in the form of statements from ordinary people, corresponded with the thematic scope of the National Petition. In April, the image of the campaign leader was introduced. Pál Schmitt, a former fencer and diplomat, is a popular public figure whose social role is associated less with politics than with success in both professional and private life. His role was to encourage the citizens to participate in the elections, saying, "We can only succeed together! We should vote for the Alliance of Young Democrats on June 13." The party slogan, "Job, home, safety," was addressed to both right-wing and left-wing voters. The party made use of all the available communication channels: street posters, television, radio, leaflets, and the press. They published the Schmitt newspaper (single issue, tabloid-like layout, easy-to-understand language and style) and organized a poster exhibition (negative campaign against the government), and Viktor Orbán—the former prime minister—delivered a mobilizing speech at the Technical University on June 6 (a week before the elections). His main message can be paraphrased thus: The Hungarian Socialist Party could be defeated only if everyone participated and voted for the Alliance of Young Democrats.

As a final round-up of the whole EU campaign, MTV1 (the public television channel) broadcast a roundtable discussion with the main representatives of the four parliamentary parties[5] in prime time, between 8:00 and 9:00 p.m.

In Hungary, the European Parliament election campaign was actually a competition between the Hungarian Socialist Party (the incumbent party) and the Alliance of Young Democrats (the opposition). The political motivation of the Hungarian voter was partially similar to, and partially different from, the other EU member states. The national circumstances tended to determine the campaign generally. The results of the elections and the public opinion polls demonstrated that the Alliance of Young Democrats gained the votes of the inhabitants of most of the rapidly developing towns. During the two-round parliamentary elections of 2002, the civilian center now mainly supported the right wing. The Alliance of Young Democrats attained more than 50% support in most of the larger towns. The villages and market towns of the rural areas with farming traditions rewarded the right wing with more than two thirds of the votes, but the Hungarian Socialist Party sometimes did not even gain 20% of the votes. The Socialists, who had previously been unshakeable, were now forced back to the support of the circle of men-in-the-street of the Kádár era. They won without question in the former citadels of socialist industrialization and the worker districts of Budapest, and they performed relatively well in the country towns of former agricultural works (Tölgyesi, 2004).

It is a fact that the success of the Alliance of Young Democrats was a result of the serious campaign errors of the Hungarian Socialist Party. The strategies and the techniques of the major governing party were inefficient: It ignored the issues of the EU, and it spoke about national political affairs only superficially.

> When it realized that the Alliance of Young Democrats had brought back the unmerciful negative campaign methodology of 2002 it could not think of anything else but two slogans. It is difficult to decide which of the two was worse, but most probably the "lie production" ad carried the palm and the great idea of the ad "Hungarian Socialist Party again!" is just the second-place winner. But the failure of the campaign's finish is just a symptom. This phenomenon can be traced back to the time when the government

started losing its support a year ago. Just 34% of the total number of the 38% of eligible voters who participated in the European Parliament elections trusts the Hungarian Socialist Party. (Mészáros, 2004, p. 5)

SUMMARY

Having analyzed the different strategies used in the 1990, 1994, 1998, and 2002 Hungarian parliamentary election campaigns and the 2004 EU parliamentary election campaign, we can conclude that Hungarian political culture needs further experimentation, exploration, and improvement. The Hungarian political palette is much too fragmented, and this creates a barrier to the necessary desire to develop a suitable forum for the debate of party leaders and the declaration of party politics. At present, the party program reaches the citizens only in implicit, hidden, and often symbolic forms in party messages.

Although the symbols of the left-wing parties have been sketchy, unskillful, and too rational, not allowing enough space for emotional influence, the right-wing parties have provided too big a dose of too many different symbols, most of which were more emotional than rational. This lack of balance made the campaigns superficial, irrational, and sometimes misleading in 2002 and 2004.

One could hardly judge the effectiveness of agenda-building, although some of the crucial social questions appeared as cue words and sentences in the mediated messages of parties (for example, family, health care, education, joining the European Union). Hungarian campaigning is colorless and rife with technical and rhetorical errors. It is a competition without any coherence, in which the citizen is very often just a means to, but not the goal in, the struggle of the parties.

NOTES

1. Four coalitions existed at that time: (a) the middle-class or liberal coalition, consisting of the

Alliance of Young Democrats and Alliance of Free Democrats in cooperation with the Agricultural Alliance and the Party of Entrepreneurs; (b) the left-wing coalition, consisting of the Hungarian Socialist Party and the National Alliance of the Hungarian Trade Unions; (c) the national conservative coalition (the governing coalition), consisting of the Hungarian Democratic Forum, Christian Democratic People's Party, and United Smallholders' Party; and (d) the right-wing radicals, which included the Hungarian Party of Truth and Life.

2. The Christian Democratic People's Party broadcast only 5 ads; the Alliance of Young Democrats–Hungarian Civic Party, 4; Hungarian Socialist Party, 2; Hungarian Democratic People's Party, 2; New Alliance, 2; Independent Small-holders's Party, 2; Union of Being Together for Hungary, 2; Hungarian Party of Truth and Life, 1; Workers' Party, 1.

3. In comparison, in 1990, 46 different ads were aired; in 1994, 15 ads; and in 1998, 12 ads.

4. Compare rates of participation: Latvia, 41%; Lithuania, 39%; Hungary, 38%; Czech Republic, 29%; Estonia, 27%; Slovenia, 26%; Poland, 21%; Slovakia, 20%.

5. Pál Schmitt, leader of the nomination list of the Alliance of Young Democrats; László Kovács, president of the Hungarian Socialist Party; Gábor Kuncze, president of the Alliance of Free Democrats; and Ibolya Dávid, president of the Hungarian Democratic Forum.

REFERENCES

Act No. 34 of 1989 on the Election of Members of Parliament. (1994, January 20). *Magyar Közlöny*, (7).

Angelusz, R., & Tardos, R. (2005). *Törések, hálók, hidak* [Breaks, nets, and bridges]. Budapest, Hungary: Demokrácia Kutatások Magyar Központja Alapítvány.

Böhm, A. (2000). A harmadik választás politikai kultúrája [Political culture in the third election]. In A. Böhm (Ed.), *Parlamenti választások 1998. Politikai szociológiai körkép. Századvég* [The 1998 parliamentary elections: Political and sociological panorama].

Constituencies and electoral districts. (2002). Retrieved January 31, 2006, from the Ministry of Interior Central Data Processing Registration and Election Office Web site: http://www.election.hu/parval2002/ve02/veeng/start1_en_ind.htm

Gallai, S., & Török, G. (2003). *Politika és politikatudomány* [Politics and political science]. Budapest, Hungary: Aula Kiadó.

Galló, B. (2002). Sokk volt és elég. A szimbólumok szerepe a kampányban [It was too much and enough: The role of symbols in the campaign]. In M. Sükösd & M. Vásárhelyi (Eds.), *Hol a határ? Kampánystratégiák és kampányetika, 2002* [Where is the end? Campaign strategies and campaign ethics]. Budapest, Hungary: Elet és Irodalom.

Gyévai, Z. (2004). Messze volt az urna [The ballot box is too far away]. *Figyelö, 25*, 14–17.

Hargitai, L. (2002). Érez vagy gondolkodik a magyar választópolgár? Politikai hirdetések összehasonlító elemzése, 1998, 2002 [Does the Hungarian citizen feel or think? A comparative analysis of similarities and differences in political advertisements]. In *Médiakutató, 7*. Retrieved 2002 from http://www.mediakutato.hu-archivum/2002/nyar

Jany, J., Ilosvai, G., & Bölcskei, J. (2000). *Médiajogi kézikönyv* [Handbook of media law]. Budapest, Hungary: Osiris kiadó.

Kapitány, Á., & Kapitány, G. (1990). *Értékválasztás. A választási pártmüsorok elemzése* [Value choice: The analysis of party election programs]. Budapest, Hungary: Müvelödéskutató Intézet.

Kapitány, Á., & Kapitány, G. (1994). *Értékválasztás. A választási és kampánymüsorok Szimbolikus és értéküzenetei* [Value choice. Symbolic and value messages in campaign programs.]. Budapest, Hungary: Societas.

Kapitány, Á., & Kapitány, G. (1998). *Értékválasztás '98* [Value choice 1998]. Budapest, Hungary: Új Mandátum Könyvkiadó.

Kapitány Á., & Kapitány, G. (2002a). *Értékválasztás 2002* [Value choice 2002]. Budapest, Hungary: Új Mandátum Könyvkiadó.

Kapitány Á., & Kapitány, G. (2002b). A választási kampánymüsorok értéküzenetei és szimbólumai [Value messages and symbols in election campaign programs.]. *Jel-Kép, 3*, 17–36.

Kéri, L. (2005). *Választástól népszavazásig* [From the campaign to election day]. Budapest, Hungary: Kossuth kiadó.

Kliphuis, J. (2002). Surprise lead for Hungarian Socialists. Retrieved 2002 from the Radio Netherlands Web site: http://www.rnw.nl

Kód Piac- és Közvéleménykutató Intézet [Code Market and Public Opinion Research Institute]. (2004). Unpublished document prepared for party leadership use.

Körösényi, A. (1999). *Government and politics in Hungary*. Budapest, Hungary: Central European University Press.

Mészáros, T. (2004). A kihívás napja [The day of challenge]. *168 óra, 16*(24), 5.

Newman, B. I. (Ed.). (1999). *Handbook of political marketing*. Thousand Oaks, CA: Sage.

Róka, J. (1994, July). *Media and elections: The role of visual manipulation in political image-making*. Paper presented at the Turbulent Europe: Conflict Identity and Culture Convention, London.

Róka, J. (1997). *Public space: From rumour through conversation to opinion-formation*. Unpublished manuscript, Central European University, Budapest, Hungary.

Róka, J. (1999a). Do the media reflect or shape public opinion? In B. I. Newman (Ed.), *Handbook of political marketing* (pp. 505–518). Thousand Oaks, CA: Sage.

Róka, J. (1999b). Party broadcasts and effects on Hungarian elections since 1990. In L. L. Kaid (Ed.), *Television and politics in evolving European democracies* (pp. 113–130). Commack, NY: Nova Science.

Róka, J. (2004). Forming political culture and marketing strategies in a central-European setting. *Journal of Political Marketing, 3*(2), 87–108.

Tarde, G. (1922). *L'Opinion et la foule* (4th ed.). Paris: Alcan.

Tölgyesi, P. (2004). *Kommentárok a választások után* [Commentary after the election]. Unpublished manuscript.

21

Fifteen Years of Televised Political Advertising Developments in Bulgaria

LILIA RAYCHEVA

A COUNTRY IN TRANSITION

The period of transformation to democracy and a market economy, which started in 1989, has posed significant social challenges to the people of Bulgaria. The transition was slowed down by delayed legislation, aggressive political behavior, and underdeveloped markets. All this caused rapid impoverishment, a high rate of unemployment, and a loss of established social benefits, such as free health care and free education. Thus the country lost the momentum generated by the quick start of democratic reforms, missed the chance to get integrated with the Central European countries into European structures, and entered the 21st century under the already launched Currency Board.

Since the turn of the century, Bulgaria has begun to improve its legislative, economic, and social situation. It joined NATO in 2004, signed the EU Accession Treaty in April 2005, and is expected to become a member of the European Union in 2007.

Currently, gross domestic product (GDP) per capita in Bulgaria equals 4108 Bulgarian Lev (BGN)—approximately €2100. The average monthly wage is 284 BGN (€145). As of 2001, Bulgaria's population was 8 million, grouped into about 3 million households. It consists of Bulgarians (84%), Turks (9%), Roma ("Gypsies") (5%), and others (2%). The large majority of the population (84%) professes the Eastern Orthodox faith, and 12% are Muslim. The population has decreased by more than a million since the last population census (which was taken in 1985, prior to the period of transition), mainly due to aging and emigration ("Census 2001," 2001).

More than a decade of political, economic, and social upheavals in Bulgaria led directly to the profound changes in the system of mass media and the trends in its development. Of all Bulgaria's institutions, it was the mass media that were the quickest and most flexible in their reaction to the transformation to democracy after 1989. The processes of decentralization, liberalization, and privatization began spontaneously, and in a short time, a completely new journalistic landscape was formed,

359

in which different patterns of media consumption and new advertising strategies were introduced. However, like the politicians (both former and newly hatched), journalists were not ready to shoulder fully their new role and the subsequent responsibilities of the Fourth Estate in a society in transition.

Many challenges were encountered in the process of establishing the new press. The tight ideological control over the mass media was replaced by economic motives. A wide range of highly varied media quickly took shape: political, popular, quality, topical, and specialized. A special group of publications was established to target foreign information consumers, and periodicals were issued in English, French, German, Russian, and Turkish. The monopoly of the state-owned Bulgarian Telegraph Agency (established in 1892) was broken by the new private press agencies, such as the Balkan Agency, BGNES, and online agencies.

The periodical press has shown a stable increase since the beginning of the millennium in the number of commercial dailies (from 36 in 1999 up to 63 in 2003, a 75% increase), and those with national coverage have increased 100%. Nondailies have marked a similarly high growth: Their number grew from 115 in 1999 to 221 in 2003 (a 92% increase). Daily newspaper reach among adults is 45%. Men seem to be greater consumers (60%) than women (31%). Cover prices are from 0.40 to 1.00 BGN (€ 0.5).

In 2002, advertising expenditures amounted to 60 million BGN (€31 million) for newspapers, 40 million BGN (€20 million) for magazines, and 200 million BGN (€102 million) for television. From 1999 to 2003, advertising revenues for the dailies increased more than 300% and for the nondailies, about 90%. Advertising expenditures in the media are expected to mark a steady growth in the coming years ("World press trends," 2004).

In contrast to the turbulent transformation in the print media, the changes in the electronic media were slower, incomplete, and lacked general consistency. After 7 years of unfruitful discussion about several bills, in 1996 the National Assembly adopted the Radio and Television Act, which was amended several times afterwards. In 2005, there were about 209 television and 118 radio channels available in Bulgaria, offered by a large number of national, regional, and local radio and TV operators. Three national TV channels and two national radio stations are broadcast for free. These and other channels are, additionally, distributed through more than 1800 cable networks and more than 20 nationwide satellite networks. Two telecommunications operators provide a digital package of program services. Radio and television broadcasting on the Internet is in embryo. The alternative of privately owned broadcast and cable radio and TV networks gravely challenged the monopoly of the State, but licensing catalyzed the process, and, although it is still rather meager, a radio and TV market was established in Bulgaria ("Current developments in," 2004).

Although the Bulgarian public is offered a highly varied media menu, expectations that the media would aid the processes of democratization in a purposeful and effective manner proved unrealistically high. They were in need of transformation themselves. Changes in ownership and the end of single-party control were not sufficient to render them professional. Although the journalism guild (for press, radio, and TV) adopted an ethical code in 2004, it failed to build the mechanisms that would sustain it, and in many cases the media react inadequately to important and publicly significant national issues, as well as to a number of professional problems. The activity of the civil-society structures proved insufficient, too. Prior to the most recent parliamentary elections in 2005, some of the most renowned PR agents had promised in public not to buy media in the upcoming campaign, thus indirectly admitting that in some of the previous campaigns, the media had been rendering political services. "Freedom of speech" and "independent journalism" were convenient buzzwords for many a nongovernmental organization disbursing the funds of European and Transatlantic institutions. The activities of these organizations, however, proved in the long run to be erratic, limited, and ineffective.

The model of democracy that was being developed in Bulgaria delegated the difficult tasks of transition to the political elite and eliminated the broad participation of the people in the process of transformation. Although superficially heterogeneous, the political and media environments (especially during campaigns) were never aware of the parameters of pluralism—or of independence. Due to this lack of awareness, the media failed to meet expectations and carry through on their chance of contributing effectively to the process of social transformation, as they failed to seek society's active participation (Gross, 2001).

In the last 15+ years, there have been three presidential elections (in 1992, 1996, and 2001), six parliamentary elections (in 1990, 1991, 1994, 1997, 2001, and 2005), four local elections (in 1991, 1995, 1999, and 2003), and the appointment of 10 governments. An encouraging sign is that the last two governments successfully completed their mandate.

The comparative stability in the executive power during the last eight years had spread relief in the political and economical development of the country. For the first time since the beginning of the democratic changes, after the parliamentary elections in 2005 the new government found such favorable starting conditions, especially in respect to the financial status of the state. The Simeon Sax Coburg Gotha government (2001-2005) left a fiscal reserve of more than 5 billion BGN, which is almost 1 billion BGN more than is necessary for the 2005 budget, and a level of unemployment of 10.95%, which is the lowest in almost 9 years ("Unemployment in July," 2005).

Nevertheless, apathy about elections started to displace the initial political euphoria in Bulgaria. After the elective boom triggered by the political changes that began in 1989, the relative share of people who refused to vote in Bulgaria gradually but unswervingly began to increase, and only half those eligible to vote voted in the local elections of 1999. Characteristically, since then, all the elections (parliamentary, presidential, and local) have been seen as an opportunity for a protest vote by the Bulgarian people against the political class. Apparently, Bulgarian voters refuse to yield to any mass media, political, or sociological propaganda, especially when it is negative. Thus they have outstripped politicians, sociologists, and the media in gaining civil self-awareness and behavior.

After the parliamentary elections of 2005, in which the electoral activity was 55.76%, seven political parties entered into Parliament, but none of them succeeded in reaching a majority. Because of imperfections in the Election Act regarding elections to National Assembly positions, it became possible for the Movement for Rights and Liberties to mobilize the majority of its emigrant electorate in Turkey (Turks living in Turkey but holding Bulgarian passports), and the Turkish vote raised it to the third position. The traditional role of this party as a balancing factor in the political arena had been considerably shaken. This happened because of the growing exasperation in society concerning the Turkish image of this party and its aggressive acquisition, after the occupation, of a great portion of preaccession European funding. The popular discontent with this party was expressed in the people's sweeping support for the newly established coalition, Ataka (Attack), which had a markedly nationalistic character. Without any special campaigning for less than 2 months the coalition was able to attract 9% of the ballots and win the position of fourth political force in Parliament. This became possible mainly through the efforts of its leader's television program of the same name, which had been broadcast over one of the cable television channels. Even without a clear policy or program, the presence of Ataka in Bulgarian society, which by now was exhausted with endless political fights, might attract more sympathizers in the future. The aggressive vocabulary it uses, however, could menace the country's unique ethnic status quo—one of Bulgaria's great achievements during the transition period.

None of the seven parties in Parliament after the last elections had the necessary majority to form a government independently. With great difficulty, 52 days after the elections and after two abortive efforts by the Bulgarian Socialist Party [BSP] and the National Movement Simeon the Second (NMSS), with destructive floods in many regions of the country, a coalition government of the BSP, NMSS, and Movement for Rights and Liberties was voted into existence with the mandate of the Movement. The three main goals uniting the newly established social-liberal coalition are European integration, accelerated economic growth, and social responsibility. The coalition faces serious political, economic, and social challenges on the way to those goals.

In the process of creating a multiparty political system in Bulgaria, which was a great democratic achievement by itself, all the elections after 1989 played an important part in laying the foundation for political marketing and campaigning, especially in the electronic media.

Televised political advertising, plus a strong press and radio involvement in defining voters' final choice, have played a significant role in election campaigns from the very beginning of the democratization of political life in Bulgaria. Thus the mass media have had a great deal of influence on the strong politicization of the Bulgarian people. The press has frequently distorted the country's political processes, yet it exerted considerable influence on public opinion (Raycheva, 1999b).

PARLIAMENT AND PRESIDENT IN THE ELECTORAL SYSTEM

Under the terms of its Constitution, Bulgaria is a republic with a parliamentary system of government. The National Assembly is composed of 240 deputies elected for a term of 4 years.

(Only the Seventh Grand National Assembly of 1990, the first after the democratic changes, consisted of 400 MPs.) Any Bulgarian citizen who does not hold a dual citizenship, who is at least 21 years old, who has not been convicted of a crime, and who is not currently in prison is eligible to run for member of Parliament. Members of Parliament represent not only their constituencies but the entire nation ("An election act for members," 2005).

The president is the head of state in the Republic of Bulgaria. He is assisted by a vice president. The president is elected directly by the people for a term of 5 years. Every Bulgarian who is a citizen by birth, is at least 40 years old, has the qualifications to run for member of Parliament, and has lived in the country for the last 5 years is eligible to run for president. The latter condition was added in 2001 partly to frustrate any possible attempts on the part of Tsar Simeon II, the Bulgarian monarch in exile who lived in Madrid, to run for head of state ("An election act for president," 2001).

The president of the Republic schedules the elections for the National Assembly and for local administrative bodies, as well as national referenda decided upon by the National Assembly. The territory of the Republic of Bulgaria is divided into municipalities and regions. The municipal council is the local self-administrative body of municipalities. The residents of the respective municipality elect its members for a term of 4 years by a legislatively set order. The mayor is the executive authority of a municipality. The town's residents or the municipal council elect him or her for a term of 4 years by a legislatively set order ("A local elections," 2003).

It could be said that the consensus achieved by political forces in the 1990 roundtable discussions about the convocation of a Grand National Assembly marked the start of legalization of democratic processes in Bulgaria. The major task of that assembly was to develop and adopt a new constitution.

Actually, the work on a legislative foundation began with the preparations for the convocation of the Grand National Assembly, which required outlining of the main parameters of future political activity in Bulgaria. Parallel with this, efforts had been made to establish rules for the organization and financing of the election campaigns. Tension was heightened not only by the pressing deadlines but by the new and turbulent political situation. The long years of one-party dominance were replaced by a host of new political parties, unions, and organizations that constantly split, regrouped, and entered into coalitions, especially on the eve of elections. By snatching the opportunity to air the campaign activity, television catalyzed this political reshuffling.

Legislation created a number of documents that legally regulated various aspects of the political parties' activities during election campaigns. One of the most sensitive and difficult areas proved to be campaign and party financing. It should be pointed out here that, from the outset of democratization, public opinion and expectations found it difficult to accept the private financial initiative in politics. This is why government institutions were entrusted with the procedure and control of this type of activity, especially in regard to political canvassing via national state-owned electronic media, where firm rules were instituted and strictly observed. After 1992, with the advent of private radio and TV stations, purchase of broadcasting time became possible under the relevant regulations. Parties took advantage of this at first timidly and then more confidently after the parliamentary and presidential elections of 2001.

As in other democracies, election campaign financing in Bulgaria is provided by two major sources: government and nongovernment sources ("A political parties," 2001).

Government funding is realized chiefly in the following forms:

- Partial advance subsidizing from the State Budget of the parties and coalitions represented in Parliament, in proportion to the votes cast for them in the previous election
- Short-term credit (usually interest free) for registered extraparliamentary forces and independent candidates
- Postelection equalization of the funds received by the parties, coalitions, and independent candidates in proportion to the votes cast for them, under an order established by the Council of Ministers

These financial rules seemed clear at first sight; however, they exhibited their weak points in time. In practice, the State outwardly tolerated the forces represented in Parliament. In contrast to this, the extraparliamentary forces and independent candidates faced enormous, complex hardships that further complicated their already difficult race with the megaparties.

According to the election laws, candidates for elective offices (in elections for parliamentary, presidential, and local positions) must report their campaign funding methods publicly, before their constituencies and the respective election commissions ("An election act for the," 1990). In the majority of cases, this law has not been observed. Moreover, debtors from earlier campaigns often encountered no barriers to financial assistance from the State for new campaigns.

Nongovernment funding is realized in the following forms:

- Membership fees: Funds accumulated from membership fees, although a regular source of income, are important only for the big parties and coalitions with well-constituted and organized local structures. In the present condition of economic stagnation they often are merely symbolic, demonstrating rather the member's affiliation with the ideology of the respective political force, than a notable contribution to a party's budget.
- Private donations: Private donations are receivable along three lines:

    — Spontaneous contributions to the party coffers to meet the general needs of the respective political force

— Sale of promotional materials (stamps, cards, posters, balloons, etc.) or tickets to specially organized events (meetings, performances, concerts, etc.)

— Fund-raising campaigns (usually before the elections). The maximum size of individual contributions is fixed by the legislative act for the respective election

- Donations from sympathizers to the respective political force are also very encouraging, especially during the most decisive campaign days. Although this type of donation is predominantly symbolic in character, sometimes ample contributions are made by individuals, either so they or their nominee will be placed on the election lists or to ensure certain economic preferences for themselves after the election.

- Sponsorships by nongovernmental Bulgarian organizations: Sponsorships actually bring in the most money, but this type of activity is also the worst regulated. Funds come either from party firms (offspring of the respective political force) or from nonparty organizations. The financial bond of the party firms with their political patrons is comparatively clear. Financial participation of nonparty firms, especially of those which dub themselves "independent," is often unpredictable. Many organizations invest in politics so they will have a say in the redistribution of national wealth in periods of decentralization, to reap the dividends. That is why often the same firm will support different political forces, depending on the probability of that party's electoral victory.

- Sponsorship from abroad: Foreign sponsorship is the most delicate element in campaign funding. Legislation states clearly that candidates for president, members of Parliament, mayors, and municipal councilors should not receive foreign aid, donations, or contributions from foreign countries or from foreign government agents or independent persons ("An election act for the," 1990). This clause of the election law is one of the most frequently violated, and violations are seldom sanctioned, irrespective of the fact that, in case of violation, the act provides for canceling the election returns and confiscation of the received sums by the State. Actually, the fact is that no political force that has managed to secure intellectual, material, or financial support from abroad has been sanctioned so far.

In spite of some already established traditions (for instance, the proportional voting system), the existing legislation was further refined so that the preparations for every election are now the same. The regulations regarding access to the state-owned national electronic mass media during election campaigns also experienced a notable change.

Thus, for example, the 1991 Election of Members of the National Assembly, Municipal Councilors, and Mayors Act contained only one article providing the right of access to the national mass media to all candidates for members of parliament, parties, and coalitions ("An act for," 1991). The mode of access was regulated by a decision of the Grand National Assembly. The 1995 Local Elections Act had already introduced 13 articles regulating the featuring of political forces in the national media during election campaigns ("A local elections," 1995). Problems arising in each election campaign were to be settled by the Central Electoral Commission (CEC) and the Council of Ministers.

The development of these decisions deserves a closer look. The 1991 regulations providing for televised election campaigning generally followed the same logic as that of the preparatory rules for the Grand National Assembly. Strictly fixed in duration and form, political advertising was allowed only on the national state-owned TV network and was financed exclusively through the State Budget. During the 1994 elections, the regional radio and television centers of the state-owned Bulgarian National Radio and Bulgarian National Television were allowed to air political campaign material as long as they observed strict regulations in regard to what candidates (who were listed in the respective constituencies) did and said on the air. Funding again came from the State Budget. The order of appearance by candidates on the national screen was determined by drawing of lots. CEC introduced another important point in its regulations for the 1997 elections: TV and radio stations and cable channels owned by individuals and legal entities could assign air time to parties, coalitions, and independent candidates under equal, previously set conditions and prices ("Decision of the," 1997).

Thus in 1997 it became possible for the first time to use the commercial broadcasters on a mass scale for campaign purposes, instead of just the national state-owned operators BNT and BNR. Although the rules applied to state-owned (public) television and radio were traditionally strict, private broadcasters, who did not have to operate under these rules, were able to avail themselves of political financial resources. The presidential elections of 2001 marked another first in election campaigning in Bulgaria: the use of the Internet for publication of analyses, online polls, and political campaigning. Since the local elections in 2003, these trends have increased. In this already competitive situation, some of the commercial broadcasters offered free time for political debates, which according to the Elections Act was not possible for public operators.

THE CHRONICLE OF TELEVISED CAMPAIGNS

The Parliamentary Elections

Since the political changes in 1989, the country has voted six times for Parliament. After the Seventh Grand National Assembly in 1991, because of the strongly politicized and economically problem-rife situation, the 36th National Assembly saw the majority of votes go to the Union of Democratic Forces; the 37th National Assembly was dominated by the Bulgarian Socialist Party, the successor of the former Communist Party; and the 38th National Assembly was dominated by the Joint Democratic Forces.

These three National Assemblies (36, 37, and 38) failed to complete their legally fixed mandates. Parliamentary crises led to preterm elections. A common characteristic of all

parliamentary elections in the country, including those for the 39th and the 40th National Assemblies (both of which completed their mandates), was that they were held in an extremely strongly politicized atmosphere and under rigorous restructuring of the political arena. In the election campaign for the 40th National Assembly, an integrated ballot paper was introduced for the first time as a replacement for the numerous party-colored ballot papers. Another innovation was the requirement for collection of at least 5000 signatures for the registration of a political party ("A Political Parties," 2005). Immediately, the number of phantom parties dropped considerably. Bulgaria's fatigue from the endless political fights, as well as the blurred boundary between left and right in the programs of the various political forces, drove the creation of four independent deputies in the first days after the formation of the 40th National Assembly.

The difference in this newest parliamentary position is that disagreement with the governing political force or which party a deputy belongs to usually does not result in resignation from the Parliament. It has been common practice since 1989 that MPs who disagree with their party do not resign as MPs but move to another party represented in Parliament or declare themselves independent.

In 1990, the Bulgarian Socialist Party won the majority in the Grand National Assembly, which adopted the new Constitution on July 12, 1991. It was the first constitution of a Western type in the former Eastern Bloc countries. Although it had many imperfections, it proclaimed that Bulgaria was governed by the rule of law and set up the fundamental principles for a civil society.

1990 marked the reestablishment of political advertising and campaigning in Bulgaria. Although political campaigning in newspapers was practically uncontrollable, the Parliamentary Commission for Radio and Television set the rules for this activity on the state-owned

National Radio and the National Television (there were no private broadcasting stations at that time yet). It was therefore in 1990 that political advertising first appeared on television in Bulgaria. It began approximately 50 days prior to the first round of the elections. According to a preliminary agreement, the campaign was organized in two forms: video ads and a political debate studio called *The Open Studio*. Both were aired in prime time for nearly an hour every working day under the common heading of *Pre-Election Studio*. This televised campaigning totaled more than 32 hours of political advertising, organized in 37 program blocks.

The election campaign for the 36th National Assembly of 1991 was shorter than the 1990 Grand National Assembly campaign. A very significant feature of the 1991 campaign was the fact that the nominees were divided into three groups: parliamentary political formations (i.e., those who had deputies in the Grand National Assembly), nonparliamentary political formations, and independent candidates. The televised part of the campaign lasted less than a month and was launched in three major forms: addresses, television ads, and debates. Strict regulations were in force again regarding the proper usage of TV time. The weekends were free from television campaigning. The 36th National Assembly was dissolved before it finished its term.

The 37th National Assembly, in 1994, adopted the Radio and Television Act. Its Article 31 required that political radio and TV programs be subjected in campaign times not only to the Radio and Television Act but also to the respective election laws ("A radio and," 1996). The rules for TV campaigning were set with a CEC decision. For the first time, then, it became possible to purchase broadcasting time on commercial channels during an election campaign. The televised part of the campaign lasted 1 month and was in two major forms: television ads and debates. The weekends were free from television campaigning.

The 37th National Assembly was also dissolved before it finished its term. After the turbulent events of January 10, 1997 (aired throughout the world), when the MPs were besieged in Parliament by the social unrest outside, and the Parliament building itself was violated, it became clear that the political space needed to be rearranged again.

The televised portion of the 1997 parliamentary election campaign for the 38th National Assembly lasted less than a month and was held in three major forms: addresses, campaign news, and debates. Possibly because it had regrouped, this National Assembly was the first one to complete its full mandate, thus giving a start to normalization in the country's political life.

In 2001, the parliamentary election campaign for the 39th National Assembly for the first time unfolded in an atmosphere of competition between the state-owned and the private media, which reflected in a rather positive manner on these media. A successful stroke was when bTV (a private broadcaster licensed for nationwide coverage) took the debates outside the capital-city studio to the people in the country. This set new challenges to the anchors. The campaign was strictly regulated by the Election Act, the Instructions of the National Council for Radio and Television, and the ordinances of the Central Electoral Commission, particularly in regard to the state-owned National Radio and National Television. Nevertheless, one could hardly claim that there was a balance of information about the different political forces in their programs. For instance, the national media tended to cover the work of government members quite uncritically and too extensively. According to the Election Act for National Assembly members, the election campaign had to be televised by the BNT and BNR in the form of inaugural and peroration addresses, campaign news, and debates. The 39th National Assembly was the second one after the political changes in 1989 that successfully completed its full mandate.

Simeon II's induction into power as prime minister of the country was predetermined after the refusal of the Constitutional Court to allow him to join the presidential race in 2001. In fact, that prompted him to found the National Movement Simeon the Second (NMSS) and join the parliamentary campaign to fulfill his statement before the media that all Bulgarians who were willing to vote for him would be able to do so. A number of circumstances supported his success, and the people gave him their confidence. The unproductive bipolar model of alternating the main political opponents was broken. A new and unusual player of royal blood emerged, who, without any firm structure, with few funds, and under conditions of political and media hostility, unquestionably won the majority vote. The Movement for Rights and Liberties was the invariable balance keeper on the political scene, even with a tsar in the prime minister's seat.

As usual, the election campaign for the 40th National Assembly, in 2005, started 30 days before and finished 24 hours before Election Day. The law required that the election campaign run by the Bulgarian National Television and the Bulgarian National Radio be in the form of television ads, debates, and campaign news. The tendency toward strict regulation of public operators, which cramps the style of their political messages, was further developed. Some of the commercial operators managed to present the otherwise tedious content of the political advertisement in a more attractive manner.

The Presidential Elections

The president has little authority in Bulgarian home policy, and his foreign political functions are mainly representative. He is regarded rather, on the one hand, as an enigmatic figure that embodies the majority ideas of style in a European context, and on the other, as a national leader in the midst of a difficult socioeconomic transition.

Besides developing and adopting the new Constitution of the Republic of Bulgaria, the Grand National Assembly completed another important task: on August 1, 1991, it elected a president. Zhelyu Zhelev, at that time the leader of the Union of Democratic Forces (and who had not been listed among the earlier candidates), was elected after a heated debate, several dramatic votes, and extensive behind-the-scenes negotiations. He immediately named General Atanas Semerdzhiev (BSP) as his vice president, which was a forthright manifestation of his willingness for national conciliation. Under the newly adopted Constitution, elections had to be held as soon as possible to let the people choose the head of state. Thus the democratic start in the election of this important institution was also marked (Raycheva, 1999a).

Bulgaria has so far managed to conduct successful presidential elections three times: In 1992 (Zhelyu Zhelev, president; Blaga Dimitrova, vice president), the Union of Democratic Forces won, gaining 52.85% of the vote in competition against 21 other nominated pairs; in 1996 (Petar Stoyanov, Todor Kavaldjiev), the Joint Democratic Forces won, earning 59.73% of the vote against 12 opponents; and in 2001 (Georgi Parvanov, Gen. Angel Marin), the Coalition for Bulgaria won, with 54.13% over 5 opponents.

The election campaign of 1992 opened in a tense atmosphere due to restructuring of the political arena. Owing to the continued strong politicization of the country, 22 pairs of candidates for president and vice president were nominated.[1] A two-round electoral system was adopted, allowing the two nominees with the highest number of votes to run in the second round.

Once more, certain regulations were introduced for the election campaign regarding state-owned television. Every nominated pair was entitled to two short public addresses (up to 5 minutes each). The two finalists were expected to have a 1-hour televised debate.

January 10, 1992, marks the first live presidential debate on Bulgarian television. The opponents were Dr. Zhelyu Zhelev, the Union of Democratic Forces candidate, and Prof. Velko Vulkanov, an independent candidate backed by the BSP. The debate was anchored by long-time journalist Dimitry Ivanov. Both candidates were supposed to have an equal amount of time to speak. The result, however, was 44 minutes for Prof. Vulkanov and 17 minutes for Dr. Zhelev (Pesheva, 1992).

The 1996 presidential elections were preceded by an escalation of social tension in the country as a result of the failures of the socialist government. On the eve of the beginning of the election campaign, Andrey Loukanov, an MP, former prime minister, and well-known public figure in the sociopolitical life of the country, was assassinated in front of his home. Contrary to the expectations of some, his tragic death postponed the start of the campaign, but not the elections. Five new articles regulating campaigning by candidates on national electronic media were added to the Presidential Elections Act. A decision of the Central Electoral Commission restricted radio and TV campaigning to the following forms: one introductory and one closing address by candidates for president and vice president registered in the CEC's lists; debates; and news coverage of the demonstrations and meetings, concerts, and other events organized by the parties, coalitions, and independent candidates. Regional radio and TV stations of the state-owned television and local and municipal radio stations could assign up to 2 hours a week to presidential canvassing, which included the time for debates.

TV and radio stations and cable networks owned by individuals and legal entities could sell airtime to all candidates at equal, previously fixed prices. Thus it became possible to purchase radio and TV airtime for political promotion, although on the local level only (Raycheva & Petev).

Thirteen pairs of candidates for president and vice president were registered.[2] A two-round electoral system was again used, allowing the two nominees with the highest number of votes to run in the second round. Only four pairs managed to collect more than 1% of the votes.

According to the adopted rules, all candidates for president and vice president were entitled to free introductory and concluding addresses (each 7 minutes long) during the campaign for the first vote. On the last day of the election campaign, they were allotted 10 minutes for balloting. The order was determined by drawing of lots, which was organized by the Central Electoral Commission.

The debates were to be televised once a week, in 120 minutes of airtime altogether, and participation in them was prepaid according to tariffs set by the Council of Ministers. The regional BNT stations received 80% of that paid to Bulgarian National Television. Those parties and coalitions represented in Parliament which had registered candidates were allotted 60 minutes, which was parceled out in proportion to their representation in Parliament. The rest of the candidates had to divide the remaining 60 minutes equally between themselves. The topics of the debates focused on national security, law and order, foreign policy, and the strengthening of the state system and constitutional order in Bulgaria under the current conditions of socioeconomic hardship.

Although the debates offered a platform from which the political forces could pointedly voice the message of their program to the voters, their conduct was apparently frustrating to their audiences. Thus the real discussion failed to take place between the candidates. For instance, although the big political forces, the BSP and the Joint Democratic Forces, had enough airtime to unfold their theses, the smaller parties could wedge themselves into the discussion only with difficulty in their narrow, 20-second time slots. In this sense, the "debate" shifted toward monologue, occasionally broken by a remark that hung in the air, unanswered.

In the period between the two rounds of voting, a 90-minute debate between the major contenders was held, funded by the State Budget. The theme of this debate was "The president as a unifier of the nation."

The coverage of candidates' campaign events was also free (i.e., funded by the State Budget). In this coverage, too, there was a requirement for equal time, the use of similar forms of coverage, and several changes in sequence. The second presidential elections in 1996 were won by the Joint Democratic Forces candidates (Petar Stoyanov and Todor Kavaldjiev).

Six president–vice president pairs were nominated in the 2001 presidential elections. The campaign took place in a competitive media environment, with broad participation among the commercial electronic media. These occasionally reacted in a more responsible way and with greater public commitment than the state-owned National Radio and National Television, wheezing in the stays of legal restrictions. Campaign regulations for radio and television did not differ in principle from the regulations of the previous campaign. This time, however, only the addresses on BNT and BNR were free of charge; the debates aired on public channels were paid for by the parties according to a rate schedule determined by the Council of Ministers. The commercial media could provide time to the candidates only under uniform prices, announced in advance.

Like the NMSS parliamentary victory, which was not expected by Bulgarian political scientists, sociologists, analysts, or the media, the winning Parvanov-Marin pair (BSP) was not regarded as a favorite even on the eve of the first round of the presidential race. NMSS failed to nominate a candidate. For the first time since the political transition, a representative of the left qualified for the presidential post, which was an articulate acknowledgment by the people that the left had changed, as well as an eloquent criticism of the former bearers of public confidence.

Seeking to justify their professional failure to forecast the election returns, many sociologists pointed out as a main reason the negative media propaganda by the candidates, which flourished in the last days of the campaign. Although Bulgarian political practice has aroused justified curiosity, so far, it has shown that negative campaigning in general repulses the voting public and redirects it to another political choice or to civil passiveness. According to the leading sociological agencies, these campaign wars explain the low voting activity (41.62%) in the first round. A considerable majority of nonvoters formed, who, in both the first and second rounds, exceeded those voting. It was this active passivity of Bulgarian citizens that swung the stakes for the sociologists.

The Local Elections

Since the beginning of the democratic changes in Bulgaria, four local elections have been held (in 1991, 1995, 1999, and 2003). The increase in participants who have registered for the elections is indicative of the rise in political activity. In the local elections of 1991, 38 parties and coalitions were registered at the Central Electoral Commission for Local Elections, while in 2003, 146 parties and coalitions registered for the local elections. The number of independent candidates was also large. The regulations for conducting a campaign for local elections were similar to those for parliamentary elections. One of the usual campaign formats was the free address on state-owned national television. All political parties and coalitions that had registered their candidates for mayors of municipalities and municipality councilors could take advantage of this free airtime. Time slots were determined by lot.

Another format for TV election campaigning on BNT, BNR, regional television centers, regional radio stations, and local and municipality radio stations was the debate. Candidates who wanted to participate in debates had to pay for the airtime according to a special rate schedule determined by the Council of Ministers before the debate was broadcast. Debate topics were determined through consultations between the participants. Commercial, national, and regional radio and television stations and cable networks were required to allow parties, coalitions, and independent candidates to purchase time under equal financial terms.

FORMATS OF TELEVISION POLITICAL ADVERTISING

Addresses

An important format in televised parliamentary election campaigns is the address to the public by parliamentary and nonparliamentary candidates. Inaugural and peroration addresses frame the campaign. Usually they are free of charge, and most frequently they are the only possible format for small parties with limited funds to present their political platform to the voters. The duration of every address is strictly regulated; usually they are about 5 minutes in length. The leader of the political formation is usually the speaker. The visual and graphic layout of the recorded addresses are made by the state-owned Bulgarian National Television and are the same for all appearances, and the sequence in which they are aired is determined by lots drawn before the CEC. In the presidential election campaigns, the addresses are also one of the main formats for political advertising. The duration is usually a bit longer—up to 10 minutes. The common disadvantage of these addresses is that when arranged in blocks (lasting for several hours because of the large number of those making addresses), they are one of the most tedious political advertising forms. Thus, instead of inspiring the voter, they are boring and irritating him or her. This is the most probable reason that this form was not offered in the last parliamentary election campaign, in 2005.

Television Ads

Television ads are one of the most popular formats for political campaigning. Televised ads became the hit of the 1991 election campaign. Ads first hit Bulgarian television in the previous elections, for the Grand National Assembly. Although they lacked experience, the production crews worked with great inspiration and produced some really good political pieces in terms of screen aesthetics. According to regulation, each ad cannot exceed 3 minutes in length. In 1991, parliamentary parties and coalitions were given the opportunity to air five video ads each on BNT, and nonparliamentary groups were allowed two each. However, not all parties had the opportunity to come out with original productions.

A swanky public drawing of lots, televised live, determined the order of the broadcasting of television ads in the 1994 parliamentary election campaign. Until the commercial television sector began to compete for these ads, the rules for ads broadcast there followed a similar pattern. The gratuitous enthusiasm of earlier elections was irrevocably gone once competition began, and the political parties and coalitions tried to outdo each other in generous offers to famous pop singers and football players. In the campaigns that followed 1994, the duration of television ads was gradually shortened, although the quality improved.

Debates

The basic format for political advertising on television in all election campaigns is the debate, which covers some of the country's most important political, social, and economic issues. According to the preset rules, debates can vary between 90 and 120 minutes. In all campaigns, the number of debates for the parliamentary candidates (6-8) has outnumbered those for nonparliamentary candidates (1-2).

Usually each debate is devoted to a current issue, such as social problems, national order and security, economic reforms, rural economy, education and culture, foreign policy, and so on. CEC determines the rules of participation.

In the first years of political debating, the discussions rather resembled a series of monologue presentations of political platforms by each of the participating parties and coalitions. This was especially true for the nonparliamentary groups: The participants were so many that, practically speaking, there was no time for any real debate to be held. Some political groups flatly refused to participate, primarily because of the ridiculous way in which the "debates" were organized. Others simply presented their statements in the narrow time slots. Because all the statements were strictly limited as to time (with an electronic clock ticking in the camera's eye), no real discussion happened. Moreover, this form of TV propaganda disgusted many voters, who found it boring and tiresome.

The invasion of commercial media into political campaigning as of the beginning of the millennium positively influenced the rules for the organization of debates on the public BNT. Thus the debates have been normalized, and television viewers now witness heated debates that help them form a clearer idea about the participating political players.

Campaign News

Since the 1997 parliamentary election campaign, another format has been added to political advertising on state-owned radio and television: campaign news. News offered a more equal presentation of the parties and coalitions, especially of those that lacked sufficient intellectual and material resources for television ads. Strict rules were agreed on before the elections concerning the number, duration, and broadcasting sequence of campaign news. Particular attention was paid to the observance of principles of objectivity and equal standing.

Campaign news reported the marches, meetings, concerts, and other events organized by the parties, coalitions, and independent candidates. Campaign news was more information than propaganda.

The inclusion of the commercial media in the election campaign allowed for more varied presentation of campaign events. At the same time, it become possible for the electronic media to openly take the side of a particular, preferred political force (for the print media, this had been the case for some time). When a cable channel aired the program *Attack*, it became the basis of a new political formation of the same name, which won the fourth position (out of seven) in the 40th National Assembly.

Table 21.1 provides a summary of the elections, parties, vote outcomes, and political communication formats used during each election cycle.

CONCLUSION

In the transition to a democratic society and a market economy, political life in Bulgaria has faced manifold social and economic difficulties. The encouraging sign is that the political processes and changes in the country are carried out peacefully, and in spite of significant differences between the political forces, their reasonable behavior has so far not allowed any display of violence.

Practically all the existing mass-media institutions have undergone changes in their management, structure, and professional programs. The mass media have also brought about a high level of politicization in the people in Bulgaria.

In line with national regulations, TV stations (both public and commercial) have successfully aired political material in 13 election campaigns (the first in 1990 for the Grand National Assembly, which adopted the new Constitution; five for Parliament, in 1991, 1994, 1997, 2001, and 2005; three for president, in 1992, 1996, and 2001; and four local elections, in 1991, 1995, 1999, and 2003). Thus, in the process of transformation to

Table 21.1   Basic Data: Bulgarian Elections

Elections	Number of Political Groups	Voting Activity	Winners	Formats of Political Advertising on TV
Seventh Grand National Assembly (1990)	40 parties and coalitions	90.79% (first vote) 90.60% (second vote)	BSP: 47.15% UDF: 36.21% BAPU: 8.03% MRL: 6.02% Zhelyo Zhelev (UDF), president; Atanas Semerdjiev (BSP), vice president	Television ads Debates
36th National Assembly (1991)	38 parties and coalitions, 17 independents	84.82%	UDF: 34.35% BSP & coalition: 33.14% MRL: 7.55%	Addresses Television ads Debates
Local (1991)	38 parties and coalitions, 17 independents			
Presidential (1992)	22 pairs of candidates for president and vice president	75.39% (first vote) 75.90% (second vote)	Zhelyo Zhelev and Blaga Dimitrova (UDF)	Addresses Debate
37th National Assembly (1994)	48 parties and coalitions, 8 independents	75.34%	BSP & coalition: 43.50% UDF: 24.23% PU: 6.51% MRL: 5.44% BBB: 4.73%	Television ads Debates
Local (1995)	64 parties and coalitions, 239 independent candidates for councilor, 1912 for mayor	46%	BSP MRL UDF	
Presidential (1996)	13 pairs of candidates for president and vice president	63.14% (first vote) 61.67% (second vote)	Petar Stoyanov and Todor Kavaldjiev (UDF)	Addresses Debates Campaign news
38th Parliament (1997)	39 parties and coalitions, 10 independent	62.40%	JDF: 52.26% DL: 22.07% ANS: 7.60% EUROLEFT: 5.50% BBB: 4.93%	Addresses Debates Campaign news

Elections	Number of Political Groups	Voting Activity	Winners	Formats of Political Advertising on TV
Local (1999)	95 parties and coalitions, 257 independent candidates for councilor, 1070 for mayor	55.06% (first vote) 54.06% (second vote)	BSP UDF BEL	Addresses Debates Campaign news
39th Parliament (2001)	58 parties and coalitions, 9365 independents	67.03%	NMSS: 42.74% JDF: 18.18% CB: 17.15% MRL: 7.45%	Addresses Debates Campaign news
Presidential (2001)	6 pairs of candidates for president and vice president	41.76% (first vote) 55.09% (second vote)	Georgi Parvanov and Angel Marin (BSP)	Addresses Debates Campaign news
Local (2003)	146 parties and coalitions, plus independent candidates for councilor and candidates for mayor	47% 57.45%(II)	BSP UDF NMSS MRL	Addresses Debates
40th Parliament (2005)	22 parties and coalitions, 13 independent	55.76%	CB NMSS MRL ATTACK JDF DSB BNA	Television ads Debates Campaign news

Note: ANS indicates Alliance for National Salvation (coalition of 6 parties, among them MRL); BAPU, Bulgarian Agrarian People's Union; BBB, Bulgarian Business Block; BEL, Bulgarian Euro Left; BSP, Bulgarian Socialist Party; CB, Coalition for Bulgaria (Bulgarian Socialist Party and coalition); DL, Democratic Left (Bulgarian Socialist Party and Political Club "Ecoglasnost"); JDF, Joint Democratic Forces; MRL, Movement for Rights and Liberties; NMSS, National Movement Simeon the Second; PU, People's Union (Bulgarian Agrarian People's Union and Democratic Party); UDF, Union of Democratic Forces.

democracy, the foundations of televised political advertisement were laid down in Bulgaria. This reserved for television the great responsibility of molding public opinion, especially in view of the fact (claimed by various sociological surveys) that Bulgarians have greater confidence in public television than in any other medium. In December 2004, BNT had the highest approval rating (74.1%), followed by Bulgarian National Radio (65.8%). The police had an approval rating of 50.7%; the army, 45.6%; the government, 26.7%; Parliament, 18.4%; and the Court, 17.1% (National Center for Research on Public Opinion, 2004).

In less than a decade, electronic media campaigning has made enormous progress. Addresses, television ads, debates, and campaign news, aired on the state-owned and commercial broadcast outlets and, lately, on the Internet have marked the advancement of political marketing.

Analysis of political advertising in election campaigns on television in Bulgaria during the period of transition prompts the following inferences:

1. Political pluralism was established in the country after four decades of one-party rule.

2. Competition among the mass media, including the Internet, is fully in progress.

3. Political advertising has been introduced in election campaigning.

4. Television is the most important medium for political campaigning.

5. New TV genres, such as political ads, political addresses, and political debates, have been introduced.

6. For the first time in Bulgarian history, a public debate between two candidates for president was aired live on television.

7. A lack of perspective in advertising strategy is felt by almost all political groups.

8. Professional inadequacy and bias has been displayed by some political scientists, sociologists, and media.

9. Voting activity is gradually declining because of the unfulfilled expectations of the voters.

10. Content analysis of televised political election campaign programs shows some interesting tendencies:

    a. Only the big political groups (such as the BSP, the Union of Democratic Forces, the Movement for Rights and Liberties, the Bulgarian Agrarian People's Union, the NMSS, etc.) have the financial and creative opportunities to produce and participate in all the forms of TV campaigning (television ads, addresses, and debates). Smaller groups have to restrict themselves mainly to addresses.
    b. Gradually, significant success in terms of creativity is being achieved in the production of television ads.
    c. The addresses to the electorate proved boring, and in the last election they were dropped.
    d. The debates developed from time-restricted, stiff statements and clumsy declarations to more vivid discussions.

Since the turn of the century, all the elections (parliamentary, presidential, and local) have reflected the changes brought about by a competitive media system and the introduction of the Internet into political campaigning. Both campaigns and election returns, however, demonstrated grave professional problems in sociological terms, and the media failed to meet the basic requirement of unbiased information and predictable airing of developments and results. The paradox is that sociological forecasts and attitudes did not correctly predict the outcomes of the parliamentary elections of 2001 and 2005 or the presidential election of 2001.

Bulgaria is still experiencing the difficulties of the transitional period. The country has achieved considerable progress toward democratization and economic growth, but the political status quo remains undetermined and unstable. The mass media, and especially television, often operate as the Fourth Estate, strongly influencing public opinion politically, economically, socially, and culturally.

NOTES

1. There were one pair from a group represented in Parliament (the Union of Democratic Forces), 18 nonparliamentary candidates, and three independently nominated pairs.

2. There were three pairs from groups represented in Parliament (the BSP, the Union of Democratic Forces, and the Bulgarian Business Block), nine nonparliamentary candidates, and one independently nominated pair.

REFERENCES

An act for members of Parliament, municipality councilors, and mayors' elections (in Bulgarian). (1991, November 28). *Official Gazette*, (98), 1.

Census 2001—final results. (2001). Retrieved January 27, 2006, from the National Statistical Institute Web site: http://www.nsi.bg/Census_e/Census_e.htm

Current developments in radio and television activities in Bulgaria (in Bulgarian). (2004, May/June). *Council for Electronic Media Bulletin*, (5-6), 1–2.

Decision of the Central Electoral Commission (in Bulgarian). (1997). (Accessible only in the archive of the Central Electoral Commission)

An election act for the Grand National Assembly (in Bulgarian). (1990, April 6). *Official Gazette*, (28), 1–7.

An election act for members of Parliament (in Bulgarian). (2005, April 12). Retrieved January 19, 2006, from http://www.paragraf 22.com/pravo/zakoni/zakoni-d/19564.html

An election act for president and vice president (in Bulgarian). (2001, October 19). Retrieved January 19, 2006, from http://www.paragraf 22.com/pravo/zakoni/zakoni-d/75.htm

Gross, P. (2001). *Entangled evolutions: Media and democratization in Eastern Europe*. Baltimore, MD: Johns Hopkins University Press.

A local elections act (in Bulgarian). (1995, July 25). *Official Gazette*, (66), 1–14.

A local elections act (in Bulgarian). (2003, October 21). Retrieved January 20, 2006, from http://www.paragraf22.com/pravo/zakoni/zakoni-d/99.htm

National Center for Research on Public Opinion (2004). Sociopolitical arrangements (in Bulgarian). (2004). Retrieved January 20, 2006, from the Bulgarian Parliament Web site: http://www1.parliament.bg/nciom/

Pesheva, M. (1992). *Television—the political machine*. Sofia, Bulgaria: Hercule.

A political parties act (in Bulgarian). (2001, March 28). Retrieved January 20, 2006, from http://www.namrb.org/izbori/Zakoni/ZPP.doc

A radio and television act (in Bulgarian). (1996, September 10). *Official Gazette*, (77), 1–14.

Raycheva, L. (1999a). The impact of television on the democratization processes. In B. Newman (Ed.), *Handbook of political marketing* (pp. 485–505). Thousand Oaks, CA: Sage.

Raycheva, L. (1999b). Political advertising in Bulgarian television (1990-1997). In L. L. Kaid (Ed.), *Television and politics in evolving European democracies* (pp. 61–85). Commack, NY: Nova Science.

Raycheva, L., & Petev, T. (2002). Mass media's changing landscape in Bulgaria (1989-1999). In D. Paletz & K. Jakubowicz (Eds.), *Business as usual* (pp. 73–109). Cresskill, NJ: Hampton Press.

Unemployment in July reached its lowest level of 10.95% for 9 years now. (2005, August 17). Retrieved January 19, 2006, from the Republic of Bulgaria Council of Ministers Web site: http://www.government.bg/cgi-bin/e-cms/vis/vis.pl?s=001&p=0138&n=000004&g=

World press trends. (2004). Paris: World Association of Newspapers, pp. 81–84.

22

Political Advertising in a "New" Democracy

The Czech Republic

JAN JIRÁK AND OTAKAR ŠOLTYS

The first post-1989 parliamentary election took place in the Czech Republic—still within the framework of the former Czechoslovakia—in 1990. The election was accompanied by a campaign. However, the election was (thanks to the unique historical context) de facto a nationwide rebuff of the pre-1989 political regime. Many political parties and associations struggled for voters' attention, using meetings, mass media, and outdoor advertising. For *many* voters, it was the first real election campaign aimed at attracting their attention and winning their votes. For *all* the people living in the country, it was their first experience with an election campaign that involved tools widely used in other democratic countries; for example, billboards and, especially, television broadcasting.

SHORT OVERVIEW OF THE POLITICAL AND MEDIA SYSTEMS

Political System in the Czech Republic

More than 10 million inhabitants live in the Czech Republic, and a free market economy operates in the country. The Czech Republic is a member of NATO and, since May 2004, a member of the European Union.

The main features of the political system of the Czech Republic have been developing within the framework of former Czechoslovakia since 1989, when the political and economical structure of the Soviet Union and the whole Eastern Bloc collapsed. Czechoslovakia remained a federation of two republics until 1992, and the democratic character of the regime was under restoration (the regime had openly declared its strong ties to the tradition of a "democratic" Czechoslovakia during and between war periods[1]). The fundamental process of privatization of industry and agriculture took place, democratic institutions were newly established, and huge properties were returned to their former owners, from whom they had been taken during the postwar Soviet dominance between 1948 and 1989 (Večerník & Matějů, 1999).

On January 1, 1993, Czechoslovakia peacefully split into two independent republics with their own political institutions—the Czech Republic and the Slovak Republic. Because the former Czechoslovakia had been a federation of two republics anyway, both new countries had most of their political institutions already organized at the time of the split, and citizens had already had their first experience with free democratic elections and with election campaigning, as well (during the parliamentary elections of 1990 and 1992).

By its Constitution,[2] the Czech Republic is defined as a parliamentary democracy, with a two-chamber Parliament consisting of the Poslanecká sněmovna (House of Representatives) and the Senát (Senate). The House of Representatives consists of 200 members, elected every 4 years, and the Senate consists of 81 members elected for 6 years; one third of the senators are elected every 2 years. The main groups participating in political struggle are political parties ("independent" candidates are also allowed to participate in elections, but their real influence is marginal, and they usually form an association of independent candidates or cooperate with one of the smaller political parties).

The leading players in the political playground are political parties in close orbit around the political center between the traditional "left" and "right." There are currently five parties in the House of Representatives, and many marginal political bodies are not represented there.[3] The two biggest political parties are Česká strana sociálně demokratická (the Czech Social Democratic Party, ČSSD, which won the last election), a traditional social-democratic party with a strong pro-EU orientation and modest welfare state political program, and Občanská demokratická strana (the Civic Democratic Party, ODS),[4] which has a more conservative orientation, some nationalistic characteristics, and a very cold approach to the European Union (the current president of the Czech Republic, Václav Klaus, one of the "founding fathers" and a former leader of ODS, is still closely related to the party). Other parties are Komunistická strana Čech a Moravy (the Communist Party of Bohemia and Moravia, KSČM) clearly a leftist party, with an electorate still identified with the pre-1989 situation; Křesťansko-demokratická unie–Česká strana lidová (the Christian Democrats), a middle-sized but quite stable centrist party (it has been a member of all coalition governments since 1990); and the Union of Freedom (Unie svobody–Demokratická unie), a marginal, neoliberal party with very few voters that is a member of the current coalition government because of the low "coalition potentiality" of both ODS and KSČM (the Union of Freedom has probably no chance to enter Parliament during the spring 2006 elections).

Financing for the political parties and their campaigns comes from a state budget (funding is granted according to the number of votes a party gains in the election, as long as it is more than 3% of the votes, and according to the number of mandates for parties represented in Parliament), from membership fees, and from sponsorship and money offered by donators. These financial resources are the foundation of several scandals that took place on the Czech political stage from 1990 to 2005.

There are several types of elections: election to the House of Parliament (every 4 years), election to the Senate (every 2 years, but because of the graduated change in senators, only in a limited number of counties), and regional and local elections (every 4 years). The election of members of the House of Representatives is understood as the most important event in the political life of the nation (for more information on the Czech political system see Strmiska, 2001, or Malíř & Marek, 2005).

The Media System in the Czech Republic

Czech Media Before 1989

To understand the depth and nature of the changes in Czech media in the 1990s, some knowledge about the Czech media system during the previous regime is necessary. The media in the former "socialistic" Czechoslovakia had a highly centralized structure with a clearly defined goal: to serve the communist power elite and to support its decisions and image. The whole system was very close to the description offered as a "Soviet model" in *Four Theories of the Press*[5] (Siebert, Peterson, & Schramm, 1963). Czech society possessed a well-developed media system that offered most of the types of media available in noncommunist countries. In the print media sector, national dailies were published mainly by the political parties (the Communist Party, People's Party, and Socialist Party).[6] There was a rich variety of regional and local weeklies and specialized magazines published in all major cities by the local and regional authorities. One type of daily was missing: the sensational paper. All broadcasting in the former Czechoslovakia was run and controlled by the State and financed via the state budget. The alternative media, *samizdats,* were marginal and, in comparison with those of other countries (for instance, Poland), underdeveloped. On the other hand, the BBC, Voice of America, and Radio Free Europe were commonly available in the former Czechoslovakia.

Changes in the Media System After 1989

After 1989, the whole media structure changed very profoundly. The system of control, based mainly on personal responsibility

(justified by the "leading role of the Communist Party" expressed in the Constitution), dissolved, and media started to operate independently of the state and in a completely new legal framework. "The new media are embedded in legal forms and social practices and are no longer a matter of hope, fear or speculation," concluded Sparks (1998, p.174) in his observations of media transition in Central Europe.

Some national dailies changed into employee shareholding companies. The former daily of the Socialistic Union of Youth, *Mladá fronta* (Young Front; after 1989, *Mladá fronta Dnes,* Young Front Today), is an excellent example. Finally, the shareholders sold their shares to owners based in other countries. The new owners were of different origin (French, Scandinavian, Swiss), and as such, they did not provoke any negative reaction from the general public. Only potential owners based in Germany were understood as a danger to the country. However, most of the Czech dailies moved into the hands of German owners during the 1990s. Currently, only one national daily, *Právo,* is owned by a Czech owner, and all the others are in the hands of foreign owners (two of them are owned by one company). New dailies appeared, too, but most of these attempts were not successful. The whole structure of regional and local print media is under the control of one owner—a midsize publishing house based in Bavaria, Germany.

Within the field of broadcasting, the so-called dual system (a system in which both public service and private commercial broadcasting operate side by side) was established both for radio and television (for details, see Jirák, 1997, p. 44). The state media established in the previous regime were transformed into public service media and formed Český rozhlas (Czech Radio) and Česká televize (Czech Television).[7] Czech Radio now offers three nationwide FM stations, one network of regional FM stations, one AM news and talk show station, and a radio service broadcast

Table 22.1   Investment in Advertising in the Czech Republic

Medium	1990	1992	1996	1998	2000	2004
Print	310	2757	4300	5000	5450	6000
TV	40	1050	3800	5300	6250	8330
Radio	8	250	710	850	985	1190
Outdoor	8	600	880	950	1015	1050
Internet	—	—	—	25	110	310
Other	8	75	210	195	210	255
Total	374	4732	9900	12,320	14,020	17,135

SOURCE: *Media and Marketing Journal* (2005).

Note: Numbers shown are in thousands of Czech crowns.

abroad. Czech Television offers two nation-wide channels: one mass audience oriented and one more minority oriented. Both public service media are financed primarily by fees paid by audience members for the ownership of functioning receivers and by the sale of some limited broadcasting time to advertisers.

Private radio and television stations also appeared after 1989. First came local and regional radio stations, then nationwide private radio stations appeared, and then television channels. Private television stations appeared in 1993, with the first (regional) commercial television financed by Silvio Berlusconi. This network, called *TV Premiéra,* was not very successful and was transformed into *TV Prima* in 1998. The real victory of commercial TV broadcasting came in 1994, when *TV Nova* started to broadcast. This entertaining mass audience TV channel (offering *Dallas* in 1994, *Who Wants to Be a Millionaire* in 2001, the equivalent of *American Idol* in 2003, and *Big Brother* in 2005) was the most successful media project of the 1990s, gaining the attention of about two thirds of viewers in ratings at the beginning and with a long-term weekly share of over 40% for more than 10 years. In 2005, after some changes in *TV Prima*'s programming, *TV Nova*'s audience share started to drop.

The advertising market opened in the Czech Republic after 1989 and has been developing extremely quickly since then. With no regard

for the ups and downs of the Czech economy (a financial crisis in 1998 resulted in an extraordinary election and a change of government), the amount of finances pumped into advertising has increased steadily (Table 22.1). The importance of advertisers as long-term and stable financial resources is one basis for their potential influence on media. In other words, the character of Czech media as "market-driven" media is strengthened by the actual economic success of the media—with all the attendant consequences (consumer-oriented journalism, the domination of "media logic" as the main code of public communication, including political advertising, etc.). In this sense, the Czech media (as established during 1990s) are a true laboratory for the future development of media in traditional European democracies.

Quite clearly, the Czech media system is a market-driven media structure deeply rooted in the trends of economic globalization and commercialization. Unlike other countries, in the Czech Republic, the process of commercialization has not been slowed down by "quality" media. The political elite, trained in understanding "media logic," see the media as suitable tools for communication with voters and are trying either to adapt to media logic or to dominate the media (especially the public service media) through laws and councils or PR techniques.

The changes in the media system mirror the development of Czech society and its communications from totalitarian to liberal systems without limits set by any dominant normative theory but using instead the ideology of the free market. The relationship between media and the political elite represents the rise of mediated politics, with all its consequences (news management, personalization of political communication, etc.).

REGULATION OF POLITICAL ADVERTISING

Political advertising is not regulated in print and outdoor media by any specific law, but it is regulated very strongly in the broadcast media. No advertising of political parties and movements is allowed on radio or television according to the Broadcasting Law (Zákon 468/1991, 2001). The only exception is during election campaigns, as will be discussed later. Political advertising is used in the print media very rarely outside of campaign periods. Outdoor advertising is used more often—especially specific, sarcastic, blaming, or accusatory messages about political rivals, which are frequently seen on billboards.

The Constitution also defines the basic principles according to which elections of all kinds are organized. Namely, the necessity of passing a special election law (volební zákon) is mentioned in the 20th article (Catch 2) of the Constitution. This "election law" is in fact a set of laws defining the specific type of election: a Czech parliamentary election law (defining the rules of elections both to the House of Representatives and to the Senate), a European parliamentary election law, and so on. Most of these laws are changed before each election (the date of the specific election is announced, organizational matters are arranged, etc.), but the rules of the election campaign and political advertising are very similar. Therefore we will summarize the main legal conditions for political advertising defined by law on a more general level and without reference to the specific versions of election laws. As an example, we

will use the 1995 election law that defines election to Parliament (Zákon 247/1995, 1995). Article 16 of this law sets the basic rules of the election campaign, with the clear idea of making the campaign fair.[8] Fairness is required by § 3, which forbids the publication of any public opinion poll results 3 days before and during election days.

The rules of the election campaign, as set in the election law, provide a framework for political advertising, as well. According to § 1 of Article 16, mayors (starostové, elected representatives of communities) are allowed to reserve a public space for political posters 16 days before election. The principle of equality of political parties and coalitions (and individual candidates, in the case of their election to the Senate) is stated in the article.

According to Article 16, § 4 in the election law, all political parties, political movements, and coalitions are allowed a total of 48 hours of free broadcast time, both on Czech public radio and Czech public television (this in fact defines the period of open, "declared" election campaigning). The broadcast time must be used during a period that starts 16 days before the election and ends 48 hours before voting begins. This free broadcast time must be divided equally among all political parties, political movements, and coalitions. The time slots for each political party, movement, and coalition are determined arbitrarily. Political parties, movements, and coalitions are responsible for the content of the message broadcast in their time slot.

By providing the rules for election campaigning, Article 16 represents an exception from the Broadcasting Law, according to which any political advertising in broadcast media is forbidden.

THE DEVELOPMENT AND USE OF POLITICAL ADVERTISING IN THE CZECH REPUBLIC

Political advertising has not been around very long in the Czech Republic. A short period of democracy in the period beginning with the establishment of Czechoslovakia (October 1918) was remarkably weakened by the Munich Treaty (September 1938) and ended with the invasion of Hitler's army (March 1939). The regular political struggle of political parties took place in that earlier period with all usual "weapons," including political advertising via print and outdoor media. The tradition of political advertising was renewed after World War II but lasted only till 1948, when Czechoslovakia was incorporated into the Soviet bloc.

Political advertising as a regular feature of political communication in democratic countries was a concept that had no place in pro-Soviet regimes, with the dominant position of the Communist Party. The "political advertising" of that period (1948-1989) has mostly aimed at mobilizing (meaning "supporting") the Communist Party, the "working people," and the "republic," or blaming enemies. Only the short period of "Prague Spring" (from January to August 1968) represents an exception, but this was too short a period for the development or renewal of a solid tradition of political advertising. Traditional political advertising was established after 1989, when the country shifted from the collapsing Soviet bloc toward the Western democracies.

The Role of Television
Advertising in Elections

Among all available communication channels, TV broadcasting is understood to be the most important one for political parties and other candidates struggling for victory during elections. The candidates are trying to present themselves not only in their legally allowed free airtime but in political debates, via various "media events," and so on. Although some parties have broadcast promotional programs, more attention has been devoted to televised debates between the competing candidates and parties (Hughes, 1999). The number of

viewers and range of popular coverage—which is truly "mass"—are highly appreciated qualities of political communication in Czech television broadcasting, monitored both by political parties and by the media. However, the mass audience was not present in front of its TV sets when campaign clips were broadcast, because public television (and public radio as well) scheduled them during the day, usually between 4:00 p.m. and 5:00 p.m. The political debates were known to be much more effective.

Academic Research and Popular
Analyses of Political Advertising

Each election has been accompanied by the publication of results by the Czech Statistical Institute and by analytical publications comparing party platforms; parties' political and sociological characteristics; territorial and general characteristics of the electorate; social, age, and other characteristics of voters of every party; and other aspects of the election (Linek, Mrklas, Seidlová, & Sokol, 2003; Šaradín, 2002). The research and analyses paid a lot of attention to political processes, including elections as a specific type of decision making, but media communication and political advertising have not been included in the surveys, despite the fundamental change in political communication that took place at the beginning of the 1990s. During the 1970s and 1980s, political campaigning was not aimed at the competing parties; the effectiveness of political advertising was focused on gaining *as much* support for the Communist Party of Czechoslovakia as possible. The paradigm change after 1989 brought democratic competition, rational selection, and existential participation into election campaigns, as well as simplification (and personalization) in the mediated political struggle, with strong tendencies to find a clear, dominating topic for each election: the 1990 election was dominated (and reduced) by the theme "refusing communism"; the 1992 election was dominated (and reduced) by the theme "standard economic reform, no third alternative on our way back to Europe"; the 1996 election was dominated (and reduced) by the theme "finishing privatization"; the 1998 election was dominated (and reduced) by the theme "stopping economic losses and beginning economic revival organized and guaranteed by state"; and the 2002 election was dominated (and reduced) by the theme "to be or not to be in the European Union" (Alan et al., 1993, p. 68).

The only academic qualitative analysis of electoral clips was published in 1993 (Alan et al., 1993, pp. 68-69). The authors offered a methodological background based on syntactical and paradigmatic relations among clips presented on TV, which led to simple classification. The classification reveals a number of functions fulfilled by the clips, and the authors add typical means to the concrete function. For instance, the function classified as "pure humanity and caring about the future" (one of the most frequent functions) is expressed by a "beautiful child," usually combined with "careful parents," mostly candidates for election, or a "typical Czech landscape," with the caring connected to saving it for future generations, as well as "young sheep, horses, cows, any possible beast that needs human care" associated with the same caring as the landscape, and so on. Another example of a function can be "education," which is accompanied by a huge library in the background and a computer (still a new phenomenon in those days) in front of the candidate. Neither the library nor the computer usually influences the quality of the talking head's speech. Almost inevitable is the function of "cultural tradition" with signs that say Prague Castle, St.Vitus Cathedral, Vltava River, or Říp Mountain (a mythological place symbolizing the settlement of Czechs in the region). This analysis has not been repeated, although the electoral clips are still an obligatory part of any Czech election campaign.

As far as we know, there is no scientific analysis of campaign debates from the perspective of political advertising. The only exception is an analysis of the quality of communication in television debates (Bozděchová, 2003). Indirectly, some information about political campaigning is included in academic research and analysis that focused on content analysis of TV news broadcasting during the 1998 electoral campaign (Schulz, Hagen, Scherer, & Reifová, 1998). Two university teams—one from Charles University, Prague, and one from the University of Erlangen-Nürnberg—prepared a research project they titled "How the Media Vote" (Schulz et al., 1998). The strongest parties in the 1998 campaign were ODS and ČSSD. The other strong parties were the Christian Democratic Union, Civic Democratic Alliance, Communist Party of Czech and Moravia, and Republican Party of Czech. As shown in Table 22.2, the time and attention given by TV stations to the political parties corresponded with their position in political discourse: ODS was the leading party of the ruling coalition, ČSSD was the main opposition party, the Christian Democrats and the Civil Democratic Alliance were right-to-centrist parties with coalition potential, the Communist Party represented the extreme left, and the Republican Party the extreme right.

Table 22.3 compares the positions of the main protagonists of ODS and ČSSD, Václav Klaus and Miloš Zeman, respectively. Václav Klaus was the prime minister for a long time; Miloš Zeman was a possible winner in the election. As can be seen from the number of camera shots in the news coverage, their position was comparable (ČT1 was slightly in favor of Miloš Zeman). Both private stations strongly preferred Václav Klaus.

CONCLUSION

The framework of political advertising in the Czech Republic is stable and the rules are widely accepted. There has been some discussion of the

Table 22.2   Party Members in the Role of Speaker

	Station (%)		
Party	CT1	Nova	Premiéra
ODS	30	32	28
ČSSD	19	22	18
KDU-ČSL	9	14	8
ODA	11	18	14
KSČM	1	4	8
SRP-RSČ	0	0	2
Others	30	10	22

Note: ČSSD indicates the Czech Social Democratic Party; KDU-ČSL, Christian Democratic Union; KSČM, Communist Party of Czech and Moravia; ODA, Civil Democratic Alliance; ODS, Civic Democratic Party; SPR-RSČ, Republican Party of Czech.

Table 22.3   Number of Shots of Klaus and Zeman in TV News in the 1998 Campaign

	Station		
Candidate	CT1	Nova	Premiéra
Klaus	47%	70%	65%
Zeman	53%	30%	35%
Total number of shots	55	55	26

SOURCE: Schulz et al. (1998), p. 132.

potential effects of legally guaranteed broadcast time and the potential effects on news coverage of election campaigns. Czech public television always announces all the rules for political ads and debates in advance.

The rules lead toward unified types of persuasive messages: stereotypical clips of talking heads and self-presentation in "debates," with no real discussion. In such an environment, any departure from the rules attracts the attention of the voters. For instance, ČSSD used an ordinary bus as a means of communication and transportation during the 1988 campaign. The ČSSD was the opposition party for several years, and its financial situation was poor, not comparable to that of ODS, the ruling party. So an old bus had to serve as the transportation to ČSSD electoral meetings. It could not

be compared with the expensive limousines and helicopters used by ODS. This disadvantage was changed into an advertising triumph by a joke based on the near similarity of the last name of ČSSD leader Zeman and the word for "potato" in the Czech and Moravian dialects, zemák. The bus was called Zemák, which amused and interested the voters, and the apparent disadvantage gained points for the 1998 election winner.

It seems likely that election campaigning is governed by the media logic of the contemporary mass media and that traditional types of political advertising are not effective. The guaranteed free airtime on public television has been shown to have particularly little impact, and the political parties and candidates participate in it for ritualistic reasons.

Election results suggest that direct contact with voters is much more effective than any communication through the mass media. The "mass communication" qualities of election campaigning will probably diminish in the future and another means of campaign communication will become dominant: the Internet, personal meetings, and direct mail are all candidates. TV advertising as a tool of persuasion may become a complementary type of communication.

On the other hand, the political debates organized by public broadcasters still serve an important agenda-building function, and the shape of the debates may gradually change. The stiff, performative character of the debates is very likely to shift toward a more Western-style form of actual discussion. This process may be delayed by the shaky position of Czech public service television, which has been weakened by the continual attempts of the Czech political elite to dominate it.

NOTES

1. The 1968 "Prague Spring" has been widely ignored by political representatives who have stated that it was just an internal struggle between factions of the Communist Party. These post-1989 representatives were probably trying to minimize any left-wing–oriented inspiration.

2. The Preamble to the Constitution of the Czech Republic (Ústava České republiky), passed on December 16, 1992, claims that the Czech Republic is *svobodný a demokratický stát, založený na úctě k lidským právům a na zásadách občanské společnosti, jako součást rodiny evropských a světových demokracií* (a free and democratic state, founded on respect for human rights and principles of civic society as a part of the family of European and world democracies).

3. To enter the House of Representatives, a party has to gain at least 5% of the votes.

4. ČSSD is a traditional political body in Czech society (established in the 1880s, swallowed by the Communist Party after World War II, and reestablished in 1989). ODS is a "new" political party, founded after 1989. It fit into the widely shared resentment against the compromised leftist thinking of the early 1990s, won the election in 1992,

formed a coalition government, and ran the country until 1996, when the prime minister was forced to resign because of a financial scandal in his party and because of the remarkable economic decline. Since 1996, ODS has been the opposition party. On the other hand, ODS won most of the mandates in the last regional election, and most of the leaders of the main administrative regions and mayors of big cities are ODS members.

5. However simplifying and biased the model is, it can be used as a good frame for the basic characteristics of the Czech media's situation before 1989.

6. There was a formal multiparty system in Czechoslovakia before 1989, but political parties were organized under an umbrella association called the National Front, and as members of this front, all parties were supposed to support the policy of the leading Communist Party.

7. The whole concept of "public service" broadcasting was inspired by the German ARD/ZDF model and the British BBC.

8. "*Volební kampaň musí probíhat čestně a poctivě, zejména nesmí být o kandidátech a politických stranách nebo koalicích ... zveřejňovány nepravdivé údaje*" (the election campaign must be held fairly and honestly, and disseminating false information about candidates, political parties, and coalitions is expressly forbidden) (Zákon 247/1995, 1995, Art. 16, § 2).

REFERENCES

Alan, J., Gál, F., Jirák, J., Kakosová, T., Kapr, J., Kotlas, P., et al. (1993). *Volby* [Election]. Praha, Czech Republic: Egem.

Bozděchová, I. (2003). K jazykové úrovni současných televizních debat [On the language quality of contemporary television debates]. In S. Čmejrková & J. Hoffmannová (Eds.), *Jazyk, politika, média* [Language, politics, media] (pp. 157–172). Praha, Czech Republic: Academia.

Hughes, E. (1999). The role of the media in the elections in the Czech Republic. In L. L. Kaid (Ed.), *Television and politics in evolving European democracies* (pp. 207–217. Commack, NY: Nova Science.

Jirák, J. (1997). The Czech Republic: Media accountability system—an unknown concept. In U. Sonnenberg (Ed.), *Organising media accountability: Experiences in Europe* (pp. 43–48). Maastricht, The Netherlands: European

Journalism Centre. Retrieved January 20, 2006, from http://www.ejc.nl/pdf/pub/mas.pdf

Linek, L., Mrklas, L., Seidlová, A., & Sokol, P. (Eds.). (2003). *Volby do Poslanecké sněmovny 2002* [2002 parliamentary elections]. Praha, Czech Republic: Sociologický ústav AV ČR.

Malíř, J., & Marek, P. a kol. (2005). *Politické strany. Vývoj politických stran a hnutí v českých zemích a Československu 1861–2004. II. díl: Období 1938-2004* [Political parties. The development of political parties and movements in Czech lands and Czechoslovakia, 1861-2004. Volume II: 1938-2004]. Brno, Czech Republic: Doplněk.

Šaradín, P. (Ed.). (2000). *Volby '98* [Election–98]. Brno, Czech Republic: Doplněk.

Šaradín, P. a kol. (2002). *Volby 2002* [Election 2002]. Olomouc, Czech Republic: Periplum.

Schulz, W., Hagen, L., Scherer, H., & Reifová, I. (1998). *Analýza obsahu mediálních sdělení* [Analysis of content of media messages]. Praha, Czech Republic: Karolinum.

Siebert, F., Peterson, T., & Schramm, W. (1963). *Four theories of the press.* Urbana: University of Illinois Press.

Sparks, C. (1998). *Communism, capitalism and the mass media.* Thousand Oaks, CA: Sage.

Strmiska, M. (2001). *Challenges of consolidation and post-communist party systems.* Brno, Czech Republic: International Institute of Political Science.

Večerník, J., & Matějů, P. (Eds.). (1999). *Ten years of rebuilding capitalism: Czech society after 1989.* Praha, Czech Republic: Academia.

Zákon 468/1991, resp. 231/2001 Sb. o provozování rozhlasového a televizního vysílání [Law on radio and television broadcasting]. (2001). Retrieved January 29, 2006, from the Czech Republic Public Administration Web site: http://portal.gov.cz/wps/portal/_s.155/701/.cmd/ad/.c/313/.ce/10821/.p/8411/_s.155/701?PC_8411_number1=231/2001&PC_8411_l=231/2001&PC_8411_ps=10#10821

Zákon 247/1995 Sb.ze dne 27. září 1995 o volbách do Parlamentu České republiky [Law 247/1995, passed September 27, 1995, on election to the Parliament of the Czech Republic]. (1995). Retrieved January 29, 2006, from the Czech Republic Public Administration Web site: http://portal.gov.cz/wps/portal/_s.155/701/.cmd/ad/.c/313/.ce/10821/.p/8411/_s.155/701?PC_8411_number1=247/1995&PC_8411_l=247/1995&PC_8411_ps=10#10821

23

Persuading Voters and Political Advertising in Turkey

BAKI CAN

W hen talking about the Turkish political system, election system, media procedures, and election campaign procedures, it can be said that the main determining factor in the way they work is the initiatives of the current leaders, not the lifestyles of the Turkish people, their values, or their expectations. There are two kinds of elections in Turkey: parliamentary elections and municipal elections. This chapter discusses parliamentary election campaigns. The president of Turkey is elected by the members of Parliament in the Great National Assembly of Turkey (TBMM).

The phrase "methods of persuading voters" is an appropriate label for all the activities during the political campaigns. For instance, an open area meeting is one of the major methods used to persuade voters, and this method retains its importance even though it may be less effective in every election.

ELECTIONS AND THE HISTORICAL PROGRESS OF THE ELECTION SYSTEM

The Turkish people are accustomed to being ruled by leaders who come to power through elections. During the period of the Ottoman State, different kinds of election systems were used during the reigns of different emperors. Furthermore, the modern Turkish people are aware of the history of elections in the Ottoman State and that approach to determining who will be in charge. Because of this extensive political history (Timur, 1986), the people of the Turkish Republic have sought to have more effective popular participation and fair election systems.

The first election under the current system took place in 1877, during the time of the Ottoman State. Since then, Turkish voters have gone to the polls 28 times for local and parliamentary elections. Six of these elections took place during the period of the Ottoman State, two of them during the foundation of the Turkish Republic, and 20 of them during the current period of the Turkish Republic. There have also been nine midterm elections for members of Parliament.

It is possible to divide the Turkish Republic elections into two periods. The first one covers the elections that took place from 1927 to 1943, with a single party, and the second one is the multiparty elections period, from 1946 to the present.

The election laws determine the rules under which elections take place. Over the years, changes in these laws have been frequent. For instance, the Kanun (law), established on April 26,1961, was changed 27 times between 1961 and 2003. Many different electoral systems have been used, and the first Turkish Republic period was characterized by single-party rule (by the Republican People's Party, or CHP) between 1923 and 1950. The Democrat Party (DP) reigned from 1950 to 1960, followed by a period characterized by military coups and numerous coalition governments until the military coup of 1997, which marked the last military intervention and is referred to as the postmodern military intervention. This intervention occurred on February 28, 1997, during a coalition of the Welfare Party (RP) and the True Path Party (DYP). The intervention did not eliminate the government directly but did not give it a chance to survive, either. From the 1997 intervention to the time of the November 3, 2002, elections, the Turkish Motherland Party (ANAP) and the Democratic Left Party (DSP), a majority coalition, were in charge (Ahmad, 1992). The Justice and Development Party (AKP) achieved power in the 2002 elections. It was surprising that the majority of the members of parliament and the high-level administrative managers elected then came from the RP.

Between 1946 and 2002, 15 parliamentary elections were held. Two of them were conducted during the reign of military governments, nine of them were held earlier than the regular election periods, and only four of them were held at their regularly specified time.

LEGAL PROCEDURES

The subjects of voter persuasion, making propaganda, and making political advertisements in Turkey are complex and not easily discussed. Some legal rules can be mentioned: The first legislation, *Seçimlerin Temel Hükümleri ve Seçmen Kütükleri Hakkında Kanun*, was passed on April 26, 1961. This law is still in effect in an amended version; it has been changed 27 times since 1961, and the last amendment was made on July 15, 2003. Of course, these amendments did not change the entire law.

During the elections, campaign propaganda can only be produced in accordance with this law. The campaign period begins 10 days before the elections and ends at 6:00 p.m. the day before Election Day. In addition to this, specific procedures must be followed, and there are regulations governing verbal messages indoors and outdoors.

Regarding written documents used for propaganda by political parties or independent candidates, it is legal to use all kinds of brochures and distribute them to the public. However, when the campaign period expires the day before the election, distributing, hanging, or selling any kind of written campaign material is illegal. It is illegal to use the Turkish flag or any kind of religious symbol or content in these written materials. An addition to this law in 1995 (para. no. 4125) states that

> During the General Parliamentary Elections; it is strictly forbidden to give presents, promotional goods, or to have them distributed, or to air any kind of broadcast that includes memoranda, surveys, or research about the opposing political parties or candidates over any kind of communication device in an attempt to persuade the voters for or against a political party or a candidate.

Using Radio and Television in Propaganda

Political parties participating in the elections can air propaganda (during specific, scheduled hours) on radio or television during the last 7 days before Election Day. These propaganda messages are produced for free on Turkish Radio and Television (TRT), which is a public broadcasting association. According to the regulations governing these free messages,

a. All political parties participating in the elections may broadcast a total of two briefings about their public programs, 10 minutes on the first day and 10 minutes on the last day of the campaign.
b. Political parties having groups in TBMM may air an additional 10 minutes of propaganda.
c. The leading political party is allowed an additional 20 minutes, and the other political parties in a coalition are allowed an additional 15 minutes.

The political parties may produce their own television ads on the condition that these do not take up more than half the party's total allotted time. Political ads prepared by other associations may also be broadcast on TRT. These ads may not be shorter than 2 minutes each and may not take longer than 10 minutes over the course of a day. The Yüksek Seçim Kurulu (High Assembly of Elections) organizes the schedule of political ads on TRT. Political radio and television briefings are broadcast at the same time on all the radio and television channels in Turkey. TRT announces the time of the briefings before they are aired.

Visual material is subject to very strict requirements. Parties are forbidden to use any kind of visual material in the background apart from the Turkish flag and the political party's flag. Male speakers must wear suits and ties, and women must wear skirt suits. On commercial radio and television channels, the broadcasts must follow TRT procedures. The order of the speakers is determined by lot (Yavuz, 1994).

The legal procedures for producing propaganda messages during elections are as noted. So far there is no legislation governing communication techniques related to cellular phones, Internet advertisements, or e-mail messages.

Media Procedures

It is useful to consider the years of the 1920s to clearly understand current Turkish media regulations. Magazines and newspapers put forth great effort to save the country from invasion by enemies (Inugur, 1982). Because of this, General Mustafa Kemal encouraged the press in many ways (Öztoprak, 1981). There was a need for the newspapers to cover the Turkish people's revolution seriously after the foundation of the Turkish Republic. With this aim, the newspaper *Cumhuriyet* was founded (Yılmaz, 2002), and many other newspapers were important to the political development of Turkey. During single-party periods, newspapers supported the leading political party. During the multiparty period, some of the newspapers started to support one party and the rest the other party. There were at least one or more newspapers supporting each political party (Kabacali, 1994).

In the 1980s, almost at the same time as other Eastern European countries, the press started to be affected by liberalization. Newspapers that were originally founded for ideological or for political purposes increasingly started to seek financial profit. Of course, newspaper publishers have always sought profit, but this objective used to come second after their primary ideological aims.

Until this period, the only concern of the newspapers had been journalism, but in the 1980s a monopolist period began. Companies or people in a variety of occupations added print media to their business portfolios. First they bought newspapers, then TV channels, and then radio stations.

Political advertisements in Turkey started in June 1977, when the Justice Party (AP) took out advertisements in magazines and newspapers. Before this date, advertisements had not appeared in the newspapers due to ideological and partisan concerns. Before 1977, advertisements were not needed, and because of new structuring, it was considered unnecessary to advertise the party being supported. In addition to this, the opposing parties did not think about advertisements either.

METHODS OF PERSUADING VOTERS AND POLITICAL ADVERTISING

Although elections have been held in Turkey since 1877, the country did not use political advertising until 1977. The AP used advertisements as a part of their political campaign for the July 7, 1977 election. In the previous hundred years, there had been several reasons for not making any advertisements or feeling the need for them. The most important reason was the political structure, because the media was organized around it. However, the phrase "political advertisements" alone does not define the subject clearly; it is more appropriate to think of this kind of propaganda as "styles of persuading voters." An examination of the most important styles used in important elections follows.

Early Elections in 1946 and 1950

In the history of elections in Turkey, the 1946 elections are considered a milestone because multiple political parties participated in the elections. In this election, CHP, which had been the leading political party since the foundation of the Turkish Republic, struggled against DP. During the political campaigning before the election, newspapers and radio were used as mass communication devices.

During the campaign, CHP, as the ruling party and with control over the radio, did not allow DP to use the radio for its campaign. In fact, CHP used it extensively for its own campaign. In addition to the leader of CHP and the Turkish president, İsmet İnönü, the prime minister and some other members of CHP made a number of propaganda speeches on the radio. The prime minister's first propaganda speech for CHP, on July 8, 1946, lasted for 50 minutes.

Before the 1946 elections, one-to-one talks with voters and open area meetings, as well as supportive newspapers, had been effective for DP. Candidates in both parties had interesting characteristics. For example, CHP had placed the names of three army commanders on their list of 23 candidates in Istanbul, two of them in the first two places. Again in Istanbul, DP placed five non-Muslim candidates on their list. (The population of non-Muslim residents was about 1%.) The 1950 elections came after an important period, and DP wanted secret voting and an open vote count to avoid putting any possible pressure on the voters.

It had seemed quite odd to some groups that the opposition parties were criticizing the government using the public's radio. However, by many it was appreciated. On the radio, representatives of the Nation Party (MP), DP, and CHP had made 10-minute speeches without being censored. These first examples following each other were very interesting.

During the political campaigns, CHP emphasized that the party belonged to Atatürk and İnönü, and they mentioned the efforts of the party. DP stated that it was time for the people to speak, and DP itself was the representative of the people.

After the elections, the 487 parliamentary seats were divided as follows: 415 for DP, 69 for CHP, 1 for MP, and 2 for independents. It was quite surprising that CHP had so low a percentage; even many ministers of the old government had failed to be reelected. A final result like this cannot be explained by a 7-day period of propaganda. Maybe this single week brought about action from what had long been in the public mind.

As in other countries, different aspects of the different elections in Turkey differ in significance. In examining the subject of voter persuasion, I must first note that the 1946 and 1950 elections were the first examples of real political campaigns. From the 1950 elections until May 29, 1960, DP had ruled the country and CHP was the leading opposition party. In the 1954 and 1957 elections, the leading and opposition parties had more liberal election campaigns. In the 1954 elections, the 541 members of parliament in TBMM broke down as 502 DP members, 31 CHP, 5 for the Republican Nation Party (CMP), and 3 independents.

A military coup took place on May 27, 1960, the first in the history of the Turkish Republic. The leaders of the coup took charge of the government. The 1961 elections were conducted in obedience to the rules of the military government.

The result of the elections under these circumstances was, broken down from the total number of 450 seats, 158 for AP (which was said to be an extension of the DP), 173 for CHP, 54 for the Republican Peasants Nation Party (CKMP), and 65 for the New Turkish Party (YTP).

Even more political parties were able to enter the Parliament in the 1965 elections, due to changes in the election system. Out of 450 seats, 240 went to AP, 134 to CHP, 31 to MP, 19 to YTP, and 11 to CKMP.

The 1970s were the peak years of left-right ideological conflict in Turkey. The anarchy started in the 1960s, resulting in 10 to 15 people being killed every day in the 1970s. The conflicts among the political parties, newspapers, the public, and even among families rose greatly. University and high school students, trade union workers, and members of ideological associations were the main groups driven into this conflict. The government was formed through coalitions, and every new leader was supporting the ones on his side and trying to isolate the others. Newspapers and magazines became totally ideological and supported specific political parties. This was their major reason for being published. On the other hand,

the government-controlled TRT tried to emphasize the revolutions of Atatürk and his idealism (Cankaya, 2000), in addition to supporting the leading parties. Under these circumstances, the supporters of different political parties, especially enthusiastic young people, attempted to persuade the public with face-to-face communication. These conversations frequently ended with discussions, arguments, fights, and even with death. During the early elections for members of Parliament on June 5, 1977, AP for the first time had used political advertisements in newspapers and magazines. These advertisements had attracted both attention and reaction. CHP had never approved this kind of campaign; for example, *Hürriyet* ran an article on May 17, 1977, about İzmir Province (which supported the CHP) that strongly criticized AP's use of political advertisements.

As the 1977 elections approached, the government was again being shared by coalitions. However, the coalition leaders were not loyal to each other. They plotted against each other and tried to steal each other's election points. Fights of leftists against rightists, and resulting casualties, rose enormously. There were days when 30 to 40 or even more were killed. In a single occasion in Mardin, four people died and 13 were injured. The AP candidate was also killed.

AP advertisements in 1977 focused on these issues, making an obvious appeal to the emotions. In a full-page advertisement published on May 19, 1977, the advertisement started with "Beloved Mom" and ended with "That is enough for this brothers' fight!"

In an advertisement published on June 1, 1977, again on a full page, the opening phrase was "For Great Turkey!" and the ad ended "The only leader for Great Turkey!"

The response to this advertisement came from CHP, with the "Our only hope Ecevit" motto (it was sarcastic). AP replied to this with a quarter-page advertisement saying that "Hope is behind a mountain but reality is right next to you!"

Because they were the first political advertisements, we have analyzed 13 newspaper
advertisements published by AP. Five of them
were full-page and the others were quarter-
page. They were plain statements focused on
specific subjects and did not include statistics,
comics, pictures, or any other figures. However,
they all had writing and one or two large AP
logos, with one at the beginning and one at the
end of the advertisement.

The content of the advertisements consisted
primarily of strong appeals to the voters to
vote for AP candidates. The party's positive
attitudes were put aside.

The "Powerful Leader for Great Turkey"
motto is an example. There are other examples
of advertisements that appealed to voters
without using negative elements. During the
coalition period elections, however, putting
the blame on the coalition partners for not
keeping their promises to the public was a
common practice.

On September 12, 1980, another military
coup took place. Military powers were once
more in charge. They had already been
involved in peacekeeping efforts, but now, with
the coup, anarchy suddenly came to an end. All
political parties, as well as the Parliament, were
abolished, all leaders were detained, and some,
along with many deputies, were put on trial.

The September 12 military coup brought a
different perspective to Turkey's political life.
The country was ruled by Bülent Ulusu, a
retired general, until November 6, 1983. All
the political parties and candidates taking
place in the 1983 elections had to get approval
from the military government. In the end, only
three parties were approved: the Nationalist
Democracy Party (MDP), the Populist Party
(HP), and ANAP. The president of MDP was
a retired general, and many of its members had
military backgrounds. Clearly, the military
powers were supporting MDP, and they were
uncomfortable with ANAP.

The November 6, 1983 elections were the
first following the 1980 military coup. They

had an important place in the history of
elections also because of the style of the campaigns. For these reasons, the 1983 campaign
deserves close analysis.

There was no passion in the open area
meetings during this campaign. Small crowds
gathered at the meeting places without enthusiasm and barely applauded the speakers, even
those from the political parties. Only the well-
decorated meeting places were getting the
attention of the public. Neither the leaders of
the political parties nor the public were enthusiastic. There was no effective leader and no
excitement. However, up until that point, the
most effective campaign tool had been these
meetings.

Perhaps the only thing that made any
significant impact during the election was the
live debate of the leaders on television on
October 22, 1983. It was the first such debate
in the political history of the country, and with
the help of this debate, the voters started to
form general opinions about the leaders and
their parties (Can, 1993). Immediately afterwards, the leaders of the political parties
started to arrange speeches and press conferences on radio and television. Newspapers
published critiques of the leaders' TV performance for days. During this election, television started to be used, along with radio,
for campaigning. Both radio and television
were public owned. There were no commercial
television or radio channels. The candidates'
discussions and conferences were broadcast
simultaneously on radio and television, starting on the evening of October 30 and ending
on the evening of November 6.

As in other elections, during the 1983 elections, there were political newspaper and magazine advertisements. ANAP's advertisements
were seen as effective, and they were two to
three pages long, with sensible statements that
attempted to persuade the voters. These advertisements, seriously lacking in emotion, were
published every 3 or 4 days. The total number
of print advertisements was very low, however.

The November 1991 parliamentary elections were also important from our perspective, particularly in regard to the appearance of the final results and the new dimension brought to political advertising during the campaign.

The only party that could still survive with the same name and the same leader after being in Parliament from the 1983 elections through the November 29, 1987 elections was ANAP. However, its share of the vote had fallen from 45.1% in 1983 to 36.3% in 1987. After the October 20, 1991 elections, ANAP's share dropped to 24%. As is discussed later, ANAP was eventually crowded out of the TBMM when its ratio fell to 5.1% of the vote, resulting in its having no members in Parliament.

During the October 20, 1991 elections, Süleyman Demirel, who had been the president of AP before the September 12, 1980 military coup, established DYP and won 178 seats out of 450. ANAP was in second place with 115 seats.

The second important point about this election is the use of the media in the campaigns. During the elections, many political advertisements appeared in the newspapers. Political parties used the national newspapers, in particular, for their advertisements. In *Sabah* alone, for example, which is one of the best-selling national newspapers, there were four full-page Social Democratic People's Party (SHP) advertisements. ANAP advertisements contained a photograph of its party leader, Mesut Yılmaz, stating that the party had done a lot when it was in charge, but it still had a lot to do. It should be noted that ANAP arranged their advertisements in consultation with the French advertiser Seguela.

In SHP advertisements, aggressive, negative messages drew attention. They were humiliating the leaders of rival parties, using cartoons. In the DYP advertisements, verbal promises were emphasized, with aggressive messages. There were reasonable statements in the DSP and RP advertisements. The RP advertisement had a photograph of the mentioned group.

As there was no interest in the open area meetings, SHP preferred to bring famous singers to its meetings, and DYP began to offer shows with popular stand-up comedians. Their task was to warm up the crowd for the party's speeches. For the first time in these elections, individual candidates for Parliament placed their own advertisements in the newspapers with the aim of increasing their chances of being elected.

The political party leaders' speeches and meetings on TRT had been very effective in influencing the voters' decisions. In these programs, the party leaders talked about their political platforms, there were scenes from their private lives, and their friends told favorable anecdotes about them. Furthermore, there were party advertisements between the speeches on both television and radio. The establishment of private channels by the leading political parties ANAP and SHP was another important advertising method during these elections. These channels, Star 1 and Mega-10, were established by Turkish legislation. The opposing parties used any available chance to handicap the two channels (this can be seen as illegally preventing illegally established channels from broadcasting). Most of the broadcasts on these channels were intended to persuade the voters, and the rest were political advertisements. Of course both channels made advertisements in favor of their own parties and their leaders. The majority of the advertisements consisted of aggressive, negative messages. The mentality noted in the past of "if my rival is perceived negatively and he fails, that will lead to my success" was highly subscribed to during the 1991 elections.

Between the October 20, 1991 elections and the November 3, 2002 elections, two other elections took place, on December 24, 1995, and April 18, 1999. These two elections have less historical importance to this study. However, I did apply a videostyle content analysis to party television ads and party-sponsored broadcasts in the 1995 elections.

This research indicated that the parties focused most of the verbal and visual aspects of the spots on the party leaders, giving the greatest emphasis to images and emotional appeals (Can, 1999).

Of greater importance is the November 3, 2002 election. To put this election in context, it is necessary to give some background information about the military intervention (coup) on February 28, 1997. This intervention started on the same day as the meeting of the National Security Council. What is really interesting about the intervention is that the president of the council was Süleymen Demirel, who was also president of Turkey at that time. He was not only one of the leaders of the political parties eliminated by the 1971 and 1980 military coups but had been prime minister both times. This intervention, later called the postmodern military coup, took place during the coalition of RP and DYP, which was led by Necmettin Erbakan, the president of RP. Once the coup had taken place, the military powers made the leading parties do what the army wanted. They reformed the new government, bringing the RP-DYP coalition to an end. First the president of ANAP, Mesut Yılmaz, and then the president of DSP, Bülent Ecevit, managed the coalition governments that ruled the country following the April 18, 1999 elections and until the October 3, 2002 elections.

In the October 3, 2002 parliamentary elections, none of the political parties involved after the 1997 military intervention earned enough votes to take seats in the TBMM. AKP, which was formed by a group of former RP deputies, won 363 seats out of 550 and formed a majority government. This result (considering both the period and the result) was, in fact, a repetition of the 1965 parliamentary elections.

The October 3, 2002 elections were quite different from the previous elections in terms of the political campaign, devices used for the campaign, message contents, aggressive attitudes, use of the media, and style of statements. Perhaps the only similarity to other elections was in the behavior of the voters, who continued not to vote for those whom they considered unsuccessful.

The most effective device in persuading the voters was television. The national channels aired propaganda about the personal character of the leaders, their ideas, and their political parties. On the program called *The Last Round With the Leaders*, broadcast over CNN Türk, the leaders of the political parties answered questions from reporters. On *Scouring Sands of Elections*, broadcast on channel D, leaders answered a reporter's questions; later, on the same show, AKP and CHP met. On *What Is Going On?* on channel TGRT, leaders answered additional questions. On *High Politics,* on channel 8, the political parties were discussed. On *The Area of Politics*, on channel ATV, second- or third-rank leaders of the parties and different representatives from the public held discussions. All of these programs were really effective for AKP, as it became the only leading party as a result of the elections. Party speeches were broadcast on the TRT television and radio channels at the same time they were aired on the other channels. Also, there were visual promotional messages in these programs. As coalition partners, DSP, the Election and Nationalist Movement Party (MHP), and ANAP received more time on TRT channels to present their messages. However, even these efforts could not help them to win seats in Parliament, and they failed to obtain the required 10% of the national vote.

By 1991, ANAP and SHP had their own television channels, focused on their own promotional messages. The new channels were established especially for this reason. During the 2002 elections, Cem Uzan, who owned a commercial television and radio network, founded his own political party, called the Young Party (GP). On his television and radio channels, he continuously aired promotional messages and propaganda for himself and his party.

As in the previous elections, the television channels, as well as the newspapers and the radio stations, continued to produce programs praising the political parties they supported and humiliating and spotlighting the faults of rival parties. This may be viewed as a symbiotic relationship between the political parties and television channels. If we add the percentages of television channels that mentioned the political parties to the positive, negative-humiliating, and sarcastic attitudes exhibited on specific television channels toward specific political parties, the result, of course, is more complex. The situation of TRT, although it maintains that it is a public channel, fair to all, is no different from that of the private channels.

No media channels, apart from the media group owned by the president of GP, were allowed to participate in GP meetings or conferences. Programs about the GP were produced and broadcast only by its own media group. Thus the party president's media group, his television and radio channels and his newspapers, acted as party broadcast organs. So blatant were the irregularities involved that his television and radio channels received 5 days of broadcast penalties due to infringement of the election laws.

During the 2002 elections, printed advertisements were also popular. However, by law, since October 22, 2002 no political advertisements have been published in the press. ANAP, DYP, CHP, MHP, and DSP made use of written advertisements quite extensively, although AKP rarely used them. In these advertisements, ANAP's efforts were for the European Union. MHP's advertisement, which appeared in *National Geographic Magazine*, was noteworthy.

The Turkish people were even less enthusiastic than in previous election campaigns about public meetings. To boost enthusiasm, DSP tried bringing singers to the meeting areas, but the results fell short of expectations. On the other hand, when GP brought popular pop stars to the meeting places and distributed free packages of food there, this was effective, especially with young people.

POLITICAL ADVERTISEMENTS AND NEW TECHNOLOGIES

The use of new technologies in the area of political communications was substantial in the October 6, 2002 elections. In previous elections, the political parties had distributed tapes of propaganda speeches and party songs. These were given to influential people in specific places who could easily reach and affect other voters around them. CDs replaced the tapes in the 2002 elections, and were handed out in greater numbers. Most of the CDs were distributed locally and, generally, for free. These CDs consisted of the history of the party, its members, political plans, and party songs.

The use of cellular phones as a campaign device was also seen in the 2002 elections. The material sent contained party slogans, pictures, and short messages. In the regional elections, the messages were more specific, such as information about special day celebrations, best wishes, and messages about the candidate. Most party members believed that these cellular messages would be effective on young voters. MHP, however, believed just the opposite. It believed that receiving messages constantly from different political parties would bore the voters and would result in negative attitudes toward the messaging party. As a result, MHP chose not to send persuasive messages to people the members did not know, although motivational messages were occasionally sent to party members.

It was observed that there was a significant increase in the use of e-mails, by both receivers and senders, in 2002. It had been very easy for the party members to obtain the e-mail addresses of people working in the public or private sector. Some of the parties also used Internet advertisements. These advertisements consisted of still or moving visuals that attracted interest. CHP used 21 Internet advertisements.

Some of the political parties had Web sites. With the help of these sites, people using computers could easily learn about the ideas, plans, and procedures of the party.

CAMPAIGN EXPENSES

Political parties run their campaign activities from their headquarters. The expenses of these activities are covered by the central party offices. These expenses are for transportation and for all kinds of advertisements, such as billboards, newspaper advertisements, letters to the voters, CDs, SMS messages, Internet advertisements, magazine advertisements, and other media. Procedures governing the expenses of political parties are determined by the Law for the Political Parties (Law 2820, Pt. 61). According to this law, party membership fees, fees from the party's members of parliament, donations, and income from fundraising activities organized by the party (Yavuz, 1994) are the important income sources for political parties.

Expenses accrued in local or city election areas are covered by donations or party income. Some expenses are covered by the party's deputy. If the deputy or the party's candidate is popular, then scores of volunteers may be ready to make donations to the party. If there is no financial support, then candidates must use their own resources. Newspapers have written that, during an election campaign, some candidates have accumulated expenses amounting to 2 or 3 years of a deputy's salary. In some regions, candidates with high risks of losing may spend more on advertisements than the total expenditures of two or three members of parliament.

One of the major expenses of political parties, local organizations, and candidates is the money they spend to personally reach out to their regional voters. Turkish people like to see the candidates or an authorized member of a political party visit their own regions, villages, streets, workplaces, and even their homes to demand votes. They would be proud of this kind of behavior. Such attempts by a candidate to make voters feel proud may increase that candidate's chance of getting those votes.

CONCLUSION

The relationships of the newspapers, magazines, and radio and television networks with the political parties have been effective in gaining positive results from the voters for the favored parties—and negative attitudes toward the rest. Also, the media have made great efforts to produce broadcasts or air news that uses photographs, comments, visuals, and so on during campaigns that can be labeled election propaganda.

Because the TRT is a public organ, its television and radio channels have always had a clear bias in favor of the current leading parties during election periods. All speeches and other types of propaganda are free on TRT channels, but airing political party advertisements outside of an election campaign is strictly forbidden.

Newspapers and magazines have different restrictions. They can print as many political advertisements as they like until a week before the elections. As there is no regulation for advertisements done through SMS, the Internet, or with other new technologies, parties are free to distribute as many advertisements as they desire.

Two points are prominent when we analyze the content of all the political advertisements. The first is the effort of political parties to turn emotions into actions. The second is negative advertising: Parties attempt to get voters to think negatively about rival parties by humiliating opponents aggressively instead of mentioning their own abilities and achievements. It is not difficult to observe the need and interest of the Turkish public for more stable, clear, and improved regulations—as soon as possible.

REFERENCES

Ahmad, F. (1992). *Demokrasi sürecinde Türkiye.* İstanbul, Turkey: Hil Yayınları.

Can, B. (1993). *İkna edici İletişimde duygu ve mantık kullanımı.* İzmir, Turkey.

Can, B. (1999). Television and electoral success in Turkey. In L. L. Kaid (Ed.), *Television and politics in evolving European democracies* (pp. 171–185). New York, Nova Science.

Çankaya, Ö. (2000). Türkiye'de Radyo Yayıncılığının Öyküsü. In E. Çakıroğlu, (Ed.), *İstanbul Radyosundan Anılar, Yaşantılar* (pp. 15–42). İstanbul, Turkey: Yapı Kredı Yayınları.

Inugur, M. N. (1982). *Basın ve Yayın Tarihi.* İstanbul, Turkey: Çağlayan Kitabevi.

Kabacalı, A. (1994). *Türk Basınında Demokrasi.* Ankara, Turkey: Kültür Bakanlığı Yayınları.

Timur, T. (1986). *Osmanlyı Kimliği.* İstanbul, Turkey: Hil Yayınları.

Öztoprak, I. (1981). *Kurtuluş Savaşinda Türk Basini.* Ankara, Turkey: Iş Bankasi Kültür Yayinlari.

Yavuz, M. (1994). *Seçim Kanunları.* Ankara, Turkey: Seçkin Yayınevı.

Yılmaz, S. (2002). *Kalemin Gücü* (Documentary), TRT 2.

24

Political Advertising in Emerging Democracies

The Philippines, Hong Kong, Singapore, Indonesia, and Malaysia

LARS WILLNAT AND ANNETTE AW

The year 2004 brought an unprecedented wave of democratic elections to the Asia-Pacific region, with nearly 1.2 billion people casting their votes ("Election watch Asia-Pacific," 2005). Many of these elections dramatically changed the political landscape of the countries in which they took place. In Indonesia, for example, almost 154 million people were able to cast a direct vote for their president for the first time.

Nonetheless, despite Asia's growing democratization, free and impartial elections are still the exception rather than the norm. Corruption, election fraud, violence, and even terrorism have undermined a large number of Asian elections in the past decade. The continued struggle for more democracy in Asia, however, has only increased the importance of the mass media as a political watchdog during elections and other political reforms. Moreover, the

trend toward more democracy in Asia has resulted in citizens who are more active politically and who demand reliable and unbiased information. It is therefore important to analyze and document the function of the mass media in the political transformation of these emerging democracies.

This chapter will focus on one particular aspect of this transformation: the role of political campaign advertising during elections in the Philippines, Hong Kong, Singapore, Indonesia, and Malaysia. Although the political systems of these five countries differ significantly and range from free in the Philippines to highly controlled in Singapore, political advertising is a commonly used campaign tool in all of them. Another common feature is the direct and indirect government controls and political biases, which come in various forms and have influenced the use and the effects of political advertising in each of these nations. Consequently, the goal of this analysis is to evaluate the significance and the impact of political advertising within the political, social, and cultural context of each of the five nations.

THE PHILIPPINES

Since the Philippines gained independence in 1946, democracy there has been marked by a series of turbulent events that demonstrate the importance of "people power" in politics. Widespread public rebellions and demonstrations ended the 21-year dictatorial rule of Ferdinand Marcos in 1986 and, after a failed impeachment trial, the presidency of Joseph Estrada in 2001. The combination of the Filipinos' high political involvement with a relatively free mass media made political campaigns an essential component of all elections in the Philippines over the past 40 years.

In fact, the media are one of the most effective means of attaining and sustaining political power in a country that is composed of geographically divided island regions (Garcia, 2003). The enormous importance of the mass media in Filipino politics has been recognized by aspiring political candidates who have used the media, and especially television, to convey information to the voters in a centralized way. No longer an exclusive possession of the affluent, television has rapidly entered most Filipino homes, indicating that a growing number of households can now be reached with political images during election campaigns (Coronel, 1998). According to a survey conducted by the Asia Research Organization in 1997, for example, 84% of Filipinos watch television (with the figure rising to as much as 97% in the capital), compared to only 81% who listen to the radio (Florentino-Hofileña, 1998).

To level the playing field for political candidates with widely different financial resources for campaigning, political advertising was banned in 1988, making it illegal "for any newspapers, radio broadcasting or television station, or other mass media to sell or to give free of charge print space or air time for campaign or other political purposes" (Electoral Reform Law, 1988). To circumvent the political advertising ban, Filipino election campaigns quickly became more creative, with candidates receiving media coverage through routine political news, talk shows, and television entertainment programs instead (Gamalinda, 1992). This trend, in turn, has contributed to extremely image-driven and personality-oriented election campaigns that put more importance on a candidate's popularity than on his or her political platform (Eaton, 2002).

Political candidates also found it fairly easy to circumvent the ban by paying reporters and columnists for favorable coverage (Coronel, 1991; Floretino-Hofileña, 1998). According to a study by the Philippine Center for Investigative Journalism, half of all the Filipino reporters who covered the 2004 election campaign said they were offered money by candidates, political parties, and other sources. Of those who were offered money, more than one third said that they actually took the money (Floretino-Hofileña, 2004). One sophisticated variant of this news-to-order journalism is the so-called attack-collect-defend-collect system (or AC-DC). First, journalists attack a candidate to collect money from his or her political rival, and then they defend the candidate originally attacked—also for a fee (Floretino-Hofileña, 1998; Garcia, 2003).

Another unexpected side effect of the advertising ban was that politicians with a background in the entertainment industry were able to spend less on their election campaigns because of their already high name recognition among voters. As a result, the number of media personalities making the transition to politics surged shortly after the advertising ban to exploit the personality-oriented culture of Filipino voters (Florentino-Hofileña, 1998; Garcia, 2003; Velasco, 1999).

The meteoric rise of former movie actor Joseph Estrada is one such classic case. Leveraging former movie roles, which often depicted him as a hero, Estrada rode on a wave of popularity that swept him from the mayor's office in San Juan in 1969, to the Senate in 1987, to the vice presidency in 1992, and finally to president of the Philippines in 1998 (May, 2002). Another media celebrity dabbling in politics was the popular actor Fernando Poe, Jr., who starred in more than 280 Filipino movies as the "champion of the weak, savior of the poor, and hope of the desperate" and ran for presidency in the 2004 election campaign shortly before his death the same year (Hoang, 2004).

Threatened by the dominance of media personalities in electoral races devoid of real political discussions, many lesser known candidates soon began to recruit movie stars and pop singers for their election rallies. In the 1992 campaign, for example, then presidential candidate Gloria Macapagal-Arroyo, along with many others, began hosting television talk shows and radio commentaries to combat the new trend of media celebrities (de Jesus, 1993). Other candidates eagerly appeared on talk shows and Filipino sitcoms (Gamalinda, 1992). Three senators even endorsed detergent, liquor, and medical products to circumvent the political advertising ban (Garcia, 2003). Taken together, these trends seriously undermined political discussions during election campaigns in the Philippines. The president of the Asian Institute of Journalism and Communication in Manila, Florangel Rosario Braid, pointedly summed up these developments by calling the Philippines a "showbiztocracy" (cited in Meinardus, 2004).

In hopes of eradicating the rampant corruption among politicians and the mass media, President Gloria Macapagal-Arroyo finally lifted the advertising ban in 2001 (Vanzi, 2000). The 2001 Fair Elections Act legalized political advertising in the mass media but also restricted the total airtime and print space that could be devoted to advertisements by each candidate. Political candidates running for national office were now allowed to purchase 120 minutes of television time and 180 minutes of radio time during the entire 90-day campaign period. Candidates running for local offices, on the other hand, were permitted to purchase 60 minutes of television time and 90 minutes of radio time during their 45-day campaign period. In addition, candidates were entitled to buy one quarter-page ad in a newspaper and one half-page in another publication three times a week during the campaign period. In return, the Fair Elections Act required the media to offer a 30% discount for television ads, 20% for radio ads, and 10% for print ads, based on the average rates charged during the year preceding the elections. The act also required that the candidate or party concerned identify all political advertisements as paid advertisements (Fair Election Act, 2001).

To prevent media personalities or celebrities from gaining an advantage over lesser known candidates during a political campaign, all films featuring actors or media personalities running for a political office were banned from public exhibition in theaters, on television, or in any public forum during the campaign. Additionally, to prevent politicians from circumventing election regulations with guest appearances on talk shows or similar indirect promotions of their political views, the Fair Election Act carefully defines "political advertisement" as

> any matter broadcasted, [*sic*] published, printed, or exhibited which is intended to draw the attention of the public or a segment thereof to promote or oppose, directly or indirectly, the election of a particular candidate or candidates to a public office. In the broadcast media, political advertisements may take the form of spots, guestings in TV shows and radio programs, live or taped announcements, teasers, and other forms of advertising messages or announcements used by commercial advertisers. (§ 1c)

In addition to the political advertisements that candidates can buy with their own funds, the Commission on Elections purchases airtime from national newspapers and the main television and radio networks, which is then allocated equally and free of charge among all candidates running for national office. Free airtime is also given to the national candidates for the broadcast of debates at the beginning, middle, and near the end of the campaign period (Fair Election Act, 2001).

Traditional mass media have been used extensively during recent elections in the Philippines, but new communication technologies, such as the Internet, played only a minor role in the recent 2004 presidential election campaign. According to a content analysis of official Web sites launched for the 2004 election, only 34% of all political candidates and political parties in the Philippines even had an official Web site (Cuevas, 2004). This, of course, is partly a reflection of the fact that only about 5% of the population in the Philippines has access to the Internet (Meinardus, 2004).

Despite the fact that new communication technologies such as the Internet are still out of reach for most Filipinos, the popularity of cell phones has influenced the way people discuss politics in the Philippines. With as many as 150 million text messages sent per day by a population of only 80 million (Meinardus, 2004), the potential of cell phones as campaign tools is enormous—especially in a country where the average voter cannot afford more expensive sources of political information. The growing influence of this new technology is exemplified in the 1999 impeachment trial of President Estrada, which focused on charges that he profited from illegal activities while in office (May, 2002). During the proceedings, cell phones quickly became a central part of a larger communication network that resulted in the impromptu gathering of protesters who demanded the resignation of President Estrada. Cell phones were also used to spread political rumors and jokes, which steadily eroded whatever legitimacy President Estrada had left during that period (Rafael, 2003). Although it is important to remember that the main purpose of cell phones is personal communication, their significance during important political events in countries that have limited alternative media sources is just beginning to emerge.

Overall, the history of corrupt and manipulated election campaigns has left many Filipino voters tired of the political intrigues that were once eagerly devoured by an audience deprived of political controversy during martial law. It is therefore no surprise that, in an already strained political climate tainted by the ideology of patronage, clientelism, and nepotism, recent elections in the Philippines have been marked by voters' deeply rooted mistrust and skepticism (Alejo, Rivera, & Valencia, 1996; Teehankee, 2002).

HONG KONG

Hong Kong's political environment has been shaped primarily by 150 years of British colonialism. The residents of this modern Asian city did not experience true democracy until the final years of colonial rule, when the British government increased its political reforms in anticipation of Hong Kong's reunification with China in 1997. In the early 1990s, the British introduced a more representative form of government in Hong Kong in the hopes that China would allow further democratization after the handover (Sing, 2003). To validate this new form of partial democracy and to ensure Hong Kong's continued democratic development, the British government assigned Chris Patten, an experienced British politician, as Hong Kong's last governor (Lau, 1998). Although many of Governor Patten's political reforms were abolished by the Chinese government after the handover, his efforts at introducing more democracy into Hong Kong have left a lasting impressing among the people of Hong Kong (Horlemann, 2003).

Despite these last-minute efforts by the British government to introduce more democracy, Hong Kong's current electoral system cannot be called fully democratic, because the chief executive and the legislature are not elected on the basis of universal suffrage (Kuan & Lau, 2002). In the recent 2004 Legislative Council (LegCo) election, for example, only half of the available 60 seats were elected directly. The remainder was selected by functional constituencies; more often than not, pro-China elites from various business and professional sectors. Likewise, the chief executive is selected by an 800-member election committee carefully chosen by the Chinese government to ensure the success of pro-China candidates in Hong Kong's elections (Cheung, 2003; Kumar, 2003; Sing; 2003).

The political changes also had a negative impact on press freedom in Hong Kong. There is no direct media censorship in Hong Kong, but most broadcast and print media are owned by large corporations with ambitious plans to expand their business into China (Lam, 2003). In view of Hong Kong's growing economic dependence on China, most media owners have ensured that Hong Kong's news coverage of China remains predominantly neutral. Indeed, many Hong Kong journalists are now practicing self-censorship by avoiding news coverage that could be construed as critical of the government in Beijing. As a result, the media have been generally cooperative with the hard-line stance and mandate of the Chinese government—despite the fact that there is no direct or established mechanism for Chinese authorities to give instructions to the Hong Kong media (Lam, 2003). The current situation is perhaps best captured by Cheng (2005), who points out that the media's "overwhelming incentive is to please—or at least to avoid annoying—the PRC authorities and their local affiliates" (p. 147). In turn, Chinese

officials, seeing the influence that the media wield among the Hong Kong public, cultivate sympathetic journalists by giving them preferred access to Chinese government officials or similar journalistic rewards.

Despite the self-censorship of Hong Kong's media, there are indications that political participation has increased among Hong Kong's residents since the 1997 handover. According to Scott (2004), two decades of political reform in Hong Kong "have created increased opportunities for political participation, with the political system having moved from one marked by colonial cooption and appointment and limited opportunities for participation in formal politics to one characterized by a heightened sense of citizenship" (p. 383). As a consequence, elections have become important political events in Hong Kong, making it necessary for political candidates and parties to adopt more sophisticated campaign strategies and presentation styles.

However, despite a growing trend toward more professional and expensive election campaigns (Ma & Choy, 2003), campaigning in Hong Kong still resembles what Butler and Ranney (1992) labeled "traditional electioneering" (pp. 5-6). Some parties have begun to adopt new technologies, such as telephone banks, to reach voters, but elections in Hong Kong are still dominated by traditional means of campaigning, such as posters, billboards, pamphlets, and public appearances by the candidates.

Ma and Choy (2003), who analyzed the campaign techniques used in the 1995, 1998, and 2000 LegCo elections, note that street-level campaigning and door-to-door canvassing are still the most popular campaign methods employed by political candidates in Hong Kong. Although it is time-consuming, personal contact between candidates and voters is relatively easy and cost-effective in densely populated Hong Kong. Moreover, it allows the candidates to meet voters directly, gather information about living conditions and local concerns, and distribute literature about their campaign (Cheng, 1996).

Recent election campaigns also saw the emergence of "mini campaign stations" that allow political candidates and volunteers to freely and directly interact with potential voters. Parties usually set up tables at densely populated public housing estates, plaster them with posters and prominent displays of the party logo, and then complete the setup with campaign music and speeches advertising the virtues of the political candidates. This rather festive atmosphere is complemented with a group of volunteers in matching attire who distribute leaflets and explain the party plat-form to passers-by (Scott, 2004).

Another popular mode of political advertis-ing in Hong Kong is the use of political banners or posters, usually found on guard railings, fences, and along busy pedestrian walkways. Political posters on private cars, trucks, public trams, and light buses, on the other hand, were first used in the 1994 District Board election campaign. By the year 2000, such vehicle advertising became a standard campaign technique, with public light buses bearing as many as six posters on each side of the bus (Scott, 2004).

Most campaign posters in the 1995 LegCo election focused on the candidates' names and pictures, but most posters in the 1998 election "chose to promote the party label rather than candidate names and personalities" (Ma & Choy, 2003, p. 355). A possible explanation for this change in focus might be the fact that the major political parties hired advertising agencies to design and produce campaign posters and newspaper advertisements for the first time in 1998. During the 2000 election campaign, however, political posters and advertisements again focused more on the can-didates rather than on the parties (Ma & Choy, 2003).

The use of political campaign posters and banners in Hong Kong has traditionally been supplemented with the distribution of pamphlets to the electorate. Given Hong Kong's strict political media advertising rules, campaign pamphlets, either distributed directly to voters or sent by mail to each household, are one of the most effective ways of reaching voters (Chan, 1993). According to a representative survey preceding the 2000 LegCo election, however, only about 15% of the respondents declared that flyers found in the mail had been influential and helpful in forming an opinion about who to vote for (Hong Kong Transition Project, 2000).

According to Ma and Choy (2003), these traditional campaign methods have historical and institutional roots in Hong Kong. In the past, popular elections were organized pri-marily at the local level (District Boards), and thus door-to-door canvassing was a cost-effective means of campaigning. Despite a substantial increase in the size of the con-stituencies that each candidate has had to cover in recent elections, personal contact between the candidates and voters remains a fixture in political campaigning. In addition, stringent restrictions on party finance prevent campaigning in Hong Kong from becoming too costly. During the 1998 election, for example, political parties and candidates in Hong Kong were permitted to spend only 46 U.S. cents on each voter during the campaign (Ma & Choy, 2003). Thus, expensive, media-based election campaigns are difficult to finance, especially for smaller parties and independent candidates.

The dominance of traditional campaign methods in Hong Kong is also explained by the fact that political advertisements are pro-hibited on Hong Kong's electronic media (Chan, 1993). Some parties found ways to attract routine media coverage by packing their campaign events with colorful parades and gimmicks such as "Batman and Robin" appearances or Chinese operas featuring singing candidates (Ma & Choy, 2003), but political advertising in the mass media is restricted to newspapers and magazines.

The use of print advertisements has, surprisingly, been extremely limited in past elections. For example, during the 1995 and 2000 LegCo elections, the two main political rivals, the Democratic Party and the Democratic Alliance for the Betterment of Hong Kong, published only a few advertisements each in the local newspapers (Ma & Choy, 2003). As indicated earlier, this obvious reluctance to advertise in the print media might be related to a strong belief in traditional campaign methods (such as public speeches and door-to-door canvassing), as well as the limited funds available for print advertisements.

In addition to traditional forms of political advertising, all major parties in Hong Kong launched Web sites in the 2000 election campaign. However, these Web sites were mostly used for the posting of basic information about the candidates and their party platforms and lacked true candidate-voter interactivity. Also, Ma and Choy (2003) note that "judging from the hit-rates, these Web sites were not influential campaigning tactics" (p. 358).

Overall, political campaign advertising in Hong Kong has come a long way in the past 10 years. Advertisements that once contained unfocused political messages, poor visuals, and cluttered designs have become more sophisticated and professional. In fact, election campaigns in Hong Kong are starting to resemble those in other Asian countries with longer histories of citizen participation and political campaigning, such as Taiwan, South Korea, and Japan. Although much of the campaigning in Hong Kong is still conducted at the personal level, new forms of campaigning based on telephone campaigns or political Web sites are likely to support a trend toward more media-based election campaigns in the near future.

SINGAPORE

Since independence from British rule in 1965, the political system in Singapore has been shaped by the rule of Senior Prime Minister Lee Kuan Yew and his close associates in the People's Action Party (PAP). Convinced that a purely Western model of democracy would lead to ethnic conflict and social unrest in Singapore's multicultural society, the government has consistently maintained that only a strong and united government can provide the leadership and policies to secure progress and prosperity in the city-state (Vasil, 2004). In addition, the ruling PAP claims that Singapore's racial and religious diversity make it necessary to limit the democratic rights and freedoms of Singaporeans—especially during elections, when there is heightened political activity and emotion (Singh, 1992; Vasil, 2004). Thus elections in Singapore are not held to determine who is to rule the country, but instead to bring together "the most gifted, innovative, well-educated and experienced men and women, who can offer Singapore a good, achievement-oriented and effective government" (Vasil, 2004, p. 110).

Singapore's economic achievements during the past 40 years have given the largely corruption-free government a high level of credibility and legitimacy among the public. Thus, although most Singaporeans wish for stronger opposition in their Parliament, only a few have a genuine desire for an alternative government (Singh, 1992). As a consequence, opposition parties in Singapore attract only limited public support and are therefore weak and fragmented (Vasil, 2004). It comes as no surprise that, in the last general election in November 2001, the ruling PAP won 82 of the 84 seats in Parliament.

Both the print and broadcast media in Singapore are tightly controlled by the government. The Singapore Press Holdings, a private media conglomerate with close ties to the government, owns all general circulation newspapers. Similarly, government-linked companies and organizations operate all broadcast television channels and almost all radio stations. Because of this indirect, but omnipresent, control of the media by the government, Singaporean journalists practice rigorous self-censorship by avoiding all sensitive issues. As a consequence, media coverage of domestic events and foreign relations issues closely reflects government policies and the opinions of government leaders ("Singapore: Country report," 2002).

Although Singapore's constitution guarantees freedom of speech and expression, political advertising is limited by a number of restrictive governmental regulations. The printing, display, and number of political advertisements, for example, is strictly controlled by the Parliamentary Elections Act. In addition, political advertisements can only be displayed during the official 9-day election campaign period. The ruling PAP maintains that a short campaign period is necessary to limit the potential for ethnic tensions and social disharmony (Vasil, 2004).

The use of the mass media during elections in Singapore is further restricted by a 1998 amendment to the Films Act that bans political advertising using films or videos, as well as "films directed towards any political end." The government justifies this ban by arguing that it prevents potentially sensationalist or emotional films from influencing the campaign. However, the ban also "has the effect of denying opposition parties, which already receive far less coverage than does the PAP in the government-influenced press and media, a potential outlet for their political messages" ("Singapore: Country report," 2002).

Political parties are given free airtime by the Singapore Broadcasting Authority in the form of prerecorded broadcasts that allow individual candidates to present their campaign and party platform. In addition, two special election broadcasts are aired during the campaign period—one program on election issues and a second, aired on the nomination day, on the candidates who will stand for election. However, these broadcasts are not open to independent candidates or parties fielding

fewer than six candidates, and as a result, candidates from smaller parties are excluded. Moreover, the amount of allocated airtime depends on the number of candidates each party is fielding. In the 2001 election, for example, these rules led to a clear advantage for the ruling PAP, which had more candidates (84) than the two main opposition parties combined (24). The PAP was consequently allotted 12 minutes of airtime for each of the two free broadcasts, and the opposition parties were entitled to only about 3 minutes of free airtime each ("Schedule for second," 2001).

Despite the fact that about 60% of all Singaporeans have access to the Internet ("Internet usage in Asia," 2005), the role of political Web sites in Singapore's recent elections has been limited. As part of the opposition, the National Solidarity Party was the first party to launch a Web site in 1995 (Seah, 2001). In response, the PAP developed the "Young PAP" Web site, which provides young Singaporeans with the opportunity to discuss political, social, and cultural issues in a Web-based discussion forum. According to the Young PAP ("Our vision," 2005), the official goal of such a discussion forum is to "help the PAP maintain its position as the mainstream political party of Singapore, by expressing the aspirations of young Singaporeans, and by recruiting supporters, members and leaders for the Party from among young Singaporeans." It is interesting to note that all major political parties in Singapore launched their official Web sites only shortly before the 2001 general election, obviously under the impression that Web sites are relatively unimportant as political campaign tools (Gomez, 2002).

Kluver's (2004) content analysis of political party Web sites during the 2001 Singapore general election shows that only four out of 21 political parties in Singapore actually maintained Web sites and that "most of them did not make use of features and content explicitly allowed by the Parliamentary Elections Act

Amendment, such as candidate biographies, frequent updates, moderated forums, and multimedia content" (p. 449). Moreover, only a few Web sites offered interactive features such as discussion forums, opportunities for active participation and volunteering, and e-mail addresses to which voters could send their views and comments. Kluver (2004) concludes, "in contrast to a perceived global trend toward the 'Internet-ization' of politics, the 2001 Singapore general election demonstrated that in spite of an advanced technological infrastructure, elections are still won and lost offline" (p. 455).

The use of the Internet for political campaigning in Singapore was severely curtailed by a 2001 amendment to the Parliamentary Elections Act aimed at regulating Internet campaigning and advertising during elections. The act allows only official party Web sites to carry political advertising, manifestos, candidate profiles, announcements of events, or party position papers (Kluver, 2004). Nonparty Web sites, on the other hand, are prohibited from displaying any political advertisements or even links to partisan Web sites. Although moderated chats and discussion forums are permitted on party Web sites, messages that are offensive or could harm the public interest, public order, or national harmony have to be removed (Tsang, 2001). Fund-raising activities and the publication of opinion polls during the election campaign are also prohibited (Tan, 2001).

The new regulations also address the use of e-mail and SMS messages for political purposes. Parties, candidates, and other election officials who send out e-mail or SMS messages with political advertisements during an election must clearly indicate the name of the sender of the message and on whose behalf these messages are sent. Since SMS messages have not been used in any systematic way by political parties in Singapore (Gomez, 2002), the government's efforts to legislate their use seems to indicate extreme anxiety about any

new form of communication that might be used for political purposes.

INDONESIA

The public revolution that shook Indonesia in 1998 ended the 32-year authoritarian regime of President Suharto and marked the beginning of the so-called *reformasi* (reformation) period. The political reforms gradually removed the myriad of business privileges and monopolies that once surrounded Suharto's inner circle and freed the Indonesian press from government control. In 1999, the Indonesian House of Representatives passed a new press law that, among other things, eliminated media licensing requirements, revoked the government's ability to ban publications, guaranteed freedom of the press, and even imposed penalties on "anyone who acts against the law by deliberately taking actions which could obstruct the work of the press" (Gazali, Hidayat, & Menayang, in press). Indonesian press freedom was also strengthened with the closure of the much-loathed Ministry of Information, "the main institutional body of state propaganda, surveillance and intimidation vis-à-vis the press" during President Suharto's rule (Heryanto & Adi, 2002, p. 54). Unfortunately, in the past few years, the Indonesian media have experienced setbacks due to widespread bribery, an increasing number of civil and criminal defamation suits brought against journalists, restrictions on reporting about ethnic conflict, and mob attacks on editorial offices (Freedom House, 2005).

In Indonesia, television is clearly the most powerful political medium, reaching more than 154 million eligible Indonesian voters spread across some 6000 islands. According to a representative survey of 1286 respondents conducted by the Asian Foundation in late 2003, two thirds of all Indonesians (66%) watch television every day or almost every day. Moreover, about half of all voters (46%)

have used television to find information about how to register and vote in elections. In contrast, only about one in 10 Indonesians relies on radio or newspapers for election information (Meisburger, 2003, p. 155).

Against the backdrop of the severe social, political, and economic problems that have plagued Indonesia since Suharto's resignation, the majority of the Indonesian media doubted that the first direct presidential election in 2004 would be peaceful and smooth (Mariyah, 2005). However, despite some administrative shortcomings and delays in the electoral preparations, the election was peaceful and democratic (EU Election Observation Mission, 2004). The success of the 2004 election was partly due to Indonesia's newly established General Elections Commission (KPU), which released a series of campaign regulations intended to organize one of the largest direct elections ever to be conducted (Gee, 2004; McBeth, 2004). Specifically, the regulations state that the campaign period for the legislative election can last a maximum of 3 weeks and must stop 3 days before Election Day. Party and candidate advertisements must be submitted to the KPU at least 2 weeks before the beginning of the campaign and can be printed or aired in the mass media only during the official campaign period. The regulations also allow political parties and candidates a maximum of one full-page advertisement per week in newspapers and two full-page advertisements per week in magazines, tabloids, and other print publications. In addition, each day during the campaign period, parties and candidates can run 10 television spots lasting no more than 30 seconds each and 10 radio spots lasting no more than 60 seconds each (Kurniawan, 2004). KPU regulations also prohibit parties and candidates from conducting a media campaign that attacks or disparages other parties or candidates and from "producing sound or visual effects that could raise fear and anxiety, from using impolite and coarse language, or material deemed

insulting to various ethnic groups or religions" (Kurniawan, 2004).

The presidential run-off between Megawati Soekarnoputri and Susilo Bambang Yudhoyono in September 2004 was accompanied by an intense media campaign blitz that lasted only 3 days—the time allowed to organize the final election run-off. The KPU granted each of the two presidential contenders 20 minutes of broadcast airtime per day to run advertisements on commercial television stations and 15 minutes of free airtime to deliver their speeches during the final days of the campaign. In addition, the candidates were able to run one half-page advertisement per day in the print media (Taufiqurrahman, 2004).

An independent report by the European Union Election Observation Mission (EU-COM), which observed the 2004 elections in Indonesia, noted that "the highly restrictive campaign regulations frequently led to efforts by both media and candidate teams to circumvent the rules through hidden and indirect candidate promotion or negative advertising" (EU-COM, 2004, p. 63). The EU-COM report also states that prior to the election, the state television company TVRI "showed a pronounced bias in favor of Megawati, devoting disproportionate amounts of coverage to positive reviews of her activities and achievements in office" (EU-COM, 2004, p. 63). Between July 14 and September 20, 2004, Megawati received more than five times as much coverage as Yudhoyono, more than half of it positive. Commercial television and newspapers, on the other hand, provided more balanced news coverage of the two candidates, with a variety of opinions expressed.

According to another study by the Institute for Studies on the Free Flow of Information, however, most of the Indonesian television campaign coverage focused on festivities and campaign preparations rather than political issues. In fact, more than 50% of the news coverage was concerned with the minute aspects of the political campaign, such as the installation of party flags, convoys, or music performances held by parties across the country (Saraswati, 2004). This particular media focus, however, may well have been a reflection of the fact that Indonesian journalists attending official campaign activities in 2004 were often met with lighthearted entertainment rather than politicians discussing their party's platforms (Saraswati, 2004).

Nevertheless, most observers of Indonesian election campaigns agree that political campaigning in Indonesia is less a contest of ideas, integrity, opinions, and political ideologies than it is a dramatic display of colorful symbols, entertainment, and freebies. This is especially the case for a common campaign technique in Indonesia, the *pawai*—a carnival of trucks, cars and motorcycles covered in the respective party colors that roar endlessly around the towns and cities. As has been the case for decades, young men dismantle the mufflers on their motorcycles and paint their faces either red (Democratic Party of Struggle of Indonesia), green (United Development Party) or yellow (Golkar) to demonstrate their political support during the campaign. Of course, the fact that parties usually provide free food and drinks to the members of these motorcycle squads only helps to increase their number and political support.

In the same spirit as the *pawai,* the festive atmosphere of a typical Indonesian election rally is often achieved with free entertainment and gifts such as "stickers, T-shirts, songs and dances, platitudes and more songs" ("Asia: A singing," 2004). In his bid to entice voters, Darwis Hamid, a parliamentary candidate in the 2004 elections, reportedly gave away packets of clove cigarettes (*kreteks*) wrapped in the green color of his United Development Party (Donnan, 2004). These gifts may seem small, but there is evidence that they might be able to persuade at least some Indonesians to vote in favor of their benefactors. According to Meisburger's (2003, p. 18) national survey

conducted shortly before the 2004 election, "about four voters in ten think that voters will be influenced if political parties offer money, food, or other gifts to voters, but only 15% think a gift would influence their own vote, while 24% are unsure."

Another unique form of political campaigning in Indonesia is based on theatrical shadow plays, known as *wayang kulits* among the locals (Ahmad, 2003). In the past, shadow plays were used by Suharto's ruling Golkar party and the opposition to depict and belittle their political rivals (Cederroth, 2004). Although shadow plays were very popular in Indonesian villages and small cities, competition from television, video, and film soon diminished their importance during national election campaigns. Nevertheless, a recent trend among Indonesian urbanites to rediscover their cultural roots has created new audiences for this traditional art in political campaigning. Attempts have been made to customize the shadow plays to the requirements of television broadcasts, so *wayang kulits* may soon become part of Indonesian election campaigns again (Ahmad, 2003).

MALAYSIA

After 22 years in power, Malaysian Prime Minister Mahathir Mohamad stepped down voluntarily on October 31, 2003. His successor, Deputy Prime Minister Abdullah Ahmad Badawi, won an overwhelming victory in the March 2004 general elections, with the ruling Barisan National (BN) coalition party winning 199 of 219 seats in the lower house of parliament ("Background note: Malaysia," 2005). This came as no surprise, because the BN has always maintained control of the Malaysian government, with the exception of a brief period in 1969 (Manikas & Thornton, 2002).

While the government of Prime Minister Badawi has proven to be more tolerant of political dissent than his predecessor

Mahathir, the country's repressive laws banning certain types of political speech remain in effect—ostensibly to protect national security and public order. Under the Printing Presses and Publications Act, for example, all domestic and foreign newspapers and television stations in Malaysia must obtain an annual operations permit from the government, which can be withdrawn without judicial review. This act also allows the Malaysian government to restrict publications containing "malicious" news or news that may threaten ethnic stability. Similarly, the Sedition Act prohibits public comment on issues defined as "sensitive," such as racial and religious matters.

Another law that has been frequently used by Malaysian officials to restrict free speech is the Internal Security Act, which allows the government to detain anyone without trial for 60 days for acting "in a manner prejudicial to the security of Malaysia." Opposition parties have accused the Malaysian government of using the Internal Security Act to restrict their political activities, and many opposition party members have been arrested under this law over the past several years (Manikas & Thornton, 2002). Political expression on the Internet has been constrained by the Communications and Multimedia Act, which requires licensing for Internet providers in Malaysia and allows legal action against "those who post defamatory and false information on the Internet."

Most political observers agree that these legal restrictions have been used to specifically target media sources that are critical of the government (Manikas & Thornton, 2002; Freedom House, 2005). In the 1999 election campaign, for example, news coverage of opposition activities such as rallies and speeches was forbidden on all government-operated electronic media outlets. Using arguments similar to those used by the Singapore government, Malaysian officials declared that news coverage and advertising supporting opposition parties and candidates would only lead to civil unrest and was therefore

in violation of several laws (Tamam & Govindasamy, in press).

Political parties and private businesses close to the ruling coalition own or control most major newspapers in Malaysia. Because of pressure from media owners and fear of legal action, many Malaysian journalists report practicing self-censorship (Manikas & Thornton, 2002). Self-censorship in the Malaysian media is often accompanied by news coverage and editorials that strongly support the government line (Freedom House, 2005) or by flattering media portrayals of the government and its policies. According to an analysis of the 1999 election coverage found in three major Malaysian newspapers, approximately half of all election news reports were biased in favor of the ruling Barisan Nasional party. In contrast, only about 10% to 15% of news stories were found in support of the opposition coalition Barisan Alternatif. The remaining coverage was either balanced or made no reference to any particular party (Wong, 2004).

As a consequence, although full-page advertisements encouraging voters to support the BN candidates were run in most major newspapers, nearly all advertising from the opposition was denied (Tamam & Govindasamy, in press). Moreover, the political advertisements by the BN relied on a full-scale "fear and scare" tactic, depicting the opposition alliance as a group of disunited, chaos-causing individuals. During the final days of the 1999 election campaign, for example, the ruling BN launched five full-page advertisements with photographs of young men smashing cars, throwing stones, and kicking trash bins, captioned with slogans such as "Don't Let Mob Rule Lead Us" and "Don't Let Hatred Win" ("Malaysia campaign off," 1999).

The prevalence of character assassinations, slander of opposing candidates and parties, and "hate politics" made the 1999 election one of the dirtiest in Malaysian electoral history (Moten, 2000). The 2004 general election was marked by a much softer, gentler campaign. This change in campaign style was mainly the result of a new advertising code of ethics that was added as an amendment to the Election Act and partially due to the more relaxed campaign style and personality of BN candidate Abdullah Ahmad Badawi. Rather than attacking its political rivals, the BN campaign in 2004 focused on portraying Badawi as a friendly and pragmatic candidate who was mostly concerned about excellence and efficiency in the civil service (Tamam & Govindasamy, in press).

As do the campaigns in other Asian countries, political campaigns in Malaysia rely extensively on traditional forms of political advertising, such as posters, leaflets, billboards, flags, and banners. Political parties in Malaysia have also distributed videotapes, CDs, and DVDs that usually feature political speeches and other events of political significance. According to Hilley (2001), these recordings are often sold at street markets and other informal outlets with a message that can be copied and passed on. In addition, political candidates often attend small public gatherings, visit public places, and distribute free food and other small gifts as they solicit votes and explain their policies.

Given the repressive media climate in Malaysia, the Internet has provided a welcome alternative medium for free and critical discussions of politics in Malaysia. In response to the public interest in the Web as an alternative news source, opposition parties in Malaysia have launched political Web sites that have captured a growing audience of young and active voters. Among the most popular Web sites are HarakahDaily.Net (http://harakah daily.net), a site maintained by the Islamic Party of Malaysia, and *Malaysiakini* (http:// www.malaysiakini.com), an online newspaper now regarded by many as one of the most important alternative sources of news about Malaysia today (Hussain, 2003).

Unlike countries where information is readily available through traditional media channels, the tight controls under which the Malaysian media operate might actually boost the political importance of political Web sites by creating a scarcity of reliable information and public mistrust of the mainstream media. Especially for the Malaysian opposition parties, which traditionally have received very little mainstream media coverage, this new medium provides direct and uncontrolled access to a limited but well-educated audience in Malaysia, particularly young voters (Mustafa, 2003). Thus it is not surprising that, according to one study, the Internet ranked third as source of political information during the 1999 campaign election, right after personal discussions and television (Aziz, Mohamad, Ghazali, & Abdul Rahman, 2000).

In addition to the Internet, the rapid spread of mobile phones in Malaysia has enabled political parties to use SMS messages to reach voters. Currently, almost 50% of the 25 million people in Malaysia use a mobile telephone service, the second highest mobile penetration in Southeast Asia after Singapore (Paul Budde Communications, 2004). During the 2004 election campaign, both the opposition alliance and the ruling party used SMS to advertise political slogans, to alert voters on election-related matters, and to communicate with campaign workers. For example, the youth wing of the United Malays National Organisation, which is part of the ruling BN party coalition, sent about 50,000 political slogans on SMS per day during the campaign ("Let the SMS," 2004). Similarly, the opposition Pan-Islamic Party of Malaysia offered information services, such as the headlines of HarakahDaily.net's top stories and notices about small gathering times and venues, via SMS (Hassan, 2004).

CONCLUSION

Without doubt, political advertising has become an essential campaign tool in the five countries analyzed here. Recent elections in the Philippines, Hong Kong, Singapore,

Indonesia, and Malaysia have been saturated with traditional and modern forms of political advertising. It is also obvious that the specific use of political advertising is highly dependent on the political, social, and cultural context found within each nation.

Overall, political advertising is tightly regulated in all the countries discussed in this chapter. Even in countries that have a relatively free political system, such as that found in the Philippines, a number of rules and regulations for political campaign advertising do exist. Although not all regulations are the same, it is fair to say that most of them limit the amount and frequency of political advertisements during election campaigns. Of course, the motivations for limiting political advertising differ greatly depending on the political system of each nation. The imposed limits in Singapore and Malaysia, for example, seem to be motivated primarily by political reasons (e.g., the dominance of the ruling party). The limits in the Philippines, on the other hand, seem to be based more on cultural and social concerns (e.g., image and celebrity-driven campaigns). The greatest threat to free elections, however, is the variety of national security and sedition laws that have been used to control media coverage and political advertising during election campaigns. The recent elections in Malaysia and Singapore show that, despite seemingly unbiased regulations controlling campaign activities, governments can easily suppress the mass media and the opposition parties with legal threats.

At the same time, it appears that political advertising regulations have been circumvented in most of the countries discussed here—with the possible exception of Singapore, where political advertising rules are enforced enthusiastically by the government. As the elections in Malaysia and Indonesia have shown, however, the ruling parties, rather than the opposition, usually are better able to undermine existing rules and regulations by using the mass media to

their advantage. Thus, instead of relying on political advertising alone, ruling parties often expect routine news coverage to reflect their point of view rather than that of the opposition. This can be accomplished through direct government controls, such as those found in Malaysia and Singapore, or by threatening and intimidating journalists and media owners, as has been documented in Indonesia. Politicians in the Philippines, on the other hand, have used the entertainment-oriented election campaigns to their advantage by appearing in campaign-unrelated television shows or, in some cases, using their celebrity status to gain favorable media coverage. Overall, it is clear that political advertising regulations in most of the five countries primarily benefit the ruling parties rather than the opposition. The one exception might be Hong Kong, where political advertising is dominated by street-level campaigning and door-to-door canvassing—forms of political advertising that level the playing field for the parties in power and the opposition.

This discussion has also shown that the potential of the Internet as an alternative venue for political information and campaigning has not yet been fulfilled. Although political Web sites have sprung up in all five nations, the impact of the Internet has been limited for various political and economic reasons. In Singapore, for example, tight regulations allow only political parties to run political Web sites, thus ruling out alternative political news sources. In countries such as the Philippines, Malaysia, and Indonesia, the impact of political Web sites is limited mainly because of the small percentage of the population in each country that has access to the Internet. The relatively small influence of political Web sites in Hong Kong, where about 71% of all people have access to the Internet ("Internet usage in Asia," 2005), seems to be determined primarily by the focus on traditional meet-the-voter election campaigns. Overall, it seems fairly certain that with rising

Internet access in Asia, political Web sites hosted by parties and alternative news sources will gain in importance. The already extensive use of more widespread communication technologies, such as cell phones by political parties in the Philippines and Malaysia, have shown that the potential of new technologies in political campaigns has not been fully used.

Finally, this overview has shown that there is an acute shortage of empirical studies that explore the character and potential effects of political advertising in each of the countries analyzed here. This is in stark contrast to the many political advertising studies found in more stable democracies, such as South Korea, Taiwan, and Japan (see chapter 17). The limited number of empirical studies can be explained at least partially by the fact that political advertising only recently became an important part of election campaigns in countries such as Malaysia and Indonesia. The Philippines and Hong Kong, however, have had more experience with political campaign advertising, and it is therefore somewhat puzzling that there are not more studies investigating the impact of this important campaign tool. Because political advertising is an essential part of free and democratic elections, it is hoped that future studies will address this shortcoming, especially in countries that are just emerging from authoritarian rule.

REFERENCES

Ahmad, C. M. (2003). Mass media in Indonesia: A short historical journey through five centuries. In M. Y. Hussain (Ed.), *Mass media in selected Muslim countries* (pp. 1–35). Kuala Lumpur: International Islamic University Malaysia.

Alejo, M. J., Rivera, M. P., & Valencia, N. P. (1996). *[De]scribing elections: A study of elections in the lifeworld of San Isidro.* Quezon City, Philippines: Institute for Popular Democracy.

Asia: A singing contest—Indonesia's election. (2004). *The Economist, 372,* 64.

Aziz, B., Mohamad, A., Ghazali, R., & Abdul Rahman, A. R. (2000). *Kajian mengenai peranan dan pengaruh Internet terhadap pada pengundi semasa pilihan raya umum Malaysia 1999* [A study on the role and influence of the Internet on voters in the 1999 general election in Malaysia]. Unpublished manuscript, Universiti Teknologi Mara, Malaysia.

Background note: Malaysia. (2005, September). Retrieved January 22, 2006, from the U.S. Department of State Web site: http://www.state.gov/r/pa/ei/bgn/2777.htm#political

Butler, D., & Ranney, A. (Eds.). (1992). *Electioneering: A comparative study of continuity and change.* Oxford, England: Clarendon Press.

Cederroth, S. (2004). Traditional power and party politics in North Lombok, 1965-99. In H. Antlov & S. Cederroth (Eds.), *Elections in Indonesia: The new order and beyond* (pp. 111–137). New York: Routledge.

Chan, J. M. (1993). Communication, political knowledge and attitudes: A survey study of the Hong Kong electorate. In S. K. Lau & K. S. Louie (Eds.), *Hong Kong tried democracy: The 1991 election in Hong Kong* (pp. 41–61). Hong Kong: Chinese University of Hong Kong Press.

Cheng, J. (1996). Political participation in Hong Kong in the mid-1990s. In H. C. Kuan, S. K. Lau, K. S. Louie, & K. Y. Wong (Eds.), *The 1995 Legislative Council elections in Hong Kong* (pp. 13–44). Hong Kong: Chinese University of Hong Kong Press.

Cheng, J.Y.S. (2005). Hong Kong's democrats stumble. *Journal of Democracy, 16*(1), 238–252.

Cheung, C. Y. (2003). Accountability and open government. In C. Loh & Civic Exchange (Eds.), *Building democracy: Creating good government for Hong Kong* (pp. 35–43). Hong Kong: Hong Kong University Press.

Coronel, S. S. (1991). Discussant: Sheila S. Coronel. In C. G. Hernandez & W. Pfennig (Eds.), *Media and politics in media: Trends, problems and prospects* (pp. 49–52). Manila: University of Philippines Press.

Coronel, S. S. (1998). *Media ownership and control in the Philippines.* Retrieved January 22, 2006, from http://www.wacc.org.uk/wacc/layout/set/print/content/view/full/1275

Cuevas, A. C. (2004). *The Internet and 2004 Philippine elections: Analysis of election campaign websites.* Unpublished master's thesis, School of Communication and Information, Nanyang Technological University, Singapore.

de Jesus, M. Q. (1993). Politicians in the press. In L. V. Teodoro & M. Q. de Jesus (Eds.), *The Filipino press and media, democracy and development* (pp. 219–221). Quezon City: University of the Philippines Press.

Donnan, S. (2004, March 16). Indonesian candidates smoke out their voters: Politically branded cigarettes are being used to woo the electorate in a country where smoking is a way of life. *Financial Times*, p. 10.

Eaton, K. (2002). *Politicians and economic reform in new democracies: Argentina and the Philippines in the 1990s.* Philadelphia: Pennsylvania State University Press.

Election watch Asia-Pacific. (2005). Retrieved January 22, 2005, from the Inter Press Service News Agency Web site: http://www.ipsnews.net/new_focus/asia_elections/calendar.asp

Electoral Reform Law of 1987, Rep. Act No. 6646 (January 5, 1988).

European Union Election Observation Mission to Indonesia 2004: Final report. (2004, November 1). Retrieved January 22, 2006, from http://europa.eu.int/comm/external_relations/human_rights/eu_election_ass_observ/indonesia/final_report_en.pdf

Fair Election Act, Rep. Act No. 9066 (February 12, 2001).

Florentino-Hofileña, C. (1998). *News for sale: The corruption of the Philippine media.* Quezon City, Philippines: Centre for Media Freedom and Responsibility.

Florentino-Hofileña, C. (2004). *News for sale: The corruption and commercialization of the Philippine media* (2nd ed.). Quezon City, Philippines: Centre for Media Freedom and Responsibility.

Freedom House. (2005). *Freedom of the press: Country reports.* Retrieved February 6, 2006, from http://www.freedomhouse.org/template.cfm?page=16&year=2005&country=6697

Gamalinda, E. (1992). Great expectations: Campaign strategies, image makers and the pursuit of the presidential candidate. In L. Kalaw-Tirol & S. S. Coronel (Eds.), *1992 and beyond: Forces and issues in Philippine elections* (pp. 284–307). Quezon City: Philippine Center for Investigative Journalism.

Garcia, E. Jr. (2003, October 31). *The mediatisation of politics or the politization of media?* Retrieved January 22, 2006, from the Konrad Adenauer Foundation Web site: http://www .kas.de/upload/dokumente/einbahnstrasse/garcia-_the_mediatisation_of_politics.pdf#search=philippines%20political%20advertising

Gazali, E., Hidayat, D. N., & Menayang, V. (in press). Political communication in Indonesia: Media performance in three eras. In L. Willnat & A. Aw (Eds.), *Political communication in Asia.* New York: McGraw Hill.

Gee, J. (2004). Indonesian presidential elections hard-fought second round. *Washington Report on Middle East Affairs, 23*(18), 3.

Gomez, J. (2002). *Internet politics: Surveillance and intimidation in Singapore.* Singapore: Think Centre.

Hassan, K. (2004, March 19). The heat is on. . . . There's SMS overload and midnight visits. *New Straits Times*, p. 64.

Heryanto, A. & Adi, A. Y. (2002). Industrialized media in democratizing Indonesia. In R. H. K. Heng (Ed.), *Media fortunes, changing times: ASEAN states in transition* (pp. 47–82). Singapore: Institute of Southeast Asian Studies.

Hilley, J. (2001). *Malaysia: Mahathirism, hegemony and the new opposition.* New York: Zed Books.

Hoang, M. (2004). The Philippines: Hail to "da king." *World Press Review, 51*(3). Retrieved January 22, 2006, from http://www.worldpress.org/Asia/1790.cfm

Hong Kong Transition Project. (2000, September). *Poll-arization: Election politics and the politicizing of Hong Kong.* Hong Kong: Hong Kong Baptist University.

Horlemann, R. (2003). *Hong Kong's transition to Chinese rule: The limits of autonomy.* London: RoutledgeCurzon.

Hussain, M. Y. (Ed.). (2003). *Mass media in selected Muslim countries.* Kuala Lumpur: International Islamic University Malaysia Research Centre.

Internet usage in Asia: Internet users & population statistics for 35 countries and regions in Asia. (2005). Retrieved January 22, 2006, from the Internet World Stats Web site: http://www.internetworldstats.com/stats3.htm

Kluver, R. (2004). Political culture and information technology in the 2001 Singapore general election. *Political Communication, 21,* 435–458.

Kuan, H. C., & Lau, S. K. (2002). Between liberal autocracy and democracy: Democratic legitimacy in Hong Kong. *Democratisation, 9*(4), 58–76.

Kumar, C. R. (2003). Election and voting systems: Perspectives on democratic governance in Hong Kong. In C. Loh & Civic Exchange (Eds.), *Building democracy: Creating good government for Hong Kong* (pp. 44–60). Hong Kong: Hong Kong University Press.

Kurniawan, M. N. (2004, January 3). Commission sets campaign rule on mass media. *Jakarta Post*. Retrieved January 22, 2006, from http://www.thejakartapost.com.

Lam, W.W.L. (2003). The media in Hong Kong: On the horns of a dilemma. In G. D. Rawnsley & M.Y.T. Rawnsley (Eds.), *Political communications in Greater China: The construction and reflection of identity* (pp. 169–189). London: RoutledgeCurzon.

Lau, S. K. (1998). *From the "through train" to "setting up the new stove": Sino-British row over the election of the Hong Kong Legislature* (Occasional Paper No. 72). Hong Kong: Hong Kong Institute of Asia-Pacific Studies.

Let the SMS battle begin. (2004, March 13). *Straits Times Interactive*. Retrieved February 6, 2006, from http://pgoh13.free.fr/sms_battle.html

Ma, N., & Choy, C. K. (2003). The impact of electoral rule change on party campaign strategy: Hong Kong as a case study. *Party Politics, 9*(3), 347–367.

Malaysia campaign off to stormy start. (1999, November 21). Retrieved January 22, 2006, from the BBC News Web site: http://news.bbc.co.uk/1/hi/world/asia-pacific/530778.stm

Manikas, P. M., & Thornton, L. L. (Eds.). (2002). *Political parties in Asia: Promoting reform and combating corruption in eight countries*. Washington, DC: National Democratic Institute for International Affairs. Retrieved January 22, 2006, from http://admin.corisweb.org/files/Manikas2003Political_Parties1093601961.pdf

Mariyah, C. (2005, October 4). General elections and triumph of pragmatism. Retrieved January 22, 2006, from the Jakarta Post.com Web site: http://www.thejakartapost.com/outlook/pol0b.asp

May, R. J. (2002). Elections in the Philippines, May 2001. *Electoral Studies, 21*(4), 673–680.

McBeth, J. (2004). A new start. *Far East Economic Review, 167*(39), 14–18.

Meinardus, R. (2004, February 2). *The media in elections*. Retrieved January 22, 2006, from the *Korea Times* Web site: http://times.hankooki.com/lpage/opinion/200402/kt2004020221073211360.htm

Meisburger, T. (Ed.). (2003). *Democracy in Indonesia: A survey of the Indonesian electorate 2003*. Jakarta, Indonesia: Asia Foundation. Retrieved January 22, 2006, from http://www.asiafoundation.org/pdf/democracy_in_indonesia.pdf

Moten, A. R. (2000). The 1999 general election in Malaysia: Towards a stable democracy? *Akademika: Journal of the Social Sciences and Humanities, 57*, 67–86.

Mustafa, K. A. (2003). The role of Malaysia's mainstream press in the 1999 general election. In K.W.F. Loh & J. Saravanamuttu (Eds.), *New politics in Malaysia* (pp. 52–65). Singapore: Institute of Southeast Asian Studies.

Our vision. (2005). Retrieved January 22, 2006, from the Young PAP Web site: http://www.youngpap.org.sg/abtus_vision.shtml

Paul Budde Communication. (2004, August 3). *2004 South East Asian mobile communications market August 3, 2004*. Retrieved January 22, 2006, from the MarketResearch.com Web site: http://www.marketresearch.com/product/display.asp?partnerid=885830502&productid=1030131

Rafael, V. (2003). The cell phone and the crowd: Messianic politics in the contemporary Philippines. *Public Culture, 15*(3), 399–425.

Saraswati, M. S. (2004, March 24). TV fail to answer campaign challenges. *Jakarta Post*. Retrieved January 22, 2006, from the http://www.thejakartapost.com

Schedule for second party political broadcasts, general election 2001. (2001, October 31). Retrieved January 22, 2006, from the Media Development Authority Web site: http://www.mda.gov.sg/wms.www/thenewsdesk.aspx?sid=275

Scott, J. L. (2004). The campaign imperative: Election strategies and the material culture of urban electioneering in Hong Kong. *Urban Anthropology and Studies of Cultural Systems and World Economic Development, 33*(2-4), 383–420.

Seah, C. N. (2001, June 26). *Cyberwatching politics: New political weapons—advertisements and Internet chatrooms, posting "false information" and advertising*. Retrieved January 22, 2006, from the Little Speck Web site: http://www.littlespeck.com/content/politics/CTrendsPolitics-010626.html

Sing, M. (2003). Legislative-executive interface in Hong Kong. In C. Loh & Civic Exchange (Eds.), *Building democracy: Creating good government for Hong Kong* (pp. 27–34). Hong Kong: Hong Kong University Press.

Singapore: Country report on human rights practices 2001. (2002, March 4). Retrieved January 22, 2006, from the U.S. Department of State Web site: http://www.state.gov/g/drl/rls/hrrpt/2001/eap/8375.htm

Singh, B. (1992). *Whither PAP's dominance? An analysis of Singapore's 1991 general elections*. Selangor, Malaysia: Pelanduk.

Tamam, E., & Govindasamy, M. (in press). Political communication practices and research in Malaysia: An overview. In L. Willnat & A. Aw (Eds.), *Political communication in Asia.* New York: McGraw-Hill.

Tan, T. H. (2001, September 1). *Confusion over Internet political advertising law.* Retrieved January 22, 2006, from the IT AsiaOne Web site: http://it.asia1.com.sg/newsarchive/09/news002_20010901.html

Taufiqurrahman, M. (2004, September 2). Poll commission completes drawing up campaign rules. *Jarkarta Post.* Retrieved January 22, 2006, from the Jakarta Post.com Web site: http://www.thejakartapost.com/yesterday detail.asp?fileid=20040902.C02

Teehankee, J. (2002). Electoral politics in the Philippines. In A. Croissant, G. Bruns, & M. John (Eds.), *Electoral politics in Southeast and East Asia* (pp. 151–202). Singapore: Friedrich Ebert Stiftung.

Tsang, S. (2001, October 18). *Singapore unveils rules for e-campaigning.* Retrieved January 22, 2006, from the ZDNet Asia Web site: http://asia.cnet.com/news/industry/0,39001143,38025935,00.htm

Vanzi, S. J. (2000, October 10). *Senate lifts political ad ban.* Retrieved January 22, 2006, from the Philippine Headline News Online Web site: http://www.newsflash.org/2000/10/hlframe.htm

Vasil, R. (2004). *A citizen's guide to government and politics in Singapore.* Singapore: Talisman.

Velasco, R. S. (1999). The Philippines. In I. Marsh, J. Blandel, & T. Inoguchi (Eds.), *Democracy, governance and economic performance: East and Southeast Asia* (pp. 167–192). New York: United Nations University Press.

Wong, K. (2004). Asian-based development journalism and political elections: Press coverage of the 1999 general elections in Malaysia. *Gazette, 66*(1), 25–40.

25

Deficient Democracies, Media Pluralism, and Political Advertising in West Africa

FRANK WITTMANN AND BABA THIAM

Since the beginning of the 1990s, several transformations have taken place in West Africa that have led to a reorganization of the political, economic, media, and social spheres. New organizational forms have manifested themselves at national conferences, in democratic changes in constitutions, in free elections, and in peaceful changes of power. These phenomena can be taken as indicators of the democratization of the West African region. This process of democratization is even more important considering the massive poverty in the area. The postcolonial state is also burdened with the task of initiating a nation-building process. In regard to ethnic diversity, this process of nation building has not yet come to an end in most countries. Because of the colonial past and structural deficits of the West African states, they require time to construct sustainable development. Initiatives such as the New Partnership for Africa's

Development can be interpreted as a sign of good governance. This partnership attests to the growing readiness of members to solve their own crises (Tetzlaff, 2004).

The introduction of multiparty systems, economic liberalization, technological innovation, and international linkage was accompanied by the privatization of information and communication technologies, the expansion of freedom of expression, and the formation of new media markets. The private media have become central vectors of public space and have pushed state media to the edge (Frère, 2005; Heyden, Leslie, & Ogundimo, 2002; Nyamnjoh, 2005). The transformation of the West African system of communication and the key role of mass media in the process of democratization have not been addressed sufficiently in communication research and political science. Especially in the West African presidential democracies, where charismatic

Authors' Note: The authors would like to express their sincere gratitude to Mohomodou Houssouba, Stephan Kuster, Heinz Nigg, and Adolphe Sanon for their input and support in compiling this paper.

417

leaders are of central importance, aesthetization, dramatizing, emotionalizing, personalizing, and adding scandal in political reporting
is not unusual. Political actors respond to the
popularization of political communication
through mass media with new mediatization
strategies. It has become common to employ
communication consultants and spin doctors.
In election periods, political advertising also
plays a role. The amount of newspaper advertising, as well as radio and television advertisements, for political candidates and parties
is low. However, indirect and surreptitious
advertisements play an important role: On the
one hand, political actors receive a lot of
media reporting; on the other hand, a large
deficit in West African journalism occurs
because of its partisan role (Perret, 2005). As
will become apparent in this chapter, the
mostly young and "deficient" democracies
(Merkel, Puhle, & Croissant, 2003, p. 1) suffer
from the fact that actors in the public arena
such as politicians, media representatives, and
religious leaders do not confine themselves to
their proper fields of function.[1] Under these
conditions, it is not surprising that the division
of powers guaranteed by constitutions does
not function smoothly in practice.

This chapter describes the political system,
the media landscape, and the role of political
advertising in West Africa. Because West
Africa is characterized by broad political,
social, and cultural diversity, we use examples
from different countries in West Africa.
However, Senegal will be covered more extensively than other countries. This is because
Senegal "is one of the first countries on the
continent that outlined a program of how to
escape the nightmare of a one party system,
which has prevailed in almost all countries
south of the Sahara" (Mbembe, 1990). The
next section offers a general overview of the
political landscape, followed by a discussion
of the new pluralism of mass media, which
contrasts strikingly with the decline of freedom of the press. Finally, we consider the

recent election campaigns in Mali, Senegal,
and Burkina Faso and the role of political
advertising in them, and we outline the perspectives of political advertising and of mediatization strategies in West Africa.

POLITICAL LANDSCAPES BETWEEN DEMOCRACY AND AUTHORITARIANISM

The democratization process initiated at the
beginning of the 1990s can be explained with
exogenous as well as endogenous factors.
More pressure has been exerted on (West)
African countries for greater democratization
after the fall of the Berlin Wall and the end of
the Cold War. This push for democratization
has been promoted by former colonial powers
and international institutions like the World
Bank and the International Monetary Fund. In
his speech in La Baule in 1990, former French
president François Mitterrand linked the payment of the development funds (of vital importance to African state budgets) to the progress
of the democratization process. Civil societies
also have pushed for democratic reforms.

Fifteen years after this push for change, the
democratization process has been mostly
disappointing. With military and political
conflicts in the Ivory Coast, Guinea-Conakry,
Liberia, Mauritania, Sierra Leone, and Togo
from 2003 to 2005, West Africa became a
place of violence and instability.[2] Neglecting
the principles of good governance, West
African nations have experienced a marked
increase in domestic political crises so that
today the political systems of only five
countries can be considered to be free: Benin,
Ghana, Cape Verde, Mali, and Senegal (Piano
& Puddington, 2005). However, only the
democracies of Ghana, Cape Verde, and Mali
are consolidated. The regimes of Benin and
Senegal embody semiauthoritarian indicators, as do those of Burkina Faso, Gambia,
Mauritania, Niger, and Nigeria, which have
been classified as not free. In these nations,

democratic values and institutions are only partly rooted in society. Ivory Coast, Guinea-Bissau, Guinea-Conakry, Liberia, Sierra Leone, and Togo are so-called failed states, with collapsing governmental institutions. No single country in West Africa has a corruption coefficient of more than 3.6 on a scale from 1 (very high) to 10 (very low) (Transparency International, 2004). Corruption and neopatrimonialism have established themselves as quasifavored modes of government. Income based on economic production and the export of raw materials usually does not get reinvested but is absorbed by a system organized on clientelism. Coming from a background of a marginal share of world trade and few foreign investments, the economies of many West African countries have come under the influence of criminalization. As a consequence, the region has become a platform for trafficking in diamonds, drugs, and people; for money laundering, smuggling, and fraud (Bayart, Ellis, & Hibou, 1999; Chabal & Daloz, 1999; Smith, 2003).

NEW MEDIA PLURALISM

In recent years, the political evolution in the West African region has reflected ambivalence. On the one hand, certain democratic standards have been introduced, such as multiparty systems, freedom of the press, and free elections. As a result of this, few democracies have succeeded in being consolidated. On the other hand, the majority of semiauthoritarian regimes managed to subvert the democratization process and destabilize their regions politically and militarily. The ambivalence of this political situation is reproduced in the mass media. Because of the external political and internal civil pressure at the beginning of the 1990s, governments have understood that a liberalized media market offers them the possibility of documenting their progress of democratization and displaying it to the outside world. Accordingly, the national communication policy has been modified and the state monopoly on information has been lifted. To provide financial support for the establishment of media pluralism, some national governments have invested funds to assist commercial mass media.

Media Important for Political and Social Communication

The radio is the most popular, credible, and important medium for information gathering in the West African region (Fardon & Furniss, 2000; Tudesq, 2002). Radio is used by more than 90% of the population. The availability of commercial, communal, confessional, national, and international radio varies according to country from 20 to 100 channels. The success of radio can be explained in that it modernizes oral tradition, furthers West African culture, promotes identity, does not exclude illiterates, elaborates local languages, and can be received without great cost. The broadcast sectors in Burkina Faso (Frère & Balima, 2003) and in Mali (Schulz, 2001) show that the stunning success of commercial and community radio is the result of original programming, innovative moderator styles, and recognition of the needs of local audiences. A good example of innovation is the interactive program. The audience can take part in the program by calling into the station. This form of program shows how private radio functions as a platform for political and social dialogue. Although public channels generally still act in favor of the governments and play only a subordinate role, international channels such as the BBC, Radio France International, Radio Televisao Portuguesa Internacional, and Voice of America have succeeded in establishing themselves in the market because of their quality of information. Generally, the radio stations are financed through advertising.[3]

Television is the second most important medium. In cities such as Abidjan, Dakar, and

Lagos, television is used so extensively that it already competes with radio as the leading medium (Tudesq, 2004). The content and the technical quality of public TV channels are so poor that local television is not valued very much by the public. It is mainly used for sports and foreign entertainment series. Many democratically elected governments have difficulties with the privatization of the audiovisual sector (Ba, 1996; Sy, 2003). The regimes reveal their semiauthoritarian character by postponing the liberalization of television, giving the thinnest of reasons. The statement by Senegalese president Wade, that television is too sensitive and dangerous to be left in the hands of anybody, has become famous. The fear of critical journalism is so great that only in Benin, Burkina Faso, Ghana, and Nigeria can one talk about a partial privatization of the television market. In all other countries, foreign channels can only be received with the installation of expensive parabolic antennas and the payment of big fees. Because of the economic depression, most citizens cannot afford these fees.

The press sector, however, is completely liberalized. Up to 50 (Burkina Faso), 70 (Senegal) and even 100 (Nigeria) different journals are sold in newspaper kiosks and on the street. In actuality, only the elite, about 10% of the population, regularly read newspapers. All in all, the printing press plays a subordinate role: Considering the illiteracy rate, up to 40% in the anglophone and up to 70% in the francophone and lusophone countries of West Africa, only a minority of the population has the reading skills that enable citizens to read newspapers written in the official languages of English, French, and Portuguese. As the medium of the opinion leaders, the press exercises certain influence on the agendas of the other mass media. Besides a fixed number of professional and regularly appearing newspapers and magazines, many periodicals are only sporadically published or do not satisfy high-quality standards (Frère, 2000; M'Bayo, Onwumechili, & Nwanko,

2000). A small, irregular, and economically disadvantaged readership, marginal advertising market, low level of income, high costs of production, and poorly maintained network of distribution have led to high turnover in journalists and to a dangerous instability in the market. These factors push many editorial boards into dependence on the informal sector and lead to corruption, fraud, and even violence. Nevertheless, some newspapers are successful in reaching an audience beyond the traditional intelligentsia, thanks to their strategies of popularization (Beck & Wittmann, 2004; Perret, 2005). This is especially true for the yellow press, which established itself a few years ago in Ivory Coast, Burkina Faso, Nigeria, and Senegal. The print media also find an even wider audience through the "press reviews" on the radio. Most West African radio stations broadcast reviews several times a day of items published in local newspapers and magazines. These reviews last 5 to 10 minutes and are aired in both the official European and African national languages. The radio personalities offer to their audience an attractive and, until now, unreachable access to print information with their intonation skills, comments, wit, and ironic humor.

The print media and the information and communication technologies are mostly limited to urban areas (Brunet, Tiemtoré, & Vettaino-Soulard, 2004; Chéneau-Loquay, 2004). Since the year 2000, all African countries have been wired to the Internet. Political actors (governments, parties, candidates) and civil society (nongovernmental organizations, trade unions, federations, pressure groups) are represented on the Internet through their home pages. Some Web surfers make use of online national, pan-African, and international mass media and news agencies. National online publications fulfill two primary functions: (a) The homepage serves as an advertising instrument that enables the media to make themselves visible, and (b) online publications also serve the great West African diaspora in Europe and North America by providing current information. However, what is online does not reflect the plurality of local mass media. The Internet is mostly used at the work place and at public cyber-cafés. In the modern cities especially, cyber-cafés have become part of the urban landscape. This phenomenon cannot hide the digital division between rich and poor, as well as between the city and the countryside. In the wide rural areas of West Africa, the Internet is practically nonexistent.

The Development of Telephony

The African mobile phone market today has the highest rate of growth worldwide. Many multinational telecommunication enterprises, such as France Télécom, Orange, and Vodafone, have set up West African companies or have formed joint ventures with them. Today, in all the countries of West Africa, there are more mobile telephones than telephones using fixed lines. Mobile phones also have changed the everyday lives of journalists. Now radio reporters are able to broadcast live from wherever they are. Specifically, elections can be more efficiently controlled if journalists are directly placed in polling stations, interviewing voters. This helps to reduce the danger of election manipulation (Institut Panos Afrique de l'Ouest, 2001). The mobile phone has changed political and social communication. The so-called *télécentres* also have become very important in West Africa. They are privately run and provide services for people who want to call per minute or even want to be called themselves in the télécentre booths. In Senegal, more than 13,000 télécentres exist (Diop, 2002; Zongo, 2000).

VIOLATIONS OF PRESS FREEDOM

Today, all West African states have a democratic constitution. Media pluralism and freedom of the press are fundamental to democratic practice. Although the pluralization of media during the last 15 years can be considered an irreversible process, this contrasts strikingly with the decrease in freedom of the press that has been going on at the same time. In 2004, violations of press freedom have been noted in all West African countries with the exception of Benin, Ghana, Cape Verde, and Mali ("Introduction Africa," 2005; Karlekar, 2005). Examples vary, from arbitrary conviction of journalists to physical harassment and the introduction of new laws that contradict all principles of freedom of the press. Through these violations, regimes aim to intimidate the media and force self-censorship on them.

Arbitrary Arrest of Journalists in Senegal

As in all other West African states, the liberty of expression and freedom of press is officially guaranteed in Senegal. "Every person has the right to express and to distribute freely his or her opinions through speech, writing and images" (Sy, Fall & Samb, 2000, p. 10). These rights are supplemented with several duties journalists have to fulfill in the practice of their profession. Written laws describe the rights and duties of media publications and professional journalists. According to the law, ethical norms such as conscientiousness, responsibility, and the right of anyone who feels attacked in the press to a counterstatement have to be observed. The National Commission for Press Cards keeps watch on whether journalists are compliant and may remove the licence card of journalists acting against the law. This licence card officially confirms the professional status of the journalist and obliges him or her to respect the ethical norms described here. The Penal Code defines offences and defamations of the press against institutions of the State, and a number of articles can be applied if national security is threatened through the diffusion of misinformation or offences against morality. Clearly, the media law in Senegal is contradictory. Freedom of the press is legally guaranteed and protected by different institutions, but there are several laws that impinge on journalistic freedom. Because of this, there has always been tension between the media and the State (Loum, 2003; Paye, 1992).

The case of Madiambal Diagne illustrates the contradictory nature of the laws, as well as the regular *and* arbitrary application of laws by authorities. In July 2004, the director of the daily newspaper *Le Quotidien* was arrested and held in custody for 3 weeks (Havard, 2004). He was charged with having published secret court documents and for disseminating false information, thus threatening national security. The documents dealt with a corruption scandal in which public authorities were supposed to have been involved. Diagne was arrested for having violated Article 255 of the Penal Code (dissemination of false information) and Article 139 of the Criminal Process Code (restriction of the journalist's right to information). The arrest of Diagne led to protests by the people, and the French government intervened. In view of the internal and external pressure, President Wade could do nothing but advise the authorities to set the journalist free.

Legal and Physical Harassment and Murder of Journalists in Ivory Coast and Gambia

After the failed coup d'état in Ivory Coast against President Laurent Gbagbo in 2002 and the breakout of a rebellion that divided the country in two, the mass media were reduced to spokespeople for the parties in conflict and even served as instruments of agitation. Nationalistic newspapers and radio channels have provoked their audiences to respond negatively to Muslim guest workers from neighboring countries, supporters of opposition politicians, French citizens, and even United Nations Blue Beret troops. The government and the rebels controlling the north of the country both practice censorship. Often, investigative, independent, and even international journalists find themselves caught between the fronts in this tense atmosphere. In 2004, three journalists were killed in Ivory Coast. Kidnapping, death threats, physical aggression, and criminal conviction are part of a journalist's everyday life. Several times, international radio channels such as Africa No 1, the BBC, and Radio France International have been confronted with bans on broadcasting and with sabotage.

In Gambia, the situation is also alarming. Since the confirmation of the authoritarian regime of Yahya Jammeh in the presidential elections of 2001, freedom of the press has continuously decreased. Although freedom of the press is guaranteed in the Gambian constitution, a Media Commission controlled by the government has been created. This commission has introduced several media laws that attempt to suppress any critical or independent journalism. In vain, the Gambia Press Union has fought the amendments to the Newspaper Act and the Criminal Code. In conjunction with this conflict, the former president of the Union, Deyda Hydara, who had been a correspondent of Agence France Press, a collaborator with Reporters Without Borders, and the managing editor of the newspaper *The Point*, was murdered in 2004.

REGULATION AND PRACTICE OF POLITICAL ADVERTISING

Press freedom is especially important in times of election. The violations described in the sections above cast doubt on whether conditions for free and fair presidential elections in Ivory Coast (2005), Gambia (2006), and Senegal (2007) will be met. In the next section, we analyze the role of political advertising in campaigns in Mali, Senegal, and Burkina Faso. These three examples show the wide range of political practice and communication within the West African region. A common characteristic of these countries lies in the insignificance of commercial political advertising. Both media attention-generating events (meetings, manifestations) and public relations (press declarations, press conferences) are more important than advertising spots on television, radio, newspaper, and billboards. In other words, the goal of political actors is to set the agenda of the mass media. Widespread partisanship among journalists in regard to both political parties and candidates helps them to succeed.

POLITICAL ADVERTISING IN A DEMOCRATIC COUNTRY

Mali

Mali is not only one of the rare consolidated democracies in West Africa but also has a liberal approach to political advertising. Since the country ousted the military dictatorship of Moussa Traoré in 1991, it has chosen a democratization path that is progressing step by step. The maturity of the democratic process has been attested to in the election of the independent candidate Amadou Toumani Touré in the presidential elections of 2002. Touré has built a government of national unity that pays special attention to policies of decentralization. In conjunction with this, in 2004 communal elections were held for the first time in Mali's 703 communities. Despite the fragmentation of the party landscape and some cases of manipulation, the election was considered a success by national political actors as well as international election observers.

The most important political campaign instruments were meetings, press declarations, billboards, and advertising spots on the radio. The candidates for mayor were visible to the public and were supported by the heads of their parties. These heads travelled not only to the different regions of the country but guided the parties' campaigns from the capital, Bamako. Public radio and television offered to all parties little but equal amounts of time for advertising. Because of the fact that the television sector is still not liberalized and newspapers play only a marginal role, radio has almost no business competition for the broadcast of political advertising spots. Political advertising spots are an outstanding source of income for many commercial and community radio channels. Therefore, businessmen regularly buy advertising time for certain parties or candidates. According to the statements of observers, political advertising has not had any decisive effect on the elections. The political reporting in the mass media was much more important for the campaign. Partisanship in the editorial sections of radio and newspaper programming occurs regularly. With regard to the fact that, in neopatrimonial systems, the mass media has a special function of critique and control, one must admit a certain deficiency in terms of transparency. The Superior Council of Communication has the task of controlling media reporting. However, in its final report, the council highlighted the neutrality of the Malian mass media and did not mention any serious offences. Moreover, the Observatory for Deontology and Ethics of the Press has not received any complaints.

Senegal: Political Advertising in a Semiauthoritarian Country

Senegal is a country with a long democratic tradition. In spite of the multiparty system introduced in 1974, former presidents Léopold Sédar Senghor (1960-1980) and Abdou Diouf (1981-2000) succeeded in establishing their Socialist Party as a quasinatural governmental party. Finally, in the presidential elections of 2000, long-time opposition politician and challenger Abdoulaye Wade of the Democratic Party of Senegal managed to win the vote. There are four reasons for this democratic and peaceful change (Cruise O'Brien, Diop, & Diouf, 2002). First, the economic crisis and the rise of social tensions have led to a serious loss of power and deteriorated image for incumbent Diouf. Second, the opposition succeeded in introducing reforms for election procedures. The founding of the National Observatory Charged with Elections in 1997 provided the basis for higher transparency in future elections. The third reason is the transformation of the religious sector, which now had politically, economically, and socially influential actors. Previously, the leaders of the Muslim brotherhoods had recommended and supported specific candidates, but they have abstained from interventions in campaigns since the beginning of the 1990s to avoid a weakening of their own position of social emancipation and modernization. Last but not least, commercial mass media played a crucial role in the election. Early in the campaign, the media exposed attempted election fraud by the former government (e.g., the falsification of voting cards). Moreover, with their critical reporting, the independent media encouraged and increased the people's will for political change. On voting day, the editorial boards guaranteed the transparency of the elections by sending a multitude of journalists to the polling stations to control the course of the elections and to disseminate first trends and results (Institut Panos Afrique de l'Ouest, 2001). Under these circumstances the government saw no possibility of falsifying the results afterwards, and Abdou Diouf had to admit his defeat.

Effecting a change of power was more difficult for Abdoulaye Wade, because Article 37 of the Electoral Code prohibits any commercial advertising during the official campaign. The only exception is the public television channel, RTS, which allocates free airtime to all parties for advertising spots. The significance of political advertising in the electronic mass media is generally marginal, and the regulations are restrictive. Together with the National Observatory, the High Audiovisual Council (HCA) watches for compliance to this law. According to law 98-09, the HCA's role is to be an impartial arbitrator in regulating the sensitive field of communication, especially during election periods.

Despite the restrictive law, all political actors in Senegal are aware of the importance of political advertising. After all, the law permits the use of all other advertising instruments, such as billboards, banderols, promotional gifts such as t-shirts and ballpoint pens, and telemarketing. The goal is to have a positive influence on the public's image of the candidate: "In the sector of political marketing, the leader becomes a product, like a package of cigarettes or a can" (Mané, 1998, p. 8). The parties have at their disposal a budget for the production and distribution of billboards (articles 43 to 46 of the Electoral Code regulate billboard advertising). Abdouaye Wade's Democratic Party of Senegal spent 15 million francs CFA on the occasion of communal elections in 1996 to promote the slogan "Dakar has chosen" on billboards. Moreover, it was this party (which in the meantime had become the government party) that introduced telemarketing in 2002. In those districts where the party was especially weak, the directory had been linked with the election lists. Consequently, approximately 50,000 prospective voters received a call with an advertising message recorded on tape by Prime Minister Idrissa Seck.

Because of the restrictive advertising regulations, the election appearances and public relations by the political actors were of great importance. The law indicates that no reporting about the political campaign and no surreptitious advertising is allowed during the last 30 days before the official campaign closes so that (a) the candidates and parties are allocated adequate airtime for their appearances, press declarations, and press conferences during the campaign and (b) the mass media serve as independent and neutral reporters. Nevertheless, these regulations are not respected by the media. A majority of the media violate the legal dispositions by acting as spokespeople for particular parties. Their partisan role is made manifest in one-sided reporting by newspapers (e.g., about the "blue marsh" of presidential candidate Abdoulaye Wade), in disproportionately long contributions by readers on political topics, and in the transmission of entire political meetings through radio broadcasts. Public TV channel RTS puts itself entirely in the service of the reigning government party. The political actors pay heavily for journalistic coverage of their activities: In Senegal, it is well known that journalists obtain lump sums for their participation in press conferences, at candidate appearances, or on campaign trips (Diouf, 2005). Although the HCA is legally required to control the campaigns and to guarantee compliance with legal dispositions, in actuality the regulation authority is not able to successfully fulfill its duties. Hence civil societal actors criticize the inefficiency of the council. For example, the human rights organization La Rencontre Africaine pour la Défense des Droits de l'Homme (the African Conference for the Defense of Human Rights, best known as RADDHO) deplores the slow but real erosion of the authority and credibility of the control and supervision boards. Moreover, Jacques Habib Sy has come to the conclusion that the work of the HCA has led to ambivalent results: "There has been, for example, no strong condemnation of the HCA in regard to audiovisual messages deemed offensive by large sectors of public opinion (references were made to ethnic or religious groups during the airtime of certain political parties and in certain electoral meetings)" (Sy, 2003, p. 69).

Burkina Faso: Political Advertising in an Authoritarian Country

Compared to that of Senegal, the regime in Burkina Faso is even more authoritarian. It often ignores democratic standards or tries to subvert them. To prove the accuracy of this statement, one has only to consider the fact that the president, Blaise Compaoré (in power since 1983), was allowed to run again for office, even though the Burkina Faso constitution prohibits another term. Five oppositional presidential candidates have sued because of this violation of the constitution, but the Constitutional Court has rejected the claim. Consequently, the opposition party candidate Herman Yaméogo decided to withdraw a few days before the elections. The campaign process was especially interesting. Due to a domestic loss of his power since 2000, the current incumbent felt compelled to build up a government of national unity. Expecting a strong campaign of opposition based on civil and social issues, the government party accordingly initiated a new tactic. In fact, it initiated a type of para–civil-societal campaign. The primary goal was to gain the public's attention through traditional civil-societal actions, such as manifestations of solidarity and support marches. The local press was supposed to report such events in detail. Moreover, the government engaged groups to travel in rural areas and issue voting cards. With regard to the mass media, legal violations concerning political advertising have been asserted, but the Supreme Council of Information has not intervened. Although the official campaign did not begin until October 20, 2005, the public television and radio channels had been broadcasting advertising spots in favor of President Compaoré months earlier. In contrast, commercial television and radio channels have respected the principle of the legal dispositions and have delayed the broadcast of advertising spots. With regard to the mass media's reporting on the campaign, a multitude of partisanships could be asserted, too. Although the public media entirely supported the campaign of the governmental party and its candidate Blaise Compaoré, the commercial media allowed a lot of editorial space for declarations, interviews, and other methods of promotion to different political actors. All in all, Compaoré spent 983 million FCFA (U.S. $1.7 million) for his campaign, whereas all other candidates disposed officially of only about 8 million FCFA (U.S. $15,000) each. To no one's surprise, under these circumstances, Blaise Compaoré won the elections with more than 80% of the votes.

CONCLUSION

Analysis of the campaigns in Mali, Senegal, and Burkina Faso demonstrates that there are great differences between the political communication practices of the countries in the West African region. One common characteristic is that electoral appearances and public relations play a much more important role than advertising. Because the television sectors are only liberalized in Benin, Burkina Faso, Ghana, and Nigeria, the significance of television is marginal overall. The primary aim of political actors is to set the agenda for the mass media. Campaign advertising takes place particularly in the editorial parts of newspapers, radio, and television. To gain the public's attention, political actors from West Africa chose media strategies similar to those in other parts of the world. The model of presidential democracy that prevails in this region (a president with a strong position of power) is susceptible to performance strategies. Charismatic presidents such as Mathieu Kérékou of Benin or Abdoulaye Wade of Senegal have successfully adopted media reporting, using aesthetization, dramatizing, emotionalizing, and personalizing techniques, as well as the addition of scandal. The campaigns of candidates and parties are carried out much more professionally than they were some years ago: Although communication specialists emphasize public relations, more and more consultants, managers, and spin doctors are engaged in the planning and realization of the campaign. For example, in the 2000 election, former Senegalese president Abdou Diouf obtained the support of French communication specialist Jacques Séguéla, whose slogan "La force tranquille" (peaceful power) had helped bring François Mitterand to power in 1981. However, the fact that Séguéla was not able to prevent the defeat of Abdou Diouf shows clearly that, at least in some countries of West Africa, neither advertising nor propaganda but political performance was decisive for success in elections. This example might be a sign that the hopes for consolidation of the deficient democracies in West Africa are still intact.

NOTES

1. The notion of deficient democracies was introduced by Wolfgang Merkel in regard to political transformation processes in Asia, Latin America, and Eastern Europe. We are applying this term in the West African context.

2. Through a peace agreement, the government in Dakar and the rebels of the Movement of Democratic Forces in the Casamance succeeded in solving their 20-year-old military disagreement.

3. However, the multinational companies that sell services and consumer products have considerably higher budgets for advertising formats such as billboards and television.

REFERENCES

Ba, A. (1996). *Télévisions, paraboles et démocraties en Afrique noir* [Television sets, satellite dishes, and democracies in black Africa]. Paris: L'Harmattan.

Bayart, J.-F., Ellis, S., & Hibou, B. (1999). *The criminalization of the state in Africa*. Oxford, England: James Currey.

Beck, R. M., & Wittmann, F. (Eds.). (2004). *African media cultures: Transdisciplinary perspectives*. Cologne, Germany: Rüdiger Köppe Verlag.

Brunet, P. J., Tiemtoré, O., & Vettraino-Soulard, M.-C. (2004). *Ethics and the Internet in West Africa: Toward an ethical model of integration*. Lawrenceville, NJ: Africa World Press.

Chabal, P., & Daloz, J.-P. (1999). *Africa works: Disorder as political instrument*. Oxford, England: James Currey.

Chéneau-Loquay, A. (Ed.). (2004). *Mondialisation et technologies de la communication en*

Afrique [Globalization and communication technologies in Africa]. Paris: Karthala.

Cruise O'Brien, D., Diop, M.-C., & Diouf, M. (2002). *La construction de l'Etat au Sénégal* [The construction of the state of Senegal]. Paris: Karthala.

Diop, M.-C. (Ed.). (2002). *Le Sénégal à l'heure de l'information: Technologies et société* [Senegal in the information era: Technologies and society]. Paris: Karthala.

Diouf, Y. (2005). Les journalistes: Des corrompus? [Journalists: Corrupt?] In M. Taureg & F. Wittmann (Eds.), *Entre tradition orale et nouvelles technologies: Où vont les mass médias au Sénégal?* [Between oral tradition and new technologies: Where is Senegal's mass media going?] (pp. 31–36). Dakar, Senegal: Enda Tiers Monde.

Fardon, R., & Furniss, G. (Ed.). (2000). *African broadcast cultures: Radio in transition.* Oxford, England: James Currey.

Frère, M.-S. (2000). *Presse et démocratie en Afrique francophone: Les mots et les maux de la transition au Bénin et au Niger* [The press and democracy in French-speaking Africa: Words and evils in the transition of Benin and Niger]. Paris: Karthala.

Frère, M.-S. (2005). Médias en mutation: De l'émancipation aux nouvelles contraintes [The changing media: Freedom and new constraints]. *Politique Africaine, 97,* 5–17.

Frère, M.-S., & Balima, S. T. (2003). *Médias et communications sociales au Burkina Faso: Approche socio-économique de la circulation de l'information* [Media and social communication in Burkina Faso: The socioeconomic approach to the circulation of information]. Paris: L'Harmattan.

Havard, J.-F. (2004). De la victoire du "Sopi" à la tentation du "Nopi"? Gouvernement de l'alternance et liberté d'expression des médias au Sénégal [From the victory of "Sopi" to the temptation of "Nopi"? The government of alternation and freedom of expression for the media of Senegal]. *Politique Africaine, 96,* 22–38.

Heyden, G., Leslie, M., & Ogundimo, F. F. (Eds.). (2002). *Media and democracy in Africa.* New Brunswick, NJ: Transaction.

Institut Panos Afrique de l'Ouest. (Ed.). (2001). *Médias et elections au Sénégal: La presse et les nouvelles technologies de l'information dans le processus électoral* [The media and the Senegalese elections: The press and new

information technologies in the electoral process]. Dakar, Senegal: Author.

Introduction Africa—annual report 2005: Continent of hope and death. (2005). Retrieved January 23, 2006, from the Reporters Without Borders Web site: http:// www.rsf.org/ rubrique.php3?id_rubrique=510

Karlekar, K. D. (Ed.). (2005). *Freedom of the press 2005: A global survey of media independence.* New York: Freedom House.

Loum, N. (2003). *Les médias et l'Etat au Sénégal: L'impossible autonomie* [The media and the state in Senegal: Impossible autonomy]. Paris: L'Harmattan.

Mané, B. (1998). *Marketing politique au Sénégal: Comment le leader fabrique son image* [Political marketing in Senegal: How the leader constructs his image]. Dakar, Senegal: Cesti.

M'Bayo, R. T., Onwumechili, C., & Nwanko, R. N. (Eds.). (2000). *Press and politics in Africa.* Lewiston, NY: Edwin Mellen Press.

Mbembe, J. A. (1990). *Afrique sub-saharienne: Enjeux de fin de siècle* [Sub-Saharan Africa: The stakes at the end of the century]. Unpublished manuscript, Université de Laval, Québec.

Merkel, W., Puhle, H.-J., & Croissant, A. (Eds.). (2003). *Defekte Demokratie. Band 1: Theorie* [Deficient democracy. Vol. 1. Theory]. Opladen, Germany: Leske und Budrich.

Nyamnjoh, F. B. (2005). *Africa's media: Democracy and the politics of belonging.* London: Zed Books.

Paye, M. (1992). La presse et le pouvoir [The press and power]. In M.-C. Diop (Ed.), *Sénégal: Trajectoires d'un Etat* [Senegal: The path of a nation] (pp. 331–377). Paris: Karthala.

Perret, T. (2005). *Le temps des journalistes: L'invention de la presse en Afrique francophone* [The time of the journalist: The invention of the press in French-speaking Africa]. Paris: Karthala.

Piano, A., & Puddington, A. (Eds.). (2005). *Freedom of the press: The annual survey of political rights and civil liberties.* New York: Freedom House.

Schulz, D. E. (2001). *Perpetuating the politics of praise: Jeli singers, radios and political mediation in Mali.* Cologne, Germany: Rüdiger Köppe Verlag.

Smith, S. (2003). *Négrologie: Pourquoi l'Afrique meurt* [Negrology: Why Africa is dying]. Paris: Hachette.

Sy, D., Fall, M., & Samb, M. (2000). *La Constitution: Quoi de neuf?* [The Constitution: What's new?]. Dakar, Senegal: Fondation Friedrich Ebert.

Sy, J. H. (2003). *Crise de l'audiovisuel au Sénégal* [The audiovisual crisis in Senegal]. Dakar, Senegal: Aid Transparency.

Tetzlaff, R. (2004). Stufen und Etappen politischer Herrschaft 1960-2002 [Grades and stages of political rule, 1960-2002]. In M. A. Ferdowsi (Ed.), *Afrika—ein verlorener Kontinent?* [Africa: A lost continent?] (pp. 33–71). Munich, Germany: Wilhelm Fink Verlag.

Transparency International. (2004). *L'indice de perceptions de la corruption 2004* [2004 corruption perception index].Retrieved January 23, 2006, from http://www.transparency.org/cpi/2004/dnld/media_pack_fr.pdf

Tudesq, A.-J. (2002). *L'Afrique parle, l'Afrique écoute: Les radios en Afrique subsaharienne* [Africa speaks, Africa listens: Radio in Sub-Saharan Africa]. Paris: Karthala.

Tudesq, A.-J. (2004). La télévision en Côte d'Ivoire [Television in Ivory Coast]. In R. M. Beck & F. Wittmann (Eds.), *African media cultures: Transdisciplinary perspectives* (pp. 241–262). Cologne, Germany: Rüdiger Köppe Verlag.

Zongo, G. (2000). Télécentres au Sénégal [Telecenters in Senegal]. In A. Chéneau-Loquay (Ed.), *Enjeux des technologies de la communication en Afrique: Du téléphone à Internet* [The stakes for communication technologies in Africa: From the telephone to the Internet] (pp. 211–223). Paris: Karthala.

26

Political Advertising in South Africa

RUTH TEER-TOMASELLI

The political landscape in South Africa has changed so dramatically in recent years that it is truly possible to give credence to the aphorism that "Yesterday was another country." The 1976 uprising and the armed struggle waged by African National Congress (ANC) cadres and associated organizations signalled the beginning of a new, highly contested and negotiated dispensation. From the mid-1980s to the end of the decade, South Africa witnessed a series of states of emergency (1985-1990), during which coercive legislation, including severe restrictions on the media, was enacted (Teer-Tomaselli, 1992). Parallel to this process, however, a process of reform was undertaken that culminated in the announcement by then president F. W. de Klerk of the 1990 release of Nelson Mandela from a 27-year prison term for sedition against the state. The final break with the past was heralded by the first fully representative election on April 27, 1994.

Thus, this survey of party campaign advertising begins with the year 1994.

Prior to 1994, the use of political advertising in the lead-up to elections was sporadic. Street posters and placards, the occasional ad hoc newspaper announcement, and pamphlets and handbills given out door to door provided the main thrust. The success of party campaigns depended primarily on the party's ability to communicate with those seen as loyal followers who would vote for and legitimize it. In this respect, campaigning during apartheid resembled earlier, premodern campaigns in Europe and America, where voting was the prerogative of the few—the educated and propertied elite or, in the case of South Africa, enfranchised whites. There was little need for widespread campaigning, as meetings, rallies, and editorials in the press of the time were deemed sufficient (Norris, Curtice, Sanders, Scammell, & Semetko, 1999, p. 5). Across the globe, the age of universal suffrage made it imperative to expand the outreach of parties, candidates, and politics in general into the realm of the mass media. With the 1994 elections, South Africa entered that age of universal suffrage.

OVERVIEW OF THE POLITICAL AND MEDIA SYSTEM OF SOUTH AFRICA

South Africa is a parliamentary democracy with an elected president, a National Assembly of 400 seats, and a National Council of Provinces that consists of nine delegations nominated by the provincial legislators. Each province is allocated 10 seats in the Council. Elections are held every 5 years, and both the National Assembly and the provincial assemblies are contested on the same day.

Elections are overseen by the Independent Electoral Commission, established in 1998 (Electoral Act No. 73, 1998). The Commission functions as both a manager and a regulator of elections, as well as organizing voter education. It favors mediation rather than judicial adjudication of disputes between parties, including those between political parties and broadcasters.

South Africa uses a system of proportional representation, and voters choose a party rather than individual candidates. Each party draws up two lists of nominated candidates—one for the National Assembly and one for provinces—in the order in which the party would like to see them in Parliament. Voters complete two ballot papers, one for the National Assembly and one for each of the nine provincial legislatures. Each ballot paper carries the list of parties, together with their logos and the faces of their leaders (to enable less literate voters to recognise the party of their choice). Candidates are allocated seats in accordance with the proportion of votes garnered by each party, and not all parties that participate in the elections attract sufficient voters to be allocated any seat in Parliament.

Introduction to the Parties

In 1994, 19 parties participated in the election: 16 in 1999 and 21 in 2004 (Independent Electoral Commission, 2006). Not all parties participated in the national election; some smaller parties stood only in particular provinces. This chapter considers the fortunes and electoral campaigns of only three parties: The African National Congress; the National Party (NP), subsequently renamed the New National Party (NNP); and the Democratic Party, subsequently renamed the Democratic Alliance. Other parties of importance, referred to but not discussed here, are the Inkatha Freedom Party, a Zulu nationalist party with a stronghold in KwaZulu-Natal, and the Independent Democrats.

The ANC, the South African Communist Party, and the Congress of South African Trade Unions formed a tripartite alliance for the 1994 and subsequent elections. Although each came from a different historical trajectory, they shared important similarities in their goals and aspirations for the new government. The ANC itself was a coalition of different, but generally like-minded, groups and organizations, including an external (and most influential) wing of diplomats, exiled professionals, political activists, and the military cadre *Umkonto we Sizwe*.

Because the ANC, Pan African Congress, and the South African Communist Party had been banned since the early 1960s, surrogate domestic organizations were formed, the most important of which were the Congress of South African Trade Unions and the United Democratic Front. The Front was itself a broad coalition of black, "colored," and Indian organisations, as well as white democrats, pressure groups, and nongovernmental organisations. The release of Nelson Mandela, the homecoming of many exiles, and the establishment in 1992 of the United Democratic Front's own election commission signalled the genesis of its change from a liberation movement to an orthodox political party.

From the outset, the ANC has been the hegemonic party with the largest number of voters: 62% in 1994, 66% in 1999, and nearly 70% in 2004. This dominance has led to a lopsided political landscape in which elections largely are about securing a two thirds majority and establishing an opposition. Following the first two elections, the ANC governed in seven of the nine provinces, with KwaZulu-Natal under the Inkatha Freedom Party (IFP) and the Western Cape Province under the New National Party (discussion follows). Both provinces were won over in the 2004 elections, largely as a result of the collapse of the NNP in the Cape and a poor showing by the IFP. Signs of growing strain within the tripartite alliance were evident from 2001 on, as the ANC moved into a more centrist position (endorsing liberal, as opposed to radical, economic policies) than its alliance partners were prepared to accommodate.

The National Party came to power in 1948. This party initially saw its aim as protecting and fostering white Afrikaner interests against both the economic monopoly of English mining capital, as exemplified in the post–World War II United Party, and the encroachment of cheap black labor. To achieve the latter, an elaborate system of social, economic, and political separation, called *apartheid*, ensured that blacks remained oppressed, while whites and, to a lesser extent, coloureds and South Africans of Indian origin received preferential access to social and economic goods and services.

In the 1994 election, the NP performed relatively well, becoming the official opposition to the ANC and gaining 20% of all votes cast. It was particularly strong in the Western Cape, where it headed the provincial government. In terms of an agreement brokered before the first elections, the NP formed an alliance with the ANC, creating a "Government of National Unity." The party pulled out of the arrangment ahead of the 1999 elections, opting to change its name to the New National Party, a strategy designed to distance itself from its apartheid past and reinvent itself as a moderate, nonracial federal party. The 1999 general election saw the party almost wiped out nationally, but it remained influential in the Western Cape. The NNP was also part of a short-lived alliance with the Democratic Party (DP), for which purpose the party changed its name to the Democratic Alliance (discussion follows). After leaving the alliance, the NNP allied itself with the ruling ANC. After repeatedly poor showings in subsequent elections, the party disbanded in 2005, and many of its members crossed over to the ANC.

The Democratic Party had been one of the all-white parties involved in parliamentary politics prior to the entrance of the new, mainly black liberation parties. The DP traced its origins back to the formation of the Progressive Party in 1959, when twelve United Party MPs broke away in disgust at their party's refusal to repudiate unequivocal racial discrimination and embrace the policies that accepted evolution toward a democratic, nondiscriminatory society in South Africa. The DP played a vital role in the negotiation of an interim constitution that includes most of its original Progressive Party principles. However, in 1994, the party won only 1.7% of the vote, securing only 10 seats in Parliament. Under the leadership of Tony Leon, the party fared better in 1999 with 9.6%, becoming the official opposition. A short flirtation with the NP in 2000 led to the party's renaming itself the Democratic Alliance (DA) and saw the DA take over the Western Cape, always an electoral battleground. In 2004, the DA consolidated its role as the official opposition, with 12.4% of the votes and 50 seats, and it remains the second largest political party in South Africa.

MEDIA STRUCTURES: PRINT

At the time of the 1994 elections, South Africa had not yet caught up with the global revolution of increasingly fragmented media and politics. Looking back, it appears that the South African media were in the death throes of a "modern" period. The rapid restructuring of media houses and the push for black economic empowerment had not yet taken place.

Campaigns for the opening of the airwaves and the neoliberal thrust taken by the Department of Communications, the establishment of the Independent Broadcasting Authority (IBA) (1993) and, later, the Independent Communication Authority of South Africa (ICASA) (2000), created a new proliferation of broadcasting channels. The "new media" of cell phones and the Internet were embryonic, and party-political Web sites would not be a feature of the elections until 1999. This made the task of political parties easier, as the media system of the time was relatively closed and easier to manage.

Prior to 1994, the printscape was dominated by two English-language media groups, Argus Holdings Limited and Time Media Limited, and two Afrikaans-language media groups, Perskor and Nasionale Pers (National Newspapers). These companies were interconnected on the Johannesburg Stock Exchange with the wider web of South African monopoly capital. The four press groups also controlled M-Net, a subscription television channel. Complex relations thus existed between the media conglomerates and other South African capital interests of the apartheid era (Teer-Tomaselli & Tomaselli, 2002, p. 131). Historically, the South African press was divided along linguistic, racial, and regional lines and showed a strong loyalty toward particular party political affiliations. The antiapartheid English language newspapers had traditionally supported the Democratic Party (in its various incarnations from the Union Party through to the Progressive Party); Afrikaans papers shared a long history with the National Party (de Beer, 2002; Domisse, 1980; Tomaselli, Tomaselli, & Muller, 1989). At the beginning of the period under review, newspapers were still heavily divided along party lines, even if there was some realization that change was inevitable. At the same time, the press was aware that future survival depended on an open-ended acceptance, if not endorsement, of the new

regime, spearheaded by the ANC. In later elections, party-political loyalty was muted, with only traces of previous fault lines visible.

The period after 1994 was one in which political, social, economic, and technological conditions were conducive to media growth (Berger, 2002, p. 152). The Argus Group began the process of restructuring in 1993, when it "unbundled" its titles in an attempt to further black economic empowerment. *The Sowetan*, aimed at black middle-class readers, was gradually acquired by New Africa Investments Ltd. (NAIL), a corporation set up to empower the newly enfranchised black business sector. In turn, the company sold the paper to another empowerment corporation, Johnnic Publishing, in 2004. With the impending ANC victory of 1994, the way was opened for foreign investment into South Africa. The Irish-based Independent Newspaper Group, owned by Tony O'Reilly, purchased the Argus Group.[1] In 1994, Johnnic purchased Times Media Limited, among other media and entertainment ventures. The NP-supporting Afrikaans newspaper chains also underwent vast changes during the early 1990s. During the 1990s, the print sector saw a deterioration in circulation and profits (Berger, 2002) before an upswing was exemplified by the larger circulation successes of the *Sowetan Sunday World*, the *Sunday Sun*, *Isolezwe*, and *Vukani* in 2002.

BROADCASTING

The overhaul of broadcasting began with the establishment of the IBA in 1993, the year before the first election in 1994. There was a strong perception that the then NP-supporting South African Broadcasting Corporation (SABC) could not be trusted to provide fair and unbiased coverage of the upcoming political campaigns. Part of the mandate of the IBA was to oversee political electioneering on the air, and to this effect, a number of regulations were promulgated (discussion follows). In

1996, the IBA merged with the South African Telecommunications Regulatory Authority to form the Independent Communications Authority of South Africa, to whom fell the responsibility of regulating and monitoring political advertisements and broadcasts.

Because only public broadcasters are required to transmit party political broadcasts, only SABC broadcasting portfolios are considered here. The SABC's radio portfolio consists of 15 public service channels, which includes one for each of the 11 official languages of the country. Lotus FM caters specifically to the large Indian community in the country, and Radio 2000, a facility station, relies heavily on sports broadcasts, as well as "easy listening" music. These public service stations provide a full spectrum of education, information, and entertainment programmes, as well as news, sports, and music. Their information-heavy formats make them ideal to carry political election broadcasts (PEBs).

The SABC's radio portfolio also includes three commercial stations. Radio Good Hope, a contemporary hit music station based in the Western Cape, aims to meet the needs of the historically coloured audiences (although this information is omitted in official descriptions of the channel). Metro fm is the largest national urban commercial station, with 3.1 million listeners, and is positioned as the primary vehicle to reach the emergent and increasingly influential black youth market. The hit music station 5 fm is iconic of the entertainment industry, aimed at an "affluent and multicultural" listenership (SABC, 2005). All three use music as the backbone of their format, but they also include limited information programming made up of news, economic indicators, traffic reports, and sports updates.

There are powerful reasons for political information to be aired on the radio. Radio enjoys several advantages over both television and print in a Third World nation, making it the most appropriate means of communication.

Most important, radio is broadcast in the home languages of the listeners, and all 11 official languages have their own dedicated stations. Radio is a medium that can keep the nation in touch with events almost as they are happening. Its relative cheapness, its immediacy, speed, and reach ensure it a secure place in the swiftly changing world of 21st-century media technology. Compared with print media, radio has far greater reach and accessibility. Throughout Africa, and indeed even in South Africa, the rate of illiteracy is high. Newspapers are expensive. Excluding a couple of recently introduced tabloids targeted at the lower end of the socioeconomic spectrum, newspapers cost the same amount or more than a loaf of bread, and to a family in marginal economic circumstances, there is little room for discretionary choice between them. At the time of the first election in 1994, the differentiation between audiences for radio and television was dramatic: 12.1 million people, or 49% of the adult population, watched television on a daily basis; 15.7 million, or 64% of the adult population, listened to radio daily ("All media and products survey," 1995). By 2005, these figures had risen to 18 million adult listeners for television and 19 million for radio (SABC, 2005). Thus, although radio remains a preeminent medium, the divide between the two electronic forms has diminished.

USE OF TELEVISION

SABC maintains two public service channels, one free-to-air commercial channel and one satellite pay channel. The public service channels broadcast in five African languages, as well as English and Afrikaans. They cover a full range of entertainment, education, and information programming. SABC 3 broadcasts only in English and targets the country's cosmopolitan and sophisticated viewers. All three channels carried significant amounts of news, discussion, and talk-show coverage of the election campaigns. These programmes were monitored by ICASA in terms of the rules of "equity" discussed later.

The only independent free-to-air television station is e-TV, launched in October 1998. e-TV is included here because it chose to flight political election broadcasts. Although the IBA Act is silent on the broadcasting of PEBs on television, e-TV invited parties contesting the 2004 election to produce short programme inserts that would be broadcast during the news bulletins (Mtimde, 2004). The frequency and number of these broadcasts were governed by the same formula laid down by ICASA for radio commercials.

Although television advertisements are not permitted, political parties have become increasingly aware of the value of televisual campaigning. To this end, most parties tailor their "road shows" to make them as telegenic as possible, including stadium rallies with the double purpose of addressing large crowds in person and creating a spectacle that will qualify for television news coverage.

REGULATIONS THAT APPLY TO POLITICAL ADVERTISING

Political party broadcasting is governed by the Independent Broadcasting Authority Act (No. 153 of 1993), the Independent Communications Authority ASA Act (No. 13 of 2000), the Electoral Code, Schedule Two, attached to the Electoral Act (No. 73 of 1998), and the Constitution of South Africa (1996). The 1994 election was conducted prior to the promulgation of the regulations governing PEBs, and transitional arrangements were made for this election (see Teer-Tomaselli, 1996, for details). Before that election, more than 150 hours of free airtime in prime radio time slots, characteristically just before or after news bulletins, were allocated to political parties. Only registered political parties, as defined in the IBA Act (1993), may place advertisements or party election broadcasts. They may be aired only during the "Election Broadcast Period," a

period beginning with the announcement of the candidates list and ending 48 hours before Election Day. The precise dates and times of the election period are gazetted for each election and are usually 10 weeks long (IBA Act 1993, Section 60[6]).

From the time of the 1999 elections, the IBA, and later ICASA, had exclusive responsibility for allocating to contesting parties time for party election broadcasts on public radio stations and on any other stations choosing to broadcast them. Broadcast advertisements are permitted only on radio. The rationale is twofold: Advertising is an expensive enterprise, making it less egalitarian than radio, and television advertising is believed to be a particularly potent form of persuasion. In addition, parties are permitted to publicise their positions through free PEBs. Further paid advertising is permitted on radio, as well as printed advertisements in newspapers, in any quantity the parties can afford.

The IBA Act defines political advertisement as a commercial, for which the medium publishing or broadcasting it can expect money or some other consideration. A PEB is defined by the same act as a direct address or message broadcast free of charge on a broadcasting service and which is intended or calculated to advance the interests of a particular political party. To ensure that all parties have a fair chance to communicate with their perspective electorate and supporters, legislation and regulations have been drawn up that allow all parties free access to radio time on the public broadcast network, worked out on an equitable basis (discussion follows).

The legislation stipulates that all parties must be treated equitably. Equitability is to be understood as *fairness* rather than *equality*. PEBs are conceived of as fulfilling the function of providing information in the public interest. Their use is based on the notion that "the public is entitled to hear more from and about political parties more likely [to affect] the electorate, nationally and provincially" (IBA Act,

1993, § 78). Thus, larger, more powerful parties are allocated more time than smaller parties with less chance of returning a sizable constituency. In allocating the precise number of slots to each party, the formula takes into account three factors: first, the need for all parties to be heard by voters who could vote for them, which serves as a numerical filter to ensure that the electorate is afforded an opportunity to hear all parties potentially exercising influence in the policy decisions affecting their lives. Second is the historical track record of parliamentary representation; third is the number of seats being contested in the current election. Because national and provincial elections take place on the same day, both parliaments are taken into account in the calculation. Points are assigned on the basis of each of these factors, but because fairness also requires that the differential between new, untested parties and established parties remains relatively low, a basic, equal allocation is given to all parties, accounting for approximately a quarter of the optimum number of points available to each party. In this way, the largest, best-established parties receive the lion's share of time allocation; nevertheless, smaller parties do receive sufficient time to be able to make their case on the national public airwaves.

The act stipulates that time be allocated on an "equitable" basis, not necessarily an *equal* basis, worked out in terms of a strict formula. Each affected broadcaster makes available four time slots of 2 minutes daily, with the caveat that this could be increased at the discretion of ICASA. The 2-minute slot may not be exceeded, and no PEBs can be aired immediately before or after that of another party or paid political advertisement. Each party, in turn, is allocated a number of such slots, depending on a range of factors.

All unused slots are forfeited and cannot be transferred to another party. The sequence of allocated slots cannot be changed or swapped by either the broadcasters or the parties concerned. All parties participating in the national and provincial elections are entitled to time for PEBs. Each party designates one person to act as liaison between the party and ICASA, who act as the agents for the PEBs. Once all the parties have notified ICASA of their wish to be allocated time, the sequence of broadcasts is decided by drawing lots.

In 1994, there was no historical record on which to base these calculations, so the formula initially depended on the number of candidates fielded by each party and, to a limited extent, on public opinion findings. According to the formula, the ANC and the NP, considered to be the two strongest contenders in that election, received almost 19 times as much time as the smallest provincial party (*Weekly Mail and Guardian,* 1994).

The regulations applying to PEB and paid advertisements are detailed and strict, and similar, with the exception of the formula for calculating the proportion of time allocated on the public media for each political party (discussion follows). The SABC is obliged to carry both PEBs and advertisements. Other broadcasters may choose whether or not to carry PEBs, but all are required to indicate their willingness (or not) to ICASA by the beginning of the broadcast election period and to abide by the regulations and requirements governing such broadcasts (IBA Act, § 59). Each broadcaster informs ICASA, in writing, of the technical standards required from the parties. The parties are responsible for the production of the advertisement or PEB, and these are subject to prior constraint by the broadcaster. Delivery must be at least 96 hours prior to broadcast, and the station may object if it believes the ad or PEB is not up to its required technical standards. The broadcast may not "contain any material that is calculated, or that in the ordinary course of things is likely, to provoke or incite any unlawful, illegal or criminal act, or that may be perceived as condoning or lending any support to any such act" (IBA Act, 1993, § 60 [3.8.2]). If the advertisement or PEB is rejected, the party has the choice of reediting it to conform to the broadcaster's requirements and resubmit it 24 hours before broadcast, or the party may appeal the objection to ICASA, which acts as mediator (IBA Act, 1993, § 60.6). If ICASA is unable to resolve the matter, it is referred to the Broadcasting Monitoring and Complaints Commission for arbitration. This commission's decision is final.

HISTORY AND DEVELOPMENT
OF POLITICAL ADVERTISING

There is no legal requirement for political parties to disclose either their sources of election funding or the ways in which it has been spent. Consequently, any estimate of spending can only be pieced together from the evidence of campaigning, based on the market value of the various media used. Following the 2004 election, the Institute for Democratic Alternatives in South Africa (IDASA) commissioned a survey of the "adspend" by the major parties in the 2004 election and a comparison with the spending in the previous 1999 election ("Elections adspend in," 2004). This "adspend" represents the amount of money spent by each of the 12 parties participating in the election on print, radio, direct mail, and outdoor advertising. Although the picture remains partial, such an exercise provides a rough guide to the choices and emphases of each party.

In 1994, large amounts of donor money were available for the elections. Nevertheless, only the ANC, NP, and DP (precursor to the Democratic Alliance) were able to afford multiple advertising spots on radio or large print media campaigns (Teer-Tomaselli, 1996). Less money was made available from outside sources in 1999, and in 2004, almost all the money was derived from internal sources. To allow political parties to inform the voting public about their choices, thus enhancing the democratic value of the campaigns, the Public Funding of Represented Political Parties Act (No. 103, 1997) allocates public funds to political parties according to a formula tied to the number of elected public representatives in each of the parties in the various legislatures.

In 1999, the ANC estimated the cost of their election efforts at R20 million (U.S. $3.3 million) for advertising and media support alone (West, 1999). This did not include street posters, at between R5 and R10 per poster (West, 1999). To this must be added the cost of backing boards and the labour used to erect and dismantle the posters. Thousands of lamp-post posters are erected in each electoral campaign. Nearly R47 million (U.S. $7 million) was spent by major political parties on the advertising campaigns in the mainstream media in 2004.[2] This represents 70% of the R66.6 million (U.S. $10 million), allocated in the 2003-2004 tax year to all political parties, up from R52 million (U.S. $7.9 million) in 1999. Most of the money received from the state would have been spent on party structures and nonrepresentative political and support staff. Taking into consideration the expensive poster campaigns not captured by the survey, "the discrepancy between the monies received from the state and the money expended on advertising indicates the extent to which political parties rely on the raising of private funds to drive their election campaigns" ("Elections adspend in," 2004).

Radio proved to be the most popular choice of medium, with the greatest amount of money, time, and effort spent there. In 1994, a total of 18,864 party political radio spots were broadcast between March 4 and April 23 ("Covering elections," 1994, p. 4). This excluded spots for voter education and party political broadcasts. The ANC placed the most commercials, running almost twice as many as the next important player, the NP. In all three periods, the trends were similar (Fourie, 2002; "Elections adspend in," 2004; Teer-Tomaselli, 1996; West, 1999). Radio also absorbed the greatest allocation of resources in 1999 and again in 2004 when R8 million (U.S. $1.3 million), or 43% of the total allocation, was spent on radio advertisements. An ANC spokesperson noted:

"Radio advertising formed a large part of our budget . . . because of its ability to reach rural areas" (West, 1999, p. 3). The DP spent more than three fifths of its budget on radio (West, 1999). In all the elections, radio advertising was heavier toward the end of the campaign (measuring from the beginning of April each time).

All major parties concentrated their advertising across the nine African language stations, as well as the SABC's commercial music station targeting black youth, Radio Metro. The two regions in which the greatest adspend on political spots occurred were those where the ANC faced stiff opposition. In KwaZulu-Natal, home to the Zulu nationalist party, the IFP, the public service formatted Radio Zulu (later renamed *Ukhozi*), attracted the largest numbers of advertisements in all three elections. The choice of radio station was due both to its large audience numbers—4.8 million weekly ("All media and," 2004)—and its location in KwaZulu-Natal province, where the election was most keenly fought. Most of these advertisements were placed by the ANC, followed closely by the IFP, indicating the seriousness with which the ANC regarded the Inkatha threat. (Ironically, IFP did not buy much advertising time, indicating its lack of resources.) In the other fiercely competitive area, the Western Cape, the music-format radio station Good Hope FM was the recipient of the most frequent advertising, indicating the strong tussle between the ANC, the NNP, and the DA in that province.

Outdoor advertising (taxis and billboards) commanded the next highest amount, with R14.4 million (U.S. $2.2 million), or 30% of the allocation in 2004. Even though this figure did not include streetlamp posters, thematically the outdoor advertisements were an extension of the poster campaigns. An original form of advertising is the plastering of minibus taxis with customised posters. This was achieved through a company known as CommutaNet, which placed advertisements on 16,000 taxis nationwide, reaching "16 million economically active South Africans"

("Elections adspend in," 2004). Again, the majority of outdoor money was spent by the ANC, with only the DA and the NNP contributing to the adspend, although at a significantly smaller level than the ANC.

Print advertising is very expensive and had to be used judiciously. Because of the large volume of political coverage in newspapers' news and editorial sections, there is a perceived danger that "party political coverage [will become] just a 'noise' to the reader," so parties use print media to "break through the noise," according to a DP spokesperson (quoted in West, 1999, p. 3). Print was relatively neglected in the 1999 campaign. Smaller parties, in particular, had much less money than the larger parties, and after initial spending, it appeared that their campaigns "had run out of steam" (West, 1999, p. 3). Only the ANC, DP, and NNP campaigned aggressively toward the end of the 1999 period. In the 2004 campaign, for which monetary amounts are easier to estimate, print media came third, accounting for R12 million (U.S. $1.8 million), or 25% of the total adspend by all parties in 2004 ("Elections adspend in," 2004). Voting is disproportionately higher among literate voters, giving parties a good return on investment for print adpsend. Print campaigns allow for expanded messages, in which parties are able to conduct sophisticated, First World–style campaigns, provide detailed manifestos, and give links to other areas of information, such as telephone call lines, Internet sites, and the like. Nevertheless, the print media have the disadvantage of a heavy urban bias, and they are only available in English, Afrikaans, and, to a lesser extent, the Zulu and Xhosa languages.

CONTENT OF POLITICAL BROADCASTING

The 1994 elections were fought by all parties on the basis of a new dispensation, of hope and great promises to come, and all the parties were eager to attract the electorate. The 1999 election was marked by the generally negative stance of parties across the political spectrum, and a far more belligerent tone dominated party political messages. In 2004, the election battles were generally muted, and very little controversy was evident. This section provides a brief overview of some of the main themes articulated by the four main parties during the three elections.

African National Congress Election

While other parties spent much time castigating their opposition, the ANC, accepting that they would win a majority, invested their money and intellectual energy in publicising their positive attributes. The campaign was a sophisticated and extensive one, devised over three interlocking campaign periods and driven by the electoral expertise of Hunt Lascaris, a top advertising agency.

The same thematics were used across different media—radio (audio), newspapers (print), and outdoor (lampposts and billboards). The core of the ANC's campaign was an information drive based on a dual philosophy. The first part was that the ANC had been largely responsible for the negotiation process, ending the logjam of the demise of the apartheid state. Implicit in this assertion was an attempt to minimise the role of other parties in the negotiation process, particularly the NP. This is significant, because it is the only stage in the campaign during which the ANC actively engaged with the assertions of the NP. The second line of attack was to outline the ANC's own blueprint for a future South Africa.

The theme of reassurance was developed further in the outdoor poster display, which used a direct, candidate-driven approach. Full page, full-colour portraits of Nelson Mandela headlined, with the ANC's name and logo, and underscored with the slogan "A better life for all. Working together for jobs, peace and freedom" were pasted on lampposts and reproduced in newspapers in great quantities

to maintain top-of-the-mind awareness in the electorate.

The ANC proved to be remarkably consistent in the next two campaigns. Assured of an overwhelming majority in each case, the party focussed on the objective of reassuring voters, both its core constituencies and the insecure, non-ANC minorities. Following the retirement of Mandela, Thabo Mbeki was elected as president of the ANC, and as such he became the president of South Africa. The ANC's campaign highlighted the continuity from Mandela to Mbeki, using the slogan "Together, fighting for change," and an iconic image of the election depicted Mandela and Mbeki clasping hands in a symbol of unity and friendship. The radio advertisements put Mbeki in the foreground, using his voice in all the English language slots and voicing over in other languages for different language-specific radio stations. Most of the themes of the 1994 election were reiterated in 1999. The ANC took credit for having achieved a truly democratic dispensation and the successful implementation of service delivery. At the same time, the party reasserted the challenges faced by the nation. The radio commercial transcribed here gives a flavor of this construction:

Thabo Mbeki: I am Thabo Mbeki, president of the ANC. I am honoured to be working with you to speed up change in South Africa. Our experience has confirmed that change does not come easily. We did away with a government created to serve a minority and formed one that serves all South Africans. The fight continues so that we can meet the basic needs of all our people. We won our freedom; today we can walk tall with pride and dignity. Together we have brought electricity, water, and other services to millions of homes. Today 750,000 additional families have a roof over their heads on land that belongs to them. But more work lies ahead. Together we must step up the fight for a better life for all; we must speed up change with renewed determination.

Narrator: Together, fighting for change. A better life for all. Vote ANC.

The 2004 election offered more of the same, with the slogan "A people's contract to create work and fight poverty." Despite its ascendant position, in 2004 the party faced three interlocking challenges. Ten years into the democratic dispensation, opinion polls persistently suggested that there were serious policy areas in which a significant body of voters, among both the ANC's loyal followers and those who were more critical, thought the government was performing badly (Calland, 2004). There was a perception that the government was failing in key areas (unemployment, crime and security, poverty, and health issues, particularly in combating the HIV/AIDS pandemic). To acknowledge the ANC's own concern and address voters' concerns, the ANC adopted a subtitle for its slogan: "A people's covenant to create work and fight poverty." The wording was significant, promising "work" rather than jobs or employment and ignoring issues of security and health.

Democratic Party–Democratic Alliance

The Democratic Party (or Democratic Alliance) has fared best of all the opposition parties in the 10 years since the democratic dispensation. It entered the 1994 election period in a very weak position. This first election was inevitably a "liberation" or *Uhuru* event of the first order. First-time black voters were loath to cast their vote for what was regarded as a marginal, liberal-white party, despite its human rights record. As an "honest broker" during the negotiation phase, the DP's traditional liberal-democratic policies were adopted by both the NP and the ANC, leaving the party with few issues that were unique unto itself (Teer-Tomaselli, in press). As a

point of departure, then, the DP attacked both the ANC and the NP on two fronts: their human rights records and, in the case of the NP, the failure of its economic policies; in the case of the ANC, its prospective economic ideals. In its opposition to the NP, the DP claimed it was the only party effectively able to provide strong opposition to the ANC, and it constantly depicted the NP in cahoots with the ANC. A full-page spread in the print media clearly articulated this message. Three quarters of the page were taken up by a luminous double bed carrying the following legend: "When the Nats get into bed with the ANC, guess what happens to you?"

Five years later, the DP went into the election with the expectation of becoming the official opposition, and once again, it took on a pugnacious stance with the slogan "The Guts to Fight Back." Poster-size advertisements blazoned this, fronted for the most part by photographs of DP leader Tony Leon, looking suitably serious and strong willed. DP radio advertisements concentrated on three issues: crime, corruption, and unemployment. In keeping with the strong-leader focus, Leon's voice was used in the majority of radio advertisements (Fourie, 2002, p. 293). A sample advertisement from this period ran as follows:

Narrator: The 132 woman raped every day will never be able to forget. The families of the average 72 South Africans murdered every day—white, black, Indian, coloured—will feel the pain for ever. The over 20 billion stolen by corrupt government officials will never be recovered. The 500,000 jobs lost may never be regained.

Tony Leon: You have the power to fight back. I am Tony Leon, Democratic Party leader. Show *your* courage. Fight back. Vote DP.

The fighting spirit that characterised the 1999 election was far more muted in the 2004 elections, when the party fought on a nuanced, almost neutral platform. The party went for uncontroversial slogans: "South Africa deserves better" and "more jobs, less crime." The "fight back" slogan of 1999 seemed to have driven the party into a political cul de sac, with "fight back" being rearticulated by the ANC into "fight black." Less inclined to fight a negative campaign in 2004, the DP seemed to realise that winning votes from erstwhile ANC supporters could not happen through explicit attack; hence the new strategy was less antagonistic and more empathetic to the mass of voters and their problems.

The National Party Campaign

The National Party began its 1994 election drive by putting the predictable theme of the ANC's communist connections and untrustworthiness into the foreground. Halfway through the campaign, attention was given to the central point that the NP had changed to the "New National Party" and that the electorate should change too. In preparation for the 1999 elections, the party went as far as to reregister under the name New National Party, abbreviated as NNP. In the final run up to the election, populist endorsements by ordinary South Africans, most of them black, were featured, emphasizing the policy points of the NP (Teer-Tomaselli, 2006). This new, multiracial NP (NNP) attempted to convince floating voters, who wanted to vote NP with their heads, though not their hearts. The campaign relied heavily on the underlying notions of "nation building" and the "rainbow coalition." An elderly black man, David Malatsi, noted in one advertisement: "With the NP it's not the color of your skin—it's what you can do that counts" (printed in *Die Burger,* 30 March 1994; *UmAfrika,* 25-28 March 1994; and the *Sunday Tribune,* 30 March 1994). Although racial origin was never overtly referred to, the impact of the photographs in the print advertisements and the accents and languages used in the radio commercials served both as iconic representations of "reality" and as indicators of race.

In 1999, the renamed New National Party attempted to shake off its associations with the pre-1994 apartheid regime. This effort was not particularly successful. Nevertheless, the NNP attacked the ANC on three grounds: (a) that its economic policy effectively excluded white and colored people, traditionally the strongholds of NP support; (b) that the ANC had lost its right to political legitimacy through making promises it could not deliver on, particularly in the areas of employment, housing, and health provision; and (c) most significantly, that the ANC were weak in the areas of safety and security. In all these areas, the NP projected its own claims and solutions, invariably fronted by its leader, Marthinus van Schalkwyk, as exemplified by the following radio advertisement:

Marthinus van Schalkwyk, with music in background:	Crime is threatening the very fabric of society. No one is safe anymore. I am Marthinus van Schalkwyk, leader of the New National Party, and there are solutions: In contrast to the ANC, the New NP says the rights of law-abiding citizens should be more important than the rights of criminals—the death penalty must be brought back. Our policy is straightforward: no mercy for criminals. Vote for the new NP and let's get South Africa working.

This was reinforced through other media, including posters with the slogan "We will bring back the death penalty," together with portraits of the leader, Martinus van Schalkwyk.

By 2004, the NNP no longer viewed itself primarily as an opposition party but aligned itself with the ANC-Tripartite Alliance. The NNP campaigned as a separate party, but its primary strategy (that of attacking the ANC) was no longer a strategic option. The task of selling cooperation with the ANC was an inimical one and proved to be a difficult objective, given that the parties' predecessors had spent so much energy on combating the ANC. "Let us be your voice," "You deserve a fair share," and "Your key to government" were the slogans that replaced the hostility of the previous elections. Each of these slogans promised that, through a partnership with the ANC (albeit a junior partnership), the NNP would be able to give its constituency some small leverage in government policy. In this way, the party was harking back to its 1994 position of suggesting that a vote for the DA was a wasted vote. In the event, a vote for the NNP was a vote wasted for the opposition, as later in 1994, the party committed political suicide, officially joining the ANC in its alliance.[3] The remaining members of Parliament crossed the floor in September 2005.

After 10 years of turbulence, in which both the face of the media and the political landscapes of South Africa have changed dramatically, it would appear that a level of stability has been achieved. At the same time, the dynamics of a parliamentary democracy seem at once to be maturing and yet still volatile. Political communications in the coming elections may face new challenges and possible expansion into other channels.

NOTES

1. For a full account of the transaction, see Teer-Tomaselli and Tomaselli (2002).

2. Print figures were assessed in house by AC Nielsen based on the size of the advertisement relative to the cost charged by the publication for advertising space. This did not take account of negotiated discounts, as these were confidential and unavailable to Nielsen. Direct mail captures those parties using the major agencies, and not mail sent directly by party personnel.

3. In an irony of historical hindsight, the National Party amalgamated with the ANC early in 2005.

REFERENCES

Covering elections. *Activate.* (1994, June-July). Auckland Park: SABC.

All media and products survey. (2004). Johannesburg: South African Advertising Research Foundation.

Berger, G. (2002). Deracialization, democracy and development: Transformation of the South African media, 1994-2000. In K. Tomaselli & H. Dunn (Eds.), *Media, democracy and renewal in Southern Africa.* Colorado Springs, CO: International Academic Publishers.

Calland, R. (2004, January 20). Election 2004: More of the same. *Business Day.*

Constitution of the Republic of South Africa, No. 108 (1996). Retrieved January 28, 2006, from http://www.polity.org.za/html/govdocs/constitution/saconst.html

De Beer, A. (2002). The South African press: No strangers to conflict. In I. E. Gilboa (Ed.), *Media in conflict: Framing issues, making policy, shaping opinions* (pp. 263–280). New York: Transnational.

Domisse, E. (1980). Afrikaans and English press: The case of the goose and the gander. *Equid Novi, 1*(2), 118–127.

Electoral Act, No. 73 (1998). Retrieved January 28, 2006, from http://www.polity.org.za/html/govdocs/legislation/1998/act73.pdf

Fourie, L. (2002). *Partybeheerde kommunikasie in die Noordwesprovinsie tydens die Suid-Afrikaanse Algemene Verkiesing van 1999* [Party-originated communications in the North-West Province during the general election of 1999]. Unpublished Ph.D. thesis, Potchefstroom University for Christian Higher Education, Potchefstroom, South Africa.

Elections adspend in mainstream media. (2004). *ePolticsSA, 7.* Retrieved January 24, 2006, from the IDASA Web site: http://www.idasa.org.za

Independent Broadcasting Authority Act, No. 153 (1993). Retrieved January 28, 2006, from http://www.polity.org.za/pdf/IndBroadAuthA153.pdf

Independent Communications Authority of South Africa Act, No. 13 (2000). Retrieved January 28, 2006, from http://www.polity.org.za/html/govdocs/legislation/2000/act13.pdf

Independent Electoral Commission (Home page). (2006). Retrieved January 23, 2006, from http://www.iec.org.za

Mtimde, L. (2004). *Broadcasters' coverage of the 2004 general elections.* Johannesburg, South Africa: ICASA.

Norris, P., Curtice, J., Sanders, D., Scammell, M., & Semetko, H. (1999). *On message:*

Communicating the campaign. Thousand Oaks, CA: Sage.

Public Funding of Represented Political Parties Act, No. 103 (1997). Retrieved January 28, 2006, from http://www.polity.org.za/html/govdocs/legislation/1997/act103.pdf

South African Broadcasting Corporation. (2005). *Annual report.* Johannesburg: Author. Retrieved January 28, 2006, from http://annual report.sabc.co.za/annual05/index.html

Teer-Tomaselli, R. (1992). *The politics of discourse and the discourse of politics: Images of violence and reform on the South African Broadcasting Corporation's television news bulletins, July 1985–November 1986.* Unpublished Ph.D. thesis, University of Natal, Durban, South Africa.

Teer-Tomaselli, R. (1996). Moving towards democracy: The South African Broadcasting Corporation and the 1994 election. *Media, Culture & Society, 17,* 577–601.

Teer-Tomaselli, R. (2006). Images of negotiation: South Africa's first democratic election as seen through party political advertising in print. *Critical Arts,* Volume 19: Double Issue.

Teer-Tomaselli, R., & Tomaselli, K. G. (2002). Transformation, nation-building and the South African media. In K. Tomaselli & H. Dunn (Eds.), *Media, democracy and renewal in Southern Africa.* Colorado Springs, CO: International Academic.

Tomaselli, K. G., Tomaselli, R., & Muller, J. (1989). *The press in South Africa.* Belville, South Africa: James Currey and Anthropos Press.

Weekly Mail and Guardian. (1994, March 30).

West, E. (1999, May 30). Parties count the cost of reaching the voters. *Business Report on Sunday,* p. 3.

PART VI

Comparisons and Conclusions

27

Television Advertising and Democratic Systems Around the World

A Comparison of Videostyle Content and Effects

LYNDA LEE KAID AND CHRISTINA HOLTZ-BACHA

Political candidates and parties in most democratic systems face the fundamental problem of how to communicate with and persuade voters to accept their leadership. Political advertising, as the other chapters in this volume have established, has become important to many democratic systems because it provides a solution to this problem that also has the advantage of being under the direct control of the party and candidate. With news coverage or debate formats, the party or candidate cannot have total control of the message conveyed to voters. As we pointed out in the first chapter of this volume, political advertising provides this necessary control, allowing candidates and parties to determine the content and style of their messages and take advantage of modern mass-audience channels (radio, television, Internet) to maximize the distribution of these promotional messages to potential voters.

Despite these fundamental advantages to political advertising (control and mass distribution), the roles of such messages, their content and styles, and their effects vary across democratic systems. In our earlier work, *Political Advertising in Western Democracies* (Kaid & Holtz-Bacha, 1995), we discussed the various media, cultural, and political system differences that affect the role such messages play in the United States, Western Europe, and Israel. The chapters in this volume expand that application to include selected democracies in Eastern Europe, Russia, Central and South America, Asia, and Africa.

Authors' Note: Some material from this chapter was presented at the British Political Marketing Conference, London, September 2003. The authors would like to thank John C. Tedesco, Daniela V. Dimitrova, and Andrew Paul Williams for their assistance with this research.

445

With so many different governmental systems (presidential vs. parliamentary, as well as combinations), electoral systems (proportional, majority, and variations on these), media systems (public, private, and dual), and cultural features (collective vs. individual societies, for instance), it sometimes seems impossible to find any common ground upon which to discuss the political communication strategies that characterize such diverse systems.

Nonetheless, we suggest that there are many commonalities, as well as differences, in how democratic leaders use communication to solicit the support of their citizenry. Research across many different countries with diverse political, media, and cultural systems has allowed scholars to understand more fully the underlying strategies and tactics that allow communication to serve the unifying and legitimizing functions that are necessary for democracies to survive. In this chapter, we bring together some of these strategies and tactics that have been used across selected democratic systems and compare their content and potential effects on citizen attitudes toward political leaders and parties.

COMPARATIVE RESEARCH ON POLITICAL ADVERTISING

The overwhelming majority of research on political advertising has been conducted in the United States, where television spots are the dominant form of communication between candidates and voters (see chapter 3 earlier in this book; also Kaid, 1999b, 2004b). Although other democracies have often been accused of "Americanization" of their political television offerings, differences in media, political, and cultural systems impose some limitations on the adoption of American practices. For instance, as we pointed out in chapter 1, many countries impose limitations on or prohibit the purchase of time for political advertising, but the United States allows virtually unlimited purchase of time. Many other systems provide free time on public channels to candidates and parties, but the United States has no institutionalized system for such free-time allocations. The results of these differences can be seen in the quantity of spots aired by candidates and parties. Although in many countries this free-time system may allot commonly 3 or 5 or 10 spots per candidate or party in an election campaign, the two major party U.S. presidential candidates, their parties, and independent groups supporting or opposing them in 2004 purchased time in the general election campaign for more than 300 spots, costing more than $600 million (Devlin, 2005; Kaid, 2005; Kaid & Dimitrova, 2005).

However, despite the dominant role of advertising in U.S. campaigns and the large amount of research on it, researchers have begun to look at the role of advertising in other countries. The past two decades have seen an increased interest in research on the political broadcasts in other countries and on attempts to compare and contrast both the content and the effects of political advertising from an international perspective. Much of this research was done in studies inspired by those of the United States but by researchers who developed their own approach (see chapter 2).

COMPARISONS OF POLITICAL ADVERTISING CONTENT

Research on the content of political party and candidate broadcasts in the United States was summarized in chapter 3 of this book (see also Kaid, 1999b, 2004b), demonstrating that the content of U.S. spots is predominantly based on issues, such as the economy, foreign policy, health care, and education. Research on other countries individually and in comparative studies has led to similar results (Plasser, 2002). For instance, British party election broadcasts seem to be similarly focused on issues (Hodess, Tedesco, & Kaid, 2000; Johnson & Elebash, 1986; Kaid & Holtz-Bacha, 1995; Kaid & Tedesco, 1993).

The importance of issue content in political broadcasts in France has also been validated (Johnston, 1991). However, the campaign spots of the two large parties in Germany have shown a stronger emphasis on candidates and their personal characteristics (Holtz-Bacha, 2000; Holtz-Bacha & Kaid, 1993; Holtz-Bacha, Kaid, & Johnston, 1994).

The concept of *videostyle* has been used frequently to describe the content of political spots. Videostyle refers to the verbal, nonverbal, and production characteristics that define how a candidate presents him- or herself to voters through political spot advertising (Kaid & Davidson, 1986; Kaid & Johnston, 2001). This concept has also been used to compare and contrast political television advertising across cultures (Kaid, 1999a; Kaid & Holtz-Bacha, 1995), in analyses not just of issue and image components but also of the valence of the ads (positive or negative), the types of appeals made (logical, emotional, or ethical), and the extent to which partisanship is important in the advertising.

With that research as background, we have extended this research on the content of political advertising internationally, to include samples of television advertising in many countries around the world. Table 27.1 summarizes the results of our content analysis,[1] using the videostyle system applied to political advertising in a number of countries throughout the world. The individual countries, the election years, and the number of advertisements used in each country are shown at the top of the table.

An important feature to remember before looking at the specific category comparisons is the nature of the ads themselves and the samples used for analysis. As we noted earlier, one of the dominant features of American-style political advertising is the 30-second spot. Many scholars are critical of the 30-second spot for its typical oversimplification of issues and absence of candidates' specific policy proposals; still, many of the countries reported here have adopted short spots as their standard. Some notable exceptions include British, French, and Spanish political ads. The British party election broadcast (PEB) standard is about 4 to 5 minutes, offers significant "opportunity" for candidate policy elaboration, and accomplishes many different objectives in a single PEB that might take several American ads to accomplish. Similarly, the French political broadcasts, known as "emissions," have traditionally been much longer than the American spots. The French emissions were generally somewhere between 5 to 15 minutes in 1988, but shorter formats were allowed in 1995 and in the 2002 spots used in the sample shown in Table 27.1. Spain also has a tradition of longer advertisements (3 to 4 minutes), although the most recent election witnessed the adaptation of the 30-second spot. Finally, the German development showed that spots became shorter over time, particularly when broadcast time had to be purchased. However, although scholars have generally noted that the longer spots provided a better opportunity for candidates to furnish more detailed campaign information, the "talking head," a flat production style that characterized the longer spots, was a deterrent to audience attention. Recent campaigns in Spain, France, and Britain alike have witnessed tremendous advances in production quality, with quick clips, music, and use of interesting cinematography. Nevertheless, the differences in length of some of the ads in various countries make the comparisons in Table 27.1 a little incongruent. However, general observations may be made from the data, offering much opportunity for comparison.

Issue or Image

Whether candidates focus on the issues or their image is probably the most widely explored content area of political spots. It is clear from Table 27.1 that the overwhelming majority of spot samples from the various

Table 27.1 Videostyle: Content and Appeals of Political TV Broadcasts Around the World (%)

Content and Appeal	U.S. 2004 (n = 170)	Greece 1996 (n = 76)	Germany 1994 (n = 52)	Russia 1996 (n = 36)	Britain 1992 and 1997 (n = 16)	Turkey 1995 (n = 9)	Poland 1995 (n = 81)	France 2002 (n = 10)	Italy 1992 (n = 41)	Israel 1992 (n = 60)	Spain 1996 and 2000 (n = 33)	Korea 1992 through 2000 (n = 138)
Emphasis of the ad												
Issues	81	42	69	58	63	33	56	80	71	50	67	47
Image	19	58	12	42	37	67	30	20	23	50	33	52
Combination	0	0	19	0	0	0	14	0	0	0	0	0
Focus of ad												
Positive	58	71	NA	72	69	89	93	90	85	58	91	82
Negative	42	29	NA	28	31	11	7	10	15	42	9	11
Dominant type of appeal[a]												
Logical	89	22	23	39	56	33	21	90	15	25	82	20
Emotional	56	64	33	47	25	55	67	70	54	40	88	33
Source credibility	16	13	4	14	19	11	12	40	31	35	49	67
Combination			40									
Political party emphasized	6	87	44	8	50	NA	4	60	7	7	27	NA

Note: NA indicates not applicable.

a. In some countries, the totals sum to more than 100% because the appeals were coded as to their presence or absence in the ads; others show the dominant type of appeal in each ad.

countries indicate that issues are the dominant focus in spots. However, there are some notable differences in issue and image focus. If ranked in order of amount of focus on issues, the United States (81%), France (80%), and Italy (71%) lead the way, with at least 70% of their spots having issues as the dominant focus. Germany (69%) and Spain (67%) are close behind the leaders, with at least two thirds of their spots dominated by issue concerns. Britain, with a 63% focus on issues, is not too far behind the issue leaders. However, what the ranking appears to indicate based on the samples from the 1990s and early elections of the new millennium is that the "traditional" westernized democracies emphasize issues more than the "evolving" democracies. In a very interesting result, the bottom six countries on the issue ranking are Russia (58%), Poland (56%), Israel (50%), Korea (47%), Greece (42%), and Turkey (33%). Although the issue emphasis percentages for Russia, Poland, and Israel are not that far off those of the more westernized democracies, the grouping of the top and bottom six countries in this ranking is interesting. Although it is logical to expect that candidates and parties in these evolving states would spend more time discussing the issues relevant to moving their young democracies toward more stability, it is very possible that the candidates and parties found it more necessary to emphasize that they were the most capable individuals or groups to move the country forward. Thus, it may be interesting to see if this issue-image distinction continues as evolving democracies become more stable and, it is to be hoped, develop parties and candidates that have more long-term credibility with their electorates.

There are also many comparisons that can be made about the specific issues emphasized in the broadcasts. For instance, in the United States during the 1990s and through 2000, the emphasis on issues almost always meant an emphasis on domestic issues, such as the economy, health care, and education. However, in 2004, only John Kerry retained this focus: Most of his spots addressed the economy (45%) and health care (48%). President George W. Bush, on the other hand, concentrated his largest percentage of television ads on terrorism and security (34%), and he discussed defense spending (22%) much more frequently than Kerry. In contrast, British PEBs in 1997 featured a mixture of domestic and foreign policy issues, with particular emphasis on Britain's role in the European Union. Likewise, in the French presidential campaign of 2002, although economic issues and children's concerns dominated, nearly half of the broadcasts mentioned international or foreign policy issues.

Positive and Negative Focus

Over many years, the United States' spots have been the most negative of any of the 12 countries analyzed. In fact, the United States and Israel have the distinction of being the two countries with the highest percentages of negative ads. A rank ordering of positive and negative content does not reveal any clear difference in the use of positive and negative ads among the stable or evolving European democracies or among the party- or candidate-centered democracies.

Five countries reached a positive advertising threshold of 85%. For example, Poland (93%), Spain (91%), France (90%), Turkey (89%), and Italy (85%) exhibited positive advertising rates well above the other countries in this study. Although these rates do not indicate that attacks do not occur in ads, they do indicate that the negative aspects of the spots are less dominant than the positive features. Three other countries grouped close together at around the 70% positive range: Russia (72%), Greece (71%), and Britain (69%). Considerably higher negative numbers are reported in Israel (42% negative) and Korea (11% negative).

As Table 27.1 shows, the German spots were not coded in a comparable method. The German coding did not dichotomize between positive and negative as a dominant ad emphasis but rather reported whether an attack was made in the ad instead of indicating whether the ad was negative or positive. On this measure, about two thirds of the German spots included some type of negative attack, whether or not the spot itself was predominantly positive or negative. Using that measure (whether an attack was made in the spot, even if negativity was not the major focus of the spot) would also increase the negative focus for several other countries. For instance, although most Greek spots were positive, 55% of them contained a negative attack on the other party or its candidate. The same was true in Turkey, where over half the spots contained some type of attack. This content analysis also fails to capture the magnitude of advertising buys for the negative ads compared to the positive ads in the various countries. For example, one thing that may increase the perception among U.S. voters that ads are so negative is the possibility that the negative ads get more exposure than the positive ads.

The overall totals in each country also mask differences between and among parties in some cases. In the United States in 2004, the overall totals show that 42% of the ads were negative and 58% were positive. In fact, only 34% of John Kerry's ads were negative, but Bush aired more than half of his ads (58%) with a negative tone. Nonetheless, it is important to remember that although a higher percentage of Bush's ads were negative, Kerry sponsored so many more total spots that he actually aired almost twice as many negative spots as did Bush over the course of the campaign (Kaid, 2005; Kaid & Dimitrova, 2005).

It is also true that more Kerry ads contained some kind of attack (71%) against Bush, even in ads that were classified as predominantly focused on Kerry's positive attributes. A similar differential occurred in the 2002 French presidential race, in which 90% of all the broadcasts were, overall, positive, but Le Pen made some sort of attack against incumbent president Jacques Chirac in 80% of his broadcasts.

One other observation may be relevant about differences in negativity in ads in different countries. Although the candidates and parties in many countries in the sample exhibit some type of attack strategy in their political broadcasts, these attacks take many different forms. In 2004, American challenger John Kerry emphasized Bush's personal qualities and character in 40% of his attacks on the president. In contrast, the negative attacks featured in political broadcasts in Britain, Germany, and many other countries focused more on the failings of the opposing party than on the specific candidate. In 1997, a British Conservative Party spot accused the Labour party of being a party "without roots," and the Labour Party used emotional music and pictures to question the Conservative Party's record on health care and social issues. Neither party's spots focused on the opposing party's standard bearer, neither Tony Blair nor John Major.

Ethos, Logos, and Pathos Appeals

We also categorized spots according to whether the dominant type of appeal or proof offered in the ad was logical, emotional, or ethical, corresponding to Aristotle's original distinctions between logos, pathos, and ethos. Broadcasts that rely on logical proof use factual information and examples and often offer statistical data to substantiate their points. Emotional proof is characterized by appeals that use language and images to try to evoke feelings or emotions such as happiness, patriotism, anger, or pride. Advertisements that use ethical appeals or source credibility rely on good character to make their appeals, including information about the qualifications, integrity, and trustworthiness of the candidate or of someone speaking on behalf of the candidate or party. When the average for all 12 countries for each appeal strategy was calculated, emotional appeals surpassed logical appeals as the most prominent proof strategies. The average percentage of emotional appeals for the 12 countries coded was 50%, compared to 44% for logical appeals and 27% for credibility appeals. The U.S. and French spots were the most likely to use logical proof, relying on this form of persuasion in 89% and 90% of their ads, respectively. Spanish spots also made frequent use of logical reasoning, which was used in 82% of their ads. Italian spots were the least likely to use logic as an appeal strategy to persuade voters. Logical appeals appeared in only 15% of Italian ads. Results from five countries (Israel, Germany, Greece, Poland, and Italy) reveal that logical appeals were used in 25% or less of their ads.

Emotional appeals were the most prominent when all 12 countries were considered. Spanish candidates used emotional proof more frequently than their peers in other democracies. Spain, with 88% for emotional appeals, far exceeds France, with 70%, the second highest country on the list. Korean ads were the least likely to employ emotional appeals. Emotional proof was the most dominant proof strategy for 8 of the 12 countries in this study. Spain (88%), Poland (67%), Greece (64%), Turkey (55%), Italy (54%), Russia (47%), Israel (40%), and Germany (33%) all used emotional appeals more than logical or ethical appeals. It is interesting that only France, the United States, and Britain were more likely to use logical appeals than emotional or ethical appeals.

Clearly, it is much more necessary for challenger candidates to establish their credibility; incumbents usually point to their past leadership successes as evidence of their credibility. However, source credibility proof was much less prevalent in the ads than logical or emotional appeals. Korea, the only Asian country in this cross-national comparison, was the only country whose candidates relied on source credibility appeals (67%) more than either logic or emotion. It is likely that this is one area in which cultural differences may have played the greatest role in differences in spot content and style. Asian culture places greater regard on respect for the wisdom and value of those with age and experience. Such traditions signify cultural differences between Eastern and Western democracies and may suggest reasons for the greater reliance of Korean political ads on ethical proof (Tak, Kaid, & Khang, 2004).

Party- and Candidate-Centered Advertising

The use of political spots as a dominant form of political communication in modern democracies has given rise to the hypothesis that reliance on televised campaigns has resulted in the diminished significance of political parties. As a result, candidates in many of the democracies analyzed here are no longer reliant on political parties to create and shape their identity. Clearly, the overt role of the party in political broadcasts remains most prominent in Greece. However, the role of the party is not very pervasive in at least five of the countries analyzed in this study. The number of spots in each country of which the content focused primarily on the political party was generally quite small in Poland (4%), the United States (6%), Israel (7%), Italy (7%), and Russia (8%). However, in countries where broadcast time is allocated to parties, the party continues to play an important role.

Parties remain relatively strong in France, Britain, and Germany, where 60%, 50%, and 44% of their respective spots emphasized the party. The allocation of time to parties in France and Britain and the proportional allocation of time in Germany put the party at the center of politics in these countries. However, as is evidenced by the ad content, the candidate can emerge as the central figure of the ads despite the party's role in securing time. A good example of this comes from Britain, where the candidate has developed into a more central character in the PEBs in the most recent election cycles. The party still remains important in the British system, but the candidate's qualities, leadership, and personal qualities have assumed a much more prominent role in the spots. "Blair: the Movie" was an example of a 1997 Labour PEB that focused directly on Tony Blair's personal qualities as the embodiment of the "new" Labour Party. Clearly the British system is balancing candidate- and party-centered interests. In the United States, the candidates have been deemphasizing the party and running campaigns as moderates for most of the last half century. Candidates campaign on the middle ground, emphasizing moderate platforms to appeal broadly to the less extreme ends of the Republican and Democratic parties. The increasing percentage of registered independent voters also points to a fairly large abandonment of the major parties in preference for issue politics. The generally low percentage of spots emphasizing the party may provide some evidence that spots are contributing to a declining emphasis on parties in democratic systems around the world, resulting in a more personalized campaign system.

COMPARISON OF POLITICAL ADVERTISING EFFECTS

Researchers and political observers have also been interested in the effects that exposure to political advertising has on the citizens in a democracy. How successful are political ads in helping citizens to form views of political leaders and parties? Of course, answers to such questions are complicated by the same types of political, media, and cultural differences that affect spot content. Individual chapters in this volume have recounted the results of research on advertising effects in individual countries where data on such questions exists.

Here we consider the results of research over the past two decades that provides some answers to advertising effectiveness in a comparative way.

Beginning with the 1988 U.S. election, which also coincided for the first time in many decades with the election of the French president, we have worked in cooperation with a number of colleagues in other countries to make some comparisons of advertising effectiveness using similar experimental techniques with similar measuring instruments.

These projects have involved experiments in conjunction with major elections in the respective countries. These experiments involved measurement of citizen attitudes toward major party candidates, exposure of these citizens to sample political advertising messages used on television by these candidates during each ongoing campaign, and then a postexposure measurement of attitudes and learning after viewing the advertisements. The studies in individual countries are reported in a number of specific papers and publications (Cwalina, Falkowski, & Kaid, 2000; Gagnère, & Kaid, 2003; Hodess et al., 2000; Holtz-Bacha & Kaid, 1993, 1996; Kaid, 1991, 1999a, Kaid, Gagnère, Williams, & Trammell, 2003; Kaid & Holtz-Bacha, 1995; Kaid & Tedesco, 1999). Because these studies used similar methodologies and similar measuring instruments (a 12-item semantic differential scale[2] to assess attitudes toward candidates), we are able to analyze these studies across time to determine if exposure to political advertising has any common effects.

As shown in Table 27.2, it is clear that exposure to political television advertising does indeed affect the evaluations of major party candidates in a number of the countries analyzed. Effects data from experimental studies were available for seven countries (United States, 1992, 1996, and 2000; Italy, 1992; France, 1992, 1995, and 2002; Britain, 1997; Poland, 1995; Chile, 1997; and Germany,

Table 27.2   Effects of Political Broadcasts on Candidate
Images Across Countries

Countries and Candidates	Pretest	Posttest
United States, 1992 (n = 50)		
Bush	4.58	5.75[a]
Clinton	4.42	4.58[a]
United States, 1996 (n = 525)		
Clinton	4.51	4.59[a]
Dole	4.48	4.34[a]
United States, 2000 (n = 906)		
Bush	4.65	4.72[a]
Gore	4.63	4.67
France, 1988 (n = 55)		
Chirac	3.50	3.35[a]
Mitterrand	4.90	4.92
France, 1995 (n = 84)		
Chirac	4.23	3.99
Jospin	4.31	4.44
France, 2002 (n = 50)		
Chirac	3.43	3.58
Le Pen	3.21	2.59[a]
Germany, 1990 (n = 171)		
Kohl	3.64	3.66
Lafontaine	4.57	4.68
Germany, 1994 (n = 202)		
Kohl	4.03	3.99
Scharping	4.31	4.44[a]
Germany, 1998 (n = 207)		
Kohl	4.32	4.32
Schröder	4.45	4.68[a]
Italy, 1992 (n = 53)		
Martinazzoli	4.49	3.59[a]
Occhetto	3.86	3.86
Britain, 1997 (n = 106)		
Blair	4.30	4.43[a]
Major	4.07	4.15
Poland, 1995 (n = 203)		
Kwasniewski	4.74	4.85
Walesa	3.76	3.98[a]
Chile, 1997 (n = 120)		
Foxley (PDC)	4.08	4.03
Allamand (RN)	4.30	4.32

Note: Numbers reflect the summary mean of the 12-item semantic differential scale, measured from 1 (negative) to 7 (positive).

a. Indicates t test between pre- and posttest score is significant at $p \leq .05$.

1990,1994, and 1998).[3] These data demonstrate that political advertising exposure can significantly affect a leader's image rating. In almost every country, this is true for one and sometimes both of the candidates and leaders. However, sometimes the direction of the change is positive, and sometimes it is negative. In the United States in 1992, the spot exposure resulted in significantly higher evaluations for both George Bush, Sr., and Bill Clinton; in 1996, Clinton's ratings increased significantly after viewing, but Bob Dole's image score decreased. In 2000, the positive effect was only present for George W. Bush; spot viewing had no effect on Al Gore's rating.

The tendency for the spots to result in significantly higher evaluations of the candidate or party leader was also true for Rudolf Scharping in Germany in 1994, for Gerhard Schröder in Germany in 1998, for Tony Blair in Britain in 1997, and for Lech Walesa in Poland in 1995. In addition to the case of Dole in the United States in 1996, a negative change after exposure was present in France, for Jacques Chirac in 1988 and for Jean Marie LePen in 2002, and for Martinazzoli in Italy in 1992. After watching their television portrayals, respondents rated them lower than before. Only in France in 1995, Germany in 1990, and Chile in 1997 did the political spot exposure fail to produce a change in one of the candidate's image scores.

In addition to the overall effects of viewing television ads focusing on the images of political leaders, it is interesting to note that in many of the cases reported here there are some intriguing gender differences in reactions to the advertising. In an earlier book, we discussed differences found in several countries (Kaid & Holtz-Bacha, 2000). For instance, women voters rated Bill Clinton (United States, 1996) and Tony Blair (Britain, 1997) much higher than they rated their opponents, Bob Dole and John Major. Overall, the gender comparisons across several countries suggest that "female voters are more likely to be affected by exposure to political spots; and, when they are, the spots are more likely to result in higher positive evaluations for the candidates than is true for male voters" (Kaid, 1997, pp. 20-21).

CONCLUSION

Overall, then, there are some well-documented similarities among countries, in both the content and the effects of political advertising. Summary findings about content comparisons indicate that

1. Most countries concentrate the content of their ads on issues. Korea and Turkey are exceptions.

2. Political broadcasts across countries are overwhelmingly positive, not negative, in their focus. The United States is the notable exception.

3. Despite the emphasis on issues and positive claims, most leaders and parties rely on emotional appeals, rather than logical or source credibility proof, to make their points. Exceptions are France, Britain, and the United States, where logical appeals dominate. Korea is the only country where source credibility appeals dominate.

4. Most parties and leaders have deemphasized the political party in their ads. France, Britain, and Greece are exceptions.

Overall, the results provide a means for comparing the contents and styles of political advertising around the world. The results do provide some evidence of the often-lamented "Americanization" process, some of which is more often labeled "professionalization" or "modernization," but they also show some of the enduring similarities of democratic system values, such as the concentration on issue information. Many of the countries analyzed in the study are what we consider evolving democracies, or democratic states where major system characteristics have changed in the past few decades.

Among the interesting trends to watch over the course of the next few election cycles in each country will be those that develop for each of the variables reported here. If support for the "Americanization" hypothesis is to be achieved, media regulation and system differences will necessitate change. For example, for French ads to more closely resemble American ads, restrictions in content and paid formats will most likely need to be eliminated or at least liberalized.

Comparisons and generalizations about the effects of political advertising are, perhaps, more easily seen in these results. Although many countries still resist the conclusion that political advertising has an effect on election outcomes, our data suggest otherwise in many situations. Across several countries with different political systems, different media systems, and different cultural characteristics, it is still possible to see similar effects from political advertising. Exposure to political television messages during a campaign can sometimes increase, and sometimes decrease, the image of political leaders. These effects also appear to have identifiable differences according to the gender of the exposed citizen.

With so many countries adopting changes in their media and governmental procedures for elections, the coming years will provide new challenges for the study of political advertising. All indications are that political advertising will remain an identifiable and important media format for communication between political leaders and the citizens they seek to govern. Future research will also find that new channels of distribution for these messages are of major importance. Many political parties and candidates in many countries are already using the Internet to distribute their political messages. This new and developing medium will provide even more opportunities for candidates, parties, individuals, and interest groups who wish to communicate directly with voters.

NOTES

1. The content analysis procedures were applied to a sample of spots from 12 countries: the United States (170 from Bush and Kerry in 2004), France (10 spots from Chirac and Le Pen in 2002), Germany (52 spots from various German parties in 1994), Italy (41 spots from various parties in 1992), Greece (76 spots from various parties in 1996), Turkey (9 spots from four parties in the 1995 parliamentary elections), Britain (16 spots from major parties in 1992 and 1997), Poland (81 spots from various parties in the 1995 presidential election), Israel (60 spots from the Likud and Labor parties in 1992), Spain (33 spots from the Popular Party and the Socialist Party in 1996 and 2000), Russia (36 spots from the presidential election in 1996), and South Korea (138 spots from the two main parties in the 1992, 1996, and 2000 presidential elections). The categories developed for the content analysis followed the procedures set forth in prior studies of videostyle (Kaid & Johnston, 2001). Trained student coders completed the coding. In all cases, coders were native speakers of the language used in the spots. Intercoder reliabilities averaged +.84 across all categories for all samples.

2. The bipolar adjective pairs making up the semantic differential are qualified-unqualified, sophisticated-unsophisticated, honest-dishonest, believable-unbelievable, successful-unsuccessful, attractive-unattractive, friendly-unfriendly, sincere-insincere, calm-excitable, aggressive-unaggressive, strong-weak, active-inactive. They were translated into the language of each country by native speakers of each language. Further explanation of the development, derivation, and use of this semantic differential scale to measure candidate image can be found in Kaid (2004a).

3. The samples for these experiments were drawn from young voters in each country and were tested as part of research projects at various universities that cooperated with the researchers during the national election campaigns in the individual countries. Details on the sample composition and characteristics can be found in the individual research studies cited in this chapter. The authors would like to thank the following individuals for their help in data collection and analysis for this project: John Tedesco (Virginia Tech University); Andrjez Falkowski and Wojciech Cwalina (Warsaw School of Social Psychology); Hans-Jörg Stiehler (University of Leipzig); Wolfgang Donsbach (Technische

Universität Dresden); Janine Retat (Blaise Pascal University in Clermont-Ferrand, France); Nathalie Gagnere; Robin Hodess, Stephan Henneberg, Nicholas O'Shaughnessy, and Ralph Negrine (Britain); Sarah Oates (Glasgow University); Markus Moke (University of Bochum, Germany); Cindy Roper (Abilene Christian University); and Gianpietro Mazzoleni (University of Milan).

REFERENCES

Cwalina, W., Falkowski, A., & Kaid, L. L. (2000). Role of advertising in forming the image of politicians: Comparative analysis of Poland, France and Germany. *Media Psychology, 2*(2), 119–146.

Devlin, L. P. (2005). Contrasts in presidential campaign commercials of 2004. *American Behavioral Scientist, 49*(2), 279–313.

Gagnère, N., & Kaid, L. L. (2003, March). *Political broadcasting in the 2002 presidential election in France: Appeals and effects for young voters.* Paper presented at the European Communication Association Convention, Munich, Germany.

Hodess, R., Tedesco, J. C., & Kaid, L. L. (2000). British party election broadcasts: A comparison of 1992 and 1997. *Harvard Journal of International Press/Politics, 5*(4), 55–70.

Holtz-Bacha, C. (2000). *Wahlwerbung als politische Kultur* [Election ad as political culture]. Wiesbaden, Germany: Westdeutscher Verlag.

Holtz-Bacha, C., & Kaid, L. L. (Eds.). (1993). *Die Massenmedien im Wahlkampf* [The mass media in the election campaign]. Opladen, Germany: Westdeutscher Verlag.

Holtz-Bacha, C., & Kaid, L. L. (Eds.). (1996). *Wahlen und Wahlkampf in den Medien: Untersuchungen aus dem Wahljahr 1994* [Elections and election campaigns in the media: Research from the election year 1994]. Opladen, Germany: Westdeutscher Verlag, 1996.

Holtz-Bacha, C., Kaid, L. L., & Johnston, A. (1994). Political television advertising in Western democracies: A comparison of campaign broadcasts in the U.S., Germany, and France. *Political Communication, 11,* 67–80.

Johnson, K. S., & Elebash, C. (1986). The contagion from the right: The Americanization of British political advertising. In L. L. Kaid, D. Nimmo, & K. R. Sanders (Eds.), *New perspectives on political advertising* (pp. 293–313). Carbondale: Southern Illinois University Press.

Johnston, A. (1991). Political broadcasts: An analysis of form, content, and style in presidential communications. In L. L. Kaid, J. Gerstlé, & K. R. Sanders (Eds.), *Mediated politics in two cultures: Presidential campaigning in the United States and France* (pp. 59–72). New York: Praeger.

Kaid, L. L. (1991). The effects of television broadcasts on perceptions of political candidates in the United States and France. In L. L. Kaid, J.Gerstlé, & K. R. Sanders (Eds.), *Mediated politics in two cultures: Presidential campaigning in the United States and France* (pp. 247–260). New York: Praeger.

Kaid, L. L. (1997, October). *Political television advertising: A comparative perspective on styles and effects.* Paper presented at the International Conference on Images of Politics, Amsterdam.

Kaid, L. L. (1999a). Comparing and contrasting the styles and effects of political advertising in European democracies. In L. L. Kaid (Ed.), *Television and politics in evolving European democracies.* Commack, NY: Nova Science.

Kaid, L. L. (1999b). Political advertising: A summary of research findings. In B. Newman (Ed.), *The handbook of political marketing* (pp. 423–438). Thousand Oaks, CA: Sage.

Kaid, L. L. (2004a). Measuring candidate images with semantic differentials. In K. L. Hacker (Ed.), *Presidential candidate images* (pp. 231–236). Westport, CT: Praeger.

Kaid, L. L. (2004b). Political advertising. In L. L. Kaid (Ed.), *The handbook of political communication research* (pp. 155–202). Mahwah, NJ: Erlbaum.

Kaid, L. L. (2005). Videostyle in the 2004 political advertising. In R. E. Denton, Jr. (Ed.), *The 2004 presidential campaign: A communication perspective* (pp. 283–299). Lanham, MD: Rowman & Littlefield.

Kaid, L. L., & Davidson, J. (1986). Elements of videostyle: Candidate presentation through television advertising. In L. L. Kaid, D. Nimmo, & K. R. Sanders (Eds.), *New perspectives on political advertising* (pp. 184–209). Carbondale: Southern Illinois University Press.

Kaid, L. L., & Dimitrova, D. V. (2005). The television advertising battleground in the 2004 presidential election. *Journalism Studies, 6*(3), 165–175.

Kaid, L. L., Gagnère, N., Williams, A. P., & Trammell, K. D. (2003, May). *Political advertising and the 2002 presidential election in*

France. Paper presented at the International Communication Association Convention, San Diego, CA.

Kaid, L. L., & Holtz-Bacha, C. (Eds.). (1995). *Political advertising in Western democracies: Candidates and parties on television.* Thousand Oaks, CA: Sage.

Kaid, L. L., & Holtz-Bacha, C. (2000). Gender differences in response to televised political broadcasts: A multi-country comparison. *Harvard Journal of International Press/ Politics, 5*(2), 17–29.

Kaid, L. L., & Johnston, A. (2001). *Videostyle in presidential campaigns: Style and content of political television advertising.* Westport, CT: Praeger.

Kaid, L. L., & Tedesco, J. (1993). A comparison of political television advertising from the 1992 British and American campaigns. *Informatologia, 25,* 1–12.

Kaid, L. L., & Tedesco, J. (1999). Die Arbeit am Image: Kanzlerkandidaten in der Wahlwerbung, Die Rezeption der Fernsehspots von SPD und CDU [Working on the image. Candidates for chancellor in electoral ads: Reception of the SPD and CDU's television spots]. In C. Holtz-Bacha (Ed.), *Wahlkampf in den Medien— Wahlkampf mit den Medien. Ein Reader zum Wahljahr 1998* [The election campaign in the media—campaigning with the media: A reader on the 1998 elections]. (pp. 218–241). Opladen, Germany: Westdeutscher Verlag.

Plasser, F., with Plasser, G. (2002). *Global political campaigning: A worldwide analysis of campaign professionals and their practices.* Westport, CT: Praeger.

Tak, J., Kaid, L. L., & Khang, H. (2004, August). *The influence of cultural parameters on videostyles of televised political spots in the U.S. and Korea.* Paper presented at the Association for Journalism and Mass Communication Convention, Toronto.

Index

About the Authors

Annette Aw is Adjunct Associate Professor in the Department of Communication at the University of Maryland University College. She is also an independent Research Consultant in Washington, DC, where she conducts media-related studies for private businesses, trade associations, and government agencies. Before working in the United States, she taught at Nanyang Technological University in Singapore from 1995 to 2001. Her research and teaching interests focus on public relations and intercultural communication in Asia and the United States. She received her Ph.D. in Intercultural Communication from the University of Oklahoma in 1994.

Kees Brants is Director of the MA program in European Communication Studies and Senior Research Fellow at the Amsterdam School of Communications Research, both at the University of Amsterdam. At Leiden University, he is Professor of Political Communication. His research interests and publications range from media policy to political communication, from media and criminal justice to the social construction of the immigration issue. With his wife, he shares an interest in World War I that some call macabre but that has resulted in two books on the history and memory of that fatal period.

Baki Can is Associate Professor in the Department of Public Relations at Ege University in İzmir, Turkey. He holds a doctorate in using reasoning and emotion in persuasive communication from Istanbul University. He specializes in the study of political communication, especially in political propaganda, voter persuasion, political advertising, and public speaking. He has written book chapters and articles related to these issues, which have been published in Turkey and the United States. He had been as a consultant for numerous members of parliament and major candidates during election campaigns. He has also worked as a consultant major of İzmir and as Adviser to the Speaker of the Grand National Assembly of Turkey.

Dan Caspi is Chair of the Department of Communications Studies and Head of the Hubert Burda Center for Innovative Communications at Ben-Gurion University of the Negev. He served as Founding Chair of the Israel Communication Association and filled several public roles, including Consultant for a communications program at Israeli Educational Television; Member of the Committee on Public Broadcasting of the Ministry of Science, Culture and Sports; and Council Member of *Bizchut*, the Israeli Human Center for People with Disabilities. He was Board Member of the Israeli Broadcasting Authority (2000-2003). He has written and coauthored several books: *Mass Media and Cultural Minorities: The Dialectics of Integration and Fragmentation* (in press); with Hanna Adoni and Akiba A. Cohen, *Due to Technical Difficulties: The Fall of the Israeli Broadcasting Authority* (2005); in Hebrew, *The In/Outsiders: The Mass Media in Israel* (1999);

with Yehiel Limor, *Media Decentralization: The Case of Israel's Local Newspapers* (1986); and, coedited with Avraham Diskin and Emanuel Gutmann, *The Roots of Begin's Success: The 1981 Elections* (1984).

Colleen Connolly-Ahern is Assistant Professor of Advertising and Public Relations in the College of Communications at Pennsylvania State University. Her research interests include the influence of culture on political communication, transnational conflicts, and apologia. She has published her research in a number of different journals in the United States and in Europe, including *Journalism Studies, Journal of Political Marketing,* and *Doxa Comunicacion.* Before returning to the University of Florida to complete her Ph.D., she worked in the publishing industry as owner of her own marketing communications firm, promotion manager for *USA Today,* and managing editor for *Marine Log,* a trade magazine.

Wojciech Cwalina, Ph.D., is Assistant Professor in the Department of Marketing Psychology at the Warsaw School of Social Psychology, Warsaw, Poland. His research specialties include political marketing psychology and analysis of media coverage. He is the author of *Television Political Advertising* (2000) and coauthor, with Andrzej Falkowski, of *Political Marketing: Psychological Perspectives* (2005). Among his publications are numerous articles in psychological and marketing journals (e.g., in *Media Psychology, Journal of Political Marketing, Journalism Studies, Polish Psychological Bulletin, Journal for Mental Changes*) and chapters in books about political marketing and mass communication (e.g., *Handbook of Political Marketing,* edited by B. I. Newman, 1999, Sage Publications; *Television and Politics in Evolving European Democracies,* edited by L. L. Kaid, 1999; *Branding and Advertising,* edited by F. Hansen & L. B. Christensen, 2003). From 1997 to 2001, he worked as a marketing specialist and campaign advisor for the Solidarity Election Action, in the Lower Silesia Division.

Andrzej Falkowski is Professor of Psychology and Marketing and Head of the Department of Marketing Psychology at the Warsaw School of Social Psychology, Warsaw, Poland. His research specialty is cognitive psychology, including consumer behavior, marketing, and political advertising. A Fulbright Scholar (University of Michigan), his publications include numerous articles in consumer behavior, political marketing, and cognitive psychology journals. He has also written numerous books and book chapters, including *Television and Politics in Evolving European Democracies* (1999), *Psychology of Consumer Behavior* (2001), and *Cognitive Psychology in Practice: Marketing and Advertisement* (2002). He was Advisory Editor of the *Handbook of Political Marketing* (1999) and is Editorial Board Member of *Journal of Political Marketing.*

Nathalie Gagnère was born and raised in Lyon, France. She received her M.A. in Political Science from Western Washington University (1991) and her doctorate from the University of Oklahoma (1998). She was the 1999 recipient of the Aaron Wildavsky APSA Dissertation Award on religion and politics. She has taught at the University of Oklahoma and Ohio University. In France, she joined the Centre de Politologie de Lyon as a Research Associate and held visiting positions at French business schools, including the Ecole Supérieure de Commerce de Rennes. More recently, she has been a freelance consultant in translation and information gathering. Her research interests have focused on European integration, political communication, democratization, economic transitions, religion, and political psychology.

Julio César Herrero is Professor of Information Theory and Communication at Universidad San Pablo CEU in Madrid, Spain, and Fellow of the Real Colegio Complutense at Harvard University. He holds a doctorate in Information Sciences, with honors, from the Universidad Complutense de Madrid, and his research specialties include political communication and campaigns. Working with the Pablo Iglesias Foundation, Herrero is an advisor to Latin American political parties in the areas of public discourse, media relations, and argumentation and debate. In addition to many conference papers, journal articles, and book chapters, he is the author of two public relations texts: *Una forma de hablar* [A form of speech] and *La comunicación en el protocolo: El tratamiento de los medios en la organización de actos* [Communication in protocol: The treatment of methods in the organization of acts].

Christina Holtz-Bacha received her Ph.D. from the University of Muenster in 1978 and is now Professor and Chair of the Communications Department at the Friedrich-Alexander-University in Erlangen-Nürnberg, Germany. Before she went to Nürnberg, she taught at the universities in Mainz (1995-2004), Bochum (1991-1995), and Munich (1981-1991). She was Guest Professor at the University of Minnesota, Minneapolis, in 1986 and Research Fellow at the Joan Shorenstein Center on the Press, Politics and Public Policy at the John F. Kennedy School of Government, Harvard University, Cambridge, Massachusetts in 1999. She is Coeditor of the German journal *Publizistik* and a member of the board of various other journals. She has cowritten and edited more than 20 scholarly books, among which are her most recent: *Massenmedien und Wahlen* (Mass media and elections, 2003); *Journalism Education in Europe and North America: An International Comparison* (2003); *Schlüsselwerke für die Kommunikationswissenschaft* (Key works in communication science, 2002); *Wahlwerbung als politische Kultur: Parteienspots im Fernsehen 1957-1998* (Electoral advertising as political culture: Party spots on TV, 1957-1998,

2000); and *Europawahl 2004* (The 2004 European elections, 2005).

Jan Jirák, Ph.Dr. (1958), is Docent and a member of the Department of Media Studies and Center for Media Studies, Faculty of Social Sciences, Charles University, Prague. He received the status of Docent (Associate Professor) in the field of Media Studies in 2002, when his thesis on media literacy was accepted. He is Adjunct Professor at New York University in Prague and Lecturer in the Faculty of Social Studies, Masaryk University, Brno. He is the author of texts on the transformation of the Czech media, a coauthor of *Introduction to Media Studies* (2001) and *Media and Society* (2003), and coeditor of *Political Communication and Media* (2000). From 1997 to 2000, he chaired the Council of Czech Public Television. He translates novels (Updike, Vonnegut, Le Carré, Auster) as well as media-related texts (McQuail, DeFleur-Ball-Rokeach, Thompson, Curran).

Anne Johnston is Professor in the School of Journalism and Mass Communication at the University of North Carolina at Chapel Hill. Her research interests include political communication, political advertising, women and politics, and diversity issues in the media. She is a coauthor of *Videostyle in Presidential Campaigns: Style and Content of Televised Political Advertising* (2001); has authored articles that have appeared in *Political Communication, Journal of Communication, Journalism Quarterly, Political Communication Review*, and *Journal of Applied Communication Research*; and has chapters in books on U.S. and French political advertising, election communication, women and politics, and media coverage of women.

Lynda Lee Kaid is Professor of Telecommunication in the College of Journalism and Communications at the University of Florida. She previously was a George Lynn Cross Research Professor at the University of

Oklahoma, where she also served as Director of the Political Communication Center and supervised the Political Commercial Archive. Her research specialties include political advertising and news coverage of political events. A Fulbright Scholar, she has also done work on political television in several Western European countries. She is the author or editor of more than 20 books, including *The Handbook of Political Communication Research* (2004), *The Millennium Election* (2003), *Political Television in Evolving European Democracies* (1999), *Civic Dialogue in the 1996 Presidential Campaign* (2000), *Videostyle in Presidential Campaigns* (2001), *The Electronic Election* (1999), *New Perspectives on Political Advertising* (1995), *Mediated Politics in Two Cultures, Political Advertising in Western Democracies* (1991), and *Political Campaign Communication: A Bibliography and Guide to the Literature* (1974). She also has written more than 100 journal articles and book chapters and more than 100 convention papers on various aspects of political communication. She has received over $1.5 million in external grant funds for her research efforts, including support from the U.S. Election Assistance Commission, U.S. Department of Commerce, the U.S. Department of Education, the National Endowment for the Humanities, and the National Science Foundation. Dr. Kaid is Former President of the Political Communication Divisions of the International Communication Association and the National Communication Association and has served in leadership roles in the American Political Science Association.

Ana Inés Langer is Tutorial Fellow at the Department of Media and Communications at the London School of Economics. She is completing her doctoral thesis on media and the personalization of politics in the United Kingdom at the same institution. Her research interests include democratic theory and communication; the role of the media in processes of political legitimation and in the development and reinforcement of democratic culture, especially in "young" democracies; and electoral campaigns. She has published articles in *Media, Culture & Society* and *The Communication Review*.

Baruch Leshem is Head of the Marketing Communication Division at the School of Communication, Sapir Academic College. He earned his Ph.D. from Université Paris 8 in 2003 after completing a thesis titled *La communication politique en Israël: Le processus de personnalisation dans les campagnes électorales télévisées en Israël de 1984 à 1999 et son influence sur le système politique* [Political communication in Israel: The process of personalization in televised electoral campaigns in Israel from 1984 to 1999 and its influence on the political system]. Dr. Leshem was Board Member of the Israeli Second Television and Radio Authority (2004-2005), and he is an active columnist for *Yedioth Achronoth*, the largest Israeli daily. He gained his professional reputation as a political adviser while working with major members of the Israeli government and participating in several election campaigns.

José-Carlos Lozano received his MA from Leicester University, England, and his Ph.D. from the University of Texas at Austin. He is Director of the Center for Communication Research, Monterrey Institute of Technology, Mexico, and a former Director of Mexico on the Executive Board of the Federation of Latin American Communication Schools. A member of the National System of Researchers of the National Council for Science and Technology of Mexico, he is also the author of numerous books and journal articles in the areas of mass, political, and international communication; one of his textbooks on mass communication theories is widely used in Latin American schools. He is a former Editor of the Mexican Communication Yearbook (volumes 1 through 4). He was appointed as his university's Televisa Research Chair in 1999; as such, he directed a massive quantitative and qualitative reception study in Mexico City, Guadalajara, and Monterrey. He is Chair of Audiovisual Media and Globalization in North America, Monterrey Institute of Technology, Monterrey, Mexico.

Gianpietro Mazzoleni is Professor of Sociology of Communication and of Political Communication at the University of Milan (Italy). He is Postgraduate Coordinator of the MSc Course in Social and Political Communication. He is Chair of the Political Communication Division (2004-2006) of the International Communication Association and Cofounder and Editor of the scholarly journal *Comunicazione Politica* (www.com-pol.it). He serves also on the editorial boards of the *European Journal of Communication* (published by Sage Ltd.) and of *Political Communication*. His main research interests are in the areas of mass communication, media policy, and political communication. Among his books are, most recently, *The Politics of Representation: Election Campaigning and Proportional Representation* (with J. Roper & C. Holtz-Bacha, 2004); *The Media in Europe* (coedited with M. Kelly & D. McQuail, 2004, Sage Ltd.); and *The Media and Neo-Populism: A Comparative Perspective* (coedited with J. Stewart & B. Horsfield, 2003).

Markus Moke, MA, Ph.D., is Researcher at the Institute for International Law of Peace and Armed Conflict at Ruhr-Universität Bochum (Germany) and coordinator of the European Master Programme in Humanitarian Action. His main fields of interest are media and humanitarian action; political communication and election campaigning, mainly in Latin America and the EU; media transition; and international media systems. He has participated in several research projects on political communication and election campaigns in the EU and Germany and on the role of mass media within the process of redemocratization in Latin American societies. He is working on a

project on the usage of media within humanitarian assistance.

Tom Moring is Professor of Communication and Journalism at the Swedish School of Social Science, University of Helsinki. He defended his doctoral thesis (*Political Elite Action: Strategy and Outcomes*) in 1990, after studies in the Department of Political Science at the University of Helsinki. His professional career includes work as a journalist, Head of Programmes, and Director of the Swedish Radio Channel of the Finnish Broadcasting Company, Yle; work as Acting Professor of Political Science, Department of Political Science, University of Helsinki; Secretary General of the European Bureau for Lesser Used Languages, Brussels (during which time the bureau established the news agency Eurolang); and Chair of the Board of the Newspaper Conglomerate HSS Media (which publishes four newspapers in Ostrobotnia, Finland). Dr. Moring has published on a wide range of issues, including articles and books on political campaigning, media, and political elite action.

Sarah Oates is Senior Lecturer in Politics at the University of Glasgow. She has published widely on the mass media, elections, and public opinion in the former Soviet Union. She is the author of *Television, Elections and Democracy in Russia* (2006) and coeditor of *The Internet and Politics: Citizens, Voters and Activists* (2005). She is Principal Investigator of a project in the New Security Challenges Programme of the British Economic and Social Research Council comparing media coverage and voter response to security issues and terrorist threats in Russian, American, and British election campaigns.

Stylianos Papathanassopoulos is Professor in Media Organisation and Policy in the Department of Communication and Mass Media, National and Kapodistrian University of Athens. He has written extensively on media developments in Europe and Greece and especially on television issues. His research interests are in European communications and new media policies, as well as media effects. His publications can be found in journals such as the *European Journal of Communication, Media, Culture & Society, Media International Australia, The Harvard International Journal of Press/Politics, Intermedia, Political Communication, Communication Review,* and *Journalism Studies.* He has also written for the trade press (*Broadcast, Television Business International, European Television Analyst, Cable and Satellite Europe*) and is Editor of the first and only communication journal in Greece, *Zitimata Epikoinonias* (Communication Issues). His most recent books are *Media and Politics: The Case of Southern Europe* (2004); *European Television in the Digital Age: Issues, Dynamics and Realities* (2002); and *European Communications: The Policies of the European Union in the Domain of Communication* (2002).

Mauro P. Porto is Assistant Professor in the Department of Communication at Tulane University, New Orleans. He holds a master's degree in Political Science from the University of Brasília, Brazil, and a Ph.D. in Communication from the University of California, San Diego. In 2002, he received the Best Doctoral Dissertation Award from the Brazilian Society of Interdisciplinary Communication Studies. His research and teaching interests include journalism, political advertising, and *telenovelas* in Brazil and Latin America. He has published on political communication in several academic journals around the world, including *Television and New Media, Communication Review, America Latina Hoy, Ecuador Debate, Media International Australia,* and *Brazilian Journalism Research.* He is working on a book about television and politics in Brazil.

Lilia Raycheva has been Associate Professor at the Radio and TV Department of the Faculty of Journalism and Mass Communication, St. Kliment Ohridsky Sofia University, since 1978. After earning her Ph.D. degree at M.V. Lomonosov Moscow State University in 1977, she was an American Council of Learned Societies Research Fellow (1980-1981) at New York University and Columbia University, a Fulbright Research Fellow and Visiting Professor (1993-1994) at the University of Oklahoma, and an Open Society Institute/HESP Research Fellow and Visiting Professor (2003-2004) at the University of Florida. During the time she was Vice-Dean of Scientific Research and International Affairs in the School of Journalism and Mass Communication, St. Kliment Ohridsky Sofia University (1998-2001), she was also Head of their Radio and Television Department (1999-2001). Since 2001, she has been serving as a member of the Council for Electronic Media, the regulatory authority for radio and TV broadcasters in Bulgaria. She is the author and editor of a number of books, articles, and conference papers on different mass communication issues and has lectured extensively at home and abroad. She has also been involved in a number of international media projects, among them the Cooperation in Scientific and Technical Research (COST) Actions of the European Commission.

Jolán Róka, Ph.D., has been Associate Professor of Speech Communication at the Eötvös Loránd University (Budapest) since 1978 and Professor and Vice General Director of Research and International Programs at the Budapest School of Communication since 2001. She was awarded the Széchényi Professor Award in 1998. As Guest Lecturer at the Századvég Political School and McDaniel College Budapest, she lectures on the history of mass media, theory of communication, cross-cultural communication, media of mass communication, interpersonal communication, and political communication. She is the author or editor of five books and 70 journal articles and book chapters and has been awarded several grants: a George Soros Grant to the School of Communication at the Pennsylvania State University (1990); IREX Grant to the Annenberg School for Communication, University of Pennsylvania (1992-1993); CEU RSS Grant (1994-1996); TEMPUS Grant to the University of Wales, Cardiff (1995); and a Fulbright Grant to Texas A&M University, Faculty of Journalism (1996-1997).

Athanassios N. Samaras holds a Ph.D. in Political Communication (Sussex University, U.K.), an MA degree in Political Communication (Emerson College, Boston), an MA degree in Communication Policy (City University, London) and a BA degree in Economics (University of Piraeus, Greece). He has been a Research Fellow at the Institute of Defense Analysis, Hellenic Audiovisual Institute, and Mediterranean Studies Foundation. He has conducted political campaigns in Greece and Cyprus. He has written extensively on political advertising, political marketing, campaigning in Greece and Cyprus, framing, and the representation of conflicts. His research interests include political communication and persuasion, political culture, news analysis, nation image making, and anti-Americanism. He is the author of the book *Television Political Advertising: A Quantitative Research Study on Greece* (2003).

Margaret Scammell is Senior Lecturer in Media and Communications at the London School of Economics. She has published widely on politics, communication, and political marketing and is the author of *Designer Politics* (1995), *On Message: Communicating the Campaign* (with Pippa Norris, John Curtice, David Sanders, and Holli Semetko; Sage, 1999) and *Media Journalism and Democracy* (with Holli Semetko; 2000).

Otakar Šoltys, PhDr., CSc., is a member of the Department of Media Studies and Center for Media Studies, Faculty of Social Sciences, Charles University, Prague. He was Researcher

in General Linguistics for 17 years in the Institute for Czech Language, Czechoslovak Academy of Sciences, then lecturer of media communication on stylistics of the Czech language and media semiotics. He is the author of texts on general linguistics (Verba dicendi and metalanguage function, Basic moods of predication) and media communication (Media and public sphere, Mytheme of light in news broadcasting).

Julianne Stewart teaches Communication and Media Studies at the University of Southern Queensland, Australia. She was coeditor, with Gianpietro Mazzoleni and Bruce Horsfield, of *The Media and Neo-Populism*, as well as coauthor of two chapters in that book. Additionally, she has published articles and presented papers on the relationship between the Australian media and contemporary government policies on immigration and security. Other areas of research interest include immigration, identity, and citizens' uses of communication technologies in a changing public sphere.

Jinyoung Tak is Professor of Mass Communication at Keimyung University in South Korea, where he is also Director of the Center for Political Communication. His research interests focus on political advertising and election campaigns. He has published in numerous journals and has authored two book chapters. He received his Ph.D. in Political Advertising from the University of Oklahoma in 1993.

Ruth Teer-Tomaselli is Professor of Culture, Communication, and Media Studies, University of KwaZulu-Natal, Durban, South Africa. She holds a UNESCO-Orbicom Chair in Communication for Southern Africa. Her research interests include the political economy of broadcasting and telecommunications in Southern Africa; program production on television; radio, particularly community radio; and the role of media in development. She has served as Director on the boards of the national public broadcasting network, the South African Broadcasting Corporation; a commercial radio broadcaster, East Coast Radio; and a community radio broadcaster, Durban Youth Radio. She is an avid gardener and nurtures a spectacular collection of bonsai trees.

Baba Thiam, Ph.D. in the Sociology of Communication, University Cheikh Anta Diop, Dakar, is the journalist in charge of production and diffusion of contents at Enda Cyberpop, Senegal, and a permanent correspondent with the Panos Institute, West Africa, in Dakar. He was a coauthor of the collective work *Entre tradition orale et nouvelles technologies: Où vont les mass médias au Sénégal?* [Between oral tradition and new technologies: Where are Senegal's mass media going?] (2005). He carries out research on the social use of information and communications technologies by populations in Senegal. He was given a media award by the Economic Commission on Africa of the United Nations in 2004.

Lars Willnat is Associate Professor at the School of Media and Public Affairs at George Washington University in Washington, DC. Before joining George Washington University in 1996, he taught at the Chinese University of Hong Kong and was a MacArthur Foundation Fellow at the Indiana Center on Global Change and World Peace. His teaching and research interests include media effects on political attitudes, theoretical aspects of public opinion formation, and international communication. He has published book chapters and articles in journals such as *Journalism and Mass Communication Quarterly, International Journal of Public Opinion Research, Political Communication, Journalism,* and *Gazette.* He received his Ph.D. in Mass Communication from Indiana University in 1992.

Frank Wittmann works as Public Information Officer for the United Nations Stabilization Mission in Haiti. Before, he was Research Assistant at the Department of Social Sciences, University of Fribourg, Switzerland. He is coeditor of the volume *African Media Cultures: Transdisciplinary Perspectives* (2004) and *Entre tradition orale et nouvelles technologies: Où vont les mass médias au Sénégal?* [Between oral tradition and new technologies: Where are Senegal's mass media going?] (2005). He is also the author of numerous articles on mass communication, cultural studies, and popular music. He has conducted empirical research in West Africa.